Handley Page Aircraft

since 1907

V/1500 second prototype J1935 in October 1918. (*G. S. Leslie*)

Handley Page Aircraft

since 1907

C H Barnes

Revised by Derek N. James

BY THE SAME AUTHOR

Bristol Aircraft since 1910

Shorts Aircraft since 1900

The first of earthly blessings, independence

EDWARD GIBBON (1789)

ISBN 0 85177 803 8

Printed in Great Britain for
Putnam, an imprint of
Conway Maritime Press Ltd,
24 Bride Lane, Fleet Street,
London EC4Y 8DR
by BAS Printers Limited, Over Wallop, Hampshire
Set in Monophoto Times
First published 1976
Second edition 1987

CONTENTS

FOREWORD

A completely representative account of Handley Page Limited could only have been written by Sir Frederick Handley Page himself. That he intended ultimately to do so is evident from the care with which all the significant archives were selected and filed at his direction by his secretary, Miss Elise McMichael, without whose diligence much essential information would have been lost. Not that his company's achievements were ever hidden under a bushel—Sir Frederick always made the most of them in his own communications and by means of the lively Public Relations Department, latterly managed by S. A. H. Scuffham, whose press releases have been unexcelled in content and lucidity. It is to Hugh Scuffham as well as Miss McMichael that the present author is principally indebted, for without their contribution a balanced picture of the adversities as well as the triumphs of the company during sixty years could not now have been presented. A popular history had already been drafted for the company's Golden Jubilee in 1959, but Sir Frederick would not approve it as it stood; after his death in 1962 it was revised for publication in 1969, but then shelved when the Jetstream production programme began to encounter difficulties.

At this point an approach by the author for permission to embark upon a less biographical complementary account of Handley Page aircraft development was well received after discussion with the former Chairman, G. C. D. Russell, and the Technical Director, Dr R. S. Stafford; a start was made on the present work with a promise of full co-operation from the firm, but the project was soon imperilled by the catastrophic collapse of February 1970. After some weeks, the liquidator, Kenneth Cork, accepted a suggestion from Sir Peter Masefield and Air Commodore F. R. Banks that Sir Frederick's archives would be of great value to the nation if handed over intact to suitable trustees, whereas they could realise little in terms of cash if sold on behalf of the creditors; the files were then presented to the Royal Aeronautical Society, which placed them on permanent loan to the library of the Royal Air Force Museum then being built at Hendon. So the book was reprieved and the author was most generously allowed access to the temporarily stored files by the Director of the Museum, Dr John Tanner, his Deputy, J. M. Bruce, and his Archivist Keeper, D. C. Brech.

During the final days at Radlett in July 1970, the author was invited to see the full range of original general arrangement linen tracings then being catalogued and packed for storage pending eventual disposal; he is most grateful to F. C. Cooper of Handley Page Ltd and Mr Saxelby of Hawker Siddeley Aviation Ltd for arranging for selected drawings to be printed before the Ozalid room ceased operation, and to S. Guyler, the liquidator's resident representative, for permission to use these prints for the purpose of illustrating this book. Though not all were suitable for direct reproduction, they served as the basis for the many accurate three-view tracings executed in a uniform style by Don Clayton, himself a former Handley Page apprentice with a keen personal interest in, and knowledge of, the company's history. His new drawings cover nearly all aircraft types actually built, as well as a few unbuilt projects, while the facsimiles of Handley Page originals are all of unbuilt projects; some loss of quality from long storage is more than outweighed by their unique archival value.

In pursuit of personal reminiscences, the author has been generously helped and encouraged by Harald Penrose who, as a Handley Page apprentice, was contemporary with Dr Stafford at Cricklewood and Northampton Engineering College (now The City University); through his good offices and enthusiasm valuable interviews were afforded with Major Cordes, 'STAR' Richards and the late Mrs Dorothy Wheeler of Sherborne, daughter of Sir Frederick's uncle George Handley of Southsea and sister of Trevor Handley; she was able to shed new light on her famous cousin's early activities and on the high affection in which he was held within the family. She recalled how her father had lent his nephew the then substantial sum of £600 in 1912, not expecting to see it back; how pleased and surprised they had been when Frederick came to Southsea in 1920 and wrote out a cheque for the loan with eight years' compound interest added, and how her father had thanked his nephew and then put the cheque in the drawing-room fire! Valuable assistance was also received from the late Lord Douglas of Kirtleside, from the late Captain A. S. Wilcockson and from H. C. Vereker, who, as a pilot in the RNAS, had the misfortune to land a brand-new O/100 in fog behind the German lines on New Year's Day 1917. For help in interpreting available data on high-speed and boundary-layer-control projects, the author is particularly indebted to John Bagley and Brian Edwards of the Royal Aircraft Establishment, Farnborough, the latter having been closely associated with Dr G. V. Lachmann in the Research Department at Radlett.

Very much help has been unstintingly given by colleagues in the aircraft industry and other long-term correspondents; in particular, the author is indebted to Chaz Bowyer, Don L. Brown, Don Clayton, Fitz Cowley, Mike Goodall, Eric Harlin, A. J. Jackson, Philip Jarrett, Eric Morgan, Philip Moyes, Denis Newman, Leo Opdycke, Jim Oughton, Elfan ap Rees, Richard Riding, Gordon Swanborough, John Underwood, Eric Watts and the late G. J. Weiss for photographs and other material, as well as to Miss Ann Tilbury late of *Flight*, Arnold Nayler of the Royal Aeronautical Society, D. C. Bateman of the Air Historical Branch (Ministry of Defence), Miss R. Coombs and E. Hine of the Imperial War Museum, Richard Simpson of the Royal Air Force Museum, E. J. MacAdam of Cranfield Institute of Technology and Gordon Bruce of Short Brothers & Harland Ltd. Finally, the daunting task of typing out some 200,000 words of manuscript was expertly and painstakingly achieved by Joy Flintoff, who, sadly, has not lived to see the finished book.

Capel Curig, March 1976 C.H.B.

FOREWORD TO SECOND EDITION

It will be very gratifying for Chris Barnes to know that a second edition of his magnificent *Handley Page Aircraft since 1907* is being published to meet the worldwide demand for it. I would like to thank, on his behalf, those members of the Handley Page Association who provided me with unique experience and help with minor modifications and updated information for this edition. They are Harry Fraser-Mitchell, Ray Funnell, Alan Dowsett, Roger Brookes, S. E. Hazell and J. Campbell. Graham Cowell and Kevin Cobb aided my research into the surviving Herald fleet and Catherine Lang, Public Relations Manager at British Aerospace Prestwick, provided details of Jetstream 31 production.

Barnwood, Gloucester. D.N.J

Origin and History of the Company

Frederick Handley Page was born at Cranham Villa, Cheltenham, Gloucestershire, on 15 November, 1885, the second of four sons of Frederick Joseph Page and his wife Ann Eliza, née Handley. Cheltenham originated in Roman times as a British village and had become a market town by 1223; it remained so until the early eighteenth century, trading mainly in livestock and malt, and sheltered to the northeast by the high escarpment of the Cotswolds—ideal grazing for a hardy and long-fleeced native breed of sheep. Then in 1716 Cheltenham's bucolic rhythm was quickened by the discovery of mineral springs and twelve years later a Pump Room and Spa were built in emulation of Beau Nash's establishment at Bath; in 1788 a visit by King George III and the ladies of the Royal Family set the seal of approval on Cheltenham as a fashionable resort. The town expanded steadily, allying the local Cotswold limestone with John Forbes' elegant Grecian style of architecture, and in 1815 grand new Assembly Rooms were opened by the Duke of Wellington to mark the final defeat of Napoleon Buonaparte. Thirty years later the Grammar School (founded in 1568), hitherto the town's sole educational establishment, faced competition from Cheltenham College, and in 1856 both were joined by the Ladies' College, whose famous headmistress, Dorothea Beale, is remembered as one who 'Cupid's darts did not feel'.

In this variegated environment of high fashion, earnest endeavour and middle-class respectability, Frederick Page senior was the hard-working proprietor of a small furniture and upholstery business and, being a Plymouth Brother, equally busy as a preacher on Sundays; his wife, of the same persuasion, came from Hampshire and was at first his only assistant. Family prayers were said daily (as was the rule in most Victorian households) and, by the time young Frederick entered Cheltenham Grammar School, he had acquired an extensive and apposite repertoire from the Scriptures; from this he continued to quote throughout his life, with devastating effect upon his adversaries and greatly to the joy of his hearers on all sorts of formal and informal occasions. To the end of his days he retained his rich, mellow (though somewhat nasal) Cotswold accent, which has been well recorded on tape for posterity to enjoy.

Some years before his school days began, the fringe effects of the Industrial Revolution had reached the Spa, now past the peak of its fame but still favoured by retired colonels and their memsahibs seeking an Indian summer on the tree-fringed lawns of Pittville and the caryatid terraces of Montpellier. Although the Cotswold woollen industry had declined as a result of greatly increased importation of Australian merino wool into Yorkshire, steam-power had replaced water-wheels in the local mills, Brindley's canals and MacAdam's turnpikes had been overtaken by the rival railway systems of Isambard Brunel and Robert Stephenson, and Cheltenham had become an important junction, initially as an end-on railhead of the broad and standard gauges. Before leaving school in 1902, young Frederick had noted recent redevelopment (including a new Town Hall and Central Spa on the site of the old Assembly Rooms) and decided that electric traction, for both railways and tramways, was the coming thing. Much against the will of his parents and the advice of his eldest brother Arthur (who was reading for the Bar), he left home for London, where he enrolled at the Finsbury Technical College for a three-year course in electrical engineering under Professor Sylvanus P. Thompson, whose perceptive and forthright method was epitomised in his famous best-seller *Calculus Made Easy* by the aphorism 'What one fool can do, another can'. Handley Page and another Finsbury student, Charles Richard Fairey, (contemporaries, but then unknown to each other) both became interested in the possibility of mechanical flight, although neither was attracted to ballooning, which had graduated from a fair-ground spectacle to a rich man's sport but (in spite of Lord Kelvin's approval) appeared to have no transport potential.

At first Handley Page experimented with flapping-wing models, with the inevitable lack of success, but, being an avid reader with a photographic memory and a strong sense of mathematical logic, soon became impatient of mere imitation of avian locomotion and began to discern an analogy between fluid motion and electromagnetic fields; in this he was thinking along the same lines as Frederick Lanchester and Dmitri Riabouchinsky, although at that date neither had published any of their findings. Graduating in 1906, Handley Page was appointed chief designer of Johnson & Phillips Ltd, a firm of electrical machinery manufacturers long established at Charlton near Woolwich. Invited to address the Institution of Electrical Engineers in May 1907, he chose as his subject *The present state of direct-current design as influenced by interpoles*, his able exposition so impressing his international audience that he was offered an attractive post with the Westinghouse Electric Company at Pittsburgh, Pennsylvania. By this time he had seen reports of the successful flights in 1905 by the Wright brothers at Dayton, Ohio, and of wind-tunnel tests on aerofoils in 1906 by Rupert Turnbull at Rothesay, New Brunswick, so he was much tempted to use the Westinghouse opportunity as a stepping stone to the pursuit of aeronautics in the New World; then he recalled the apparently advanced age level of the audience at his lecture, reckoned that he was too young to attain the quick promotion he sought in so well-entrenched a field as electric traction, and decided to continue the study of aviation on his home ground.

In 1907 he joined the Aeronautical Society of Great Britain, then in low water and ruled by a self-elected council which had failed to grasp that aviation had already arrived and was no longer the fictional fantasy of Prince Rasselas. He was particularly interested in the experiments of the pioneer artist-engineer José Weiss, who for many years had made and successfully flown gliders of various sizes having wings with a curved leading edge, upturned and swept-back flexible tips, and thickness and camber diminishing outwards from the centre. Weiss had arrived at this shape, which he protected under British Patent No. 17150 of 1908, from a study of soaring eagles in the Tyrolean Alps, and found that it ensured a high degree of both lateral and longitudinal stability, similar to that of the seed-leaf of the Javanese plant *Zanonia macrocarpa* studied by Igo Etrich in Germany during the same period. On 28 January, 1908, Handley Page wrote to the Society's Secretary, Colonel J. D. Fullerton, RE, 'With reference to the experiments I have carried out, the results I have obtained are mostly of a qualitative and not quantitative nature. Sufficient data has not been obtained under varying conditions to enable a paper to be brought out. I should much prefer to have a conversation on the subject with Mr Weiss, with whom I am as yet unacquainted, and I should esteem it a great favour to be put into communication with him. I should then be in a better position to judge whether anything I have done is of any value, as I know in other classes of engineering work that one's own researches are usually very small in other people's eyes'. As a result of this letter he was invited to join the Society's 'Wings Committee' to assist Major R. F. Moore, a retired Sapper with several ornithopter patents to his name dating from 1890, and during 1908 they worked together on the experimental measurement of the lift and thrust available from a pair of flapping wings, each of 7·5 ft span and a total area of 45 sq ft, derived by scaling up three times the flight organs of an Indian flying fox, *Pteropus giganteus*; the results of these experiments were published in the *Aeronautical Journal* in January 1909.

Handley Page met José Weiss for the first time on 8 February, 1908, when he was invited to Houghton House, near Amberley, Sussex; three weeks later Weiss spent the week-end at 60, The Crescent, Charlton, and returned again on 27 March after reading a paper to the Aero Club. As a result of these meetings Handley Page became a shareholder in the Weiss Aeroplane and Launcher Syndicate, formed on 10 June, 1908, and spent a week-end at Amberley ten days later. Then Wilbur Wright arrived in Europe to give demonstrations of practical flying at Le Mans in August 1908, and Handley Page's enthusiasm for aviation so outran his caution

Weiss monoplane and launcher at Fambridge in December 1908.

that he initiated experimental work at Johnson & Phillips without proper authority; unfortunately his directors interpreted his mistaken zeal as attempted embezzlement and he was dismissed, his place being taken by his assistant Archibald R. Low (who two years later was to join the emergent aircraft industry at Bristol). Perhaps this was what Handley Page expected, for he lost no time in setting up in business on his own account in a shed and office at 36 William Street, Woolwich, where he accepted a commission to design and build a so-called 'quadruplane'—more precisely, a tandem biplane—for G. P. Deverall Saul (an enthusiastic but impractical inventor), incorporating the latter's ideas on automatic stability. He engaged a former Johnson & Phillips patternmaker named Tucker as his first employee, but had no adjacent flying ground, so in December 1908 he went to inspect the facilities then being publicised by Noel Pemberton Billing at Fambridge, Essex, where he found José Weiss completing his first powered monoplane and delighted to renew their acquaintanceship. Handley Page then agreed with Weiss to take a stand at the following year's Aero & Motor Boat Show at Olympia, using the Weiss monoplane as centre-piece, and to make Weiss a structurally improved wing for his next glider, in return for which he was to be allowed to use the Weiss patent in any of his own designs; Weiss forbore to stipulate any financial consideration for this informal contract and Handley Page saw no reason to suggest one in an arrangement which brought mutual advantage to both parties.

The much-advertised Fambridge flying ground soon proved to be too rough and remote for Handley Page's purpose and he then went to see the flying ground leased by the Aeronautical Society adjacent to Dagenham Dock in Essex, which in an earlier access of enthusiasm it had acquired for the use of members, but then found a white elephant. This was little better than Fambridge, but much nearer the Woolwich Free Ferry he found at Creekmouth, and was able to lease, a similar piece of marshland with a corrugated iron shed owned by Samuel Williams & Co Ltd, thus acquiring a rudimentary factory and small adjacent ground, with flying rights over $2\frac{1}{2}$ miles of even rougher marshland extending eastward along the north bank of the Thames from Barking Creek to Dagenham Dock, alongside the London, Tilbury & Southend Railway; the right to fly over this area conferred no right of entry on to the land itself and he was often to become involved in claims for trespass on alleged meadowland from which,

Handley Page's first glider at Barking in 1909.

Frederick Handley Page on his first experimental glider in 1909.

nevertheless, he was unable to prevent his 'factory' being invaded by stray cattle. Part of the marsh near Barking Creek had been built up above the original level some years earlier, by dumping blue clay spoil excavated during the building of the London Underground railways; further east, only a small area of the Aeronautical Society's Dagenham ground was usable, comprising 500 yards of by-road and a small cinder-filled plot designated as the 'starting track'; in the end, the Society was unable to raise by voluntary subscription the £400 or so required for further levelling and after several months of indecision agreed on 14 January, 1910, to accept Handley Page's offer of £40 for the three sheds already standing at Dagenham Breach, which he forthwith removed and re-erected at Creekmouth. It has been said that Handley Page raised the initial capital for his venture by playing poker on the commuter trains in and out of Fenchurch Street—certainly he was remarkably dexterous with a pack of cards and in later years his post-prandial prestidigitation was as popular an entertainment as his oratory—but in fact he built up his resources by extremely frugal living and maximum use of the Woolwich Free Ferry to eke out the profit from manufacturing airscrews and small accessories for experimenters who lacked the necessary skill and facilities; he supplied the twin propellers for the Willows No. 2 airship which flew from Cardiff to the Crystal Palace in August 1910, and many others of smaller size.

The sloping dykes at Creekmouth were suitable for gliding experiments and Handley Page began his personal attempt to fly by making a simple *canard* monoplane glider, having both foreplane and mainplane of Weiss shape, with a triangulated frame to carry the pilot's seat below the mainplane and an undercarriage comprising three bicycle wheels, two behind and one in front; to save weight, the airframe spars were built up of parallel pairs of spruce laths spaced at intervals by blocks; the wings were skilfully constructed of properly jointed spruce by Tucker, instead of the bamboo crudely lashed together with whipcord employed by Weiss. Handley Page duly exhibited the Weiss monoplane on Stand No. 30 at the Society of Motor Manufacturers & Traders' Aero and Motor Boat Show at Olympia on 17 March, 1909, together with a 12 ft span unmanned Weiss glider and a description of the Deverall Saul machine, which itself was not

Barking works in June 1909, with Deverall Saul quadruplane outside shed.

far enough advanced to be shown, although the show catalogue contained a highly optimistic artist's impression of its appearance in flight. The Weiss monoplane, with only a 12 hp Anzani engine to drive its two propellers, never flew, and Handley Page failed also to leave the ground in his own glider, as did his first two premium pupils Cyril W. Meredith and Arthur Dukinfield Jones. In May the Deverall Saul quadruplane was finished and Handley Page attempted to fly it along the Dagenham 'starting track', but without success even when assisted by a towing motorcar—its own engine only developed 8 hp! This in no way damped his enthusiasm and on 17 June, 1909, he turned himself into a private limited company for the specific purpose of aeronautical engineering, the first such company to be registered in the United Kingdom; styled simply Handley Page Limited (a title that was to remain unchanged for 61 years) it had an authorised capital of £10,000 in 500 shares of £20 each, the three other directors being his eldest brother Arthur and two engineers, Francis Dalton and W. G. Magdalen; its initial subscribed capital was £500.

The new company's first activity was to build a larger shed at Creekmouth with its name displayed in large enough lettering to be read at a glance from passing trains. Deverall Saul ordered a two-seat version of his quadruplane and two other commissions were received, one from

The enlarged shed at Barking, built after storm damage in 1910.

Alexander Thiersch of Plumstead for a monoplane wing and control surfaces to suit a machine he was building to demonstrate a novel control system, and the other from W. P. Thompson of Freshfield, Lancashire, for a patented 'pendulum-stability' biplane. Concurrently with these two 'outside' jobs, Handley Page began the design and construction of his first tractor monoplane, intended for the 1910 Olympia exhibition. This featured the structurally improved Weiss wing, with no means of lateral control because of its presumed automatic stability, and was powered by a 20 hp Advance vee-four air-cooled engine driving a Handley Page two-bladed airscrew copied from a design by Weiss. This monoplane, Type A, was covered with blue rubberised cotton fabric and consequently was known as the *Bluebird*. The biplane, though basically of Thompson's layout, had been much simplified in design by Handley Page, so was listed as Type B; when it was damaged on its first outing and immediately afterwards wrecked by part of the works shed collapsing in a gale, Handley Page promptly disowned it and dubbed it the *Scrapheap*.

Frederick Handley Page in *Bluebird* in April 1910.

Though still unfinished in March 1910, the *Bluebird* was duly shown at Olympia and favourably commented upon by more experienced aviators, although the general criticism was that its Demoiselle-type cruciform empennage was too small to be effective. Like most small motor-cycle air-cooled engines of its day, the Advance gave its full power only for a minute or two after being persuaded to start; at first it was too cold to run up to speed, then it overheated rapidly unless the aeroplane could actually be kept moving at not less than 30 mph. With immense patience and tenacity, and not a little physical courage, Handley Page tried day after day to achieve the elusive coincidence of wind speed and direction, engine revolutions and temperature, and c.g. location and elevator angle to trim, which alone would get him airborne; at last, on 26 May, 1910, he hit the jackpot and took off for a brief straight hop; after several adjustments, a few more hops were accomplished, but Handley Page was entirely self-taught and between his own lack of piloting skill and the absence of any means of checking the wing's inherent tendency to overbank, the first attempt to change direction ended in a crash. Thiersch had had better luck on the Kent side of the Thames marshes, at Belvedere near Erith; having just managed to leave the ground in April, he flew a full 1,200 yards on the same day as Handley Page's first hop, but his luck ran out soon afterwards and his novel monoplane was wrecked, never to fly again.

Handley Page was less easily discouraged and set about rebuilding the *Bluebird* with several improvements, including additional bracing for the wing and undercarriage, warping for lateral control and a 25 hp Alvaston water-cooled flat-twin engine; thus remodelled, it became Type C, but it was no more successful than in its first form, and after a brief trial with a 50 hp Isaacson radial engine, which was too heavy, Handley Page set it aside to begin work on a larger monoplane for the next Olympia show. Meanwhile Thompson had sent his assistant, Robert C. Fenwick, to rebuild the Type B biplane, for which Handley Page had disclaimed further liability, although he offered facilities at Barking for repairs to be made by Thompson, who had formed his own company, Planes Limited, to continue its development at Freshfield. After reconstructing and dispatching the airframe of Type B by rail to Liverpool, for completion at Freshfield, Fenwick stayed on awhile at Barking to help Handley Page with his new monoplane, Type D, in which the fuselage was a boat-built monocoque very beautifully planked with mahogany veneer, instead of the earlier fabric-covered framework. In November 1910 he returned to Freshfield to fly the rebuilt Type B, now renamed the Planes Ltd Biplane, and on the 29th not only made a successful first flight but went on to complete the simple circuits, climb to height and dead-stick landing required to qualify for a Royal Aero Club aviator's certificate. Having gained this, he returned to Barking as Handley Page's first test pilot, while Handley Page himself, recognising his own lack of flying aptitude, devoted himself to improving not only the standard of design and manufacture of aeroplanes but also the status and qualifications of members of the Aeronautical Society, particularly the rules governing the election of members to the Council. A regular attendant at the Society's meetings, Handley Page was an outspoken critic of the oligarchic system whereby Council members were self-elected, as though the Society were a dining club disguised as a learned society, rather than the technically orientated professional institution it should have been.

Much criticism had arisen from the failure of members to support the Dagenham flying ground scheme (there were only about six others besides Handley Page who regularly visited it) although, in fairness, many members belonged also to the Royal Aero Club, which offered (through the generosity of Frank McClean) very much better amenities at Eastchurch, since moving from their first club-house at Mussel Manor. The Society's equivalent of Frank McClean was Patrick Y. Alexander, who continually injected new finance into the Society's ever-lean bank account from his large private inheritance, which, alas, was not self-regenerating like McClean's and suddenly expired some twenty years later, leaving him in desperate straits from which his many friends in the aircraft industry rescued him with tact and dignity. Patrick Alexander had put up one quarter (£100) of the initial experimental ground donation fund and Handley Page had been among the dozen or so other members to subscribe over £5—the remainder of the fund was made up of guineas and half-guineas given in an almost derisory spirit by those who considered the Society to be moribund. When the scheme failed, Handley Page became the very articulate leader of a revolt among the younger and better technically-trained members against the existing state of affairs; early in 1911 a committee of enquiry was charged with framing new rules for the election of both technical and non-technical grades of membership, and when these were at last reluctantly accepted by the old Council in September 1911, Handley Page was among the sixteen members elected to serve on the new one.

Concurrently with the reform of the Aeronautical Society, Handley Page became extremely active in more directly remunerative side-lines, including technical journalism and lecturing. Following his early paper, jointly with Major R. F. Moore, reporting the 'Wings Committee's' experiments with flapping wings in 1908, he had written for *Flight* a critical assessment of the new aeroplanes flown at the 1910 Reims meeting, noting the reduced camber of the later Blériot monoplanes; in the same journal he advertised the availability from stock of a range of cast aluminium strut sockets and similar fittings. As an evening class lecturer, he returned to the Finsbury Technical College to give a short course in electrical engineering; there he read that the Northampton Polytechnic Institute at Clerkenwell was seeking a lecturer in aeronautical engineering, to bring its existing syllabus (introduced in 1909) up to the more advanced level offered by A. P. Thurston at the rival East London College at Mile End. So far, the Northampton Institute's aeronautical lectures had been shared by the Principal, Dr Mullineux Walmsley, with his Head of Mechanical Engineering, Charles Larard (neither of whom had any direct knowledge of aviation) and Léon Blin Desbleds, whose experience was limited to ballooning. Desbleds had left to join the staff of the Regent Street Polytechnic and a large increase in the Northampton Institute's enrolment for the 1910–11 session made the recruitment of more lecturers imperative, so Handley Page's application for the aeronautical vacancy was welcomed by Larard, who had begun the course single-handed in October. Handley Page's lectures commenced on 13 January, 1911, after he had secured Dr Walmsley's support in equipping a laboratory with a wind-tunnel and flow visualisation apparatus, in addition to the usual drawing office and workshop facilities; he also succeeded in transferring to the Institute, no doubt without financial loss, the Type C airframe as the basis of a practical construction exercise, including the installation of a 30 hp engine of unspecified type; naturally any design problems at Barking needing wind-tunnel experiments could be more quickly and cheaply investigated at Clerkenwell than in the National Physical Laboratory at Teddington. Handley Page already accepted premium pupils at Barking, the first two being Meredith and Dukinfield Jones, followed by Elvison and A. A. Fletcher, who later became chief designer first to Martin & Handasyde at

Brooklands and then to Warren & Smiles (The London & Provincial Aeroplane Co) at Hendon and Stag Lane.

Meanwhile the Type D monoplane was completed at Barking in time for the third Aero Show at Olympia, where it appeared on Stand No. 73. Barking had proved too rough for regular use as a flying ground and Handley Page had rented part of a playing field, 1,000 yards long by 500 yards wide, some six miles to the north at Fairlop. Here Robert Fenwick tried in vain to take off with the 35 hp Green engine loaned for the Olympia show, so when Type D failed to find a buyer in spite of its low price of £450, Handley Page fitted it with the 50 hp Isaacson already obtained for Type C, and entered it for the *Daily Mail* Circuit of Britain race in July. With the new engine, Type D took off easily at Fenwick's first attempt on 15 July,

Close-up of Type D at Olympia in April 1911.

one week before the race, but he crashed it on landing and Handley Page was grievously disappointed at having his hopes dashed after so much effort. Having first ascertained that Fenwick was unhurt, Handley Page turned on him furiously and sacked him on the spot; no doubt he would have re-engaged him next day, but Fenwick too was aggrieved, since the accident was not his fault, and departed equally in anger, eventually returning to Freshfield; both Dukinfield Jones and Meredith were keen to qualify as pilots and the former left Handley Page soon afterwards to join the Melly School at Liverpool, while Meredith got his chance six months later when he was allowed time off to gain his brevet at Eastchurch; but for the moment Handley Page had no pilot and in any case it would have been impossible to repair Type D in time for the start of the race on 22 July. Soon afterwards the brothers Henry and Edward Petre (whom their friends at Brooklands had nicknamed respectively 'Peter the Monk' and 'Peter the Painter' after two contemporary criminals) came to consult Handley Page about their own experimental monoplane, which they had just crashed. Edward Petre agreed to join Handley Page as test pilot and to assist with design, and the repair of Type D began at Barking, whence it emerged with a new fabric-covered fuselage and a liberal coating of lanoline anticorrosive paint on all metal fittings; on seeing it thus, Petre dubbed it *The Antiseptic* and later *The Yellow Peril*; he made a few short flights on it at Fairlop, but it was soon set aside in favour of an improved two-seat monoplane, whose Weiss-type wing incorporated the results of Rupert Turnbull's research on reflexed aerofoils; it was powered by a 50 hp Gnome rotary engine and designated Type E. Petre took a hand in the design, under Handley Page's supervision, and may even have taken up a few £20 shares in the Company, but he had at first no qualifications as either pilot or designer apart from his irrepressible enthusiasm, and received only a token salary.

While the design of Type E evolved, supported by wind-tunnel tests which formed part of the practical coursework at the Northampton Institute, Handley Page (aided by a £600 loan from his uncle, George Handley of Southsea) began the next stage in expanding his business. In rebuilding the Barking works shed after gale damage he had enlarged it to 10,000 sq ft and had given up his Woolwich premises. Next he rented an office—little more than an accommodation address, with a single clerk in charge—at 72 Victoria Street, London, S.W., right among the big fish, with Vickers Ltd a near neighbour and the two senior engineering institutions a short walk away on the edge of St James's Park; the Aeronautical Society was just across the street at No. 53, so he was a frequent visitor there, especially when he had just spotted a likely customer entering the Society's door. He advertised his range of accessories from this address and began to take up agencies for new products, such as Martin & Handasyde's patent dope (to which the trademark 'Martinsyde' was first applied). Then in March 1912 an opportunity occurred which he seized with alacrity: Horatio Barber, designer of the tail-first Valkyrie monoplanes built by his company, the Aeronautical Syndicate Ltd, announced the liquidation of his business after having built some twenty aeroplanes; he presented the four best Valkyries to the newly formed Army Air Battalion and instructed Harrods to sell all the rest of his stock, except tools, where it lay at Hendon. The advertised auction sale never took place, because Handley Page made an acceptable cash offer for the entire catalogue and within three weeks had sold off most of the items, including three Valkyries and the Viking biplane, at a comfortable profit, after retaining several 50 hp and 70 hp Gnome engines and spares for them, for his own immediate use; the sheds at Hendon and most of the materials were bought by George Holt Thomas, to become the nucleus of the Aircraft Manufacturing Company, itself the precursor of the de Havilland enterprise.

By mid-April Type E was finished and Edward Petre flew straights on it at Fairlop on the 26th—he had not yet flown in a closed circuit and was in fact still teaching himself to fly. He made rapid progress, in spite of gusty weather, and eventually flew from Fairlop to Barking, but crashed on arrival, fortunately without irreparable damage. Within a few weeks Type E had been rebuilt and taken back to Fairlop, with its original white rubberised wing covering replaced by yellow doped fabric. On 24 July, 1912, Petre qualified for his RAeC certificate (No. 259) at Fairlop, his flights being officially observed by Tom O'Brien Hubbard and Charles

G. Grey; so Handley Page could at last claim to have trained a pupil in his own flying school. Handley Page had in fact already obtained a foothold at Brooklands at the end of May, by taking over from Howard Flanders the selling rights for Flanders monoplanes and the agency for the Flanders flying school. Three days after gaining his certificate, Petre flew Type E from Fairlop to Rainham and thence along the course of the Thames to Kew, landing at Brooklands 50 minutes after taking off; his distance flown was 55 miles. So Handley Page arrived at the Mecca of contemporary aviation and his new monoplane, with its blue fuselage and mustard yellow wings and tail, was much admired by the resident fraternity as the (second) *Yellow Peril*. It was not, however, his only new monoplane, for as soon as the provisional rules for a military aeroplane competition had been announced in December 1911, Handley Page had begun work on an improved version with side-by-side seating for pilot and observer, being assisted in its design and construction by Edward Petre's elder brother Henry ('Peter the Monk'). It was to be flown in the trials at Larkhill on Salisbury Plain in August by 'Peter the Painter', but arrived almost too late to compete. The delay was due to two factors, one being the imminent removal of Handley Page's factory from Barking to larger premises at Cricklewood, within easy reach of Hendon, where a flight shed had been reserved; the other was Henry Petre's presumption in designing and manufacturing two alternative pairs of wings, since he preferred orthodox straight leading and trailing edges to the curved Weiss shape; the straight pair, on his instructions, were fitted for the first flight of the military monoplane (Type F) without reference to his younger brother who, when informed, left Henry in no doubt as to Handley Page's certain reaction to such arrogance, and the Weiss-type wings were hastily substituted before Handley Page's next visit to Barking. Type F was unlucky in the military trials, because the 70 hp Gnome was not in good tune and Petre was forced to land down wind on his second flight, causing more damage than could be repaired on site. Early in September the works moved from Barking to converted riding stables (of 20,000 sq ft) at 110 Cricklewood Lane, off the Edgware Road between Kilburn and Hendon. Although advertised for sale as a ready made aircraft factory, the Barking site was never used again for aviation and in later years was engulfed by Barking electricity power station.

Handley Page's main reason for needing new premises was the expansion expected from an invitation from the War Office to build B.E.2a biplanes designed by Geoffrey de Havilland at the Royal Aircraft Factory at Farnborough, this type having been adopted as the standard aeroplane for the new Royal Flying Corps; large contracts were due to be placed with established manufacturers and Handley Page was determined to be in the picture. In the event, only five B.E.s were ordered in the first batch, and the special alloy steels specified proved so difficult to obtain in the small quantities needed that delivery of the first three was severely delayed, the last two being cancelled by mutual consent, since Handley Page preferred to stick to the methods and materials he already knew; furthermore, Type E was flying right in the public eye at Hendon, where it attracted the attention of many leading Service pilots, notably Lieutenant Wilfred Parke, RN, who considered that Type F would be a useful scout for naval purposes, and was anxious to fly it when repairs were completed. The Petre brothers by this time had left Handley Page, Henry being chosen to head a British mission to inaugurate the Australian Flying Corps and its flying school at Point Cook, while Edward became test pilot to Martin & Handasyde at Brooklands, and was to be killed on Christmas Eve in a Martinsyde monoplane, while attempting in bad weather to fly nonstop from Brooklands to Edinburgh; Robert Fenwick had already died during the military trials in August on Planes Ltd's second product, the Mersey monoplane designed by himself; but the worst blow of all was the deaths of both Wilfred Parke and his passenger, Arkell Hardwick, in Type F at Wembley on 15 December, 1912. Parke's confidence in the machine's excellent stability had led him into placing undue reliance on its 70 hp Gnome, which had never been a good runner, and was in even worse condition than usual on the fatal morning, when he and Hardwick took off from Hendon; it failed in a situation—down draught over the lee of some tall trees—where a stall and spin in the attempted forced landing were inevitable. Undoubtedly this tragic accident profoundly influenced Handley Page's future philosophy, which, more than ever, put safety before speed and impelled him to seek out means of reducing, or if possible eliminating, the loss of control at the stall which was to prove the worst killer of all in the four years of aerial warfare ahead. Wilfred Parke was a natural pilot of exceptional skill and promise, whose methodical approach to test-flying was reflected in a detailed critical log which he called *Aviaticanda*, extracts from which were published after his death. The loss of Alfred Arkell Hardwick was equally grievous, although he was not a pilot, because he was a man of exceptional talent and vigour, who had sailed round the world more than once as an apprentice (he had survived a passage round Cape Horn during which one wave had washed him overboard and the next had cast him back on deck); he had also served in the Mashonaland police, worked on the Nile irrigation scheme, hunted big game and traded ivory in Kenya and Nigeria, and spent a year in the United States, before joining Handley Page Ltd as assistant manager in 1911; he was a man after Handley Page's own heart and Handley Page grieved for him as for a brother.

Handley Page was always interested in improvements to control systems and ready to help anyone with a promising idea in this direction. During the summer of 1912 he had been approached by a Japanese engineer, T. Sonoda, for whom he had built a conventional heavily-staggered straight-

Sonoda biplane at Hendon in August 1912.

winged biplane resembling the French Zodiac design. It crashed early in its career at Hendon, but the next few months brought a War Office ban on monoplanes being flown by military pilots, following several accidents during army manoeuvres. Handley Page did not believe that monoplanes were inherently more dangerous than biplanes, and on 15 January, 1913, read a paper to the Aeronautical Society and the Royal United Services Institution, entitled *The comparison of monoplanes and biplanes, with special reference to the stresses in each type*, drawing the overall conclusion that monoplanes were most economical up to a wing area of 275 sq ft, but biplanes were superior for larger sizes. He rebuilt a Blériot-type Radley & Moorhouse monoplane for the Australian pilot Sydney Pickles; then refurbished the *Yellow Peril* in February 1913 as his only available exhibit for the fourth Olympia show (where it was seen and commended by King George V), before taking it back into the works for major modifications, including the substitution of ailerons for warping and a revision of the tail unit. These design changes were the first contribution of George Rudolph Volkert, who had attended Handley Page's aeronautical lectures in addition to the normal three-year mechanical engineering degree course he was taking at the Northampton Institute. On graduation in 1912, having already put in vacation work at six shillings a week, he accepted Handley Page's invitation to become chief designer at Cricklewood, at the princely (but then not totally inadequate) salary of fifteen shillings a week.

By Easter 1913 the *Yellow Peril* was rebuilt in its revised form and Handley Page had found a new test pilot in Ronald Whitehouse, who took up his official duties and made his first flight on the *Yellow Peril* on 1 May; its handling was so much improved with ailerons that ten days later Sydney Pickles flew it to Winchester for an exhibition flight at the polo ground and back again on the 17th just in time for Whitehouse to share with him two appearances in the Hendon race meeting that week-end. Meanwhile Volkert was quietly busy in his one-man stress office on the design of a new

Ronald Whitehouse in *Yellow Peril* at Hendon in August 1913.

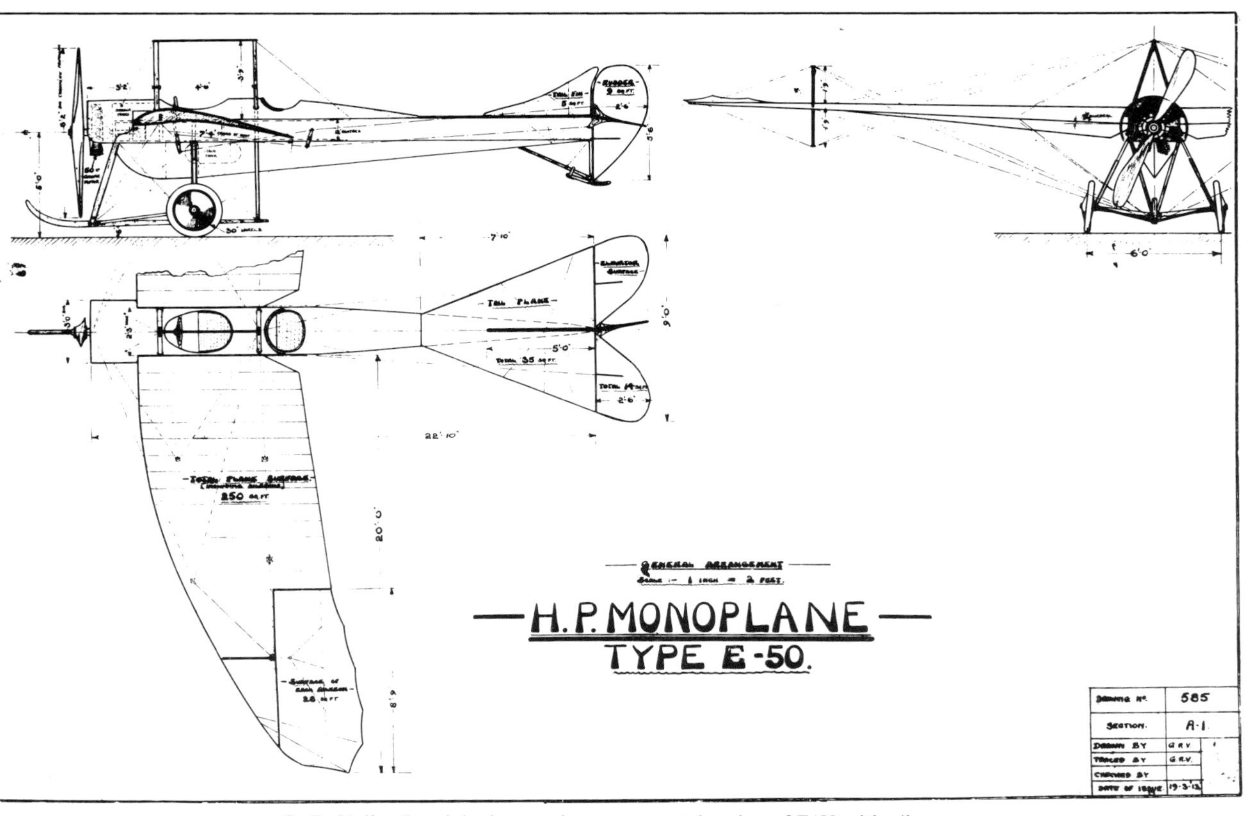

G. R. Volkert's original general arrangement drawing of E/50 with ailerons.

biplane (Type G) using the revised Weiss-type wing, with aileron controls, in a tandem two-seat layout which made use of the better features of the B.E.2a, without getting involved in material supply problems. Before completion it was bought by the Northern Aircraft Co, of which Rowland Ding was chief pilot; it had originally been schemed as a Green-engined float seaplane, but the Admiralty showed no interest and Handley Page then offered it to Ding as a landplane for exhibition flying on account of its ability to fly slowly and alight in restricted spaces. While Type G was being completed, Handley Page agreed to lend the *Yellow Peril* with Whitehouse to fly it, for exhibition flights already booked and contracted for at Buxton, Leicester, Mansfield and Lincoln in June, Hull in July, and Burton-on-Trent in August; most of these were four-day programmes, including races and more or less spectacular stunts, such as bombing with flour-bags. At Hull Whitehouse damaged the monoplane, but repaired it in time to defy a ban on Sunday flying threatened by a local sabbatarian minority.

A few weeks after this tour ended, Handley Page made one of his very rare financial mistakes; in an argument on the virtues of automatic stability between himself and Noel Pemberton Billing, the latter claimed that anyone with any sense could learn to fly a standard aeroplane in a single summer day; Handley Page retorted 'Rubbish!', upon which Pemberton Billing wagered £500 that *he* could do so, and Handley Page accepted the challenge; however, Pemberton Billing soon found that no flying school would accept him as a pupil on such terms, so he forthwith bought an ancient Farman from Maurice Ducrocq, and cajoled Harold Barnwell into giving him the essential minimum of instruction. Barnwell sent him solo at Brooklands after a few circuits and bumps, and having obtained an official RAeC observer to witness the next stage in the proceedings, Pemberton Billing managed to complete the prescribed certificate tests by the skin of his teeth, before sitting down to a well-earned breakfast. Handley Page meanwhile had begun a few reluctant taxying runs at Hendon in the *Yellow Peril*, and was much relieved to hear at lunchtime of Pemberton Billing's triumph; he paid up as though it really gave him pleasure to do so, for it would have cost more to replace the only aeroplane he possessed at that date, had he wrecked it; Pemberton Billing meanwhile had continued flying after breakfast, with a ciné operator in attendance to record his prowess.

Type G was first flown by Whitehouse on 6 November and by 12 December had proved so successful that he flew it across country from Hendon to Farnborough for official performance tests by the Royal Aircraft Factory; the only modification officially recommended was a small change in tail area, whereupon Handley Page got Whitehouse to fly it with the tailplane and fin removed altogether, to show that the automatically stable wing made fixed tail surfaces unnecessary. In a lecture to the Kite and Model Aircraft Association at Caxton Hall on 9 January, 1914, Handley Page referred to Professor G. H. Bryan's recent book on stability, giving equations of motion which could be used to predict full-scale behaviour from model tests; he also surveyed the earlier work of Eiffel, Rateau, Alphonse de Gaumont, Ludwig Prandtl, Riabouchinsky, and Stanton of the NPL, and paid particular tribute to Rupert Turnbull, whose wind-tunnel results with reflexed trailing edges he had applied to the original Weiss wing in such a way as to ensure that the centre of pressure always moved forward with increasing angle of attack. Two weeks later

Princess Löwenstein-Wertheim and Rowland Ding in G/100 at Hendon in May 1914.

Handley Page attended Leonard Bairstow's lecture to the Aeronautical Society on *The Stability of Aeroplanes*, enlivening the subsequent discussion by demonstrating a stable model which looped when thrown hard, but performed a tail-slide when not thrown fast enough. He enunciated the principles of inherent stability as (a) a small longitudinal moment of inertia, to be obtained by grouping the major masses as near the centre of gravity as possible, and (b) a large self-righting moment consequent upon any alteration of the aeroplane's attitude in relation to its flight path, provided adequately by the Handley Page wing shape and very little impaired by removal of the fixed tail surfaces. An enlarged 200 hp Salmson engined biplane (Type L) derived from Type G was built in 1914 to the order of Princess Ludwig of Löwenstein-Wertheim to attempt a direct crossing of the Atlantic, for which the *Daily Mail* offered a prize of £10,000. Though practically complete in August, it was never flown and was later dismantled to make room for the giant twin-engined bombers which became familiar enough later to secure a place in the *Concise Oxford Dictionary* for the noun 'Handley Page', defined as 'Type of large aeroplane'.

As soon as hostilities commenced on 4 August, 1914, Handley Page offered his factory and resources to both the War Office and the Admiralty; Brigadier General Sir David Henderson (DGMA) thanked him formally and declined his services, still displeased with his earlier failure to supply B.E.2s punctually, but Commodore Murray F. Sueter, Director of the Air Department, Admiralty, at once called him and Volkert to a meeting to discuss plans for bombing and coast patrol aeroplanes. The Air Department's technical genius, Harris Booth, was convinced of the need for a really long-range heavy patrol bomber, capable of attacking the German High Seas Fleet in its base at Kiel before it ever put to sea, to say nothing of the growing number of Zeppelin airship sheds springing up along the Friesian coastline. Meanwhile Commander Charles Rumney Samson had taken a scratch naval squadron of aeroplanes and armoured cars to Flanders in an attempt to prevent the German occupation of Antwerp, but they were too late and too few to do more than rescue a small proportion of the fleeing Belgian population. Samson had signalled home to Sueter 'What we want here is a bloody paralyser to stop the Hun in his tracks' and this was the message that Sueter gave to Handley Page after seeing Volkert's schemes for converting Type L (or its twin-engined equivalent. Type M) into the bombing role; Handley Page also proposed a small quickly produced scout, Type N/80, with an 80 hp rotary engine, but Sueter brushed this aside, since he was already promised ample supplies of similar

Frederick Handley Page in 1914 (*left*) and George Rudolph Volkert CBE, Chief Designer 1912–21, 1924–31 and 1935–48.

types by Sopwith and Blackburn. Handley Page set out with Volkert and Harris Booth to design a much larger twin-engined biplane, designated Type O/100. There had been only one earlier aeroplane of comparable size, Sikorsky's *Il'ya Mourom'etz* with four 100 hp Argus engines, which had flown at Korpusny, near Petrograd, on 25 February, 1914, with fifteen passengers in addition to its designer-pilot. Frederick Lanchester had predicted that the 'square-cube law' would prevent aeroplanes from being successfully flown in sizes much larger than those already existing, but Handley Page knew that the Farman brothers, Doutre and Lioré in France, and Sopwith in England, had all made satisfactory hollow spars and struts, with considerable weight-saving which made nonsense of the square-cube law. By careful attention to detail design and scrupulous testing to destruction of every part drawn, to check its stress calculations, Handley Page and Volkert, assisted by Francis Arcier, achieved their design target weight in an aeroplane of 100 ft span, which could meet the Admiralty specification.

By February 1915, the structural design was established and the Admiralty ordered four prototypes; Handley Page insisted on an advance of £20,000 and, having got it, took it to the local branch of Barclay's Bank and demanded an overdraft of the same amount, failing which he proposed to take his account elsewhere; he got the overdraft too! With only twelve men on his payroll, work went on seven days a week, 9½ hours a day; seeing the excellent progress, Murray Sueter increased the order to twelve and soon afterwards ordered a further 28 machines; more workers were taken on to make details and assemble components, which were taken along the Edgware Road to the 40,000 sq ft Lamson factory at Kingsbury, opposite Colindale Avenue; here a 4 ft wind-tunnel was later installed, to supplement the programme already undertaken at the Northampton Institute, whose aerodynamicist R. O. Boswall took charge of the many tests needed to ensure good stability and control qualities as well as the required performance. By the end of November the payroll had risen to 150 and the Rolls-Royce repair depot in Cricklewood Lane and the skating rink on the Broadway had been taken over; the first prototype was ready at Kingsbury for final assembly, and some of Hendon's famous white iron railings had been removed in readiness for the arrival of 'the world's biggest aeroplane'. The engines installed for the early flights were the second and third examples of the new Rolls-Royce 250 hp, later named Eagle; in the ensuing months these were steadily developed to produce 320 hp, which soon improved the O/100's rate of climb and ceiling to an extent that made armouring against fire from the ground unnecessary, although more petrol tankage was needed; at the same time, the bomb load was increased, using patent bomb slips of Handley Page's own design, and four Lewis guns were installed for self-defence. Early in June 1916 the third O/100 on test at Hendon was flown to a height of 7,180 ft with twenty passengers in addition to the pilot, Clifford B. Prodger.

First deliveries to the Royal Naval Air Service training squadron at Manston were made in October 1916, and the first full squadron, No. 7, flew out from Manston to Coudekerque in April 1917. From then on, as experience grew, the O/100 was increasingly engaged in night bombing, though unsuccessful in daylight, and further squadrons were formed. In May and June 1917 a single O/100 was flown by stages to Mudros in the Aegean, whence Squadron Commander Kenneth Savory and his crew of four bombarded the German and Turkish headquarters in Constantinople, and the warship *Goeben*, on 9 July; further raids were made in September in the same machine by Lieutenant Jack Alcock and his crew, all of whom were taken prisoners by the Turks when forced down by artillery fire into the Gulf of Xeros.

By this time, an improved version, the O/400, with nacelles of smaller size and drag, and larger fuel and bomb loads, had been flown, initially with 320 hp Sunbeam Maori engines; it was ordered, with 360 hp Rolls-Royce Eagle VIII engines, into large-scale production, far beyond the capacity of the existing Cricklewood Lane and Kingsbury works; to meet this challenge, a new factory was built on eleven acres at Somerton Road, Cricklewood, with a drawing office fronting Claremont Road and an adjoining aerodrome of 160 acres at Clitterhouse Farm, on land compulsorily acquired by the Crown as part of the industrial expansion organised by Sir William Weir at the Ministry of Munitions (in their post-war claim for compensation the Ecclesiastical Commissioners sought £43,575 from the Crown, but the Courts awarded them only £31,320); concurrently, smaller components were widely sub-contracted to furniture

O/400 fuselage built by British Caudron at Cricklewood, showing fuel tanks and vertical bomb stowage.

and joinery makers in Kilburn, Willesden, Tottenham and Edmonton. Handley Page had already brought in his younger brother Theodore from the family business at Cheltenham to assist Meredith, and in February 1916 had engaged as works superintendent R. S. Hubbard, who had previously managed the aviation department of William Beardmore & Co at Dalmuir on the Clyde, having served his time with Fairfield's and visited America and Japan while working on submarines. When the United States, after much wavering, decided to join the Allies, the Handley Page O/400 was one of the two large bombers (the other was the Caproni) selected for home production, and Handley Page's American colleague William Workman headed a select team of skilled men sent from Cricklewood to the Standard Aircraft Corporation's new factory at Elizabeth, New Jersey. Handley Page was keen to have American-built O/400s flown across to Ireland, if at all possible, in view of the heavy shipping losses from U-boat attacks in the

Design staff at Cricklewood in 1918; (*left to right*) L. J. H. Richards, C. H. Parsons, Luscher, (next three not identified), M. Lewin, A. Lewin, G. R. Volkert, F. A. Arcier, Lasham, S. T. A. Richards, Sñr Lima. (*S. T. A. Richards*)

Atlantic, and he instructed Workman to attend conferences on this project at Springfield, Mass, in November 1917, but the operation did not materialise.

Throughout the first three years of exceptional wartime activity, Handley Page's energy was prodigious; far from withdrawing from his many outside activities, he increased his support of both the Aeronautical Society and technical education, bringing them closely together whenever possible; nor did he neglect his own philosophical recreation in his brief but regular hours of relaxation. During 1915, while sharing the design and check-stressing of the O/100 with Volkert and Arcier, working often till the small hours, he still found time to read the whole of Gibbon's *Decline and Fall of the Roman Empire*; like most grammar schools founded in the reign of the first Queen Elizabeth, Cheltenham had instilled into Handley Page a sound appreciation of Latin and Greek, both of which he could construe with some facility; consequently he enjoyed the esoteric footnotes in these tongues in which Edward Gibbon had sought to conceal the pithier morsels of Roman scandal from the vulgar gaze, and in later years would translate them with zest for his more privileged friends. In February 1917 he lectured to the Aeronautical Society on *The Case for the Large Aeroplane* illustrated with photographs of the O/100 in production, and a month later he initiated at St Peter's Hall, Cricklewood, in association with the Aeronautical Society, a series of local lectures by such notable speakers as Bertram G. Cooper on *General Design Principles*, E. F. Relf on *Aerofoils and Fluid Flow round Bodies*, Arthur Fage on *Airscrews* and Frank Barnwell on *The Modern Aeroplane*, having cajoled Geoffrey de Havilland into occupying the chair on the last occasion. Nor did he neglect to read the contemporary technical press, and when *Flight* was so unwary in September 1916 as to print 'The Curtiss Aeroplane Co of Buffalo are, as far as we are aware, the first private firm to install a modern wind-tunnel for experimental research work', its editor, Stanley Spooner, received an immediate rocket from Handley Page and next week stated 'Mr Handley Page is to be reckoned amongst the earliest subjugators of the air. He has always been original and well ahead in most things that matter in aviation up-to-dateness. Therefore we gladly give space to his forethought in having long since erected and had running a wind-tunnel, by means of which a good deal of research has been carried out. In fact, as he very modestly puts it, in reference to an airism last week giving the initiative in this respect to the Curtiss Co, "I think we can safely challenge other private firms as to priority in this respect".'

Concentration on the O/400, for which large new contracts were placed late in 1917, did not preclude Handley Page from tackling other quite different projects for the Admiralty. Type P, a single-engined ship-borne triplane bomber with a 320 hp Sunbeam, was little more than an outline sketch, but a small two-seat biplane scout to specification N.2a was awarded a contract for six prototypes known as R/200, having the 200 hp Hispano-Suiza engine. Convertible to either twin-float or deck-landing form, the first two were tested as seaplanes by Gordon Bell from the Welsh Harp late in 1917 and the third was evaluated as a landplane at the Isle of Grain in 1918, the other three being cancelled because of a shortage of Hispanos and the adoption of the rotary-engined Parnall Panther to fill the role. Meanwhile Handley Page, encouraged by Sir William Weir, had tendered to a new requirement for a long-range heavy night bomber capable of attacking distant German strategic targets, including Berlin itself, from bases in East Anglia and Bohemia (Czechoslovakia). After a short delay due to disagreement on bombing policy between the Air Board and the Ministry of Munitions, three prototypes and a hundred production aircraft of Type V/1500, with four Rolls-Royce Eagle VIII engines, were ordered from Handley Page Ltd, initial production being allocated by Sir William Weir to the ship-building yards of William Beardmore & Co at Dalmuir, and Harland & Wolff at Belfast, although design and development were to remain the responsibility of the parent company. Volkert and Arcier, with four senior assistants, moved to Belfast, where Handley Page visited them every week-end to do the check-stressing, returning to Cricklewood on Mondays with all the Irish hams and bacon he could carry.

V/1500 production at Dalmuir works of William Beardmore & Co Ltd in 1918.

Within six months, with all hands working eleven hours a day except on Sunday afternoons, the first V/1500 was ready to be erected and flown at the new airfield at Aldergrove, but this was not yet commissioned; the unassembled components of the first prototype were thereupon shipped to Cricklewood, where it was erected and first flown by Captain Vernon Busby in May 1918; but on its thirteenth flight on 8 June he and four others on board were killed when it crashed at Golders Green; the single survivor was Colonel Alec Ogilvie, Controller of Technical Design at the Air Board, who was in the tail gunner's cockpit and escaped with a broken arm and severe bruises. Eventually three V/1500s were fully operational at Bircham Newton on 9 November, ready to be flown to Berlin by No. 166 Squadron, RAF, but the signal to take-off was not given before the Armistice was signed two days later. Although the V/1500 was thus prevented from fulfilling its intended function as the world's first strategic bomber, the third prototype did after all see brief active service in 1919 by flying to India for operational trials and, whilst there, bombing the arsenal at Kabul during the third Afghan war.

Four days after the Armistice, a party of journalists visited Cricklewood works and saw V/1500s in production, with a new one having just completed its acceptance test flight; on the spur of the moment Handley Page invited the party to experience for themselves the ease and safety of aerial travel; after being fitted out in a motley array of borrowed warm clothing, the journalists (including Geoffrey Watson the official war artist and Arthur Mee the children's encyclopaedist) and several employees—forty passengers in all—clambered aboard the vast empty fuselage and were taken up to 6,500 ft by Clifford Prodger; at that date this was the largest number of people ever airborne in one aeroplane, which was also carrying fuel for six hours. Handley Page's plans for civil aviation in peacetime were indeed already matured some months before Armistice Day, and he greeted the end of hostilities with none of the misgivings of those who saw only the prospect of cancelled contracts, closed factories and widespread unemployment. In the discussion following George Holt Thomas's paper read to the Aeronautical Society on 29 May, 1917, on *Commercial Aeronautics*, Handley Page had disagreed with the lecturer's advocacy of small single-engined aircraft and had said 'When one considers that a load of over six tons has been carried on some machines, it is evident that it is possible to either fly long distances or carry considerable weight for commercial purposes . . . comfort could be supplied for passengers, which was an aspect that should not be neglected, . . . and space could also be provided for mails . . . .' In April 1918 he had raised an additional £100,000 of capital by a banker's debenture charged on the company's plant and buildings; then in January 1919 he converted Handley Page Ltd into a public company and in March the new directors issued 500,000 preference shares of £1 each, which were quickly taken up. The existing ordinary capital stood at £150,000 and contracts in hand totalled £1,787,000, of which £1,301,000 were still to be executed and thus liable to cancellation under the standard break clause; nevertheless, gross profits had risen steadily during the war years from just under £7,000 in 1915 to £22,026 in 1916, £40,783 in 1917, and no less than £224,758 in 1918, and there were no debentures except with the Bank; on the other hand the effects of Excess Profits Duty and cancelled contracts had not been computed at that date, and the final net profit was only a fraction of the gross. Over half of the 794 O/400s and 60 out of 210 V/1500s ordered had been completed before the break clause operated, though many of these, on account of their size, went straight into storage after being flown a mile or two to Hendon. Handley Page had modifications already drawn for converting both O/400s and V/1500s for civil use at very low cost, and in March a furnished cabin mock-up of the former was put on show at Selfridges in Oxford Street. He proposed to form separate companies to operate aerial transport services in all parts of the world where sufficient traffic potential existed, and believed that 'the government should provide the necessary aerodromes and leave the rest to commercial enterprise.' The first such company, Handley Page Transport Ltd, was incorporated in London on 14 June, 1919, with capital of £200,000 wholly owned by the parent company; operations had begun six weeks earlier under the new Air Navigation Regulations effective from 1 May, using minimally converted O/400 bombers to distribute newspapers

Royal visitors at Cricklewood on 7 April, 1919; (*left to right*) the Prince of Wales (later King Edward VIII), Frederick Handley Page, Wing Commander Louis Greig (Equerry to Prince of Wales), Theodore Page and Prince Albert (later King George VI).

as well as to carry passengers. As early as December 1918, the Royal Air Force had started a priority passenger service between Hendon and Paris using D.H.4s and O/400s, two of the latter, named H.M. Air Liners *Great Britain* and *Silver Star*, being specially furnished for members of the government attending the Versailles Peace Conference. In January 1919 a diplomatic and military airmail service had begun with O/400s between Marquise and Cologne, and the London–Paris courier service, with its home base switched in March from Hendon to Kenley, was doubled; valuable experience of cross-Channel operation was obtained and eight O/400s shared the service with two dozen smaller aircraft, maintaining over 90 per cent regularity until the end of October. A civil conversion of the O/400 was first flown at Cricklewood on 4 April, 1919, and three of them were available to carry 800 joy-riders over London during the Easter holiday, when the Air Ministry gave temporary and belated permission for local passenger flights.

On the first official day of civil aviation, three ex-RAF pilots co-opted by Handley Page (Lt-Col Sholto Douglas, Major E. L. Foot and Lieutenant Walker) began carrying passengers and newspapers from Cricklewood to Manchester and Scotland, and also dropped newspapers at many centres by parachute; a week-end passenger service to Bournemouth began with much *éclat* on 5 June, but faded out on 18 August for lack of support. Throughout the summer, joy-riders were taken up daily at Cricklewood to see London from the air, 2,500 of them having free flights at the expense of the *Daily News*. After a press demonstration flight between Hounslow and

Le Bourget on 25 August, Handley Page Transport Ltd began a regular service on this route with a link service between Cricklewood and Hounslow, on 2 September; and in a proving flight on 26 August the first women passengers across the Channel on a public service airliner were Mrs Sholto Douglas (whose husband was at the controls) and Miss Gertrude Bacon, the celebrated balloonist who had also been the first Englishwoman ever to fly—at Reims in 1909; she did not, however, aspire to emulate Sylvia Boyden and Nellie Gibson, who regularly used Guardian Angel parachutes to drop from O/400s for propaganda and entertainment. A second cross-Channel service began in October, to Brussels, but Handley Page's interests were world-wide, and as early as April 1919 he had scooped a contract to supply six fully-furnished ten-passenger airliners (designated O/7) to the Chinese Ministry of Communications, under the very nose of Sir Basil Zaharoff and his carefully protected Vickers interests in the Far East; the first was assembled and flown at Peking on 6 December, 1919, six months before the arrival of the first of the forty Vickers Vimys shipped out to recapture the Chinese market. In September, Handley Page won a monopoly concession to operate a passenger and airmail service across Brazil linking Buenos Aires with Pernambuco, intending to employ twenty-four O/400s over 2,700 route miles in eleven stages, but this scheme was frustrated by political intrigue and came to nothing; similar plans for South Africa and India led in due course to the formation of Handley Page South African Transport Ltd at Cape Town in February 1920 and the Handley Page Indo-Burmese Transport Co at Calcutta in June 1920, while from Bombay came a private order for an O/7, luxuriously furnished in pink silk for the Thakur Saheb of Morvi. In the first year of commercial operation

Interior of O/10 passenger cabin.

ending 30 April, 1920, Handley Page aircraft all over the world flew 100,188 miles carrying 4,460 passengers and 35 tons of parcels, mostly of small bulk but high value, such as silks, jewellery, cosmetics and drugs; their journeys took them through Britain, France, Belgium, Holland, Poland, Scandinavia, Spain, Greece, India, China, South Africa and the USA. But this was only the beginning of Handley Page's peacetime enterprise.

Early in 1919 Handley Page had bought up the Norman Thompson Flight Co, makers of flying-boats at Middleton-on-Sea, Sussex, and followed this relatively trivial transaction by a deal of staggering immensity. Enormous stocks of new and unused aircraft, engines, components and accessories, delivered to the Ministry of Munitions too late for active service, had been congregated at the National Aircraft Factories at Waddon, Castle Bromwich, Heaton Chapel and Aintree, and an Aircraft Disposals Board had been set up at Waddon to auction off these stores. This the Board began doing in a haphazard manner which competed unfairly with the legitimate aircraft industry and was likely to have serious repercussions on public safety; on the one hand, airframes built to a relaxed wartime emergency standard of quality were being converted for joy-riding by shoestring barnstormers and, on the other, useful spares needed by more responsible operators were being sold by weight as firewood and scrap metal. Questions were asked in Parliament and eventually the government agreed to hand over the entire stock to any competent aircraft company or syndicate capable of regulating the resale of the material in a safe and satisfactory manner. Handley Page put in his bid and on 4 March, 1920, the Aircraft Disposal Company Ltd was registered with £600 capital; on the 18th this company appointed Handley Page Ltd as its sole agent and acquired the entire stock of the Aircraft Disposals Board for £1,000,000, plus 50 per cent of all profits on the future sale of over 10,000 airframes, 30,000 engines, and stores which included 1,000 tons of ball bearings, 100,000 magnetos and 350,000 sparking plugs; the purchase money was raised on 5 March by an issue of debentures to the value of £1,080,000 charged on the company's property and, on completing the deal, Handley Page sailed for New York, to assess the prospect of doing business in America. Through the agency of William Workman, who had promoted on his behalf the American Handley Page Corporation at Ogdensburg, NY, in September 1919, he arranged for suitable aircraft to be shipped to New York, and put in a tender for an airmail contract between New York and Chicago proposing, if successful, to carry passengers and cargo also; but here he overplayed his hand for, on 10 July, in the New York Law Courts, the Wright Aeronautical Corporation obtained from Federal Judge Chatfield a perpetual injunction against the sale or use in the USA of any foreign-built aircraft embodying features infringing Wright patents; this, of course, included the use of warping or ailerons to maintain lateral control, so the whole American Handley Page enterprise was killed at one blow, the only two aircraft already shipped being impounded by Customs. At home there was a similar reaction from A. V. Roe & Co, who obtained an injunction in the Chancery Division restraining the Aircraft Disposal Co from selling any goods not of their manufacture as 'Avro' goods, although they did not object to such goods being described as 'of Avro type'. After these initial setbacks, the Aircraft Disposal Co settled down to five years of moderate prosperity, resulting in many valuable orders in later years for replacement aircraft of new types from customers who, but for their initial A.D.C. bargains, would never have bought British at all. Between 1920 and 30 July, 1925, (when the company was reconstituted as A.D.C. Aircraft Ltd to manufacture a new range of engines designed by Frank Halford) 2,000 aircraft and 3,000 engines had been sold and more than £1,250,000 (three times as much as expected originally) returned to the Treasury under the profit-sharing agreement; in 1923 the Aircraft Disposal Co absorbed the Martinsyde Co and for a few years continued to develop its products. Indeed, the Aircraft Disposal Co at one time threatened Handley Page's own position at the head of Handley Page Ltd, for in March 1921 the value of Handley Page Ordinary £1 shares had slumped to one shilling and he was accused by A.D.C. shareholders of having spent £400,000 of their money on promoting air transport services in India, South Africa and Brazil, all of which had failed; an equal amount was owed to the Bank of Scotland and it was the latter which arranged for Handley Page to remain as managing director provided the bank and A.D.C. were each allowed to nominate two new directors to the Handley Page Board, including Lt-Col J. Barrett-Lennard as chairman for six years. This arrangement cost Handley Page the voluntary sacrifice of £179,000 in royalties nominally due to him from Handley Page Ltd, but undoubtedly saved the company from extinction and enabled him to stay at the helm and pursue, as vigorously as a shoestring budget allowed, an experimental programme designed to improve safety and economy in both civil and military aviation; this activity stemmed from the discovery, through improved wind-tunnel techniques, of the slotted wing as a means of realising Handley Page's aim of taking the danger out of stalled flight, which was responsible for so many fatalities during take-off and landing—a problem which was to grow worse every year for a decade until a simple and reliable automatic slot mechanism could be developed and widely adopted. Today, the slot principle is the universally preferred means of obtaining lift augmentation and adequate control at low speeds, although its initial application had been a slow and painstaking business; but persistence was rewarded and before the slot master patents expired in 1938 they had earned more than £750,000 in royalties.

Both slotted wing research and the conversion of serviceable wartime aircraft were additional to the normal pursuit of fresh Air Ministry contracts, but these were few and far between, and new post-war designs and prototypes emerged only rarely from Cricklewood works; the former payroll of over 5,000 had been drastically cut to less than 100 and it was impossible to justify retention of the whole eleven acres of factory floor space; most of it was let off to other industries, as were the nearby factories of the British Caudron and Alliance companies, which had contributed major components to the O/400 and V/1500 production lines in 1918; half a mile away at Temple Road, another wartime plant, the Nieuport & General Aviation Co, closed its doors, later to become part of the motor accessory works of S. Smith & Sons; and Handley Page turned over a large part of the Somerton Road South Shop to motor-car assembly for the Dudley firm of A. Harper Sons & Bean Ltd, who in 1919 began marketing a family four-seater, the 11·9 hp Bean, which enjoyed several years of popularity before being taken over by Hadfields of Sheffield. The Bean car production contract included the complete manufacture of coachwork and final assembly of chassis and mechanical components, and was expected to be worth £750,000 at a time when the actual profit on aircraft work for 1919 was no more than £51,285, of which £30,000 had to be reserved against the future demand (as yet unassessed by the Treasury) for Excess Profits Duty. Another project was the production of the small Anzani-engined Eric Campbell sports saloon, but this was less successful, and indeed the whole motor-car enterprise lost money in the end. In the lean years that followed the car assembly shop was let to Armstrong Siddeley Motors Ltd as a service and repair depot, and to Hooper's the coachbuilders, whose customers ranged from Indian Rajahs to the City of London, (for which they maintained the Lord Mayor's coach). By contrast the tenant of the former works canteen at the far end of Somerton Road, a one-time Cricklewood Lane barrow-boy named Smith, used these premises to manufacture potato crisps, with such success as to become himself a millionaire and his product a household name and nearly a staple diet.

Even as the war ended, one O/400 (C9713) was being progressively modified to incorporate some of the improved structural and aerodynamic features of the V/1500, which itself was soon found to be too big and costly for the commercial traffic needs of the time. Thus was evolved a new post-war multi-engined airliner, Type W, destined not only to replace the O/7 in the Handley Page Transport fleet, but also to render valuable service in the Belgian Congo and New Guinea under the severest tropical conditions of heat and humidity. So well selected and protected were these wooden airframes that they gave trouble-free service for many years and justified Handley Page in delaying to the last moment the inevitable change to all-

W.8 in the Paris Salon in December 1919.

Robert Bager, Test Pilot 1919–20 (*left*) and Geoffrey Hill, Test Pilot 1919–23. (*Both I.W.M.—Crown Copyright*)

metal construction that the Air Ministry began to enforce as a condition in all new contracts after 1924. The prototype W.8 made its maiden flight in December 1919, just in time to fly to Paris for exhibition in the first post-war Salon de l'Aéronautique, whence it flew back to Cricklewood after the show. It was entered in the 'large aeroplane' class of the Air Ministry civil aircraft competition held at Martlesham Heath in August 1920 and, flown by Major H. G. Brackley, won the highest award of £8,000. In 1923 a military variant, the Hyderabad (W.8d) was adopted for No.99 night-bombing squadron of the Royal Air Force and an enlarged three-engined derivative, W.9, was tendered in both commercial and military transport forms for use in the Middle East on the Cairo—Baghdad—Karachi mail route pioneered by the RAF; only the civil version was ordered, but this was retained on the cross-Channel service of Imperial Airways which, in 1924, had been formed by merging Handley Page Transport with its three British competitors to form a 'chosen instrument' to which a Treasury subsidy could be paid. The W.9a Hampstead gave excellent service after its original Armstrong Siddeley Jaguar engines had been replaced by Bristol Jupiters, and ended its days in the New Guinea goldfields, in the worst environment that any wooden aeroplane could be expected to survive. Imperial Airways also operated four twin-engined W.10s, derived inversely by 'civilianising' the Hyderabad bomber, while the latter, re-engined with Bristol Jupiters, emerged as the Hinaidi bomber and Clive troop-carrier. Both these were developed into all-metal versions, Hinaidis remaining in service with four RAF squadrons until 1936, while two metal Clives gave a good account of themselves at Lahore, then in India. Concurrently there had been a succession of prototypes, many designed to exploit the slotted wing, beginning with the Type S single-seat deck-landing fighter and the Type T (Hanley) torpedo-bomber and its two-seat variant the Hendon; the Handcross single-engined day bomber; the Hamlet short-range civil transport; the Harrow naval torpedo-bomber and the Hare high-altitude day bomber. All but the Handcross incorporated progressively improved slot-and-aileron devices, giving positive lateral control at high incidence and steep angles of descent, the Harrow and Hare finally having simplified

Tom Harry England in the Hamlet in 1927.

automatic leading-edge slots near the upper wing-tips only. This was the device that in 1928 was adopted for all RAF aircraft and secured an immediate dramatic reduction in 'stall-and-spin' fatalities after the RAE had failed to produce an acceptable form of linked slot-and-aileron control, and most other air forces throughout the world followed the Air Ministry's example.

After the financial crisis of 1921, when for several months no new aeroplanes were being built and William MacRostie, the works foreman, had only eight apprentices and five men to supervise, the company had remained in business only by drastic economies, including the release of Volkert to join the Sempill mission to Japan, where he held a technical commission in the Imperial Japanese Navy and survived the Tokyo earthquake of September 1923. S. T. A. Richards took his place as chief designer and several tenders were prepared hopefully for the Air Ministry, but the latter could do little to encourage new transport designs.

Volkert had returned from Japan in 1924 to design the Hare and H.P.38, followed by a fleet of very large airliners, exceeding even the V/1500 in span, for Imperial Airways; from 1932 until after war began in 1939, eight of these H.P.42s flew on the European, African and Middle East routes with unfailing regularity—though not much faster than the W.8—carrying thousands of passengers many millions of miles in unprecedented comfort and without any loss of passengers' lives. In consultation with Handley Page's gifted production manager, James Hamilton—like Hubbard, an ex-

Beardmore man—Volkert adopted a Warren-type biplane structure which avoided rigging errors and expense, thus reducing repair and maintenance costs to a fraction of those of the V/1500. Alternative three- and four-engined layouts had been tendered to meet Imperial Airways' specification, and the H.P.42, with four Bristol Jupiters, had been chosen. Not wanting to waste a basically sound design, Handley Page then offered the three-engined variant to the Air Ministry as a bomber-transport (H.P.43) and obtained a prototype order, but on test it proved too slow for the role and was rejected. The low price paid for Handley Page Transport (£17,166 in cash plus 34,344 £1 shares in Imperial Airways) had been a disappointment in 1924, contributing to a net loss on the year's trading of £25,000, but this was retrieved in 1925, when royalties rose from £448 to £5,652 (reflecting the growing importance attached to the slotted wing) and a net profit of

Hinaidi and H.P.42 mock-up at Olympia in July 1929.

£27,600 was declared; in 1927 Barrett-Lennard retired from the chairmanship of the Board to concentrate on the affairs of A.D.C. Aircraft Ltd, in which Handley Page had relinquished his former interest, and in March that year the capital of Handley Page Ltd was reduced from £650,000 to £206,644 by writing down the 150,000 ordinary shares from £1 to 1 shilling each, the 497,860 preference shares already taken up from £1 to 8 shillings each, and cancelling £245,000 arrears of dividend and £2,140 in forfeited preference shares; this brought the issued share capital within the net valuation of the assets-less-liabilities and no call for cash was needed. It was the turn of the tide in the company's fortunes, for the automatic slot had just been adopted by the Air Ministry although Handley Page had to be content with a lump sum award of £100,000 (less £16,000 in tax) from the Royal Commission on Awards to Inventors, in compensation for the Crown's right of free user; in terms of research effort and cost, this compared unfavourably with the earlier post-war award by the Royal Commission of £30,000 for the Type O and Type V aeroplanes. Six months later the United States Navy adopted the auto-slot, paying for the

Tom Harry England ready to take off with Harold Bolas to demonstrate the automatic slot on Bristol Fighter F4967 at Cricklewood on 18 November, 1927, with Col Seely at port wingtip.

perpetual user a royalty of one million dollars (then worth about £200,000 sterling). Similar licences were later acquired by the Swedish, Australian, Canadian and South African governments, and by individual manufacturers, both military and civil, in France, Germany, Italy, Japan and the USA. Much of the credit for the promotion of the slotted wing was due to the unflagging efforts of Handley Page's test pilots, Squadron Leader Tom Harry England and Captain James Cordes, who demonstrated not only Service prototypes at Cricklewood but also slotted versions of the de Havilland Moth and similar light aeroplanes in several energetic and extended European sales tours. Perhaps the most convincing demonstration of the scientific application of slots and flaps was the

Wing Commander Vernon Brown explains the auto-slot to members of Cambridge University Air Squadron during summer training at Old Sarum in 1929. (*Central Press*)

Guggenheim Safe Aircraft Competition promoted at Mitchel Field, Long Island, USA, in 1929, in which the two finalists out of over fifteen entrants were both liberally slotted and flapped biplanes of nearly identical performance; the winner of the $100,000 prize had been the Curtiss Tanager, by virtue of a commodious enclosed cabin and floating ailerons which gave a marginal advantage over the H.P.39 'Gugnunc' in speed range. This adjudication incensed Handley Page because Curtiss had not, at that time, negotiated a licence to use the Handley Page slot patents; he sued the Curtiss company for infringement, and they in turn accused him of illegally importing into the United States a foreign aircraft in defiance of the perpetual injunction granted by Judge Chatfield in July 1920. Eventually Curtiss admitted technical infringement and Handley Page withdrew his action, each side paying its own costs; as Edward P. Warner, one of the Guggenheim competition judges, counselled: 'The disappointment felt in British aviation circles at the defeat of the Handley Page entry should be tempered by satisfaction at this striking demonstration of the value of slotted wings.'

S. T. A. Richards, Chief Designer 1921–24 (*left*) and Dr G. V. Lachmann, Consultant 1922–24, Experimental Designer 1929–31 and 1935–39, Chief Designer 1931–35, Director of Research 1953–65.

Much of the success of the slotted wing stemmed from the enlightened collaboration existing between Handley Page and Gustav Victor Lachmann, a former German Air Force pilot, who had invented even earlier than Handley Page a wing with multiple slots, for which a German patent was refused until at last Lachmann persuaded Professor Prandtl to prove its effectiveness to the patent examiners by a wind-tunnel demonstration (to pay for which Lachmann had to borrow £50 from his mother). After studying aeronautics at Darmstadt Technische Hochschule and gaining a Doctorate from Göttingen University, Lachmann had become chief designer to the Schneider and Albatros firms in turn, and in 1926 went to Japan as technical adviser to the Ishikawajima works at Tokyo, one of whose products was an A.D.C. Cirrus engined light biplane which in 1931 was flown across Siberia and Russia to Europe. Lachmann first met Handley Page (after previous correspondence) in Berlin in 1921 and again at a gliding competition at the Wasserkuppe in 1922; instead of wrangling over the priorities of their inventions, as lesser men might have done, they agreed to continue working independently but in harmony; in 1929 Lachmann joined Handley Page Ltd, bringing with him not only up-to-date knowledge of the aerodynamic research of Betz and Ackeret, but also a thorough understanding of the tension-field theory of structural design developed by Herbert Wagner from his experience at the Rohrbach works; this was at a time when Handley Page urgently needed to change over from traditional space-frame construction to stressed-skin methods; the day of the braced biplane, even in so clean a form as the H.P.50 Heyford bomber, was over, and the change was strikingly illustrated soon after Lachmann took charge of technical development, relieving Volkert of some of the more pressing problems that arose in the transition to streamlined monoplanes with retractable landing gear, variable-pitch airscrews and supercharged engines.

Heyfords of No.99 Squadron being inspected by King George V, attended by the Prince of Wales and the Duke of York, at the Jubilee Review of the Royal Air Force at Mildenhall on 6 July, 1935.

Lachmann was eager to design an all-metal cantilever wing of low drag and weight, and incorporated it in his first prototype, H.P.47, with encouraging results; then he designed a similar larger wing to match the fuselage and tail unit of the H.P.43 and the resulting H.P.51 was resubmitted for official trials, which were so promising that Handley Page received an order off the drawing board for 100 interim bomber-transports (H.P.54, also named Harrow) for the RAF expansion scheme initiated in 1935. Another feature of the H.P.47 was its slender low-drag tubular rear fuselage (originated in Germany by Messerschmitt and adopted in France

King George VI inspects models and components of the H.P.54 Harrow at Cricklewood in 1937, accompanied by *(left to right)* Viscount Swinton (Air Minister), S. R. Worley (Chairman) and Frederick Handley Page (Managing Director).

by Breguet and Potez) which offered minimum masking of the rear gunner's field of fire; this was applied to the next of Lachmann's designs, the H.P.52 which, as the Hampden, was one of the first RAF bombers in action when the second world war began in 1939; it had half-span leading-edge slots and large-area slotted trailing-edge flaps, giving a phenomenally low landing speed and quick take-off. The Handley Page slotted-wing patents were soon to expire, so ending a valuable source of income without which the company might have been forced to close down in the leanest years.

In 1928 the Air Council had bought a Genet-engined Avro Avian III, J9182, which they lent to Handley Page Ltd for auto-slot development and one of Jim Cordes' first assignments, on joining the company as assistant test pilot, was to ferry this machine from Woodford to Cricklewood. From the train to Manchester Cordes watched the weather steadily deteriorating as he went north and found visibility marginal on arrival, but England assured him on the phone that it was quite good near London, so Cordes took off, following the railway line south. As the March afternoon wore on the mist thickened and near St Albans he decided to land while he could still see to do so safely; he chose a large level field between the railway line and Watling Street north of Radlett, where the railway and road converged.

Two chief test pilots go aboard—J. L. Cordes entering a Hampden at Radlett in 1938 (*left*), and H. G. Hazelden before the maiden flight of Victor prototype WB771 at Boscombe Down on Christmas Eve 1952 (*right*).

After taxying to the lee of a hedge he switched off and walked to a farm nearby; the farmer, named Slaughter, helped him to park the Avian for the night and together they adjourned to the Black Horse, whence Cordes phoned to report his whereabouts. After finishing his journey next morning, he told Handley Page that his landing place looked possible for a future aerodrome, but the suggestion was not seriously considered at first. Six months later it had become increasingly evident that Cricklewood was too small and surrounded for larger and faster aircraft, and Handley Page then began urgent negotiations for the purchase of a triangular open site of 154 acres at Colney Street, where a modern factory could be built with ample room for future expansion; by June 1929 it was already being used for flight testing, after earlier diversions to Stag Lane and Hendon, and soon afterwards building of a production flight hangar began there. The Hendon and Hampstead Councils had for some years urged the company to cease flying at Cricklewood, partly because of complaints of low flying and noise, and partly because more land was urgently needed for building development. The sale of Cricklewood aerodrome to the Golders Green Development Corporation realised over £100,000, and the company agreed to vacate the airfield on 8 November, 1929; the new owners then put up a fence along their boundary, cutting off the airfield from the factory and warning the company of the severe penalties attached to any interference with the fence. In spite of strenuous efforts to complete all the various aeroplanes which still had to be flown after having slots installed, one remained undelivered at the final hour; it was the Latécoère 25 biplane, F-AISB of Cie Générale Aéropostale. Insufficient space for take-off remained on the factory side of the fence, so timber ramps were built on both sides; then the Latécoère was wheeled across and flown away at the crack of dawn, without the ramps or the aeroplane coming into contact with the fence. Radlett aerodrome was officially opened by Prince George (later Duke of Kent), who flew there from Northolt on 7 July, 1930, when

Hinaidis and the Gugnunc at Radlett in 1929.

the many distinguished guests included Lord Trenchard. On that occasion the remains of the *Yellow Peril* and the fuselage of the first H.P.42, G-AAGX *Hannibal*, were both on view in celebration of the company's 21st anniversary ten days later; *Hannibal* made its first straight flight at Radlett on 11 November, 1930, flown by England and Cordes as co-pilots. Following the eight H.P.42s came the production of 124 Heyford 'express' night bombers; then, from 1935 onwards, came the first really large-scale production since 1918, with orders for 100 Harrows and 500 Hampdens from Handley Page, a further 770 Hampdens being built by English Electric at Preston, 160 by Canadian Associated Aircraft and 150 (of the Hereford, a variant with Napier Dagger engines) by Short & Harland Ltd at Belfast. To finance this large expansion, the company's capital was increased in 1936 to £323,609, a year later to £448,074 and in 1938 to £572,539.

Ready for dispatch to the RAF—Hampdens at Radlett in 1938.

The climate in the aircraft industry had changed in 1935 with dramatic suddenness, following the Air Staff's decision in May to increase the RAF's bombing strength from 41 squadrons to 68 within the next two years. This resulted from the inability of the Geneva Disarmament Conference to agree on sanctions against Japan after her invasion of Manchuria in 1932, and the subsequent impetus given to Adolf Hitler to claim *lebensraum* for the German republic, of which he had become chancellor in 1933. With Germany instead of France now the potential enemy, with whom 'parity' had to be maintained, the Air Staff had already ordered the development of high-performance monoplanes to supersede the RAF's outdated biplanes, but it was not till March 1935 that Hitler himself told Anthony Eden and Sir John Simon how far ahead of parity the Luftwaffe had already grown, and the Cabinet decided to expand the RAF regardless of the League of Nations' attempt to limit the size of bombers. In February 1936 new classes of heavy bombers, both twin- and four-engined, were specified to follow the stop-gap types already ordered and Volkert's H.P.56 twin-Vulture-engined monoplane was one of the two P.13/36 tenders accepted. When the Vulture ran into development trouble, the H.P.56 was modified to take four Merlins, becoming the H.P.57 Halifax; this proved to have a better overall performance than the Short Stirling designed to B.12/36, although marginally inferior to the Lancaster, which A. V. Roe later evolved from the twin-Vulture Manchester by the same kind of surgery as had converted the H.P.56 into the Halifax.

Immediately war with Germany began in September 1939, the government's shadow factory scheme, already planned, came into operation; Hampdens were already in production by English Electric at Preston, with a parallel line of Herefords from Short & Harland's shadow factory at Belfast, and further contracts were placed for Hampdens to be produced in Canada. Meanwhile, at Cricklewood, the existing first contract for 100 Halifaxes was doubled, and 200 more were ordered to follow the final Hampdens at English Electric. In the spring of 1940 the Cricklewood orders were increased to 400 and a London Aircraft Production Group was formed to co-ordinate Halifax production by the London Passenger Transport Board and their sub-contractors. At first the management of this group was offered to Handley Page for a fee of £36,000, with final assembly at Radlett, but delays in extending the factory led to LPTB themselves managing a new final assembly shadow factory at Leavesden, near Watford.

Plans to produce the Halifax in Canada to follow the Hampden were abandoned when the Atlantic U-boat blockade intensified and two more shadow factories on Merseyside took on Halifax manufacture, one at Speke, Liverpool, being managed by Rootes Securities Ltd and the other at Errwood Park, Stockport, by Fairey Aviation, each starting with a batch of 150. All the firms concerned were experienced in administration and manufacture on the scale required and were fully competent to work independently provided they received the necessary technical information from the parent firm, which thus became consulting engineer for the whole project and supplied all necessary drawings, jigs and flow charts. This required an outside-production office, set up under the chief draughtsman at Cricklewood, J. W. Ratcliffe, assisted by Trapmore of the sub-contracts office, and housed in a new 'austerity' building sandwiched between Claremont Road and the main shops; later a northern office was set up at Preston to support the three firms in that region. The Cricklewood draughtsmen, whose total numbers never exceeded 90 at any one time, produced 13,000 aircraft drawings and 4,000 more for jigs and tools in just over 200,000 man-hours, in time for the Halifax final design conference to be held on Boxing Day 1941.

Expansion at Cricklewood meant building over every available square yard not reserved for access roadways. This created an acute drainage problem, because the old Clutterhouse Farm land had always been waterlogged in winter and now that it was covered almost continuously with concrete and tarmac it was difficult to get rainwater away in a heavy storm; consequently 'Archdale Alley' was often flooded. The Rolls-Royce car service department had long since vacated the old running sheds, but Armstrong Siddeley Cars and Ranton (successors to Hooper) were reluctant to move to the smaller alternative accommodation available. Even Smith's Crisps were forced to leave the old 1918 canteen, which was restored to its original use. The Radlett flight sheds had already been extended during Hampden production and the Colney Street area would have been further developed, but for the wartime necessity for dispersal; so new flight sheds were built at the north end of the aerodrome at Park Street, causing the original owner of the land, Slaughter, to move a few miles south down Watling Street so that his home, New Parkbury Farm, could be demolished. Several cottages in Colney Street suffered the same fate, not without some distress to the older occupiers. The aerodrome itself was extended north across Stroud Wood, which was felled and levelled, through the embankment of the disused Midland Railway branch (whose Park Street bridge remained in isolation across Watling Street) almost to the bank of the little river Ver. On an area now more than doubled, tarmac runways were laid in the standard wartime triangular pattern and telegraph wires flanking the LMS main line were buried underground. When all available space at Cricklewood had been occupied, other premises were requisitioned, including Metro-Goldwyn-Mayer's film studios at Boreham Wood and the Car Mart depot at Neasden. Armstrong Siddeley, having left Cricklewood under protest, had taken over part of the Phoenix telephone factory at Colindale, whence they were horrified and dismayed to be evicted on MAP orders to make room yet again for Handley Page's exploding empire.

At the Leavesden shadow factory, the LAP Group received complete rear fuselages from the Chrysler works at Kew, outer wings, nacelles and engine cowlings from Park Royal and White City, tail units and flaps from the Express motor works at Enfield, and front fuselage shells from Duple Bodies at Hendon; these last components went on to the LPTB works at Aldenham for fitting out before delivery to Leavesden, where the centre sections were also assembled from details and sub-assemblies manufactured in the main LPTB works at Chiswick. The Leavesden shadow factory had originally been assigned to de Havillands, who were to have come into the LAP Group at the beginning, but dropped out to concentrate on Mosquito production and eventually reoccupied Leavesden for this purpose, when the Halifax line ended there in 1945. Co-ordination of supplies between the London factories and those at Preston, Liverpool and Stockport was managed by a committee which met monthly at the Central Hotel, Birmingham, usually under the chairmanship of Thurstan James, who was Director-General of Halifax Production at MAP and later editor of *The Aeroplane*. J. W. Ratcliffe, as usual, represented Handley Page Ltd, whose resident liaison engineer at Preston, F. D. Crowe, also attended; later Crowe joined English Electric as assistant chief designer of the Canberra jet bomber, and renewed his association with Ratcliffe in reverse, when Handley Page undertook limited production of Canberras in 1950–52. All the Halifax contractors from outside the aircraft industry

Winston Churchill and Clement Attlee with a Halifax I during a tour of RAF Bomber Command in 1942.

learned a good deal about light alloys, but in return taught Handley Page quite a bit about interchangeability, especially in the early days. Altogether 6,176 Halifaxes were built in 27 versions by 51,000 men and women in 41 group factories and 600 subcontractors' works, between 1940 and 1946. At the peak of production in 1944, between 38 and 42 Halifaxes were turned out every month by the 500 or so final assembly and flight shed employees at Radlett under their inexhaustible Scots superintendent, William McRostie, and his four assistants Cleaver, Knight, Norman and Whitman. Miraculously the firm escaped serious damage or dislocation by enemy action, with only broken glass at Cricklewood and one bomb dropped amongst parked Halifaxes at Radlett. There were several V 1 flying bomb scares, but no direct hits.

But manufacture was not the whole of the war effort; the pre-war service department had been managed by J. W. Walker and his site supervisor Penfold; by 1940, Hampden production had been entirely transferred to English Electric, who managed site repair parties based at Tollerton, Nottingham, and passed the worst damaged aircraft to the Civilian Repair Organisation at the LMS railway works at Derby, transport of these being handled easily by 43 Group's Queen Mary trailers. Breaking down Halifaxes to minimum-sized components for road transport would have wasted valuable manpower apart from the risk of contaminating hydraulic circuits by breaking pipe joints unnecessarily. With the volume of casualties expected from Nos. 4 and 6 Groups it was necessary to have a fully-equipped repair depot in Yorkshire and this was set up in July 1940 at Rawcliffe, adjoining the York city airport at Clifton. Eric Pickston with thirty picked men from Cricklewood had one Bellman hangar commissioned in time to receive the first crashed Halifax from Linton-on-Ouse and, as more work flowed in, the Rawcliffe depot expanded to six hangars, and then to nine more at Water Lane on the opposite side of the airfield. Halifaxes were brought in by road by No.60 MU RAF, at Shipton-by-Beningbrough, and flown out after repair, modification or overhaul from Water Lane. Most of the workpeople were locally recruited and ranged from coachbuilders to chocolate makers and market gardeners from York, and dock labourers from Hull. One hangar was destroyed and another damaged in the 'Baedeker' raid on York, but this was the only serious interruption. By the end of the war the Service and Repair Organisation employed 2,700 at Rawcliffe and Water Lane, and another 350 in mobile repair parties using ninety assorted vehicles for repairs on site. 320 Halifaxes were completely rebuilt at Rawcliffe and nearly 1,700 others were repaired or overhauled, including 240 flown in from North Africa for major inspections and flown out again. Yet there were only two quite minor accidents, one of them due to over-enthusiasm by 'Specky' Smith, who was supposed to taxy Halifaxes to dispersal after repair, but preferred to do so with the wheels off the ground; for this 'clanger' he was suspended from duty, but had to be re-employed after three days because nobody else could cope with the job quickly enough; he was thereafter forbidden to use more than two engines at a time.

Although the majority of Halifaxes were bombers, many were adapted for coastal, meteorological, heavy transport, paratroop and glider-towing duties; and the Halifax was the only glider-tug approved to tow the Hamilcar heavy assault glider into action on D-Day and at Arnhem. When war ended, many Halifax transports were modified for civil use, twelve (known as Haltons) being specially converted and furnished as airliners for BOAC by Short & Harland Ltd at Belfast. Halifax freighters quickly proved their value in the Berlin Air Lift, mostly in the hands of civil operators, but by this time they had been superseded in front-line service by the Hastings and Hermes, respectively the military and civil versions of a pressurised passenger and cargo transport developed from the basic Halifax airframe; the prototype Hermes crashed on its maiden flight in

Halifax II towing Hamilcar prototype. (*I.W.M.—Crown Copyright*)

Wheeling out the Manx at Radlett in October 1945, with a late production Halifax A.IX in the background. (*Associated Press*)

The Halifax fleet of Bond Air Services at Southend during the Berlin Air Lift.

Hastings following Haltons at Colney Street in 1947.

December 1945, but 25 of the later lengthened Hermes IV, with nosewheel landing gear, were ordered by BOAC for their Empire fleet and remained in service for a further term with charter operators; 152 Hastings were built and served all over the world as transports with the RAF and RNZAF until the end of 1967, several remaining thereafter as radar trainers for V-Bomber aircrews. Two Hermes V prototypes were flown with Bristol Theseus turboprops in place of Hercules piston engines and contributed usefully to turbine flight development in its early stages.

Hastings C.1 TG605 and C.2 WD477 of No.36 Squadron above Kilimanjaro during the Kuwait operation in 1961. (*M.O.D.—Crown Copyright*)

While Hastings and Hermes production provided bread-and-butter for a reduced post-war work force at Cricklewood and Radlett, many other advanced projects were examined and a Handley Page proposal in 1946 for a very fast subsonic bomber led to the drafting of the V-Bomber specification B.35/46 and to the eventual design and production of the H.P.80 Victor bomber, which formed a major component of Britain's nuclear deterrent for ten years, before continuing into the 1970s as a high-speed refuelling tanker. In 1948 an opportunity was taken to expand in the commercial aviation field by acquiring the Reading factory and design organisation of Miles Aircraft Ltd, then in liquidation; this latest take-over in Handley Page's history included completion of the existing production line of Miles Marathon feeder-liners, a few of which saw revenue-earning service in West Africa and Burma, although most were converted into navigational trainers for the RAF. The subsidiary company formed to take over the Miles interests, Handley Page (Reading) Ltd, continued for fifteen years as a separate design and production organisation, bringing out in turn the H.P.R.2 primary trainer, the H.P.R.3 Herald airliner with four piston engines and its more successful development, the H.P.R.7 Dart-

Victors on the Colney Street assembly line in 1955.

Herald with two turboprops, of which fifty were built for operators in all parts of the world; the Herald competed successfully with the Avro 748 as a potential tactical freighter, and was, in fact, preferred by RAF Transport Command, but Handley Page resolutely refused to compromise with the government, when pressed to merge with other aircraft firms under the Sandys plan of 1957, and in due course the contract went to his rival, a member of the Hawker Siddeley Group.

A further important activity since the war, which deserved more active official support than it received, was the company's sustained research, under Lachmann's guidance, into a practical method of boundary layer control, using suction over the whole wing surface to reduce cruising drag and improve range. Formidable structure and material difficulties were overcome and very high L/D ratios were achieved in full-scale flight, but after 1962 the hope of official sponsorship receded and three years later,

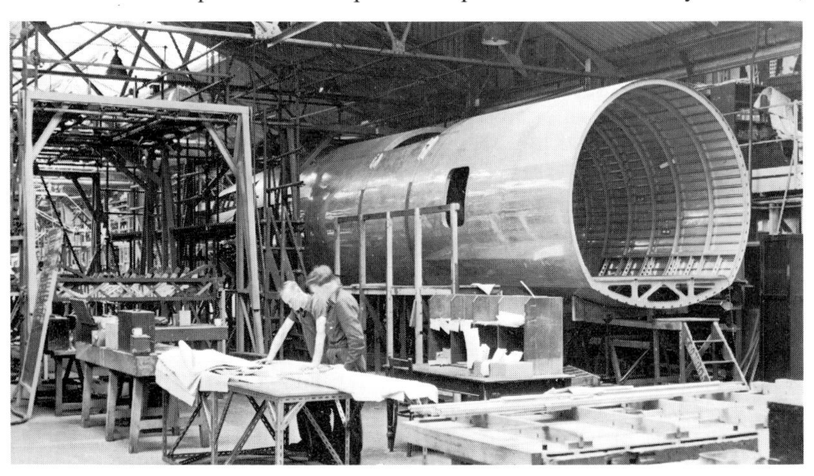

The first Herald prototype in its jig at Woodley in 1954.

Last-minute view of the first Dart-Herald prototype before its engine fire en route to Farnborough on 30 August, 1958. (*Flight*)

when Lachmann retired, the programme was terminated, although similar research was successfully continued in America. The company contributed various design studies to the Supersonic Transport Advisory Committee, in addition to designing and building for the RAE the H.P.115 experimental slender delta monoplane for low speed handling research, which provided essential information for the Concorde project.

Sir Frederick Handley Page, as he had become in 1942, devoted his later years to a multitude of interests, in spite of declining health; chief amongst them, as always, was technical education, and, with Sir Roy Fedden, he was instrumental in founding the College of Aeronautics at Cranfield, remaining chairman of its governing body until he died. He was determined to secure the future of his company on a stable basis and in 1951 nearly £750,000 of reserves were converted into paid-up ordinary stock, raising the capital to £1,319,329. It was mainly for the sake of his long-service employees that he rejected offers to merge with one or other of the big groups; had he been assured, by adoption of the military Herald and reinstatement of cancelled Victors, of a continuing future for his firm, he would have agreed to a merger with Hawker Siddeley, early in 1962, but the offer was bungled by political ineptitude and the opportunity passed with his death on 21 April, 1962.

Under George Russell's chairmanship, the directors of Handley Page Ltd decided to maintain Sir Frederick's lifelong principle of independence, and the company successfully weathered several periods of anxiety and financial stringency to emerge six years later into the civil aviation field encouraged by the world-wide acclaim accorded to its latest venture, the H.P.137 Jetstream; this was a small but sophisticated pressurised transport of outstanding versatility, neatly contrived to fill a real but hitherto unnoticed gap in the spectrum of commercial roles, and with potential utility in a military capacity. In parallel with aircraft manufacture, several aspects of industrial diversification had been successfully exploited, enabling a new range of research and production facilities to be built into a functional but efficient modern factory at Radlett, to be concentrated after 1967 on the future of the Jetstream. At its Diamond Jubilee on 17 June, 1969, with a nominal capital of £2,500,000 and a payroll of around 5,000, the company seemed set for a further period of aeronautical pioneering, but within hours of this anniversary it found itself severely short of ready cash to meet the rapidly escalating cost of getting the Jetstream into production and profitable operation. Although orders and options stood at a total of 182 aircraft, last-minute airworthiness difficulties delayed certification and only a temporary injection of £2·5 million from the principal creditors, Cammell Laird and Barclays Bank, saved the Radlett plant from peremptory closure. Meanwhile the cost of developing the Jetstream, initially computed at £3,000,000, had risen to three times this amount and by the time full certification was in sight in August the bill had topped £13,000,000, representing a break-even requirement for 1,000 Jetstreams to

Sir Frederick Handley Page with Air Cdr Vere Harvey MP and (*left*) the Hon George Ward MP (Parliamentary Under-Secretary of State for Air) after a demonstration flight in the first Victor in September 1953. (*Flight*)

William MacRostie MBE, Works Foreman 1918—Works Director 1958 (*left*) and G. C. D. Russell, Apprentice 1918—Chairman 1966.

be sold instead of the 400 originally estimated. Although the Treasury agreed to contribute £1,500,000 to offset rising development costs, the Ministry of Defence declined to place any immediate production order, and on 8 August, 1969, Handley Page Limited went into voluntary liquidation, Barclays Bank appointing a Receiver. On 16 August the Receiver formed a new company, Handley Page Aircraft Ltd, whose object was solely to continue Jetstream production, all other activities, including non-essential research, being ruthlessly terminated. By 12 September agreement had been reached in principle for a further capital injection of £5 million by K. R. Cravens Corporation, the American owners of the International Jetstream Corporation formed a year earlier to handle sales and service in the New World.

Final negotiations were delayed until the Ministry of Defence had given an assurance that the new company would be an acceptable contractor even if it became American owned. This was forthcoming at the end of November 1969, when Cravens Corporation agreed to acquire Handley Page Aircraft Ltd (the new company) and to repay the £13,000,000 owed by Handley Page Ltd (the old company) through instalments linked to sales of Jetstreams to be manufactured at the rate of five or six per month initially; in addition Cravens provided £2 million as the first instalment of working capital for the new company and a contract to convert eighteen Victors to the tanker role was confirmed. On 31 December, 1969, all assets, work in hand and a payroll of 2,800 were transferred from the old to the new company, with an assurance that when the latter had earned and repaid the accumulated debt, the old company's shareholders would receive a 10 per cent interest in the new company.

So might the Handley Page name have survived, at the price of surrendering the independence that Handley Page had so vigorously professed and fiercely defended all his life, but in February 1970 Cravens' principal American financial backer withdrew its support and on 27 February applied for the compulsory winding up of Handley Page Aircraft Ltd. On 2 March all employees arriving at Radlett were sent home, with the exception of a minimal skeleton staff and product support group to maintain continuity of service for Heralds and Jetstreams as well as the Victors of the RAF. The tanker conversion contract for the Victors already at Radlett was transferred in April, to Hawker Siddeley Aviation at Woodford, who temporarily took over product support management at Radlett, but on 1 June both the old and new Handley Page companies finally ceased to exist. Sales of plant and machinery began in July and final clearance of the factory premises was completed by September, so that the whole site could be sold for industrial redevelopment.

In little more than eight years from their founder's death, the works of Handley Page, a legend in his lifetime, had suffered the same fate as those of Ozymandias, King of Kings; fortunately the more important archives were preserved, through the good offices of the Royal Aeronautical Society and the Royal Air Force Museum, for future students of aviation to contemplate with sympathetic fascination, but, one may hope, without the despair experienced by those personally involved in the 1970 débâcle.

'Farewell! a long farewell to all my greatness!'—Jetstream T.1 XX476 over the hills of Ayrshire in 1973 while on test from Prestwick.

Tucker on the first glider at Creekmouth in 1909.

Early Single-Seat Monoplanes A, C and D (H.P.1, 3 and 4)

Soon after publication of José Weiss's flexible wing patent (No.17150) on 14 August, 1908, Handley Page began building his *canard* glider, with the help of his first employee, Tucker, and his first two premium pupils, Cyril W. Meredith and Arthur Dukinfield Jones. With this apparatus he hoped to emulate the Wright brothers by teaching himself to fly. His attempts to take off from the sloping dykes adjoining Barking Creek were unsuccessful, but at least he learned the necessity for a long skid to bridge the many ditches lying in wait to trip and break an unprotected wheeled chassis; these would have been fatal to an unguarded airscrew. For his first powered machine he may have been unduly bold in choosing a tractor monoplane, but it was cheaper to build than a Wright or Voisin-type biplane, and his primary aim was to fly at minimum cost. Nevertheless, he employed only the best quality spruce, ash, steel plate, piano wire and stranded cable in the construction of his first aeroplane.

The wing, of Weiss's patent shape, had a stiff inner box with four parallel spars and chordwise ribs, with flexible ribs extending radially from the outer ends of the spars. In view of the automatic stability claimed by Weiss, warping for lateral control was deemed unnecessary, and the inner ends of the spars were pinned to the top longerons and wire-braced above to a central vertical kingpost and below to the chassis. The fuselage was boat-shaped, with four longerons tapering to the stern; the two lower longerons converged halfway back to the tail, so that the rear fuselage section was triangular, and the two upper longerons were reinforced at the forward end to act as bearers for the 20 hp Advance vee-four air-cooled engine; a small petrol tank was strapped across the top longerons in line with the leading edge of the wing. The engine was direct-coupled to a 6 ft 6 in diameter two-blade airscrew copied by Handley Page from a design by Weiss for Lascelles & Co; Handley Page was not prepared to buy what he could make more cheaply himself and had begun selling his own popular range of airscrews, enabling him to undercut Lascelles' prices. The control surfaces comprised a cruciform tail unit, combining elevator and rudder and mounted on a universal joint, as in Santos-Dumont's *Demoiselle*. The wing, fuselage and empennage were covered with blue-grey rubberised fabric, and the chassis had a central channel-section ash skid, with a resilient ash cross-axle carrying a lightweight wheel at each end, having tension spokes radiating from wide hubs designed to resist side loads; the axle was stiff enough to carry the static weight while taxying and taking off, but flexible enough for the skid to take the main landing impact.

This first monoplane, Type A or *Bluebird*, was still unfinished when exhibited on Stand No.82 at the second Olympia Aero Exhibition in March 1910, with a price tag of £375, and although the critics were kind no customers came forward. The general opinion was that the empennage was too small and, indeed, on its first trials the elevator power was insufficient to prevent the skid digging into the ground when the engine was opened up; but this was countered by reinforcing the axle and moving it 4 inches forward, at the same time adding a small triangular fixed tailplane.

Bluebird after addition of tailplane in May 1910. (*G. S. Leslie*)

Thereafter the rudder was effective for ground steering at 15 mph and the elevator at 20–25 mph; but it was not until 26 May, 1910, that Handley Page became airborne, only to sideslip into the ground on his first attempt to turn across wind. This indicated the need for positive lateral control to correct overbanking, so during reconstruction Handley Page incorporated wing warping and enlarged the rudder. The single top kingpost was replaced by a twin-strut pylon; the axle was shortened and further reinforced, and the temperamental Advance was replaced by a 25 hp Alvaston flat-twin water-cooled engine driving a heavy square-tipped airscrew; a rectangular multitube radiator was mounted above the engine edge-on to the slipstream and slightly to the left of the centreline so as not to interfere with the pilot's view. But the *Bluebird*, thus modified and now known as Type C, refused to fly in spite of its more powerful engine; so Handley Page next installed a 50 hp Isaacson five-cylinder air-cooled radial, which necessitated further strengthening of the fuselage front-end and chassis, the outer ends of the axle being braced to the upper longerons

Bluebird rebuilt as Type C in 1910 with Alvaston engine, with wings of Type D in background. (*G. S. Leslie*)

by struts incorporating rubber-cord shock-absorbers. This was completed late in 1910, by which time Handley Page had begun work on a new monoplane, Type D, so the modified *Bluebird* was set aside, eventually reappearing in the Northampton Polytechnic Institute's aeronautical laboratory at Clerkenwell, as an instructional airframe.

Type D was designed specifically for the 1911 Olympia Aero Show and work on it began at Barking in October 1910. Robert Fenwick assisted Handley Page with it, and probably designed the fuselage, which was a mahogany semi-monocoque, planked like a carvel boat. Type D resembled Type C, but had a lengthened skid to support the tail, also a divided rudder and single elevator hinged to an integral tailplane. The pilot's controls comprised a handwheel for warping, mounted on a fore-and-aft lever for the elevator and a foot tiller-bar for the rudder; his instruments comprised fuel and oil tank pressure gauges, an aneroid altimeter and, optimistically, a compass, but no airspeed indicator. For the show, Handley Page had borrowed a 35 hp Green four-cylinder vertical water-cooled engine, installed in the nose with tubular radiators below on each flank; the aeroplane was offered for sale at £450 with free flying lessons for the buyer, and was extremely well-finished, but there were no takers. Having to return the Green engine when the show ended, Handley Page had only the 50 hp Isaacson from Type C available, and found it impossible to mount this on the monocoque fuselage, so he had to build a new fabric-covered fuselage; in fact he built a second complete Type D airframe, but kept the wings and tail unit in reserve as spares. On completion, Type D was entered in the *Daily Mail* Circuit of Britain race to be held on 22 July, 1911, with Fenwick as pilot; but he crashed it in landing after its first flight at Fairlop on 15 July and Handley Page, incensed, sacked him on the spot. Type D was quite easily repaired, using the spare components, though not in time for the

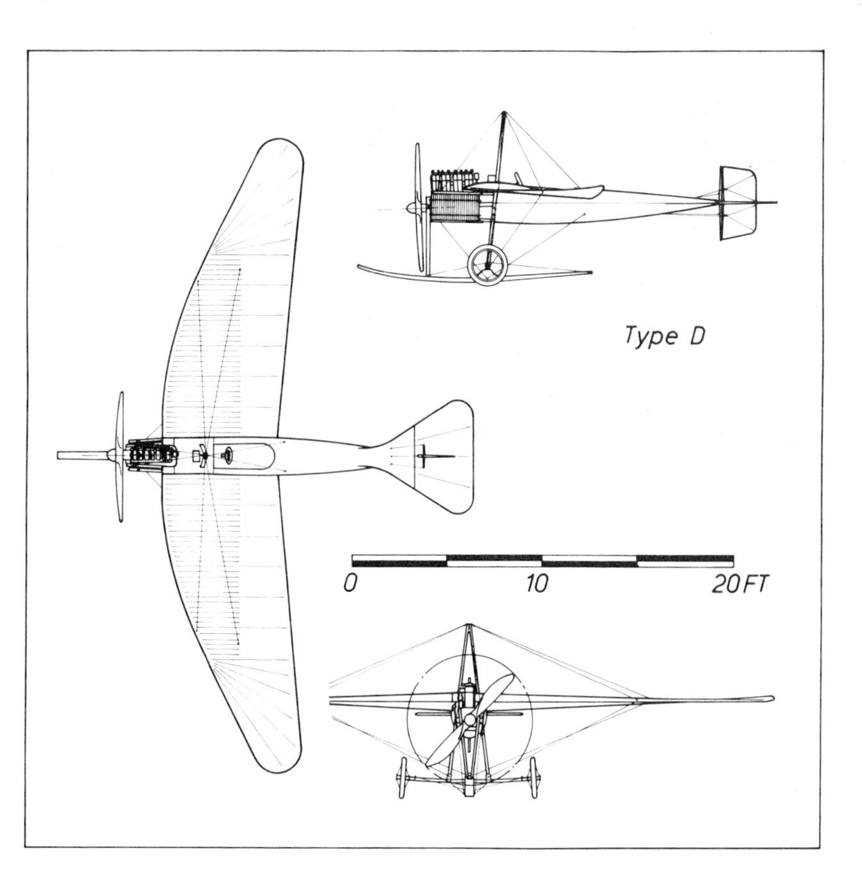

Type D with Green engine at Olympia in April 1911.

race, and in due course re-emerged from Barking works with its wings and tail varnished yellow and all its metal fittings coated with anti-rust paint; Handley Page's new pilot, Edward Petre, named it *The Antiseptic*, although it was also known in the works as the *Yellow Peril*, after the current nickname for Gold Flake cigarettes. Petre flew it several times at Fairlop, but by this time Handley Page had received the results of further wind-tunnel work by Rupert Turnbull on reflexed aerofoils, and had improved on the original Weiss wing shape sufficiently to attempt a passenger-carrying monoplane, which was more likely to appeal than a single-seater.

Monoplane A

(20 hp Advance)

Span 32 ft 6 in (9·9 m); length 20 ft 6 in (6·25 m); wing area 150 sq ft (13·9 m²). Empty weight 300 lb (136 kg); loaded weight 450 lb (204 kg). Speed 35 mph (56 km/h). Pilot only.

Monoplane C

(25 hp Alvaston)

Span 30 ft (9·15 m); length 21 ft (6·4 m); wing area 150 sq ft (13·9 m²). Empty weight 250 lb (113 kg); loaded weight 450 lb (204 kg). Speed 35 mph (56 km/h). Pilot only.

Monoplane D

(35 hp Green)

Span 32 ft (9·76 m); length 22 ft (6·71 m); wing area 156 sq ft (14·5 m²). Empty weight 420 lb (190 kg); loaded weight 600 lb (272 kg). Speed 40 mph (64 km/h).

Monoplane D

(50 hp Isaacson)

Empty weight 440 lb (199 kg); loaded weight 620 lb (281 kg). Speed 50 mph (80 km/h). Pilot only.

Early Two-Seat Monoplanes E, F and H (H.P.5 and 6)

With Edward Petre's unflagging energy and enthusiasm in the Barking factory, and a wind-tunnel readily available at the Northampton Institute, Handley Page made quick progress with the design of a tandem two-seat monoplane, Type E, hoping that it might be suitable for the Army aeroplane competition promoted by the War Office in the closing weeks of 1911; but when the proposed rules were announced, he declared the specified gliding angle (even if capable of being measured in actual flight) to be unattainable and the prize money much too small to compensate for the effort entailed. Then the stock of the Aeronautical Syndicate Ltd, including several 50 hp and 70 hp Gnome engines with spares, came on to the market and Handley Page snapped it up at a bargain price; having taken his pick and sold the remainder at a fair profit to George Holt Thomas, Handley Page was left with an ample supply of new materials and decided to complete Type E as a demonstration machine and to build an improved

Yellow Peril at Brooklands in July 1912 after flying from Fairlop.

monoplane to match the War Office specification as closely as possible; to assist with the latter he enlisted the aid of Edward Petre's elder brother Henry. The best of the ex-ASL 50 hp Gnomes was installed in Type E on completion in April, and on the 26th Edward Petre flew it for several straight hops at Fairlop. Before long he was flying circuits and by the end of June was confident enough to fly six miles across country to the Barking works; considerable damage resulted in the unavoidably difficult landing on rough ground, but the engine was unharmed and the machine was improved during the necessary rebuilding. As soon as repairs were completed, Petre's qualifying flights for a Royal Aero Club certificate (No.259) were officially observed at Fairlop by Tom O'Brien Hubbard and C. G. Grey on 24 July. On 27 July he flew Type E from Fairlop to Brooklands via Rainham and along the course of the Thames to Kew; this was the only legal route across London since flying over built-up areas was prohibited, and his time for this tortuous passage of 55 miles was 50 minutes, in gusty weather but helped along by an easterly wind.

As it first appeared at Brooklands, Type E was a handsome monoplane, similar to Type D (as rebuilt) but more robust. The two-spar crescent wings had extended flexible trailing edges near the wing-tips, somewhat in the Etrich style, and the fuselage was basically a rectangular frame of four ash longerons, tapering to a vertical wedge at the tail and extended below by a deep curved keel to form a deep belly of triangular section; it was wire-braced and fabric-covered, being faired by decking and stringers to a more or less streamline form. The cabane structure comprised two inverted V-struts rising from the wing spar root fittings and joined above the centreline by a horizontal tie-rod; at the outer ends of the rear spar, the wing was braced by kingposts to restrict spanwise flexure, leaving the wing-tips to twist in response to the warp control. The small rear cockpit was occupied by the passenger, while the pilot in the larger front cockpit had the same type of handwheel and central control column as in Type D. The original grey rubberised fabric had been replaced during rebuilding by linen tautened and proofed by cellulose nitrate dope, and smartly finished in yellow varnish for the wings and tail, and blue varnish for the fuselage, specially produced by Jenson & Nicholson Ltd whom Handley Page had encouraged to experiment with cellulose lacquers after their success in producing 'Robbialac' enamels for bicycles and automobiles. At Brooklands it quickly acquired Type D's earlier soubriquet *Yellow Peril* which pleased Handley Page but has often confused latter-day historians. The tail surfaces consisted of a slender triangular tailplane with divided semi-elliptic elevators and a rudder of similar shape, with a long narrow fixed fin above the tailplane. The sturdy landing gear comprised a central skid and two wheels carried on centre-hinged swing-axles and spring-loaded telescopic struts, together with a long resilient tailskid. In front of the pilot's cockpit and under the decking behind the engine mounting plate were installed side by side a pair of cylindrical tanks, for petrol to starboard and oil to port, each having a vertical sight glass in the rear end; the petrol tank was pressurised by air from a handpump at the pilot's right hand, near the magneto switch; the only instruments were an engine tachometer in the centre dash panel between the tank ends and a petrol feed air-pressure gauge on the port side. The engine was carried on an overhung mounting and enclosed above in a partial cowl whose function was primarily to prevent oil being thrown back on to the pilot's goggles.

Type E remained at Brooklands during August while the military trials on Salisbury Plain claimed a temporary diversion of interest, and during this period Handley Page moved his factory from Barking to Cricklewood, with a flight hangar at Hendon, to which Type E should have been flown on 28 September to join a review by Major Carden, RE; but Petre was indisposed and on 5 October Lieutenant Wilfred Parke, RN, ferried it across from Brooklands to Hendon and was so well pleased that he continued flying it next day for some hours, taking up several passengers including Mrs de Beauvoir Stocks and Eric Clift, the latter having installed a compass of his own design. On the following Sunday, 13 October, Parke took up a dozen passengers, including Robert Blackburn and the Hendon aerodrome manager Richard Gates; then he took up two children (a total live load of 367 lb) for 20 minutes and finally flew to Brooklands with Mr Nicholson of Jenson & Nicholson, before returning to Hendon; during these two week-ends at Hendon, Parke had carried 28 passengers. He flew it again on 20 October, making a careful assessment of its handling and stability, and Handley Page invited several other pilots to sample it, but on 31 October one of them, Desmond Arthur, flew too low and scraped the railings, breaking the airscrew, one wing-tip and one landing wheel.

During repairs at Cricklewood, a revised fin of triangular shape was fitted and Type E's first flight in this form was made by Sydney Pickles on 1 February, 1913, and after several circuits he reported a distinct improvement in its flying qualities. Next day Pickles was up at dawn taking up three passengers for short joy-rides, before setting out with Cyril Meredith, newly appointed works manager, to fly to Barking. Although the wind had risen to 20 mph at ground level, they made a start, but found half a gale higher up, blowing from the southeast, and after 30 minutes in the air had only succeeded in reaching Sudbury, a mere five miles from Hendon and in the wrong direction; so they abandoned their journey and returned to their starting point in six minutes; this was a striking demonstration of

Yellow Peril with ailerons and modified fin at Hendon in May 1913.

the value of automatic stability in rough weather. Type E then returned to the works to be cleaned up for exhibition at the 1913 Olympia Aero Show which opened on 14 February. A Stolz Electrophone, for communication between pilot and passenger, was installed and this was favourably noted by King George V when he visited stand No.54 after declaring the show open. The Handley Page show brochure was decorated on its front cover with a perspective outline sketch of Type E—the first drawing made by George Volkert at Cricklewood, but he immediately followed this up with a scheme to convert the lateral control from warping to ailerons. As soon as this design was complete, a new pair of wings with ailerons was made and these were fitted during April; on 1 May Type E was flown for 45 minutes by the firm's newly appointed staff pilot Ronald Whitehouse, who reported that the ailerons had cured the former tendency to roll from side to side in level flight. On 10 May Pickles flew it again, via Brooklands and Farnborough, to take part in exhibition flights at Winchester polo ground, returning on the 17th in time for the Hendon race meeting, in which he flew

Ronald Whitehouse taking off in *Yellow Peril*.

in the 16 miles cross-country handicap, followed by Whitehouse in the speed handicap. On the 25th Whitehouse burst a tyre while landing, without any damage, and on the following Sunday he took up his mother for her first flight, which she much enjoyed.

A fortnight later Whitehouse began a series of exhibition flights in provincial towns, starting with Buxton, Leicester and Mansfield, moving on to Lincoln for a week, then into Yorkshire to Hull and Beverley. Most of these four-day programmes included races and more or less spectacular stunts, such as bombing with flour-bags. Unrehearsed incidents were inevitable and at Hull Whitehouse was forbidden to fly within the city boundary on Sunday 13 July, the Mayor having invoked the Lord's Day Observance Act of 1625, with the support of the Wesleyan mission and the Hull Education Committee; on the previous evening Whitehouse had decided to defy the ban, but then, as if by divine intervention, had taxied into a watery ditch, breaking the skid and airscrew; he wired urgently to Hendon for spares, which arrived by train next morning after he had worked all night stripping the damage, and by Sunday evening he was airborne once more, to the cheers of 7,000 Sabbath-breakers, some half of whom had had their names taken by the police; however, on finding that the display had taken place outside the city limits, the Hull magistrates declined to issue summonses, and were perhaps swayed by the legal argument that, under a much earlier Act, a monoplane might be held to be an arrow, which made the assembly a perfectly lawful archery practice. Whitehouse's effort was indeed exceptional, for the engine had been entirely submerged for over four hours during initial salvage; in return his admirers in Hull presented him with a purse of gold sovereigns. After four days at Hull, he continued his tour and concluded with four days at Burton-on-Trent over the August Bank Holiday week-end. He then flew Type E back to Hendon, where Handley Page reluctantly prepared to fly it himself in consequence of his ill-advised wager with Noel Pemberton Billing on 17 September, but was fortunately relieved of this trial by ordeal by Pemberton Billing's early success.

By this time Type E had carried several hundred passengers and had flown several thousand miles across country, so was due for a major overhaul. With his new Type G biplane nearing completion, Handley Page agreed to make Type E available to George Beatty, who had just

Yellow Peril in the Beatty Flying School at Hendon after conversion to single-seater in 1914.

inaugurated a flying school at Hendon, with Édouard Baumann as assistant chief instructor. For this purpose it was converted into a single-seater with the rear cockpit deleted and the cabane modified to a pyramid structure; at the same time the original landing gear was replaced by a twin-skid cross-axle chassis of B.E.2 pattern; some time earlier a simplified rubber-sprung tailskid had been fitted. Intended for use by advanced pupils who had gone solo, Type E was first flown as a single-seater on 4 July, 1914, by Baumann and a week later his best pupil Ruffy began flying it solo, but with the outbreak of war in August it was requisitioned, only to be rejected as unfit for Service use, although its engine was retained. After being returned to Cricklewood it was stored for many years, being brought out in July 1919 to take part in the 'Victory Parade' which celebrated the signing of the Versailles Treaty, and later again at the official opening of Radlett aerodrome by Prince George in July 1930. Thereafter it hung in the rafters above 'Archdale Alley' until 1940 as one of Handley Page's most cherished relics; then works manager James Hamilton, urgently needing more space, unwarily consigned it to the incinerator without the owner's knowledge (and had his knuckles rapped later), but it had already become so decrepit that continued preservation would have been difficult.

In contrast to Type E, the contemporary military trials monoplane, Type F, was short-lived and unlucky from the beginning. Technically, it was an advance on Type E and followed closely the requirements of the War Office specification in respect of good view and protection for pilot and observer, who sat side by side in a deep commodious cockpit, with unobstructed all round vision in the upper hemisphere and additional downward view through the 'Cellon' covered entry hatch alongside the observer in the port seat. The 70 hp Gnome rotary engine was fully enclosed, for silence, in the streamlined nose, with central air entry around the airscrew boss and exhaust and air exit diffused through multiple slots in the under belly. The crescent wing, with warp control, was very stiff from root to a kingpost at 60 per cent of the semispan and braced by stranded steel cables to a cabane of regular pyramid shape, formed by two triangular frames hinged to the upper longerons alongside the cockpit and joined at the apex by a pair of $\frac{5}{8}$ inch bolts; thus the wings could be quickly assembled and their cables tensioned simply by bolting up the two halves of the cabane. The front spar was 10 inches deep at the root and the planform of the wing was lenticular without the tip chord extension of Type E. The rudder was polygonal, without a fixed fin, and the large tailplane, nearly semicircular in plan, carried small separate elevators. The fuselage had flat sides and was faired above and below to give minimum drag. The very robust landing gear had swing axles and telescopic spring struts as in Type E and the long central skid was intended to support the tail while taxying, but it was found necessary to add a tailskid of crossed rattan hoops in the early Blériot style. The pilot's instruments comprised an Elliott airspeed indicator, a tachometer, fuel tank air pressure gauge and a Clift compass. Within the general layout sketched out by Handley Page, the design of Type F was detailed by Henry Petre, who was nominated to fly it in the military trials (No.28), but he distrusted Handley Page's crescent wing and had a second pair of wings made with equivalent sweepback but straight leading and trailing edges. The machine was the last to be built at Barking, and while Handley Page and Edward Petre were preoccupied with moving to

F/70 at Hendon in November 1912.

Cricklewood, Henry Petre had the straight wings assembled for the first flight; but Edward warned his brother of the consequences of disagreeing with Handley Page on so important a matter and had the crescent wing reinstated in time to be seen and approved by Handley Page on his next visit. But Henry declined to fly it except with straight wings, so Edward took his place and the monoplane was transported to Larkhill, packed in a crate as specified, almost too late for acceptance.

There had been no time for a previous test flight and its engine, one of those bought from the Aeronautical Syndicate, was not as well tuned as could have been wished, but on the afternoon of 21 August, 1912, it was brought out of its hangar at Larkhill and flown successfully in very blustery

F/70 flying at Hendon on 17 November, 1912.

weather, showing the same wallowing tendency as Type E in its pre-aileron days; while taxying back to the hangar, the skid caught a tussock in the turf and the monoplane nearly stood on its nose, but settled back without damage. Next morning Petre brought it out again for a short check flight before starting the official 3-hour endurance test, but the engine misfired after take-off and cut out completely as he turned downwind; he had no other choice than to alight near the Bristol sheds, overrunning almost into the chains surrounding them, finally having to swerve to avoid bystanders; while across wind, a 30 mph gust lifted one wing, smashing the other and the landing gear. So Type F was out of the competition; inspection showed it to be beyond repair on site to fly back to Hendon, so Handley Page had the expense of taking it back by road. New wings and landing gear were manufactured at Cricklewood, and Type F was flown again on 9 November by Wilfred Parke, who had been waiting a month for the opportunity. He liked it so much that he flew it almost daily thereafter, with mounting enthusiasm, and recommended it as a potential scout for naval use. On the 17th he took up W. E. de B. Whitaker of *The Aeroplane*, and had carried over fifty passengers by the end of the month. On Sunday 24 November, Parke flew it across country to Brooklands with Handley Page's cousin,

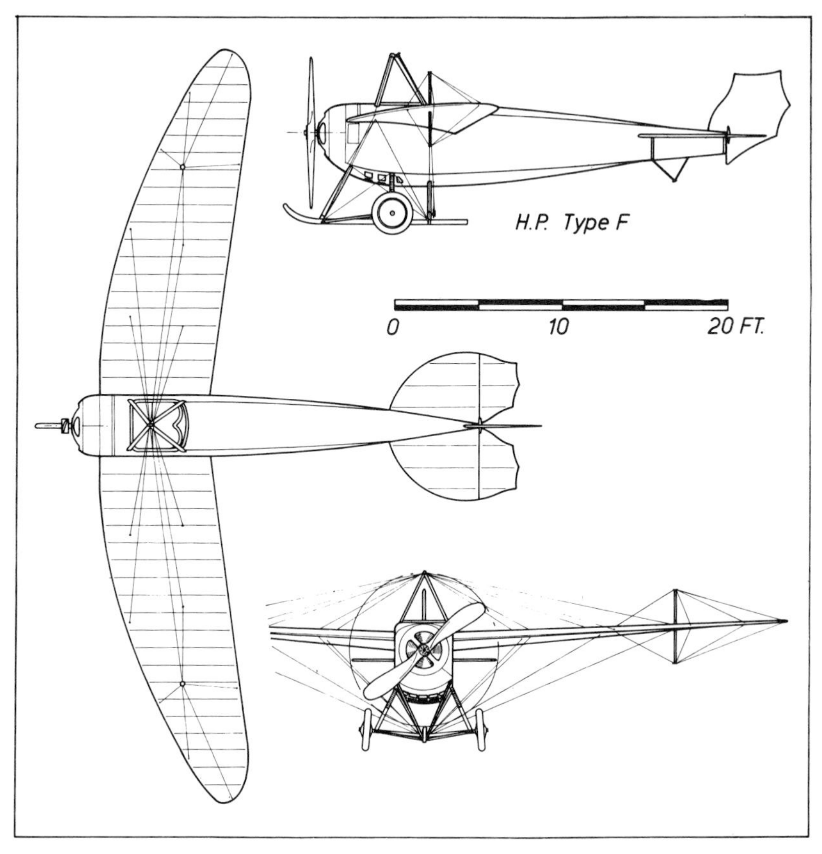

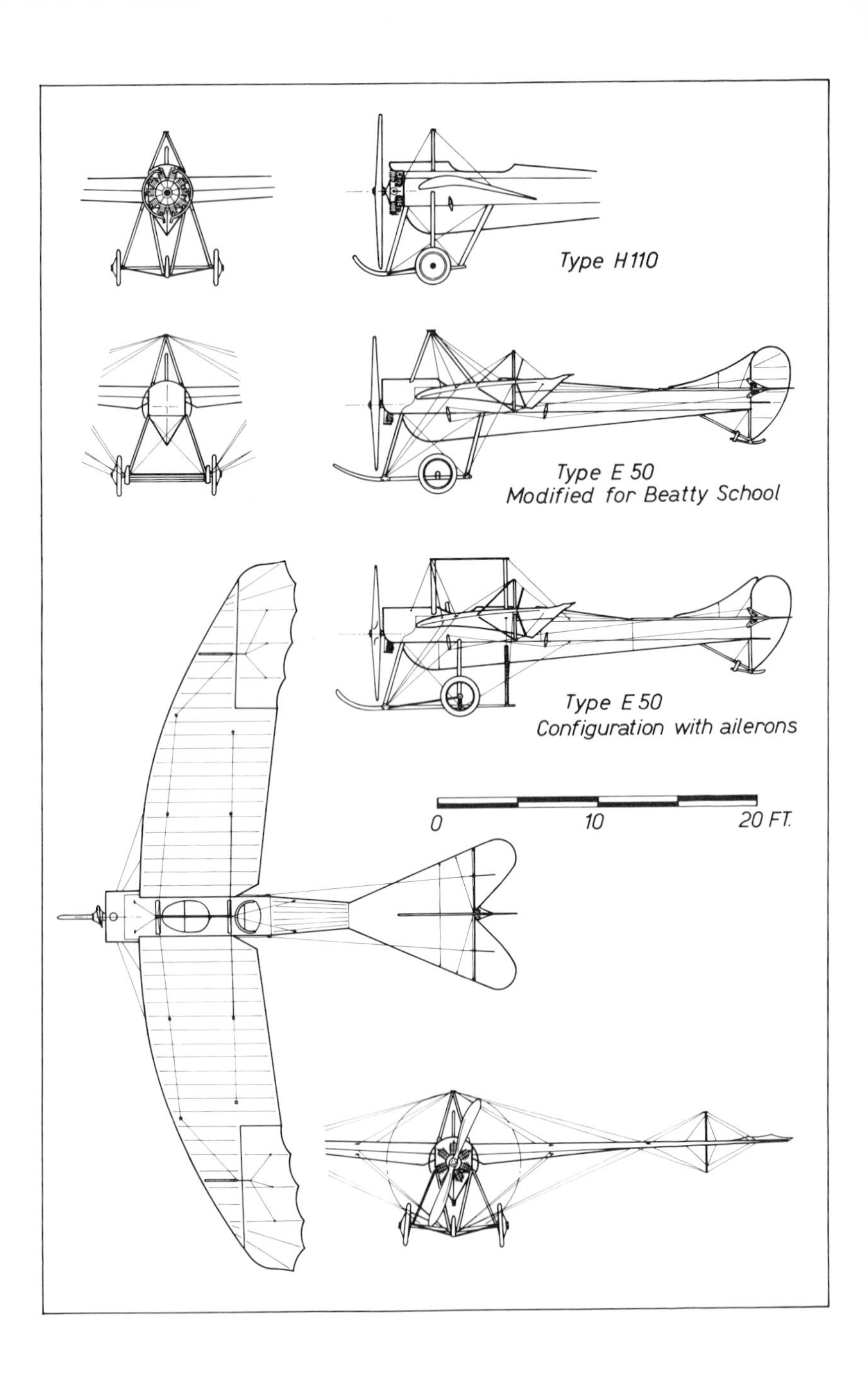
Type H110
Type E 50
Modified for Beatty School
Type E 50
Configuration with ailerons
0
10
20 FT.

Trevor Handley of Southsea, as passenger, but had to land in a ploughed field at Sunbury-on-Thames with a choked petrol pipe; Trevor Handley completed his journey by road, but Parke managed to clear the stoppage and took off solo, arriving at Brooklands in time to fly his passenger back to Hendon and thereafter to take up twelve passengers (including René Desoutter) for short flights. On the following Saturday, 30 November, Parke again flew to Brooklands, this time with Tony Fletcher, Handley Page's erstwhile apprentice, now with Martin & Handasyde. Helped by a northeaster gusting to 45 mph at ground level, as measured by the Hendon anemometer, the 23 miles were covered in only 14 minutes, at a ground speed of 99 mph.

A week later, Parke flew back to Hendon in driving mist with less than one mile visibility, locating the aerodrome from a fleeting glimpse of the Welsh Harp reservoir; on this occasion his passenger was Handley Page's works manager, A. Arkell Hardwick, and a new tailskid of B.E. pattern had been substituted for the cane hoops. C. G. Grey was at Hendon next day to watch Parke flying Type F in gusty conditions; he noted the effectiveness of the crescent wing in restoring an even keel after repeated upsets, and remarked that the engine sounded very rough, but Parke did not consider this to be serious. On 15 December, with Hardwick once more in the passenger seat, Parke took off from Hendon, intending to fly to Oxford, but the engine was giving much less than its normal power. He gained height slowly, but was only a few hundred feet up at Wembley, when the engine failed completely while crossing a belt of trees; these created a downwash which gave Parke no chance of recovering from the stall and incipient spin caused by the sudden loss of thrust, and both men were killed in the crash. So ended two promising careers and Handley Page's immediate prospects of supplying scouts for the Royal Navy; the War Office had already imposed a ban on monoplanes and was prepared to purchase from British contractors only biplanes of the Royal Aircraft Factory's design. The designation H was used, somewhat anomalously, for a projected Type H-70, drawn by H. A. Petre, which appeared to be identical with Type F, and had a 70 hp Gnome (drg. No.542); also for Type H-110, drawn by G. R. Volkert as an improved version of Type E, with a 110 hp Anzani radial and both seats in tandem within a single elongated cockpit, the main fuel tank being moved aft (drg. No.590); it seems that these were prepared for presentation to the Admiralty on the recommendation of Wilfred Parke.

E/50

(50 hp Gnome)

Span 42 ft 6 in (12·9 m); length 28 ft 2 in (8·6 m); wing area 240 sq ft (22·3 m^2). Empty weight 800 lb (363 kg); loaded weight 1,300 lb (590 kg). Speed 60 mph (96 km/h); endurance 3 hr. Pilot and passenger (tandem). (Length after rebuild as single-seater 27 ft (8·23 m)).

F/70

(70 hp Gnome)

Span 43 ft 6 in (13·7 m); length 30 ft 2 in (9·2 m); wing area 250 sq ft (23·2 m^2). Empty weight 850 lb (386 kg); loaded weight 1,450 lb (657 kg). Speed 55 mph (88 km/h). Pilot and observer (side by side).

Type B at Barking in October 1909. (*G. S. Leslie*)

Early Biplanes B, G, K, L, M and N (H.P.2, 7, 8, 9 and 10)

The first biplane made by Handley Page was not of his own design, although he contributed a very substantial amount of alteration before it became a practical proposition, and so acquired the company designation of Type B. It was the invention (rather than design) of a Liverpool patent agent, W. P. Thompson, who had registered several ingenious methods of adjusting wing area and centre of gravity position as a means of control and manoeuvre. Unfortunately he had no idea of economy in structure weight and proposed to use tubular frameworks with ordinary plumber's screwed joints. He took out six aeronautical patents of no real merit between 1893 and 1908 and had evolved a biplane layout with both pilot and engine below the wing to ensure 'pendulum stability'. He met Handley Page in 1909 and commissioned a prototype, which was built at Barking as a biplane of orthodox spruce and fabric construction; much of the work was done by Thompson's assistant Robert Fenwick, who was very much more aware of the problems and pitfalls than his employer, and insisted on having long tail booms carrying a biplane elevator and a pair of rudders. Type B was completed in October 1909 and originally had two propellers mounted level with the lower wing and chain-driven by a 60 hp Green engine installed below the wing, with the pilot seated ahead of the engine. The undercarriage comprised a pair of main landing wheels under the wing on either side of the pilot's seat, small outrigger wheels under the wing-tips, and a tailskid. Fenwick attempted a flight at Barking, but almost at once the main wheels buckled, and while repairs were in progress the factory shed was partly demolished by a gale, causing further damage. Handley Page considered Type B to be a failure and not worth repairing, but allowed Fenwick to rebuilt it at Thompson's expense, and in spite of its derisory nickname of 'The Scrapheap' Fenwick succeeded in making good most of the damage during the spring and summer of 1910, finally sending it by rail to Freshfield, Lancashire, where Thompson had equipped a flying ground and registered his enterprise as Planes Limited. Before completion, Fenwick added ailerons and improved the tail unit; he also discarded the chain-driven twin propellers in favour of a single one direct-coupled to the engine. On 29 November, 1910, Fenwick was rewarded for his efforts by calm weather in which he succeeded in flying far enough and high enough to qualify for Royal Aero Club certificate No.35. A few days later, when the weather broke, he crashed, but the machine was once more repaired and eventually flown from the sands at Formby; but by this time its origin had been forgotten and Handley Page was glad to forget it.

The second Handley Page biplane resulted from the War Office ban on monoplanes being flown by the Royal Flying Corps, after a spate of accidents in the late summer and autumn of 1912; in consequence the only War Office contracts offered to British manufacturers were for B.E.2a biplanes designed at Farnborough and Handley Page had moved from Barking to Cricklewood in expectation of a substantial share in this programme. He was disappointed to find that only five B.E.2as were required in his first order and exasperated when he tried to buy the small quantities of special high tensile steel required by the Royal Aircraft Factory specification; the large armament and shipbuilding firms like Armstrong Whitworth and Vickers already held ample stocks, but Handley Page resented being charged high prices for small offcuts and refused to accept any further B.E.2a orders unless much larger contracts were offered. Two of the five B.E.2as were delivered after some weeks' delay in making good the critical shortages and meanwhile Handley Page had engaged George Volkert as chief designer and instructed him to develop a biplane as good as the B.E.2a, but using the materials already at hand and the experience gained with the Type E and F monoplanes; the third B.E.2a was not completed till 1914 and the other two were cancelled. While the new biplane, Type G, was under construction in 1913, the design was shown to a

G/100 with brass-tipped Chauvière airscrew at Hendon in November 1913.

pupil of the Beatty School at Hendon, Rowland Ding, who, with Lindsay Bainbridge and others, had taken over the Lakes Flying Co from Captain Wakefield at Bowness-on-Windermere and restyled it the Northern Aircraft Co; they were expanding their seaplane school and Ding offered to buy Type G on completion provided it could be equipped with floats. Accordingly it was given a twin-skid chassis, but Handley Page persuaded Ding that as a landplane it would be excellently suitable for exhibition flying from public open spaces, where crowds of spectators could be equally dangerous to the aircraft and themselves. Originally intended to have a Green engine of 100 hp, Type G needed only a very short take-off and landing distance, with steep initial climb and approach. It was derived mainly from Type E, having a closely similar fuselage and tail unit; the upper wing was almost the same as Type E's in its final state with ailerons, while the lower wing was similar to Type F's wing, but with a smaller aspect ratio. The upper wing was made in two halves butted together at the centre line, while the lower wing was in one piece from tip to tip; the wings were staggered, with spruce interplane struts arranged in 3-bay formation, with the fuselage mounted at mid-gap. Only a single strut could be accommodated at the outboard position because of the taper, and to prevent wing-tip torsion the leading edges were braced to this strut by steel tubes. The twin-skid chassis was robust and carried a straight rubber-sprung cross-axle with two Palmer wheels. The engine actually installed was a 100 hp Anzani ten-cylinder air-cooled radial of less weight than the Green, driving a two-blade Chauvière airscrew with brass-sheathed tips; petrol and oil for 4 hours were carried in tanks on the decking forward of the front cockpit, which was roomy enough for two passengers on a short joy-ride. As in the B.E.2a, the pilot occupied the rear cockpit, where he had the usual controls, the aileron handwheel being mounted on an arched frame hinged from the lower longerons, instead of a central column; at first there was no decking between the cockpits.

In this form it was first flown by Ronald Whitehouse just before dusk on Thursday 6 November, 1913; he began with several slow short straights, then made a circuit and finally invited Cyril Meredith (now Handley Page's manager in succession to Hardwick) into the front seat for a trip. A further flight was made on Sunday the 9th, when Whitehouse recorded one of the first bird-strikes by decapitating a partridge, which was later retrieved and enjoyed for supper, the metal-clad airscrew being undamaged. By the 26th, he had progressed to flying for over an hour at 3,000 ft, where the motion was so steady that Ding, in the front cockpit, wrote a long letter without difficulty; later the same day he took up Meredith again, and Lindsay Bainbridge, the nominal owner-to-be. Final acceptance tests were made on 12 December, when Whitehouse climbed with two passengers to 3,000 ft at 300 ft/min and cruised at that height for 20 minutes; next, with one passenger and full load, he was timed over a measured course at 70 mph maximum and 35 mph minimum, and the same afternoon he flew across country to Farnborough for official performance measurements. He returned on the 14th via Oxford and Prince's Risborough, narrowly avoiding the cords of two advertising kites as he came in to land over Colindale Avenue. The only modification suggested by the Royal Aircraft Factory was a small increase in tailplane area, and Handley Page's predictably perverse reaction was to instruct Whitehouse to fly the biplane

G/100 at Hendon in March 1914 with revised outer wing struts and Garuda airscrew.

with tailplane and fin removed altogether, to show that the crescent wing with reflexed trailing edge made fixed tail surfaces unnecessary for stability.

During February and March various improvements were incorporated, including increased tailplane and reduced fin area; decking was added between the cockpits, and the outer leading edge bracing tubes, which vibrated in flight, were shortened to form braces at the top and bottom of the outer struts; a Garuda airscrew replaced the original heavy Chauvière since the metal sheathing was only necessary on a seaplane. Whitehouse flew Type G to check these modifications at Hendon on 23 April and again with Ding as passenger two days later; then Ding (who had gained Royal Aero Club certificate No. 774 two days previously) took formal delivery on the 29th and flew across country to Ealing and back. Repeating this trip on 2 May, he landed heavily and broke the twin-skid landing gear, which was remade as a simpler V-type, a silencer being fitted to the somewhat noisy twin exhausts at the same time. These repairs were finished on 17 May and

Princess Löwenstein-Wertheim and Rowland Ding in G/100 at Hendon in May 1914, showing silencer and simplified chassis. (*G. S. Leslie*)

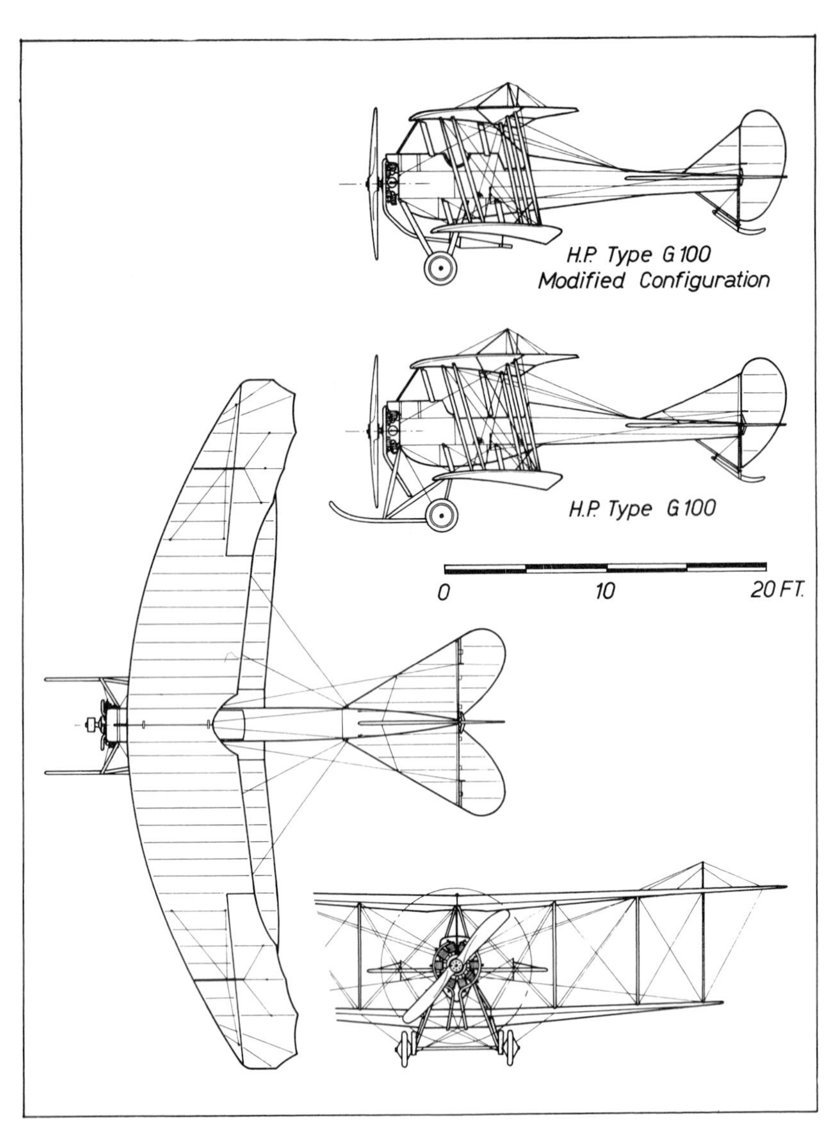

on the 21st Ding was asked to fly Princess Ludwig of Löwenstein-Wertheim (formerly Lady Ann Savile, a well-known society sportswoman) from Hendon to Paris; they ran into fog which grounded them, off course, at Eastbourne for six hours; taking off again when it cleared, they reached Dover just after 4 p.m. and Calais 15 minutes later; there the Princess decided to continue to Paris by train, while Ding put up in Calais for the night and flew back to Hendon in the morning. Although no time had been saved, because of the weather, the Princess was delighted with air travel and forthwith enrolled as a pupil at the Beatty School of Flying at Hendon.

Satisfied with his new biplane, Ding began his first barnstorming tour on 26 May by flying to Lansdown racecourse at Bath to give displays during Whit-week. He should have returned to Hendon on 6 June to compete in the Aerial Derby, for which he was entered as No.8, but trade at Lansdown was so prosperous that he stayed there and so escaped the fog which ruined the race round London, though he encountered it a few days later over the Cotswolds on his way north to Yorkshire, where his next engagements were booked. Flying almost blind on a compass course, with one cylinder misfiring, he groped his way at a steady 35 mph until further progress was impossible; then he 'felt' his way down into a barley field near Stroud without damage. When the mist cleared, he found he had settled on the only level open space in several miles of thick woodland and steep grassy slopes. During June and July he toured Yorkshire, giving displays at fairs and garden fêtes and taking his wife and six-year-old daughter as passengers from point to point; in the two months after leaving Hendon he flew 10,000 miles and took up 200 passengers, 78 of them at Harrogate, where he operated from The Stray with spectators thronging round the machine in large numbers. On 21 July he moved on to Gosforth Park, Newcastle-upon-Tyne, staying there nearly a week; on the 27th he started his return

Crowd surrounding G/100 at the Stray, Harrogate, in July 1914.

southwards too late to reach Northallerton, his intended goal, so he had to land in darkness at Willington, Co Durham, completing the stage next morning. He always made full use of the biplane's short take-off and landing capabilities, but in the Northallerton carnival on 29 July his chassis hit an obstruction while landing with a passenger; no one was hurt, but the machine nosed over and had to go back by rail to Hendon for repairs. While these were in progress, war began with Germany, and Hendon aerodrome was commandeered for the Royal Naval Air Service; Type G was requisitioned and emerged resplendent in clear-doped linen, with a Union Jack and serial number 892 painted on each side of the rudder, to be pressed into service as a trainer, but its resemblance to the much publicised Etrich Taube frequently drew the fire of trigger-happy Territorials; because of this hazard it was further marked with red circles on the wings, which became the standard marking for RNAS aircraft for a few months, till superseded by the well-known tri-colour roundels and rudder stripes. It was flown regularly from November onwards by F. Warren Merriam, who

G/100 in RNAS markings at Hendon in November 1914. (*G. S. Leslie*)

was chief instructor of the RNAS flying school at Hendon. During its rebuilding, it had been given a longer belly fairing, which much improved its appearance and performance, but on 2 January, 1915, the engine failed and in the ensuing forced landing it collided with a parked Avro, breaking several wing struts. Repaired once more, it was flown by Merriam early in May and remained in use at Hendon for both training and anti-Zeppelin patrol; for the latter warlike purpose the pilot was issued with a Service revolver, but never had occasion to use it. In June it accompanied the RNAS school to its new base at Chingford, but soon after arrival 892 crashed again, and was finally written off in August. By then, its legal owner Lindsay Bainbridge had been killed and it is believed that Rowland Ding, to whom he bequeathed it, was allowed to reclaim the Anzani engine for use in the Blackburn Land/Sea monoplane, which he began flying at Bowness-on-Windermere in October.

From Type G was derived the third Handley Page biplane, designated K/35, a small single-seater, with a 35 hp Y-type Anzani engine. Intended for solo pupils of the Beatty and similar schools, it was designed by Volkert in December 1913. Initially all the wing and tail surfaces followed the planforms of Type G closely, from which it was scaled down by a factor of 3/4, resulting in an upper wing span of 30 ft and total wing area of 225 sq ft. In January 1914 the tail unit was redesigned on the lines of the B.E.2a and the landing gear was also revised, but construction of Type K was postponed to allow Type G to be developed and repaired, and finally discarded in favour of the fourth Handley Page biplane design, L/200, a much more ambitious project intended to compete for the *Daily Mail*'s £10,000 prize for the first direct nonstop flight across the Atlantic. This machine was built during the summer of 1914 to the order of Princess Ludwig of Löwenstein-Wertheim, who proposed to accompany Rowland Ding as co-pilot on the flight. It seems to have been derived directly from K/35 by doubling its linear dimensions to give a span of 60 ft and wing area of 900 sq ft; its well-streamlined fuselage contained tanks for 350 gallons of petrol, with 35 gallons of oil and equivalent water, and the crew occupied side-by-side seats with dual controls in an enclosed cabin, which contained a third seat as a rest station. The chosen engine was a 200 hp Canton-Unné

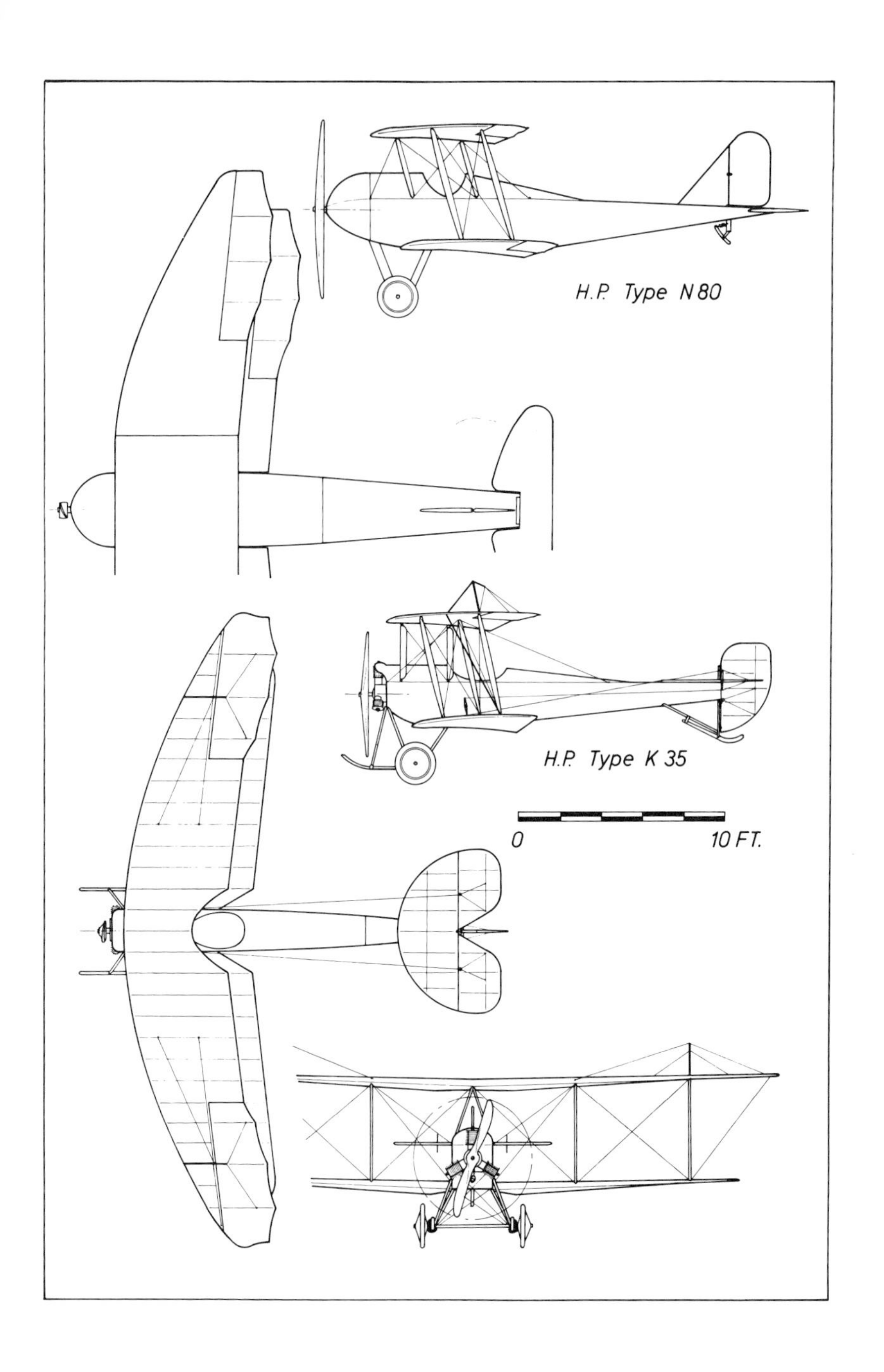
H.P. Type N 80
H.P. Type K 35
0
10 FT.

water-cooled radial built by Salmson, but this had not been delivered before war broke out; when it did arrive from France, it was promptly requisitioned by the Admiralty and so the L/200, though virtually complete, remained unassembled and was never flown. Handley Page offered it to the Admiralty as a potential coastal patrol aeroplane or seaplane, in which two extra seats could be accommodated by reducing the fuel capacity to 120 gallons. L/200 was estimated to be able to fly at 80 mph for 23 hours and to have a minimum safe speed of 43 mph; it was priced at £2,750.

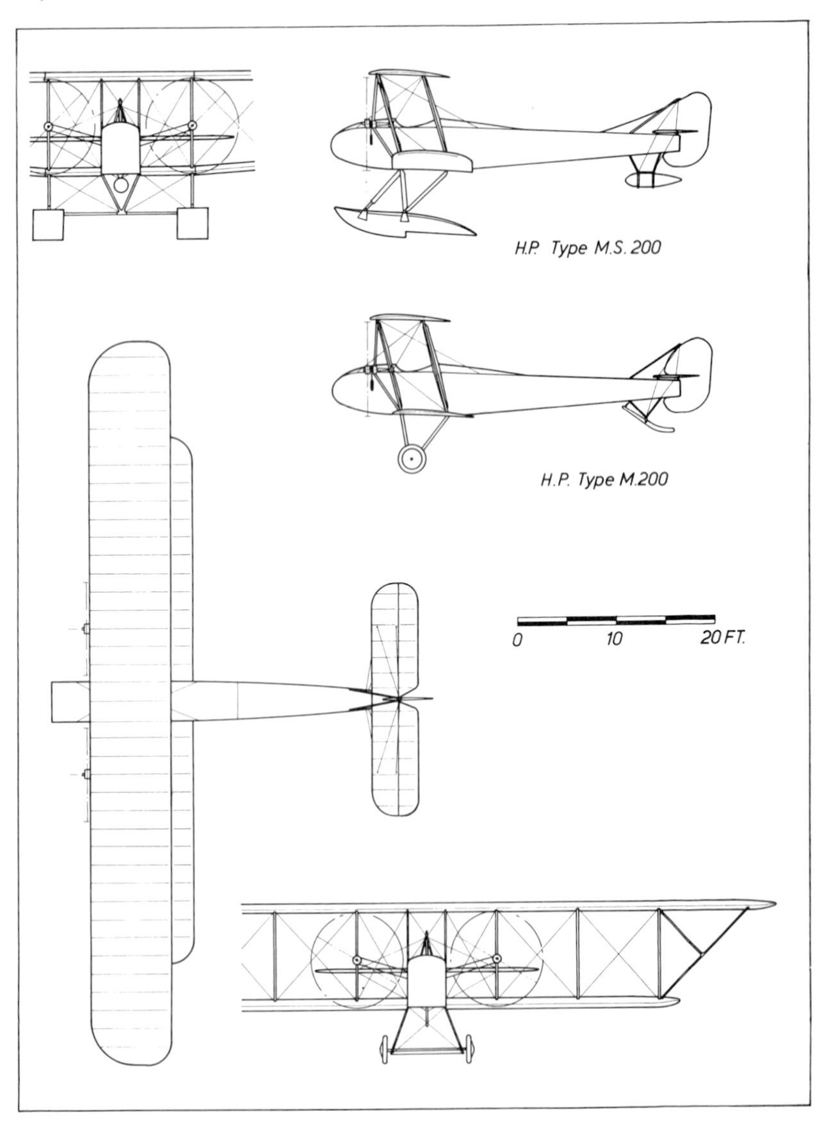

On 10 August, 1914, when it was known that all 200 hp engines had been commandeered by the Admiralty, Handley Page offered to install two 100 hp engines in the wings; then he tendered on 24 August, a version with two similar engines in the nose, at £2,300 on wheels or £2,750 on floats. Type M/200 and its seaplane variant MS/200 were staggered biplanes with straight wings of 70 ft span and two water-cooled 95 hp Salmson radial engines mounted coaxially nose to nose, with chain-drive to a wing-mounted outboard tractor airscrew on each side of the fuselage. No drawings or photographs of the L/200 have survived, as they were searched for without success in February 1920, when they were needed as evidence in support of Handley Page's claim for compensation before the Royal Commission on Awards to Inventors in respect of Crown user of the Handley Page O and V type aeroplanes. The M/200 and MS/200 drawings only came to light in recent years when the archives relating to this claim were searched. Type N/80 was a proposed side-by-side scout biplane derived from K/35, having the same crescent wings with a parallel centre section inserted; it was intended to have an 80 hp Gnome engine but the design was abandoned incomplete in January 1915. On 3 September, 1914, Captain Murray Sueter had written to Handley Page 'It is not proposed to order any seaplanes of the designs in question [L & M] at present', and he declined on 1 February, 1915, to change this view, even though Handley Page offered to assemble the L/200 immediately with straight wings.

G/100

(100 hp Anzani)

Span 40 ft (12·2 m); length 27 ft (8·23 m) with skids, later 25 ft 1 in (7·65 m); wing area 384 sq ft (36 m²). Empty weight 1,150 lb (521 kg); loaded weight 1,775 lb (805 kg). Speed (max) 73 mph (117 km/h), (min) 35 mph (56 km/h); climb to 3,000 ft (915 m) in 10·5 min; endurance 4 hr. Pilot and one or two passengers.

K/35

(35 hp Anzani)

Span 30 ft (9·15 m); length 20 ft 6 in (6·25 m); wing area 225 sq ft (20·9 m²). Empty weight (est) 500 lb (225·5 kg); loaded weight (est) 680 lb (308 kg). Speed (est) 65 mph (104 km/h). Pilot alone.

L/200

(200 hp Salmson)

Span 60 ft (18·3 m); length 41 ft (12·5 m); wing area 900 sq ft (83·6 m²). Empty weight (est) 2,800 lb (1,270 kg); loaded weight (est) 6,000 lb (2,720 kg). Speed (est cruise) 80 mph (128 km/h), (est min) 43 mph (69 km/h); endurance (est) 23 hr at 80 mph. Two pilots with dual controls.

M/200 and MS/200

(Two 95 hp Salmson)

Span 70 ft (21·38 m); length 37 ft 6 in (11·45 m); wing area 950 sq ft (88·3 m²). Empty weight (est) 3,000 lb (1,360 kg); loaded weight (est) 5,000 lb (2,270 kg). Speed (est) 75 mph (120 km/h). Crew four.

N/80

(80 hp Gnome)

Span 32 ft 6 in (9·9 m); length 24 ft (7·32 m). Pilot and observer side by side.

O/100 and O/400 (H.P.11 and 12)

Handley Page Ltd had been in business for five years when hostilities flared up on 4 August, 1914, but its total output—eight aeroplanes of its own design and six more (including three B.E.2as) to customers' designs—compared unfavourably with nearly 100 turned out by Short Brothers and over 200 by Bristol during the same period, to say nothing of rapidly increasing output from Sopwith and Vickers. The difficulties experienced (and exasperation expressed) over the B.E.2a contract had not endeared Handley Page and the War Office to one another, but nevertheless Handley Page offered the resources of his factory at 110 Cricklewood Lane to both Army and Navy without reservation. An inter-Service struggle for control of all aircraft manufacture having begun, it was to be expected that reluctance by one Service to place contracts would be promptly matched with enthusiasm by the other; so Captain Murray Sueter was quick off the mark in calling Handley Page to a discussion of naval aircraft requirements.

At the Air Department headquarters above the Admiralty Arch, Handley Page and Volkert displayed drawings of the L/200 and sketches of its proposed twin-engined variants, M/200 and MS/200; but Sueter's technical adviser, Harris Booth, preferred a very large seaplane for coastal patrol and dockyard defence, capable also of bombing the German High Seas Fleet before it ever left the safety of its anchorage at Kiel, and had already ordered prototypes from J. Samuel White & Co of Cowes. In view of Commander Samson's urgent call from Flanders for a 'bloody paralyser' to hold back the German advance on Antwerp, Handley Page offered to build a land-based machine of this size, and very quickly a specification was drafted, discussed and agreed for a large twin-engined patrol bomber designated Type O, with a span of 114 ft and defined by general arrangement drawing No.628A.1; this specification was issued on 28 December, 1914, as the basis for a contract for four prototypes serialled 1372–1375. It called for two 150 hp Sunbeam engines, 200 gallons of petrol, 30 gallons of oil, a bombsight and six 100 lb bombs, a Rouzet W/T transmitter/receiver and a crew of two, with armour plate to protect all these items from small arms fire from below. Wing loading was not to exceed 5 lb/sq ft, but a top speed of 65 mph and ability to climb to 3,000 ft in 10 minutes were required. The aeroplane, with wings folded, had to be housed in a shed not larger than 70 ft square by 18 ft high and the sole defensive weapon was to be a Lee-Enfield Service rifle with 100 rounds of ammunition. The idea for this imaginative and practical 'battleplane' was fully approved and largely inspired by the First Lord of the Admiralty, Winston Churchill, whose enthusiasm for flying was a sore trial to his surface-bound colleagues, both naval and parliamentary; its specification was almost completely achieved, only the wing loading and overall height being exceeded in the final result, whose performance and utility in turn greatly exceeded the original requirements.

Geometrical simplicity was one of the keys to low structure weight, and Handley Page's crescent wing gave way to an unstaggered straight-edged biplane layout for both mainplane and tail unit. Early in the discussions the problem of wing-folding resulted in the span being reduced to 100 ft, the slight increase in wing loading being offset by the prospect of 200 hp engines being available, but the Admiralty forbade any indication of horsepower in the revised type designation, which became O/100 by reference to the span; a surviving manuscript note from Meredith to Volkert dated 25 January, 1915, and headed 'O/300' may indicate the cause of the Admiralty's concern over nomenclature. The rectangular-section fuselage was straight-tapered from wing to tail, with the top longerons horizontal. Forward of the wing the fuselage was short, with a blunt 'chin' surmounted by a glazed cockpit enclosure having a large V-shaped Triplex glass windscreen, rectangular Cellon side windows and a Cellon roof panel with an open hatchway; through this the observer could aim his rifle over a wide field of fire from a standing position almost astride the pilot's seat, which was an ordinary cane garden chair. A 10-gauge manganese-steel armour plate protected the cockpit floor and the sides had 14-gauge armour-plating up to sill level, this assembly being known in the works as 'The Bath'. The pilot's controls comprised a large handwheel for the ailerons mounted on a tubular column rocking fore-and-aft for the elevators, and the usual rudder-bar; the narrow vertical instrument panel obscured very little of the excellent forward view. In designing the control surfaces, great care was taken to relieve the pilot of all unnecessary loads, the ailerons and elevators being aerodynamically balanced by full-chord horns taking in most of the bluntly rounded wing and tailplane tips; there were no ailerons on the lower wings, which were 15 ft shorter than the upper at each tip to give ground clearance when folded, the top overhang being braced by a triangular kingpost above each outer pair of interplane struts. The balanced twin rudders were pivoted between the tailplane rear spars and there was no fixed fin. Volkert preferred rigid tubular trailing edges to Harris Booth's favourite flexible cord or cable, and restored the aileron area lost in reducing the overall span by locally increasing the chord so that the ailerons extended behind the fixed trailing edge, giving a characteristic planform to the upper wing. The lower wing-tips were at first drawn square, but Harris Booth insisted on rounding them to reduce drag. The two engines rotated in opposite directions to cancel out torque effects and were mounted midway in the gap as close to the fuselage as clearance for 11 ft four-blade airscrews would permit; each nacelle comprised a 100-gallon petrol tank made from 14-gauge armour plate, carried on two groups of steel-tube struts, with the engine bearers cantilevered in front of the tank and a long conical fairing attached at the back; this fairing had originally been blunt, but Harris Booth requested a long pointed tail, which was found to complicate the wing-folding and later shortened again. Each engine had armour plate underneath and at the sides and its radiator was mounted vertically above the petrol tank. In the original design, the undercarriage was of the well-established Farman pattern, with pairs of wheels on short axles tied by rubber cord to short fore-and-aft skids supported by struts directly below the nacelles, so that the weight of the engines and fuel was immediately above the wheels and local offset loading was avoided.

At Harris Booth's request, a model of this layout was tested in the National Physical Laboratory wind-tunnel and found generally satisfactory, but detail structural design was more difficult, as Volkert found when he needed to stiffen the ailerons torsionally to take the reverse loading of the horn-balance tips; the solution he adopted was to reduce the horn area forward of the hinge, the resulting square-cut horn balance being found quite adequate; in fact it avoided the severe overbalance encountered by the Royal Aircraft Factory on the original ailerons of the B.E.12a and F.E.9. The aerofoil section was RAF 6, and the wing was built round two spruce spars of rectangular section, spindled out to I section between strut attachments; the close-pitched ribs, though of light section, were very stiff when assembled. The hollow spruce compression struts between the front and rear spars were made from two spindled out rectangular pieces glued with their hollow faces together, the joints being reinforced lengthways by thin oak tongues (Patent No.138006). The interplane struts were similar but had nose and tail fairings built on, the whole assembly being wrapped in glued linen tape before final varnishing. For ease of storage and erection, and to avoid using very long spars when Baltic and Scandinavian timber became scarce, the mainplanes were made in nine sections, the upper mainplane comprising the centreplane, two outer planes and two tip extensions, while the lower comprised two half centre planes and two outer planes. The fuselage was manufactured in four separate portions—front, centre, rear and tail—the latter two being permanently assembled with a scarfed and fish-plated joint in each longeron. All longerons and struts were carefully matched in cross-section to the local loads and, where extra thickness was necessary to provide stiffness, the members were built up, like the wing struts, from spindled halves glued together. Joints and strut fittings were fabricated from mild steel plates, ingeniously folded and brazed together, with fretwork holes between lines of maximum stress to save weight; nevertheless they were simple to produce in quantity with semi-skilled labour. To begin with, all internal bracing, and external bracing outside the slipstream, was by stranded cables, which naval artificers knew how to splice, although streamlined wires were required in the tail and centre bays. A sample of every part was weighed and tested to destruction to confirm weight and stress calculations, and numerous detail improvements were made as construction of the four prototypes proceeded, with sufficient lead-time between them to permit progressive refinement.

On 4 February, 1915, the basic design was substantially agreed by Captain W. L. Elder, including the substitution of new 250 hp Rolls-Royce vee-twelve engines for the original Sunbeams, as their greater power was obtained for less than a proportionate weight increase. On 9 February the contract was amended to cover four prototypes, 1455–1458, and eight production aircraft, 1459–1466. Initially it was intended to carry the bombs horizontally in a rotating cage enclosed in the fuselage, but as soon as the first few bombs had been released the cage became unbalanced and impossible to rotate. So a system of bomb suspension and release was devised which allowed up to sixteen 112-lb bombs to be hung from nose-rings in the same space as eight would have occupied in the cage. Concentration of the bomb load in the fuselage necessitated spanwise distribution of the landing gear, so the original design, with short cross-axles, was replaced by two separate chassis units with the outer wheels under the nacelles and the inner wheels under the longerons, with a clear space between units for the release of bombs. To accommodate the length of shock-absorber cord needed to prevent its extension being limited by the inextensible cotton-braiding, it was wrapped round the spreaders of telescopic struts of the type pioneered by A. V. Roe in the Avro 504, which the revised O/100 chassis resembled in principle; each unit had a vestigial central skid, reduced to a horizontal steel tube, with a braced swing axle on each side of it and a shock absorber strut on the outside of the wheel on each axle; the shock absorbers were faired by sheet metal casings and in production aeroplanes vertical steps were formed in the two innermost fairings to allow a clear path for the bomb tails. The bomb release gears (Handley Page Patent No.17346 of December 1915) were mounted on four cross-beams in the fuselage above the bomb-cell floor, which was a square grid or 'honeycomb' with sixteen spring-loaded flaps separately pushed open by each bomb as it fell; under active service conditions, these flaps soon became worn and were more easily replaced by brown paper glued across the grid openings. Bombs could be dropped singly, in pairs, in salvoes of four, or all together. The revised landing gear, nacelle structure and wing hinges were covered by Patents Nos.17066, 17067, 132478, 140276 and 144867, all dated December 1915.

Two views of 1455 at Hendon in December 1915, showing original radiators and enclosed cockpit, taken by the late H. R. Busteed. (*H. J. Penrose*)

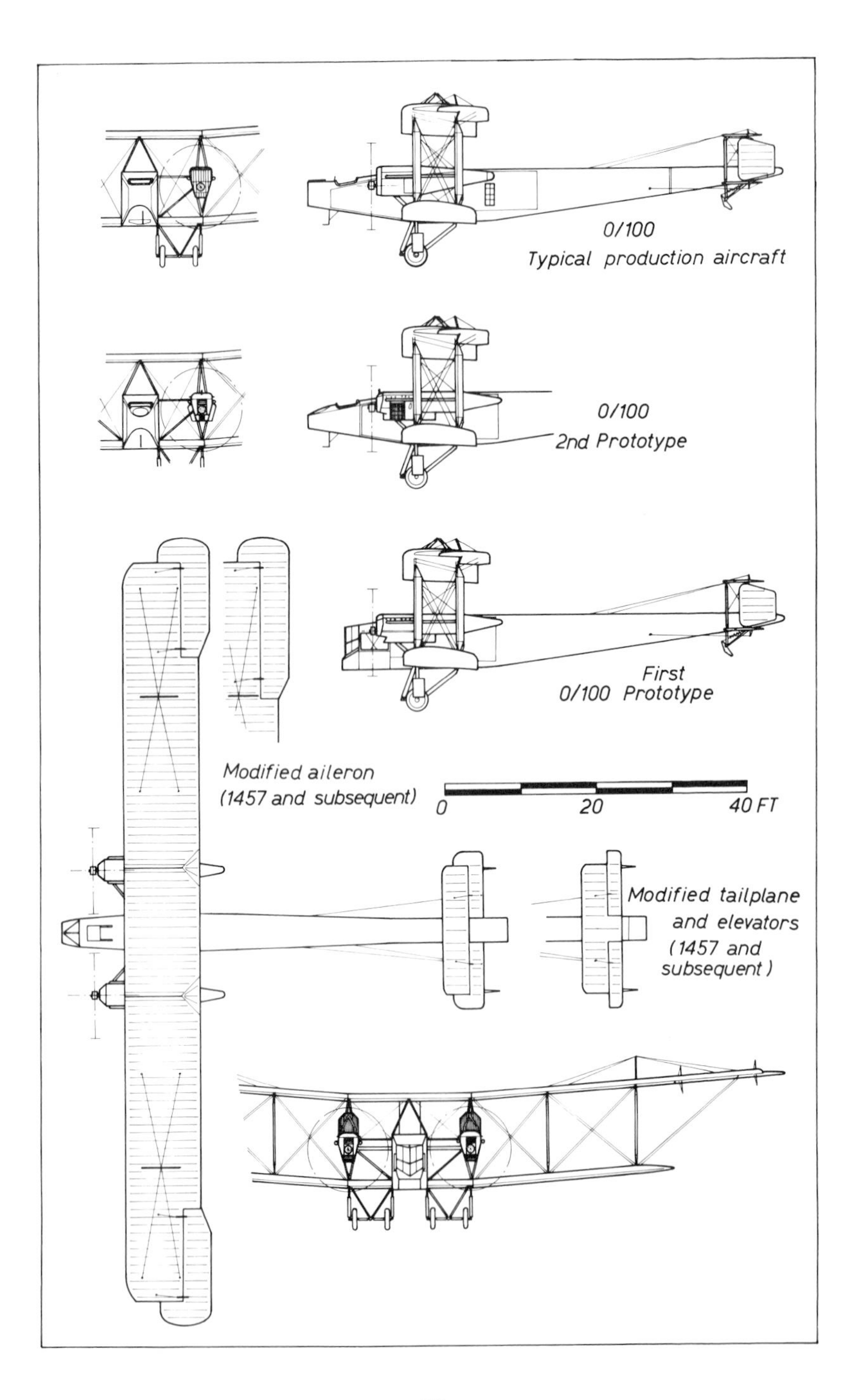
0/100
Typical production aircraft
0/100
2nd Prototype
First
0/100 Prototype
Modified aileron
(1457 and subsequent)
0
20
40 FT
Modified tailplane
and elevators
(1457 and
subsequent)

The first prototype, 1455, was finished at Cricklewood during November 1915 and its components were taken to the requisitioned Lamson factory at Kingsbury for final erection; the complete fuselage was joined up at Cricklewood and towed along Edgware Road to Kingsbury by Handley Page personally in his Arrol-Johnston drop-head coupé. Late at night on 9 December two teams of naval ratings wheeled the assembled prototype, with wings folded, out on to the tramlines of Edgware Road; almost at once two tyres burst and had to be replaced; they were of the early beaded-edge pattern and were easily twisted off the rim. The procession restarted and all went well as far as the corner into Colindale Avenue, where the other two tyres burst. Overhead tramwires, telephone wires and gas lamp standards had already been removed on Admiralty orders and there was a reasonably clear passage along Colindale Avenue, but near the Hendon aerodrome entrance by the Silk Stream the way was blocked by trees in several front gardens. Calling for a ladder and a handsaw, Handley Page himself climbed up and removed the offending branches, taking no notice of protests from bedroom windows. None of these unfortunate residents ever claimed damages, but in due course the Gas Light & Coke Company sent Handley Page Ltd a substantial bill for the cost of removing and reinstating their street lamps; blandly Handley Page referred them to the Admiralty, stating that it had been a naval operation, not a commercial one, and eventually Their Lordships paid up. The three-quarter-mile journey had taken five hours and a further week had to be spent in final rigging and engine tuning, but by the morning of 17 December, 1915, there stood at Hendon, ready to fly, an aeroplane whose span was not much less than the total distance covered by Orville Wright's first flight at Kitty Hawk, twelve years earlier to the day.

As the first two engines (Rolls-Royce numbers 2 and 3) had no turning gear, the only means of starting them was by pulling the airscrews round by hand; they could not be reached from ground level and it was unsafe to erect scaffolding or ladders close to moving blades, so a double ramp was contrived, which enabled a naval rating to run up one side within reach of the lowest blade and swing it as he passed down the other side. With a team of men it was thus possible to get the engines primed, after which they were started by turning the hand-magneto, provided the sequence was quickly carried out. Shortly before 2 p.m. on 17 December Lt-Cmdr J. T. Babington and Lt-Cmdr E. W. Stedman (formerly of the NPL staff) taxied to the downwind end of Hendon aerodrome, turned ponderously into wind and opened the throttles; to their relief they took off at 50 mph, flew straight and landed well short of the boundary. Overnight a number of slack bracing wires were tightened and next day another take-off was made, but Babington found that acceleration beyond 55 mph was negligible because of excessive drag. Handley Page blamed the large flat honeycomb radiators and Rolls-Royce recommended changing them to vertical tube units mounted on either side of the nacelle. So 1455 had to be grounded for two weeks while work went on night and day throughout the Christmas holiday, being finished in time for a third flight on New Year's Eve. This time performance was much better and handling could be assessed at up to 65 mph; the ailerons and elevators were found to be heavy though effective, but the rudders were seriously overbalanced and their chord had to be extended 3 inches by strips added at the trailing edges. Control friction was high, particularly in the aileron circuit, and elasticity in the cables allowed random movements of the ailerons and elevators which the pilot had no means of damping out. The aileron controls were much improved by deleting the original internal cable and pulley system and substituting conventional external cables with longer levers on the ailerons. Impatient at the delay caused by these modifications, Murray Sueter ordered Sqn Cmdr A. M. Longmore to ferry the machine to Eastchurch forthwith and on 10 January, 1916, he and Stedman took off from Hendon without waiting for further trials; all went well apart from loss of power in the port engine, due to partial magneto failure, and some windscreen misting. A few days later Longmore began maximum speed tests, but at 70 mph the tail began to vibrate and twist violently, and he had to throttle back and land promptly. On inspection considerable damage was found in the rear fuselage structure, with badly warped longerons locally crushed by strut-ends, bowed struts and all cables slack. Handley Page and Volkert were quickly on the scene and drew up repair schemes for local reinforcement and reduction of the offsets which caused torsional stresses. The bowed struts were stiffened with kingposts and local crushing was eased by means of hardwood facings at the butt-joints. Unfortunately these modifications did nothing to check the tail vibration and a new weak point was found at the attachment of the wings to the bottom longerons, causing the angle of incidence to vary during taxying, so that take-off became impossible. This was cured by replacing the stranded cables in the fuselage by swaged tie-rods of high-tensile steel, and 1455 could then be flown consistently provided its speed did not exceed 75 mph, beyond which tail oscillation

Handley Page and Lieut Commander J. T. Babington in the cockpit of 1456.

1456 at Manston in May 1916. (*G. S. Leslie*)

began once more. At the request of the Eastchurch pilots, the cockpit enclosure was removed, having already shown signs of collapse, and in the second prototype, 1456, the whole front fuselage was converted to a long tapered nose, with an open cockpit for the two crew members side by side and provision for a gunner's cockpit in front of them. Deletion of the Triplex windscreen and armour-plate 'bath' saved over 500 lb in weight and the new nose was made long enough to keep the c.g. position unchanged, the new bottom longerons being swept up at the same angle as the upper ones were swept down. The new pilot's position was 12 ft ahead of the wing leading edge, tending to exaggerate his control responses, and this was a further factor to be reckoned with in improving stability. In 1456 the whole nose back to the rear of the pilot's cockpit was clad with plywood, but in 1457 and subsequent O/100s the plywood area was restricted to the curved part of the nose cockpit, the flat flanks being fabric-covered. Most of the nacelle armour was also discarded, although the weight of the tanks could not be reduced immediately. With a much strengthened fuselage structure incorporating massive reinforcement across the lower wing roots, 1456 was ready to be flown early in April 1916 by Clifford B. Prodger, an American who had come to Hendon a year earlier as chief instructor at the Beatty School and later formed a syndicate with Sydney Pickles and Bernard Isaacs for free-lance test-flying. Handley Page had attributed the tail oscillation to elevator over-balance and on 1456 the elevator horns were cropped square in the same way as the ailerons, so he was gratified when Prodger reported that the first flight up to 75 mph was quite steady. On 23 April, with ten volunteers aboard, Prodger climbed to 10,000 ft in just under 40 min and Handley Page invited the RNAS to witness acceptance trials on 7 May, when he called for sixteen volunteers to emplane and Prodger flew them to 3,000 ft in 8½ min; a few

1457 at Hendon in June 1916, showing aft crew station and elevators with fabric removed from horn balance. (*G. S. Leslie*)

days later Prodger improved on this by lifting twenty Handley Page employees to 7,180 ft, and on 27 May the RNAS took formal delivery and flew 1456 to a new aerodrome at Manston, which was more spacious than Eastchurch. During this flight it was difficult to maintain a compass course and evident that extra fin area was needed to compensate for the longer nose. This was contrived quickly by covering in the panel between the fore and aft inner tailplane struts above the starboard upper longeron. On 30 May high speed tests were begun again, but the tail oscillation recurred at 80 mph and above. Furthermore, there was an elevator 'kick' at take-off with full load which started the oscillation at a much lower speed, although this could be avoided by accelerating immediately after 'unstick' while still in the ground cushion. The machine was still directionally unstable, but an attempt on 19 June to cure this by rigging the rudders with 'toe-out' only made matters worse. By this time, the tail oscillation problem had been referred by the Admiralty to the NPL and F. W. Lanchester agreed that the cause could not be simple structural weakness; he suspected dynamic resonance between engine vibration and the fuselage structure, but static tests on the third prototype, 1457, with the engines running at various speeds on the ground, proved negative. 1457 had a very stiff, completely redesigned, fuselage structure and was first flown on 25 June; it had a third crew position amidships, so Lanchester took the opportunity of flying in it with Babington next day, when the trouble began as soon as the speed reached 80 mph. He observed that the tail oscillation, at a frequency of about 4 cycles/second, caused the whole empennage to twist by as much as 15 degrees from the neutral position; he calculated that such a deflection would need a force of more than a ton to be applied at each tailplane tip if produced by a static test—a couple far greater than the pilot could apply through his controls. He deduced that this could only be caused by anti-symmetric movement of the port and starboard halves of the elevators, whose only interconnection was through long springy control cables, which ran separately to fairleads halfway along the rear fuselage; it was, in fact, one of the earliest reported cases of aero-elastic coupling. In R & M 276 Lanchester recommended positive interconnection of the two halves of each elevator; removal of the horn-balance area forward of the hinge-line (as first suggested by Handley Page himself) but retention of the full elevator span; also means for adjusting tailplane incidence during flight and extra bracing wires between both ends of the outer struts and the upper longerons. These measures were completely successful and the Admiralty, which had temporarily regretted having increased the original order from four to twelve in February 1915, had now vindicated its decision on 11 April to order a follow-on batch of twenty-eight (3115–3142) at a price of £4,375 each, under contract No.CP 69522/15/X.

The fourth prototype, 1458, the first with a one-piece upper elevator, also had provision for armament, with a Scarff ring at the nose cockpit, two gun-pillars at the mid-upper position and a quadrant mounting to fire under the tail from the rear floor hatch, but was otherwise completed quickly to the same structural standard as 1456 and restricted to training duties. It was also the first to be fitted with 320 hp Rolls-Royce Mark III engines—newly named Eagles—which were installed before delivery from

Engine runs at Cricklewood on 1458 with new nacelles in September 1916.

Hendon to Manston on 20 August. In the first twelve O/100s, 1455–1466, initially built with armoured nacelles, the nacelle tail fairings were long and tapered nearly to a point; they were hinged to the rear of the petrol tank and had to be swung inboard when the wings were folded, to clear the outer-plane bracing cables. In the second batch, 3115–3142, these fairings were shortened and blunted to clear the cables and could remain fixed. Wind-tunnel tests at the NPL in July 1916 showed a slight increase of drag with the shortened tail, but also that minimum drag was obtained with the nacelle reversed to point its tail upstream! It had been necessary to add an aerofoil section fuel gravity tank above the engine to avoid air-locks, and from 1461 onwards the total fuel tankage was increased by installing a cylindrical overload tank of 130 gallons in the fuselage above the bomb compartment; this increased range, but the higher take-off weight then

1458 at Manston in October 1916. (*G. S. Leslie*)

necessitated a change in the size of the Palmer tyres from 800 × 150 mm to 900 × 200 mm. Early in 1917 a shortage of Rolls-Royce Eagles was threatened and the third O/100 of the second batch, 3117, was built with 320 hp Sunbeam Cossacks, but these were heavier than Eagles for the same nominal power. 3117 was then sent to Farnborough for trials with uprated 260 hp RAF 3a engines after the War Office had staked a cautious claim in February 1916 with contract No. AS. 1198 for twelve O/100s (B8802–B8813) to be built at the Royal Aircraft Factory with these engines.

On completion of their acceptance trials, 1456 and 1457 remained at Manston as the nucleus of a Handley Page Training Flight formed in September 1916, while 1455 was rebuilt to production standard and 1458 was tested with new nacelles of lower drag and lighter weight. These had frontal honeycomb radiators with vertical shutters and deeper fuel tanks, no longer made of armour plate, giving a capacity of 120 gallons per nacelle or a total overload capacity per aircraft of 370 gallons; alternatively sixteen 112-lb bombs could be carried with the nacelle tanks full. Meanwhile the earlier nacelles were retained in production aircraft up to 3120 as these emerged from Kingsbury to be flown from Hendon to Manston, where

3117 at Cricklewood with Sunbeam Cossacks, showing original exhaust stacks through upper wing. (*G. S. Leslie*)

they were armed and equipped for issue to RNAS units in France. Initially, the only such unit was the 'Handley Page Squadron', commanded by Sqn Cmdr John Babington from August 1916 and assigned to the 3rd Wing at Luxeuil-les-Bains, whence it was intended to raid steel foundries and chemical plants in the Saar valley. Babington himself, with Lieutenant Jones and Sub Lieut Paul Bewsher as crew, flew 1460 to Villacoublay at the end of October, having been preceded by 1459, which continued to Luxeuil according to plan; but Babington had to land in a very small field soon after taking off en route for Luxeuil, the resulting damage being repaired on site after some weeks' delay. Meanwhile Lieutenant Waller in 1461 had force-landed at Abbeville with engine trouble en route for Villacoublay, but

3117 at Manston in July 1917, showing Sunbeam Cossacks with modified exhausts. (*National Aviation Museum, Canada*)

returned to service in December 1916. Only 1459 and 1460 were operated from Luxeuil by the 3rd Wing and the first O/100 action recorded was on the night of 16/17 March, 1917, when Babington in 1460 bombed an enemy-held railway junction southwest of Metz. The next two O/100s, 1462 and 1463, were due to leave Manston for Villacoublay on Christmas Eve 1916, but were delayed by minor engine trouble; on New Year's Day 1917 they took off once more within 15 minutes of each other, but found unbroken cloud over the Channel. Sub Lieut Sands in 1462 reached Villacoublay by dead reckoning, but Lieutenant Vereker in 1463, with Lieutenant Hibbard and three other crew, went astray because of a compass error and on descending to an altimeter reading of 200 ft could find no break in the cloud, so they climbed back to 6,000 ft where they spent some time trying to

3119 at Cricklewood in April 1917.

fix their position. With fuel running low, they had to come down again and were able to land in clear air after sighting a church spire at an altimeter reading of 500 ft. They left their aircraft to enquire their position, but found too late that they were behind the German lines at Chalandry, near Laon; they hurried back to make an immediate take-off, but were met by an infantry patrol; in fact Vereker had already climbed up the entrance ladder, but was hauled down by the seat of his breeches, so he had no chance to set fire to the machine. Thus 1463 was captured intact, but Vereker refused to fly it again, so it was dismantled for transport to Johannisthal, where it was re-erected after detailed examination. Marked with the German Eisenkreuz, it was paraded with other captured Allied aeroplanes and is reputed to have been flown to 10,000 ft by Manfred von Richthofen at Essen in a demonstration before Kaiser Wilhelm II; but, before its performance could be fully assessed, it crashed after its aileron cables had been inadvertently crossed during maintenance work.

When the 3rd Wing at Luxeuil was disbanded to provide urgently needed reinforcements for the Royal Flying Corps on 30 June, 1917, 1459 and 1460 were sent to join the 5th Wing at Coudekerque, whence daylight raids were made daily along the Belgian coast against U-boat bases at Bruges,

1463 at Chalandry after capture on 1 January, 1917. (*H. F. Cowley*)

Zeebrugge and Ostende, and later against other targets such as the long-range heavy shore batteries emplaced by the Germans along the dunes from Westende and Middelkerke to the Dutch frontier at Sluys. The first unit to operate at full strength was No.7 Squadron RNAS formed by combining O/100s from Luxeuil and Manston with the Short bombers remaining in 'B' Squadron of the 4th Wing after its Sopwith $1\frac{1}{2}$ Strutters had been transferred to the RFC. On 25 April four O/100s bombed and sank a German destroyer and damaged another, but 3115 was shot down into the sea off Nieuport and three of its crew of four were captured. After this, daylight sorties by O/100s were suspended and all efforts were concentrated against the docks at Bruges and the Zeebrugge canal where

First O/100 to arrive at Coudekerque in June 1917 was 3116. (*G. S. Leslie*)

U-boats were repaired and revictualled. At first only moonlight raids were possible, the first being on 9 May, but by September night-flying training had so improved that only the worst weather prevented operations every night. The submarine pens, like the shore batteries, were strongly protected with concrete and progressively heavier bombs were needed to make any impression; apart from the Short 184 seaplanes of the Dover Patrol, only the O/100 could effectively carry the 520 lb 'light case' and 550 lb 'heavy case' bombs developed for these targets. On 28 July the 5th Wing was strengthened by the formation of No.7A Squadron at Coudekerque, which later became No.14 Squadron and was trained exclusively for night bombing. It took over several of No.7's earlier aircraft, including 1459, 1461 and 1462, as these were replaced from the second production batch, including 3116, 3118, 3123, 3125 and 3127. In September one flight of four O/100s from No.7 was detached to Redcar to protect shipping entering and leaving the Hartlepools, where U-boats had been active inshore; on 21 September Flt Lieut Lance Sieveking (later well known in broadcasting) in 3123 dropped four bombs on a U-boat lying on the sea-bed, without apparent result; the flight remained at Redcar till 2 October, when it moved to Manston. Several of the O/100s in use at this time had Scarff rings amidships and in all of them the nose Scarff ring was mounted below the level of the pilot's cockpit.

Lance Sieveking's 3123 *Split-Pin* at Redcar in September 1917. (*G. S. Leslie*)

In the spring of 1917 the Admiralty decided to conduct operational trials with the six-pounder Davis gun against the growing menace of inshore enemy submarines; this was a single-shot double-ended recoilless weapon, firing an explosive shell from the 'active' barrel and a dispersible fragmented charge of equal mass (a mixture of lead shot and vaseline) from the 'recoil' barrel; it was breech-loaded in the middle and electrically fired, being normally aimed at 30 to 60 degrees below horizontal to avoid damage to the aircraft from the recoil charge; it was mounted on a strong outrigged bracket on the nose, where it was not easy to reload in the air. On 7 September, 1917, 3127 was sent to Redcar with 50 rounds of ammunition,

Davis gun installed on 3127 at Redcar in September 1917. (*G. S. Leslie*)

after earlier firing tests at Manston, using a prototype mounting bracket made by the Admiralty workshops at Battersea; blast damage to the upper wing had resulted at first from the recoil charge and had been overcome in July by raising the mounting and nose cockpit rim by 8 inches. In August, the same modification was applied to 1459, 1461 and 1462 and six-pounder Davis guns were fitted in them for urgent use at Coudekerque, but in December Dunkirk reported that the installation was not a success and in February 1918 the four guns and unspent residue of 500 rounds were withdrawn from service. Meanwhile the raised cockpit rim became a production modification from 3131 onwards (having also been fitted to 3124) and continued as a standard feature until the spring of 1918.

Early in 1917 the Dardanelles campaign had reached stalemate and Commodore Murray Sueter, transferred to the Mediterranean, called for a heavy long-range bomber to attack the enemy cruisers *Goeben* and *Breslau*, which had entered the Bosphorus soon after the declaration of war with Turkey in 1914. At first Sueter's request was for a floatplane conversion of the O/100, because so much of the route from Mudros to Constantinople lay over water, but Handley Page resisted this proposal, and Sueter then ordered Handley Page to design and build folding wings for two Porte F.3 flying-boats, to be allotted serials N62 and N63 under contract No.AS.17562. The wing design was completed and paid for, but construction was cancelled on 10 December, 1917; the designation Type T given to this project was also cancelled, as was Type S allotted to the O/100 seaplane. In May 1917 Sueter decided to divert 3124 from its intended Davis gun trials for urgent use by the 2nd Wing at Mudros against *Goeben* and *Breslau*, which would seriously threaten shipping in the Mediterranean if they could escape from the Dardanelles. On 22 May, 3124, fresh from the Cricklewood production line and specially equipped at Hendon, was flown to Manston and left next day for Mudros in a 2,000-mile dash via Villacoublay, Lyons, Fréjus, Pisa, Rome (Centocelle), Naples, Otranto and Salonika in a flying time of 55 hours. Mudros was reached on 8 June and the crew comprised Sqn Cmdr Kenneth Savory DSC, Flt Lieut H. McClelland, Lieutenant P. T. Rawlings, Chief Petty Officer Adams and Leading Mechanic Cromack; in addition to hammocks and other personal gear, they carried a full set of aircraft spares including a stripped-down engine and two airscrews; the latter, being four-bladers, would not go

Savory's 3124 at Otranto en route for Mudros, with spare airscrews lashed to the fuselage. (*C. A. Hall via Chaz Bowyer*)

inside the fuselage and had to be lashed on top of it. They made good progress to Otranto, where they found a collection of spares urgently needed at Mudros, so these were taken on board too, but the take-off weight then exceeded $6\frac{1}{2}$ tons and Savory was unable to climb high enough to cross the 8,000 ft Albanian mountains. After two attempts to surmount this inhospitable terrain, Savory was compelled to offload the additional spares at Otranto and, after installing the spare airscrews in place of the original ones, succeeded in reaching Salonika at the third attempt, although the radiators froze and the crew were in danger from rifle shots from Albanian marksmen. The final stage to Mudros was uneventful and, but for the abortive starts and returns at Otranto, the flying time would have been only 31 hours. After thorough servicing at Mudros, Savory made two attempts to bomb Constantinople, on 3 and 8 July, both failing because of headwinds which compelled returns to base after reaching the Sea of Marmora, although other targets were bombed en route. On 9 July a third attempt succeeded, Constantinople being reached after a flight of $3\frac{1}{4}$ hours; arriving just after midnight, Savory circled over the city for half an hour at 1,000 ft, dropping eight 112-lb bombs on the *Goeben* in Stenia Bay, two more on the steamer *General* (being used as the German headquarters) and the last two on the Turkish War Office. In spite of a broken oil pipe which compelled him to shut down one engine on the homeward flight, Savory brought 3124 safely back to Mudros at 3.40 a.m. and was awarded

B9446, the first Cossack-engined 'intermediate' O/100, at Cricklewood in November 1917. *(I.W.M.—Crown Copyright)*

a Bar to his DSC for the exploit. On 6 August 3124 bombed Panderma and for the rest of the month flew anti-submarine patrols in the Aegean, then on 2 September attacked Adrianople railway station with success; finally on 30 September Flt Lieut Jack Alcock, with Sub Lieuts S. J. Wise and H. Aird as crew, took off to bomb railway yards near Constantinople, but after 1½ hours they were met by anti-aircraft fire and one engine failed from a broken oil-pipe; in the attempt to return to Mudros they were forced to ditch in the Gulf of Xeros near Suvla Bay and, although 3124 floated for over two hours, they were not seen and eventually had to swim ashore, finally reaching Constantinople as prisoners of war.

Trials of 3117 at Hendon and Manston with RAF 3a engines proved disappointing, so contract No.AS.1198 was suspended and replaced by AS.20629/17 for six Cricklewood-built machines (B9446–B9451) with Sunbeam Cossacks; these were not used operationally and represented an interim stage between the O/100 and its later development, the O/400, retaining most of the features, including the nacelle tanks, of the former; one at least was used as a trainer by the Australian Flying Corps at Halton and some were issued to the Wireless Flight at Netheravon; yet another was inspected by King George V when he visited the new works at Cricklewood early in 1918. The concurrent trial installation of two 260 hp Fiat A.12bis engines in 3142 in July 1917 was a one-off job specifically ordered at the

The only O/100 with Fiat A.12bis engines was 3142, intended for Russia in November 1917.

request of the Russian government, but it crashed early in its trials at Martlesham Heath, just before the October revolution ended Russia's participation in the war; it is notable for having had a simplified four-wheeled landing gear of the pattern employed on the V/1500 and, later, the W.8. In October 1917, 3117 was flown more successfully at Farnborough after being converted to take four 200 hp Hispano-Suizas arranged back to back in tandem pairs in an installation contrived by Major Percy Bishop, Chief Inspector of Engines, AID; the pilot for these trials was Captain Frank Courtney and the main reason for them was that Hispanos were available at a time when Eagles were not. Initial flight tests showed a lower performance than predicted, because the slipstream effects of tandem pairs were not well understood, and the project was abandoned; however, wind-tunnel experiments with tandem airscrews of various diameters and pitches indicated that the front tractor should be of greater diameter and finer pitch than the rear pusher, and this was taken into account in the design of the four-engined Handley Page V/1500; this

3117 at Farnborough in November 1917 after installation of four Hispano-Suizas. (*RAE—Crown Copyright*)

principle had already been deduced by Horace Short at Eastchurch as early as 1911, but had remained unpublished and was apparently not known at Farnborough. The most significant development was made on 3138 at Martlesham Heath by Babington and Stedman and by September 1917 this machine had been progressively modified to become the prototype of a much-improved model, the O/400. Tested initially with 320 hp Rolls-Royce Eagle IVs, it was next flown with 275 hp Sunbeam Maoris, pending the arrival of up-rated Eagles. On 14 August, 1917, after discussion since January, contract No. AS.22434 had been awarded for one hundred 0/400s (C3381–C3480) with either Rolls-Royce Eagles or Sunbeam Maoris and production had begun at Cricklewood, but with definite results from 3138 still awaited from Martlesham, it was cancelled six days later. The first few sets of Cricklewood-built components were then sent to Farnborough so that twelve urgently-needed O/400s could be handbuilt under contract

3138 at Martlesham Heath before progressive modification into prototype O/400. (*G. S. Leslie*)

3138, the O/400 prototype, flying with Sunbeam Maori engines at Martlesham Heath in April 1918.

C3487, the first production O/400, completed at the Royal Aircraft Factory in March 1918. (*I.W.M.—Crown Copyright*)

No.AS1198 as C3487–3498, in place of B8802–B8813, while the new Handley Page factory at Somerton Road, Cricklewood, was being finished and tooled-up. Later in 1918 the Royal Aircraft Establishment (as the Factory had by then become) received contract No.35A/88/C.43 for twelve more O/400s, which were given the reinstated serials B8802–B8813, but were built to an advanced modification standard; two of these, B8810 and B8811, were used in October 1918 to test the improved 'Raftite' doping scheme.

The principal differences between the O/400 and O/100 were the substitution of 360 hp Rolls-Royce Eagle VIII engines, both rotating the same way, increased structural strength and bomb-load, and a completely revised fuel system. Final approval of the Eagle VIII was held up till December 1917 because Rolls-Royce could not produce the numbers required in both right- and left-handed versions. Then technical agreement was reached quite simply when it was shown that the counter-rotation principle, first expounded by the Wright brothers and slavishly followed by the Technical Design department of the Air Board, was, in fact, the underlying cause of directional instability in the O/100, as well as a severe handicap to increased production and serviceability. The torque effects were quite easily dealt with by offsetting the central fin, which was made adjustable on the ground; this resulted in its being repositioned a few inches farther aft than in the O/100. In the O/400's revised fuel system, the nacelle tanks were deleted and all the fuel was contained in two 130-gallon fuselage tanks and two 15-gallon gravity tanks in the centre-section leading edge. Petrol was pumped up from each main tank to its associated gravity tank by wind-driven pumps located just inside the fuselage, with horizontal rotors having four Pelton cups exposed two at a time through dumb-bell-shaped slots in the fabric panels on each side; an alternative scheme employed a pair of air-turbine wheels mounted horizontally on top of the fuselage, one for each tank, but these were out of the slipstream and stopped working during ground runs. In later production, Vickers or Rotherham air pumps driven by windmills were mounted on brackets in the slipstream. The new nacelles incorporated large-capacity front radiators with horizontal shutters and were short enough for a single large interplane strut to be used between the mainplane rear spar hinges in place of the former tubular framework; this saved both weight and drag, putting up the maximum speed to 95 mph and the ceiling to 13,000 ft.

A new Allied offensive began in Flanders on 31 July, 1917, and Nos.7 and 7A Squadrons, RNAS, had the task of disrupting the supply of enemy munitions and stores from Germany to the Ypres sector, in addition to their continued attacks on aerodromes and submarine pens around Bruges and Ostende. Fourteen O/100s set the pattern on 16 August by dropping more than nine tons of bombs on Thourout railway junction; between 2 and 5 September they followed up with 18 tons on the docks at Bruges, to which the enemy retaliated with a succesion of night raids by Gotha bombers on Kent and London, followed by a sustained assault on Coudekerque, which was under almost continuous attack from 23 September to 2 October. In spite of considerable disruption and hurried dispersal to avoid further damage, the RNAS were able to drop nearly ten tons of bombs on the Thourout–Lichtervelde–Cortemarck railway triangle on 25 September, and on the 29th 3130 of No.7 Squadron, crewed by Flt

Cmdr H. G. Brackley, Sub Lieut Bewsher and A/M Wardrop, flew 250 miles in bright moonlight to plant four 250-lb and eight 65-lb bombs on the important Meuse railway bridge at Namur. On the same night, another O/100, specially armed with five Lewis guns and crewed by a pilot and four gunners, patrolled at 10,000 ft in the path of Gotha bombers returning from a raid on England; during the four hours that this patrol lasted, three Gothas were met and two were engaged; one which passed within 150 ft dived away when attacked and was believed to have landed in Holland. This was probably the earliest use of the tactics so effectively developed 27 years later by 100 (Bomber Support) Group, RAF.

In two preliminary raids on London on 13 June and 7 July, daylight formations of Gotha bombers had caused many civilian casualties in the City and East End, raising a public demand for similar action against Germany, which was intensified when the enemy's night raids began on 2 September. Although the Admiralty and War Office were opposed to purely retaliatory bombing of civilian targets, the Admiralty had always favoured strategic bombing of the Saar and Ruhr steel industry, centred round Krupps of Essen, as a means of depriving the U-boat fleet of replacements and repairs; the public outcry over the raids on London at last convinced the Air Board of the effectiveness of night bombing and it was agreed that more Handley Page O/400s should be ordered, both to re-equip existing squadrons in Flanders and for a new strategic force, the 41st Wing, RFC, to be based (as the 3rd Wing RNAS had earlier been) in the Vosges region around Nancy, south of the Metz salient. The first heavy bomber unit to be sent there was 'A' Squadron RNAS, formed at Manston in September 1917 from the nucleus of four O/100s detached from Coudekerque to Redcar earlier in the year. Under the command of Sqn Cmdr Savory, 'A' Sqn. arrived at Ochey on 17 October, 1917, with a complement of twelve O/100s, including such veterans as 1455 (the first prototype rebuilt), 1458, 1459, 1465, 1466, 3120, 3123, 3126 and 3127; this last was still piloted by Flt Cmdr F. K. Digby and had been flown by him with No.7 Squadron continuously since its first delivery to Coudekerque on 25 May. It remained in Digby's charge at Ochey, went on to lead a raid on Mannheim on 24/25 January, 1918, and then, in a flight lasting 8½ hours, the first raid since 1914 on Cologne; the latter exceptional feat, on 24/25 March, 1918, earned Digby a DSO; 3127 survived rebuilding, after a later forced landing, to take part in the final attack on Frescaty aerodrome on the night of 10/11 November, 1918. Not all the squadron's O/100s were so long-lived; of the last four to be issued, 3140 crashed and 3141, flown by Sub Lieut Geoffrey Linnell, was shot down in the squadron's first raid on Saarbrücken on 25 October, 1917, only a few days after arriving from Manston, while 3139 never arrived at all, having crashed on take-off from Manston on 3 November. Of the original dozen, the first, 1455, was destroyed on the ground at Ochey by enemy action in February 1918 and the last, 1466, returning from a raid on Frankfurt-am-Main on 22 August, 1918, was burnt out after a forced landing one mile short of Ochey, when a landing flare set light to petrol leaking from a shrapnel-punctured tank.

Many requests came from RFC squadrons for Handley Pages to replace their veteran F.E.2bs for night bombing, but the Air Board was still reluctant to order them until Sir William Weir brought up evidence from the 5th Wing RNAS showing a lower casualty rate and higher target accuracy at night than with single-engined D.H.4s by day. 'Naval A' was the only twin-engined strategic night-bomber unit to operate on the Vosges sector until the formation of the Independent Force, RAF, in June 1918. It remained at Ochey till March 1918, being renamed No.16 Squadron RNAS on 8 January and 216 Squadron RAF on 1 April, by which time it had begun to receive some of the first O/400s to enter service. When the Gotha night raids on London and Kent began in September and official policy on night bombing was reversed, one hundred and fifty O/400s (C9636–C9785) were ordered from Cricklewood, together with one hundred (D4561–D4660) from the Metropolitan Wagon Co and fifty (D5401–D5450) from the Birmingham Carriage Co. To these contracts were added, early in the new year, fifty (D8301–D8350) from the British Caudron Co (neighbours of Handley Page Ltd at Cricklewood) and fifty (D9681–D9730) from Clayton & Shuttleworth at Lincoln. The first twenty O/400s did not arrive in service till April 1918, yet by the end of August over two hundred had been issued to the RAF. The expanded production programme to equip new squadrons from the spring of 1918 onwards was more than even the enlarged Cricklewood factory could cope with, and was therefore shared with firms which had already gained some experience as sub-contractors for smaller types of aircraft. A great deal of organisation and planning was necessary to ensure standardisation of methods and materials between all the contractors in view of their differing background and traditions, but agreement was finally reached in a meeting at Cricklewood on 17 January, 1918, at which the Royal Aircraft Factory and Cubitts Ltd (managers of the new National Aircraft Factory No.1 at Waddon) were also represented. Two further batches of twenty were ordered from the Birmingham Carriage Co (F301–F320) and Handley Page Ltd (F3748–F3767) in May, and on 5 June a first batch of one hundred (F5349–F5448) was ordered from Waddon, which was to be the final assembly line for components supplied by numerous sub-contractors in the furniture and building industries. It was clear that the demand for Eagle VIIIs would greatly exceed available production so provision was made for both the last batch from Cricklewood and those from Waddon to be equipped with American Liberty 12 engines as soon as these became available. In all these later batches the nose gunner's cockpit reverted to its original low level and permanent maintenance platforms were fitted above the engines to aid daily servicing.

In Flanders, activity became intense in March 1918 as the Germans mounted a counter-offensive against the Ypres salient and the RNAS squadrons with the British Expeditionary Force were kept at full stretch. No.7A had been renumbered No.14 in December 1917 and No.16's place was filled by a new squadron, No.15, formed in March from both Nos.7 and 14; all three remained based at Coudekerque and No.15 was trained specifically for night bombing, although during its first few weeks it shared in combined air and naval operations aimed at blocking the entrances to Ostende harbour and the Zeebrugge canal. With the merging of the RNAS and the RFC to form the Royal Air Force on 1 April, 1918, the former naval Wing and Squadron numbers were increased by 60 and 200 respectively, so that the 5th Wing RNAS became the 65th Wing RAF, to which Nos.207, 214 and 215 Squadrons belonged. In their last operation under the White Ensign on 26 March, Nos.7 and 14 Squadrons combined to attack Valenciennes and neighbouring railway targets. On 11 April seven O/100s of Nos.214 and 215 Squadrons were detailed to bomb the Mole and coastal batteries at Zeebrugge, to distract attention from a naval force which attempted to block the harbour entrance; in particular 3129 of 214 Squadron, flown by Captain J. R. Allen, Captain Bewsher and Lieutenant Purvis, was to patrol along the coast in advance of the others, releasing 112-lb bombs at intervals to draw the enemy's anti-aircraft fire. Unfortunately the latter was too accurate and after 2½ hours on patrol one engine stopped and the aircraft failed by a few hundred yards to reach the coast at Nieuport; Allen was swept out of the cockpit and drowned, but Bewsher and Purvis were rescued by a coastal motor boat from Dunkirk.

O/400 of No.207 Squadron at Ligescourt on 29 August, 1918.

Meanwhile rain and mist had blanketed the coast and only three of the other six bombers managed to find targets, one of them having to land beyond the Dutch frontier, where its crew were interned; the naval force also was called off because of the weather, but on the night of 22/23 April returned to make the famous St George's Day raid on Zeebrugge, which bottled up twelve submarines and 23 motor torpedo boats in the canal. On 9 May a second attempt was made to block Ostende harbour by sinking the old cruiser *Vindictive* across the entrance and seven O/100s from No.214 Squadron co-operated by dropping six 550-lb and eighty smaller bombs on the German shore batteries; once more these attacks were almost frustrated by the sudden arrival of sea-fog and four returning crews failed to locate Coudekerque and had to land elsewhere, but only one aircraft was seriously damaged.

Early in June heavy enemy counter-attacks on British aerodromes were stepped up, Coudekerque being bombed for 3½ hours on 5/6 June and two hangars burnt out, although no aircraft were totally lost. The RAF

Maintenance work on O/400 of No.214 Squadron at Coudekerque on 1 June, 1918. *(I.W.M.—Crown Copyright)*

retaliated on 10 June, when 214 Squadron dropped three 550-lb bombs on the Zeebrugge sea-lock, 34 smaller bombs on the Bruges canal and 20 on Thourout junction. This was a sequel to experimental night raids in O/400s by Captain Cecil Darley and Captain T. A. Batchelor, using a silent gliding approach from 9,000 ft to within 80 ft of the target; the aim was to release simultaneously one bomb close to each lock and a third midway between them, so that the combined under-water blast would burst open the lock gates. For this operation Captain Batchelor had designed a special low-altitude bombsight and had carefully rehearsed its use with the aid of a full-scale model of the target marked out on the ground at Cranwell, where Darley and both crews had attended a special briefing. On the first attempt the two aircraft were spotted during their approach and heavily engaged at 500 ft by anti-aircraft guns, Batchelor and his observer being wounded and barely able to return to a safe landing at Coudekerque. Darley and his crew escaped personal damage, and on 28 May in C9666 he repeated the silent attack successfully with three 520-lb light case bombs from 200 ft, a subsequent photograph showing one of the gates being changed. Though successful in principle, such attacks could only close the canal for a few days and 10 June was the last raid until more effective 'SN' bombs of 1,650-lb became available; the first of these was dropped on a target at Middelkerke by C9643 flown by Sergt Dell of 214 Squadron on the night of 24/25 July, 1918. By this time No.215 Squadron had been re-equipped with O/400s and transferred to the Independent Force, after a brief rest and retraining sojourn at Netheravon, so Nos.207 and 214 remained the only O/400 squadrons attached to the British Expeditionary Force until September, when they were joined by No.58 on its conversion from F.E.2bs, its first O/400 being received in August.

In the south No.216 was joined in August by Nos.97 and 115 as well as No.215, all newly equipped with O/400s and located around Nancy. No.97 was to have had special training at Netheravon in new wireless techniques, including direction-finding, but finally went to France as a normal bombing squadron; like No.215, it was based at Xaffévillers, with No.115 nearby at Roville-aux-Chênes. For the more distant targets O/400s flew singly or in pairs, notable raids being made by two aircraft of No.216 on Cologne on 21/22 August and by two of No.215 on the Badisch Anilin und Soda Fabrik at Mannheim on 25/26 August, when direct hits were scored from only 200 ft. Also at Xaffévillers, No.100 Squadron converted from F.E.2bs to O/400s, receiving C9697 on 13 August; with No.216, this unit came temporarily under French Army orders during September, when they moved from Ochey to Autreville and Villesneux to support the French and American counter-offensive against the German threat to Paris, being particularly valuable to the Americans in the battle for St Mihiel; after this detachment they resumed strategic bombing from Xaffévillers, where the five squadrons formed the 83rd Wing of the VIII Brigade, Independent Force, RAF, and were the true precursors of Bomber Command. By September production of new O/400s was more than keeping pace with

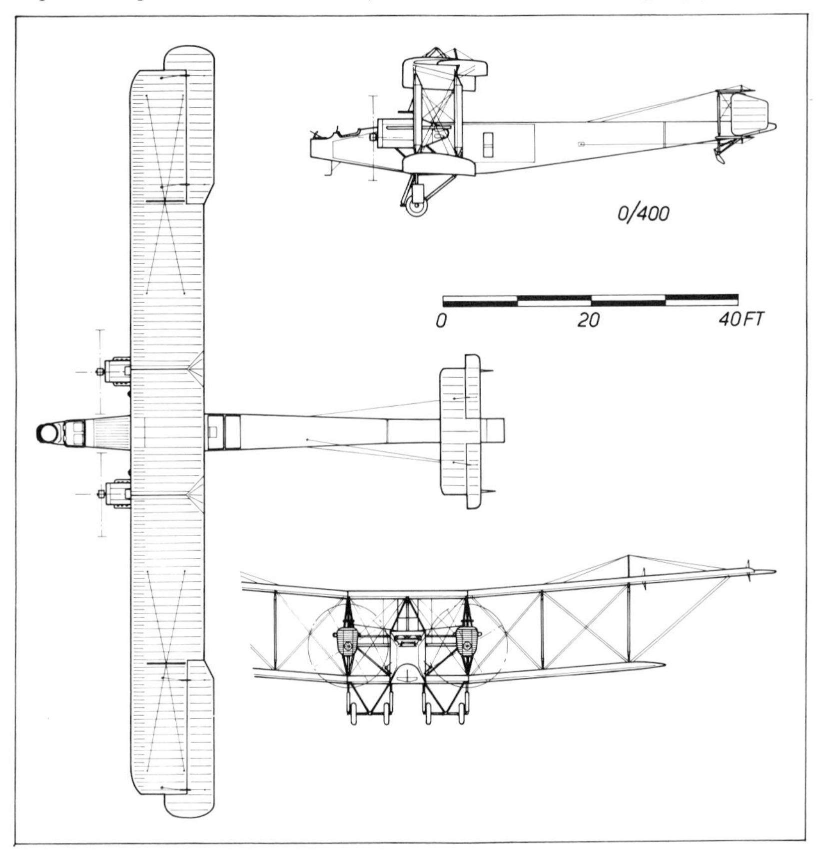

demand and only two further contracts were awarded, No.AS.34499 for fifty (J2242–J2291) to the Birmingham Carriage Co and No.AS.35429 for seventy-five (J3542–J3616) to the Metropolitan Wagon Co, both of which firms drew their labour force from the same district and delivered their products to the same Acceptance Park at Castle Bromwich. Unfortunately not all contractors were equally efficient or happy in their labour relations, a state of affairs reflected by the fact that when the Armistice came on 11 November, 1918, the Birmingham Carriage Co had completed and delivered thirty-four of their final batch, while Metropolitan Wagon had not begun theirs. In September, October and the first ten days of November, in face of very adverse weather and well-defended targets, the five Handley Page squadrons of the 83rd Wing dropped 350 tons of bombs, including eleven 1,650-pounders, on key installations in the Saar and Ruhr basins, as far afield as Essen and Cologne, yet the number of O/400s airborne on any one night was never more than forty. In September, the average weight of bombs dropped by each of the five squadrons was 26 tons, compared with 9½ tons by the single-engined D.H.4 and D.H.9 squadrons of the Independent Force; the greatest individual weight dropped in the same month was 37½ tons by the pioneer No.216 Squadron.

Handley Page operations were by no means confined to the Expeditionary and Independent Forces, and in the summer of 1918 a single O/400, C9681, following the Mediterranean trail blazed by Savory the previous year, was flown from Cranwell to Egypt in five days. This machine had been delivered new to Martlesham Heath and later detached to Cranwell for experiments by Captain Batchelor leading up to his and Darley's low-level attacks on the Zeebrugge lock gates; it retained the special low-altitude bombsight developed by Batchelor, now to be put to good use on another

O/400 with 1,650-lb SN bomb on Gledhill slip.

front. During 1917 the force sent earlier to Egypt to protect the Suez Canal had advanced into Palestine against the occupying Turkish armies; with meagre but vigorous air support, General Allenby, after significant victories at Beersheba and Gaza, had recaptured Jerusalem just before Christmas. His advance towards Damascus was opposed in the Jordan valley by three Turkish divisions, well supported by German aircraft based at Jenin and Deraa, and No.1 Squadron, Australian Flying Corps, had moved to Ramleh to restore the balance. Meanwhile T. E. Lawrence, the enigmatic egyptologist newly-gazetted as Colonel, was busy behind the Turkish lines organising Bedouin irregulars led by Sherif Feisal of Hedjaz, particularly in wrecking the railway which carried supplies from Damascus to Amman. Lawrence needed rapid communications between Feisal and Allenby, so he requested, and received, two of No.1 Squadron's newly

Ross Smith's O/400 C9861 with two Bristol Fighters of No.1 Squadron, Australian Flying Corps, at Haifa after the capture of Damascus in October 1918. (*Australian War Memorial*)

acquired Bristol Fighters; at the same time he suggested that one or more heavy bombers were urgently needed. So on 28 May, 1918, Brig-Gen A. E. Borton flew C9681 from Cranwell to Manston, where he picked up Major A. S. C. MacLaren, and continued by Savory's route to Otranto, thence by Suda Bay and Sollum to Heliopolis, finally arriving at the RAF base at Kantara on the Suez Canal on 8 August. After being serviced, C9681 was flown to Ramleh on loan to No.1 Squadron AFC, arriving there on 29 August. Piloted by Captain Ross Smith, it was promptly put to logistic use to carry one-ton loads of petrol, oil, spares and ammunition to Azrak, Lawrence's special flight base, where its arrival profoundly improved Arab morale impaired by recent enemy bombing; like wildfire the news spread that 'Allah has sent us THE aeroplane of which these others are foals' and C9681's mere presence was enough to unite the many independent Bedouin clans into a dedicated and invincible army. An early blow in the Battle of Nablus was struck by Ross Smith when C9681, with sixteen 112-lb bombs, took off an hour after midnight on 19 September, 1918, to score direct hits on the Turkish headquarters and central telephone exchange at El Afule, thus preventing the whole of the Turkish Seventh and Eighth Armies in the Plain of Sharon from getting wind of Allenby's movements for two vital days. Ross Smith returned that evening, and again early next day, to knock out the railway and aerodrome at Jenin. On the 21st the nine-mile column of the Seventh and Eighth Armies retreating towards the Jordan was trapped in the narrow defile of Wadi el Far'a and slaughtered by three squadrons of fighters from Ramleh; the O/400 took no direct part in this daylight action, but finally obliterated the enemy's remaining aerodrome at Deraa with a ton of bombs on the evening of the 23rd; meanwhile it had been airlifting more fuel and supplies from Ramleh, thus greatly speeding Allenby's advance to Damascus, where Feisal's columns entered in triumph on 1 October. For a few days C9681 remained at Haifa, thereafter flying back to Ramleh and thence to Kantara, whither Borton had meanwhile ferried from England the second O/400, C9700, to be sent to Egypt.

C9700 at Provin before being flown to Kantara in November 1918 by Brigadier-General Borton. (*C. A. Hall via Chaz Bowyer*)

During these same last days, the Germans had begun a fast retreat in Flanders and on 18 October Brackley flew No.214 Squadron's C9696 from St Inglevert to St Pol where he had the privilege of taking up King Albert and Queen Elisabeth of the Belgians to witness from the air the Allied reoccupation of Ostende, Ghent and Ghistelles, although on that day Bruges was still held by the enemy. On the 24th, No.214 Squadron flew in formation from St Inglevert to Quilen and thence on the 30th to Camphin in readiness to join with No.58 at Provin and No.207 at Ligescourt and Estrées-en-Chaussée in the final assault on Germany. Both these squadrons had effectively used 1,650-lb 'SN' bombs against railway targets at Valenciennes and Namur in September and October, No.207 alone dropping seventeen of them—more than the whole Independent Force in its nightly attacks on the Saar, Ruhr and Rhineland industries, where target priority was given to railways first and blast furnaces second. Austria signed an Armistice on 3 November, when O/400 squadrons prepared to move to eastern bases near Prague, within 200 miles of Berlin, but the total end of the war eight days later saved the German capital from actual assault. On the final night, 10/11 November, all eight O/400 squadrons, in appalling weather, sent out a total of twenty-six aircraft, railway targets being taken by five from No.58 and seven from No.214 at Louvain, and six from No.214 at Namur; Nos.97, 100, 115, 215 and 216 dispatched single machines against aerodromes at Morhange, Metz-Sablon, Lellinghen and Frescaty; No.216's representative at the last target was the O/100 veteran 3127 with 400 operational flying hours on its log, rebuilt after a forced landing and 'as good as new'.

In the last weeks of the war, new developments in night flying were impending; all national markings had been revised to exclude white circles or stripes for some months past, although the P.C.10 khaki-drab all-over colour scheme remained standard, relieved only by bright white vertical lines, considered invisible at a few hundred yards, which reinforced the standard arrows indicating the lifting and trestling points on the fuselage.

3126 in dappled night camouflage at Orfordness in 1917. (*H. F. Cowley*)

In an attempt to find an 'invisible' colour scheme trials had been made at Orfordness with a 'dappled' O/100 (3126) as a result of which a dull green colour showing minimum reflection in searchlight beams was evolved as the well-known Nivo finish; this was adopted as standard in June 1918 for Home Defence night fighters, but was not available for bombers until October, so few of the O/400s on active service in France carried this scheme; it was to be seen, however, on the long-range training aircraft of No.1 School of Navigation and Bomb-dropping at Stonehenge and Andover. About this time the High Altitude Drift Sight Mk IA was superseded by the Wimperis Course Setting Bombsight, incorporating a compass, which was to remain standard, with minor improvements, for another twenty years. The CSBS was originally mounted on the nose in the same position as the HA IA, but for the worst weather No.214 Squadron, and later the others, preferred a new position below the navigator's seat, adjacent to the permanently-fitted negative-lens drift sight, since the front cockpit was rarely manned at night. Some O/400s had two, three or four spotlights tilted downwards and a variation of this for very precise low-level attacks was to have the beams set to intersect at the required height, thus anticipating the method employed 25 years later by No.617 Squadron's 'Dam-Busters'. It was intended to fly secret service agents and saboteurs on to German aerodromes in Alsace-Lorraine, using either

Calthrop 'Guardian Angel' parachutes, or ladders in a quick 'touch-and-go' landing; the first operation was planned for the December full moon, but by then the war was over. In April 1918, when many pilots recuperating from front-line operations were employed in ferrying new aeroplanes to France, No.1 (Southern) Aircraft Repair Depot at Farnborough had fitted out an O/400 with sixteen inward-facing bench seats in place of the internal bomb-racks, with flat rectangular fuel tanks below the seats, for use on a proposed return ferry service between Marquise and Lympne. In an alternative Handley Page 'ferry-bus' scheme at Cricklewood, sixteen B.E.2c-type semicircular wicker seats were strapped to the floor in two circles, so that passengers sat with their feet together as in an Army bell-tent, and could then play pontoon. An auxiliary petrol tank had already been adopted for long-range flying, to fit on top of the fuselage, and it was practicable to use this alone in place of the normal internal tanks for short cross-Channel flights, thus making more room inside for passengers. The Farnborough scheme was used by the Parachute Experimental Unit under Major Orde Lees, but the return ferry service never materialised and eventually the aircraft was reconverted to its bomber role. The Cricklewood 'ferry-bus' scheme, however, was applied from August 1918 onwards to several newly-built O/400s used for officially-sponsored flights by foreign and Empire press correspondents at Hendon. Only one O/400 squadron, No.207, was allocated to the Army of Occupation after the Armistice, and this unit flew from Carvin to Merheim on New Year's Day 1919, moving on to Hangelar in May until its return to England in August. Nos.97, 115 and 215 returned to Ford, Sussex, in February and March 1919, while No.100 was posted to Baldonnel, Ireland, in September 1919, becoming a Bristol Fighter squadron in January 1920; the remaining three waited in France for orders to proceed to Egypt.

Meanwhile, on 13 December, the 86th (Communication) Wing had been formed at Hendon to provide quick transport between London and Paris for Cabinet Ministers and other officials engaged in negotiating the Peace Treaty at Versailles; it had eight O/400s on its strength, of which two (or possibly three) were specially converted for VIP passengers and finished all over in aluminium dope, with small roundels instead of stripes on the rudders. These were designated 'H.M. Airliners'—the first official recognition of this term—D8326 being named *Silver Star* and another *Great Britain*; a third is said to have been named *Silver Queen*, but in the absence of photographic evidence this is unconfirmed, as this was then a popular nickname for any large aeroplane (or airship) of that colour, and was given to both the Vickers Vimys which shared the first Cairo–Cape flight. *Silver Star* had a cabin for six passengers round a circular table and was upholstered with chintz-covered loose cushions; it had a large square window, with curtains, in each side. *Great Britain* was less luxurious, with eight side-facing leather-covered seats along the port side and four small square windows on each side. The arrangement in *Silver Queen* is not known, although the remainder of the eight aircraft also had side-facing bench seats, but retained their Nivo colour scheme. The 86th (Communication) Wing moved from Hendon in May 1919 and then comprised No.1 (Communication) Squadron at Kenley and No.2 (Communication) Squadron at Buc, near Paris, only the former having O/400s; traffic diminished after signature of the Peace Treaty and the Wing was disbanded

Silver Star at Cricklewood in April 1919 showing large cabin window.

in October. Additionally No.214 Squadron was employed in the early months of 1919 to carry military mails between Cologne and the Armistice Commission at Spa. The first airmail flight was made by Major Brackley on New Year's Day 1919 from Camphin, via Carvin, Lens, Arras, St Pol and Hesdin, to Ligescourt, but from 5 January the O/400s were only used nonstop between Marquise and Cologne, with D.H.9s taking the shorter stages.

Great Britain at Cricklewood in April 1919 showing small cabin windows.

C9700 wrecked by cyclone at Lahore in April 1919. (*C. A. Hall via Chaz Bowyer*)

The second O/400 flown from England to Egypt by Brig Gen Borton, C9700, had meanwhile pioneered the airway from Egypt to India, leaving Heliopolis on 30 November and flying via Damascus, Baghdad, Bushire, Bandar Abbas, Charbar, Karachi and Nasirabad to reach Delhi on 12 December. The credit for this flight has been wrongly attributed to the battle-scarred C9681, but in fact C9700 was the only O/400 to fly all the way from England to India. It wore roundels on its rudders instead of stripes, indicating that it was carrying Major-Gen W. G. H. Salmond, GOC RAF, Middle East, to survey the airmail route to India. The crew consisted of Ross Smith as co-pilot with Borton, and Sergts J. M. Bennett and W. H. Shiers of the Australian Flying Corps. The flight to Delhi was completed almost without incident, thanks to good advance planning of supplies of petrol, oil and spares at landing grounds en route; the only repair needed was to minor damage to the undercarriage after a heavy landing at Bandar Abbas, and Bennett and Shiers took this in their stride. On 16 December C9700 was flown on to Allahabad, and next morning to Calcutta, where the starboard wing-tip sustained slight damage from a tree while taxying in after landing on the maidan. In February Borton and Ross Smith continued their route survey to Burma by sea, while C9700 was flown to Ambala and Lahore for patrol duties along the North West Frontier, where in March Afghan rebels were threatening trouble; but soon after arriving at Lahore it was destroyed on the ground by a sudden storm.

Preparations were being made at home to develop an Empire-wide airmail and transport service as soon as international air-traffic regulations could be agreed, and the RAF made valuable contributions towards improved safety, particularly in night flying, until Treasury intervention curtailed expenditure on these activities. No.1 (Communication) Squadron at Kenley, in its daily London–Paris service, was gaining operational experience of scheduled night flying, maintaining radio contact throughout, and No.1 School of Navigation and Bomb-dropping at Andover began a series of training flights round the British Isles. In one of the first of these, two O/400s, piloted by Captains Stewart and Snook, left Andover on 19 April at 2.20 a.m. each with a crew of seven; flying along the coast from Brighton to the Wash via Dover, Great Yarmouth and Hunstanton, they reached their first refuelling stop at Waddington by 9 a.m. Taking off again at 12.30 p.m. they continued via Cleethorpes, Whitby, Sunderland and Berwick-upon-Tweed to arrive for the night at Turnhouse by 7 p.m. Next day they left at 11.30 a.m. and flew via Dundee, Aberdeen, Longside (Fraserburgh), Inverness and the Great Glen to their second night-stop at Aldergrove, arriving at 7.30 p.m. Resuming on the third day via Dublin, Anglesey, Aberystwyth and Cardigan to their third night-stop at Tenby, they took off at 4 a.m. on 22 April to fly home via Ilfracombe, Bodmin, Plymouth, Torquay and Portsmouth to a landing at Andover at 10 a.m. Regrettably, another O/400 (F3758), starting a similar flight, had crashed in flames at Weyhill on take-off at 2 a.m. that same morning, killing the pilots Major Batchelor and Captain Adkins and three of their crew, two survivors being injured. Major Batchelor's death was a severe loss to the peacetime RAF, as his contribution to navigational training was very great; his part in developing low-level bombing at Cranwell has already been mentioned and probably his most important invention was the Batchelor Mirror for training bomb-aimers. Another notable flight, this time by a double crew in a single O/400 (F3750, which at the time bore the legend LAST DAYS on its sides) was made by Major K. R. Park and Captain Stewart (pilots), Major B. E. Smythies and Lieutenant Wilson (navigators), with a crew of two wireless operators and three engine fitters, at the end of April. They followed the established coastwise route to Waddington and intended to make Longside for the night, but rain and low cloud over the Cheviots forced them to put down at Turnhouse. Next day they resumed their planned course via Aberdeen, Longside, Inverness and the Great Glen to the Mull of Kintyre, but found Aldergrove completely fog-bound. Arriving over Belfast at 7 p.m. with petrol running low, Major Park brought off a masterly cross-wind landing on Harland & Wolff's wharf at Queen's Island in a space only 400 yds long by 50 yds wide. Next day, to lighten the machine as much as possible, Park took off solo, having sent the rest of the crew by road to Aldergrove, where he landed to pick them up; the flight was then continued via Dublin, Pembroke (night-stop), Bodmin, Plymouth and Bournemouth to land at Andover at 9.30 a.m. on

Major K. R. Park with his double crew at Andover after flying F3750 *Last Days* round the British Isles in April 1919. (*J. M. Bruce*)

the fourth day; this flight covered 1,600 miles in 30 hours, averaging 66 mph and 450 miles per day. Just previously another O/400 from Andover had flown nonstop to Baldonnel in 6½ hours, by dead reckoning entirely in darkness.

Such experience was urgently needed when the Allied Armistice Commission awarded the mandate for the administration of Palestine to Britain; this revived an age-long dispute incapable of just solution, for the Arabs had been encouraged to win their freedom from the Ottoman Empire by Winston Churchill's promise, via Lawrence, that they would be given land in the Jordan valley; but the same territory had also been assigned by Arthur Balfour to the Zionist Jews of Europe, who were determined to build a new State of Israel in the Promised Land. Fifty years later this conflict was to become even more acute, but in 1919 the first essential was to enforce the mandate and secure peace by military occupation, in both Palestine and the other ex-Ottoman territory of Mesopotamia. In March 1919, No.58 Squadron was ordered to move to Egypt, and for the first time, in view of the difficulty and cost of packing O/400s for transit as deck cargo, it was decided that the squadron should fly out in formation, using the route already pioneered by Savory and Borton. So ten O/400s of 58 Squadron left their Belgian base at Provin on 3 May and flew to Paris, thence via Lyons, Marseilles, Pisa, Centocelle, Foggia, Taranto, Valona, Suda Bay, Sollum and Amria to Heliopolis, where they arrived on 2 July after many vicissitudes and several casualties. Meanwhile Nos.214 and 216 had received similar orders; No.214 left Camphin on 1 July and seven of its ten aircraft (including C9666 flown by Second Lieutenant C. A. Hall) had arrived at Abu Sueir by 2 August; No.216 left Marquise on 10 July in three flights, the first of which crashed en route; the remainder struggled through to Kantara by mid-October. All three squadrons became part of the Middle East Training Brigade, but only at the cost of eleven pilots killed, including Captain Cecil Darley, another veteran of the silent raids on Zeebrugge. Accusations in Parliament by Sir William Joynson-Hicks of inefficient maintenance, and a complaint that thirty-two O/400s had been picketed out at Hendon unprotected from heavy rain in March, brought a rejoinder from his old adversary, General Seely, that these were not the aeroplanes involved and that in any case they had all been repaired at an average cost of £52 each.

Coincidentally with the departure of 58 Squadron from Provin, Col T. E. Lawrence, who had been in attendance at Versailles, decided to return urgently to Egypt and, as was his way, 'thumbed a lift' with Lieutenants Prince and Spratt in D5439 of 'B' Flight when they called at Marquise to join formation with other O/400s flying from Hendon. The aerodromes along the Mediterranean coast were in a bad state of repair and the O/400 nearly overturned in landing at Pisa, but damage was averted; next day, 17 May, the flight proceeded, but D5439 arrived very late at Centocelle and crashed while attempting to land in the dusk. Prince was killed outright, Spratt died on arrival in hospital, and A/M Tomlin died later; the fourth crew member was less badly injured and Lawrence broke a collar-bone and several ribs. He was visited in hospital by King Victor Emmanuel, who arranged for adequate treatment and comfort, and Lieutenant Carl Dixon, the American pilot of C9745 of 'B' Flight, remained to attend the inquest and funeral. Although far from fit to travel, Lawrence insisted on flying on with Dixon when he resumed his journey; they reached Taranto and Valona safely, but came to grief at Suda Bay, and Lawrence was stranded once more, this time for a month. Then the Canadian crew of F318 of the 86th (Communication) Wing at Kenley was ordered to take another Middle East expert, Harry St. John Philby, very urgently to Cairo. Leaving Lympne on 21 June, Lieutenants Yates and Vance, with mechanics Stedman and Hand, set out to deliver their very important passenger to Cairo in record time. Refuelling at Lyons, they landed for the night at Marseilles and punctured two tyres taxying out to take off at dawn next day. In spite of this delay, they reached Pisa for the night and flew on to Centocelle and Taranto on the 23rd. On take-off next morning the starboard fuel pump failed, so that none of the petrol in the aft tank was available; there was not enough in the forward tank alone to reach Suda Bay, so they diverted to Athens, which was an hour nearer, but south of the Gulf of Corinth their fuel gave out and Yates pulled off a very marginal landing on a rocky plateau, puncturing one tyre and breaking the tailskid. They had no jack, but local villagers lifted the tail while the skid was repaired, and Yates then taxied the aircraft to a position where the punctured tyre overhung a pot-hole and could be removed for repair; then they transferred 3 hours' fuel from the aft tank to the forward one, took off in the bare 50 yards available and reached Athens with Stedman and Hand manning the handpumps. Next morning both engines cut on take-off because of water in the carburettors and all the petrol had to be drained and strained through chamois leather—delaying them another ten hours. At last on the 25th they got airborne, using the handpumps all the time, but halfway to Crete a blade cracked on the port airscrew and its engine had to be throttled back to reduce vibration; they arrived at Suda Bay with only 600 ft in hand. There Lawrence helped them to take an airscrew from C9745 and, in return, Philby invited him to join his party. Because of the extra weight and high ambient temperature they made two abortive attempts to take off on the 26th and then incurred four hours' delay from water in the carburettors; when at last they were airborne, they could not climb high enough to clear the mountains of Crete, so Yates flew round to the south of the island and set a course for Sollum, which they reached in 4 hours by dead reckoning, to Lawrence's great delight. By this time the external control cables were frayed and the fabric was worn through in

F318 at Heliopolis in June 1919 after flying from Lympne in 36 hours.

patches, but they decided to risk flying 6 hours across 500 miles of desert direct to Heliopolis, arriving $1\frac{1}{2}$ hours after sunset and taking another 40 minutes to find the aerodrome; F318's flying time of 36 hours in a total elapsed time of five days was a new record, the previous best being Borton and MacLaren's in C9681. A month later another O/400 of the same batch, F304, had to ditch off Spezia and its pilot, Lieutenant Collinge, was drowned, although his navigator and two sergeants were rescued. Other casualties along the route in July were C9714 and D4591, which crashed in Italy, and C9743, destroyed by a gale at St Raphaël. Such were the conditions faced by fifty-one crews of these three squadrons on the first long overseas movement by the Royal Air Force; small wonder that only twenty-six arrived, leaving a trail of fifteen wrecked and ten abandoned O/400s along the Mediterranean shores.

Salvaging engines from the O/400 which crashed at Abu Hamed on 4 April, 1920. (*G. S. Leslie*)

In the later months of 1919 No.58 Squadron began to replace its O/400s with Vickers Vimys, but two notable long-distance flights were achieved in September, one to Baghdad via Damascus using radio, and the other to Khartoum; the latter may have been an unannounced attempt to fly to the Cape in stages, but the O/400 was still at Khartoum in February 1920 and was offered to (and declined by) Brackley and Tymms as a replacement for G-EAMC*; it was in a run-down state and in an ill-advised attempt to fly back to Heliopolis, it crashed at Abu Hamed on 4 April killing all its crew (Flying Officers Barclay and Sibley, Sergt Wadey and AM2 Meldrum). No.58 Squadron's last five Handley Pages remained with the unit after it had been renumbered 70 Squadron on 1 February, 1920, and in June 1920 one O/400 was employed on a twice-weekly desert reconnaissance in liaison with the Camel Corps, who were trying to check Bedouin gun-running; as a further experiment, in September, one of No.70 Squadron's O/400s successfully air-lifted a mountain gun weighing half a ton and demonstrated this operation to the AOC, Sir Geoffrey Salmond, at Almaza. At least four O/400s remained on the strength of 70 Squadron during 1921 and took part in an air display at Heliopolis on 3 March; two of these were later lent to Wing Cmdr P. F. M. Fellowes to supply fuel and rations to the motor convoy which first ploughed the furrow marking the desert airmail route to Baghdad; one of them was wrecked at Ramleh at the end of May and the other was scrapped later in the year. Meanwhile 214 Squadron had been disbanded at Abu Sueir in February 1920 and in October 1921 the O/400s of 216 Squadron were replaced by D.H.10s; among the last in service was C9666, formerly bearer of the battle honour *Zeebrugge*.

* See pages 157–8

At home O/400s still flew on liaison duties, notably to Baldonnel in Ireland, and on 17 December, 1920, J2259 ditched in the Irish Sea off Holyhead, the crew of five all being rescued by the Elder Dempster cargo ship *Ijakaty*. Another had come to grief on 11 January, 1920, while pegged down for the night at Werrington, near Peterborough, when a gale had uprooted it and blown it across the Great Northern Railway mainline; the southbound *Flying Scotsman* was held up by it for 80 minutes and the wings were sawn off to save time in clearing the track. No fewer than fourteen O/400s were equipped for trials with the Aveline auto-stabiliser, a French device which in reasonably smooth air could hold an aeroplane on a steady course for up to two hours without intervention by the pilot, but could not cope with repeated gusts. In the RAF Tournament at Hendon in July 1920 and again at the Pageant there a year later, an O/400 flown by Flt Lieut Cecil Rea from Martlesham Heath demonstrated various pyrotechnic devices, including smoke and incendiary bombs developed at the Isle of Grain by Sqn Ldr J. K. Wells. Although the 'Geddes Axe' interim report stated that O/400s were no longer on RAF charge in October 1921, a few had, in fact, been retained for miscellaneous and experimental duties after being superseded in squadron service by Vickers Vimys and D.H.10s. In July 1922 two O/400s were detailed to drop eight 9-lb practice bombs each in simulated attacks on the old battleship *Agamemnon* while steaming at 10 knots under radio control off the Isle of May in the Firth of Forth; one had to return to Leuchars, but the other scored two direct hits and six near misses from 8,000 ft, arousing much animosity in the Royal Navy, who resented the RAF's control of naval flying before the independent Fleet Air Arm was formed. One or two O/400s had survived as the equipment of Lt-Col L. F. Blandy's Wireless Testing Park at Biggin Hill, and one of them may have been J2260 which paid several visits to Croydon in 1922 for night landing practice without ground aids; the first was on 2 March for preliminary tests, then on 5 April it flew with eight technicians (one of whom was P. P. Eckersley, later the BBC's first chief engineer) to test lighting and wireless facilities at Lympne and St Inglevert; these tests culminated in a demonstration to Sir Sefton Brancker, the new Director of Civil Aviation, of night flying between Croydon and Le Bourget on 1 June.

J2260 of the Wireless Testing Park, Biggin Hill, during night navigation trials at Croydon in April 1922.

J2260 was equipped with Holt landing flares, improved navigation and identification lights and the latest Marconi radio telephone and direction-finding aids. A Martlesham O/400 reappeared twelve months later to make a farewell appearance as dispenser of coloured smoke in the final item of the RAF Pageant at Hendon on 30 June, 1923, but the last two O/400s were in use at Farnborough as late as 1 August, 1923, when Flying Officer Junor crashed one while testing a gyro-stabilised rudder control system; at that date C9773 was still in commission, after completing slipstream exploration trials in the hands of Flying Officer Howard Saint, who later became test pilot to the Gloster Aircraft Company.

So far only British production has been considered, but the O/400 was one of the only two European multi-engined bombers selected for mass production in America after the United States joined the Allies in April 1917, the other being the Caproni Ca.46. In June Colonel Raynal C. Bolling arrived in Europe with a commission to select suitable types of aircraft and in August a set of O/400 drawings was sent to McCook Field, Dayton, Ohio, where the US Signals Corps Engineering Division designed a modification scheme to substitute the new Liberty 12 engine for the Rolls-Royce Eagle. Like the D.H.4 and D.H.10, the O/400 was strong enough to accept this engine change with advantage, although some other selected types, including the Bristol Fighter and S.E.5a, were too light. In January 1918 a sample airframe was shipped to McCook Field; this was in fact B9449, an 'intermediate' O/100 in which most parts were the same as in O/400, those which were different being painted red. The change of engine delayed production to the extent that, of the first batch of five hundred O/400s ordered from the Standard Aircraft Corporation of Elizabeth, New Jersey, only 100 sets of components (each 85 per cent complete) were ready to be shipped to Liverpool before Armistice Day; of these, 70 sets were dispatched in five ships, but only ten sets reached their destination; the second batch of 1,000, ordered in August 1918 for the equipment of 30 US squadrons in Europe, was cancelled before any work began on it. In November 1917 a conference at Springfield, Mass, had considered the possibility of flying Standard-built O/400s across the Atlantic to Aldergrove, and Handley Page was very keen to have this done, but the project was later given up. The first O/400 (almost certainly B9449 reworked) to emerge from the Standard Corporation's new factory at Bayway, NJ, was tested first by Colonel the Master of Sempill and Captain E. B. Waller and ceremonially launched with a bottle of champagne on 6 July by Mrs Mingle, wife of Standard's president; immediately afterwards it was again taken up by Colonel Sempill, accompanied by Captain E. L. Austin and General L. Kenly, in the presence of Major Gen. Brancker, Sir Henry Fowler, W. A. Chamberlain of Handley Page Ltd and W. H. Workman, who was Handley Page's agent in America. Because of the existing indigenous cotton crop and the scarcity of flax, a specially developed scoured cotton fabric (similar to madapalam) was used instead of Irish linen, and this required cellulose acetate dope, which was in short supply, instead of the more plentiful nitrate dope; for the first few flights the dope scheme was unpigmented and finished with clear varnish; the name *Langley* was painted on each flank and also across the nose, together with crossed Union Jack and Old Glory. The nose cockpit was of the high (Davis gun) pattern, with a Scarff ring mounting a yoked pair of Marlin 0·300

Langley at Wilbur Wright Field in 1919. (*US Air Force*)

calibre machine-guns. After handing over in August for flight trials, the *Langley* was repainted all over in olive-drab, with red-blue roundels and full red, white and blue rudder stripes, but retained its nose and flank decorations. During the next twelve months a Bayway-built O/400 was assessed against a new Glenn Martin G.M.B. prototype, and the first of two Caproni Ca.46s also built by Standard. All three were destroyed at Hazelhurst Field, Long Island, on 28 July, 1919, when the base was struck by a hurricane. The *Langley* itself was stored at Wilbur Wright Field, Dayton, in November 1919; it never had a serial number.

A Standard-built Liberty-engined O/400. (*US Air Force*)

Gallopin' Goose at Kelly Field, Texas, in 1921, compared with a Martin MB-1. (*US Air Force*)

Apart from the ten sets of components actually shipped to Liverpool, to be completed at Gorse Mill, Hollinwood and Lilac Mill, Shaw, and shipped back to New York after the Armistice, only three more O/400s were assembled in 1919 for Service trials by the US Air Service; at least one of these retained the raised nose cockpit, but twenty others with the later low gun-rings were held in store; one O/400 stationed at Kelly Field, San Antonio, Texas, was numbered 32 and had a *Gallopin' Goose* emblem painted on the nose. In 1920 seven of those in store, serials 62445–62451 were recommissioned at Langley Field, Hampton, Virginia, for trials with experimental 2,000-lb armour-piercing bombs, made at McCook Field to the order of General William Mitchell. On 21 July, 1921, after the US Navy's F5-L flying-boats had failed to make any impression with 520-pounders on the 3-inch deck armour and 12-inch belt armour of the former German battleship *Ostfriesland*, while anchored in Chesapeake Bay, the US Army sent in six Martin MB-5s and a single O/400 (probably 62448), each with a 2,000-pounder 11 ft 6 in long and 18½ inches in diameter, packed with 1,000 lb of TNT. Flying 98 miles from Langley Field to the target ship, they attacked in line astern with the Handley Page last; all six of the Martins' bombs scored direct hits and the seventh, from the O/400, finished the job as the ship began to sink. In September 1921 an even more powerful 4,000 lb bomb was successfully dropped by 62448 at the

Standard-built 62448 over Aberdeen proving range with 4,000-lb bomb in September 1921. (*US Air Force*)

Aberdeen, Maryland, proving range. Such demonstrations of the vulnerability to air attack of heavily armoured but unescorted battleships made 'Billy' Mitchell a marked man in US Navy circles and the vendetta leading to his court-martial and dismissal, followed too late by posthumous recognition, is a matter of history.

In the confusion following the Armistice it was inevitable that application of the break clause to cancel contracts not already started by that date, superimposed on the breakdown in labour relations which had occurred earlier in several of the Waring group of factories, should have left some of the production records incomplete. The best attempt at elucidation was made by the Royal Commission on Awards to Inventors in 1920, when Handley Page's claim to compensation in respect of Crown user of the O and V types was investigated. In the pleadings it is recorded that a total of 840 O-type aircraft was ordered, of which 600 were manufactured and paid for by the Ministry of Munitions and 476 were delivered to Service units and stores depots. These totals include forty O/100s, six intermediate

F5349 being erected by US Air Service personnel at Ford Junction in October 1918. (*I.W.M.—Crown Copyright*)

O/100-400s (*i.e.* B9446–B9451) and 281 O/400s manufactured by Handley Page Ltd; and 273 O/400s by other contractors. Taking into account the known cancellations under the break clause, it is evident that Handley Page Ltd received payment for 120 more O/400s than were originally ordered from them. It is known that Handley Page Ltd erected the British Caudron batch of fifty and that Cubitts' National Aircraft Factory No.1 at Waddon was closed down on 31 December, 1918, without having delivered any O/400s, but that seventy of the Cubitts batch were in fact completed, being assembled at Cricklewood from components manufactured by Cubitts' sub-contractors; it is a reasonable assumption that Handley Page Ltd were credited with the manufacture of these seventy in the final reckoning; only the first, F5349, had Liberty engines, which were installed at Ford Junction, Sussex, in October 1918 by American personnel, who also erected the aircraft. This appears to have been the only British-built Liberty-

F5349 with Liberty engines at Cricklewood in February 1919; in the pilot's cockpit is the Crown Prince of Sweden, with Lt-Col Ormonde Darby beside him. (*I.W.M.—Crown Copyright*)

engined O/400, and was test-flown at Cricklewood early in 1919. The British totals stated do not include the total of American production, which was officially recorded as 107 delivered and 1,393 cancelled.

By comparison with the D.H.10 and Vickers Vimy, which superseded it in post-war RAF service, the O/400 was outdated and outpaced, but should not be too harshly judged. In 1914, the O/100 was a bold embodiment of the most advanced state of the art of its day; after early troubles had been overcome, it succeeded far beyond its creators' hopes and its critics' fears, but most of its success was due to progressive improvements in its Rolls-Royce engines. Without the constraint and compulsion of standardised wartime production schedules, there might well have been a case for developing and refining the airframe to gain more speed, increased bomb load, higher ceiling and longer range, to say nothing of an assured single-engine capability. There were schemes to reduce drag by simplifying the landing gear and tail arrangement and it is believed that the single O/400 manufactured by Harland & Wolff, J1934, was a prototype in which the longerons were McGruer tubular spars, as in the V/1500. A relatively small change in wing section from RAF 6 to RAF 15 would have enhanced the O/400's overall performance in 1917, and it might then have competed with the D.H.10 and Vimy; it accepted Liberty 12 engines without structural change and a successful civil conversion of D5444 to Napier Lions (as G-EASO) in 1920 showed how its post-war service, both military and commercial, could have been prolonged.

Handley Page and Volkert may have considered this possibility, but were wiser than to risk new wine in old bottles; instead, they developed the W series, combining the experience and best features of both O and V. So the O/400 remained virtually unchanged in the changing environment it had done much to create, and not till Fairey Hendon monoplanes arrived in 1936 did the RAF again have land-based bombers of 100 ft span in squadron service.

O/100

(Two Rolls-Royce Eagle II or IV or two Sunbeam Cossack)

Span 100 ft (30·5 m); length 62 ft 10 in (19·2 m); wing area 1,648 sq ft (153 m²). Empty weight 8,000 lb (3,630 kg); maximum weight 14,000 lb (6,350 kg). Speed 76 mph (122 km/h). Crew four.

O/400

(Two Rolls-Royce Eagle VIII or two Sunbeam Maori or two Liberty 12-N)

Span 100 ft (30·5 m); length 62 ft 10 in (19·2 m); wing area 1,648 sq ft (153 m²). Empty weight 8,200 lb (3,720 kg); maximum weight 14,000 lb (6,350 kg). Speed 97 mph (156 km/h); ceiling 8,500 ft (2,625 m); endurance 8 hr. Crew four.

P/320 and R/200 (H.P.13 and 14)

By the end of 1916, the Royal Naval Air Service had accepted the technique of flying-off land aeroplanes from the deck of a seaplane carrier as feasible for active service; single-seat scouts were already replacing float seaplanes for short-range attacks on Zeppelin sheds sufficiently near the coast and the Admiralty invited tenders for larger ship-based bombers, both single- and two-seat, in category N.1a. One such was the Handley Page Type P, designed to carry a crew of two, two machine-guns, four 100 lb bombs, and cameras, but no wireless, with a speed range of 50 mph to 115 mph and climb to 10,000 ft in 20 min. Originally sketched as a biplane for which the intended 200 hp Hispano-Suiza engine was not available, a change was made to the much heavier 320 hp Sunbeam Cossack, which in turn required a large increase in wing area to maintain the same wing loading; since the overall dimensions also had to be kept within close limits, Volkert solved the problem by redesigning this machine, P/320, as a triplane. Two prototypes, N519–N520, were ordered, but cancelled almost at once, after which a fresh start was made with a smaller biplane, Type R/200, when at last a supply of 200 hp Hispano-Suizas had been assured for it.

The R/200 was a small two-seat reconnaissance-fighter intended to operate either as a seaplane or from the decks of HMS *Furious* and *Argus*, on which deck landing techniques were being developed during 1917. The specification, in the Admiralty N.2a category, defined dimensional limits to suit the carriers' hangar space, emphasising interchangeability and ease of maintenance at sea. The engines specified were the Bentley B.R.2 rotary or the 200 hp Hispano-Suiza, which were both in mass production for the Admiralty and War Office. Volkert chose the latter engine and obtained a contract for six prototypes, N27–N32, in the summer of 1917, with a

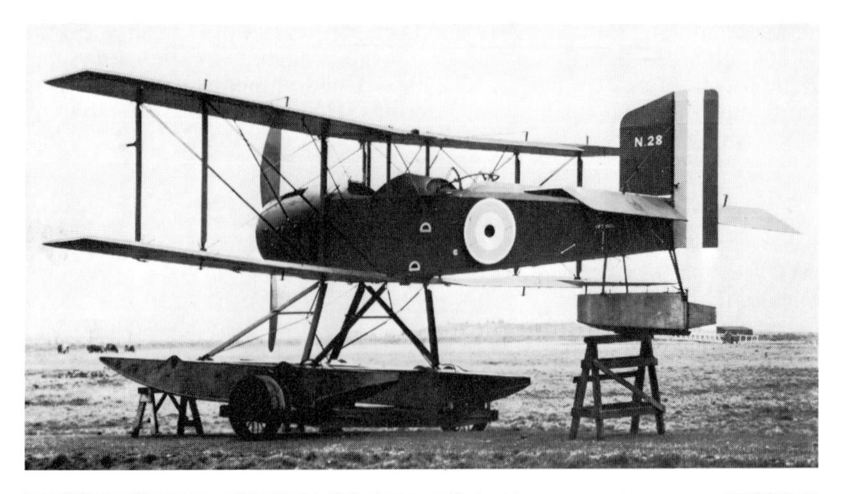

Two views of the second R/200, N28, at Grain in December 1917. (*I.W.M.—Crown Copyright*).

promise of an initial production batch of twenty to follow. Soon afterwards, his involvement with a new heavy bomber project necessitated his delegating the detail design of the R/200 to Leslie Richards, who evolved a neat single-bay biplane of economic construction, with identical upper and lower wings, having 2 degrees dihedral and no stagger; the whole trailing edge aft of the rear spar was taken up by ailerons and camber-changing flaps on both wings. Not only were the ailerons and flaps all of equal span and area, but the port ailerons were interchangeable with the starboard flaps and vice versa. The same principles governed the design of the tail surfaces, where the rudder and each elevator were identical, as were the fin and each half of the tailplane; such comprehensive interchangeability was expected to speed production of components and reduce the variety of spares needed on board ship. The fuselage was a flat-sided wire-braced girder with four spruce longerons and perpendicular struts, stringers being used only to form the curved decking. The pilot occupied the forward cockpit under the centre section and had conventional controls, with the aileron cables arranged to intersect the wing hinge centres so that tension in the circuit was maintained whether the wings were spread or folded. The flaps were pulled down symmetrically, by means of a separate handwheel alongside the pilot, against the tension of rubber cords anchored to the top of the front spar of the upper wing.

The geared 200 hp Hispano-Suiza vee-eight water-cooled engine was neatly installed with a circular front honeycomb radiator and louvred detachable aluminium cowling panels. There were no exhaust manifolds and the petrol in the main fuselage tank between the cockpits was pumped to a small gravity service tank set into the centre-section leading edge. The observer's cockpit, with its Scarff ring for a Lewis gun, was aft of the centre section and afforded a good all-round view and field of fire for self-defence. The landing gear comprised interchangeable sea and land chassis, the former having twin carvel-built mahogany floats with single steps and shallow V-bottoms, together with a tail float having a strong central skeg and a water-rudder operated directly from the pilot's rudder bar by separate cables; the main floats were rubber-sprung, but not the tail float. The alternative wheeled chassis had simple V-struts, with a rubber-sprung cross-axle; the tailskid also was rubber-sprung. The third and fourth prototypes were to be delivered with wheels and the other four with floats. Meredith had arranged for most of the work on the production batch to be

Two views of N29 at Grain in March 1918.

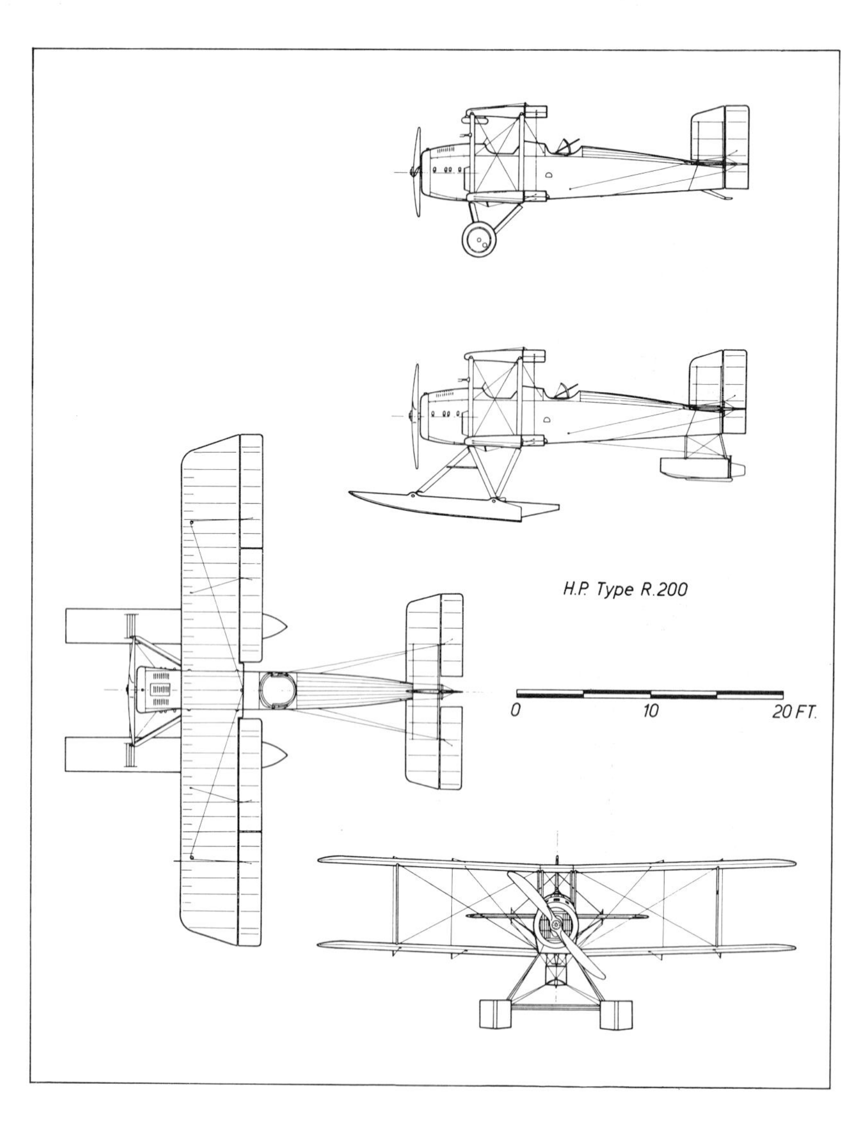

sub-contracted, with final assembly in requisitioned premises in Cricklewood Lane, as the main factory was fully occupied, and it is believed that serials N6080–N6099 were reserved for production aircraft.

The first two seaplanes, N27 and N28, were tested at the Welsh Harp reservoir at Hendon in December 1917 by Gordon Bell, who ferried them to the RNAS testing station at the Isle of Grain, where the first landplane, N29, also arrived in February 1918; but in view of the overriding priority of O/400 and V/1500 production at Cricklewood the remaining three prototypes and all the production R/200s were cancelled in March 1918. The performance, as tested at Grain, was not outstanding and in general the R/200 was considered inferior to the Parnall Panther, which was faster, lighter and even smaller, with the further advantage that its B.R.2 engine was reliable, whereas the Hispano-Suiza suffered badly from reduction gear and crankshaft failures. Possibly the R/200 could have been refined and improved, but for the more urgent demands of the V/1500.

R/200

(200 hp Hispano-Suiza)

Span 36 ft (10·97 m); length (seaplane) 29 ft 8 in (9·1 m), (landplane) 25 ft 6 in (7·77 m); wing area 390 sq ft (36·2 m²). Empty weight 1,882 lb (853 kg); maximum weight 2,990 lb (1,355 kg). Speed 93 mph (150 km/h); ceiling 12,000 ft (3,710 m). Pilot and observer.

V/1500 (H.P.15)

Ever since the formation of the Royal Flying Corps in 1912, it had been the Army's consistent view that military aircraft should be used only for reconnaissance, to report back the enemy's disposition, which the artillery would then destroy so as to clear the way for the infantry's advance. The idea that aircraft could themselves destroy and occupy was not taken seriously by the War Office, which held that the RFC was to be employed strictly at the discretion of the army commander in the field. The Admiralty, being accustomed to bombardment and blockade, was willing to accept bombers as alternative to long-range guns, provided that they could attain a better level of performance and reliability than the fragile aeroplanes so far available. For this reason Admiral Jellicoe had fought the Battle of Jutland without the carrier *Campania* and her fourteen seaplanes, and it was left to the relatively junior officers of the RNAS to demonstrate the value of bombing enemy submarine bases along the Belgian coast and to extend this activity to the Saar and Ruhr steelworks where submarine manufacture really began. The Handley Page O/100 and O/400 were the only bombers capable of carrying a worthwhile bomb load to targets, such as Mannheim and Cologne, 250 miles or more from the nearest French base at Nancy, and by early 1917 the naval members of the Air Board had drafted two specifications for night-bombers capable of flying at least 500 miles: A.3(b) for a large aircraft carrying a bomb-load of 3,000 lb at 100 mph and A.2(b) for a smaller one carrying 500 lb at 115 mph. Confident from his experience in evolving the O/400, Handley Page was already designing a new bomber of twice the weight, powered by two of the new 600 hp engines being developed by Rolls-Royce (as the Condor) and Siddeley-Deasy (as the Tiger) and scheduled for production early in 1918. Before this design could be formally offered to meet specification A.3(b), the military members of the Air Board, at a meeting on 23 June, 1917, vetoed all new orders for night bombers, claiming that they diverted effort from the real job of reconnaissance and artillery spotting on which aircraft should properly be engaged, a view that Major-Gen Trenchard, C-in-C RFC, vigorously opposed. The new Controller of the Technical Department at the Air Board, Major John Buchanan, having been informed from naval sources that neither the casualty rate nor bombing accuracy in RNAS squadrons was worse by night than by day, had the question reconsidered a week later, with the support of Sir William Weir, and was allowed to invite and accept tenders to both specifications; then on 7 July, enemy bombers raided London for the second time and the War Cabinet had to take urgent action to restore public confidence. General Smuts was charged with reorganising the flying services and recommended amalgamation of the RNAS and RFC into a single Royal Air Force, with Trenchard at its head. In August 1917, orders were given to Vickers Ltd for three prototypes to A.2(b) and to Handley Page Ltd for three prototypes to A.3(b), the latter being designated Type V and covered by contract No.AS.22690 for serials B9463–B9465.

Type V was schemed initially as an enlarged equal-span version of the O/400, of twice its weight and carrying more than twice its useful load. It had to accommodate a minimum crew of three in the nose, with the best possible communication between pilot and bomb-aimer, and to carry up to twenty-eight 112-lb bombs suspended vertically on removable racks inside the fuselage. In October 1917, in view of the strict secrecy of the project and lack of drawing office capacity at Cricklewood, Handley Page arranged, with Sir William Weir's help, for the design work and prototype manufacture to be undertaken at Belfast by Harland & Wolff Ltd, who supplied twenty draughtsmen and a large number of fitters and carpenters, normally employed on the interior furnishings of luxury ocean liners but transferred to aircraft work for the duration of the war. Volkert went to Belfast in charge of the project, taking with him Francis Arcier as his chief assistant and four senior designers, including S. T. A. Richards (younger brother of Leslie Richards and an ex-Great Western Railway apprentice from Swindon) who a year earlier had been personal assistant to Handley Page. The Admiralty lent Captain T. M. Wilson RN, who undertook all the stressing, which Handley Page himself checked during visits to Belfast every week-end; they all worked twelve hours a day from Monday to Saturday, and four hours on Sunday mornings when Handley Page joined them, starting from a preliminary layout drawn on squared paper by Richards under Handley Page's guidance. With the double aim of saving weight and avoiding the use of long lengths of spruce, all the longerons and struts, except in the extreme nose of the fuselage, were made from hollow spars of circular or streamline section, rolled up from laminated spruce in the manner patented by the Southampton yacht builder McGruer. This resulted in a very slender but strong structural space-frame, of larger cross-section, but little greater length, than the O/400. There were upper and lower gun mountings amidships as on the O/400, and a catwalk along the port side gave interior access to a gunner's cockpit in the extreme tail. Instead of separate cylindrical fuel tanks, a large internally-braced rectangular tank of 1,000 gallons capacity was designed to fit exactly into the upper half of the centre fuselage above the bomb-carriers, so that all the disposable load was as near as possible to the centre of gravity, maintaining constant trim under all conditions of loading. The wings, of 2,800 sq ft gross area, were generally similar in construction to the O/400's, but had hollow box spars and were of equal span; as the lower dihedral had to be great enough to ensure ground clearance when folded, the upper wing remained flat.

Originally the aircraft was designed for two Rolls-Royce Condors in nacelles cantilevered forward from the front spar, but late in 1917, when Condor development was delayed to give priority to Eagle VIII production, Henry Royce advised Handley Page to redesign for tandem pairs of Eagles instead; in this form the design became V/1500, in reference to the total horsepower of the four engines. Trials of an O/100 (3117) with two tandem pairs of Hispano-Suizas at Farnborough, although not entirely conclusive, had confirmed that the rear propeller should be smaller in diameter and coarser in pitch than the front one of the pair, which allowed ample clearance for a four-blader to work within the available gap forward of the wing trailing edge, but since the c.g. of the tandem pair was now above the front spar instead of well forward of the leading edge, it was necessary to sweep back the outer wings. The tail unit was a high aspect ratio biplane, with four unshielded rudders pivoted between the front spars and separate struts aft of the rudders between the rear spars; the rudders were aerodynamically balanced, without fixed fins, and the elevators were rigidly interconnected from side to side. Various landing gears were schemed to cater for the concentrated weights of the engines outboard and the bombs and fuel inboard; some included wheels recessed into the fuselage and wings, mounted on railway-style horn-plate suspensions (jettisonable for ditching), but finally four equally-spaced wheels in a transverse row were disposed in two pairs, with a faired shock-absorber strut and rear radius tube inboard of each wheel and a cross-axle and diagonal bracing tube for each pair. This arrangement was as serviceable on rough ground as the O/400's, but simpler to maintain and manufacture. The Palmer wheels were 5 ft in diameter and cost £135 each, and were calculated to provide two tons buoyancy for ditching. The tailskid, made from a single baulk of ash, was shod with a steel plate and sprung by several skeins of rubber cord. The span of 126 ft was large compared with the fuselage length and resulted in a substantial increase in overall length with wings folded, but wind-tunnel tests predicted adequate longitudinal and directional stability. The ailerons, of high aspect ratio, were balanced by inset triangular horns, imposing less torsional stress than in the overhung O/100 design. The controls were conventional, with a 2 ft diameter wheel on a long column, together with a 2:1 pulley gear which reduced pilot effort but required correspondingly large travels; this gear could be locked out at the pilot's option. The pilot occupied the starboard half of the cockpit, with eight petrol cocks and carburettor jet levers in a vertical stack on the sidewall and two pairs of throttle levers, for forward and aft engines, arranged, as in the O/400, to control port and starboard engines differentially by rotating the knobs. The engines were uncowled, with a common rectangular oil tank sandwiched between them on the bearers and the four rectangular radiator matrices were combined into a single block mounted above the fuselage and occupying half the centre-section gap. The cooling system included reserve water tanks in the upper centre-section, which also contained gravity tanks to which the petrol pumps delivered fuel from the main tank. As in the O/400, the engine controls were connected from the fuselage to the engines by concentric torque tubes encased in streamline fairings.

The Air Board decided to place production orders in advance of the prototype's first flight and on 27 January, 1918, Harland & Wolff received contract No.35A/185/C.74 for twenty V/1500s, E4304–E4323. To speed up the layout of the controls and bomb gear, a centre fuselage mock-up was made at Cricklewood and shipped to Belfast via Fleetwood on 2 February, 1918. A site near Crumlin, Co Antrim, for final assembly hangars was inspected and agreed on 28 February by Lord Pirrie, chairman of Harland & Wolff, and four days later Sir William Weir held a conference at the Alexandria Works, Belfast, to which he invited A. J. Campbell, general manager of William Beardmore & Co Ltd of Dalmuir on the Clyde. It had already been decided that as Handley Page Ltd's new factory at Cricklewood was fully occupied with O/400 production, the second V/1500 order should be placed with Beardmores, who on 13 March, 1918, received contract No.35A/315/C200 for twenty aircraft, E8287–E8306; their proposal to substitute 500 hp BHP Atlantic engines for Eagles was expected to enhance the overall performance. Like Harland & Wolff, Beardmores were well established Admiralty contractors and were already engaged in rigid airship construction on the Renfrewshire bank of the Clyde at Inchinnan; they had their own aeroplane design office at Dalmuir under George Tilghman-Richards and were fully competent to undertake the alternative engine installation. Sir William Weir had become Director General of Aircraft Production in February and was much concerned by the constant risk of labour disputes under the stress of food rationing and coal shortages, so the Beardmore contract was an insurance against delays at Queen's Island and vice versa; but in fact no strikes were threatened in either shipyard at that time and it was the building contractor's delay, due to both disputes and bad weather, at the Crumlin aerodrome (later named Aldergrove) which threatened the first flight of the V/1500 first prototype. The carefully planned isolation and secrecy of its final assembly and trials had to be abandoned early in March and the completed components of B9463 were urgently shipped to Cricklewood for erection and test at the new 160-acre aerodrome at Clutterhouse Farm. The fuselage parts arrived at London Docks on 12 March and were sent on by barge to Cricklewood, and the crated mainplanes and other components were ready at Belfast Docks on the 27th, but no ship was available during the next two days, so on the 29th they were sent by mail steamer to Stranraer and railed to Euston, where Handley Page collected them personally by lorry to save transferring them to the Midland Railway for Cricklewood. The final batch of parts arrived on 12 April and nine days later—only six months from the commencement of design work—the first V/1500 was ready to be flown by Captain Vernon E. G. Busby, a Service test pilot of Herculean physique but tender years from Martlesham Heath.

He made the first straight flight, at a height of 10 ft on 22 May, accompanied only by Jack Hathaway, a former Beatty School instructor, as mechanic. Finding a slight nose-heaviness, Busby decided to carry an extra man in the tail on future flights, the volunteer for this duty being Francis Kappey, a Handley Page apprentice who was waiting to join the Royal Air Force. Four flights were made on 25 May, with Hathaway, Kappey, Volkert and S. T. A. Richards aboard, and Busby climbed to 3,000 ft and recorded a full speed of 101 mph, gliding speed of 70 mph and stalling speed of 38 mph. In spite of the wind-tunnel predictions, the V/1500 was directionally unstable, with ailerons and elevators very heavy and rudders too light. However, Busby did not consider the machine

Rigging checks on B9463 after erection at Cricklewood in April 1918. (*upper: J. M. Bruce*)

dangerous and on 27 May two more flights were made with a full petrol load of 7,300 lb; for the second of these the elevator 2:1 gear was brought into use and three more passengers—General Brancker, General Ellington and Colonel J. G. Weir (brother of Sir William)—were invited aboard, while Lord Pirrie was among the official spectators; ballast was carried to make up the design gross weight of 12½ tons and General Brancker took a turn at the controls; on this flight Richards was instructed to walk aft along the cat-walk during take-off, so as to reduce the elevator control load for rotation. The sheer size of the V/1500 posed many problems and it was found that when the wings were folded the vertical fuselage struts to which they were latched became permanently bowed outwards; this was simply corrected by interconnecting the mid-points of the two struts by a tension wire across the fuselage. Another difficulty arose from the proximity of the folded wings to the ground, which damaged the aileron control levers, although these had been kept as short as possible and thereby increased cable tension and friction in the aileron circuit. Above all the big central radiator caused excessive drag and disturbed the airflow over the tail. Busby considered the elevator control to be too light with the 2:1 gear in circuit, and objected to the control travel being doubled, so it was removed for the ninth flight on 29 May, the 15 cwt aileron cables having been replaced by 20 cwt to reduce stretch and backlash. For the tenth flight on 30 May, Busby was accompanied by Commander Bartley of the Admiralty and six other passengers, and detected an incipient spin during a right turn at 2,000 ft. Suspecting aileron overbalance, he had the triangular horn balances cut off, but on the eleventh flight, on 2 June, he could find no difference in handling and agreed to Handley Page's request to reinstate the balances, since wind-tunnel tests had shown no possibility of overbalance. It had taken only an hour to cut off the horns, but nearly a week was needed to put them back, so the twelfth flight was delayed till 8 June, by which time also the elevator levers had been lengthened. After a 15 minute flight with only Hathaway in the tail, Busby landed to report a marked improvement in handling and announced his intention of climbing to 10,000 ft; he took off almost immediately on the thirteenth flight, after taking aboard four more passengers, comprising a second mechanic, Colonel Alec Ogilvie, Ogilvie's assistant Bertram G. Cooper (formerly secretary of the Aeronautical Society), and George A. Cooper of Harland & Wolff. Heading due north, the aircraft had climbed to 1,000 ft over Golders Green when it turned left and the engines were heard to stop. Possibly Busby was faced with fuel starvation to all four engines and attempted to turn back to the aerodrome, but, being still in a climbing attitude, the machine stalled and spun into the ground, fortunately on allotments and not on the adjacent houses. Busby, Hathaway, Bertram Cooper and the second mechanic, who were all in front, were killed instantly before fire broke out, and the other two were saved through being in the tail cockpit. Although not burned, and quickly rescued, Colonel Ogilvie was taken to Mount Vernon Hospital with a broken arm and severe bruising, but George Cooper had serious head injuries and died within ten minutes from arterial haemorrhage. The fire that followed consumed all evidence of the cause of the disaster, which was a serious setback to the programme; this had assumed very great importance and urgency with the formation of the Independent Force, RAF, for the strategic bombing of more remote German targets, including Berlin. Ironically, it was Ogilvie himself, in the course of his official duties, who had delayed the Belfast production line in April by insisting that 250-lb bombs must be carried vertically as well as 112 lb; this required the main fuel tank and bomb suspension beams to be raised 7 inches from their formerly agreed position and affected all aircraft other than the three prototypes.

B9463 at Cricklewood in June 1918 before its fatal last flight.

A third production contract, No.35A/1455/C.1528 for ten V/1500s, F7134–F7143, had just been awarded to the Alliance Aircraft Co to manufacture complete aircraft to be test flown by Handley Page Ltd at Cricklewood and these incorporated the revised bomb beam height and so were to be given priority for delivery to the RAF, but there had been labour disputes in several of the Waring & Gillow factories (of which Alliance was one) and it seems that this problem, together with the loss of the first prototype, led to Handley Page Ltd taking on the final assembly of details and components manufactured by Alliance, making up various shortages and incorporating modifications as necessary. Harland & Wolff were instructed to ship the two remaining prototypes and the first three production aircraft to Cricklewood, commencing their own final assembly with the fourth production machine, E4307, scheduled for September. The second prototype was shipped from Belfast on 17 June and meanwhile the first Beardmore V/1500, E8287, had been erected at Inchinnan, in the large airship hangar. It had the same tail unit as the prototype and a similar

The first Beardmore-built V/1500, E8287, at Inchinnan in September 1918 with original tail unit and Galloway Atlantic engines (*H. F. Cowley*)

central radiator block; curiously, it was marked with roundels instead of stripes on the rudders. Its direct-drive Galloway-built BHP Atlantic engines were faster-running than the Eagles and their airscrews turned in the opposite direction. It probably was not flown with the original radiator arrangement, in view of the high drag experienced on the first prototype, and remained grounded for some weeks while flight tests of the second prototype at Cricklewood were made to determine the modifications needed before entry into squadron service. These were discussed urgently during the third week in June and on the 19th Handley Page was informed that an operational crew of nine would be required, comprising captain/bomb-aimer, two pilots (one navigating while off duty), one air-mechanic in charge of engines and fuel system, one wireless operator and four gunners (one each in nose, tail, mid-upper and mid-lower stations).

B9464 at Martlesham Heath as delivered from Cricklewood in August 1918. (*G. S. Leslie*)

Following satisfactory flight tests at Martlesham, early in July, by Major Savory on an O/400 (C9713) fitted with a new design of aileron, with the horn-balance deleted and full-span aerodynamic balance secured by means of back-set hinges, this type of aileron was adopted for all V/1500s; at the same time the aileron levers were repositioned inside the gap so that they could be made long enough to reduce cable tension and pulley friction, without risk of damage from the ground or the hangar roof. In the hope of further reducing turbulence over the tail, the engines were completely cowled in sheet aluminium nacelle panels resembling airship gondolas and of good streamline form, with a pair of tall narrow radiators at the front, arranged side by side to form a single octagonal matrix with a vertical separator on the centreline; in the nacelle top panel was a water header tank acting as a steam trap and condenser, and the suggestion for this nacelle may have originated from Beardmores, as an improvement to their Atlantic installation.

Thus modified at Cricklewood, the second prototype was ready for flight testing on 3 August by Clifford Prodger, who found that, although the aileron controls were considerably lighter, directional and longitudinal instability remained, due mainly to variation of downwash with speed and throttle opening. An attempt to remedy this was made by adding a central fin above the tailplane and a tapered fairing behind the tail cockpit, but neither remedy effected a cure and the tail fairing ruined the tail-gunner's field of fire. The fin and tail piece were removed before delivery on 29 August to Martlesham Heath, where the leading edges of the rudders were stripped of fabric to reduce the balance area, again without effect. After brief trials with no fewer than twelve pitot heads arranged to sample the airflow round the tail, the machine returned to Cricklewood on 6 September and the nacelle cowlings were removed, which immediately improved handling and saved nearly 500 lb of weight; meanwhile, wind-tunnel tests on modified tail surfaces showed that positive stability could be obtained by completely redesigning the tail unit with 50 per cent larger gap, four fixed fins with plain rudders hinged to them, and longer elevator levers to reduce cable tension. So large a series of modifications necessitated not only the use of new components but also substantial contract cover, as a result of which the second and third prototypes, built as B9464–5, acquired new identities as J1935–6. With its new tail unit J1935 was officially accepted at Martlesham Heath late in September and was joined early in

B9464 at Cricklewood with extra fin and tail fairing in September 1918. (*D. C. Clayton*)

B9464 at Martlesham Heath in September 1918 with enlarged tail unit and nacelle panels removed. (*I.W.M.—Crown Copyright*)

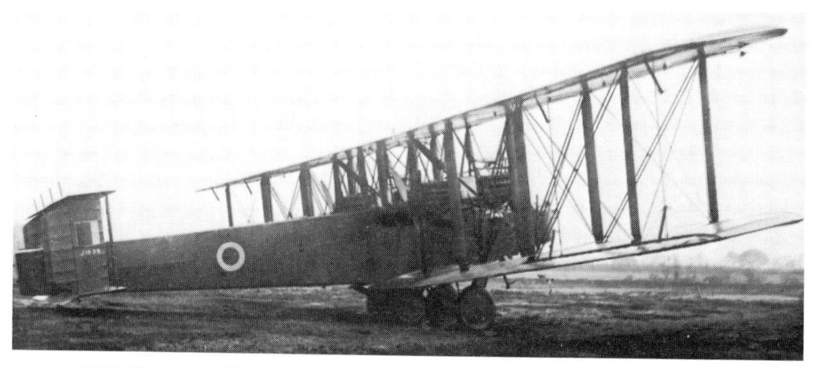

J1935 (formerly B9464) in Nivo finish at Martlesham Heath in October 1918. (*I.W.M.—Crown Copyright*)

October by J1936, brought up to the same standard. Both were equipped with Scarff gun rings at nose and tail and pillar mountings above and below the midships station, all for Lewis guns, but in August it was proposed to install one or two 37 mm shell-firing Coventry Ordnance Works (COW) guns, either singly above the top centre section or at the nose and tail stations, as a defence against pursuing fighters. J1936 was allotted for these and similar armament trials at Orfordness and also made brief tests with a three-inch mortar in the mid-upper cockpit, which lobbed shells over the tail. In September provision was requested for carrying four 550 lb or two 1,650 lb SN bombs horizontally on Gledhill slips, and already a 3,300 lb 'block-buster' had been manufactured for later use, although no carrier for it had so far been designed. At the same time the 86th Wing, Independent Force, was brought into being, in great secrecy, at Bircham Newton, near Hunstanton in Norfolk, where two new V/1500 squadrons, Nos.166 and 167, were formed under the command of Wing Cmdr Redvers H. Mulock.

Due to the time taken in clearing J1935 for squadron service, and the effect of the necessary modifications on the several production lines, deliveries of V/1500s were delayed till the end of October and only three had arrived at Bircham Newton by 5 November; these are believed to have been F7134 and F7135 built at Cricklewood and the first Beardmore machine E8287, fully modified with enlarged tail unit and with its Atlantic engines replaced by Eagles immediately after arrival from Inchinnan. This change was due to an Air Board decision on 31 October to standardise Rolls-Royce Eagle VIIIs for all V/1500s and to cancel production of the Atlantic. Neither the Napier Lion nor the Siddeley-Deasy Tiger, which were more powerful than the Eagle, were available in sufficient quantity, and even the Eagle was still prone to cooling system troubles in spite of its long period of service in O/400s. The Cricklewood production line was programmed to deliver three V/1500s in October, four in November, eight in December and thereafter fifteen per month, and new contracts had been awarded in July and August for 30 more from Beardmore, 40 more from

E8287 at Inchinnan with revised tail unit in October 1918. (*G. S. Leslie*)

Clifford Prodger in the cockpit of E8287 at Inchinnan in October 1918, showing Galloway Atlantic installation. (*G. S. Leslie*)

Handley Page and 40 from Grahame-White Aviation, making a total of 160 on order. Production machines from different makers exhibited minor variations, notably in the pitot-head position; Handley Page-built V/1500s had plain tubes supported by a long lightweight mast taken vertically through the floor immediately below the pilot's airspeed indicator in the middle of the dashboard. Beardmore machines had a short mast with an Elliott or Ogilvie pitot head attached, at the same location, but for some reason Harland & Wolff machines had a mast of intermediate length set about 2 ft further aft. Another small difference was that Beardmore machines had less plywood cladding round the nose cockpit, the fabric side panels being extended forward to oblique lacing strips.

As already mentioned, Harland & Wolff's first three production V/1500s had been built with small tails, like the prototypes, and were shipped to Cricklewood for final modification and assembly. Probably they were aggregated with the Alliance machines and lost their identity, and the first V/1500 to be flown at Aldergrove seems to have been E4307, which was programmed for delivery early in October but delayed for over a month. The three V/1500s which had already reached 166 Squadron suffered many teething troubles, mainly due to engine vibration and bursting of rubber hose joints in the petrol, oil and water pipes. However, on 9 November two of them were ready to carry bomb loads of 1,000 lb each into Germany, intending to penetrate as far as Berlin if possible and prepared to land in either Czechoslovakia or neutral territory if fuel was insufficient for the

Harland & Wolff delivered E4307, their first complete V/1500, to Aldergrove in the first week of November 1918, but it was not flown till 20 December.

return journey. But the raid was called off because of bad weather, giving the Rolls-Royce team an opportunity of changing all eight engines before the next raid, planned for 48 hours later, and the new engines were all ready to be started when the Armistice was signalled just before midday on the 11th. All the factories immediately went on three or four days' holiday and all overtime ceased thereafter with the result that E4307, nearly ready for flight test by Captain Henshaw at Aldergrove on Armistice Day, was not in fact flown till nearly six weeks later. Nevertheless, until the Treasury stepped in to curtail costs, both the Royal Air Force and the manufacturers were anxious to continue development of the V/1500 along lines already discussed and agreed. Already the third Cricklewood machine, F7136, had been designated as an extra prototype, with widened radiators forming regular hexagons, redesigned cylindrical header tanks and the nacelles lowered by 2 ft, not only to improve performance and stability (as found by experience with the D.H.10A), but also to allow the later substitution of

A Harland & Wolff-built V/1500 of No.166 Squadron at Bircham Newton early in 1919. (*Real Photographs*)

F7136, the third Cricklewood-built V/1500, in which Clifford Prodger took forty passengers aloft on 15 December, 1918; this aircraft featured lowered nacelles and was intended for installation of Napier Lions.

Napier Lion engines, which had a higher thrust line. On 15 November, 1918, when normal work had been resumed at Cricklewood, F7136 had just been loaded with 6 hours' fuel for its first flight, when a party of 28 journalists arrived on a sponsored visit, escorted by Handley Page himself; on the spur of the moment he invited them, and a dozen employees, to sample the delights of flying for themselves and produced fur-lined flying clothes for them all. Clifford Prodger then took off and climbed to 6,500 ft with a total complement of 40 passengers sitting at two levels inside the vast empty fuselage, making up a live load of 6,022 lb; sharing the tail gunner's cockpit were Handley Page's secretary, Miss Spiess, and Dorothy Chandler of the design office. Unfortunately F7136 did not survive to become a Lion test-bed, but crashed near Waltham Cross in January 1919, and F7140 was then allotted to replace it, remaining at Cricklewood without armament until Lions became available and meanwhile being used to test an adjustable tail incidence gear.

Wing-folding arrangement and lowered nacelle of F7136.

Pilot's controls of V/1500. (*M.O.D.—Crown Copyright*)

On 20 December Clifford Prodger was at last able to test Harland & Wolff's first complete V/1500, E4307, at Aldergrove. After an entirely satisfactory first flight of one hour, he ferried it next day nonstop to Bircham Newton. He came back to fly the next Belfast machine, E4308,

Cricklewood-built F7135 at Bircham Newton, showing early-type radiator on starboard nacelle and revised hexagonal type on port nacelle. (*Real Photographs*)

from Aldergrove to No.2 (Northern) Repair Depot at Coal Aston, Sheffield, on 18 January, 1919; later it was flown to an exhibition at No.9 Aircraft Acceptance Park, Newcastle-upon-Tyne, before delivery to Bircham Newton, where it joined F7137 and F7138 from Cricklewood both with the new hexagon radiators and header tanks, but retaining the standard high engine position; there also was F7135, with an original radiator on the starboard side and a new one on the port side, being flown to investigate various overheating and air-lock troubles which had caused F7134 to crash. Meanwhile, on completion of its stay at Orfordness, the third prototype, J1936, had been prepared and equipped at Martlesham Heath for an ambitious long-range flight to Egypt and India.

J1936 in India in March 1919. (*C. A. Hall via Chaz Bowyer*)

It retained its original radiators and cooling system and had full tricolour stripes on each rudder to make its nationality plain in the event of a forced landing. Across the nose it bore the name *H.M.A. Old Carthusian* chosen by its pilot, Major A. S. C. MacLaren; his co-pilot was Captain Robert Halley and their distinguished passenger was Brig-Gen N. D. K. McEwen; the remaining crew members were Sergts Smith, Crockett and Brown. Leaving Martlesham Heath on 13 December, 1918, they were delayed by fog at Le Bourget for several days, but then continued via Marseilles and Pisa, arriving at Centocelle (Rome) on the 19th and Otranto next day. There they picked up nine passengers for Malta on the 21st and on the 22nd flew 1,050 miles nonstop over the sea from Malta to Mersa Matruh, landing in torrential rain, which flooded the cockpits and induced General McEwen and the other passengers to continue to Cairo by train from the railhead. The crew dried the machine out and on Christmas Eve reached Heliopolis, where General McEwen resumed his flight to India. They started well on 29 December with a nonstop stage of 850 miles across the desert to Baghdad, but next day their luck changed and they faced a strong headwind, which reduced their ground speed to 50 mph; after a few hours they had to land at El Amara with a disintegrated wind vane on a fuel pump, which could not be repaired till they reached Bandar Abbas, after using hand pumps, with frequent landings, all along the north coast of the Persian Gulf. On 13 January, 1919, the wind changed and they took off for Jask, hoping to reach Karachi in a single stage next day, but after making fair progress along the coast of Baluchistan on the 14th, the port rear engine overheated and seized up, blowing off one cylinder, and eventually the reduction gear broke away, taking the four-blade propeller with it, fortunately without serious damage to the wings. They landed safely on the hard beach at Ormara, 150 miles short of Karachi, and on the 16th managed to take off again on three engines after discarding most of their load of spares, equipment and clothing to reduce weight; then, 35 miles from Karachi, an oil pipe broke on the starboard rear engine; nevertheless they reached their goal that day with only their front engines in action, thus completing the second through flight from England to India, the honour of making the first having gone to Borton in the O/400 C9700 which had preceded J1936 by five weeks. After repairs and much-needed rest, Halley flew J1936 on to Delhi, Ambala and Lahore, where he arrived on 29 March, having flown 7,000 miles from Martlesham Heath. After a few days C9700 arrived at Lahore, having been sent to intervene in Afghan hostilities on the North West Frontier, if possible by bombing the rebellious Amir Amanullah's stronghold at Kabul; but in April the O/400 was wrecked on the ground by a sudden storm and only the V/1500 was left to do the job, although it had been judged incapable of climbing over the Khyber Pass with maximum fuel load in addition to several 250 lb bombs. Nevertheless, it was carefully serviced and flown to its advanced base at Risalpur, whence on 24 May Captain Halley and his observer Lieutenant Villiers took off at 3 a.m. and climbed precariously over the Pathan Hills to Jalalabad, where they found a tail wind to speed them to Kabul. They spent ten minutes over the target and scored several direct hits on the Arsenal, incidentally breaching the outer wall of Amanullah's harem. With their load lightened, they returned safely to Risalpur after a round flight of 400 miles over the most difficult terrain in the world. This was the first and only warlike action

Wing Commander R. H. Mulock with aircrew of No.166 Squadron at Bircham Newton, under the Belfast-built V/1500 in which they flew for nearly 12 hours in April 1919 before Nos.166 and 167 Squadrons disbanded. (*M.O.D.—Crown Copyright*)

by any V/1500, but it was so effective that it ended the revolt and, in a political conference later at Rawalpindi, the Afghans were reported to have been 'very much impressed'. J1936 was not flown again because of damage by termites to the wing spars, but its fuselage survived for some years as the squadron office at Risalpur.

Had the war in Europe continued, V/1500s would have been employed in the spring of 1919 to fly from bases near Prague, where the 87th Wing was planning to attack Berlin direct with the 3,300 lb 'block busters' round which the A.3(b) specification had been drafted. As the war had ended so soon, the 86th Wing organised simulated sorties to test the capacity and reliability of the V/1500 and on 22 May, 1919, one of 166 Squadron's aircraft, carrying a crew of five officers and three mechanics, flew nonstop from Bircham Newton for 11 hr 33 min over a 'figure eight' course of 836 miles, via Birmingham, Southport, Manchester, Lincoln, London, Felixstowe, Great Yarmouth and Hunstanton, landing back at Bircham Newton at 7.40 p.m.; the take-off weight was 24,890 lb and average speed 72·8 mph. Another such flight was planned for August, but by this time the Versailles Peace Treaty had been signed and strict economy was the order of the day. The 86th Wing was disbanded and its V/1500s transferred to the 71st Wing, whose trial squadron, No.274, was formed at Bircham Newton in May and later based at Hawkinge, its main purpose being to develop methods of coastal patrol and long-range transport that would be relevant to the peacetime duties of the Royal Air Force. No.274's aircraft were generally of a later modification standard exemplified by E8293 and F8281–F8290; these had strengthened landing wheels, adjustable tail incidence and an improved cooling system which retained the hexagonal radiator shape, but had the header tanks raised so as to supply the rear engines without interruption in a prolonged dive; also the shutters were arranged in three vertical rows per radiator instead of one, and the double filler orifice was extended upwards to increase the head of water during manoeuvres.

Up till Armistice Day, total orders for V/1500s (excluding the three prototypes) amounted to 160, viz:

Harland & Wolff	20	E4304–E4323
Beardmore	20	E8287–E8306
Alliance	10	F7134–F7143
Beardmore	30	F8201–F8230
Handley Page	40	F8281–F8320
Grahame-White	40	H4825–H4864

Of these, 100 were cancelled in December 1918, namely F8201–F8230, F8291–F8320 and H4825–H4864, from which it is seen that Handley Page Ltd received a direct contract only for ten, F8281–F8290. Yet Handley Page Ltd are known to have delivered, and received payment for, thirty-five V/1500s, while 'other contractors' were credited with only twenty-five. It is evident, therefore, that Handley Page Ltd assembled at Cricklewood not only the ten Alliance machines in addition to their own ten, but also fifteen which can only have been transferred from the Harland & Wolff and Beardmore contracts. Surviving records do not indicate with certainty which individual aircraft these fifteen comprised, but photographic evidence suggests that E8287–E8295 were flown out from Inchinnan and the

F7141 at Cricklewood in May 1919.

Last Cricklewood-built V/1500, F8290, showing raised water header tanks of latest engine installation.

Beardmore-built E8295 at Inchinnan before delivery in May 1919. (*G. S. Leslie*)

Beardmore-built E8290 at Hendon on 17 May, 1919, after being flown nonstop from Inchinnan in 6½ hours by (*inset*) Clifford Prodger and Bernard Isaacs. (*G. S. Leslie*)

remaining eleven delivered as spares. E8290 was flown from Inchinnan to Hendon by Clifford Prodger on 17 May, 1919, while he also ferried three V/1500s from Aldergrove in the same month: one to Bircham Newton on 3 May, and two to Hawkinge on 13 and 24 May; these were additional to E4307, flown to Bircham Newton on 21 December, 1918, and E4308 to Coal Aston on 18 January, 1919, as already noted, and were presumably E4309–4311; it seems likely that Harland & Wolff received payment for only the first five and that the remaining twelve (E4304–E4306 having already been shipped to Cricklewood for final modification) were taken over by Handley Page Ltd as spare components at Aldergrove. Probably as many as fifty were in progress at the time of the cancellations, although Grahame-White had not begun any manufacture and Beardmore had not

J6573 with Napier Lions at Martlesham Heath in 1920. (*J. F. Brown*)

started to assemble their second batch. Before the Versailles Treaty there had certainly been an intention to order fifty Lion-engined V/1500s, J6523–J6572. Some of these were to have had metal wing spars for tropical service, but in August the smaller and more economical Vickers Vimy was adopted and the V/1500 order was revoked; however, the Air Ministry agreed to purchase one Lion-engined machine, J6573, for trial purposes nominally to replace F7140, which Handley Page had been allowed to borrow for an attempt on the direct Atlantic crossing in June. J6573 was assembled and modified from spare components at Aldergrove, where it

Napier Lions installed in J6573 in September 1919.

was test-flown on 3 September, 1919, by Major Keith Park, who then ferried it from Aldergrove to Hawkinge on 22 September at the high average speed of 140 mph. It was flown at Martlesham Heath between May 1920 and March 1921, but the intended full performance trials at 28,000 lb were not completed and it was scrapped in June 1921. At least two other V/1500s were collected from Aldergrove in June 1920 by RAF pilots including Lt-Col Sholto Douglas and Major Keith Park, and a formation of three was seen at the RAF Tournament at Hendon on 3 July, 1920, when one of them carried in its tail cockpit Miss Sylvia Boyden, making her thirteenth drop with a Calthrop 'Guardian Angel' static-line parachute. Sholto Douglas, who led this flight, with Keith Park and Flt/Lieut Naish in charge of the other two machines, took off straight over the Royal Box, but King George V was 'not amused' and Douglas later received a resounding 'rocket' from Sir Hugh Trenchard, to whom the King had complained.

In spite of early proposals by Handley Page to convert the V/1500 for commercial use, none was ever civil-registered and only three 'near-civil' demonstrations were made. In the first of these, F7139 was sent on an officially sponsored goodwill flight to Spain, flown by Major Cecil Darley, with Lieutenant Kilburn as co-pilot, Lieutenant Murray as navigator, and three sergeant-mechanics. They left Manston on 6 May, 1919, for a first stop at Pau, intending to fly via San Sebastian and Vittoria to Madrid, but bad weather ruined the schedule and heavy rain stripped the fabric covering of the two starboard airscrews between Pau and Biarritz. At San Sebastian another severe storm prevented Darley from landing, so he returned to Biarritz, where he made a difficult landing on the shelving beach. Nevertheless, at the next attempt on 11 May, they reached Madrid in 1 hr 40 min and then flew on to Barcelona and back carrying seven passengers including Colonel Sanday, the British military attaché; during the next fortnight F7139 was based at Cuatros Vientos and made several more flights over Madrid, including one for King Alfonso XIII when Darley flew over the Alcalá at a height of 200 ft. On the return flight on 29 May, the airscrews again suffered damage from heavy rain, but the Pyrenees were crossed safely at 6,000 ft en route for Pau. Then, two miles offshore at Biarritz, the starboard rear reduction gear seized, throwing off the propeller and carrying away two interplane struts and tearing a large hole in the top wing. With this severe damage, Darley was unable to hold up the right wing by means of the ailerons, but managed to retain enough control to attempt a landing on the steep beach. This time he had a cross-wind and could not prevent the machine from swinging down the slope and plunging 30 yds into the sea. The incoming tide soon broke up the wreck, but the engines were recovered later and Darley was able to save a packet of correspondence he was carrying from King Alfonso, though not the hamper of carnations intended for delivery the same day from Queen Ena to Queen Mary.

Before this unlucky flight began, the next machine of the same batch, F7140, hitherto reserved as a future Lion test-bed, had been loaned free of charge by the Air Ministry to Handley Page for a new bid to win the *Daily Mail*'s £10,000 prize for the first direct crossing of the North Atlantic—the same prize that Rowland Ding and Princess Ludwig of Löwenstein-Wertheim had intended to compete for in the L/200 of 1914; this prize had not been won before the war and was now revived. The V/1500 was entered by a syndicate of Handley Page's old friends, Vice-Admiral Mark Kerr, Lt-Col E. W. Stedman and Major Tryggve Gran, the Norwegian polar explorer who had accompanied Captain R. F. Scott to the antarctic in 1911 and had flown a Blériot monoplane from Scotland to Norway in 1914; apart from Handley Page's own contribution, generous material support was promised by Rolls-Royce Ltd and several other companies. The syndicate's chosen pilot was the Canadian ace, Lt-Col Raymond Collishaw, who expected to be demobilised early in 1919; but he was recalled to command the RAF contingent in the White Russian Expeditionary Force at Archangel, so another pilot had to be found; this time Major Herbert Brackley, latterly CO of No.214 Squadron in Flanders, was invited and accepted. Also in the team as meteorologist, though not in the flight crew, was a young Cambridge physicist, Major Geoffrey Ingram Taylor. With his customary attention to detail, Brackley left nothing to chance and on 2 April began extended flight trials at Cricklewood to obtain optimum fuel consumption, and reliable airspeed indicator position errors, using the long vertical radio mast on the nose to carry several pitot heads which could be selected in turn and compared; apparently the standard Handley Page location was the best. For F7140, Volkert had designed an internally braced double-size 2,000 gallon petrol tank which completely filled the centre bay of the fuselage and raised the all-up weight to 32,000 lb. Brackley estimated that this was enough for 30 hours flying and that only 1,700 gallons would be needed for the flight from Newfoundland to Ireland if the wind were right and an economical cruising speed could be held. Aft of the tank were three air bags for emergency flotation and each of the crew had electrically-heated clothing; the engine oil and reserve water tanks were also jacketed to prevent freezing.

By 14 April Brackley was satisfied with his fuel consumption figures and next day F7140 was dismantled and crated for shipment from Liverpool to St John's on ss *Digby*, which had just returned after taking across the rival Sopwith competitors, Harry Hawker and Mackenzie-Grieve. In Newfoundland, Stedman had already leased the best available pasture on the east coast, at Harbour Grace about 60 miles from St John's, and on 2 May Admiral Kerr sailed by ocean liner to Halifax, NS, with the other crew members, who now included Frank Wyatt of the Marconi Co as wireless operator, so as to leave Tryggve Gran free to navigate by star fixes and relieve Brackley and Kerr at the wheel. The W/T set installed was powerful enough to maintain contact with Handley Page at Cricklewood via the Marconi station at Chelmsford. ss *Digby* docked at St John's on 10 May and F7140 was uncrated at Harbour Grace on the 12th, when one of the McGruer longerons was found to be damaged; this was spliced and final erection in the open air began on 21 May, being very much hampered by stormy weather. After a brief handling flight on 8 June, Brackley attempted

F7140 at Harbour Grace on 13 June, 1919. (*G. S. Leslie*)

a five-hour test on the 13th, but landed after 1½ hours with the engines boiling, so decided to wait for new radiators of the latest pattern, which were already on their way in ss *Digby*; the ship docked next day, having been held up by thick fog 200 miles from St John's, and the radiators were sent on urgently to Harbour Grace by the narrow-gauge railway. They were installed and found satisfactory in the third test flight on 18 June, but meanwhile Jack Alcock and Arthur Whitten-Brown, the last to arrive on the scene, had flown their Vickers Vimy from Lester's Field to Clifden on 14/15 June and won the prize.

F7140 on test after repair on site at Parrsboro. (*I.W.M.—Crown Copyright*)

Handley Page thereupon cancelled the Atlantic flight and instructed Mark Kerr to fly nonstop to New York instead. So on 5 July Brackley, Kerr, Gran, Wyatt, H. A. Arnold (fitter) and C. C. Clements (rigger) took off at 5.55 p.m. in an attempt to fly 1,000 miles to Hazelhurst Field, Mineola, Long Island, intending to greet the airship R34 on her arrival there. Two hours after starting, the port front and starboard rear engines began boiling and had to be throttled back; soon after midnight the starboard front engine also began to overheat and an oil-pipe joint broke. Arnold climbed out on to the nacelle, but could not stop oil pouring out of the engine and soon after 2 a.m. the engine seized, with a connecting rod breaking through the crankcase. Both Gran and Arnold climbed out to the nacelle twice more to prevent other parts coming adrift, while Brackley cruised around over the lights of a township until daybreak three hours later. He made a good landing on a small racecourse, but hit a fence and then a hummock, collapsing one wheel and tipping the aeroplane on to its nose, which was crushed, although no-one was hurt; the place was Parrsboro, Nova Scotia, and after coming to survey the damage Stedman decided to repair it on site and resume the flight to Long Island as soon as possible, but Gran and Wyatt had to leave the crew and return to England.

Spare components, including a complete nose section, undercarriage and starboard bottom wing, were shipped to Halifax in ss *Caterino*, arriving there on 21 August and being sent on by rail to Parrsboro, where repairs were completed in the open by 1 October with satisfactory test flights during the following week. Then on 9 October, flown by Kerr and Brackley, with Arnold, Clements and three other fitters and riggers as crew, and three journalists and a film cameraman as passengers, F7140 (having had a bulldog badge painted on its nose by the *Boston Globe*'s staff artist) took off at 11 a.m. and landed in total darkness at Greenport, 96 miles short of Mineola, just over twelve hours later, with fuel nearly all gone after a flight of 800 miles against strong headwinds. The aircraft was refuelled next morning but continuing strong wind and heavy rain prevented take-off till fine weather arrived on the 13th, when Mitchel Field, Mineola, was reached in 65 min. Fourteen flights were made over New York City between 17 October and 4 November, with such distinguished passengers as the Governor of New Jersey and the President of the Aero Club of America, Laurence Driggs, as well as many businessmen, journalists and film magnates. Hearing that King Albert and Queen Elisabeth of the Belgians were staying in New York, Kerr and Brackley sent them a pressing invitation to sample a flight in F7140, but it came too late to be accepted. Next, a commercial demonstration was arranged in conjunction with the American Express Company, to fly a 1,000 lb payload of baggage, newspapers and urgent parcels nonstop from Mitchel Field to Chicago. Taking off at 7 a.m. on 14 November at a gross weight of 29,000 lb Kerr, Brackley and their crew of three, with three passengers, were over Delaware in two hours and reached Ithaca by midday, against strong headwinds at 5,000 ft. Over the Alleghenies three hours later, the starboard rear engine boiled nearly dry and after ten minutes of anxiety Brackley landed safely

F7140 over Long Island in October 1919, with 'bulldog' badge on nose.

two miles from Mount Jewett, Pennsylvania. A burst water pipe joint was repaired next day and they took off again at 2.5 p.m. on 16 November, intending to refuel at the Glenn Martin factory at Cleveland, where William Workman was to meet them; but they mistook their landmarks and landed instead on North Randall racecourse, east of the city, and in their final run sheared off both wing-tips in trying to steer between the judge's stand and the timekeeper's stand, which were marginally too close together; the cargo was then transferred to the railroad and F7140 was dismantled and not flown again, Brackley and Stedman returning to England from Halifax NS on 9 December.

During F7140's protracted Odyssey in America, a third V/1500 had made a brief public appearance in Europe. Though not positively identified, this machine was one of the last to be built by Harland & Wolff and was on charge of No.274 Squadron at Bircham Newton; it was lent to Handley Page Ltd for exhibition at the First International Air Transport Exhibition at Amsterdam (ELTA) in July and August. On 19 July Lt-Col Sholto Douglas flew it from Cricklewood to Brussels in 3 hours for demonstration to King Albert, and on via Soesterberg to Amsterdam on the 24th. Although level and sufficient in size, the exhibition aerodrome was in a polder (reclaimed land below sea level) and heavy rain had made soft patches in it. On arrival the V/1500 sank axle-deep into the sandy soil and had to be lifted on to baulks of timber, then towed to the exhibition hall on a specially laid road of sleepers; in the hall, it was by far the largest exhibit; only one wing could be unfolded, and then only after slots had been cut in the wall for the wing-tips to protrude. When the show closed on 18 August a great deal of re-rigging was necessary before it could be cleared for flight and then a long delay ensued from flooding of the aerodrome after continuous rain; meanwhile Douglas had resigned from Handley Page Transport Ltd and another approved pilot had to be found to ferry it back to England. Finally on 30 October, it was flown off by an RAF sergeant-pilot at minimum weight to a dry field at Vreeswijk near Utrecht, where passengers were taken on for a 2½ hour flight to Hounslow, for Customs clearance before returning to Cricklewood. This flight and the Mineola to Cleveland flight were the nearest approach to commercial utilisation attempted with the V/1500 and in neither case were fares or freight fees charged. Like its contemporary the Bristol Pullman triplane, the V/1500 was too big and costly to operate while traffic remained sporadic and unpredictable, and it could not have survived the lean years that civil aviation was soon to face. In October 1920 Handley Page proposed a return to the original twin Condor-engined concept with two variants, to meet specifications D of R Type 4A for a long-range bomber and D of R Type 12 for a troop carrier with reduced tankage for 400 miles and a fuselage adapted to seat 25 troops; in each case standard V/1500 components were to be used as far as possible, with square-section hollow-longerons in place of McGruer spars and the innermost bay of the outer wings deleted, reducing the span to 105 ft. Low cost and rapid production were promised, using existing jigs, but the Air Ministry ordered prototypes of the Vickers Virginia and Victoria for these two roles, mainly because they were smaller and used more economical Napier Lion engines.

The V/1500 story would be incomplete without mentioning a sequel to Handley Page's claim from the Royal Commission on Awards to Inventors

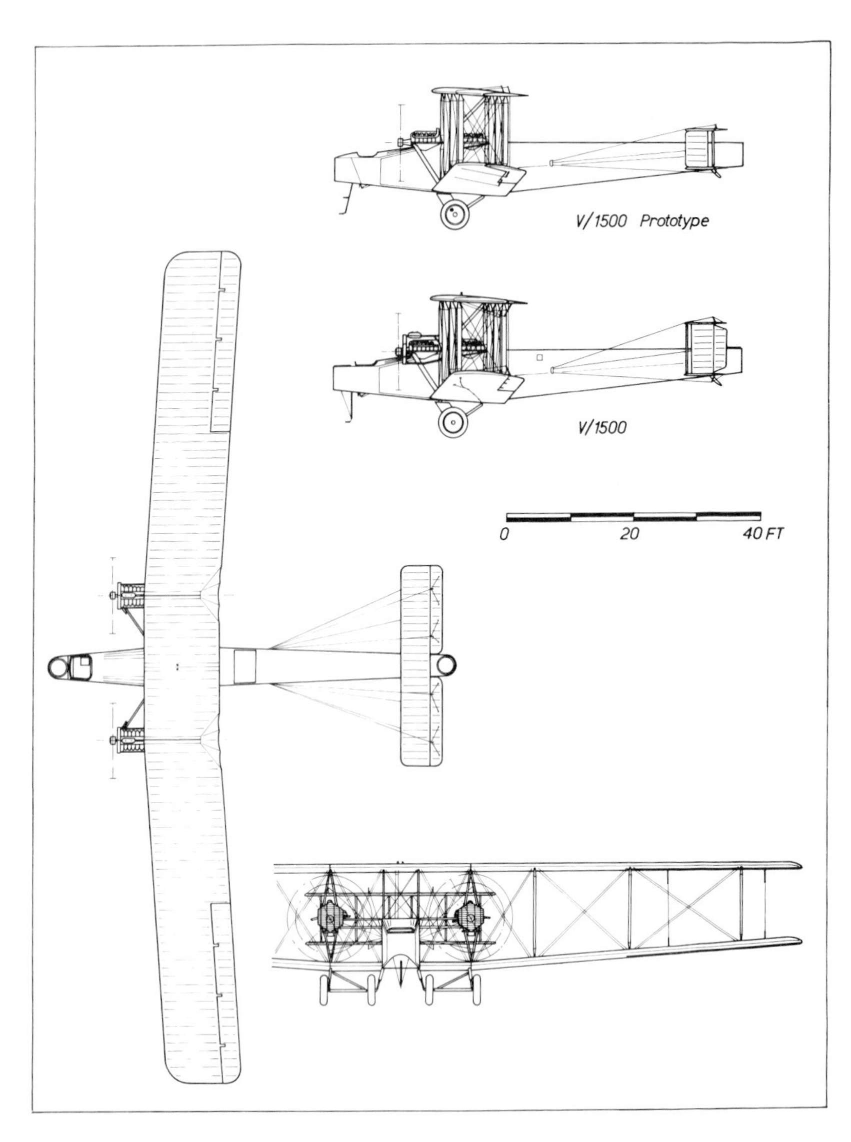

for Crown user of his wartime patents, including No.139230 of 15 March, 1918, for the tail-gunner's cockpit. In December 1922 the Royal Commission awarded £30,000 to Handley Page Ltd in respect of the complete designs of both O and V types (for which the total claim had been £500,000). This brought an immediate reaction from the Receiver in Bankruptcy for Chessborough J. H. Mackenzie-Kennedy, designer of the derelict Kennedy Giant at Northolt, who faced a serious deficiency arising from the Treasury's claim for Excess Profits Duty. Kennedy claimed prior invention of the tail gun cockpit, while working in Russia with Igor

Sikorsky, and that designs he had submitted to the Admiralty in August 1917 had been improperly disclosed by the Air Board to Handley Page. The Patent Office had apparently granted him patent No. 166184 the day after 139230, drawing attention to the priority of the latter, but the Receiver sued the War Office for £171,000 in royalties due on 166184, plus £156,506 damages, being Handley Page's profit from 139230; the aggregated claim would have just discharged Kennedy's bankruptcy, but in February 1923, when the action came to trial, Mr Justice Russell dismissed it.

V/1500

(Four Rolls-Royce Eagle VIII or four Galloway Atlantic or four Napier Lion IB)

Span 126 ft (38·4 m); length 64 ft (19·5 m); wing area 2,800 sq ft (260 m²). Empty weight 17,600 lb (8,000 kg); maximum weight 30,000 lb (13,600 kg). Speed 99 mph (160 km/h); range 1,300 miles (2,090 km); endurance 17 hr; ceiling 11,000 ft (3,400 m). Bomb load 7,500 lb (3,400 kg). Crew six.

O/400 Civil Transport Variants

As early as October 1916 George Holt Thomas, proprietor of the Aircraft Manufacturing Co at Hendon and Handley Page's principal competitor, had staked a claim for British post-war commercial aviation by registering a subsidiary, Aircraft Transport & Travel Ltd, with a capital of £50,000. He was an advocate of medium-sized single-engined aeroplanes, in preference to Handley Page's twins, and Handley Page missed no opportunity of proclaiming the contrary view in favour of a modified O/400 capable of carrying six-ton loads and accommodating a dozen or more passengers in reasonable comfort in an enclosed saloon. In May 1917 the Air Board set up the Civil Aerial Transport Committee to examine the possibilities and needs of post-war commercial aviation, although hostilities were expected to last at least two more years; and in January 1917, Lord Montague of Beaulieu, during a visit to Delhi, had forecast an air route to India as a peacetime priority task. His view was endorsed by the report of the Civil Aerial Transport Committee to the Air Council in February 1918, recommending development of aerial transport services by the State and stressing the need for Empire air route surveys. With the war ending unexpectedly soon in November 1918, official plans had only partly matured and the government was immediately faced with urgent industrial and social problems arising from the cancellation of munitions contracts. In the ensuing chaos, a Ministry of Reconstruction was set up to redeploy labour and capital into useful channels; in industry, everyone looked to his own survival, as the first exuberance and relief of the Armistice gave way to anxiety in the prevailing environment of unemployment, bankruptcy, demobilisation and accumulation of unwanted 'warlike stores'. On the Service side, there was a good deal of enthusiasm, particularly in the Independent Force, for the immediate conversion of the medium and heavy bomber squadrons into transport units; on 13 December the 86th (Communications) Wing RAF was formed at Hendon under Lt-Col

Primrose to operate a few O/400s (as 'H.M. Airliners') and smaller types for carrying mails to the army in Flanders and at Cologne; a month earlier Holt Thomas had announced his intention to start a civilian air service between London and Paris immediately after the Armistice, but was prevented from doing so by the Defence of the Realm Act, which effectively reserved all flying to the armed services until new legislation could introduce civil aviation under formal parliamentary control; furthermore there were complicated issues of international law to be negotiated with neighbouring countries.

Satisfied that Holt Thomas could not obtain a monopoly of civil aviation, Handley Page concentrated on the most economic ways of adapting both the O/400 and V/1500 to commercial use, giving priority to the former. The cancellation of current production contracts had left a large number of newly delivered O/400s at Hendon and Cricklewood, which were no longer needed by the RAF, and Handley Page had no difficulty in buying back from the Ministry of Munitions, at rather less than cost, a batch of sixteen. Only four of these were already completed, the others being still in the final stages of manufacture and thus more readily modified for transport purposes. The four comprised D8350, the last of a batch of fifty manufactured by the British Caudron Co as sub-contractor to Handley Page Ltd, and F5414, F5417 and F5418, the last three completed of the batch transferred to Cricklewood from Cubitts National Aircraft Factory No. 1 at Waddon, which had closed down at the end of 1918. Neither passengers nor mails could be carried until the Air Navigation Bill became law, but Handley Page was in close touch with Fleet Street and had made the most of officially sponsored press visits to Cricklewood during the later stages of the war; an obvious application of air transport, which did not conflict with the Post Office mail monopoly, was the rapid delivery of newspapers from London and Manchester to provincial cities. In collaboration with Major Orde Lees, the Air Ministry's parachute specialist, these four O/400s were converted to carry parcels of newspapers on their bomb racks, to be dropped by 'Guardian Angel' static-line parachutes. The existing 'honeycomb' grid of sixteen bomb cells was replaced by six larger cells, while rudimentary 'ferry-bus' seats were installed forward and aft of the bomb bay (which retained the internal fuel tanks above), so that up to seven passengers could be carried in tolerable comfort in addition to one or two in the nose-gunner's cockpit.

The Air Navigation Bill 1919 received the Royal Assent on 27 February and Handley Page celebrated this occasion by exhibiting the fuselage of an O/400, mocked-up (with club lounge chairs) as a saloon for sixteen passengers, at Selfridges in Oxford Street; he also gave a luncheon party at Prince's Restaurant, where he announced the formation of a new subsidiary, Handley Page Transport Ltd, to operate passenger, freight and mail airliners adapted in the manner shown in the mock-up. He proposed to start with a London–Paris service; then, as experience and traffic grew, to extend the route to Lyons, Marseilles, Turin, Florence, Rome and finally Brindisi, to connect with P & O ships to Port Said and India. In March 1919 a twin-float seaplane version of the O/400 was planned, probably for Mediterranean use, and Boswall tested several float shapes in the wind-tunnel; as Type S, this layout had already been investigated for Murray Sueter two years earlier. Meanwhile through the good offices of Godfrey

Isaacs of the Marconi Company, Handley Page had been invited to tender for the supply of several twin-engined aircraft to carry a payload of ten passengers plus 1,800 lb of cargo, urgently needed by the new republican government of China, which had set up a Ministry of Communications to combat the bandits and pirates who preyed on travellers by land and water. The Chinese authorities saw aircraft as a means of both policing their vast territories to eliminate banditry, and improving commerce between isolated regions more quickly than by building new roads and railways; they were fully aware of recent advances in wireless telegraphy and proposed to coordinate wireless and aviation to the limit of the techniques available at that date. The first job of these aircraft would be to transport the bulky wireless ground stations to their locations in the hinterland, in the absence of any ground access whatever. In April 1919 Handley Page's Chinese agents, the Peking Syndicate, confirmed a contract for six aircraft as specified and these were converted from the twelve uncompleted O/400 airframes already reserved on the halted production line at Cricklewood; only one of them, J1934, already had a Service serial allotted, this being nominally a contract replacement for the sample O/400 airframe sent early in 1918 to the Standard Aircraft Corporation of Elizabeth, New Jersey.

The new transport design, called O/700 (later O/7), was generally similar to the O/400 and retained all its main components, but the internal fuel tanks were deleted and new fuel tanks were installed in extended nacelles, in the manner of the original O/100. The fuselage cross-bracing tierods were replaced by diagonal tubular struts at each frame, from the upper longerons to the middle of the floor, giving a narrow but adequate central gangway between facing pairs of wicker armchairs arranged in five rows, with seven rectangular Cellon windows in each fuselage side wall. There were seats for one or two additional passengers in the nose cockpit, now fitted with a raised coaming and windscreens, and these were accessible from the crew cockpit, which in turn was entered from the main cabin through a door in the bulkhead behind the cockpit; in the O/7 this bulkhead was the same height as the cabin roof, unlike the 'limousine' transport conversions from existing O/400 bombers, which retained the downward slope of the upper longerons and convex decking between them. The new fuel tanks were larger than those of the O/100 and a small gravity service tank was installed above each nacelle under the top wing. The main cabin was entered by a full-height door in the port side, with a window in it so that there were effectively eight windows on the port side and seven on the starboard.

It was obviously impracticable to define and promulgate Air Navigation Regulations immediately after the Royal Assent in time for civil flying to commence on 1 March, although Sir Woodman Burbidge of Harrods took a chance on it by chartering a flight from Hendon to Brussels and back, without being prosecuted. Handley Page thought 1 April was a possibility, since the International Convention on Air Navigation had begun sitting at Paris to sort out the legal tangle of international sovereignty and transit rights. So the four converted O/400s were hurried forward and the first (F5414) was flown at Cricklewood on 4 April; by then the commencing date had been put back to 1 May and both Handley Page and Holt Thomas protested against this delay in permitting commercial flights within the United Kingdom, even though the international difficulties were appreci-

O/400 passenger conversion D8350 at Cricklewood in June 1919.

ated. At the last moment the Air Ministry relented to the extent of allowing local passenger flights by approved operators at specified aerodromes during the Easter holiday week-end; and D8350, F5414 and F5417, piloted respectively by Lt-Col Sholto Douglas, Major Leslie Foot and Captain Geoffrey Hill, were kept busily employed at Cricklewood taking up 800 of the many spectators for half-hour joy rides over London. In addition, two of Major Orde Lees' team, 'Professor' Newall and Miss Sylvia Boyden, demonstrated the 'Guardian Angel' parachute with jumps from 1,200 ft. F5418 was test flown soon after Easter and all four were surveyed and approved for awards of the first four British Certificates of Airworthiness, dated 1 May, 1919; No.1 was issued to F5414, No.2 to F5417, No.3 to D8350 and No.4 to F5418. Pending international agreement on registration markings, these four O/400s displayed their existing serial numbers painted as large as possible on the fuselage sides.

First away from Cricklewood, and the third British civil aircraft to begin operation on 1 May, was D8350 with eleven passengers, flown by Lt-Col Douglas to Manchester (Didsbury) in 3 hr 40 min against a stiff headwind; next day Douglas attempted to fly on to Aberdeen via Carlisle, Dundee and Montrose, intending to drop newspapers at each place and to stop overnight at Edinburgh, but bad weather forced him to return after 100 miles and delayed the flight till the 5th, when it was successfully completed, 1,500 lb of newspapers being conveyed in a total distance of 370 miles; on this trip Major Orde Lees left the aeroplane by parachute over Aberdeen in order, as he said, 'to drop in on a friend there'. Returning on the 6th with Mr Blackwood, the Edinburgh publisher, as his only passenger, Douglas had to make a precautionary landing in bad weather near Penrith, but took off again later and reached Didsbury the same day without further incident. Meanwhile on 3 May, with eight assistants aboard to sort and release packets of newspapers, Major Foot flew a round trip of 170 miles from Hounslow, probably in F5417, over Brighton, Eastbourne, Hastings and St Leonards, returning to Cricklewood after 2¼ hrs without landing en route;

on the 6th he made a similar circuit to deliver newspapers to Bristol, Exeter and Plymouth, covering 310 miles in just under 5 hr. Further newspaper flights were made by Foot to Southampton, Bournemouth, the Isle of Wight and Portsmouth, and by Lieutenant Walker to South Wales and Filton and back, both on 9 May; by Walker to Southend and Clacton on the 10th and to Norwich, Cromer and Great Yarmouth on the 11th; and by Douglas to Castle Bromwich via Nottingham, Northampton and Lichfield on the 12th, returning to Cricklewood the same day. Meanwhile Captain W. Shakespeare had begun flying newspapers from Didsbury to Glasgow in F5414 on 3 May, and on the 12th was returning to Didsbury with Major Orde Lees and Sylvia Boyden, together with his fitter Bill Crisp and rigger George Marchmont, when he had to make a forced landing with engine trouble at Harker, a few miles north of Carlisle. The trouble was soon rectified but the aircraft crashed in attempting to take off from the small field in which it had landed and was considerably damaged; Orde Lees, Marchmont and Crisp in the rear fuselage were only shaken, but the two in front had to spend a few days in Carlisle hospital, Miss Boyden having several front teeth knocked out. Only the rear fuselage and tail unit of F5414 was found to be worth salvaging for return to Cricklewood, but this was sufficient to preserve the legal identity of the rebuilt airframe which emerged two months later, having been converted to the full O/7 standard in the process; it was, in fact, the only previously flown O/400 to be so converted, its original C of A having lapsed at the end of May and being replaced by a new one, No. 165, dated 14 August, 1919.

As a result of these experimental flights, most of which had been sponsored by the *Daily Mail* and *Evening News*, Handley Page planned to extend his operations and appointed Lavington Brothers and Leopold Walford (London) Ltd as his official passenger and freight agents for services in all parts of the world; but international flights were still prohibited until conditions had been agreed by all the nations involved, so Handley Page meanwhile accepted an invitation from Bournemouth corporation to operate a week-end summer service leaving Cricklewood each Friday and returning each Monday. This service was inaugurated on 5 June by Walker in D8350, which had been brightened up by having its nose painted red, but over such a short distance the O/400 could show no net gain in block speed over the excellent service already provided by the London & South Western Railway, and the experiment ended on 18 August, by which time international agreement had been obtained at Paris. One of the results of regular joy riding flights at Cricklewood was a complaint from the MCC of low flying over a cricket match at Lord's on 18 May, for which Handley Page Transport Ltd's general manager, E. J. Bray, expressed contrition in acceptable terms; although already operating by this date, Handley Page Transport Ltd was not in fact formally incorporated till 14 June. Meanwhile Handley Page had sent Major Ivor Bellairs to Brazil to report on the possibility of running an airline between Buenos Aires and Pernambuco, a project strongly mooted in Rio de Janeiro and São Paulo.

On 5 July, 1919, the first of the six new O/7s for China was tested by Captain Geoffrey Hill, who climbed to 1,500 ft with eighteen passengers, representing a gross weight of 12,800 lb; at this height he found it possible to fly level with one engine throttled back. This machine, not having a previous identity, was given the maker's mark HP-1, and was also allotted the temporary civil mark K-162, which it never carried; this in turn was superseded by the registration G-EAGN when its C of A No.149 was awarded on 8 August, but by this time it was already crated for shipment to Shanghai. The other five also were shipped on completion, HP-2 and HP-3 being dispatched on 25 August, HP-4 on 6 September, and HP-5 and HP-6 on 20 September. Meanwhile the surviving tail end of F5414 had been 'rebuilt' as a virtually new O/7 early in July and, while still unfurnished, was equipped to test a new Marconi radio-telephone, for which purpose it carried aerial masts at the nose and tail. It is believed to have flown from Hounslow to Paris and back on 15 July, during the concessionary period of civil flying from 13–20 July granted in connection with the signing of the Versailles Peace Treaty. Thereafter its furnishings for fourteen passengers were completed and about 12 August it was flown to Brussels by Major Menzies and thence to the ELTA exhibition at Amsterdam, with a forced landing at Breda en route. At the ELTA aerodrome Menzies landed safely on the soft polder, but the O/7 became bogged down while taxying in and tipped up on its nose, breaking the wireless mast; six hours were spent in salvage, but it was then found to have suffered no other damage, although the condition of the aerodrome made the proposed flying demonstration impossible. For this flight to Amsterdam it carried no marking on the fuselage except the Handley Page trade mark 'scroll', but to comply with the latest ICAN edict its rudders were marked with the national letter G and the serial displayed above and below the wings was changed to G-5414. The three other civil O/400s were also converted for full passenger service, retaining the internal fuel tanks and having a cabin for six passengers aft of them, with a door on the port side and four windows on each side; the original mid-upper gunner's floor was retained as 'an observation platform with a sliding roof,' the latter serving also as a ditching exit. Two windows were provided on each side forward of the mainplane, where two further

The first O/7, HP-1, at Cricklewood in July 1919, showing long nacelles and full-height forward end of cabin. (*I.W.M.—Crown Copyright*)

F5414 at Cricklewood after being rebuilt as an O/7 in July 1919, showing Marconi R/T aerial masts at nose and stern. (*G. S. Leslie*)

passenger seats were installed; as long as the rear cabin was full, one or two more passengers could be carried in the nose cockpit, which was fitted with coaming and windscreens as in the O/7, and was particularly recommended to 'those who prefer to travel in the open.' A proving flight of the first such conversion, marked G-5417, was made by Captain Shakespeare with several passengers from Hounslow to Brussels and Amsterdam on 21 August; he returned on the 25th, when he became the first man to have breakfasted in Amsterdam, lunched in Brussels and dined in London all in one day. All four of the original machines then received new registration marks in the all-letter style preferred by ICAN, the O/7 G-5414 becoming G-EAAF, and the O/400s G-5417, D8350 and F5418 becoming G-EAAW, G-EAAE and G-EAAG respectively; the last three were temporarily named *Flamingo, Vulture* and *Penguin*.

On 25 August, 1919, international civil flying became legal and Holt Thomas was first away with a scheduled Aircraft Transport & Travel service from Hounslow to Le Bourget. Handley Page, though not quite ready for scheduled operation, laid on a proving flight in G-EAAE, which was the third aircraft to leave Hounslow for Paris that morning; the pilot was Major Leslie Foot and his seven passengers were invited journalists. They reached the cabin door by means of an ordinary step ladder, of which Handley Page had bought six for one guinea as his basic airport equipment. They returned next day, landing at Lympne to clear Customs, in order to fly straight on to Cricklewood without calling at Hounslow. Lt-Col Douglas also flew to Le Bourget on the 25th in G-EAAF, returning next day with his wife and Miss Gertrude Bacon as his only passengers, who thereby became the first women to cross the Channel in a certificated civil airliner, even though it was not yet in scheduled service. Handley Page had hoped to begin regular operation on 1 September, but had to start one day late, when Lt-Col Douglas again flew from Cricklewood, via Hounslow, to Le Bourget in G-EAAF. In anticipation of increasing traffic on the Cricklewood–Paris route and of the complementary service to Brussels that he proposed soon to commence, Handley Page bought in from the Aircraft Disposals Board a further twelve O/400s stored at Castle Bromwich, including seven built by Birmingham Carriage Co and three built by the Metropolitan Wagon Co, none of them having been flown since their half-hour acceptance tests. Two of these, J2249 and J2250, were converted for passenger service forthwith, becoming G-EAKF and G-EAKG, to the same standard as G-EAAW. The Brussels service began on 23 September on three days a week, but on the 28th a railway strike began at home which disrupted both inland passenger and mail traffic, and cross-Channel rail and boat services. On 29 September the Postmaster General authorised AT & T to carry mail between London and Paris and Handley Page Transport to do the same between London and Brussels, while the RAF was called in to carry inland mail between principal centres; the strike

Civil O/400 G-EAKG of Handley Page Transport Ltd climbing out of Cricklewood.

ended on 6 October, but Handley Page managed to retain the Brussels airmail concession, and had also helped AT & T to clear some of the backlog of mail for Paris. Civil aviation had surmounted this crisis and Handley Page Transport Ltd looked forward to steadily increasing traffic in the months to come; on 2 October another O/7 (HP-7) received its C of A, becoming G-EANV; this was the first of the second half dozen new machines, which Handley Page hoped to sell abroad at the full price, so he withdrew it from cross-Channel service after a few running-in flights and began conversion of five more of the Castle Bromwich O/400s to the more utilitarian passenger standard of G-EAAW; these were J2251 (G-EALX) and J2247 (G-EALY) in October, J2248 (G-EAMA) in November, and J2243 (G-EALZ) and D4623 (G-EAMB) in December. During the same period several O/400s from the same stockpile were modified for demonstration and record-breaking purposes. Earliest of these was G-EAKE (ex J2252), which was a minimal conversion with ten seats, but without extra windows, for a Scandinavian demonstration tour by Captain

J. Stewart and Major Tryggve Gran, the latter having returned from Canada after Brackley's misfortune with the V/1500 at Parrsboro. Leaving Cricklewood on the afternoon of 24 August, they reached Soesterberg for the night and flew on to Copenhagen and Århus before flying on to Norway, where they had a considerable welcome, taking up over 450 passengers at Christiania (Oslo), but came to grief at Lillesand on 6 September when one engine cut after take-off and caused a crash landing between two houses; none of the eight persons on board was injured and the aircraft was rebuilt after a long delay, eventually being flown 350 miles to Stockholm on 28 June, 1920; returning next day, Gran and his co-pilot Carter, after flying 80 miles in heavy rain, had to land at Örebro and damaged one wing, which they patched up; but on take-off next day one engine cut and G-EAKE was burnt out, though without any serious casualties. More fortunate was an expedition to Poland by Captains Herne and McNaught Davis in G-EAMD (ex D4633), leaving Cricklewood on 10 December and arriving via Cologne at Berlin (Spandau) the same day; there they had to wait ten days for permission to fly on to Warsaw, where they arrived on the 20th, and in January gave a series of official exhibition flights; this resulted in the sale of G-EAMD to the Polish Government, which proposed to run airmail services from Warsaw to Danzig and Cracow, with a possible extension through Ukraine to Kiev; six O/400s were ordered, but political difficulties soon afterwards caused them to be cancelled. An enthusiastic reception had been given to Captain Shakespeare, who flew G-EAAW to Athens on 30 October to take part in an exhibition of British industrial products; his route was Paris–Lyons–Pisa–Rome–Benevento–Taranto and on 1 November he took up the King of Greece for a flight at Tatoi near Athens.

One other O/400, believed to be C9704, had been flown, as HP-17, by Major E. L. Foot on a special charter from Hounslow to Madrid in August 1919 about the time that Handley Page tendered for the airmail service across Brazil. Having refuelled at Bordeaux for the stage to Vittoria, Foot was forced by engine failure to land in a maize field at Durango, striking a telegraph pole which damaged one wing. With wings folded HP-17 was towed by two oxen through the narrow streets of the village to a larger field, where repairs were begun and spares ordered from Cricklewood. After several months of delay and frustration, it was made airworthy and on 6 March, 1920, R. H. McIntosh flew it back to Hounslow via Vittoria, Tours and Le Bourget in the record time of 13½ hours; it was then dismantled, for use as spares for G-EAAF, when the latter was withdrawn from the Handley Page Transport fleet in May 1920 and shipped to New York in anticipation of operating charter flights between there and Chicago; but this enterprise was killed by Judge Chatfield's injunction against importation of foreign aircraft into the USA. On arrival G-EAAF was impounded by Customs, but was later released to the Curtiss Engineering Division at Curtiss Field, Garden City, Long Island, where it was renovated in 1921 and flown for exhibition purposes by Curtiss pilots in 1922 and 1923.

Further afield Major Ivor Bellairs had won for Handley Page the Brazilian government's concession to fly passengers and mails between Pernambuco and Buenos Aires on a four-day schedule in eleven stages totalling 2,725 miles in each direction, for which a fleet of twenty-four

O/400s would be needed, but this plan was frustrated by political intrigue, and the only O/400 (probably HP-29) to arrive in Brazil was later flown in Argentina by Lieutenant Charles Eardley Wilmot, who organised a Handley Page flying school at El Palomar during 1920. Similar activity in South Africa by Captain S. Wood proclaimed the formation of Handley Page South African Transports Ltd to operate a passenger and airmail route between Cape Town and Johannesburg. In November 1919 the O/7 G-EANV was withdrawn from the cross-Channel service and shipped to Cape Town in RMS *Durham Castle*, together with the eighth new O/7 en route to Calcutta as G-IAAA. Major Menzies was put in charge of flying operations at Young's Field, Wynberg, where G-EANV was re-erected in January. This aeroplane had been named *Pioneer* on arrival, but commercial pressure caused it to be emblazoned with the legend *Commando* for its first flight; this was not a change of name, but the trade mark of the brandy that it was advertising across its ample wing span. The first flight of 103 miles from Wynberg to Saldanha Bay, with thirteen passengers and a crew of three, was made by Major Menzies on 12 February, but while returning on the 16th the aircraft ran out of fuel in the Karoo near Sutherland, having flown off course due to a compass error over the Hex River ironfields. After a successful forced landing, petrol was brought to the spot and the flight was resumed as far as Beaufort West on the 22nd. Five minutes after take-off next morning, tail flutter developed when the port rudder post came out of its bearing socket and *Pioneer* spun slowly down from 300 ft fortunately without injuring any of the ten people on board. As a result of this accident, the Cape Town–Johannesburg airline project was abandoned for the time being and although G-IAAA was erected at Wynberg, it was flown only to display the *Commando* advertisement and was repacked for shipment to Calcutta as soon as this contract had been fulfilled; meanwhile it had been hoped that another O/400 would have succeeded in flying all the way from England to Cape Town.

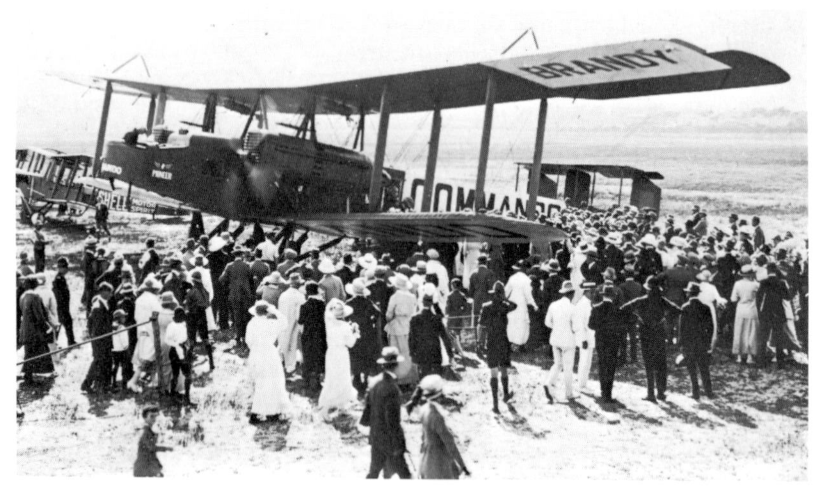

Pioneer at Wynberg before being flown to Beaufort West in February 1920.

G-IAAA at Calcutta in March 1920 after being shipped from Cape Town.

After the £10,000 prize for the first direct crossing of the North Atlantic had been won by Jack Alcock and Arthur Whitten-Brown in June 1919, the *Daily Mail* had offered a similar prize for the first continuous flight from England to Australia; this had been won by Ross and Keith Smith in December and the *Daily Mail* then put up a further £10,000 prize for the first through flight from Cairo to Cape Town. Since both the previous prizes had been won with Vickers Vimys, it was natural that this type should also be chosen by two of the entrants for the African flight; a Vimy Commercial, flown by Captains Cockerell and Broome, was financed jointly by Vickers Ltd and *The Times*, while a Vimy bomber, flown by Lt-Col Pierre Van Ryneveld and Flt Lieut Quintin Brand, was officially entered by the South African government. Handley Page was determined not to let Vickers have the field to themselves and persuaded the *Daily Telegraph* to share the cost of entering an O/400, to be flown by Major Brackley, who had stayed too late with the V/1500 in America to take part in the Australian competition, but had returned to England shortly before Christmas. The *Daily Telegraph*'s special correspondent, Major Charles C. Turner, was to join the flight at Cairo and the other crew members were Captain Frederick Tymms (navigator), Sergt R. Knight (engine fitter) and Jack Stoten, a Handley Page rigger, who had flown with Brackley in the V/1500 from Parrsboro to Cleveland. The O/400, G-EAMC (ex D4624), was a standard bomber with armament removed and high compression Rolls-Royce Eagle VIII engines installed to improve performance in the tropics. After a test flight at Cricklewood with Geoffrey Hill on 17 January, 1920, Brackley and his crew took off on the 25th, intending to fly 500 miles to Lyons, but unbroken cloud over France compelled them to land at Marquise, whence they edged their way through patchy fog to Le Bourget next day; on the 27th they reached Istres a few hours after Cockerell and Broome had left, but on the 28th bad weather forced them to shelter for two days at St Raphaël. They had fine weather for the stage to Centocelle on the 30th and reached Brindisi early next afternoon, but on 1 February, while starting for Athens, the machine taxied into a boggy patch on the edge of the aerodrome. Immediately Stoten and Knight jumped down with spades to dig out the sunken starboard wheels, but the airscrew was still turning and struck Stoten a fatal blow on the head, breaking two blades in the process; he was dead on arrival in hospital. Attempts to obtain a serviceable airscrew in Taranto and Athens proved fruitless and finally a new one was brought from Cricklewood by Stoten's replacement Corporal Banthorpe, who fiercely repelled a threat by the French railway guard to saw pieces off the blade tips when the train was stopped by insufficient clearance under a low bridge. Banthorpe arrived at Brindisi on 17 February and the flight was resumed next morning. They left Athens on the 19th on the 470-mile oversea stage to Sollum, steering by the sun, and flew 400 miles across the desert to Heliopolis next day. At Cairo they found Van Ryneveld and Brand, who had crashed their first Vimy, while Cockerell and Broome had reported arrival at Mongalla. After necessary repairs at Heliopolis, Brackley and his crew reached Assiut on the 23rd and Aswan next day, after a very rough ride through sandstorms and turbulence, complicated by a defective fuel pump. Taking off before 7 a.m. on the 25th, while the air was still cool, they made good progress, passing Abu Hamed in four hours, but twenty minutes later, while flying at 8,000 ft, tail flutter forced them to come down without delay. The rudders were partly jammed by the elevators and Brackley was unable to turn fully into wind before touchdown; the undercarriage collapsed and Brackley was shaken, but nobody else was hurt. They were five miles north of Shereik station on the railway line to Atbara and 200 miles from Khartoum. While the engines were being salvaged by the RAF, Brackley tried to ascertain the source of the flutter, but found nothing definite; probably it was the same rudder bearing defect as had afflicted G-EANV in Cape Province, and later in the year Notice to Ground Engineers No. 13 of 1920 drew attention to a risk of fatigue failure at this point on all civil variants of the O/400.

In contrast to disappointing results with O/400s in Scandinavia and Africa, and political frustration in Brazil, the six O/7s shipped to China made a good beginning. The first was erected at Nanyuan aerodrome and flown over Peking on 6 December, 1919, in a three-hour test flight, carrying fourteen passengers and 1,200 lb of sand ballast to a height of 6,200 ft, where the air temperature fell to −20 deg C. In spite of this intense cold, the Chinese government representatives Mr K. Y. Wei and General Tsing, who were in the front cockpits, praised the machine's steadiness and comfort and the landing was made 'in failing light in an aerodrome festooned with Chinese lanterns,' according to one eye-witness. By the end of February all six were ready and began proving flights, but the first official airmail service was not flown from Peking to Tientsin and back till 7 May; this was the first occasion on which letters posted by 5 p.m. in Tientsin had been delivered at 8 p.m. in Peking on the same day; among the fifteen passengers were again Mr Wei and General Tsing, also the British Minister at Peking, Mr B. F. Alston, and members of the Legation staff. Unfortunately the service was interrupted by the outbreak of civil war, with the result that three of the Handley Pages at Nanyuan were taken by General Tsao Kun to his headquarters at Paotingfu, while the other three, together with most of the Vickers aeroplanes, were removed to Mukden by General Changtso-lin; both warlords refused to release them on the grounds that the Treaty Powers had broken their agreement not to import military material during

The first O/7 air mail flight about to leave Peking for Tientsin on 7 May, 1920, with B. F. Alston and staff of the British Legation.

the civil war, although, in fact, all the aircraft had been supplied strictly for commercial purposes before the fighting began.

After the early arrival in 1919 of both the O/400 C9700 and the V/1500 J1936 in India, there was a lengthy hiatus before the Indian government announced regulations similar to the British Air Navigation Regulations and attempted to run an airmail service between Karachi and Bombay, using D.H.10s operated by No.97 Squadron RAF; this began in January 1920, but was suspended after six weeks because of the high cost and interruption of schedules. Meanwhile Handley Page had proposed a Calcutta-based air transport company with adequate facilities, in the expectation of being invited to tender for airmail services when these were offered to civilian contractors. The ninth new O/7 was shipped to Calcutta in November 1919, to become G-IAAB on the Indian civil register and G-IAAA arrived some weeks later from Cape Town. A working party under Mr Fford erected them on the Ellenborough racecourse soon after the RAF airmail had been suspended. Handley Page proposed to carry passengers on the airmail routes and if possible to fly at night to avoid excessive heat and turbulence, especially during the south-west monsoon season. On 5 March, 1920, Captain Clarke arrived in Bombay after flying G-IAAB from Calcutta in 17 hours flying time, carrying a crew of three, three passengers and three journalists; during the next two months demonstration flights were made from both cities and over 1,400 passengers were carried, including senior naval and army officers, and various rulers. Amongst the latter was His Highness Sir Waghji Ravaji, the Thakur Saheb of Morvi, a small but progressive independent state in Kathiawar, north of Bombay Presidency. He had already installed a metre-gauge railway to handle his extensive grain and cotton crops, and became an enthusiastic advocate of aviation after his first flight. As a result of these first demonstrations, Handley Page had three more O/7s modified for service in India, with improved cabin ventilation and silk upholstery; the first

HP-11 (G-EAPA) at Cricklewood in January 1920, finished in aluminium dope with blue nacelles and pink silk interior trim for Handley Page Indo-Burmese Transport Ltd.

of these to arrive at Calcutta in May was HP-11 (G-EAPA), specially finished in sun-resistant aluminium dope externally, with blue nacelles and pink silk interior trim. HP-11 had been originally prepared in December 1919 as the standby exhibit for the Paris Salon in case the new W.8 failed to keep its date, but was not needed on that occasion. HP-10 (G-EAQZ) and HP-12 (G-EAPB) followed in June, soon after the incorporation of the Handley Page Indo-Burmese Transport Company at Calcutta, with an authorised capital of 1·5 million rupees and Lt-Col Ivo Edwards as managing director; its objects were to secure 15-year contracts for the carriage of airmails from the Indian Post Office, associated with short-range passenger and freight services, and to operate a factory and flying school, also a new hotel, at Calcutta. In promoting this ambitious scheme, Handley Page had fallen into the error of reckoning without the Asiatic temperament and the monsoon weather. To cover the route of 1,200 miles between Calcutta and Bombay an enormous capital outlay was necessary, not so much to prepare landing grounds every 150 miles as to maintain them through all the vagaries of the Deccan climate, which reduced them alternately to quagmires and dust-bowls as the rains came and went. Local labour was unreliable and the railways opposed any competition to their monopoly of long-distance travel, so the airline never really got off the ground; only a fraction of the authorised capital was subscribed in cash and the Indian government, having burnt their fingers on the Karachi–Bombay airmail, refused to subsidise any private undertaking. Although few records remain, it seems that the Ruler of Morvi took up a large proportion of the shares actually subscribed and was allotted HP-11 for his private use, with the registration G-IAAC. While an aerodrome was being prepared at Morvi, HP-11 was flown at Calcutta on various charters; on one occasion it flew over the city dropping leaflets, which were promptly seized in the air and carried off by crows and kites. It is also recorded that on 17 October, 1920, Charles Manson Mann was married to Vera Kathleen Gardner while flying over Calcutta at 6,000 ft in a Handley Page; the passengers included eight guests in addition to the clergyman and bridal party. This event almost certainly took place in HP-11, but this aeroplane was destroyed on the ground by a gale soon afterwards; a replacement was ordered urgently from Cricklewood. Thereafter the Handley Page Indo-

Burmese Transport Co restricted its activities to short-range charter and express parcel work, using D.H.9s except when a full Handley Page load was offered, but liquidation became inevitable in July 1921 and all the company's assets were sold by auction in September to the Calcutta motorcar firm, G. McKenzie Ltd.

At home, Handley Page Transport Ltd had maintained their share of cross-Channel traffic since the end of the rail strike in October 1919 and now offered numbered bookable seats on both the Paris and Brussels routes, also lunch baskets at three shillings each. On 22 October, 1919, their newly recruited pilot, Captain Robert Henry McIntosh, late of No.214 Squadron and No.1 (Communication) Squadron, flew to Paris and back the same day carrying express freight, which was becoming an important item. The company soon proved its ability to carry safely and speedily such items as news films, scientific instruments, antiques and exotic flowers, all of which were vulnerable in rough handling by rail and sea; it had obtained an exclusive contract from Harrods to carry their imports of new dresses from Paris. In October 1919 Lt-Col Sholto Douglas resigned to return to the RAF and was succeeded as general manager by Major George Woods Humphery; in March 1920 Major Brackley became chief pilot on his return from Khartoum. On 10 January, 1920, Cricklewood was approved by the Home Secretary as a Port of Entry, although Customs facilities were not available until 17 February; meanwhile positioning flights from Cricklewood to Hounslow had to be maintained, with such occasional passengers as presented themselves. On one such flight on 3 February W. F. Jones had to land G-EALY with engine trouble in the Old Deer Park at Richmond, but flew out again without difficulty after rectifying the defect. Meanwhile, the Brussels service ceased until direct flying from Cricklewood could begin. Season tickets were offered on the Paris route at £120 for ten return flights to encourage a larger proportion of passengers, but it was soon evident that thrice-weekly freight services were paying better than daily passenger flights. In March 1920, Handley Page brought off his famous £1,000,000 deal to acquire all the assets and stock of the Aircraft Disposals Board for ten per cent of their original cost and during the next six months thirteen more O/400s were selected for the Handley Page Transport Co's fleet and modified to a standard approximating to the O/7, with similar nacelle fuel tanks and full length payload accommodation in the fuselage. A further O/400, G-EASO (ex D5444), was specially prepared for an attempt to win a prize of £10,000 offered by the *Daily Express* for the first flight to India and back carrying a payload of not less than 1,200 lb. It was to be flown by Major A. S. C. MacLaren and Captain J. A. Barton, with Sergt Major H. H. Perry as rigger and R. G. Smith of Napiers as fitter, since it was the first and only O/400 to have Napier Lions installed in place of Rolls-Royce Eagles; by 14 May it was ready to start from Waddon, having been named *Old Carthusian II* in memory of MacLaren's earlier flight to India in the V/1500 J1936, but the RAF reported Arab unrest in the Cairo–Baghdad sector and the Foreign Office prohibited the competitors from flying beyond Egypt; consequently the attempt was called off and G-EASO went back into storage after its borrowed Lion engines had been removed. In March 1920 the first six new O/400 civil conversions, G-EASL (ex C9699), G-EASM (ex C9731), G-EASN (ex D4611), G-EASX (ex F308), G-EASY (ex D4614) and G-EASZ (ex F310) emerged from

The only Napier Lion engined O/400 was G-EASO *Old Carthusian II* in May 1920.

Cricklewood as O/11s, having their fuselages unfurnished, for carrying cargo and mails, except for a small cabin for three passengers at the aft end and seats for two passengers in the nose cockpit. The first three were mainly employed on the new airmail contract to Brussels and Amsterdam, but when the summer tourist traffic increased in June G-EASY and G-EASZ were further modified to the former O/7 standard, with seats for ten passengers and windows the whole length of the cabin, being then designated O/10. These were so immediately successful that a further seven O/10s were converted from O/400s in July and August: G-EATG (ex D4618), G-EATH (ex D4631), G-EATJ (ex F307), G-EATK (ex J2262), G-EATL (ex F312), G-EATM (ex D4609) and G-EATN (ex J2261); G-EASX remained in reserve as an O/11 till October, when it was the only

G-EASL, the first O/11 cargo conversion for Handley Page Transport Ltd.

immediately available replacement for the Thakur Saheb of Morvi's O/7 in India. It was urgently trimmed and furnished in pink silk to the same standard as HP-11, but at the Thakur Saheb's request was painted pink externally as well as inside, the nacelles being blue as before; this striking colour scheme was executed in a high gloss varnish and inevitably the machine was known in the works as 'The Pink Elephant'. With its conversion number HP-34 on the tail and the re-issued Indian registration G-IAAC, it was test flown at Cricklewood and granted C of A No.426 on 15 October, 1920, being the last civil O/400 variant to receive one. It was shipped to Calcutta in eleven crates at the end of November and flown to Morvi by Captain A. F. Muir early in 1921 but its subsequent history is obscure, since the Thakur Saheb died without issue in July 1922; Morvi then joined neighbouring states in a federation whose allegiance to either India or Pakistan remained undecided at the partition in 1947 and not resolved until the Rann of Cutch dispute was settled in 1969.

G-EASX, the last O/10 for India, was a replacement for G-EAPA; not only was it trimmed in pink silk, but it was also painted all over in pink for the Thakur Saheb of Morvi.

The three original O/11s gave good service in the Handley Page Transport Co's fleet, which by December 1920 had carried over 4,000 passengers in a total mileage of 320,000 without a single fatality, but on 14 December Robert Bager took off in the (limited) easterly direction at Cricklewood in G-EAMA, failed to clear a tree on the boundary and crashed into a back garden at Childs' Hill. Bager and his mechanic J. H. Williams were killed, together with the two passengers in the front cabin, but the three other passengers escaped through the rear cabin windows before fire broke out; Eric Studd, the sole occupant of the nose cockpit, was thrown clear, but when the rescue party arrived he was nowhere to be found and was feared lost in the wreckage; next day he was seen in Paris, having no clear memory of how he got there; apparently he had been knocked out in the crash and on recovering consciousness in the garden had remembered only that he had to go urgently to Paris, so he had taken the Underground to Victoria Station and travelled on the boat train via Dover and Calais.

The loss of G-EAMA was an indication that the O/400 had not enough performance in reserve to maintain scheduled flights under adverse weather conditions and, moreover, that, as engines and airframes wore out with use, their performance was likely to deteriorate further. In a tour of Switzerland during September to explore the route beyond Paris to Basle and Zürich, Walter Hope had found G-EATL difficult to handle in valley cross-winds and down-draughts and on 14 September the pilot of G-EASL had been reported for flying over Golders Green at only 100 ft; residents in Kilburn complained that Handley Pages taking off in a southwest wind flew low enough to blow soot down their chimneys, while one newspaper correspondent claimed that it was dangerous even to stand up on the top deck of a tramcar between Cricklewood Broadway and the Welsh Harp! To add to Handley Page's troubles he had been sued in America by the Wright Corporation for infringement of the Wright patents and prohibited from starting a proposed air freight service with O/400s to be supplied by the Aircraft Disposal Co. At home, both Handley Page Transport Ltd and their compatriots AT & T and the Instone Air Line, had lost traffic to the French airlines, which received a substantial government subsidy and could thus undercut the true economic fares. The Cricklewood–Amsterdam route had to be abandoned at the end of October and on 17 November the Paris passenger service was reduced to three days a week; a month later AT & T suspended their operations permanently and finally all British commercial air traffic ceased on 28 February, 1921.

Two days later, Winston Churchill, Secretary of State for Air, appointed Lord Londonderry as chairman of a committee set up to examine the question of subsidies for cross-Channel air services. Terms were agreed within a fortnight and Handley Page Transport, now managed by Edward Cogni, began flying to Paris again on 19 March, Instone following suit two days later; the new fares were £6-6s single and £12 return, the same as the French airlines were charging. First away under the new agreement was W. L. Hope in G-EATM with seven passengers, but traffic was slow to return and in April, when their Cs of A expired, the three O/11s, G-EASL, 'SM and 'SN, were scrapped and the two original O/10s, G-EASY and 'SZ, were shipped to Calcutta, but arrived too late to be re-erected before the demise of the Indian company. Meanwhile Handley Page had gone to America and George Volkert had accepted an invitation to join Colonel Sempill's naval mission to Japan. Under pressure from the residents of Cricklewood and Hendon, the Air Ministry requested Cogni to transfer Handley Page Transport's operations to the new air terminal at Croydon, which had replaced Hounslow in March 1920; Cricklewood ceased to be a Customs airport on 29 May, 1921, the last service out being flown by McIntosh in G-EATM the day before. The service from Croydon was maintained by G-EATK, 'TM and 'TN, the last of which had earlier been equipped with an Aveline automatic stabiliser for test by Brackley. It was soon found that O/10s had much more difficulty in taking off from Croydon than from Cricklewood; indeed, on the first flight out of Croydon with a southwest wind curling over the Purley ridge, Wilcockson was barely able to get airborne with eight passengers and was forced back to the ground near the waterworks with the engines still at full throttle; later it was found that the cargo hold had been overloaded in error. Handley Page was still detained in America, but called in Colonel W. A. Bristow of Ogilvie & Partners to investigate the loss of performance, which was traced to bad maintenance, rather than age or mishandling. The permitted number of passengers,

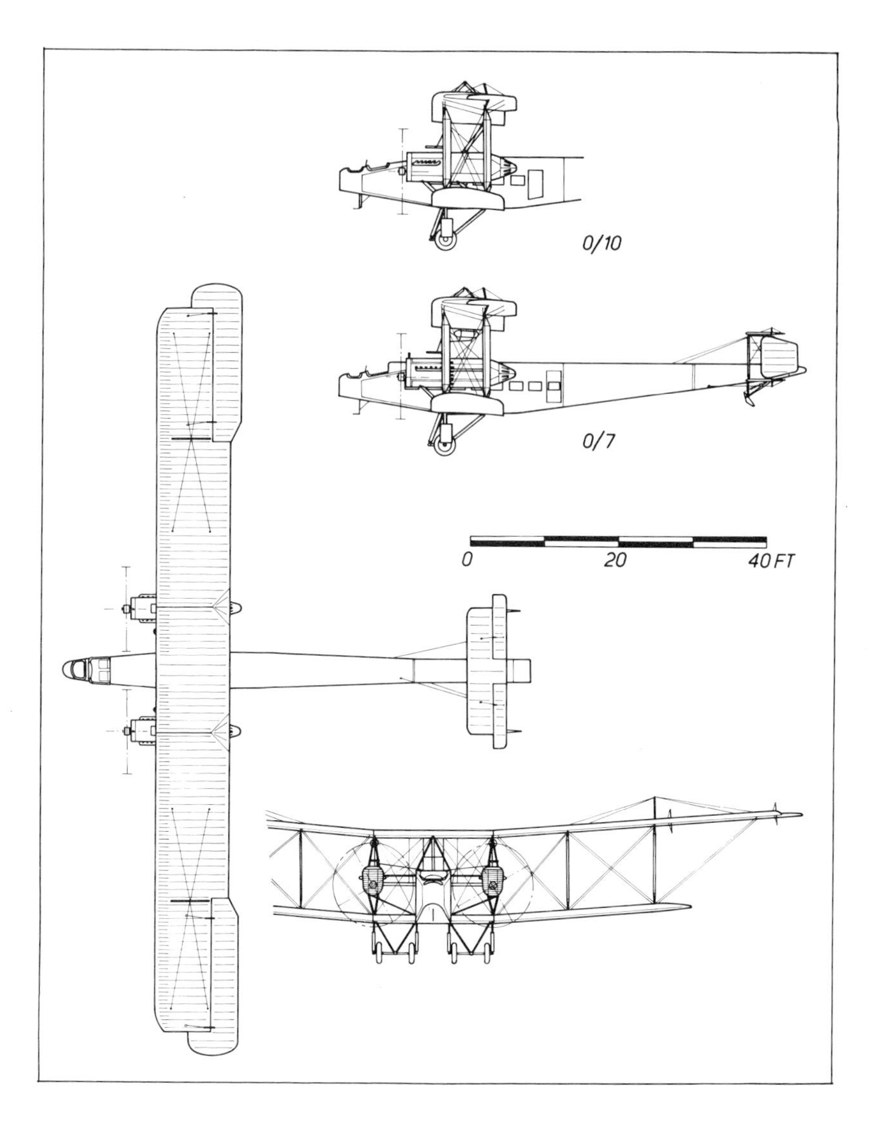

already reduced from eleven to eight, was temporarily still further restricted to five and on 21 June, H. H. Perry (who had been appointed chief pilot to the Aircraft Disposal Co on leaving the RAF) flew G-EAKG to Martlesham Heath for check weighing and to get an official ruling on the permissible number of passengers. Colonel Bristow had found variations of up to 500 lb between the weights of individual machines, due to differences in wireless equipment and repair schemes, while the Aveline auto-control in G-EATN accounted for 150 lb. Soon there were changes in the maintenance staff and the new engineering manager, W. P. Savage, by careful re-rigging and engine tuning, regained some of the lost performance. Air Ministry approval was eventually given for eight passengers to be carried with full Marconi radio installed, for pilots were reluctant to save weight by reducing radio equipment, which was compulsory on cross-Channel flights for weather information as well as position checks. How valuable radio had become was indicated on 20 October, when McIntosh, with Dismore as his radio operator, flew in from Paris with six passengers in G-EATH, and was 'talked down' by Colonel Bristow to a safe landing at Croydon in dense fog, which had grounded all other incoming air traffic at Tonbridge. This widely reported incident earned McIntosh his famous nickname 'All-weather Mac', but many years later he confessed that in actual fact he had lost his trailing aerial in a tree on the North Downs near Sevenoaks, so his wireless was 'dead' before the talk-down began. His actual method when, as on this day, the fog blanket was shallow enough, was to fly above it till he could see the tops of the two towers of the Crystal Palace at Sydenham; by lining these up and letting down to 200 ft for 4½ miles while flying at a steady 65 mph, he could arrive at Croydon airport with great precision. Previously, radio telephony had been used on 20 November, 1920, to instruct a Handley Page pilot to land at Croydon instead of Cricklewood; on 26 November, 1920, to order a similar diversion, but then to countermand it, with a safe landing at Cricklewood assisted by rocket signals; and on 15 January, 1921, to request rockets and a searchlight for a landing after dark at Lympne, the call being made from mid-Channel. The fleet was halved in 1921, for G-EAAG and G-EASL had been written off after crashes in April 1920, G-EAAE and G-EAKG were scrapped in August 1920 and 'KF, 'LY, 'LZ and 'MB two months later. After Bager's fatal crash in 'MA in December, the next casualty was G-EALX in April 1921, scrapped after a heavy landing which made repair uneconomic, but several other mishaps were survived by the aircraft involved. Thus on 2 November McIntosh, with three passengers from Paris on board, landed G-EATM safely at Crowhurst after shedding the starboard reduction gear and airscrew; after a new engine had been installed, he flew it back to Croydon on the 5th; but three days later exactly the same thing happened to him in another O/10 inbound from Brussels, while over the coast near Folkestone at only 600 ft, below heavy cloud; with five excitable passengers in a state of panic running up and down the length of the cabin, he nevertheless managed to land safely in a field full of cattle, just short of Lympne. Both W. L. Rogers and Gordon Olley claimed the record of seventeen forced landings between Croydon and Paris in a single journey, and normally the O/400 was easy to handle in such an emergency, with its exceptionally low wing loading of 8 lb/sq ft. However, it was sensitive to large longitudinal movements of the centre of gravity, as McIntosh found on an unscheduled flight in an O/10 bringing back a crew of fitters and riggers, who decided to play darts in the empty cabin and caused violent changes of fore and aft trim. With a cruising speed of less than 80 mph it was difficult to maintain schedules in winter against headwinds, as for instance on 2 January, 1922, when an O/10 spent over 5 hours en route from Le Bourget to Croydon in face of a northerly gale. Only four days earlier, McIntosh and Wilcockson had taken off from Le Bourget in similar conditions in 'TN and 'TM respectively at the same time—11.20 a.m. 'TM's engines overheated, so Wilcockson landed at Berck-sur-Mer to cool off and had just disembarked his passengers when a

G-EATK at Filton on 5 February, 1922, after installation of Bristol Jupiters; in the cockpit are (*left*) Gordon Olley of Handley Page Transport Ltd and (*right*) Arthur Suddes of the Bristol Aeroplane Co Ltd.

sudden gust cartwheeled the aircraft on to its back and wrecked it. McIntosh, who had been about to land to render assistance, just had time to change his mind and bang the throttles wide open—'TN went up like a lift to 3,000 ft and reached Croydon after a journey time of 4 hr 35 min. G-EATM was a write-off that day, leaving only 'TH and 'TN available, since 'TG, 'TJ and 'TL were being overhauled and 'TK had been flown to Filton by McIntosh on 21 December for Bristol Jupiter air-cooled radial engines to be installed for service trials; this job was completed by the end of January, but meanwhile McIntosh had crashed 'TN at Senlis, between Beauvais and Le Bourget, in a fog blanket forecast as having cloudbase at 300 ft, but in fact continuous down to ground level. With only two passengers aboard and Dismore as radio operator, he was groping his way down, expecting to break cloud over Le Bourget, whence he could get no radio reply; he was knocked out and his feet were trapped between the floorboards and the rudder bar. Dismore, though in pain with three broken ribs, checked that the two passengers were only shaken and the three of them managed to free McIntosh, who expected fire to break out at any moment. He was unable to walk for several months and G-EATK, with its Jupiters installed on 5 February, was collected from Filton by Gordon Olley. For a few weeks only G-EATH remained serviceable for regular schedules and, to augment the Handley Page Transport fleet, the Air Ministry loaned the Bristol Ten-seater G-EAWY and D.H.18 G-EAWX previously assigned to Instone. With a total of 850 hp for take-off, G-EATK had a much enhanced performance and could be flown at full weight with either Jupiter dead; it was demonstrated before the Air Conference delegates at Croydon on 6 February and flown by Olley to Le Bourget on 16 March for further demonstrations to French officials in

G-EATH at Plough Lane, Croydon, after overhaul for the Paris–Basle–Zürich route in 1923. (*I.W.M.—Crown Copyright*)

support of the licence to manufacture Jupiters then being negotiated between the Bristol and Gnome-Rhône companies. Olley flew it back to Croydon on the 23rd and on to Filton next day, the Jupiters then being removed and the Eagles reinstalled. Although the Jupiters saved 900 lb in empty weight and G-EATK could climb to 3,000 ft in 6¼ min at a gross weight of 12,000 lb, the remaining O/10s were considered to be too nearly obsolete for such rejuvenation to be worth while; so G-EATK was withdrawn from use on 9 June, when McIntosh, returning from convalescence, flew it to Cricklewood for storage; it was scrapped there at the end of the year, together with G-EAAW, 'TG, 'TJ and 'TL; only G-EATH was kept serviceable at Croydon to supplement the W.8bs which had taken over the principal schedules in May and June. Although not regularly flown in passenger traffic, G-EATH was overhauled a year later and opened a new extension service from Paris to Basle and Zürich on 16 August, 1923, being again flown by McIntosh, with Sir Sefton Brancker and Sir Francis Festing among the passengers; for two months it flew out on Mondays, Wednesdays and Fridays, returning on the alternate weekdays, but in spite of a joint Anglo-Swiss subsidy the service was reduced to once weekly after the summer season ended in October.

Thereafter G-EATH, nominally in reserve, was picketed out in the open at Plough Lane and steadfastly resisted the worst the weather could do, until it was finally broken up in June 1925 when the site was cleared. It was thus the only O/10 to pass into the ownership of Imperial Airways in March 1924 and by then had long outlived the last O/400 in RAF service or anywhere else, although there was an unconfirmed report of G-IAAA (HP-8) having survived the Indian débâcle of 1921, to reach Egypt (presumably as deck cargo) in 1924; it appears also that G-EAAF was still extant in the USA in 1925, when it was on view at the National Air Races at Roosevelt Field.

O/7, O/10 and O/11

(Two Rolls-Royce Eagle VIII)

Span 100 ft (30·5 m); length 62 ft 10 in (19·2 m); wing area 1,648 sq ft (153 m²). Empty weight 8,326 lb (3,800 kg); maximum weight 12,050 lb (5,470 kg). Speed 97 mph (156 km/h); endurance 7½ hr. Crew two. Passengers O/7-fourteen, O/10-twelve, O/11-five.

W/400, W.8, W.8b and W.8c (H.P.16 and 18)

From the beginning of 1919, Handley Page realised that adaptation of the O/400 bomber as a transport could not produce a satisfactory post-war airliner, whatever its value as a means of generating traffic and enthusiasm for the new mode of travel. For one thing, the internal tubular bracing, which replaced tie-rods in the cabin, was a hindrance to passengers and prevented seats from being placed in the best positions. So in February 1919, when Volkert, assisted by S. T. A. Richards, began sketching layouts for a new project known as Type W, the first consideration was to eliminate internal bracing in the cabin altogether. At first it seemed that this could be done only by restricting the cabin length to 12 ft, and this would have needed a width of at least 5 ft 6 in to accommodate twelve seats, in four rows of three abreast. This, in turn, would have meant placing the two engines further apart and so increasing yaw with a single engine failure; the ability to maintain height with one engine dead was certain to be marginal and any increment in trim drag was most undesirable. The problem was solved by replacing the central cabane struts by braced vertical struts, whose longeron attachments were braced to the top and bottom ends of the engine struts. This made internal bracing across the middle of the fuselage unnecessary and allowed a longer cabin of 22 ft, with forward and aft frames stiffened at the corners. The internal cabin width could then revert to 4 ft 6 in as in the O/400, accommodating forward-facing pairs of seats in as many as eight rows, if desired, with a central gangway. To provide full height throughout the cabin, the bottom longerons were curved to taper less abruptly aft of the wing and the fuselage was deepened to 7 ft, with the crew's cockpit lowered and the nose cockpit deleted; pilot opinion was strongly opposed to an enclosed cockpit and no attempt was made to incorporate one.

For the wing layout, Volkert proposed to use the V/1500 style with equal span, four ailerons and dihedral only on the lower wing, giving a gap of 11 ft at the centre and 8 ft 6 in at the tips, while retaining the O/400's original chord of 10 ft and area of 1,650 sq ft; this resulted in a span of 85 ft. At a meeting on 3 March, 1919, Handley Page approved this suggestion and ordered a set of the new wings for C9713, an O/400 which had been used at Cricklewood and Martlesham Heath for V/1500 development; since July 1918 it had had hornless balanced ailerons of the V/1500 type on its original upper wings; it made three satisfactory flights on 31 March with a simplified undercarriage of V/1500 pattern, the pilot being Lieutenant Carruthers, who flew it again in April with the new wings for speed and climb tests at 12,000 lb before taking it to Martlesham for official tests and instrument calibration. Meanwhile a new monoplane tail unit, with the stern tapering to a vertical knife-edge, was designed and made up, ready for assembly to C9713 when it returned from Martlesham; in the event it was flown on to Farnborough for airspeed calibration, which

C9713 at Cricklewood in March 1919 with new landing gear and balanced hornless ailerons, before installation of equal-span wings and single tail. (*I.W.M.—Crown Copyright*)

was completed on 22 May. On 19 May the test figures from Martlesham confirmed Volkert's prediction and Type W was finalised with a fuselage width of 5 ft and variable tailplane incidence. Possibly with the intention of having it ready for the forthcoming First International Air Transport Exhibition (ELTA) at Amsterdam in August, Handley Page pressed on with as full as possible a conversion of C9713 to the new standard, retaining the original main fuselage and centre section, with the Eagles in nacelles extended to include new fuel tanks of 110 gallons each, with a 10-gallon gravity service tank above each, as already designed for the O/7. Carruthers was no longer available and Geoffrey Hill was ill with influenza when C9713, modified to 'W/400' standard, was ready for flight. Lt-Col Sholto Douglas, chief pilot of Handley Page Transport Ltd, was therefore instructed by Handley Page to take Hill's place, which he did under protest since Handley Page had declined to pay any bonus for test-flying. Douglas flew C9713 on 22 August, 1919, and confirmed the performance predicted from Boswall's wind-tunnel tests but asked for the controls to be geared-up $1\frac{1}{2}$ times to improve response. It was already too late for it to appear at ELTA even if a special C of A could have been rushed through.

It has been suggested that C9713 was converted in stages to become the Type W prototype, which appeared in November 1919 carrying the number HP-15 in the sequence applied to civil conversions of O/400s, but company records show that both these aircraft co-existed for nearly a year; on 8 March, 1920, C9713 was being regularly flown at Cricklewood for routine testing of such experiments as a two-wheeled chassis, slewed engines (to improve directional control with one engine throttled), slotted exhaust pipe silencers, and triple fins and rudders (which had been allowed for in the original monoplane tail design). Arthur Wilcockson flew it on engine-out trials with a single rudder at the end of March 1920 and was waiting in April for a windy day on which to check weathercock effect on cross-wind taxying. A new main fuselage of Type W design had been ordered for C9713 on 24 February, 1919, but had not been incorporated in that aeroplane before it was taken out of service at the end of July 1920; it is likely that this new fuselage became the nucleus of the Type W prototype in May 1919, having initially been included in the production sequence as HP-15. C9713 never had a civil registration, remaining the Air Ministry's property on loan to the company, thanks to good relations between Handley Page and the new Director of Research, Sir Robert Brooke-Popham. The Type W prototype came very near to the ideal 'Large Transport Aeroplane' envisaged by the Civil Aviation department of the Air Ministry, when it promulgated rules for a Civil Aircraft Comfort and Safety Competition, to be held at Martlesham Heath and Felixstowe in August 1920.

In the final design of Type W, it had been hoped to install a pair of 400 hp Cosmos Jupiter air-cooled radial engines instead of the Eagles, and clearance for 12 ft diameter airscrews had been obtained by narrowing the upper half of the fuselage immediately aft of the cockpit; at the same time the centre-section span was reduced by 2 ft, with the engines mounted on the outboard side of the outer struts, thus maintaining the same distance between engine centres as on the O/400. Jupiters were not available because the Cosmos company's original contracts had been cancelled after the Armistice and, in reinstating a prototype order for six Jupiters, the Air Ministry had stipulated a more severe type test for civil use; instead of Jupiters, the Air Ministry agreed to lend a pair of 450 hp Napier Lions, since there was considerable official support for Handley Page's enterprise. With more power available, Volkert reduced the wing area, giving a span of 75 ft, but (as in the earliest days of the O/100) retained the original aileron area by extending the aileron chord. The elevators, like the ailerons, were aerodynamically balanced by setting back the hinges, but a substantial horn balance was retained for the rudder, another sample of which was tested on C9713 in November 1919. In this form, the prototype was designated W.8 and allotted the civil registration G-EAPJ. Hill was still off flying duty and Douglas had resigned rather than undertake further test-flying, so Handley Page decided to delay the first flight until the furnishings had been completed to exhibition standard. They included wall-to-wall carpet, pelmets and curtains for the eight openable circular Triplex

W.8 G-EAPJ nearing completion at Cricklewood in November 1919.

windows along each side, a clock on the forward bulkhead and several small electric candelabra on the walls. The sixteen cane seats all faced forward and were upholstered with plush-covered cushions, each passenger having an adjacent window; the cabin was entered by an outward opening door at the aft end on the port side, with a toilet compartment adjacent to the aft bulkhead, behind which was a cargo hold accessible through a floor hatch. An interesting facility at first was the provision of port-holes in the floor to enable passengers to view landmarks, but they proved unpopular and were soon deleted.

Structurally, the W.8 incorporated all the best features of both the O/400 and V/1500, retaining folding wings with hollow box spars and employing hollow compression struts and longerons, though not of the McGruer tubular pattern, which had given trouble through shrinkage allowing the strut fittings to loosen and rotate. All steel fittings were rust-proofed and stove enamelled, and the wooden members were thoroughly protected with copal varnish. Had Jupiters been available, the fuel and oil tanks would have been installed in circular section nacelles of good streamline form, but with the substitution of Napier Lions it became necessary to lengthen the nacelles, still keeping the circular section; the engines were fed from small cylindrical gravity tanks under the upper wing as in the O/7, fuel being pumped up to them from the main tanks. Finished all over in white Emaillite, the W.8 was rolled out for its first engine runs in November 1919. Geoffrey Hill was still unfit for flying, so 20 years old Robert Bager, of Handley Page Transport Ltd, undertook the first test flight, which lasted 20 minutes, on 2 December. He was entirely satisfied with the W.8's handling and, on the morning of the 4th, took off at 11.30 for Hounslow to clear Customs before flying on to Le Bourget, which he reached in the record time of 110 minutes; en route he overtook the regular O/400, which had left Hounslow 40 min before him and was to land at Le Bourget ten minutes after him. Late at night a few days later, with wings folded, the W.8 was towed 12 miles on its own wheels to the centre of Paris and into the Grand Palais on the Champs Élysées, where the Handley Page working party, under foreman William MacRostie, was completing the stand to the satisfaction of Edward Cogni, publicity manager, and J. B. Richard, the company's Continental agent. When the VI-ième Exposition In-

The W.8's original tall fin and rudder was later reduced in height.

The W.8 at Olympia in July 1920, showing revised fin and rudder.

ternationale de Locomotion Aérienne opened on 19 December, the W.8, in a prominent central position, dominated the smaller exhibits, being matched in size only by the Farman Goliath, and was universally admired, not only for its sparkling white finish and luxurious interior furnishings, but also for its structural ingenuity, which banished all internal bracing from the capacious saloon. After the exhibition closed on 4 January, 1920, some time necessarily elapsed while the W.8 was extricated from the Grand Palais and returned by road to Le Bourget, whence Bager flew it back via Hounslow on 22 January in 130 min, bringing MacRostie and his party home to Cricklewood in time for the company's annual staff dinner at the Connaught Rooms on the 24th. The W.8 was not flown again until the end of March, when Geoffrey Hill was pronounced fit for flying duties, having spent his latter weeks of convalescence on various wind-tunnel experiments. Soon after beginning a series of carefully graded handling tests, he asked for reduced fin and rudder height without changing the original chord, to improve directional stability and control with one engine throttled back. By the end of April he had completed performance measurements at full weight with varying c.g. positions, the load being made up with water ballast carried in three tanks supported by a strong wooden framework laid on the cabin floor. On receiving Hill's report, Handley Page at once arranged for a demonstration climb to service ceiling with full payload to be officially observed for a possible world record claim; on 4 May Geoffrey Hill and his engineer, 'Nigger' Knight, flew G-EAPJ to a height of 4,276 metres (nearly 14,000 ft) with a payload of 1,674 kg (3,690 lb), equivalent to 26 passengers, in a flight from Cricklewood lasting 80 min. Although this flight did not qualify for homologation by the FAI, the Royal Aero Club recognised it as a British record and awarded a Certificate of Performance on 18 May, 1920. A few days later the W.8 was due to appear at Brussels for demonstration to King Albert of the Belgians, to whom the Aircraft Disposal Co were presenting a specially equipped touring conversion of a Bristol Fighter for his private use; there was great enthusiasm in the running shed to get the W.8 ready after various small modifications had been done, and, as soon as work on the port engine was finished, Knight started it while the starboard engine installation was still in progress, to save time. Unfortunately a panel-beater, in replacing a nacelle cowling panel, had had to disconnect the port throttle linkage and had inadvertently reversed it in reconnecting it, so that when Knight tried to slow the engine down its speed increased and the aircraft, still trestled on the starboard side, tilted on to its nose with the rudder rising into the roof girders; apart from a broken airscrew, little damage was done, but the W.8's visit to Brussels had to be postponed.

At the beginning of the year, the Air Ministry had announced a competition to promote comfort and safety in the design of civil aircraft, offering prizes totalling £64,000 for the best entries in three classes: large aeroplanes, small aeroplanes and amphibians. The competition was originally scheduled to begin on 1 June, 1920, but on receiving complaints from the SBAC that this would prejudice the Aero Show being held at Olympia in July, the Air Ministry agreed to postpone the starting dates to 1 August for the landplane classes and 1 September for seaplanes. A week before the Olympia show opened on 9 July, the W.8 once more made a road journey on its own wheels, with wings folded, this time from Cricklewood down Edgware Road and Park Lane to Hyde Park Corner and thence along Knightsbridge and Kensington High Street to Olympia, which was reached without incident before the morning rush-hour began. Again the W.8 occupied a dominating central position, on Stand 49, but had to share the honours for size with the Bristol Pullman triplane and the slightly smaller Vickers Vimy Commercial. The W.8 had been refinished in glossy white, with black nacelles and black lining along the edges of the fuselage, and its registration marks painted out, which greatly enhanced its appearance; the only external embellishment was the company badge on the nose and on each side of the fin. Its furnishings were acclaimed by a large number of visitors and on its return to Cricklewood after the show closed on the 20th it needed further refurbishing, but it was found that the brilliant gloss had to be stripped off ruthlessly to save a serious weight increase and only a light finishing coat could be permitted for the competition flying. So it emerged from the shops for its next test flight on 1 August finished in a light pea-green colour, the result of mixing Nivo dope with a minimum of gloss white; it retained this colour for the remainder of its life.

G-EAPJ's pilot for the Air Ministry competition was Major Herbert Brackley, who had been appointed chief pilot of Handley Page Transport Ltd in March 1920, soon after returning from Egypt. He found it handled well, with remarkable climb and speed, and flew it to Martlesham Heath on 3 August, but next day one of the airscrews was found to be defective and could not be rectified until Friday the 13th. Next morning, Brackley began the prescribed reliability and economy test, but after 2¾ hours the fabric at the port hinged trailing edge of the upper wing began to strip and vibrate in the slipstream, and when three of the tail-ribs broke he had to land. All through Sunday and Monday work continued to repair the ribs and renew the fabric, but just as the job was finished, in the afternoon, one of the riggers fell off a trestle and through the trailing edge of the lower wing, breaking two of the hinge ribs on this wing also, so they had to work throughout the night to complete this repair. On Tuesday the 17th the W.8

G-EAPJ at Martlesham Heath in August 1920. (*J. F. Brown*)

was ready for flight again and Brackley completed the high speed test at 118 mph, and next day the economy and reliability test with two flights of 3½ hr each. Bad weather and low cloud then interrupted flying till Saturday the 21st, when Brackley began the single-engined test, but had to give up after half an hour; on Monday he flew for 35 min with the starboard engine switched off losing 150 ft of height and then for half an hour with the port engine off without loss of height. Next day he completed the short take-off and slow flying tests satisfactorily, but failed to demonstrate uncontrolled flight for 5 min as required, in spite of repeated attempts at several different altitudes, his best time being 3 min. On the 27th, having achieved half an hour with starboard engine off without losing height, he completed the landing tests over a 50 ft barrier of balloons, and on the 28th made a final attempt to improve on his slow speed, which he got down to 55·2 mph; after this he flew the W.8 back to Cricklewood with eleven passengers, including the competition judges and rival competitors. The results were announced a month later, when the judges withheld the first prize of £20,000 in the large aeroplane class, but awarded the second prize of £8,000 to Handley Page and the third prize of £4,000 to Vickers for their Vimy Commercial; their reasons for not giving the W.8 the first prize were that it had failed to demonstrate sufficient stability in uncontrolled flight and that none of the competitors offered the radical advance in design that the Air Ministry had wished to elicit.

Handley Page had hoped to put the W.8 into immediate revenue earning service, and a C of A was granted on 7 August, 1920, but the Napier Lions were still on loan and there were none available for sale, so the machine could only be used for such flying as was authorised by the Air Ministry. The next opportunity of showing its paces occurred on 13 October, when the International Air Conference visited Croydon aerodrome for a display of the latest types of civil aircraft. The W.8 and an O/400 arrived from Cricklewood in formation, the O/400 being already at maximum speed, but over the aerodrome the W.8 accelerated to its own maximum speed with spectacular effect, leaving the O/400 standing. But by this time all British air services were losing revenue to subsidised French operators, who could afford to charge only half the true economic fare needed to show a profit; consequently, even when Napier Lions became available for sale, Handley

Page Transport Ltd could not find the purchase money for a pair for the W.8; the possibility of hiring Jupiters from the Bristol Aeroplane Company had led to the registration of a second W.8 as G-EAVJ on 6 September, but construction never began of this machine (W.8a), which was to have had slotted wings. With the withdrawal of the Cricklewood–Amsterdam service at the end of October and total cessation of British civil air traffic four months later, the government was forced to act and a new phase began on 19 March, when subsidies recommended by the Londonderry committee enabled the Cricklewood–Le Bourget service to be restarted at the same

Wind-tunnel model of projected W.8a with Cosmos Jupiters, full-span slots and flaps. (*I.W.M.—Crown Copyright*)

fares as the French airlines. After further unsuccessful attempts to replace the Napier Lions in G-EAPJ, which the Air Ministry had handed back to the makers after removing its engines, S. T. A. Richards proposed a version, W.8b, with Eagle VIII engines which, though of lower power, could carry nearly the same payload at a slightly reduced cruising speed; this nevertheless gave a useful margin against the worst headwinds and enabled flights to be completed within the maximum time limit permitted for payment of the subsidy, which the O/400s could not always achieve. Meanwhile, both Brackley and Volkert had joined Colonel The Master of Sempill's naval aviation mission to Japan, and had been succeeded by R. H. McIntosh as chief pilot of Handley Page Transport Ltd, and S. T. A. Richards as chief designer.

G-EAPJ with overwing fuel tanks at Plough Lane, Croydon, in July 1922.

At last two Napier Lion IBs were obtained for G-EAPJ, which was overhauled and flight-tested again on 29 August, 1921, by H. H. Perry. On the same day he ferried it across to Croydon, now the Customs terminal for Handley Page Transport Ltd as for other British operators, and for the remainder of the week it was flown by the other pilots, who all expressed enthusiasm for its handling and performance. Another month elapsed while the Civil Aviation department of the Air Ministry deliberated its approval for public transport, and there was disappointment when its C of A was endorsed for a maximum load of only twelve passengers, but on Wednesday 20 October Perry was ready to fly the first service to Paris, only to be grounded by the fog which, as already related, 'All-weather Mac' alone succeeded in penetrating with his famous blind arrival that day. Next day at 2.25 p.m. Perry took off from Croydon on a 125-minute maiden flight to Paris with all seats occupied and G-EAPJ, now named *Newcastle*, was thereafter flown in regular service. On 15 November seven passengers were booked for the morning flight to Paris, including Sir Henry White-Smith and J. D. North, who had been invited to join Handley Page en route to the Paris Salon. Their pilot was the Cockney W. L. Rogers, who insisted on leaving punctually at 11.10 a.m. although Handley Page had been delayed and in fact arrived in time to see the W.8 receding over Purley. Three weeks later Arthur Wilcockson brought off an emergency landing near Beauvais after one airscrew and reduction gear had broken adrift; fortunately, spares were ready to hand and the W.8 was flown back to Croydon without passengers next day. An order for three W.8bs, to specification 16/21, was agreed in November and G-EAPJ, having been overhauled at Cricklewood, was retained there for flight trials with its Lions restricted to Eagle VIII power ratings, to provide performance data for the W.8b, so was not available for demonstration at the second Air Conference display at Croydon on 5 February, 1922.

Meanwhile, the three new W.8bs were making quick progress through the works, but when the first emerged it looked too sombre in a new livery of silver-doped wings and tail, with a black fuselage relieved only by gold lining along the edges. Before sending it to Croydon, Handley Page had the colour scheme changed to silver, with black lining and lettering, although the first W.8b, G-EBBG, retained its gold lining at first and G-EAPJ remained pea-green even after its wing and tail fabric had been renewed. The main differences between W.8b and W.8, apart from the change of engines, were the continuous rectangular windows along each side of the saloon, instead of separate round port-holes, and the removal of the fuel tanks from the nacelles to the top of the upper wings, which reduced the risk of fire and provided a simple and reliable gravity feed to the engines without using pumps; the wing-folding facility was also deleted to save weight and improve the wing root strength. Although ICAN had standardised a cockpit layout with the pilot on the port side and the engineer or radio operator on the starboard side as early as November 1919, this rule had not been enforced on the O/400 civil variants or the original W.8, which had inherited the opposite layout from the O/400 bomber; in spite of its having been designed three years after promulgation of the ICAN standard, the W.8b retained the pilot in the right-hand seat,

Interior of W.8b passenger saloon.

G-EBBH flew as *Melbourne* for only a week before being unveiled as *Prince George* at Croydon on 16 May, 1922; G-EATH survived as the last O/10 till 1924. (*K. A. Winkley*)

apparently because Handley Page Transport pilots were accustomed to it and resisted any change. Since the number of passengers was still limited to twelve, the front bay of the saloon was partitioned off as a cargo compartment in addition to the main hold aft of the entrance door, and this permitted easier adjustment of the centre of gravity during loading.

After its first flight by Wilcockson at Cricklewood on 21 April, 1922, G-EBBG was flown to Croydon and thence to Martlesham Heath for official C of A trials, in which it took off easily with 300 lb overload; it was flown back to Croydon on 3 May by Harold Payn. Although the full C of A was not issued till June, G-EBBG went into immediate service, its maiden flight to Paris being made by Wilcockson with eight passengers on 4 May; returning next day, he made a precautionary landing at Lympne because of bad weather and broke the tailskid, but managed to repair it temporarily so as to fly direct to Cricklewood after sending his passengers on by train. On the 5th he also flew G-EBBH, the second W.8b, for the first time and delivered it to Croydon on the 9th. During their first short period of service, these two W.8bs were named *Bombay* and *Melbourne* respectively but on 16 May they were unveiled as *Princess Mary* and *Prince George* by the new Director of Civil Aviation, Sir Sefton Brancker, performing his first official duty at Croydon. In a well-attended ceremony, Sir Sefton confessed to being a purist who thought that transport should be dissociated from manufacture, but hoped that Handley Page Transport Ltd might be the exception to this rule. In reply, Handley Page felt he was addressing a Salvation Army meeting and although he did not intend to lead those present in praise and prayer, he thought they should praise Sir Sefton for his past and pray for his future; during the subsequent joy-riding by the guests, one flight was made in G-EBBG with 25 passengers on board. Although the W.8bs came out 150 lb below their estimated weight, it was found necessary to strengthen the landing gear to avoid damage from taxying on rough grass and this absorbed some of the weight saving. The

G-EBBG entered service with Handley Page Transport Ltd on 4 May, 1922, as *Bombay*, but became *Princess Mary* twelve days later.

G-EBBI *Prince Henry* taking off from Croydon in 1922.

third W.8b, G-EBBI, named *Prince Henry*, was delivered from Cricklewood to Croydon on 2 June and entered service on the 7th, being flown to Paris that day and back the next day by McIntosh, followed by out and return flights by Olley on the 9th and 10th. G-EBBI incorporated further weight-saving modifications and had an appreciably better performance than the other two, so it was chosen to compete in an international aviation meeting at Evère, Brussels, held by the Belgian Aero Club on 23–26 June; this event included a competition to select a commercial airliner to be operated the next year by the newly formed Société Anonyme Belge pour l'Exploitation de la Navigation Aérienne (SABENA). Flown to Brussels on the 24th by R. H. McIntosh and Leslie Foot, with Handley Page and Cogni among the twelve passengers, G-EBBI scored a runaway win in all its classes on 26 June, well ahead of the French ace, Sadi Lecointe, in a single-engined Nieuport-Délage. King Albert and his sons, Prince Leopold and Prince Charles, watched the events and took a keen interest in G-EBBI's performance. As a result of this demonstration, SABENA order-

The fourth W.8b, O-BAHK, built at Cricklewood for SABENA. (*Pierre Regout*)

ed two modified W.8s from Cricklewood and its associated manufacturing company SABCA acquired a licence to manufacture others of the same type, to equip the SABENA fleets in Europe and the Belgian Congo.

On 30 June W. L. Rogers flew G-EAPJ back from Cricklewood after an extensive overhaul and demonstrated its ability to fly and manoeuvre on either one of its Napier Lions alone; with all four W.8s in service, traffic increased substantially and 'PJ, being the fastest, was frequently chartered for additional flights to carry full loads; only one O/10, G-EATH, was still held in reserve by Handley Page Transport and the borrowed Bristol Ten-seater G-EAWY and D.H.18 G-EAWX were returned to the Air Ministry at the end of June. On 19 July Leslie Foot flew 'PJ from Croydon to Le

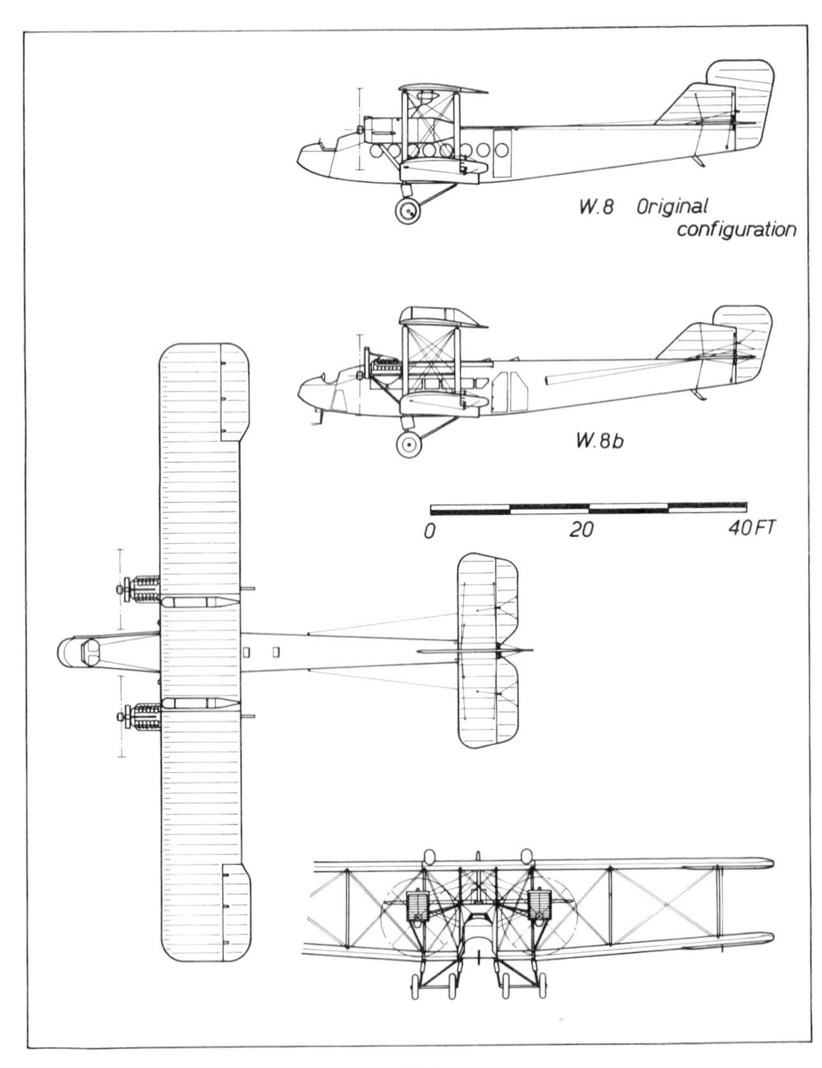

Bourget in 102 minutes, thus improving on Bager's maiden flight for the first time; a month later it was withdrawn for further modifications including installation of overwing gravity fuel tanks of W.8b type and removal of the long nacelle cowling panels; at this stage it was renamed *Duchess of York*.

Meanwhile, Sir Sefton Brancker had sought to rationalise the British airlines, to prevent waste of subsidy through competition on the same routes, and from 1 October Handley Page Transport Ltd was given the sole responsibility for the London–Paris route, with a future extension to Basle and Zürich, and withdrawn from the Brussels, Amsterdam and Cologne routes. As a result, the Instone Air Line, on the advice of Colonel Bristow, proposed to adopt an improved W.8c carrying sixteen passengers and powered by 390 hp Rolls-Royce Eagle IXs; this was similar to the W.8b as supplied to SABENA with gravity fuel tanks slung under the top wing to reduce drag. Taking advantage of this development, W. P. Savage, chief engineer of Handley Page Transport, next year converted 'BG, 'BH and 'BI to carry fourteen passengers by removing the baggage locker at the front of the saloon and putting in an extra pair of seats, although the side windows were not correspondingly extended. At the end of October, Larry Carter had a double engine failure in 'PJ near Tonbridge, but with adequate height in hand he managed to reach Penshurst for a safe landing; after this it was decided to convert 'PJ to Eagle VIIIs; this proved to be a long job, from which it did not return to service till the end of April 1923, an attempt to use direct-drive Eagles (to avoid the frequent reduction gear failures) having proved unsuccessful. With Eagle VIIIs, 'PJ's performance was equal to the standard W.8b's, but its payload was slightly lower because its empty weight was higher; only six months later, on 22 November, 1923, flying towards Paris near Poix, Wilcockson ran short of fuel on one engine, probably from a leak in the tank, and in trying to reach Le Bourget on the other engine, its radiator boiled dry and it seized up; Wilcockson made a perfect landing in an apparently suitable field, but failed to notice a sunken road, into which 'PJ dropped its nose and wheels, to be wrecked beyond repair. The three W.8bs all had longer lives, the only casualty being G-EBBG, which was destroyed in a precautionary landing in very rough weather near Abbeville on 15 February, 1928, after nearly four years'

G-EBBG in the blue livery of Imperial Airways in 1924. (*K. A. Winkley*)

service with Imperial Airways. G-EBBH was honourably retired three years later and G-EBBI lasted till October 1932, having, in its ten years' service, flown half a million miles in 5,473 hours. All three were repainted in the Instone-style royal blue and silver livery adopted by Imperial Airways on its formation in April 1924, but reverted to a silver lined with dark blue scheme in 1927 when the livery was changed again. After 'BH had been withdrawn from use in 1931, 'BI was leased to Aviation Tours Ltd for joy-riding and display work, in the course of which it visited Croydon several times in 1932.

W/400

(Two Rolls-Royce Eagle VIII)

Span 85 ft (26 m); length 63 ft (19·2 m); wing area 1,650 sq ft (153 m²). Maximum weight 9,770 lb (4,430 kg). Speed 94 mph (151 km/h). Crew two.

W.8

(Two Napier Lion IB)

Span 75 ft (22·9 m); length 60 ft 3 in (18·4 m); wing area 1,456 sq ft (135 m²). Empty weight 8,000 lb (3,630 kg); maximum weight 12,250 lb (5,610 kg). Speed 115 mph (185 km/h); range 500 miles (805 km); ceiling 18,000 ft (5,560 m). Crew two. Passengers twelve (later fourteen).

W.8b

(Two Rolls-Royce Eagle VIII)

Span 75 ft (22·9 m); length 60 ft 1 in (18·35 m); wing area 1,456 sq ft (135 m²). Empty weight 7,700 lb (3,490 kg); maximum weight 12,000 lb (5,450 kg). Speed 104 mph (167 km/h); range 500 miles (805 km); ceiling 10,600 ft (3,280 m). Crew two. Passengers 12–14. The figures for the W.8c (two Rolls-Royce Eagle IX) were the same as for the W.8b except that it had accommodation for sixteen passengers and had a maximum weight of 13,000 lb (5,900 kg).

Hyderabad, Hamilton, Hampstead and W.10 (H.P.24, 26, 27 and 30)

In October 1920, in response to Air Ministry invitations to tender to specifications D of R4 for a long-range bomber, D of R9 for a coastal defence torpedo-bomber and D of R12 for a troop-carrier, Handley Page Ltd put forward, among other proposals, designs for all three roles derived from the Napier Lion engined W.8, but without result until two years later, after the W.8b had entered commercial service, when tenders were invited to specifications 31/22 and 41/22. The first of these called for a twin-engined night bomber to replace the D.H.10 and Vickers Vimy, for although the Vickers Virginia had already been adopted for two RAF squadrons, a lighter alternative was being sought for operational comparison with the single-engined Avro Aldershot which then equipped No.99 Squadron. Under the designation W.8d, S. T. A. Richards and C. D. Holland evolved a four-seater to carry two 550-lb bombs, or an equivalent load of smaller bombs, together with three Lewis guns mounted on Scarff rings at the nose and mid-upper positions and in a rear-firing ventral position. The wings,

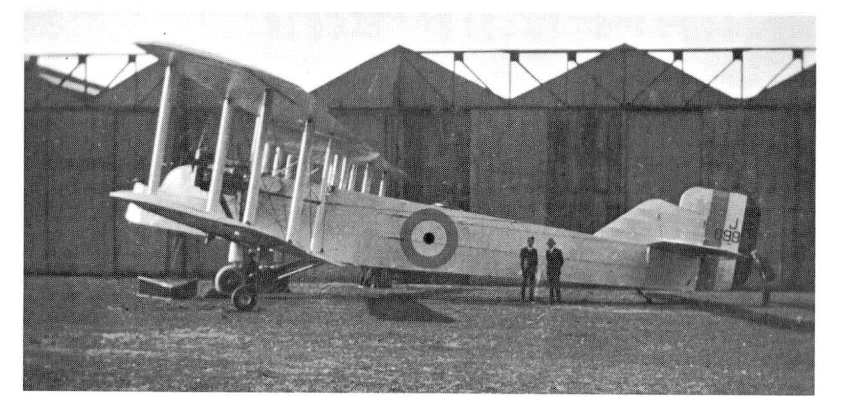

The prototype Hyderabad, J6994, at Cricklewood before its first flight in October 1923. (*S. T. A. Richards*)

J6994 in the New Types Park at the RAF Pageant at Hendon in June 1924.

J7745 of the first production batch with original fin and rudder in 1926; later it became the prototype Hinaidi. (*Flight*)

tail and landing gear were similar to the W.8b's and the fuselage was the same size, with separate cockpits for two pilots in tandem ahead of the wing, affording a good all-round view unobstructed by the front gunner/bomb aimer, whose cockpit was at a lower level; the engines were Napier Lion IIBs installed without fairings and the gravity fuel tanks were slung under the top wing as in the W.8c. The prototype, J6994, ordered on 13 January, 1923, under contract No.369332/22, was first flown by Arthur Wilcockson in October 1923 and in the course of Service trials at Martlesham Heath was found to have a considerably better performance, with the same military load, than its rival, the Virginia III J6993. As a result, a first production batch of fifteen, J7738–J7752, was ordered for the re-equipment of No.99 Squadron at Bircham Newton and the W.8d was officially named Hyderabad. Progress with this batch was slow and in 1924 the Air Ministry called the firm to account for the delay; this was attributed to financial difficulties between Handley Page Ltd and the Aircraft Disposal Co, who held most of the available cash, but in December 1924 the impasse was resolved by making Handley Page Transport Ltd contractually responsible for completing the Hyderabad order. An outcome of this transfer was a request from SABCA for a licence to manufacture Hyderabads in Belgium, but the Air Ministry refused to allow this when it became known that SABCA had been approached by the Russian government. Handley Page had already been reprimanded for allowing details and drawings of the Hyderabad to appear in the Italian technical press while still on the Secret List, but he was able to satisfy the authorities that no leakage had occurred via the firm.

The second tender, to specification 41/22, was for a three-engined derivative, W.9, for service in the Middle East as a military or civil transport. The proposed engines were Armstrong Siddeley Jaguars of 385 hp each, two in the wings and one in the nose; in the military variant, one 500-lb bomb was to be carried externally under the fuselage, or two 250-lb under the wings, and a mid-upper Scarff ring and ventral gun-mounting were provided as in the W.8d; as no front gunner's cockpit was possible, the pilot had a fixed synchronised Vickers gun firing through the middle airscrew disc. The cabin could be variously furnished to carry up to sixteen passengers or troops, and large side doors permitted stretcher cases, spare engines, fuel drums and similar bulky stores to be loaded. The tender proposed full-span leading-edge slots, slotted ailerons and trailing-edge flaps, to improve take-off and climb under tropical conditions, the wing chord being constant and greater than in the standard W.8 series. The civil variant was identical in overall dimensions, but was more comfortably furnished, including meal service, and had no armament or other military equipment. An alternative civil version, for routes other than the Middle East, was covered by specification 42/22, which differed from the 41/22 civil version only in deleting weight allowances for food and water from the payload. No immediate prototype order was awarded for the W.9 in either role, but the obvious advantages of three engines for operation over undeveloped routes, such as desert or rain forest, commended the layout to both the British and Belgian civil aviation authorities; SABENA, in particular, needed maximum reliability for their proposed Belgian Congo route and one of the two versions of the W.8 chosen for manufacture by SABCA was the three-engined W.8e, having an Eagle IX in the nose and a

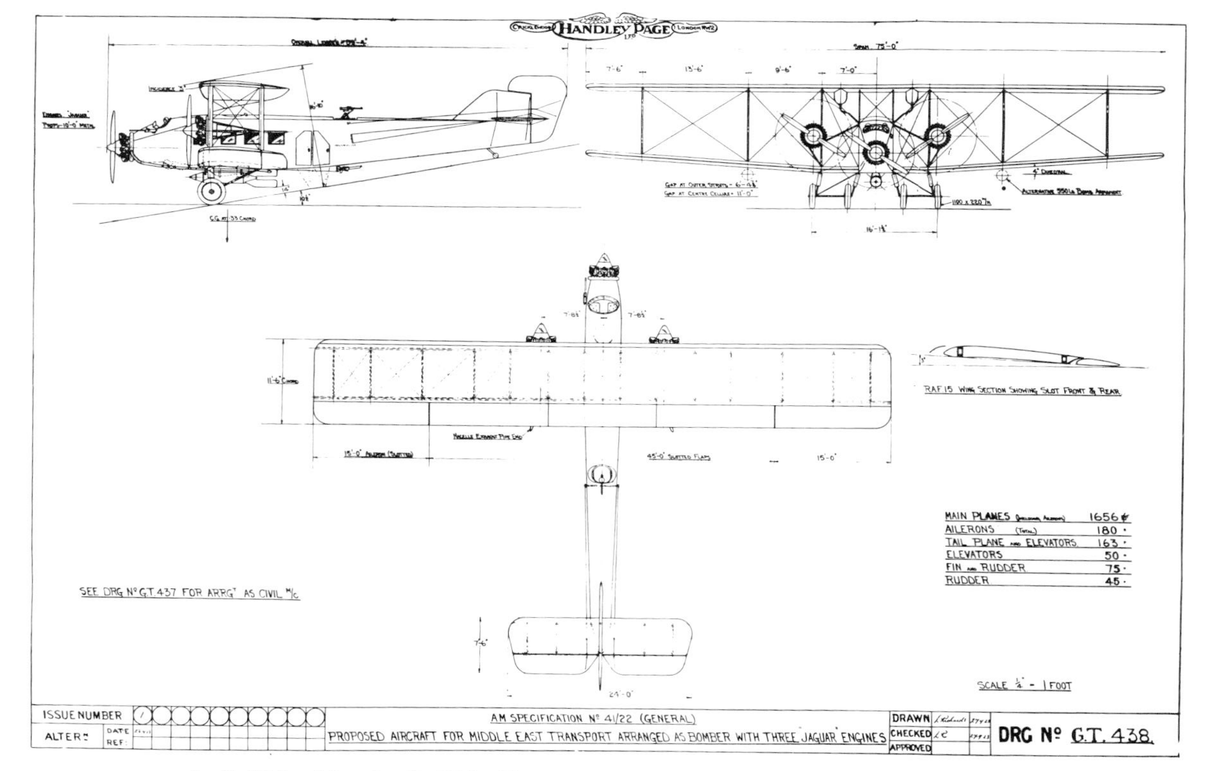

Leslie Richards' project for W.9 military transport to Specification 41/22. (*S. T. A. Richards*)

Prototype W.8e O-BAHG flying near Cricklewood in May 1924.

240 hp Siddeley Puma in each wing position, the assumption being that, in the event of a single engine failure, height could be maintained by the two Pumas symmetrically, or by the Eagle and one Puma in spite of extra drag from the yawed rudder. One W.8e, O-BAHG, was built at Cricklewood alongside a W.8b, O-BAHK, for delivery to SABENA, for whom eight W.8es and three W.8bs were ordered from SABCA. At the same time the Air Ministry, at the instigation of Sir Sefton Brancker, ordered a prototype W.8f for operational trials on the London–Paris–Zürich air route; this was first proposed with a Napier Lion in the nose and two Pumas in the wings, but to save cost the Air Ministry preferred to accept an Eagle IX instead of the Lion, the agreed price being £8,000 with engines and instruments supplied free on embodiment loan; the W.8f, registered G-EBIX, was given the type-name Hamilton in accordance with official naming policy. Both

O-BAHG at Cricklewood showing engine arrangement. (*S. T. A. Richards*)

O-BAHZ at Croydon in 1929.

the three-engined prototypes were first flown at Cricklewood by Arthur Wilcockson, O-BAHG on 25 April, 1924, and G-EBIX on 20 June, 1924, the latter being finished in the livery of Imperial Airways Ltd, although not released for revenue service until 3 November.

On SABENA's Brussels–Rotterdam–Amsterdam and Brussels–Basle services the Cricklewood-built W.8b O-BAHK was joined by SABCA-built O-BAHJ, 'L and 'M, while O-BAHG undertook prolonged reliability and fuel consumption trials prior to commencement of the W.8e service in the Belgian Congo from Kinshasa to Luebo, for which a fleet of eight, O-BAHN to O-BAHU inclusive, was built by SABCA for delivery early in 1925, followed by two more, O-BAHY and 'Z for the European routes. In view of the long delay incurred by crating and shipping these large aircraft to the Congo, SABENA decided to attempt a through flight with one of

O-BAHO *Princesse Marie-José* at Evère before flying to Kinshasa in 1925.

them, O-BAHO, which was inspected on completion on 3 February, 1925, by King Albert and named *Princesse Marie-José* by his eldest daughter. The crew comprised Lt Aviateur Edmond Thieffry in command and flying as navigator, Léopold Roger as pilot and Joseph de Bruycker as engineer. Leaving Evère on 12 February, they were forced to land by bad weather at Dijon and again at Lyons next day, but pushed on to Perpignan on the 15th, Oran on the 16th and Colomb Bechar on the 17th. Thereafter their progress was slower, but they crossed the Sahara safely from Wallen to Gao and reached Niamey on the 25th, leaving again on 1 March for Tessowa and Zinder, where they had to divert from their planned route to avoid floods near Lake Chad. Between Fort Lamy and Fort Archambault they had to land once more because of fog on 13 March but next day reached Bangui, where a thorough inspection was made before entering the final stage over tropical rain forest. They arrived at Kinshasa on 3 April, having flown 5,000 miles in thirteen stages spread over 51 days, with no defects apart from slight vibration from one airscrew due to warping in the intense heat and humidity of the final stage. This pioneering flight, though a magnificent feat in itself, demonstrated that ferrying by air would not save delivery time and, in fact, O-BAHN arrived by sea in time to be erected and flown at Kinshasa on 9 April. Thieffry and de Bruycker then returned to Belgium, while Roger remained to begin the 530-mile Kinshasa–Luebo service on 25 April with a flight of 6¾ hours carrying five passengers and 420 lb of mail. The return flight on 28 April took five minutes less, but SABENA decided for safety reasons to operate in future with two aircraft within sight of each other and the first such flight was made by O-BAHN and 'P on 6 June; by the end of June four W.8es were in service, with two in reserve and two more in transit by sea.

Meanwhile, proving flights with G-EBIX had shown the desirability of having three engines of equal power, so the W.9 project was re-examined as a possible competitor with the Armstrong Whitworth Argosy for adoption as Imperial Airways' standard airliner on the Cairo–Baghdad–Karachi

O-BAHN, the first SABCA-built W.8e, was shipped to the Belgian Congo. (*Pierre Regout*)

The W.8f Hamilton G-EBIX at Cricklewood in June 1924.

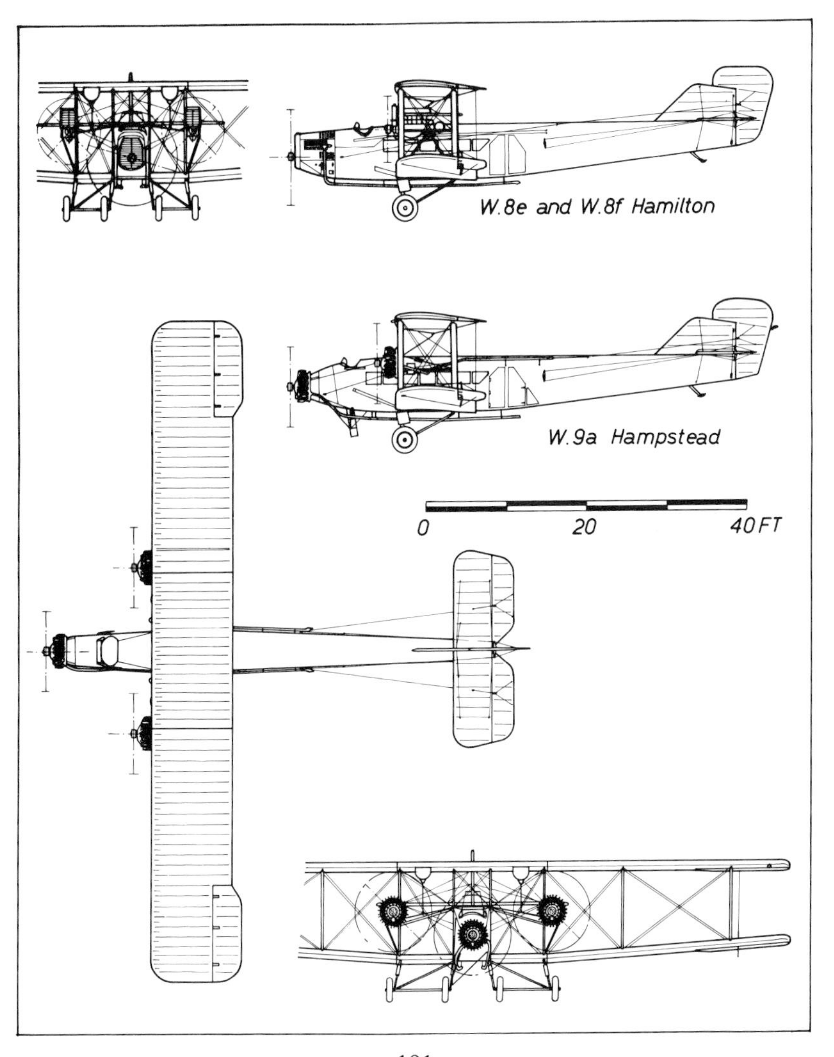

route, due to be relinquished by the Royal Air Force. The proposed military W.9 had not been accepted as a suitable alternative to the Vickers Victoria in Nos. 70 and 216 bomber-transport squadrons, and in agreeing to support manufacture of a prototype of the civil W.9, the Air Ministry insisted on the retention of as many standard Hyderabad components as possible, particularly the wings, tail unit and landing gear. This ruled out the high-lift slotted and flapped wing design, but the necessity for increased lift remained and this was obtained by adding 4 ft to the span of the centre section, bringing the overall span to 79 ft and increasing the track of each undercarriage unit by 2 ft; at the same time the overlap of the three airscrew discs was eliminated, to meet a complaint by Imperial Airways of the

The W.9a Hampstead G-EBLE with Jaguar engines at Cricklewood in October 1925.

excessive vibration encountered in G-EBIX. Thus modified, the W.9a was put in hand early in 1925 and, named Hampstead and registered G-EBLE, was first flown at Cricklewood on 1 October by Captain W. G. R. Hinchliffe of Imperial Airways. It was furnished for fourteen passengers together with a toilet and a large cargo hold, and was the first of the W type to conform with the six-year old ICAN ruling that the pilot should occupy the port side of the cockpit. After early defects in the exhaust system had been rectified, Hinchliffe delivered it from Cricklewood to Croydon on 19 October, carrying as passengers Handley Page, Colonel H. W. S. Outram and Major C. C. Turner; they were met on arrival by Imperial Airways' chairman, Sir Eric Geddes, who himself had a demonstration flight later in the day. To save sending the Hampstead to Martlesham, its certification tests were flown at Croydon by Flt Lieut Oddie of the RAE and the C of A was granted on 20 January, 1926, after a redesign of the rudder had been agreed and put in hand. In November 1925 Imperial Airways proposed to order five Hampsteads at a price of £10,500 each, provided they had metal fuselage structures, but the firm could not guarantee early enough delivery and the order was then offered to the de Havilland company, whose D.H.66 Hercules took over the Cairo–Basra route in January 1927; the price paid for G-EBLE was £9,200.

The Hampstead's overall performance was excellent and it could maintain a rate of climb of 200 ft/min with any one engine stopped; with any two engines stopped, its rate of descent could be limited to 200 ft/min, equivalent to a distance of 7½ miles from 2,000 ft. Unfortunately it was found tiring to fly because of directional instability, caused by the horn balance of the rudder being snatched from side to side in the slipstream of the central engine. This had been noticed, though not to an objectionable degree, on the W.8f, but pilots of No.99 Squadron RAF had complained of it on the Hyderabad as a source of error in bomb aiming, and wind-tunnel tests had already begun at Cricklewood, first on a triple-rudder scheme and then, more simply, on a plain rectangular rudder balanced by being mounted on backset hinges in the same way as the ailerons and elevators. Using a triangular fin of the same area as the original one, satisfactory stability was obtained in the wind-tunnel, but when tried out on the Hampstead, this fin was found to be too large; then it was discovered that the model had been made with too short a fuselage, so the full-size fin had to be cropped to the same chord as the tailplane, making the lower half of the leading edge vertical. After flight testing on Hyderabad J7752, the new fin and rudder were applied to the W.9a and the next five new Hyderabads with complete success and adopted retrospectively on G-EBIX and all eleven of SABENA's W.8es. Two years later Hyderabad J7748 was tested at Farnborough with the fin removed altogether and a full-span servo-tab on the rudder trailing edge, to test the value of Flettner's patent, but no further service trials were proposed.

O-BAHY at Croydon in 1928.

Concurrently with the Hampstead's early flights, Imperial Airways became short of multi-engined aircraft for their cross-Channel services and placed an urgent order with Handley Page Ltd for four improved versions of the W.8, insisting on delivery before 31 March, 1926. As time was short, no attempt was made to develop a new design, but a civil version of the Hyderabad was derived, using existing components with a W.8 front fuselage grafted on, the result being designated W.10. Like the Hampstead, the W.10 accommodated fourteen passengers and had the pilot's seat on the port side; it also had the basic Napier Lion installation (though with long exhaust pipes to reduce noise), differential aileron controls and

Hubert Broad flying the first W.10, G-EBMM, at Cricklewood on 10 February, 1926.

Interior of W.10 passenger saloon.

rubber-in-compression undercarriage of the Hyderabad, together with the revised fin and rudder, on which Imperial Airways insisted. Initial cost was saved by installing overhauled Napier Lions removed a year earlier from former Daimler and Instone D.H.34s and Vickers Vulcans. Using standard Hyderabad components, production went ahead in advance of drawings and there was some alarm when at a late stage in erection the Stress Office discovered that the top longerons adjacent to the cabin door and toilet were apparently below strength; but further inspection showed that the suspect members were not hollow, as assumed by the stressman, but solid to provide for the Scarff ring mounting on the Hyderabad, so all was well. The first W.10, G-EBMM, made its maiden flight at Cricklewood in the hands of Hubert Broad on 10 February, 1926, and received its C of A on 5 March;

Hampstead and W.10s ready for commissioning by Lady Maude Hoare at Croydon on 30 March, 1926.

the next two, G-EBMR and 'S, were certificated four days later and the fourth, G-EBMT, on 13 March; all four were handed over to Imperial Airways at Croydon on 30 March when, with the W.9a, they were ceremonially named by Lady Maude Hoare, wife of the Air Minister; G-EBLE was named *City of New York* and G-EBMM and 'R–'T were named *City of Melbourne, City of Pretoria, City of London* and *City of Ottawa* respectively. G-EBMR was first into service and the other three followed in time to cope with the emergency caused by the General Strike which began on 4 May, on which day Captain O. P. Jones flew the Prince of Wales back from Paris in G-EBMM after all the regular boat and train services had ceased. Previously, on 16 April, Captain Franklyn Barnard, inbound from Paris with a full load of passengers in G-EBMR, had an unpleasant encounter when struck by lightning between Beauvais and Poix; a large patch of fabric was burnt off one lower wing and the adjacent aileron was damaged; all the nearby bonding was fused, the compass was put out of action and one engine misfired because of a depolarised magneto; nevertheless he made a safe landing at Lympne.

With its new rudder the Hampstead was faster than the W.10s, but there was still a good deal of fuselage vibration unless the middle engine was kept at part throttle. Nevertheless some fast times were recorded, as on 6 March, when McIntosh flew from Croydon to Paris in 98 min; this was reduced to 89 min on the 10th, but on the 21st, returning from Paris with Freddy Dismore at the controls, and thirteen passengers, the Hampstead shed its starboard airscrew and damaged the adjacent wing while still over the Channel, but was landed safely at Littlestone. On 10 April another engine seized soon after take-off from Croydon, a safe circuit and landing being achieved on two engines, so in June three modified Jaguars were installed in an attempt to cure the persistent lubrication failures; the trouble seemed to be infectious, for on 19 June one of the hitherto blameless Eagles of W.8b G-EBBI also seized, while crossing the Channel at 1,000 ft under a low cloud base, inbound from Amsterdam. Captain Horsey found himself unable to clear the cliffs at Dover and with great skill scraped in over the roof tops of the town to a precarious landing in a small meadow beyond. With the Jaguar's troubles still not completely cured, and impressed by recent endurance demonstrations by a Bristol Jupiter VI in a Bloodhound which had flown over 25,000 miles without having to break seals affixed by the AID at the beginning of the trial, Imperial Airways' chief engineer, G. W. Hall, accepted the Air Ministry's loan of three Jupiter VIs to replace the W.9a's Jaguars for 250 hours flying on regular service. The change was made at Filton in the second week of July, with immediate improvement in both performance and reliability; in fact at the end of the 250 hours in May 1927, the cost of replacements on all three Jupiters amounted to only £14.1s, most of which was for items, such as split-pins, which could not be

The Hampstead at Filton in July 1926 after installation of Bristol Jupiter VI engines, showing gas-starter behind cockpit.

G-EBMM at Croydon in 1928 in Imperial Airways' revised livery. (*Real Photographs*)

re-used after top overhaul. The W.9a had been hired for a period in March 1927 by Sir Alfred Mond, to enable him to attend a series of nearly coincident conferences in France, Belgium and Germany and, after its engine inspection, went back into regular airline service, usually flown by Colonel Freddy Minchin. On 27 June while returning from Paris to Croydon he was forced to make a crash landing near Biggin Hill when all three engines cut simultaneously from fuel starvation; both undercarriages and the starboard wings were smashed, but, thanks to their interchangeability with Hyderabad spares, the damage was assessed as repairable at Croydon and the W.9a was back in service by the end of October, as a standby for the three Armstrong Whitworth Argosies which had taken over the first-class traffic from the W.10s. The latter, indeed, had barely filled the breach caused by the late delivery of the Argosies, for on 10 October, 1926, G-EBMR had had to land with a broken oil pipe en route from Brussels and was dismantled on site for repair at Croydon, where it received further damage when its temporary hangar collapsed under a heavy snowfall on 2 February, 1927, necessitating its return to Cricklewood until the end of March. Only eleven days after 'MR's misfortune in Belgium, G-EBMS was lost when Dismore with ten passengers suffered a sudden engine failure and had to ditch in mid-Channel; fortunately all the passengers were rescued by a nearby trawler, the only casualty being a Pomeranian dog, but there was a good deal of criticism of the inadequacy of the life-jackets provided and of the absence of a dinghy or raft big enough to support all on board. On Christmas Eve, the same fate nearly befell 'MM en route from Cologne, when an exhaust manifold burst and burned through the adjacent water hoses. The pilot, Jimmy Youell, landed at Ostend, sent his six passengers on by sea, had the manifold patched up and took off again with only his wireless operator and engineer aboard, climbing to 7,000 ft before leaving the coast. The manifold burst again in mid-Channel, as he had expected, but he was able to reach Lympne with 4,000 ft in hand. 'MR was back in service in time to join with the W.9a in the 'guard of honour' which escorted Charles Lindbergh into Croydon from Paris on 29 May, 1927, after his sensational first solo crossing of the Atlantic, and the three W.10s continued in regular scheduled and charter flights for a further two years, together with the Hamilton, G-EBIX, now named *City of Washington*; in August 1928 the latter was tested with an experimental rainproof windscreen designed to preserve visibility through a shielded slot; this

G-EBIX modified to W.8g with Rolls-Royce F.XIIA engines at Croydon on 8 September, 1930. (*K. A. Winkley*)

device proved useless and was abandoned, and when the Eagle IX and Pumas became time-expired in 1929 G-EBIX was rebuilt to the W.10 standard, but with two Rolls-Royce F.XIIA engines instead of Napier Lions, being then designated W.8g. This compensated Imperial Airways to some extent for the loss of G-EBMT, which Captain R. P. D. Brailli was forced to ditch three miles off Dungeness on 17 June, 1929, after engine failure in mid-Channel while outward bound for Zürich. Four of his eleven passengers were drowned, thus spoiling the Handley Page fleet's record of 3,900,000 passenger-miles flown without injury or loss of life. A court of inquiry under Sir Arthur Colefax found that the engine failure was due to fracture of big-end bolts made from mild steel instead of high-tensile steel, but improperly marked as the latter, and Imperial Airways was censured both for this and for the inadequacy of the means of escape from the waterlogged cabin. In consequence of this disaster, Imperial Airways ruled that from 18 September, 1929, all cross-Channel passenger services would be operated solely by three-engined aircraft, the twin-engined Handley Pages being restricted to overland routes such as Paris–Zürich, and to cargo services. Unfortunately this rule only applied to fare-paying passengers and on 30 October, 1930, G-EBIX flew into high ground in fog near Neufchatel, while homeward bound on a relief service with three privilege passengers and three crew. The pilot, J. J. Flynn, had already had a narrow escape on the 18th, with six passengers aboard, when G-EBIX had suffered a total electrical failure, losing wireless and instrument panel lights after entering cloud at 1,500 ft, with daylight nearly gone. On that occasion he had landed safely at Croydon, but his luck failed at Neufchatel and he was very severely injured, with one leg amputated in the crash, which also killed his engineer, F. H. Mason, and two of the passengers; in spite of having both legs crushed, the third passenger, F. B. Tomkins, crawled for over a mile to get help, which arrived in time to save 'Paddy'

Flynn's life; subsequent inspection confirmed that the Rolls-Royce engines were in no way responsible, and they were later installed for a short period in G-EBMR, but removed when due for overhaul.

G-EBMM and 'MR were retired from Imperial Airways in 1933 and sold to Sir Alan Cobham for flying display work and experiments in flight refuelling. Fitted as a tanker, 'MM was used to refuel Sir Alan's Airspeed Courier G-ABXN after taking off from Portsmouth on an attempted nonstop flight to India on 24 September, 1934, 'MR being stationed at Malta to provide the second refuelling, which was itself successful, although a defective throttle linkage soon afterwards caused the Courier's flight to be abandoned. Immediately after the initial refuelling Captain Bremridge had flown 'MM to Ford to have the tanks removed and seats re-installed in order to rejoin the National Aviation Day programme, but near Aston Clinton a tailplane bracing bolt fractured, causing loss of control, and the pilot and crew perished in the ensuing fire. G-EBMR was sold in Malta two months later and the first SABCA-built W.8b, OO-AHJ, which had been brought to Ford in 1932 as an addition to Sir Alan Cobham's joy-riding fleet, with the British registration G-ACDO, was scrapped without being re-erected. The SABENA W.8es had given excellent service in the Congo before being superseded in 1932 by Fokker monoplanes, and such was the quality of their protective varnish that they survived the rigours of the tropical rain forest with no more than the normal amount of maintenance and repair. Their good reputation resulted in the W.9a, no longer needed by Imperial Airways in March 1929, being sold to Leslie Urquhart for use by his newly formed Ellyou Goldfield Development Corporation in New Guinea. It was shipped to Port Moresby and re-erected, less outer wings, in six weeks by local labour under the supervision of W. R. E. Satchell and pilot G. I. Thompson; after being towed several miles from the dock to the temporary airfield, the wings were rigged and Thompson flew it 240 miles to the main base at Lae and thence to Salamaua for cargo carrying over an 8,000 ft mountain range to the goldfield at Wau, itself 3,500 ft above sea-level; it was transferred to Guinea Airways in October 1929, becoming VH-ULK on the Australian civil register. Over the next six months Thompson and his engineer McMurtree completed 250 round trips, but during the 251st on 30 May, 1930, with a cargo mainly of bully beef, canned soup and condensed milk, they flew into dense cloud and severe turbulence; losing control they spun and crashed in the jungle near the summit of the range. Although missing for six days, they survived by broaching their cargo, much of which they traded to the local tribesmen, who were reputed to be cannibals, but proved quite friendly.

During its first three years of service in No.99 Squadron, the Hyderabad had earned very good opinions from RAF crews, particularly after the modified rudder had been standardised. Following delivery of the first batch of fifteen with Lion IIB engines, two further batches with Lion Vs were ordered, eight (J8317–J8324) for 99 Squadron in June 1927, and eleven (J8805–J8815) for a second squadron, No.10, formed under Wing Cmdr Harry Busteed at Worthy Down in November 1927; No.99 Squadron took an active part in the annual Air Exercises in July and August, operating singly from Bircham Newton and from a detached flight at Kenley. A third and final batch of eleven Hyderabads, J9293–J9303, was ordered in 1928, but in fact the last six were built as Jupiter-engined

Hyderabads of No.99 Squadron with revised fin and rudder *en route* to the RAF Display at Hendon in June 1928. (*D. I. Newman*)

J9296 of No.99 Squadron being refuelled at Upper Heyford. (*D. I. Newman*)

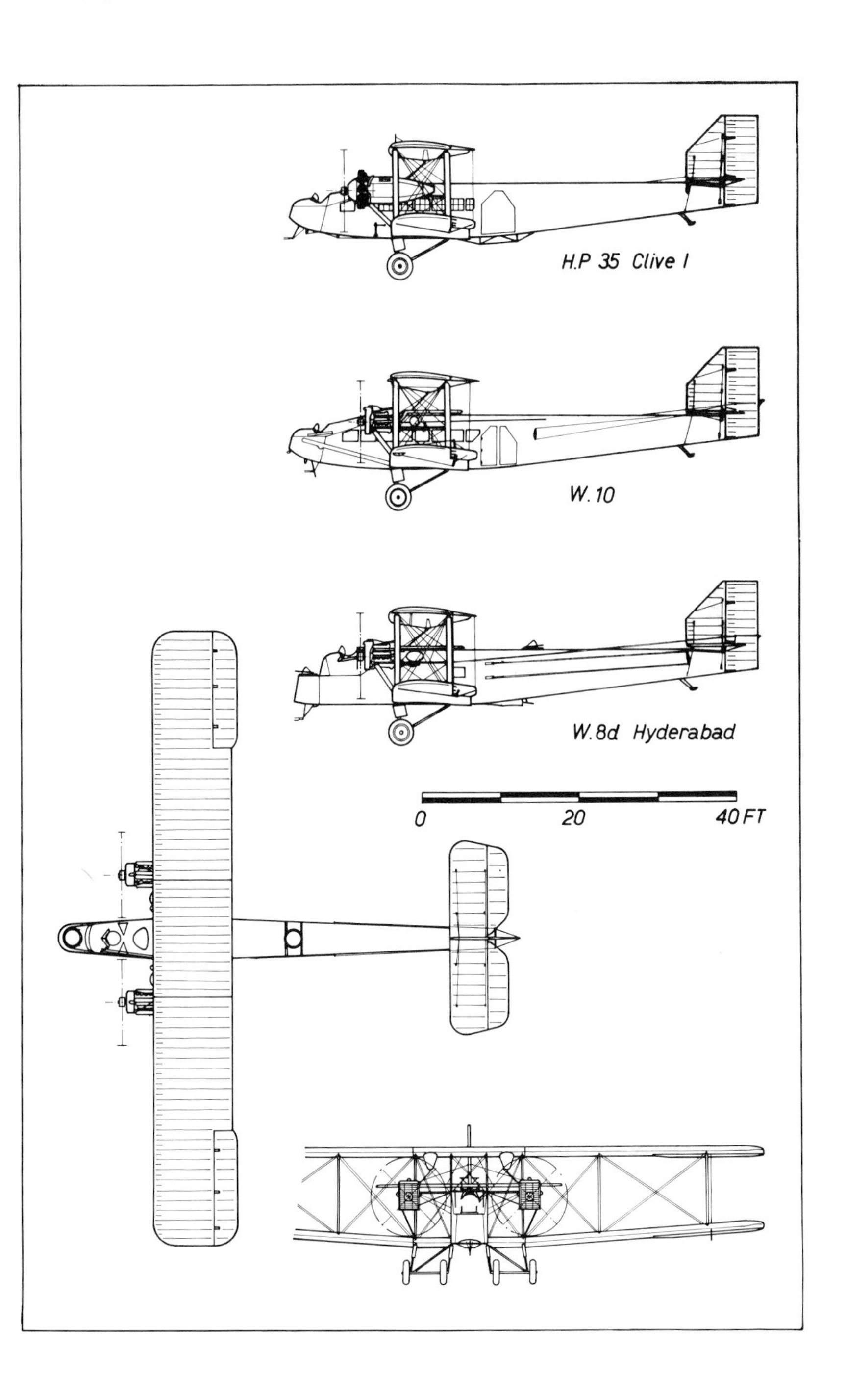
H.P 35 Clive I
W. 10
W. 8d Hyderabad
0
20
40 FT

Hinaidis, to replace J9031–J9036, ordered under contract No.790318/27 as Hinaidi Is, but issued initially as Hyderabads while Jupiters were temporarily in short supply; they were converted to Hinaidis during repair or overhaul in 1928–9. J9031 achieved temporary fame in No.99 Squadron by flying nonstop from Upper Heyford to Turnhouse on 12 October, 1928, and on 15 February, 1929, survived a forced landing on Harrow School playing fields, demolishing rugby goal-posts and careering downhill into a tree—but it was not a write-off and only one of the crew was injured; in fact, the Hyderabad seems to have been unique in RAF service in its total freedom from any fatality.

W.8d Hyderabad

(Two Napier Lion IIB or V)

Span 75 ft (22·9 m); length 59 ft 2 in (18·05 m); wing area 1,470 sq ft (136·5 m²). Empty weight 8,900 lb (4,040 kg); maximum weight 13,600 lb (6,160 kg); bomb load 1,100 lb (500 kg). Speed 109 mph (175 km/h); range 500 miles (805 km); ceiling 14,000 ft (4,325 m). Crew four.

W.8e & W.8f Hamilton

(Two Siddeley Puma and one Rolls-Royce Eagle IX)

Span 75 ft (22·9 m); length 60 ft 2 in (18·38 m); wing area 1,456 sq ft (135 m²). Empty weight 8,600 lb (3,900 kg); maximum weight 13,000 lb (5,900 kg). Speed 103 mph (166 km/h); range 500 miles (805 km); ceiling 13,000 ft (4,020 m). Crew two. Passengers twelve.

W.9 41/22

(Three Armstrong Siddeley Jaguar IV)

Span 75 ft (22·9 m); length 59 ft 4 in (18·13 m); wing area 1,656 sq ft (153·8 m²).

W.9a Hampstead

(Three Armstrong Siddeley Jaguar IV or three Bristol Jupiter VI)

Span 79 ft (24·1 m); length 60 ft 4 in (18·42 m); wing area 1,564 sq ft (145·5 m²). Empty weight 8,364 lb (3,790 kg); maximum weight 14,500 lb (6,570 kg). Speed 114 mph (183 km/h); range 400 miles (645 km); ceiling 13,500 ft (4,180 m). Crew two. Passengers fourteen.

W.8g (Converted from W.8f)

(Two Rolls-Royce F.XIIA)

W.10

(Two Napier Lion IIB)

Span 75 ft (22·9 m); length 59 ft 4 in (18·13 m); wing area 1,470 sq ft (136·5 m²). Empty weight 8,100 lb (3,675 kg); maximum weight 13,780 lb (6,250 kg). Speed 100 mph (161 km/h); range 500 miles (805 km); ceiling 11,000 ft (3,400 m). Crew two. Passengers sixteen.

Hinaidi I prototype, converted from Hyderabad J7745, at Martlesham Heath in June 1927.

Hinaidi and Clive (H.P.33, 35 and 36)

Early in 1927 one of the first batch of Hyderabads, J7745, had its Napier Lions replaced by French-built Gnome-Rhône Jupiters with Farman reduction gears, before any geared Bristol Jupiters were available from Filton. The conversion took place at Martlesham Heath, where Sqn Ldr T. H. England flew it first on 26 March. It was shown in the New Types Park at the RAF Display at Hendon in June with the new name Hinaidi, bearing the display number 4. In September it returned to Cricklewood for production Bristol Jupiter VIII engines to be installed and was then flown to Egypt and India for tropical trials, which involved a lengthy development programme to control oil temperature. In spite of its all-wood construction, it stood up to desert climatic extremes very well both at Heliopolis and later in India, where it operated successfully from Arawali on the North West Frontier, 3,700 ft above sea level. As a result of these

Hinaidi I J9033 was used for trial installations of armament and radio equipment at Martlesham Heath and Cricklewood.

Clive I J9126, combining features of the wooden Hinaidi I and W.10, at Martlesham Heath in June 1928. (*M.O.D.—Crown Copyright*)

trials, this variant was adopted as a replacement for the Hyderabad in Nos.10 and 99 Squadrons, with the type name Hinaidi I. Two new prototypes, J9030 and J9126, were ordered under contract No.786340/27, the first being a replacement for J7745 and the second having a W.10 fuselage for trial as a troop-carrier for use in India, to meet specification No.C.20/26. J9126 had a mid-upper Scarff ring like the Hinaidi and external bracing to the cabin floor to permit two spare engines or fuel tanks to be loaded. The Air Ministry wished the transport variant to be named Chitral, but Handley Page objected and insisted on a name more representative of the Indian Empire being chosen, and eventually the name Clive was agreed. The Clive I, of all-wood construction, took the air at Cricklewood in February 1928, by which time the first issues of Hinaidis to the RAF had begun; furthermore the last three of these, J9301–J9303, had experimental metal fuselages, in which steel tubes replaced spruce members.

Soon after receiving their first Hinaidis, No.99 Squadron complained of tail heaviness and requested new engine mountings to bring the engines forward, since the Jupiters were lighter than the Lions when installed. This was found impracticable and the RAF then suggested sweeping back the outer wings as had been done in later variants of the Vickers Virginia, by

J9126 with mocked-up nose gunner's station as development prototype for Clive II in 1929.

Second Clive II J9949 at Lahore in 1934. (*M.O.D.—Crown Copyright*)

inserting extension links in the front spar attachment points. Volkert agreed and estimated a maximum sweep of 2½ degrees, but hoped ¾ degree might be enough, so J9033 was converted at Martlesham in September 1928 and found satisfactory with 2½ degrees; this was standardised for production, with all-up weight restricted to 13,190 lb as for the Hyderabad and the maximum of 14,500 lb allowed only as a ferrying overload. Later the sweepback was increased to 5 degrees on all Hinaidis to permit 14,500 lb as the normal all-up weight of the metal versions. After its initial trials, the Clive was given a similar sweepback and an extended nose containing a mocked-up gunner's cockpit, with a Scarff ring and provision for a bomb-sight; this layout was eventually approved as the basis of contract No.911523/29 for two all-metal H.P.35 Clive IIs, J9948–J9949, equipped to carry seventeen fully-armed troops and a large variety of other loads, including stretcher cases, bombs, drums of petrol and oil, or three spare engines. A feature of all three Clives was that the windows were covered with fine-mesh gauze instead of Cellon sheet, so as to provide maximum ventilation without admitting sand or mosquitoes. The Clive I

Clive III G-ABYX in service with Sir Alan Cobham's National Aviation Day in 1933.

never went to India, but reverted to its original state with the nose extension removed, together with other armament, and was then furnished to W.10 standard, with Cellon windows, for the Air Council's proposed London–Belfast passenger service, as the Clive III, G-ABYX. In this form it was first flown by Major Cordes at Radlett on 5 September, 1932, its C of A being issued four days later. The Belfast scheme never matured and in April 1933 the Clive III was sold to Sir Alan Cobham, who used it for joy-riding, demonstration parachuting and flight-refuelling experiments, until it was scrapped two years later after carrying 120,000 passengers; in 1933 alone, G-ABYX carried 23,945 joy-riders in National Aviation Day displays, 1,008 of them in 48 flights on one day.

J7745 at Peshawar in January 1929 during the relief of the British Legation at Kabul. (*M.O.D.—Crown Copyright*)

The original Hinaidi J7745, doped aluminium for tropical service, was used as the personal transport of Sir Philip Sassoon during his official tour of RAF stations in India, while Under Secretary of State for Air; thereafter it served till 1934 alongside the Clive IIs with the RAF Heavy Transport Flight at Lahore, where it had been based since sharing with No.70 Squadron's Vickers Victorias the evacuation of civilians from the beleaguered British Embassy at Kabul during the rebellion against King Amanullah of Afghanistan in December 1928. This operation was completed on 25 February, 1929, after 586 passengers had been air-lifted in 82 flights over the 10,000 ft mountains to Peshawar, without a single casualty during very severe winter conditions. J7745's contribution comprised eight flights to Kabul and back, carrying 38 passengers and five tons of their baggage; Flt Lieut Anderson had flown it at short notice to Peshawar from Hinaidi near Baghdad in one of the longest overland ferry flights carried out by the RAF at that date; as J7745 was not equipped for night flying, a hurricane lamp had to be used to illuminate the pilot's instruments for landing after dark.

All-metal Hinaidi II prototype (Type M) J9478 in 1930.

One all-metal Hinaidi prototype (Type M), to specification B.13/29, was ordered as J9478 and first flown by Major Cordes at Cricklewood on 8 February, 1929. Built concurrently with the two Clive IIs, with which it had many components in common, it had 5 degrees of sweepback on the outer wings and was equipped with Handley Page automatic wing-tip slots; these had been fully tested in 1928 on Hyderabad J8813 (the only Hyderabad to be so fitted), but were not approved for use on early Hinaidis with wooden wings, whose front spars were not strong enough. Pending completion of J9478's Service trials, a new production design, H.P.36, was agreed for a batch of thirty-three metal Hinaidi IIs, K1063–1078 and K1909–1925, ordered in 1929 for the re-equipment of Nos.10 and 99 Squadrons, whose Hyderabads were re-issued to two newly-formed Special Reserve cadre squadrons, No.502 (Ulster) Squadron at Aldergrove (who retained them

The only slotted Hyderabad, J8813, on test at Radlett in 1928. (*Flight*)

till February 1932) and No.503 (County of Lincoln) Squadron at Waddington (who kept them till 1933 and then exchanged them for Hinaidis for a further two years). In June 1929 a variant, Hinaidi III (H.P.44) with Armstrong Siddeley Jaguar engines, was prepared as an insurance against shortage of production Jupiters, but not needed. Both design and manufacturing problems delayed final approval and the first of the batch, K1063, was not ready to be flown by T. H. England as a definitive Hinaidi II till 25 November, 1931. By that time a production procedure for all-metal aircraft had been firmly established and the wood-working era at Cricklewood had ended.

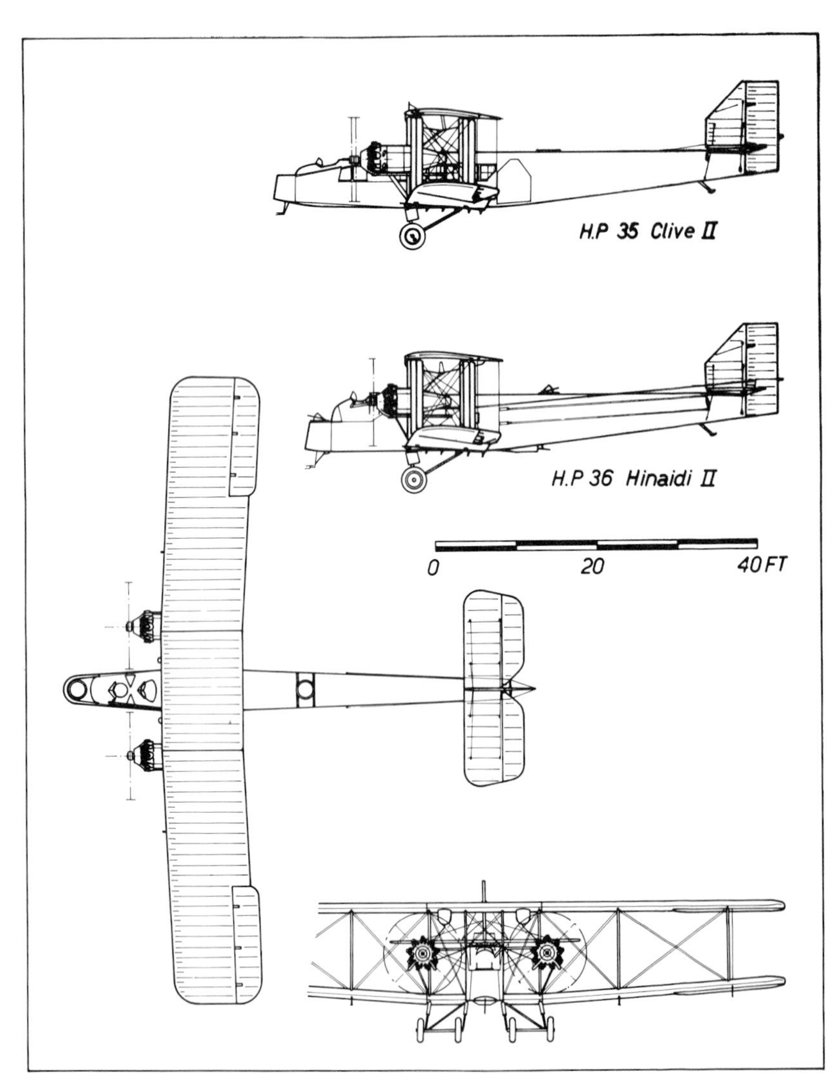

Production Hinaidi II K1909 of No.503 (County of Lincoln) Squadron at Waddington in 1934. (*I.W.M.—Crown Copyright*)

Unlike the Hyderabad, which for several years was a popular participant in the RAF Displays at Hendon, the Hinaidi never appeared there apart from J7745's debut in 1927. Both types provided valuable Service training during the lean years of appeasement, but were hardly a match for even the 1914-vintage manually-controlled 120 cm searchlights which still equipped the Territorial units of the Royal Engineers, who spent a week of their summer holiday each year co-operating in the annual air exercises. The last Hinaidi was withdrawn from use in No.503 Squadron in October 1935 and altogether 116 biplanes of the W type were built, including those by SABCA in Belgium.

H.P.33 Hinaidi I and H.P.36 Hinaidi II

(Two Bristol Jupiter VIII or VIIIF)

Span 75 ft (22·9 m); length 59 ft 3 in (18·09 m); wing area 1,471 sq ft (136·5 m²). Empty weight 8,040 lb (3,650 kg); maximum weight 14,500 lb (6,570 kg); bomb load 1,450 lb (657 kg). Speed 122 mph (196 km/h); range 850 miles (1,368 km); ceiling 14,500 ft (4,490 m). Crew four.

H.P.35 Clive I and II

(Two Bristol Jupiter VIII)

Span 75 ft (22·9 m); length (I) 59 ft 2 in (18·05 m), (II) 63 ft (19·22 m); wing area 1,471 sq ft (136·5 m²). Empty weight 8,100 lb (3,675 kg); maximum weight 14,500 lb (6,570 kg). Speed 111 mph (178 km/h); range 765 miles (1,232 km); ceiling 12,600 ft (3,890 m). Crew three. Troops seventeen. Figures for the Clive III were the same as for the Clive I except that it had accommodation for two crew and sixteen passengers.

The Handley Page Slotted Wing: H.P.17, H.P.20, Hanley (H.P.19) and Hendon (H.P.25)

In April 1911 Frederick Handley Page read to the Aeronautical Society of Great Britain a paper entitled *The Pressures on Plane and Curved Surfaces Moving through the Air*, in which he analysed the scanty wind-tunnel results then available and attempted to define a law relating lift to angle of incidence. He noted that, with a wing of moderate aspect ratio (6·25), lift increased approximately linearly up to 10 degrees incidence, but then levelled off, while the lift of a square wing (aspect ratio 1·0) continued to increase with incidence up to nearly 40 degrees—a fact already well-known from kite-flying experiments—but its drag was disproportionately high; consequently a high aspect ratio was desirable to achieve quick take-off and economical level flight. He suggested that loss of lift at high incidence was due to high-pressure air escaping from under the wing past the trailing edge into the region of suction above the wing, this effect being generally recognised and described as 'burbling'. Using the wind-tunnel at Kingsbury in 1917, Handley Page and his aerodynamicist R. O. Boswall tried to combine the low drag advantage of high aspect ratio with the delayed stall associated with low aspect ratio by separating a normal narrow wing into discrete square areas by means of chordwise slots, but found the result disappointing and incapable of being improved by varying the proportions of the slots and their disposition spanwise. At some point in these entirely empirical experiments, someone—whether Handley Page himself or Boswall or one of the carpenters is not clear—had the idea of cutting a spanwise slot parallel to the leading edge, sloping upwards and rearwards, at about the quarter-chord line. The first experiment, using RAF 15 aerofoil section, gave a spectacular lift increase of 25 per cent; with an improved shape of slot in RAF 6 section this was raised to over 50 per cent, with only a slight increase in drag; moreover the 'burble' was postponed till 25 degrees incidence was exceeded. Numerous experiments continued during 1918 and 1919, using various shapes of single slot, whose location chordwise was found to be critical on thin aerofoils; cascades of two, three, four, five, six and seven slots formed in a thick cambered aerofoil (RAF 19) were also tested; with six slots at 45 degrees incidence the lift coefficient was doubled, but structural limitations with the materials available precluded any immediate prospect of using greatly increased wing loading for commercial application. Even if a sufficiently stiff and strong cascade wing had been feasible, it would have been difficult to provide the very wide range of variable incidence necessary to maintain an acceptable flight attitude for a passenger aircraft.

Handley Page realised early on that the slotted wing was an extremely valuable invention, so he kept its principle strictly secret until patent applications had been accepted by both the British and United States

Patent Offices. To avoid premature disclosure, he did not seek protection of the original fixed slot until he was ready also to cover a movable slot, which could be opened and closed by the pilot. The master patent for this controllable slot, No.157567, was granted on 24 October, 1919, and a corresponding American patent was obtained soon afterwards. At the end of 1919 Boswall resigned in order to take up a teaching appointment at Manchester University, and his place as leader of the wind-tunnel research team (comprising Miss Chandler and Messrs Reynolds, Pirrie, Hall, Miles, Campbell and Fossett) was taken by Captain G. T. R. Hill, MC, on his demobilisation from the RAF. Geoffrey Hill, who with his brother Roderic had built a glider in their pre-war schooldays, came to Cricklewood primarily as a test pilot after the resignation of Sholto Douglas; but he was also keenly interested in aerodynamic research, particularly in the attainment of improved safety during take-off and landing. He was thus well-qualified for the task of correlating wind-tunnel and full-scale flight tests on the slotted wing. Unfortunately he had been a victim of the notorious influenza epidemic of 1919 and was still unfit for flying at the end of that year, but he began wind-tunnel work during his convalescence and was keen to try out the invention on an actual aeroplane.

In February 1920 a D.H.9 biplane (H9140) with a Siddeley Puma engine was acquired very cheaply from the Aircraft Disposals Board and its performance in its original state was carefully measured. Then full-span slats were attached to both upper and lower mainplanes in front of the leading edges so as to form slots, which were then covered over by strips of doped-on fabric. Late in the afternoon of 31 March, 1920, G. T. R. Hill began a series of short flights at Cricklewood, watched by other pilots of Handley Page Transport Ltd, including Gordon Olley, Leslie Foot and W. L. Rogers. After each flight, fabric was progressively removed to expose the slots and the slow-flying qualities of the aeroplane were effectively demonstrated, so much so that on the final flight Wilcockson landed very steeply and slowly in front of the hangar doors, into which he was prevented from drifting by Meadows, the erecting shop foreman and others, who caught hold of a wing-tip while the machine was still airborne and swung it to safety.

Concurrently with these tests, a model wing was sent to the National Physical Laboratory, who confirmed the effectiveness of the slot in delaying stalling at high incidence, thereby increasing the effective lift. Handley Page then applied to the Air Ministry's Director of Research (Sir Robert Brooke-Popham) for an experimental contract to cover further slot development, and an effective demonstration in H9140 by Geoffrey Hill on 22 April was witnessed by Lord Londonderry (Under-Secretary of State for Air) and Sir Frederick Sykes (Controller-General of Civil Aviation); immediately after this demonstration, the undercarriage of H9140 was made 12 inches taller to increase the ground angle. In the House of Commons on 18 May, Captain Wedgwood Benn asked whether the Air Ministry intended to acquire the invention so as to make it available to all aircraft manufacturers, and received a negative reply from Winston Churchill. Three more patents (Nos. 166428, 166429 and 166430) were granted on 16 June, 1920, to cover control gear and slot mechanisms, and these were further extended to multiple slots by patent No.172109 dated 31 August, 1920. By this time the Air Ministry had agreed to allow RAE pilots to make brief trials and H9140 was sent to Gosport for simulated deck landings by Sqn Ldr Roderic Hill, who also flew it on to and off the deck of the aircraft-carrier *Argus* while at anchor in Spithead. Roderic Hill confirmed his brother's opinion and reported a stalling speed in level flight of 38 mph with the engine throttled to 800 rpm, a gentle sink in engine-off gliding flight at 65 mph, rudder still effective down to 45 mph and lateral control equal to that of an unmodified D.H.9. In tests at Farnborough on 11, 14 and 20 September, 1920, Hill and his colleagues Flt Lieut Jack Noakes and Flying Officer J. F. T. Barrett assessed the take-off run as 110 yd and landing run as 190 yd, no better than a standard D.H.9, but attributed this to the difficulty of making use of a high angle of attack at touch-down in spite of the main undercarriage having been lengthened. On 21 October a press demonstration was given by Leslie Foot at Cricklewood

In 1922 Handley Page Ltd reconditioned fifteen D.H.9As for the RAF in Iraq; this is J7027. (*Chaz Bowyer*)

and the occasion was fully reported in the world's newspapers; further trials took place at Farnborough on 31 January, 1921, with H9140 matched against a standard D.H.9 (D5755), both aircraft having been loaded to the same wing loading (7·7 lb/sq ft). Since H9140 had had its wing area effectively increased to 468 sq ft by the leading edge extensions, it had to carry 250 lb more than D5755, but nevertheless returned a stalling speed of 44·5 mph against the standard D.H.9's 51 mph, representing an increase of 30 per cent in maximum lift coefficient. In connection with trials on HMS *Eagle* proposed in November 1920, the Air Ministry had offered to pay the cost of converting a D.H.9A biplane in the same manner, provided it could be equipped with variable incidence; serial J6906 was reserved for this project, but the variable incidence scheme could not be designed in the short time allowed. Handley Page proposed instead a monoplane conversion of the D.H.9A, having a thick-section semi-cantilever plywood-covered wing equipped with full-span movable leading-edge slats and ailerons arranged to open slots at the hinges when lowered. This development of slotted ailerons and flaps was covered by patent

Fixed leading-edge slot on the H.P.17 in April 1920.

No.176909, dated 21 December, 1920. The Air Ministry would have preferred to convert a Bristol Fighter, because of the extensive performance data already acquired on this type by the RAE, but the D.H.9A was easier to modify and they agreed to spend £5,000 on the experiment.

The slotted monoplane conversion had a slightly tapered thick wing of 47 ft 6 in span, to match the fuselage and tail unit of D.H.9A F1632 and was designated X.4B; it was later recorded as H.P.20 and the slotted D.H.9 as H.P.17. The monoplane was first flown, with the slot closed and sealed, at Cricklewood by Arthur Wilcockson on 24 February, 1921, with further

H.P.17 with lengthened undercarriage about to be flown by Major E. L. Foot in a demonstration of controlled stalled flight at Cricklewood on 21 October, 1921.

flights on 1, 7, 10 and 11 March. After this the slot mechanism was made operable, by pivoting the slat about its leading edge, and in this form it was flown on many occasions by Geoffrey Hill as well as Wilcockson. High aerodynamic loads in flight made the mechanism difficult to operate reliably, but after a satisfactory test on 6 September, 1921, the monoplane was considered ready for official trials and given the serial J6914; it was taken on Air Ministry charge under contract No.225504/21 on 25 October and was to be delivered to Farnborough after acceptance at Cricklewood; the pilot assigned to this task was Frank T. Courtney, but on his first flight with the slot fully open, he hit the ground in a steep slow landing, cracking a bottom longeron; during repairs, an aileron control wheel was substituted for the standard D.H.9A column and the addition of a covered observer's

H.P.20 slotted monoplane in February 1921.

cockpit was authorised, but seems not to have been installed before the aircraft was dispatched in February 1922.

During the whole period of early development of the Handley Page slotted wing, a parallel investigation had been made, quite independently, by the German engineer-pilot, Gustav Victor Lachmann. He had transferred from the cavalry to the flying corps in 1917, and had stalled and spun-in during an early training flight, breaking his jaw. In hospital he had time to ponder on the cause of his accident and on means of preventing stall, concluding that a cascade of small aerofoils within a normal wing profile might have better low-speed properties than the equivalent single aerofoil. To study this idea, he made a simple wing model and rigged up an electric fan to entrain cigarette smoke over it, so as to obtain a crude form of flow visualisation. Satisfied with the result, he drafted a patent specification as early as February 1918, some weeks before Handley Page's first application, but his agent, Otto Kattler, was unable to convince the German Patent Office that the invention would work. In spite of repeated applications, the examiners refused to accept the principle and Lachmann, on leaving the Service, had let the matter lapse and become a student at the Darmstadt Institute. It was quite by chance that he saw an account of the Cricklewood demonstration on 21 October, 1920, and immediately challenged Handley Page's priority in the invention. Still the German Patent Office refused to consider his claim, in spite of the grant of a British patent to Handley Page, unless he could prove his invention experimentally. He then approached Professor Ludwig Prandtl at Göttingen, who agreed to do the necessary wind-tunnel tests for 1,000 marks (£50); Lachmann had nothing like this sum to spare, but his mother lent it to him and the result of the Göttingen tests (63 per cent increase in lift with two slots) convinced the patent examiners, who then granted the original application back-dated to February 1918. Handley Page recognised that his own patent was being challenged, but also knew that Lachmann could not afford to contest any infringement in the courts, so the two inventors met for a discussion in Berlin and reached an amicable arrangement advantageous to both parties. Lachmann agreed to share his patent rights with Handley Page, who in turn agreed to employ Lachmann as a consultant for three years, to keep him in touch with German aeronautical developments; at the same time, each party was to be free to exploit his own inventions in his own country. This arrangement guaranteed Lachmann a useful addition to his income, and at a trivial cost to Handley Page because of the prevailing low value of marks in terms of sterling. Lachmann had gone into the Opel motor car factory after graduating, but was not happy there and soon left. The agreement with Handley Page allowed him to work under Prandtl at Göttingen, where he could develop the slotted wing in the foremost wind-tunnel in Europe. There Lachmann analysed and tested a whole family of 'X' monoplane projects, of which the X.4B was the first full-scale example to fly. In spite of the priority of Lachmann's patent, it is clear that Handley Page could have had no knowledge of it until after his own patent had been granted. Other inventors, including Prof Alfredo G. Leigh and A. P. Thurston, had claimed earlier priority than either Lachmann or Handley Page, and it is true that both had experimented with 'pilot planes' before 1914, but they failed to exploit the leading edge slot as a means of maintaining lift at high angles of attack. Even Handley Page and

Hanley I N143 in the experimental department at Cricklewood in December 1921. (*S. T. A. Richards*)

Lachmann differed in their aims, for Lachmann was chiefly concerned with improving safety, while Handley Page hoped to use much higher wing loadings.

In particular, Handley Page saw its application to deck-landing aeroplanes and took the first opportunity of tendering to specification 3/20 (D. of R 8) for a single-seat deck-landing torpedo-carrier. This tender, for which George Volkert revived the designation Type T, had been accepted late in 1920, when three prototypes, N143–N145, were ordered under contract No.313750/20 for competitive trials against three prototype Blackburn Darts. Type T was officially named Hanley, but the detail design had not been finalised when Volkert decided to join the Master of Sempill's naval air mission to Japan, so it was taken over by S. T. A. Richards, who became Handley Page's chief designer when Volkert left in March 1921. The three Hanleys were of straightforward wooden construction and were built in one batch; as in the O/400, the longerons were hollow and made from two lengths of spruce glued together, with their

The second Hanley I N144 at Cricklewood before its somersault. (*S. T. A. Richards*)

internal faces spindled out to give a varying cross-sectional area while preserving a constant external square section, so that the same standard metal fittings could be used at all strut joints. In their original form (Mark I) the Hanleys had Napier Lion IIB engines of 450 hp, robust three-bay folding wings and separate main undercarriage units with long-travel oleo shock absorbers, arranged to leave a clear central space for the torpedo; details of the torpedo gear were not agreed with the Air Ministry until some weeks had elapsed after the aircraft themselves had been completed. The leading edges of both upper and lower wings carried movable slats extending across the full span; these were of the pivoted type developed on the X.4B monoplane, and the ailerons, at first with plain hinges, were later arranged to form slots at their leading edges as they moved below the neutral position, but no separate trailing-edge flaps were fitted inboard of the ailerons. The rudder was horn-balanced, but not the elevators. All three Hanley Is were finished in December 1921 and first flown by A. S.

The third Hanley I N145 in April 1922 after transferring torpedo gear from N144.

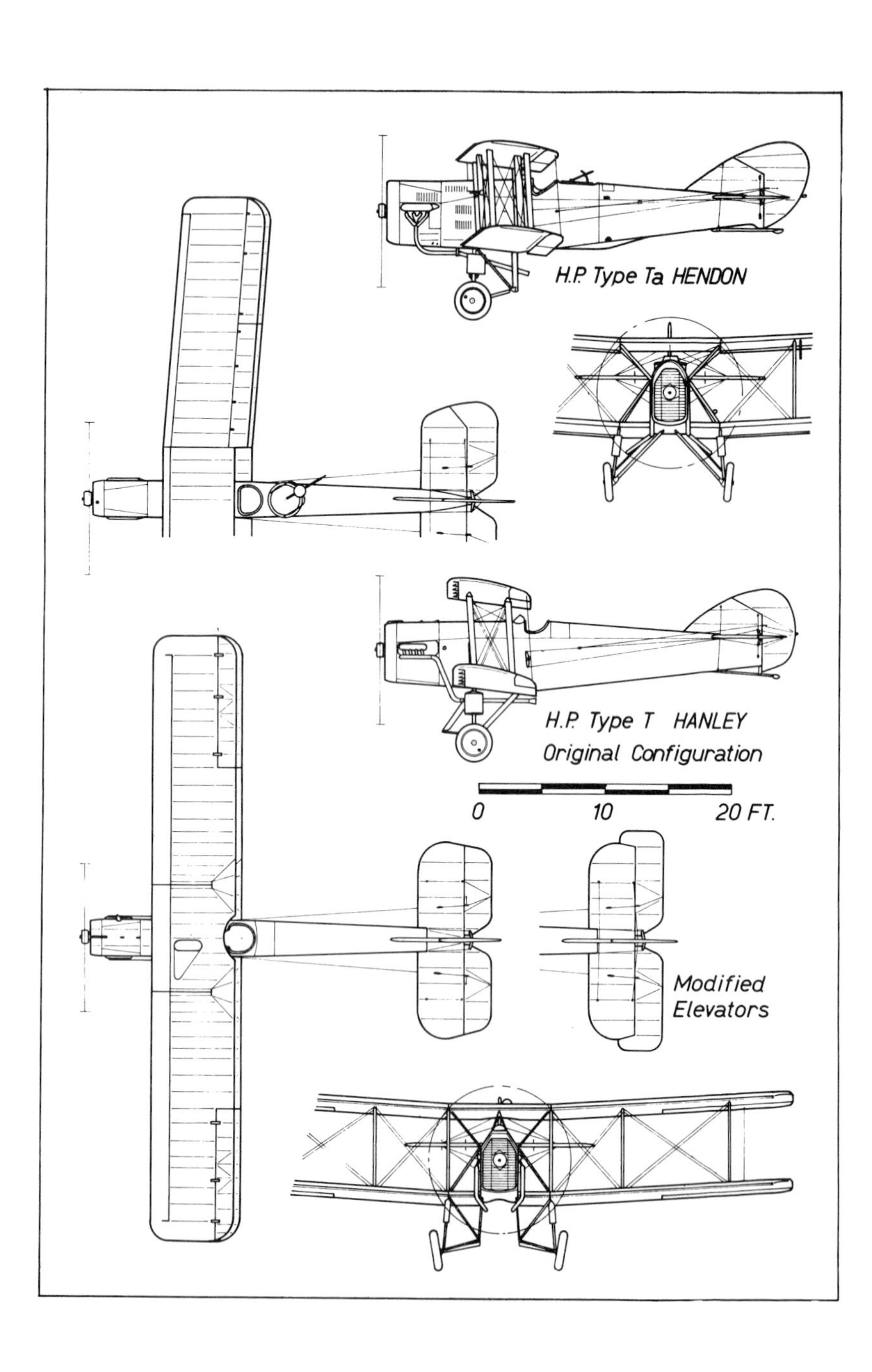
H.P. Type Ta HENDON
H.P. Type T HANLEY
Original Configuration
0
10
20 FT.
Modified
Elevators

Wilcockson at Cricklewood early in 1922, N143 on 3 January, N144 on 24 February and N145 on 23 March. After minimal manufacturer's trials, N143 was flown to Martlesham Heath on 11 March by Harold Payn, but damaged its chassis and lower wing in April, when it was returned to Cricklewood with a preliminary assessment indicating that its performance was too low and controls not well harmonised, but could be made acceptable by modifications to reduce drag and improve handling. Meanwhile N144 had somersaulted on landing at Cricklewood on 17 March and while it was being repaired its torpedo gear and Mk.VIII torpedo were transferred to N145, which went to Martlesham on 26 April to complete the performance trials begun by N143. These confirmed a disappointing maximum speed of 97 mph at 3,000 ft and a service ceiling of 10,550 ft with slots closed and 9,700 ft with slots open (A&AEE Report M.300b); on 23 May N145 went on to Gosport for dummy deck-landing trials, returning to Cricklewood at the end of September, when Wilcockson made eighteen flights to compare Martinsyde and Watts-Lang airscrews under varying conditions.

N143 at Cricklewood in December 1922 after conversion to Hanley II.

While being repaired at Cricklewood, N143 was extensively modified in order to eliminate the more obvious sources of drag, and was tested by Wilcockson on 4 December, 1922, as the Hanley Mk.II. It retained the original pivoted slats, but now had new wing-tips, an improved cabane with the inboard pairs of interplane struts deleted, a much simplified landing gear, slotted ailerons, and improved cable runs having the elevator rockshaft levers inside the fuselage covering instead of exposed to the slipstream; the upper and lower slot controls were also interconnected. Wilcockson flew it in this form from Cricklewood to Le Bourget on 8 December, landing at Croydon to clear Customs and at Kenley for an hour because of morning fog. From Le Bourget the Hanley II was towed into

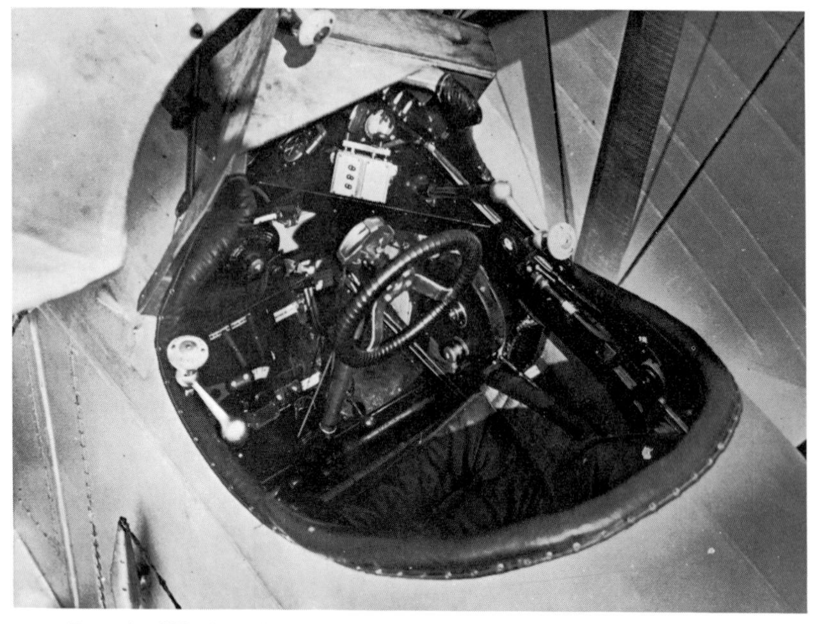

Controls of Hanley I showing separate upper and lower slot-operating handles.

Paris with its wings folded; its wheel-bearings overheated and had to be doused with water at frequent intervals. On arrival at the Grand Palais in the Champs Élysées, it was exhibited complete with a dummy torpedo, whose nose had been painted red to represent the warhead. At the end of the show, the Hanley returned to Le Bourget by road and on 6 January, 1923, Wilcockson flew it to Brussels for a demonstration at Evère, which was somewhat spoiled by difficulty with engine starting, since no Hucks starter was available and the airscrew was too high to be swung by hand from ground level. In the end, MacRostie used a broom to push the lower blade over compression while Wilcockson vigorously cranked the hand-magneto, and eventually the Napier Lion fired. Wilcockson's flight back on 15 January, 1923, was uneventful and his impressive arrival at Croydon was enhanced by a stiff breeze which enabled him to sink almost vertically before touching down, and to climb out equally steeply en route for Cricklewood after clearing Customs. Wilcockson flew N143 again on 7 February, 1923, after differential aileron controls and larger horn-balanced elevators had been fitted. On 4 April it returned to Martlesham Heath for Mark II Service trials, which included detachment to Gosport and brief deck-landing trials on the aircraft-carrier *Argus*. A & AEE Report M.336a of June 1923 showed a substantial gain in performance resulting from the cleaner design, with a top speed of 115 mph and a service ceiling of 14,700 ft; the new ailerons enabled full lateral control to be maintained down to the stall with slots open, giving a slow approach and short landing run; but the very large change of trim between the 'slots open' and 'slots closed' conditions necessitated a wide range of tail incidence adjustment and a tall main undercarriage was needed to compensate for the high angle of attack at minimum speed. This tail-down attitude spoiled the pilot's view for landing and also made torpedo handling more difficult than it should have been. Flying the Hanley II to the limit of its capability was no mean task for a solo pilot, for he had a dozen different controls to juggle with; apart from the normal flying controls (with wheel for ailerons), the tailplane incidence was variable through an unusually wide range; there were also rudder bias, engine throttle, mixture and ignition advance; radio, torpedo release gear and, finally, irreversible screw-jack crank handles for the upper and lower leading-edge slots. In their pivoted form, the slats were quite difficult to move under aerodynamic loading and had a high drag, even when closed, because of the cavity they formed behind the leading edge. A series of wind-tunnel tests during the last weeks of 1922 and early months of 1923 resulted in an improved slot shape, formed by movement of the slat on parallel arms swinging sideways, which allowed the slat to fit snugly against the leading edge of the wing when closed and so eliminated the gap and the consequent drag.

In February 1923 this pattern of slot gear was installed on N145, which also received the same general clean-up as N143 and was designated Hanley Mk.III when resubmitted to Martlesham Heath on 1 April, 1923. It was found that the minimum level speed was reduced by 8 per cent with slots open, giving a much lower take-off speed, adequate control down to the stall and very little trim change, although there was no difference in take-off and landing runs whether slots were opened or closed. The main defect of the swinging linkage was that much of the benefit was lost through the need to provide cavities in the wing leading edge to receive the links when folded sideways. The uneven airflow past these cavities caused back-lash and flutter, with some risk of asymmetric operation which would have been dangerous near the ground; so all slat movements had to be synchronised through continuous torque-tubes in the leading edges, which added to the already high friction load. In July ground handling was improved by lengthening the undercarriage radius rods and the Hanley III, entered for the revised torpedoplane competition to specification 32/22, performed much better than previously (A & AEE Report M.349); but not well enough to beat the Blackburn Dart, which scored decisive points with

N145 as Hanley III at Martlesham Heath in April 1923.

Hanley III N145 at Martlesham Heath showing improved flush-fitting slots. (*I.W.M.—Crown Copyright*)

its massive tubular centre-section structure and was adopted as the standard torpedo-bomber for the Fleet Air Arm.

Early in 1922 Handley Page had received an enquiry from a Russian trade mission for a slow-flying deck-landing naval torpedoplane as part of an aviation development programme being pursued after the main problems of reconstruction arising from the Bolshevik revolution of 1917 had been surmounted. Through the Anglo-Russian Co-operative Society agency (registered in Great Britain as Arcos Ltd) permission was obtained to export the second Hanley I, repaired but unmodified, together with one similar new Hanley I, to Leningrad, where a naval engineer, V. I. Bekaur, was developing a torpedo stabilised in the air by a tail-parachute and radio-controlled in the water. In the early months of 1923 MacRostie accompanied these two Hanleys to Leningrad, to supervise their re-erection by Russian mechanics, with whom he could communicate only by gestures. Working conditions were intensely cold, with several feet of snow and a raging malaria epidemic. When the radio had been installed, MacRostie found that his carefully selected set of valves brought from Cricklewood had been exchanged for duds and replacements had to be obtained from the Marconi Company at Chelmsford. The Russian pilots flew the Hanleys competently enough, but they insisted on MacRostie flying with them to read instruments and adjust radio and torpedo controls. Since the Hanleys were single-seaters, MacRostie had to spend many uncomfortable hours lying prone on a makeshift plywood floor under the pilot's feet, observing torpedo targets through a hole in the fabric through which blew an icy oil-laden blast; the exhaust pipes were swept down to run parallel with the torpedo to help to warm its motor compartment, but no engine heat seemed to reach MacRostie on his freezing perch. Eventually he escaped by an illegal route to Sweden and got back to Cricklewood in time to supervise N143's final public appearances, first at the RAF Pageant at Hendon in June 1923 and then at the International Aero Exhibition at Göteborg (Gothenburg) in July, from which it was shipped back to Cricklewood in September and returned to Martlesham to complete the Mark II trials. At about the same time Bekaur's experiments at Leningrad were interrupted when N144 crashed and was rebuilt as a two-seater with an enclosed observer's cockpit; the second Russian Hanley was similarly modified and both appear to have remained in service till 1926. To counteract the rearward shift of c.g., an extra bay was added to the front fuselage to move the engine forward.

The fourth Hanley I being completed at Cricklewood for export to Russia in 1923.

By July 1923 Handley Page had become desperately short of work and, faced with having to lay off 200 skilled men, he besought Sir Geoffrey Salmond, AMSR, to allot new prototype contracts, or at least allow the sale of N143 to the Greek government in the hope of obtaining further export orders. This could not be permitted, but a proposal for a two-seat variant was regarded more favourably, provided it could carry a torpedo or two 550-lb bombs and incorporated a prone bomb-aimer's position. Meanwhile, on completion of its Mark III trials in August 1923, N145 was flown back from Martlesham to have its chassis realigned and a hand starter installed, before going to Gosport for deck trials on HMS *Argus* in October; after these it came back into the works to have its rear fuselage strengthened. It was paraded before the assembled Dominion Premiers at Croydon on 10 November and flown thence to Martlesham, where it was written off charge in 1924. The advantages of a two-seat version of the Hanley had not escaped notice by the Air Ministry; both operationally and for experimental work a second crew member was useful, so a two-seat Hanley III, Type Ta, officially named Hendon, was defined by specification

37/22 Fleet Reconnaissance project drawn by Leslie Richards. (*S. T. A. Richards*)

25/23 for an interim torpedo-bomber, pending the arrival of the more advanced designs tendered to specification 21/23 for a Dart replacement. Two other Hanley variants, proposed in July 1923 but not built, were (a) a single-seat bomber to carry a single 2,300-lb SN bomb instead of a torpedo; and (b) a two/three-seat ship's reconnaissance plane to meet specification 37/22, as an alternative to a completely new 37/22 design powered by a Jaguar engine and equipped with a wheeled chassis interchangeable with a twin-float amphibian gear for deck-landing; this design was excluded from tender by the Air Ministry because some of the relevant papers were inadvertently left on an Underground train and Handley Page was severely reprimanded for a breach of the Official Secrets Act; prototypes ordered to the same specification were the Blackburn Airedale, Fairey Ferret and Hawker Hedgehog, none of which achieved production status. In spite of this lapse, six Hendons, N9724–N9729, were ordered under contract No.452299/23 dated 27 November, 1923, which indicates Handley Page's unfailing ability to make friends and influence them, even from the 'dog-house'.

Hendon I N9724 at Martlesham Heath in August 1924 with dummy torpedo and front ballast on underwing bomb-racks, before the wings were swept back.

The Hendon I retained the same slots and controls as the Hanley III, the main difference being the longer fuselage, which included a forward extension of the engine mounting to balance the observer and his Scarff ring-mounted Lewis gun immediately aft of the pilot; the latter had a synchronised forward-firing Vickers gun, although the Hanley, like the Blackburn Dart, had carried no defensive armament at all. N9724 was first flown by Arthur Wilcockson at Cricklewood on 7 July, 1924, and went to Martlesham Heath for official full-load trials in August. It was found to be tail-heavy with the torpedo aboard and ballast weights had to be strapped to the forward ends of the underwing bomb-racks to allow the maximum level speed tests to be flown. The tail-heaviness was eliminated by sweeping back the outer wings through 5 degrees on all six Hendons, the last three during manufacture and the first three by modification after first flight. They were test-flown at Cricklewood without torpedos, N9725 by Gordon Olley on 26 July, N9726 by Wilcockson one week later, N9727 by W. L. Rogers on 23 August and N9728 and N9729 early in September by

N9727 taxying at Cricklewood with flaps lowered.

Olley and Rogers respectively. All were reported to handle well at light load, but none could match the minimum speed of the Hanley III either near the ground or at altitudes up to 6,000 ft. At the end of its full-load trials in October (A & AEE Report M.398) N9724 was returned to Cricklewood and in November Sqn Ldr Watkins from Gosport flew N143 and N9724 in a programme of comparative tests for high speed with slots sealed and low speed with slots fixed open, concluding that the Hanley III was better than the Hendon I, the reason being the effect of the open observer's cockpit and its bomb-sight hatch below rather than any difference in the slots themselves. In February 1925 Flt Lieut G. M. Bryer visited Cricklewood to fly N9724 at various loadings and with ailerons rigged 5 deg or 10 deg down to simulate variable-camber flaps; a total of eight variations and 45 landings, compared with seven landings on a standard Hendon I, N9727, showed that a reduction of 3 to 5 knots and better lateral control with a flatter glide was possible on N9724 with drooped ailerons.

Next, an improved slot gear with vertical link motion was installed, the type thus modified being designated Hendon II. Bryer flew N9724 as a Hendon II with a new undercarriage and both 1,077-lb and 1,600-lb torpedoes on 13 and 16 June, 1925, and reported it better than any Hendon or Hanley previously tested. Two more Hendons, N9725 and N9727, were converted to Mark II standard, the latter being flown by Wilcockson on 11 August, 1925, first with ailerons rigged normally and then with them drooped, which gave a further useful reduction in landing speed. The next step was to install slotted flaps inboard of the ailerons, and to link the ailerons with the outer slats at each wing-tip. This was done on N9727, converting it to Hendon Mark III, which in August 1925 demonstrated a much better low-speed attitude and improved pilot's view when landing, due to the reduced angle of attack resulting when the flaps were lowered. In September 1925 N9727 was attached to the carrier *Argus* for deck-landing trials, which were continued during the following month on *Furious*, when successful landings were achieved without the use of arrestor wires, although a 1,400-lb torpedo was being carried. N9727 was thereafter retained at Cricklewood for a lengthy series of tests with small variations of slot/aileron linkage geometry; results with a cam-gear in March 1926 were less satisfactory than a direct connection to the slat, set to begin opening with the aileron neutral and fully closed with the aileron up, which was tested in May. The successful development of the Hendon III and its slot-and-flap gear was largely due to George Volkert, who had rejoined the firm as chief designer after returning from Japan at the end of 1923, and to his experimental draughtsman S. G. Ebel, who, with George Russell in the wind-tunnel, was the first to appreciate the importance of making the closed slot airtight at its leading edge, while leaving a small gap or vent at the trailing edge; this ensured a consistent point of reversal of air loads on the slat, thereby achieving a snap action without lag or flutter, and eventually led to the automatic slot which needed no mechanical control.

This final stage had not been reached in July 1926, when N9727 was equipped with a new control device, the 'interceptor', consisting of a spanwise narrow-chord hinged plate or spoiler normally lying flat under the trailing edge of the outer slat in its closed position. At large angles of attack near the stall, lateral control by means of a slot and aileron linkage was insensitive and potentially dangerous; but if the tip-slots were allowed to remain open and the interceptor was raised vertically by the up-going aileron, very fine control of the airflow through the slot was obtained without any inertia lag due to slat movement. N9727, with interceptors fitted and the aileron linkage disconnected, was effectively demonstrated by Wilcockson at Cricklewood on 20 July, 1926, to a party of Air Attachés and technical journalists; Handley Page had enthusiastically telephoned them on the previous Sunday morning, urging their immediate attendance that day; he never shared his father's devout persuasion, nor was he a successful golfer, so the Sabbath was just another working day to him, but his guests had other commitments and could not oblige till Tuesday. Next day the

Hendon III N9727 launching torpedo at Spithead during deck trials on *Furious* in October 1925. (*Real Photographs*)

Hendon III's linked slots, flaps and ailerons. (*I.W.M.—Crown Copyright*)

Hendon III was flown by a group of invited test pilots, including Piercey of Glosters, Openshaw of Westlands, Franklyn Barnard of Imperial Airways, Bulman of Hawkers, Payn of Vickers, Frank Barnwell of Bristols and Lankester Parker of Shorts, to whom Handley Page expatiated on the merits of his new invention and announced that N9727 was the first aeroplane to have landed over the bow of the *Argus* while steaming downwind. Though the pilots' opinions of the device were generally favourable, the Air Ministry was still not convinced that it was the answer to the mounting toll of stall-and-spin accidents to D.H.9As and Bristol Fighters in India and the Middle East, which accounted for the majority of flying fatalities in the Royal Air Force that year; meanwhile, the RAE strove to produce a mechanism which would be more reliable than the Handley Page gear, and R. McKinnon-Wood led a small team of aerodynamicists at Farnborough in developing a hinged 'pilot-plane' for use in conjunction with trailing-edge flaps; this was sufficiently different from the Handley Page invention to be granted patent No.289517 in January 1927, and was naturally preferred by the Treasury since it would, if successful, avoid substantial claims for compensation for Crown user in lieu of royalties. In fact, the pilot-plane itself was ineffective, but the RAE linkage, when applied to the Handley Page slot-and-aileron geometry, worked rather better than Syd Ebel's own mechanism.

Shortly before fitting the interceptor control, N9727 had been flown at Cricklewood on 8 July, 1926, by Flying Officer Howard Saint and H. L. Stevens of the RAE to assess the Handley Page slot-and-aileron gear, and this had sufficiently impressed them for a test programme to be undertaken at Farnborough in 1927 by Stuart Scott-Hall. Elaborate (for that time) instrumentation was provided, including a self-recording inclinometer, flap position indicators and a suspended air-log (remote pitot-static head) for accurate airspeed measurement. The Hendon III was allotted to the RAE after the interceptors had been removed and was first climbed to 10,000 ft over Worthy Down to check that the Napier Lion could be restarted by diving after having been stopped for partial glides to be made at 50 mph. In the next flight, a standard glide with flaps down was fully observed and recorded with engine switched off, followed by a dive with slots closed and flaps up to restart the engine as before, but on pulling out of the dive the port upper slat began to chatter severely and on landing the three middle support brackets were found to have failed, both the end ones being cracked also. N9727 was forthwith grounded and returned to Cricklewood by road somewhat in disgrace, while discussions began with the object of equipping an initial batch of the RAF's D.H.9As and Bristol Fighters with the RAE slot-and-aileron gear, at the urgent request of Wing Commander J. A. Chamier, who was determined to put an end without further delay to the continuing toll of tropical take-off casualties. Then, in October 1927, came the dramatic break-through to the automatic slot, which was to be universally adopted as a simple but essential safety feature, and was declared by C. G. Grey to be as important to aviation as the pneumatic tyre had been to land transport.

H.P.17

(Siddeley Puma)

Span 45 ft 9 in (13·96 m); length 30 ft 1 in (9·18 m); wing area 468 sq ft (43 m^2). Maximum weight 3,610 lb (1,635 kg). Maximum speed 96 mph (154 km/h); minimum speed 38 mph (61 km/h); ceiling 15,000 ft (4,640 m). Pilot and observer.

H.P.19 Hanley

(Napier Lion IIB)

Span 46 ft (14 m); length 33 ft 4 in (10·17 m); wing area 562 sq ft (52·2 m^2). Maximum weight 6,444 lb (2,920 kg). Maximum speed 116 mph (187 km/h); minimum speed 55 mph (88 km/h); ceiling 15,000 ft (4,640 m). Pilot alone.

H.P.20

(Liberty 12-N)

Span 47 ft 6 in (14·5 m); length 30 ft (9·15 m); wing area 500 sq ft (46·4 m^2). Maximum weight 6,500 lb (2,950 kg). Pilot alone.

37/22

(Armstrong Siddeley Jaguar III)

Span 46 ft (14 m); length 31 ft (9·45 m); wing area 330 sq ft (30·6 m^2). Maximum weight (est) 4,200 lb (1,910 kg). Crew three.

H.P.25 Hendon

(Napier Lion IIB)

Span 46 ft (14 m); length 34 ft 6 in (10·51 m); wing area 562 sq ft (52·2 m^2). Maximum weight 6,970 lb (3,160 kg). Maximum speed 110 mph (177 km/h); minimum speed 55 mph (88 km/h); ceiling 9,500 ft (2,940 m). Crew two.

S-1 in the Cricklewood experimental shop in September 1923. (*S. T. A. Richards*)

Ship's Fighter Type S (H.P.21)

In 1921 the United States Navy had begun to develop deck-landing techniques, and invited tenders from European as well as American designers. Among the roles specified was Class VF, a single-seat fighting scout armed with two machine-guns and capable of operating either from the deck of a carrier or as a seaplane. Handley Page saw his chance of applying slots and flaps so as to obtain a very quick take-off and short landing run, together with the high speed attainable by a monoplane with nearly double the wing loading of a biplane having the same minimum speed. In August 1921 S. T. A. Richards began the layout of a very advanced low-wing cantilever monoplane designated Type S (subsequently listed as H.P.21), with a relatively thick Göttingen wing profile recommended by Lachmann, having full-span leading-edge slots with sheet duralumin slats, and full-span slotted ailerons arranged to droop symmetrically when the slots were open. The airframe was a three-ply monocoque, fabric being used only to cover the ailerons and elevators, and the fuselage was divided into two components just aft of the wing trailing edge, the two parts being joined by six quickly detachable bolted fish-

Rear view of S-1 showing zero dihedral and full-span droopable ailerons. (*I.W.M.—Crown Copyright*)

plates; Richards preferred this to the hinged fuselage of the Parnall Panther, although it served the same purpose. All the controls were operated by light-alloy push-pull tubes and bell-cranks, the ailerons having a differential gear to provide a normal antisymmetric movement with symmetric droop superimposed by linkage to the slot mechanism.

Initially, a rigid strutted undercarriage was proposed, with a faired cross-axle sprung by rubber cord in the traditional manner, but Volkert's reports from Japan of deck-landing experience with Parnall Panthers showed the necessity for a long-stroke oleo landing gear, and Richards introduced this modification early in the manufacture of the prototypes. By February 1923 Lachmann had completed wind-tunnel tests at Göttingen, mechanical tests were in progress at Cricklewood, and G. S. Baker at the NPL's Froude water tank was testing model floats designed by W. H. Sayers, who had earlier collaborated with Linton Hope at Port Victoria and Grain. The airframe was stressed for an engine of 400 hp, and in any production

S-1 at Cricklewood ready for first flight, with spinner removed and original tail unit.

machines it was intended to install the Armstrong Siddeley Jaguar, but in the prototypes, to save time and cost, the Bentley B.R.2 rotary of 230 hp was used, being readily available from the Aircraft Disposal Company. The three prototypes, known at Cricklewood as S-1, S-2 and S-3, were allotted US Navy serials A-6402, A-6403 and A-6404, and Ogilvie & Partners were retained as consultants to supervise manufacture and testing at Cricklewood, with Major R. H. Mayo reporting personally to Commander R. H. Towers, USN. S-1 was completed in August 1923 with a flat, slightly tapered wing, a plain fin and rudder, and a large hemispherical spinner; this had to be removed because of vibration during the first engine runs. The two Marlin 0·300 cal guns, with their Aldis sight and ammunition, were not installed, nor were the Very pistol, parachute and basket containing two pigeons, which together made up the prescribed operational load of 350 lb.

The first flight, planned for 9 a.m. on 7 September, 1923, in the presence of Commander Towers, was delayed till late afternoon, because Arthur Wilcockson had been detained in France by a forced landing in an O/400 the previous day. At 5.40 p.m. he took off from Cricklewood aerodrome with slots open but aileron droop inoperative, unstuck in 5½ seconds, climbed well during a single 15-second circuit, misjudged his approach and overshot, then made an extra circuit and a good three-point landing. For his second flight, next morning at 10.30, the fuel load had been increased from 12 to 15 gallons; he took off quickly and flew wide circuits for 8 minutes, then landed very fast with the tail up, bouncing heavily and finally ground-looping through 180 degrees; he reported that the rudder was completely ineffective for ground steering and that, in level flight, petrol siphoned into the cockpit from the fuel tank vent pipe, which was forthwith extended upwards by 5 inches; at the same time the swivelling ball on the end of the tubular tailskid was removed to improve tracking. Two hours later he made a third flight of 15 minutes, again flying in wide circuits and finally landing more slowly and with less swing; he was able to close the slots while in flight, without any appreciable change of trim, and opened them again before landing, but attempted no other manoeuvres. Wilcockson, normally a Handley Page Transport pilot flying O/400s, was beginning to get the feel of his lively little mount and Handley Page was well satisfied to let him make gradual progress, but Bob Mayo was impatient on behalf of Towers and, hearing that F. P. Raynham was available, prevailed upon Handley Page to engage him, because of his unrivalled experience of high speed seaplanes. So, on 10 September, Raynham took off at midday, climbed to 1,000 ft and tried banked turns to port and starboard. On landing he reported that rudder control was dangerously deficient and agreed with Mayo that more wind-tunnel tests were needed before flying was resumed; he confirmed that the ailerons and elevators were satisfactory. Four days later, S-1 re-emerged from the experimental shop with the fin cut off square at the top and surmounted by the horn balance of an enlarged rudder. The aileron-drooping linkage, previously disconnected, was made operable by the pilot for the first time and Raynham took off at 11.15 a.m. He found no improvement in directional control, but considered the rudder now to be over-balanced. Handley Page suggested increasing the keel area, but Raynham disagreed and considered the keel area to be right but with its centre of pressure too far aft. Then followed an

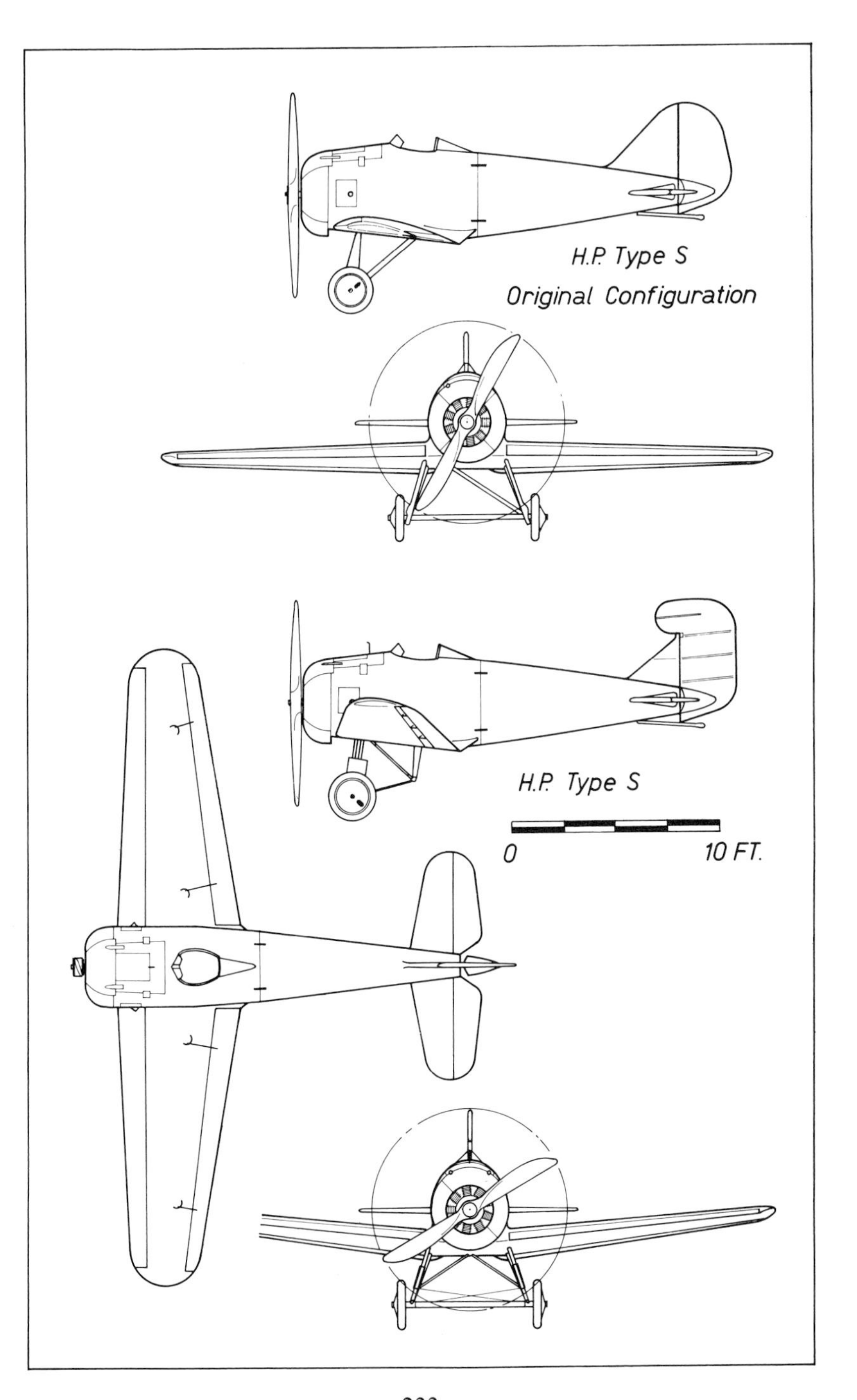
H.P. Type S
Original Configuration
H.P. Type S
0
10 FT.

S-2 at Cricklewood showing dihedral wing, with forward half of S-1 in background. (*S. T. A. Richards*)

extraordinary series of modifications, illustrating how little was understood about directional stability at that date. First the top of the rudder was cut down to reduce the balance area and then three vertical fins were added, one above the fuselage in front of the pilot and one on each side of the fuselage below the wing. After a 20-minute flight on the afternoon of 17 September, Raynham reported a slight improvement in rudder control, but was still unable to yaw the machine through more than 30 degrees with the rudder alone; moreover, in attempted flat turns to starboard, the top fin set up severe engine vibration. The engine rear mounting was stiffened and the tail fin area was still further reduced by cutting it down to a small triangle. For the seventh flight, at noon on 1 October, the top front fin was removed but the other two were retained, and Raynham then found directional control slightly improved; half an hour later, after the remaining three-ply tail fin covering had been stripped off, he flew again but could detect no difference, so the trials were suspended while more wind-tunnel tests were made. On 16 October S-1 was brought out again, this time with the top

S-2 at Cricklewood showing slots open, ailerons drooped and large balanced rudder.

front fin *in situ* but the two underwing fins deleted, and an entirely new triangular tail fin and rudder of high aspect ratio standing 6 ft above the fuselage; even with full rudder applied, Raynham was unable to yaw through more than 20 degrees, while the front fin again caused engine vibration, which disappeared when this fin was removed for the tenth flight, and on the afternoon of the same day Raynham reluctantly agreed to fly the monoplane with two large fins attached above the wing at half-span on each side. These fins were bolted to the spars and braced to the fuselage by tubular struts, their leading edges being in line with the engine back-plate. Raynham found the rudder response slightly improved and then agreed to try Handley Page's suggestion of a 300-lb ballast weight lashed to the axle to lower the c.g. and the wing fins removed. Taking off at 3.35 p.m. for the twelfth flight, Raynham found the rate of climb good and made several flat turns, but landed very fast and ran a long way after touch-down. Finally, for the thirteenth flight (the fifth that day) the ballast was removed and the gap at the tailplane root was sealed with doped fabric, but the gap was not the source of the trouble and trials were again suspended for a complete

S-2 at Martlesham Heath in March 1924 after Raynham's miraculous escape, with S-1's rudder replacing the original and ballast weights attached to undercarriage.

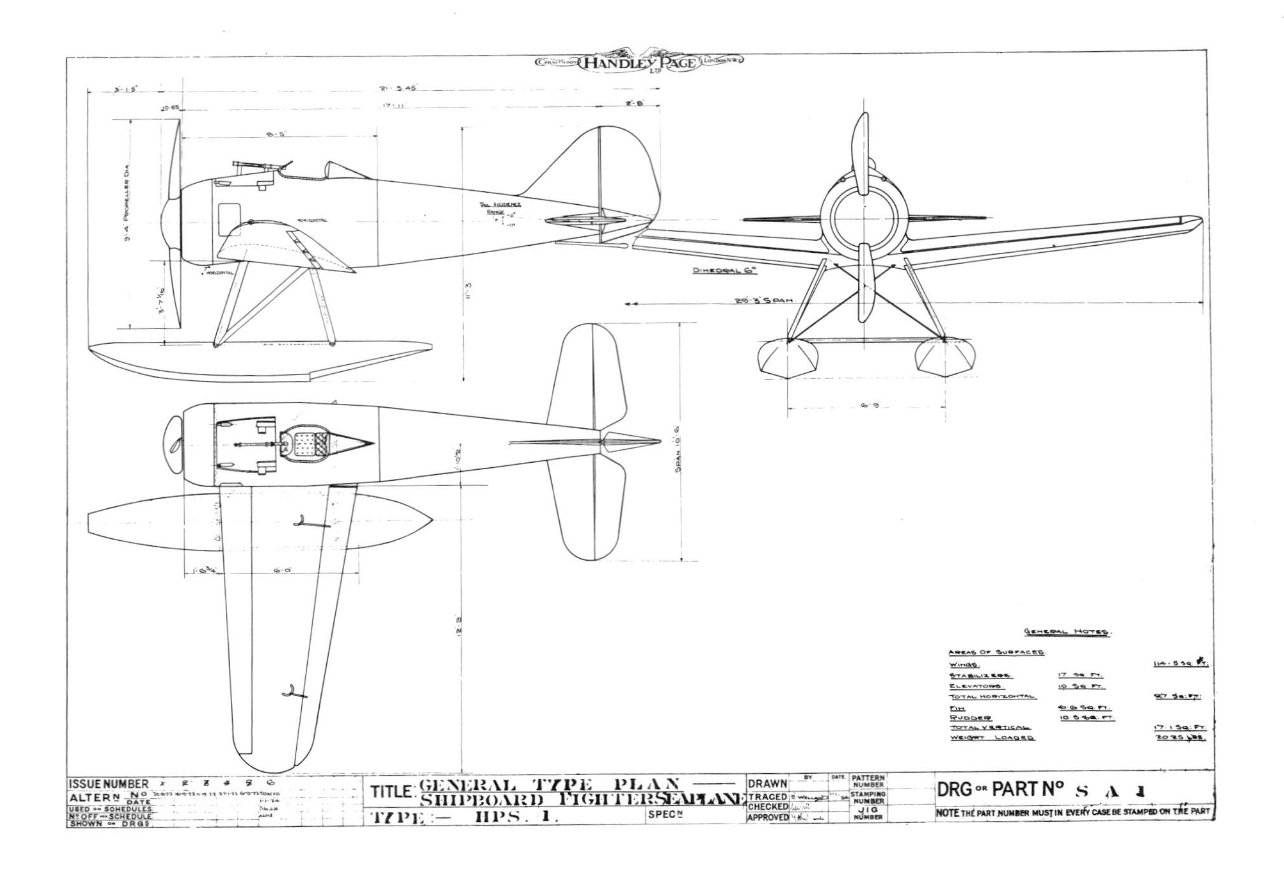
HANDLEY PAGE LTD
CRICKLEWOOD LONDON N.W.
3'-1·5"
21'-5·45
10·65
17'-11
2'-8"
8'-5"
9'-4" PROPELLER DIA.
3'-7 1/16
TAIL INCIDENCE RANGE
HORIZONTAL
11'-3
DIHEDRAL 6°
28'-3" SPAN
6'-9
SPAN 10'-6"
1'-10 1/2
1'-6 3/4
6'-0
12'-3
GENERAL NOTES.
AREAS OF SURFACES
WINGS 114·5 SQ. FT.
STABILIZERS 17 SQ. FT.
ELEVATORS 10 SQ. FT.
TOTAL HORIZONTAL 27 SQ. FT.
FIN 6·6 SQ. FT.
RUDDER 10·5 SQ. FT.
TOTAL VERTICAL 17·1 SQ. FT.
WEIGHT LOADED 2025 LBS.
ISSUE NUMBER
ALTERN NO. DATE
USED ON SCHEDULES
NO OFF PER SCHEDULE
SHOWN ON DRGS
TITLE: GENERAL TYPE PLAN — SHIPBOARD FIGHTER SEAPLANE
TYPE:— HPS. 1.
SPECN
DRAWN
TRACED
CHECKED
APPROVED
BY
DATE
PATTERN NUMBER
STAMPING NUMBER
JIG NUMBER
DRG OR PART NO S A 1
NOTE THE PART NUMBER MUST IN EVERY CASE BE STAMPED ON THE PART

Floats for S-3 under construction at Cricklewood in 1923.

new investigation of directional stability; Raynham expressed a preference for an Avro-type balanced rudder without a fin, while Mayo thought the fuselage tail-cone built into the rudder might be the culprit.

Construction of the other two monoplanes was confined to the fuselages, while an urgent request was sent to Lachmann at Göttingen to investigate the directional stability of the S-1 model he already had in his wind-tunnel. His reply in December recommended what should have been an obvious remedy—a substantial dihedral angle for the wing. Since the front fuselage and wing were built as an integral structure, the existing S-1 could not be modified without an unacceptable weight penalty and it is possible that Handley Page had shied away from this obvious solution to avoid cost and delay, but since it now appeared to be the only one, 6 deg dihedral was introduced and incidence was increased to 7 deg on 2 January, 1924, and the second and third monoplanes were built to this revised design. S-2 was completed in February 1924 and taken by road to Martlesham, where Raynham found it completely satisfactory with a small tail fin and horn-balanced rudder; he clocked up an excellent full-throttle performance over the measured speed course at over 146 mph but during the second flight to improve on this he suddenly found himself flying at 2,000 ft without any elevator control. He managed to keep on a steady course while he felt around for the cause of the defect, which he soon identified as a disconnection of the bottom of the control column from the elevator push-rod. He was just able to grasp the loose end of the push-rod below the seat and thus brought the machine in for a good final approach, controlling the engine by the magneto switch with his free hand, but was unable to see out of the cockpit at touch-down; this caused him to bounce several times and finally the airscrew touched the turf and the machine turned over on to its back; it was a magnificent effort and Raynham well deserved his miraculous escape from injury. S-2 was returned to Cricklewood and repaired, using S-1's rudder, but when it went back to Martlesham to resume full-load trials for the US Navy there had not been enough time to install all the specified military load. To make up the missing 300 lb, ballast weights were clamped to the chassis radius rods, but their inertia load at touch-down caused the undercarriage to collapse and S-2 was wrecked beyond repair. The US Navy then cancelled the contract which was several weeks behind schedule and S-3, intended for test as a seaplane, was never completed, although its Linton-Hope floats had been successfully tank-tested and were nearly ready to be rigged.

Performance estimates and strength calculations had been prepared for more powerful engine installations, including the Armstrong Siddeley Jaguar and 300 hp Hispano-Suiza; a Napier Lion version was tendered to specification D of R6 for a single-seat fleet fighter for shipboard use, in both amphibian and deck-landing forms, but this competition was won by the Fairey Flycatcher, with the Parnall Plover as runner-up, both having air-cooled radial engines. An ambitious study was also made of a seaplane version with an up-rated Lion installed with two Lamblin radiators under the fuselage, as a possible competitor in the 1923 Schneider Trophy race; its estimated top speed in this form was 170 mph and the fuel tank and pilot would have been moved 12 inches aft. The Hispano-engined landplane was estimated to reach 166 mph at sea level, 156 mph at 10,000 ft and have an initial rate of climb at sea level of 1,950 ft/min—a remarkable performance in 1923 for a fighter capable also of landing on a deck at only 45 knots. Four years later the basic design was reconsidered for possible tendering to the Bolivian government to meet their Class 5A Scout specification, for which a Gnome-Rhône Jupiter IV engine was required. With its wing area increased to 155 sq ft and gross weight to 2,754 lb, this proposed variant would have attained 150 mph at 13,400 ft and 128 mph at its service ceiling of 25,000 ft, while still being able to land at 55 mph with slots open and ailerons drooped to 20 degrees; this competition was won by the Vickers 143 biplane, which was equally fast but could not match the Handley Page monoplane's estimated ceiling and rate of climb.

H.P.21

(B.R.2)

Span 29 ft 3 in (8·93 m); length (landplane) 21 ft 5½ in (6·55 m), (seaplane) 24 ft 7 in (7·49 m); wing area 114·5 sq ft (10·62 m²). Empty weight 1,320 lb (599 kg); maximum weight 2,030 lb (922 kg). Maximum speed 146·5 mph (235 km/h); minimum speed 44 mph (71 km/h); ceiling 21,000 ft (6,500 m). Pilot alone.

Sayers motor-glider (No.23) attempting a take-off at Cricklewood with bungee assistance.

Handley Page - Sayers Motor Gliders (H.P.22 and 23)

In his reports to Handley Page, Gustav Lachmann had described the revival in post-war Germany of gliding and low-power flying resulting from limitations imposed by the Versailles Peace Treaty in July 1919. For ten years after this date the total power of any aeroplane built in an ex-enemy country was to be restricted to 200 hp, although this rule was later relaxed to permit engines of up to 200 hp *each* in multi-engined commercial aeroplanes, before being cancelled finally in 1929. One result of the ban had been to encourage the sport of motorless soaring flight in several suitable localities that existed in Germany, such as the extensive sand dunes at Rossiten on the Baltic coast and the windward slopes of the Rhön mountains above Gersfeld, at the Wasserkuppe. The sport attracted enthusiastic young flyers from all the universities and technical institutes, where they formed their own gliding clubs, from which the most skilled exponents pooled their experience in a syndicate for experimental motorless flying—the Rhön-Rossiten Gesellschaft, presided over by Dr Wolfgang Klemperer and Dr Willy Georgii of Aachen. In September 1921 Handley Page attended one of the competitions at the Wasserkuppe at Lachmann's invitation and reported on it in *The Aeroplane*, thereby starting a wave of enthusiasm for gliding in Britain. Although the Air Ministry declined to act on Handley Page's suggestion that the Aachen, München and Hannover gliders should be bought for demonstration by Klemperer, the *Daily Mail* was quick to encourage the new movement and promoted a competition in 1922 at Itford Hill in Sussex, which attracted many of the star pilots of the RRG, including Martens and Hentzen on their successful Hannover Vampyr sailplane. One of the British entries was a monoplane similar to the Vampyr, designed jointly by W. H. Sayers (technical editor of *The Aeroplane*), Frank Courtney (a veteran freelance test-pilot) and Sqn Ldr Maurice Wright (a senior test-pilot at Martlesham Heath). This glider, known as the S-C-W, was constructed by the Central Aircraft Co at Kilburn and appeared at the Itford meeting in October 1922, but was wrecked when its tent-hangar was blown down before it had made any competition flights under official observation.

Following the Itford meeting, the Air Ministry invited tenders for a two-seat sailplane to specification 47/22, in the hope of acquiring an economic means of promoting 'airmindedness' without needing Treasury support, and Handley Page was awarded contract No.446453/23 for one prototype, J7233; later the conditions were found to be impossible to achieve and Handley Page and others expressed a strong preference for using small motor-cycle engines installed in ultra-light single-seat aeroplanes. The Air Ministry at first declined to encourage this trend, but later agreed to purchase for trial at Martlesham the most successful competitors for a £500 prize offered by the Duke of Sutherland for the greatest distance flown on one gallon of petrol in a meeting to be held at Lympne in October 1923. The *Daily Mail*, not to be outdone, offered a further £1,000 for an exactly similar performance round a 12½-mile triangular course, and additional prizes of £500 and £150 respectively were to be awarded for the fastest time over 30 miles and the greatest number of laps; in all these classes the Royal Aero Club stipulated a minimum qualifying distance of 400 miles in order to eliminate freak competitors. A total of 28 entries was received, including three monoplanes built by Handley Page at Cricklewood to the design of W. H. Sayers, who was concurrently developing floats for the seaplane version of the Type S scout monoplane. Of basically similar design to the S-C-W glider, Nos.23 and 25 had a span of 36 ft 6 in and wing-loading of 2·75 lb/sq ft, while No.26, competing in the high-speed class, was loaded to 8 lb/sq ft on a wing of only 20 ft span equipped with full-span leading-edge slots and variable-camber trailing-edge flaps; all three had fixed slots in their ailerons to ensure effective lateral control at very low speed. Earlier in 1923 the Air Ministry had ordered a prototype single-seater—the English Electric Wren—which Maurice Wright had flown more than 80 miles on one gallon, and Handley Page was confident that his 36 ft version would do even better.

Initial tests of the first machine, No.23, were disappointing; when it failed to leave the ground with its 397-cc ABC flat-twin air-cooled engine, a 500-cc Douglas was substituted, but with no better success. The engine was mounted on a pylon in a miniature nacelle in front of the pilot, who received the full benefit of an oil-laden slipstream into his open cockpit under the leading edge of the wing, which was mounted flat on the top longerons of the fuselage. When No.23 refused to take off, even with assistance from four men hauling on a rubber-cord launching catapult, Handley Page called Sayers and Harold Boultbee together, and Boultbee devised a drastic but effective remedy for No.25. He lowered the wing to a 'shoulder' position below the top longerons and increased its incidence to 7 degrees; at the same time he faired the 397-cc ABC engine into the fuselage nose and covered the cockpit opening with a hinged lid with only two small 'peepholes' for the pilot to see through; he also moved the two internally-mounted landing wheels forward, for their original position under the front spar had probably done as much to prevent take-off as the low wing incidence and the chronic unreliability of the engine. The enclosure of the

No.25 with Harold Boultbee's modifications to increase lift and reduce drag.

Handling test at Lympne in October 1923.

No.26 at Cricklewood in September 1923, showing small slotted wing.

cockpit on No.25 was only feasible because the pilot chosen to fly it was Gordon Olley, who was much smaller and lighter than Wilcockson. At first, Handley Page was unwilling to offer him any bonus in addition to his basic pay as a Handley Page Transport pilot, but Olley stuck out for one and finally Handley Page agreed to give him one-third of any prize-money he could win at Lympne, but nothing extra if he failed. The 'high speed' machine, No.26, was generally similar in layout to No. 23, but had a pylon-mounted 750-cc vee-twin Blackburne engine, larger wheels mounted externally on a wider axle and a larger horn-balanced rudder. No.25, in spite of having the smallest engine, was the only one of the three to fly, mainly because of its more efficient aerodynamic shape and Olley's light weight; competitors were allowed catapult assistance with bungee cord for take-off and on the first trial at Cricklewood Olley found himself heading straight for the London, Midland and Scottish Railway's marshalling yard at Brent, behind an erratic engine which was liable to stop at any moment; he said afterwards that he could only hope to find a flat wagon to land on when his engine failed.

Gordon Olley flying No.25 at Lympne on 11 October, 1923.

At Lympne on 11 October he managed to complete nearly 40 miles (three laps) of the course at full throttle, but then had to retire with loss of power due to a loose valve-rocker bracket. Two days later, on the final day of the competition, he tried again, but was blown on to the ground by a down-gust just after take-off, smashing one side of the wing, so he got no bonus in the end. No.23 had been scratched from the competition and No.26 could not be got ready in time, although it was later bought by the Air Ministry as J7265 under contract No.488791/24 for tests on its slot gear; it was sent to Martlesham early in 1924, but remained unassembled for several months, during which it became rain-soaked and warped, being finally condemned as unsafe and burned. Neither of these designs was allotted a letter symbol in the current drawing office list, but later they were listed as H.P.22 with the large wings and H.P.23 with the small wing. Handley Page did not regard them as serious projects and, in the financial stringency of 1924, decided against building a two-seater for the Air Ministry's light aeroplane competition at Lympne later that year, although Boultbee had detailed the G.A. of a shoulder-wing design for it.

Two years later, when the de Havilland Moth had been adopted as the standard trainer for several Air Ministry-approved flying clubs, a Handley

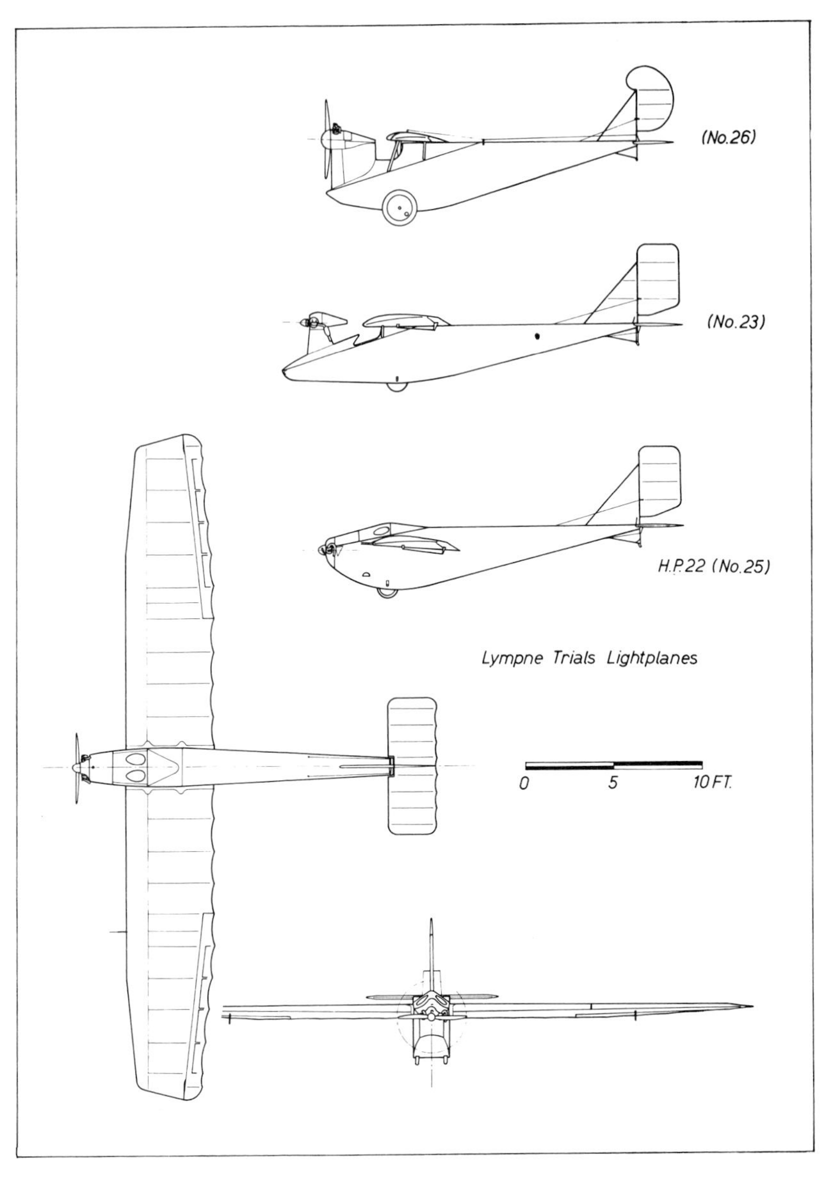

Page apprentice, A. P. Hunt, then assisting G. C. D. Russell in the wind-tunnel, became one of the first ten pupils to be taught to fly on the Moth at Stag Lane and remarked to Boultbee how cold the open cockpits were in winter. Boultbee then invited Hunt to collaborate in the design of a light cabin monoplane he was scheming and for the next two years they worked at home in the evenings to produce the complete drawings of this project. In 1928 Boultbee and Hunt both resigned from Handley Page Ltd to build a prototype at Burton-upon-Trent, forming the Civilian Aircraft Company Ltd and calling their design the Civilian Coupé. It was completed and flown in thirteen weeks and appeared at many flying events. Five more Coupés were manufactured at Hedon, Yorkshire, of which the third, G-ABNT, remained in existence till 1972.

H.P.22

(397 cc ABC)

Span 36 ft 6 in (11·13 m); length 21 ft (6·4 m); wing area 161 sq ft (14·9 m^2). Empty weight 250 lb (113 kg); maximum weight 430 lb (195 kg).

H.P.23

(750 cc Blackburne)

Span 20 ft (6·1 m); length 17 ft (5·18 m); wing area 62 sq ft (5·76 m^2). Empty weight 320 lb (145 kg); maximum weight 500 lb (227 kg).

C/7 Handcross and D/4 Transport (H.P.28 and 29)

In 1919 Winston Churchill, holding dual office as Secretary of State for both War and Air and faced with the monumental task of reconstructing the peace-time Army and Royal Air Force, at minimum cost yet remaining capable of enforcing the terms of the Versailles Treaty, had said: 'Civil aviation must fly by itself!' This was not so arrogant a rejection as it sounded and its implementation by wise and sympathetic Directors of Research at the Air Ministry, such as Sir Robert Brooke-Popham, allowed reasonable scope for the design of transport aeroplanes to benefit from technical advances in military aviation. In particular, the aircraft industry was assured that new types of aero-engines would be available for airline purposes after stringent testing to ensure their suitability for military use, and the same principle applied to the provision of first-grade materials, reliable instruments and constantly improving wireless equipment, crude though this last was to begin with. So there was a close affinity between military and civil projects during the whole decade after Versailles, and Handley Page Ltd was one of several firms which explored the civil application of each forward step in the state of the art arising from military requirements.

In April 1920 the Air Ministry invited tenders from the aircraft industry for both twin- and single-engined long-range bombers, defined very broadly by specifications D of R4A and D of R4B respectively; the designs chosen for prototype testing and eventual squadron service were the Vickers Virginia and the Avro Aldershot, the former having two Napier Lion engines and the latter a single Rolls-Royce Condor. The prototypes flew in 1922, by which time the peace-time role of the RAF had been firmly established by Sir Hugh Trenchard in defiance of the worst cuts inflicted by the 'Geddes Axe', and a forward policy of scientific research and technical development had been agreed, with a very small but realistic budget assured as a vote within the annual Air Estimates. This allowed a second round of tenders to be invited for a wider variety of roles, including specifications 31/22 and 41/22, already mentioned as the origins of the Hyderabad and the Hampstead. There were also 40/22 for a single-engined European transport and a revision of D of R4B for an improved single-engined day bomber to follow the Aldershot. The original D of R4B requirements had been widely defined and both A. V. Roe and de Havilland, whose tenders were accepted, had taken a full bomb-load of 2,000 lb and the Condor engine as the basis for very large biplanes carrying a crew of three or four, but extended service trials of the Aldershot with No.99 Squadron had shown up many objections to using single-engined machines for long-range night bombing; the role was then split between twin-engined night bombers and smaller single-engined day bombers.

Having successfully tendered the W.8d (Hyderabad) to specification 31/22, Handley Page turned his attention to the design in parallel of a pair of single-engined weight-lifters, the revised D of R4B day bomber and the European Transport, 40/22, in the hope of evolving airframes sufficiently alike to share major components other than the fuselage. The existing single-engined commercial biplanes used by Aircraft Transport & Travel Ltd were naturally of de Havilland origin; specifications 17/21 and 18/21 for a Lion-engined nine-seater and an Eagle-engined eight-seater had been drafted round the D.H.29 monoplane and D.H.32 biplane proposals, and

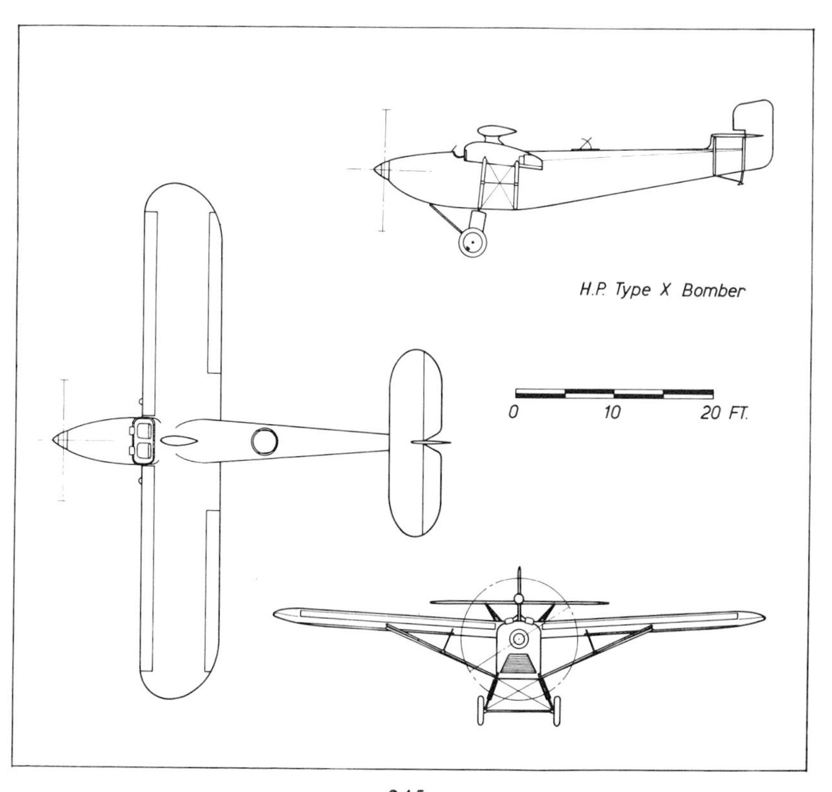

H.P. Type X Bomber

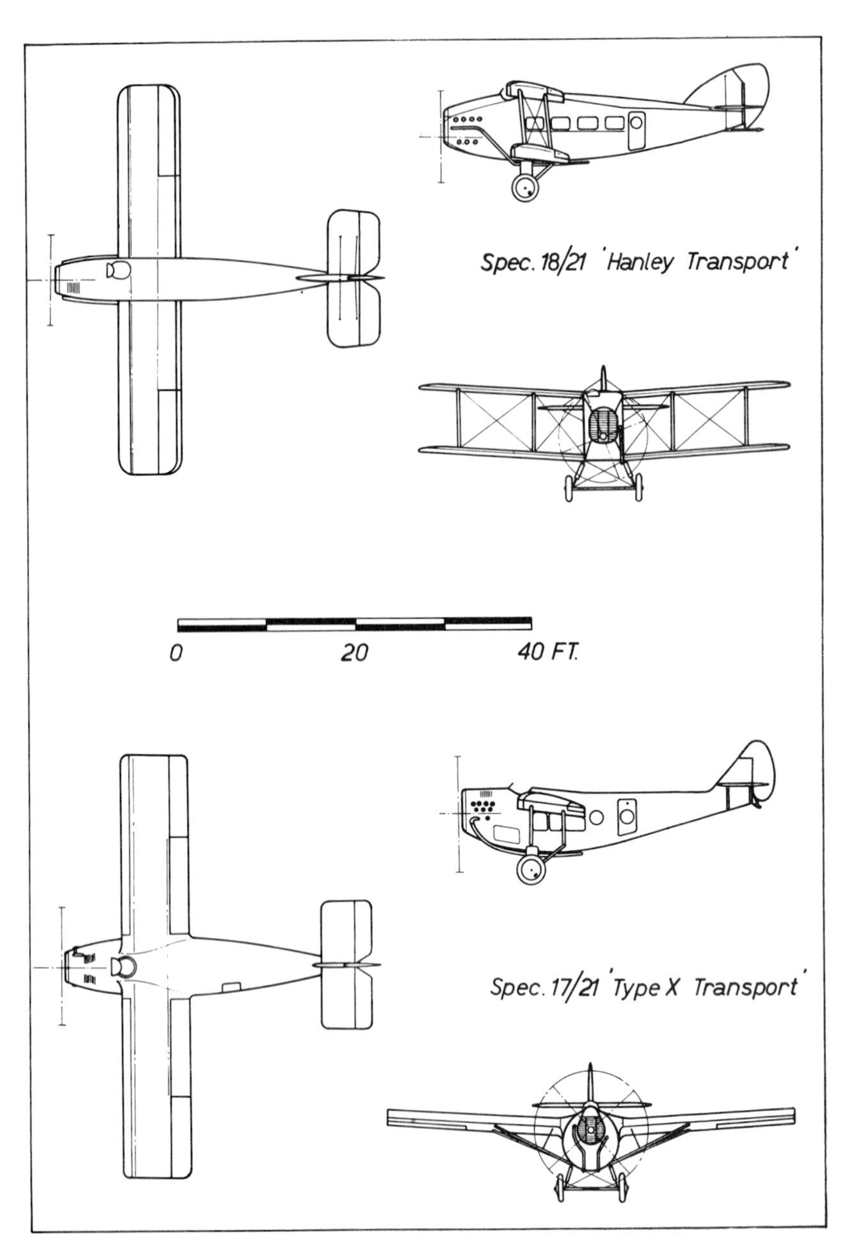

other firms had been invited to tender. Vickers Ltd designed the Vulcan, which was ordered by the Instone Air Line, and in December 1921 similar projects were investigated by Handley Page, though no formal tender was submitted; the eight-seater was to be a flat-sided cabin biplane using standard Hanley III wings, but the nine-seater was a much more advanced semi-cantilever monoplane incorporating the Type X layout, on which Lachmann had just reported wind-tunnel results from Göttingen; to match the expected high efficiency of the thick (Göttingen 390) wing with its leading-edge slots and trailing-edge flaps, the fuselage was to be of optimum streamline shape and circular cross-section, using the wooden monocoque construction evolved in France by Blériot-Spad and Breguet from the pre-war Deperdussin and later German prototypes surrendered to the Allied Armistice Commission. The monoplane was arranged with a high tailplane to avoid interference from wing downwash turbulence at minimum speed and this gave it a good ground angle for short take-off and slow landing as well as easy entrance for passengers from ground level. A similar wing and tail arrangement was proposed for a lightweight D of R4B monoplane bomber to carry a crew of two and internally stowed load of six 112-lb bombs on the power of a Napier Lion installed with a buried radiator below in a low-drag cowling, faired by a large pointed spinner on the airscrew. The original general arrangement drawing No.XA-1 issue 1 dated 28 March, 1922, showed square-tipped wings of 48 ft span, with bracing tubes from semi-span to the bottom longerons and a raised rectangular tailplane and horn-balanced rudder; three months later, issue 3 of the same drawing showed elliptical wing and tailplane tips, with the span increased to 50 ft, but the wing area unchanged at 382 sq ft. The design obviously owed something to the D.H.29, having a nearly identical undercarriage, and a technical minute dated 29 April, 1922, records that wing-root interference reported on the D.H.29 was being taken into account in the development of the X Bomber; this programme was controlled by Basil W. Townshend under the overall supervision of S. T. A. Richards, Volkert being still in Japan. Neither of the transports could be finished in time to meet the specified prototype delivery date of 31 May, 1922, the monoplane being abandoned in February 1922 and only the biplane proceeding. In June the Vickers Vulcan was reported to have flown at 105 mph, faster than the 'Hanley Transport' biplane's best predictions, so this also was stopped in order to concentrate on the bomber. By the end of October a total of 117 wind-tunnel tests had been run on the X project, comprising 58 wings, six fuselages, five fuselages plus undercarriage, one fuselage plus tail unit and 47 complete aircraft models. On 26 March, 1923, Townshend was asked to estimate D of R4B performances for two biplanes and the X monoplane, the biplane alternatives being (a) conventional two-bay, RAF 15 section, 48 ft span, aspect ratio 7·7, 575 sq ft at 12 lb/sq ft, and (b) a cantilever single-bay of Airscrew 4 (thick) section, 52 ft span, aspect ratio 12, giving a chord of only 4 ft 4 in and a total area of 433 sq ft, loaded (as for the monoplane) at 16 lb/sq ft; in each case the all-up weight was to be 6,900 lb. The monoplane came out with the best top speed of 122 mph compared with both biplanes at 118 mph but the Air Ministry still had doubts about the acceptability of monoplanes for squadron service and investigation continued on a biplane of intermediate aspect ratio. In August 1923 a definitive revision of D of R4B was issued as specification 26/23, calling for a Rolls-Royce Condor III instead of a Napier Lion, together with alternative loads of a single 550-lb bomb or two 250-lb bombs, plus a crew of two with fuel and oil for 500 miles. In October Volkert returned from Japan, having survived the Tokyo earthquake which ended Sempill's mission, but he did not immediately rejoin Handley

Page, and it was under S. T. A. Richard's supervision that a tender for the Condor-engined bomber was submitted as Type C/7; after Volkert's return to Cricklewood a few weeks later, three prototypes, officially named Handcross, were ordered under contract No.445076/23, serials J7498–J7500 being allotted in July 1924.

On 25 October, 1923, specification 40/22 for the single-engined European airliner was revised to call for a Jupiter or Condor engine and a minimum of ten passengers. To this Handley Page replied in November with a new design (GT450) having a Jupiter IV and equal-span two-bay wings of RAF 6A section, 50 ft 6 in span and 6 ft 9 in chord, totalling 615 sq ft in area; they had full-span leading-edge slots and trailing-edge slotted flaps for maximum safety in landing. At an all-up weight of 6,750 lb the wing loading was 11 lb/sq ft and power loading 17·8 lb/hp, promising maximum speeds of 111·5 mph at sea level and 109 mph at 3,000 ft, a sea-level rate of climb of 560 ft/min., service ceiling of 10,300 ft and landing speeds with slots open and flaps down of 39·5 mph with engine on and 45 mph with engine off; without slots and flaps in operation, the engine-off stalling speed was 59 mph. The crew of two occupied an open cockpit ahead of the upper wing and eight passengers, each with 55 lb of baggage, were accommodated in the cabin. Volkert showed this design, D/4, to W. P. Savage of Handley Page Transport Ltd, on 1 December, but Savage raised many criticisms, not only disliking the proposed pressurised fuel system, but also needing a bigger tankage to avoid having to refuel en route against normal winter headwinds; he also insisted on an economical cruising speed of at least 100 mph as well as complete night-flying equipment and continued to call for a ten-passenger payload. That some attempt was made to improve the D/4 is shown by an uncompleted pencil G.A. drawing by C. D. Holland dated 7 April, 1924, intended apparently for submission to the newly-formed Imperial Airways Board. This showed the D/4 with RAF 15 wings of 52 ft span and 7 ft 3 in chord; the fuselage occupied the full gap and was well-faired, with both the decking and under-belly curved in side elevation and the sides slightly convex in cross-section. The passenger cabin was furnished with a double aft-facing bench seat across the forward bulkhead, plus eight staggered forward-facing single seats; there were W.8b-type continuous windows along each side and an entry door aft on the port side, with a toilet compartment and baggage locker adjacent; the overall length was 39 ft and design gross weight 7,100 lb, but the D/4 project lapsed when the Air Ministry decided to order the Avro 563 and D.H.54, both with Condor engines, for trials with Imperial Airways as twelve-seaters. The C/7 and D/4 designs were listed retrospectively as H.P.28 and H.P.29 in Volkert's revised type numbering system.

Detail design of the Handcross under Richards was straightforward once the reduced permissible stress levels and stricter timber grading insisted upon by the RAE had been taken into account, and the layout was finalised as a three-bay biplane of 60 ft span with equal span but lower chord less than upper. The upper wings were flat and the lower had constant dihedral so that the gap tapered from 7 ft 9 in at the fuselage side to 6 ft 3 in at the wing-tip. The wings did not fold, but were detachable from the 13-ft centre section at spar joints adjacent to the inner interplane struts, the centre section upper mid-rib being joined to the top longerons by a cabane structure. The fuselage was conventional, with the pilot's cockpit high under the cabane and ample working space for the bomb-aimer, who had easy access to a prone bombing station below the pilot, and alternative defensive stations with a mid-upper Lewis gun mounted on a Scarff ring aft of the wing trailing edge and a lower Lewis gun in a shielded position aft of the prone station. the Condor drove a 15-ft diameter two-blade Leitner-Watts hollow steel airscrew, with blade angle adjustable on the ground, and was cooled by a frontal radiator with vertical shutters; petrol was carried entirely in gravity tanks similar to the Hyderabad's, with aerofoil-section extensions above the top surface of the upper wing. The 550-lb bomb was recessed into the port side of the fuselage belly fairing and the pilot had a fixed synchronised Vickers gun firing forward from the decking on the starboard side. The structure was mainly of spruce, but a metal fuselage was required in any production version that might be ordered, with metal wings and tail unit to be introduced retrospectively. The divided undercarriage, of 13 ft 6 in track, had long-stroke rubber-in-compression shock absorbers with oleo damping, as had the tailskid. The rudder and elevators were horn-balanced and the ailerons, on the upper wings only, had back-set hinges, but no slot gear was installed, although this would have been considered for production aeroplanes.

Handcross J7498 at Martlesham Heath in February 1925.

The first Handcross, J7498, was flown by Hubert Broad at Cricklewood on 6 December, 1924, and after completing manufacturer's flight trials to 19,000 ft with full load on New Year's Day was ferried to Martlesham Heath by Sqn Ldr Tom Harry England, CO of No.22 Squadron, the official trials unit. In March 1925, while being flown by Flt Lieut Capon, its engine seized up at 17,000 ft and he managed to land without damage to the aircraft, although the engine was wrecked and had to be changed; it was ready to fly again on 7 April and completed performance trials in June, when A & AEE Report M/406 was issued. By February both the others, J7499 and J7500, had been flown at Cricklewood by Hubert Broad, but without gas-starters, so J7499 was allotted to RAE Farnborough for a programme of experimental radio trials, while J7500 was retained at Cricklewood for modifications arising from the official trials of J7498. There had been complaints from Martlesham of centre-section vibration at various speeds and a more rigid diagonal strut drag bracing in the cabane was requested, but Volkert visited Martlesham with Handley Page on 18 May to investigate the trouble and found the existing structure quite

Side view of Handcross J7498 in February 1925, showing original fuel tanks.
(*I.W.M.—Crown Copyright*)

adequate; he traced the trouble to buffeting when the angle of attack exceeded 7 degrees. The raised petrol tanks were thought to cause breakaway of the airflow over the wing, so new tanks with a flush top surface and enlarged capacity under the wing were installed in J7500 before completion and retrospectively in J7498. Regulation of airflow through the radiator was another source of trouble, as the original outlet louvres in the cowling were inadequate and large round holes had to be cut in the side panels to prevent overheating during ground running and taxying, but these allowed the engine to freeze up at altitude, so blanking plates were made to close the holes selectively until the best arrangement was found by

Handcross J7500 at Cricklewood in 1925 with revised fuel tanks.

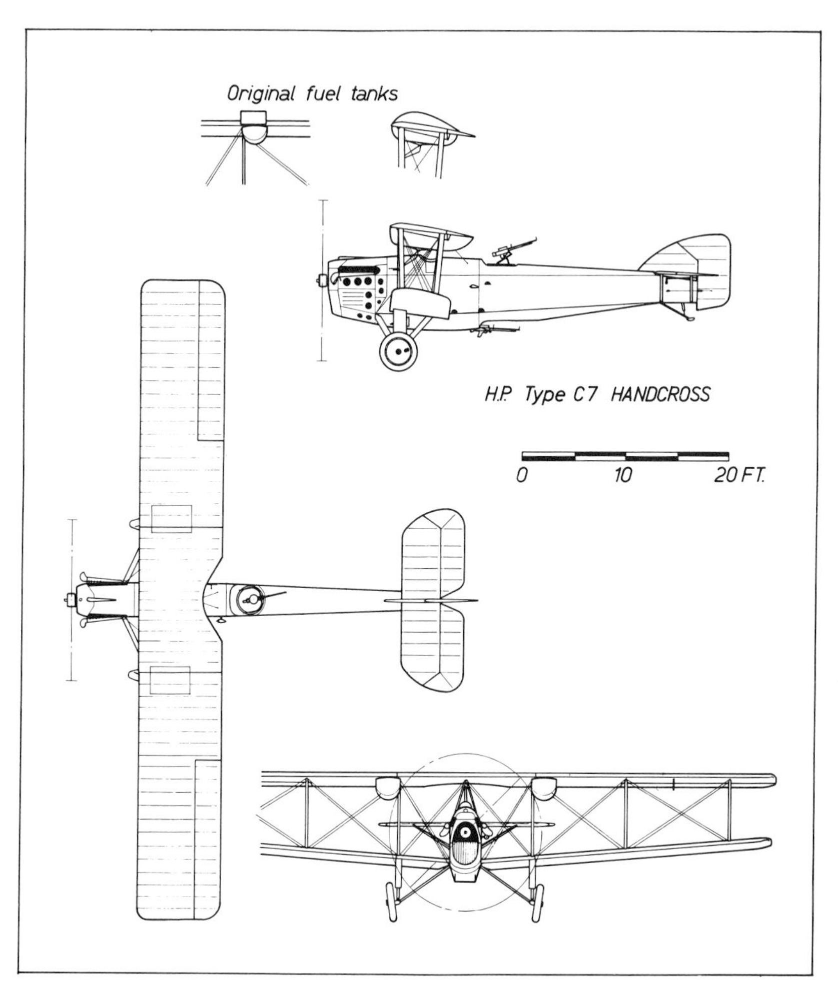

trial and error. Flames from the original backswept exhaust pipes dazzled the pilot at night and it was suspected that carbon monoxide could enter the cockpit, so the pipes were replaced by new 'ram's horn' manifolds exhausting at the forward end; also the lower gun position had to be faired over with fabric because the intense draught between the upper and lower openings rendered the gunner's station useless. The third Handcross remained at Cricklewood till 1926 as a trial installation hack, but J7499, transferred from Farnborough to Martlesham in 1925, was still in use by the Armaments Trial Flight in 1928. Like the Bristol Berkeley, another unsuccessful entrant in the 26/23 competition, the Handcross was flown with a variety of two- and four-blade wooden airscrews for comparison with the Leitner-Watts initially installed. The competition was won by the Hawker Horsley, which fulfilled not only the 26/23 role but later the coast defence torpedo-bomber specification 24/25; design work on the Handcross ceased in October 1925 and a proposed torpedo-bomber variant, to be named Hanwell, was dropped in favour of an alternative version of the Harrow for the 24/25 role, to which the name Hanwell was transferred in June 1926.

X Bomber
(Napier Lion IIB)

Span 50 ft (15·25 m); length 39 ft 8 in (12·1 m); wing area 382 sq ft (35·5 m^2). Maximum weight (est) 6,100 lb (2,760 kg). Speed (est) 122 mph (196 km/h). Bomb load 672 lb (305 kg). Crew two.

X Transport
(Napier Lion IB)

Span 46 ft 6 in (14·19 m); length 36 ft 9 in (11·15 m); wing area 360 sq ft (33·4 m^2). Maximum weight (est) 4,410 lb (2,000 kg). Crew two. Passengers nine.

H.P.28 Handcross
(Rolls-Royce Condor III)

Span 60 ft (18·3 m); length 40 ft (12·2 m); wing area 788 sq ft (73·2 m^2). Empty weight 5,215 lb (2,360 kg); maximum weight 7,500 lb (3,400 kg). Bomb load 550 lb (250 kg). Maximum speed 120 mph (193 km/h); minimum speed 53 mph (85 km/h); range 500 miles (805 km); ceiling 19,250 ft (5,950 m). Crew two.

H.P.29 Transport
(Bristol Jupiter IV)

Span 52 ft (15·86 m); length 39 ft (11·9 m); wing area 640 sq ft (59·5 m^2). Empty weight (est) 5,215 lb (2,360 kg). Maximum weight (est) 7,100 lb (3,220 kg). Cruising speed (est) 100 mph (161 km/h). Crew two. Passengers ten.

Hamlet
(H.P.32)

The abandonment of the D/4 biplane in April 1924 was followed by a renewal of interest by the Air Ministry in the earlier fully-slotted monoplane proposal and specification 23/24 was issued to define a six- or seven-passenger air-taxi or charter aircraft with three engines of a total power of 400 hp. To meet this requirement the de Havilland Co sketched out, but did not tender, their D.H.55 biplane with three 140 hp Airdisco engines, while Handley Page submitted a monoplane suitable as a landplane for inter-city charter work in Europe or, as a float seaplane, in the less developed territories of Canada and South America, where isolated small centres of population occurred along inland waterways. The type symbol D was transferred to this project, of which one prototype was ordered in July 1924 for research into short take-off and landing performance, with the proviso that it should be adaptable to use one, two or three engines. Named Hamlet and initially equipped with three 120 hp Bristol Lucifer IV three-cylinder radial engines, it was in fact furnished to an 'executive' layout with

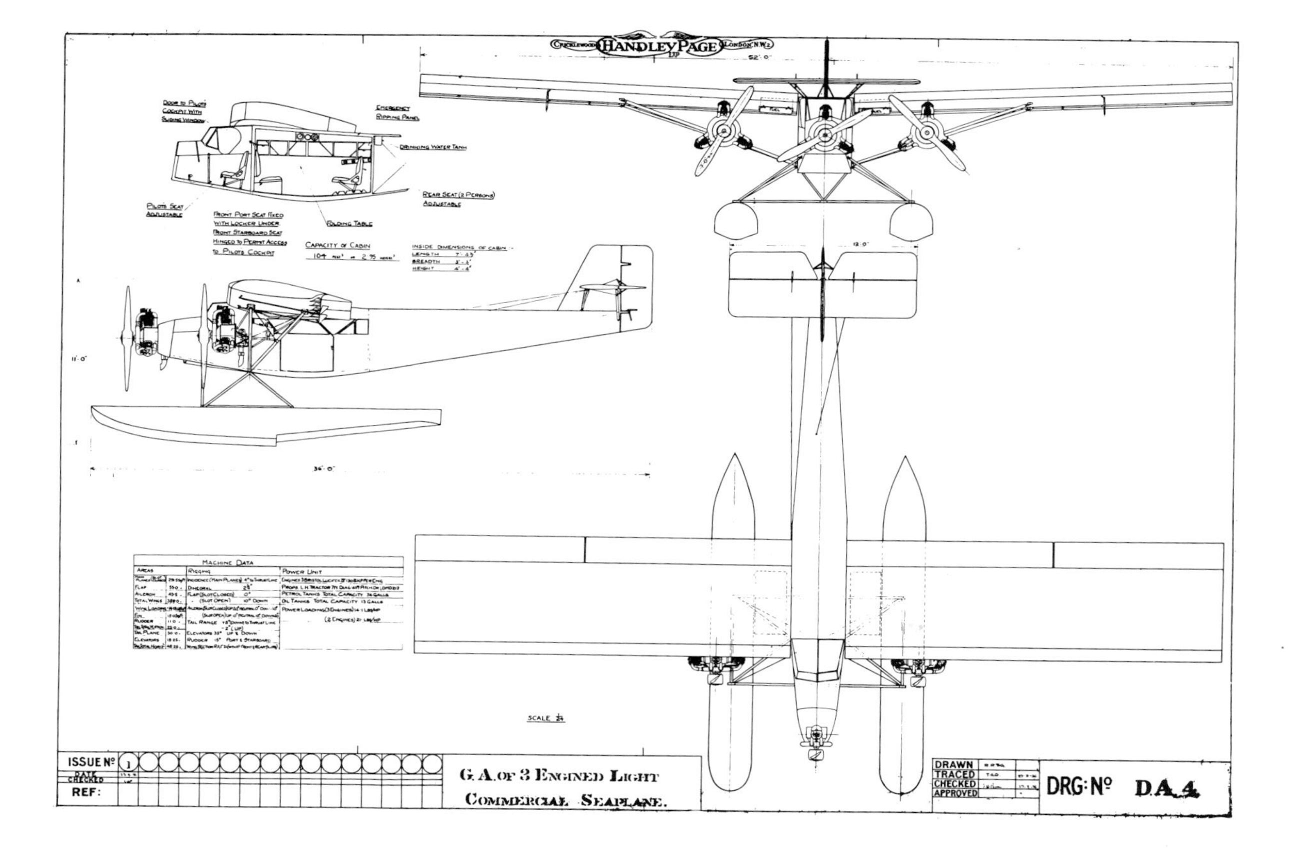
CRICKLEWOOD HANDLEY PAGE LTD LONDON, N.W.2
52'-0"
Door to Pilots Cockpit with Sliding Window
Emergency Ripping Panel
Drinking Water Tank
Rear Seat (2 Persons) Adjustable
Pilots Seat Adjustable
Front Port Seat Fixed with Locker Under
Front Starboard Seat Hinged to Permit Access to Pilots Cockpit
Folding Table
Capacity of Cabin
104 feet³ or 2.95 metre³
Inside Dimensions of Cabin -
Length 7'-4½"
Breadth 3'-1"
Height 4'-4"
12'-0"
11'-0"
36'-0"
Machine Data
Areas
Rigging
Power Unit
Flap 55·0
Aileron 43·5
Dihedral 2½°
Flap (Slot Closed) 0°
(Slot Open) 10° Down
Rudder 11·0
Tail Plane 30·0
Elevators 18·25
Elevators 35° Up & Down
Rudder 15° Port & Starboard
Petrol Tanks Total Capacity 34 Galls
Oil Tanks Total Capacity 13 Galls
(2 Engines) 21 Lbs/HP
SCALE 1/24
ISSUE Nº 1
DATE
CHECKED
REF:
G.A. OF 3 ENGINED LIGHT COMMERCIAL SEAPLANE.
DRAWN
TRACED
CHECKED
APPROVED
DRG: Nº D.A.4

four lounge seats and a folding table in addition to the crew of two; the cabin fittings included electric lights and a drinking water dispenser. The relative proportions and positions of the wing and tailplane were exactly the same as proposed by Lachmann for the earlier Type X projects on which so much wind-tunnel data had been collected, but there was still considerable doubt as to which aerofoil section would give the best results. The 'Airscrew 4' section at first favoured needed a very large leading-edge slat of T.64 section to match it, resulting in a high structure weight; for a time it seemed that only outboard control slats could be tolerated and that high lift for landing and take-off would have to rely entirely on slotted flaps inboard of the ailerons. Lachmann naturally preferred his own 1900 section or Eiffel 385, but in April 1925 the NPL tested the new RAF 31 section with a front slot and this was accepted as the best choice available. Wing structure weight was not the only problem, for the Lucifer was notoriously rough-running, in spite of Fedden's reassurances, but it weighed only 325 lb bare against 452 lb for the smoother-running Airdisco vee-eight of equal power; Frank Halford had evolved this from the war-surplus RAF 1a, of which the Aircraft Disposal Company still held large

Hamlet with three Lucifers at Cricklewood in October 1926. (*Flight*)

stocks. The semi-cantilever wings had square tips and a pronounced dihedral in the fashion set by Rohrbach in Germany; they were braced by pairs of streamline steel tubular struts from mid-span to the bottom longerons, as in the original X design, with the outboard engine mountings and oleo-leg top fixtures integrated into tubular space-frames below the wings. The wide-track undercarriage was divided and twin floats carried on triangulated struts could be substituted for wheels.

The Hamlet was one of the first British aeroplanes to have an enclosed 'flight deck' in the modern style, featuring sliding side windows and a V-shaped windscreen with an electric wiper on the port side; it also had mudguards round the landing wheels, but no brakes. With its flat-sided fuselage finished in royal blue, aluminium-doped wings and tail and the registration mark G-EBNS painted on the fuselage in white, it was first flown solo by Arthur Wilcockson on 19 October, 1926, with slots locked open. After a satisfactory initial flight he took MacRostie aboard for a second trial in which the slots and flaps were operated, but the mechanism proved too stiff for the pilot alone and MacRostie had to stand beside him

The Hon Stanley Bruce, Prime Minister of Australia, and Mrs Bruce, escorted by Air Commodore C. L. N. Newall, viewing the Hamlet at Croydon on 21 October, 1926, themselves viewed from the pilot's seat by the Master of Sempill. (*Flight*)

to turn the large handwheel controlling the gear. Two days later, after the gear had been eased, Wilcockson flew the Hamlet to Croydon for a demonstration to the assembled Dominion Premiers, who were attending a conference at Westminster. The Hamlet's furnishings attracted so much interest and favourable comment that Handley Page remarked that he ought to have charged a shilling a head for admission and covered his expenses. Unfortunately the middle Lucifer vibrated excessively, so that the pilot could not read his instruments at full throttle and on arriving back at Cricklewood after the display one of the middle engine's bearers was

Hamlet landing at Cricklewood on return from Croydon on 21 October, 1926. (*Flight*)

Hamlet in May 1927 with twin Lynxes and modified tail unit. (*Flight*)

found to have fractured. It was repaired before the next flight on 25 October, but after landing the same thing happened again and a scheduled demonstration to Sir Sefton Brancker at Hendon had to be cancelled. It was decided to replace the Lucifers with Armstrong Siddeley Mongoose radials, as with five cylinders instead of three they were much smoother-running, but it was not possible to obtain quick delivery of them.

The Hamlet was then extensively modified to accept two Lynxes in wing nacelles, with the middle engine deleted and the nose rounded off to provide additional baggage space. At the same time the fin area was reduced by cropping the upper leading edge and the rudder chord was increased. It was

Short take-off at Cricklewood by modified Hamlet.

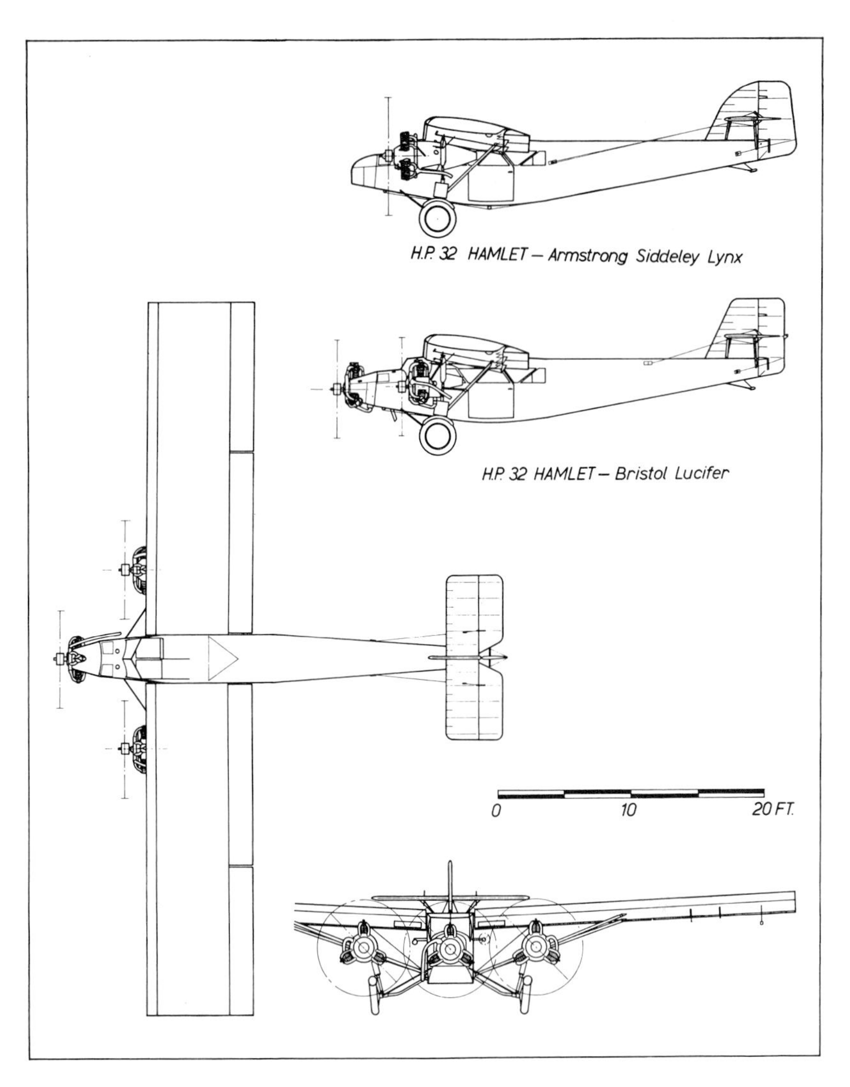

flown thus on 19 May, 1927, by Tom Harry England, who found it now devoid of vibration; the ailerons and elevators were heavy, but the rudder was lighter, though still not powerful enough to permit turning against a throttled engine. The undercarriage was smooth in action and he took off with MacRostie as passenger and with slots open, finding them easy to close in level flight without undue force being needed. On 20 May he flew the Hamlet again for the benefit of *Flight's* photographer John Yoxall, after the control gearing had been improved. On 23 May he flew it with two passengers and found handling satisfactory but considered it to be underpowered, with a poor initial rate of climb in spite of its steep take-off attitude and a strong tendency to turn to starboard. It was then decided to disconnect the control slots from the ailerons and to fit a cambered fin, with which it went for handling trials at Martlesham and appeared in the parade of new types in the RAF Display in June.

By September a set of three Mongoose engines was available, but delivery was delayed till January 1928 while contract cover was arranged. They were finally installed in March, but England had meanwhile reported very adversely on erratic slot operation and inadequate lateral control; he suspected aileron reversal due to wing torsion and refused to fly the Hamlet again until this had been investigated. Eventually, in August, the Air Ministry agreed to buy it as it stood and on 25 September it was delivered by road to the RAE: apparently it was never flown at Farnborough and was scrapped there in 1929. Lachmann's contract as consultant to Handley Page had expired in 1925, before the Hamlet was completed, and he went to Japan two years later, so he had had no say in the Hamlet's flight trials.

H.P.32 Hamlet

(Three Bristol Lucifer IV or two Armstrong Siddeley Lynx III or three Armstrong Siddeley Mongoose I)

Span 52 ft (15·86 m); length 34 ft 10 in (10·65 m); wing area 388 sq ft (35·1 m²). Empty weight 3,105 lb (1,409 kg); maximum weight 5,000 lb (2,270 kg). Speed 118 mph (190 km/h). Crew two. Passengers 4–6.

Note: Length of seaplane version: 36 ft (10·97 m)

Harrow (Type E) and Hanwell (H.P.31 and 31A)

Apart from its onerous and generally ill-equipped task of policing the mandated territory of Iraq and the turbulent frontier between India and Afghanistan, the primary role of the RAF in peacetime was the air defence of the United Kingdom and its naval bases at Gibraltar, Malta, Aden and Singapore. Only at home and later at Singapore was it thought necessary to employ land-based torpedo-bombers to repel possible invasion from the sea, the Mediterranean dockyards being in effect part of the fleet and relying on ship-based aeroplanes for air cover. This, at any rate, was the view of the Air Staff in the early years of peace, before the Fleet Air Arm regained some of the autonomy the RNAS had lost in the formation of the RAF in April 1918. The divergent claims of the RAF who flew the aircraft and the Royal Navy who deployed the carriers resulted in conflict and delay in defining the types and roles required for deck-flying and some, though not all, of the prototypes evolved were far from bird-like in appearance, with performances usually inferior to their land-based counterparts. With an unused stock of 1,650-lb and 2,300-lb SN bombs still in store after the Armistice and the example of General Mitchell's success in sinking the heavily armoured *Ostfriesland* in Chesapeake Bay, the concept of using heavy bombs rather than torpedoes to repel invading warships was economically attractive and for some weeks during the summer of 1923 a short-range shore-based single-seat 'SN Bomber' derived from the Hanley seemed a possible new requirement; but the naval preference for the underwater weapon prevailed and early in 1924 specification 21/23 was issued for a two-seat replacement for the Blackburn Dart, combining the ability to carry either an 18-in torpedo or three 520-lb bombs at short range with up to 12 hours' endurance for area reconnaissance at sea. To navigate in all weathers and return to a moving carrier required a full-time observer, but a third crew member was incompatible with the improved performance and weapon load demanded. Furthermore the span was limited to 46 ft by the size of the *Eagle's* lifts and folding wings were essential for hangarage below the flight deck. The Handley Page Hendon, though a two-seater, had much too short a range and could only be regarded as an interim type for trial and training purposes, so a new design, Type E, was derived from it. First thoughts in February 1924, as shown in drawing No. GT 282, were for alternative landplane and seaplane torpedo-bombers, powered by either a Rolls-Royce Eagle IX or a Napier Lion II; a similar day-bomber tendered, but not built, to meet a Belgian Army requirement in March 1924 would have had either a Lion or a Liberty engine; a year elapsed while details of equipment were worked out because of indecision within the Air Ministry, but eventually Type E was tendered on 21 August, 1925; the preliminary arrangement drawings by Harold Boultbee (GT 478–487) showed a clean biplane with both wings equal in span, unstaggered and with 4½ degrees dihedral on the upper wing only, the lower wing being flat, so that the gap increased from 6 ft 8 in at the parallel centre-section to 8 ft at the tips. The wings were unswept and square-tipped, with full-span slots along both upper and lower leading edges and slotted flaps extending from the ailerons to the centre-section end-ribs.

The centre-section, of slightly less than 10 ft span, had a pair of interplane struts between the end-ribs on each side, a pair of short vertical struts on the centreline and streamline tie-rod bracing throughout; this gave a very stiff box structure with minimum drag in the slipstream and least interference with the pilot's view for torpedo aiming. The single-bay outer wings were hinged to fold at the rear spars to a width of 18 ft; the wing section was Handley Page 6/15, derived from RAF 6 and RAF 15, and incidence was 7 degrees. The divided 'double tripod' landing gear had long-stroke oleo legs and inboard extensions of the stub axles carried snap-link hooks for engaging with the longitudinal arrestor cables then used on the Royal Navy's carrier decks. The incidence of the rectangular tailplane was adjustable through a wide range and the low aspect ratio fin and rudder were of the same shape as on the Handcross, the rudder and elevators having shielded horn balances. A 470 hp Napier Lion V engine was installed as low in the nose as clearance for its 11-ft two-blade airscrew would permit, so that the pilot still had a clear forward view over the sloping cowling when approaching to land at a high angle of attack. The two cockpits were close together in raised decking, the observer having a Lewis gun on a Scarff ring and adequate enclosed working space behind the pilot's seat for navigation and radio operation. The pilot had a fixed Vickers gun synchronised to fire forward through the airscrew disc and the main petrol tank of 145 gallons was suspended inside the fuselage between the pilot's cockpit and the engine firewall, with a 15-gallon gravity tank set flush within the port half of the upper centreplane. The main fuel was jettisonable to provide buoyancy for ditching, to supplement the inflatable bags in the rear fuselage. As in the Handcross, a flat frontal radiator was mounted vertically under the engine reduction gear and had controllable shutters; long exhaust tail-pipes were swept down to lie parallel to the torpedo as far aft as the wing trailing edge and the engine side cowling panels incorporated numerous louvres.

Handley Page's tender to specification 21/23 was successful and two prototypes, N205 and N206, were ordered under contract No.528239/25, for competition against two Blackburn Ripon Is, N203 and N204, and an Avro 571, G-EBNW, which the Air Ministry declined to order but agreed to test as a private venture. The design was finalised in March 1926 after approval of the mock-up and was officially named Harrow I. It was agreed that N206 should be tested as a seaplane and have metal spars and separate slot controls for the two leading edges; in fact, two sets of metal floats were ordered from Short Brothers and were to be quickly interchangeable with the wheeled chassis of both prototypes. The Harrow's slot and flap operating gear was similar to that developed on the Hendon III, the outer (control) slats being linked to the ailerons and the inner (lift) slats being linked to the flaps. The aileron linkage was adjusted so that very little slat movement occurred when the aileron moved up from its neutral position, but full opening was obtained when the aileron moved down below neutral.

N205 was weighed on 18 March, 1926, and on 24 April Hubert Broad made the first two flights of ten minutes' duration each; the water temperature rose quickly and he asked for the lower cowling to be cut away to increase the airflow through the radiator. He made a third flight on 27 April, when the flaps were lowered fully to 14 degrees, but found the mechanism very stiff and asked for an extra handle on the flap control lever at 180 degrees from the first, which gave insufficient purchase at certain angles. He also recommended increased rudder travel and a shorter tailskid to improve taxying. After a fourth flight at light load on 3 May, he handed over to Arthur Wilcockson, who flew next at full load for an hour and a quarter, climbing to 8,000 ft, but the engine again overheated and finally the oil tank burst. This was repaired and on the 14th he resumed flying with

Harrow N205 with Napier Lion VA at Cricklewood before covering.

a Hendon airscrew fitted for comparison with the original; three flights were made that day and on the 21st he completed the initial handling with a climb test lasting 100 minutes, but added two flights on the 22nd to compare landing speed with flaps up and down; it was 40 knots in each case. N205 was then cleared for deck-landing trials at a weight of 7,840 lb and on the 31st Sqn Ldr Watkins from Martlesham took off light from Gosport and landed on the deck of HMS *Furious* off the Isle of Wight. A torpedo was attached and Watkins then made six take-offs and landings in a relative wind of 30 knots, after which the torpedo was detached and he flew back light to Gosport; he reported the Harrow's deck handling and performance to be less lively than the Hendon's and N205 was returned to Cricklewood for further control adjustments. Wilcockson resumed testing on 22 June and on the 29th flew a maximum speed trial at full weight, clocking 107 kt at 1,000 ft altitude. At full speed the rudder was much too heavy, but after further flights on 3 July and 5 August it had been improved; the ailerons also became lighter after the slot mechanism had been eased, but the engine still overheated. After a height test on 23 August, N205 went to Martlesham, but was damaged in a heavy landing a few days after arrival, so had to be sent back to the works for repairs.

Second Harrow, N206, at Martlesham Heath in January 1927.

Meanwhile N206 had reached completion and Wilcockson flew it light on 30 October and then at full load for 75 minutes on 1 November; he found it better than N205 except that the slot gear was unduly stiff. On 3 November he made two flights with the top slot open and the bottom closed, with both flaps linked to the top slot. This improved lateral control, the ailerons being effective down to the stall, but the aircraft was nose heavy and fell away more quickly in the stall than with both slots open, so he considered both slots to be essential for deck flying. In December N206 went to Martlesham to replace N205 and on 10 January, 1927, Handley Page and Volkert called on Sqn Ldr Tom Harry England, CO of the handling squadron (No.22) and discussed the Harrow with him and Flt Lieuts Massey Hilton, Vaughan-Fowler and S. N. Webster, who had all flown it. During this meeting, it seems that Handley Page mentioned to England that he was looking out for a really good permanent test pilot, instead of having to rely on freelances like Broad (who had by this time joined de Havillands) or Wilcockson (who was now fully committed to

Imperial Airways and had to obtain special leave to fly for Handley Page.) After consideration, England, who was essentially ambitious and dynamic, decided that a peacetime Service career was less attractive than the one Handley Page had to offer and in April resigned from the RAF to become the company's technical adviser and chief test pilot, his immediate task being to improve the Harrow for extended competition with a later version of the Blackburn Ripon, which had emerged as the winner of the 21/23 first round in June 1927 and secured a Mark II prototype contract based on the new 530 hp Napier Lion XI. No new Harrow prototype was ordered, but the company was authorised to improve N205 by installing a Lion XI. As a first step, Volkert suggested that the rear cockpit of N206 should be covered in and on 9 and 10 May England flew it seven times in this condition, deducing that the performance could be much improved by lowering the Scarff ring and aft decking. On 13 May, with these alterations made, he found the speed increased to 106 kt, with a noticeable improvement in rudder and elevator lightness, so he asked for a similar reduction in the height of the forward decking; this was quickly contrived and on the 16th was found to have added another knot to the top speed.

By this time N205 had been rebuilt at Cricklewood with a Lion XI engine, in which the carburettors had been moved to the rear so as to allow a slimmer nose cowling and better forward entry; a half-drum Anderton-Brown radiator with semi-conical front shutters, as used on the Vickers Virginia, was located under the engine. The substantial drag reduction and higher power, taken together, were estimated to increase the Harrow's top speed to 128 mph and the service ceiling to 11,650 ft at a gross weight of 7,100 lb, using RAF 31 wing section instead of 6/15, but in fact the aerofoil section was never changed. The Harrow was inspected by Sir Hugh Trenchard during a visit to Cricklewood on 23 March and Wilcockson flew it on 4 April, but found it very tail-heavy and in trouble with a boiling radiator. The engine was then changed for a slightly more

N205 at Martlesham Heath with Napier Lion XA in May 1927. (*I.W.M.—Crown Copyright*)

Side view of N205 with Napier Lion XA.

powerful Lion XA and the c.g. was carefully checked when the machine was weighed on 18 May. England flew it at Cricklewood on 21 May, with Oswald of the performance department as observer; he reported a quick take-off and responsive handling, with none of the former vibration, but the radiator still boiled and on the ground the slots needed more than the strength of one man to pull them halfway open, beyond which they moved easily. For the second and third flights on 23 May longer exhaust pipes were fitted and the radiator shutters were removed, which cured the boiling, so England made a further flight at full load, using only the upper wing slot. He found N205 delightful to handle in this condition and after making partial climbs to 3,500 ft and slow speed tests at full load on 24, 30 and 31 May he recommended removal of the lower slot for official trials at Martlesham, but considered a larger radiator essential. On 2 June Wilcockson confirmed England's findings in two flights using both slots and one with only the top slot. Next day England made two attempts to climb to service ceiling, but each time the radiator boiled although the shutters had been removed; in the cooler evening air he reached 10,000 ft, but the engine then got too cold during the descent. Two weeks previously N206 had been flown back to Cricklewood for the fuselage decking to be permanently modified to give a 10 per cent reduction in cross-sectional area and on 4 June England flew it at 108 kt at 1,500 ft, but five days later he tested it with dummy side radiators of the Blackburn Ripon II type and found that these cost 4 knots off the top speed. Service trials of N206 were then completed at Martlesham (A & AEE Report M/470) and it was returned to Cricklewood because its cooling system was judged to be inadequate for seaplane trials at Felixstowe; these had been cleared by the Ripon I N204 earlier in the year and the Air Ministry now wished N206 to be employed on slot research to extend the work done on the Hendon III

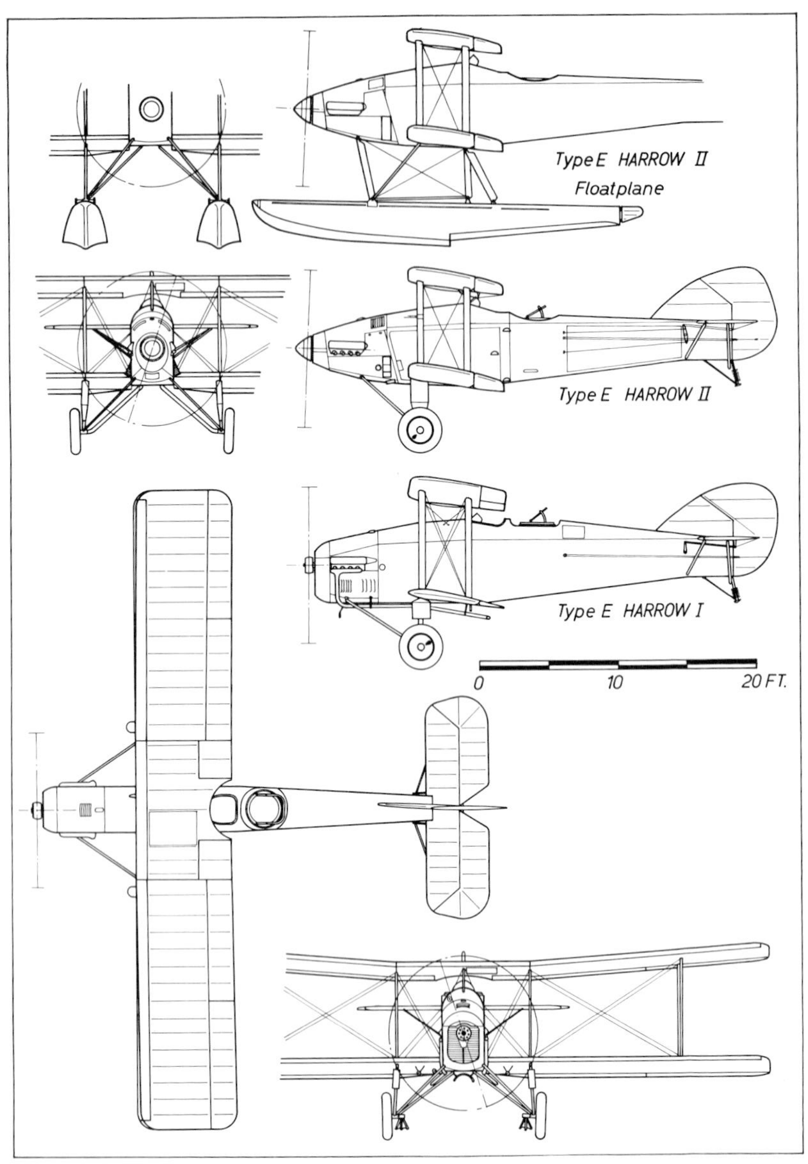

N9727 during the year before. So while N205, with a Lion XA and a larger rectangular radiator, went to Martlesham, N206 was retained at Cricklewood during August and September for trials with Syd Ebel's latest automatic wing-tip slots, with R. S. Stafford flying as observer to record slot openings at various angles of attack. N206 was flown to Martlesham on 24 September for a demonstration of the auto-slots to H. L. Stevens, who was most enthusiastic and considered that at last means had been

N205 in interceptor-controlled stalled flight with slots open and flaps lowered in October 1927. (*Flight*)

N205 as Harrow II flying fast and low at Cricklewood.

N205 as a seaplane at Felixstowe in July 1928. (*I.W.M.—Crown Copyright*)

found to make it impossible for a pilot to spin inadvertently. On the 30th England flew N206 back to Cricklewood for a final test to decide whether or not the lower ailerons and flaps should be made inoperable, as a result of which it was agreed that N205's lower flaps should be fixed but that all four ailerons were necessary for lateral control below 55 knots.

After this date N206 was declared surplus to Air Ministry requirements and dismantled for storage at Cricklewood, but N205 was modified to a new Mark II standard, with equal dihedral on both wings, a much slimmer nose shape and retractable side radiators of the same type as the Ripon II's. England first flew it thus on 5 October, 1927, and found its handling excellent, with a much improved view over the nose and obviously less drag, since speed was slow to fall off when the throttle was closed. During this period it was temporarily fitted with interceptors, but the installation was not entirely successful and subsequent development and demonstration of this device was transferred to the slotted Cirrus Moth G-EBXG. The Harrow II was demonstrated at Martlesham on 9 October to the Chief of the Air Staff, Sir Hugh Trenchard, before the second round of the 21/23 competition against the Ripon II and Avro Buffalo II. After further alterations to the auto-slots to delay early opening, N205 underwent a series of full-load trials with a torpedo, some with a Fairey-Reed metal airscrew in place of the standard wooden one. In March 1928 the Martlesham trials were completed and N205 went to Felixstowe, where the float chassis was fitted for trials as a seaplane and demonstration to the Finnish and Argentine Air Attachés, but in June it was in trouble with tail damage from spray and on 23 August, 1928, N205 was written off charge after being declared unfit for RAF service as a seaplane. There was a proposal to reassemble N206 for permanent exhibition in the Science Museum at South Kensington as an example of slot and flap gear development, but in the end one of the upper wings with auto-slot installed was presented personally by Handley Page to Highgate School and the rest of the airframe was scrapped.

Concurrently with the conversion of N205 to Mark II standard in September 1927, a variant with a Bristol Jupiter VIII engine was designed

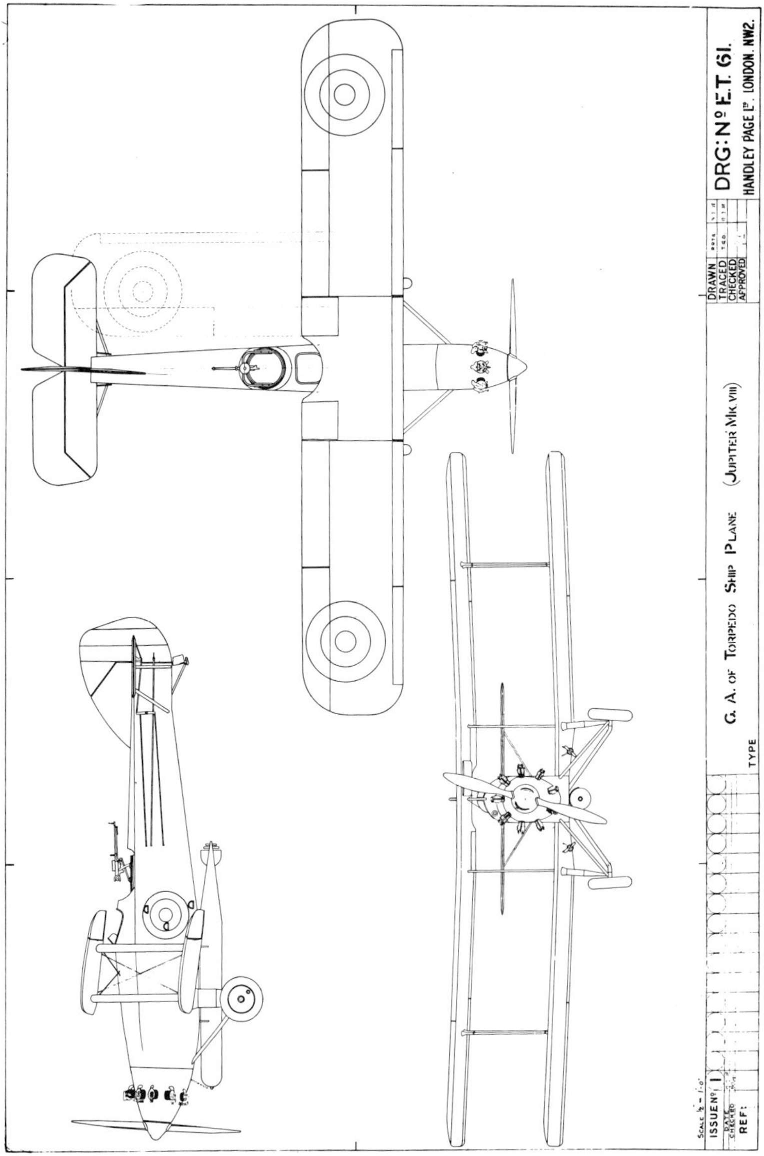

Hanwell project.

for a tender to specification 24/25 in competition with the Blackburn Beagle and Vickers Vildebeest; this was a shore-based torpedo-bomber primarily for use at Singapore and was known at Cricklewood as the Hanwell, this name having been proposed earlier for a torpedo-bomber version of the Handcross when the 24/25 requirement was first issued. After a year's discussion, the Hanwell project was dropped in favour of the Hare, since the latter showed better promise of meeting the same specification.

H.P.31 Harrow I

(Napier Lion VA)

Span 44 ft (13·42 m); length 33 ft 9 in (10·3 m); wing area 563 sq ft (52·2 m^2). Empty weight 4,403 lb (2,000 kg); maximum weight 7,140 lb (3,240 kg). Speed 115 mph (185 km/h); range 440 miles (709 km). Crew two.

H.P.31 Harrow II

(Napier Lion XIA)

Span 46 ft (14·02 m); length 34 ft 10 in (10·62 m); wing area 591 sq ft (54·9 m^2). Empty weight 4,125 lb (1,870 kg); maximum weight 7,310 lb (3,316 kg). Speed (landplane) 126 mph (202 km/h), (seaplane) 123 mph (198 km/h); range 450 miles (725 km); ceiling 15,300 ft (4,730 m). Crew two.

H.P.31A Hanwell

(Bristol Jupiter VIII)

As Harrow II except: Empty weight (est) 3,950 lb (1,790 kg); maximum weight (est) 7,000 lb (3,177 kg). Speed (est) 130 mph (209 km/h).

Hare (Type H) (H.P.34)

The Hare was an entirely new design to meet specification 23/25 for a short-range high-altitude day bomber, using a supercharged Bristol Orion engine. The aim was to produce a fast but easily maintained biplane to replace the Hawker Horsley and Fairey Fawn in squadron service. Although the specified armament and total bomb-load were virtually the same as for the Handcross, a single 550-lb bomb was not called for and it was hoped that the air-cooled engine would avoid some of the cooling troubles that had plagued both the Handcross and the Harrow. Early difficulties with the Jupiter VIII installation in the prototype Hinaidi had been overcome and the Orion was essentially a Jupiter with an exhaust-driven turbine coupled to a supercharger developed at the RAE. Identified in the drawing office as Type H, the Hare was a cleaner design than the Harrow, having a well-shaped fuselage without excrescences, a simple cross-axle landing gear and high aspect ratio staggered wings of RAF 31 section braced entirely by struts in a sesquiplane formation, with narrow-chord wide-span differential ailerons on the upper wing only; external wire bracing was confined to six short tie-rods in the centre section and undercarriage. The layout, begun by Harold Boultbee in December 1926, was approved for issue to the experimental shop in July 1927, four months after the award of contract No.716900/26 for a single prototype (J8622) to compete against three other prototypes—the Hawker Harrier J8325, Gloster Goring J8674 and Westland Witch J8596; the last was the only monoplane and all four were substantially of wooden construction although the winning design had to be capable of production in all-metal form if ordered for squadron service. Boultbee's strut-braced wing for the Hare was suggested by specification 20/25 for an army co-operation biplane designed for easy maintenance in the field; another interesting minor feature was the flexible cable trailing edge of the lower wing, which Boultbee considered to be less liable to damage by man-handling than the usual small-diameter tubing.

Hare with original tail unit, short fuselage, cross-axle undercarriage and Gnome-Rhône Jupiter at Cricklewood in February 1928.

By November 1927 development difficulties with supercharger surging had caused the Orion to be cancelled and an unsupercharged Jupiter VIII was substituted, but this too was delayed in production for some months and the first engine to be installed in the Hare was one of the two French-built Gnome-Rhône Jupiters discarded from the prototype Hinaidi J7745 when prepared for tropical trials in September 1927. The Hare was weighed with this engine and a four-blade airscrew on 22 February, 1928, and flown for the first time by England on the 24th. He recorded a top speed of 144 mph and stalling speed of 54 mph, finding the rudder overbalanced at high speed, ailerons satisfactory, elevators heavy and gliding angle exceptionally flat. Two more trials were made on the 27th, but the second ended early because the pilot's seat collapsed during a fairly tight turn, causing England to land heavily and the Hare had only run 15 yds before the undercarriage collapsed. During the ensuing repairs the rudder horn-balance area was reduced and the elevators were made lighter; a Bristol Jupiter VIII arrived from Filton in time to replace the French engine and England flew again for 20 min on the evening of 27 June. The rudder and elevators were still heavy, and the ailerons also at 140 mph; furthermore the wing struts on the port side vibrated, which they had not done previously. For the next flight on 2 July the ailerons were rigged up 3 degrees and found to be lighter but less responsive; the strut vibration had increased and at minimum speed the rudder was masked by the tailplane.

On 3 July, with the ailerons rigged up 5 degrees, England reached a true airspeed of 152 mph at 5,000 ft, but the seat structure and strut vibration were still troublesome. On 17 July Cordes flew it, with Oswald as observer to record climbs to 5,000 ft and 10,000 ft, and noted that further cropping of the horn balance had cured the rudder of hunting but made it much heavier; strut vibration had been reduced by adding temporary tension cables and was recognised as originating from the engine. A new tailplane and elevators were fitted, but showed little improvement when flown by Cordes on the 24th, although the engine was running more smoothly, and Volkert then decided to lengthen the fuselage by nearly two feet. England flew the Hare thus modified on 21 August and found manoeuvrability much improved, although the large fin area prevented a continuous side-slip being held. Smaller elevators were fitted for a flight by Cordes on the 24th and the plain upper wings used so far were exchanged for a new set with full-span leading-edge slots installed; they were manually controlled by the pilot and not linked to the ailerons. On 30 August Cordes flew with increased elevator balance area and found that the Hare would now fly hands-off at all speeds; on 1 September he did a full load test flight including stall turns, half-rolls and loops at 5,000 ft, but the engine was becoming rough again and the opportunity was taken, during top overhaul, to fit a new high aspect ratio rudder and a smaller cambered fin; these were found to give a marked improvement when the Hare was flown again on 19 September.

At this point England suggested to Volkert that the Hare could be readily adapted to meet the coast defence torpedo-bomber specification 24/25 and could carry a 2,000-lb torpedo at a gross weight of 6,960 lb, compared with a current estimate for the slower Hanwell project of 6,850 lb. Volkert checked the strength and performance for this role and found them adequate, but pointed out that necessary modifications would include a split undercarriage, flotation bags, torpedo gear, slinging gear, fuel jettison valves and a more comprehensive selection of alternative bomb loads, all of which would add substantially to the structure weight. The Air Ministry were willing to accept the Hare for the torpedo-bomber competition after trials as a day bomber, but insisted that a two-blade airscrew must be fitted because the four-blader interfered with the firing of the front gun at maximum rate; they also agreed to order and test a metal fuselage for the torpedo role, but since the latter was shore-based, folding wings would not be necessary. From August 1928 the Hare was based at Stag Lane for tests with various changes of tailplanes and elevators, but on 23 October England condemned a new horn-balanced set after a single perilous circuit and the design finally approved reverted to unbalanced elevators of reduced area with an increased overall tailplane span. With this tail unit, differential ailerons, oleo-legs lengthened by insertion of 4-inch extension tubes at the top to give clearance for a larger two-blade airscrew and new Palmer wheels with pneumatic brakes, England flew from Stag Lane to Cricklewood on 17 November after performing a series of loops, rolls and stalls at speeds ranging from 140 mph to 50 mph, with the control slots working automatically. It seemed that at last the Hare was ready for Martlesham, but on the 20th, while trying fast tail-up landings with auto-slots locked, England crashed at Cricklewood, apparently because the wings with slots locked were much more easily stalled than the original plain wings had been. On this occasion, after touching down very lightly, the port wheel collapsed and the Hare cart-wheeled, damaging both lower wings and the port upper; petrol poured out of the tank vents while inverted, but fortunately there was no fire because England had cut the ignition in time and no exhaust pipes were fitted.

The Hare was soon rebuilt with a Jupiter VIII borrowed from the Clive I, a smaller fin, new ailerons of reduced span but increased chord, and wing dihedral increased from 2 to 3 degrees. Cordes flew it on 10 December and thought it handled well, but England felt unsafe and had the ailerons changed again; by 14 January, 1929, the lateral control was satisfactory but engine vibration with the two-blader was very severe; it was no better when first a Wapiti airscrew and then one from the Harrier were tried, so the second Jupiter VIII from the Clive I was substituted and vibration was then much reduced. Summarising the many aileron changes during the past year, Volkert noted that they had gone back to the original wide span, but with area increased from 21 sq ft to 31 sq ft. On 23 February England visited Martlesham and reported that all the other 23/25 and 24/25 competitors had arrived except the Blackburn Beagle and that all were being offered with a 550-lb bomb, so Handley Page decided that the Hare too must carry one; this meant the immediate fitting of a stronger undercarriage and a divided one was contrived by deleting the cross-axle and adding outboard bracing struts between the wheel centres and the front spars of the lower wings. A divided long-stroke undercarriage for the torpedo role had been schemed by Boultbee in December 1928, with the top ends of the oleo-legs attached to the upper longerons and the swing-axles and radius rods hinged from the middle of the fuselage underside; this would have catered for higher vertical velocities, but could not be manufactured in time for use on the prototype, although it would be available for production aircraft.

In its revised form, the Hare was flown on 6 April by Cordes who found taxying better with the slightly wider track, but braking erratic; on the 10th he flew with a 550-lb bomb under the port wing and after further minor changes to the ailerons to cure a list first to port and then to starboard, the Hare eventually reached Martlesham on 10 June, remaining there till the end of September. It was flown mainly by Flying Officer Denny and Flt Lieut Stuart Culley, who recommended further testing with a supercharged Jupiter X engine, which Culley had lately tested in the Vickers 177 fighter; this would restore the performance originally expected with the Orion and would also improve the Hare in the 24/25 role using full-span lift slots. In October the Hare returned to Cricklewood for installation of a Jupiter X before final trials as a day bomber. England flew it with a four-blade airscrew on 14 November, but found vibration of the wing main struts very severe. A week later, after full-span roller-track lift slots had been installed, he began a series of short take-off and landing tests at the new aerodrome at Radlett; these continued through December and January, while various adjustments of venting were tried out to cure erratic operation. Throughout this period, excessive vibration occurred whenever a two-blade airscrew was used and Handley Page pressed the Air Ministry to accept the Hare with a four-blader. On 28 February, 1930, Cordes began tests at an overload of 6,670 lb, using the longest run then available at Radlett, as a result of which he recommended that full torpedo-load trials at 7,000 lb

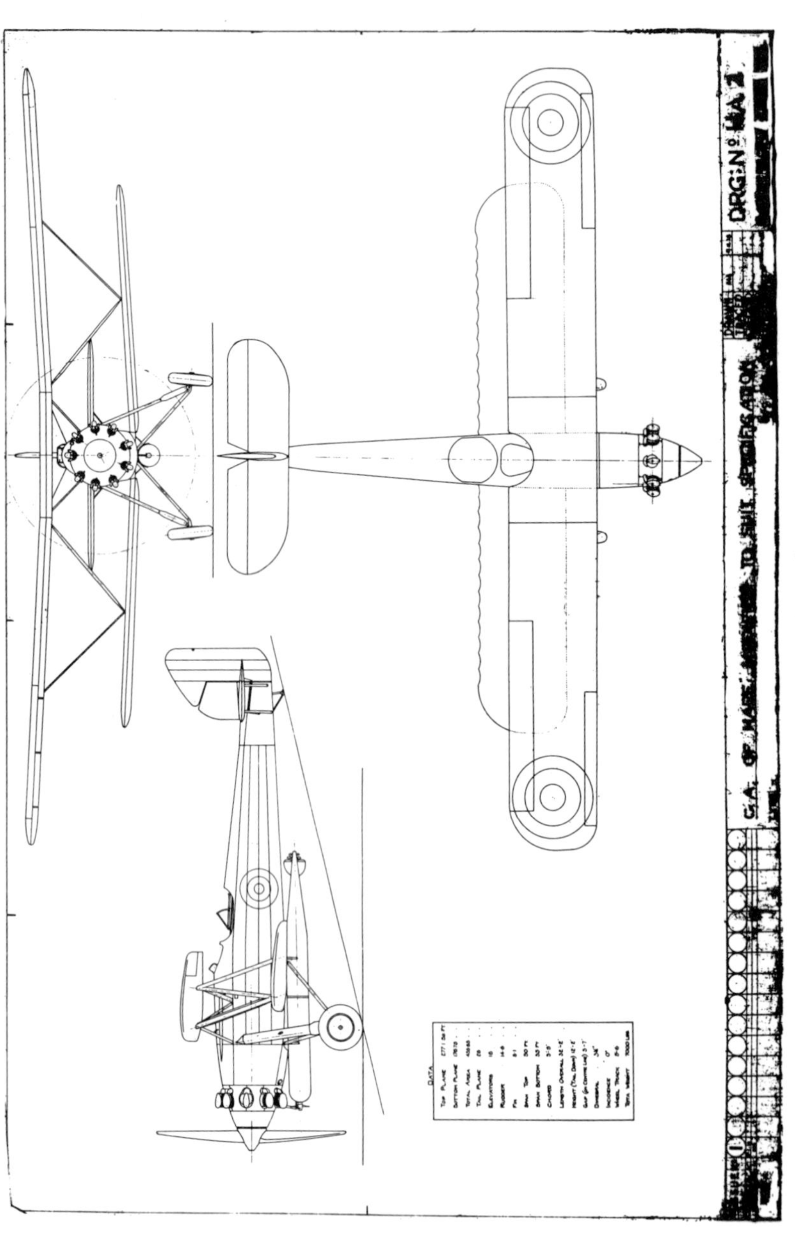

First torpedo scheme for Hare.

Hare with full-span slots and divided undercarriage at Radlett in April 1929.

should only be done at Martlesham until further levelling at Radlett was possible.

Full load trials were completed by England on 29 March, 1930, after a new Jupiter XFS engine with a four-blade airscrew had been fitted; the Hare was then given a nine-element Potts oil cooler before going to Martlesham for trials with one 520-lb bomb (23/25 revised normal load), two 520-lb bombs (23/25 extra load) and 2,000-lb torpedo (24/25 normal load). Meanwhile the original 23/25 contestants had been outclassed by a new contender, the Hawker Hart metal-framed day bomber built to specification 12/26; this had proved superior to the Fairey Fox II and Avro Antelope matched against it, so the Air Ministry had lost interest in the Hare as a day bomber and intended to restrict its trials at Martlesham to the torpedo role, in competition with the Beagle and Vildebeest. At the end of June Sqn Ldr Goodwin began the Hare's handling flights at Martlesham, but on 3 July a piston seized during a climb to 16,000 ft and he had to make a dead-stick forced landing at the Pulham airship station. The only available Jupiter XF at Martlesham was the one in the Vickers 177; this engine was sent to Pulham by road and installed in the stranded Hare, which flew back to Martlesham but overheated during the low-level ferry flight of only 30 miles, so on the 23rd the Hare went back to Cricklewood without an engine to be modified for installation of an Armstrong Siddeley Panther II.

By this time the Air Staff had virtually decided to choose the Vildebeest, as it had a better rate of climb than the Hare with the 2,000-lb torpedo, although the Hare was the faster of the two without it. England's first flight in the Panther-engined Hare lasted only a few minutes on 21 September, as the oil quickly overheated; this trouble recurred on the second flight three days later, but was corrected by adding two extra elements to the Potts oil-cooler and fitting a Townend ring cowling; the tests continued with both single and double rings, but overheating persisted throughout the dozen

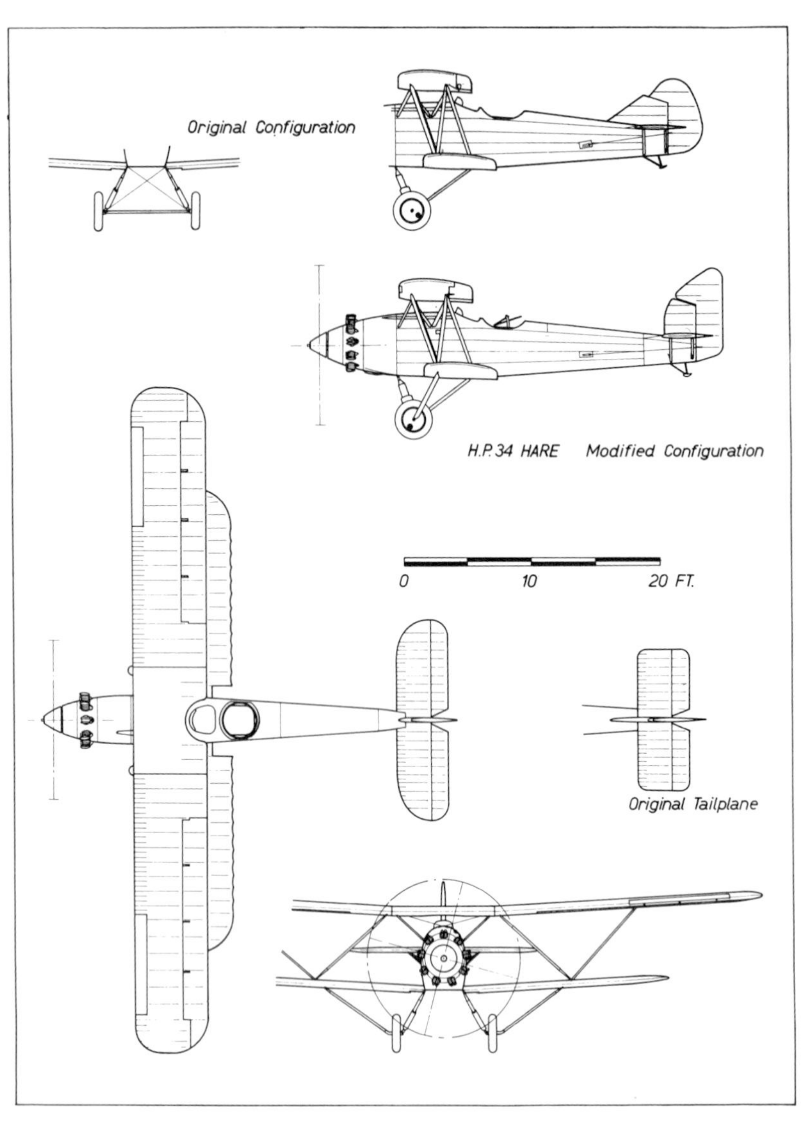

flights made during October and by the end of that month the Hare had still not been cleared to go back to Martlesham. Meanwhile the Vildebeest had been chosen to replace the Horsleys at Singapore and emphasis was being placed on a new requirement for a deck-landing torpedo-bomber to specification M.5/28, based on a Rolls-Royce Kestrel engine. Still the Air Ministry wanted the Hare for experimental flying with full-span slots, though they declined to provide a new Jupiter XFBM engine which Handley Page requested to replace the Panther, in the hope that the comparison would help to decide which engine should be adopted for the

Hare re-engined with Panther at Martlesham Heath in September 1930. (*I.W.M.—Crown Copyright*)

Western version of the new four-engined airliner for Imperial Airways being built at Cricklewood. The Hare was finally delivered to Martlesham in June 1931, but was rarely flown and in 1932 was put up for sale by tender and bought by J. N. Addinsell, who hoped to adapt it for a long-distance flight he was planning. It was registered to him as G-ACEL and removed to Hanworth in March 1933, but the project was abandoned and the remains of the Hare, much damaged by vandals, were scrapped in 1937. Somehow the Hare just missed its cues all through its career, in spite of its undoubted talent, probably because, as Lachmann pointed out in 1931, no advantage in take-off and landing performance could have been expected from full-span slots in the absence of flaps.

H.P.34 Hare

(Bristol Jupiter VIII or X or Armstrong Siddeley Panther)

Span 50 ft (15·25 m); length 32 ft 2 in (9·8 m); wing area 454 sq ft (42·1 m^2). Empty weight 3,050 lb (1,383 kg); maximum weight (Bomber) 5,720 lb (2,590 kg), (Torpedo) 7,243 lb (3,280 kg). Speed (Bomber) 152 mph (244 km/h), (Torpedo) 145 mph (233 km/h); range 1,000 miles (1,610 km); ceiling 20,000 ft (6,190 m). Crew two.

Panther-Hare with single Townend ring at Radlett in 1931. (*Flight*)

Fleet Fighter Type F (H.P.37)

Early in the life of the Hare a water-cooled alternative to the Orion engine had been considered and in 1927 a parallel design, Type F or H.P.37, was begun for a two-seat fleet fighter to specification O.22/26. It was to be of all-metal construction and powered by a Rolls-Royce F.XIS water-cooled engine, with wire-braced two-bay wings of nearly equal span and unequal chord, the aerofoil section being RAF 31. Equipped with auto-slots in front of the narrow-chord ailerons, the wings were arranged to fold about the inner pair of interplane struts, leaving the inner bays to form a wide centre-section with short struts at the mid-rib, as in the Harrow. The rectangular fuselage of welded steel tube was faired to an oval section and a retractable deeply-finned radiator was installed under the engine, which was closely cowled, with a large conical spinner; the overall appearance was similar to the contemporary Fairey IIIF, although there were fewer resemblances in detail. The mock-up was inspected by Sqn Ldr Brand on 29 November, 1927, and in response to his criticisms a new layout was produced in March 1928, with the fuselage lines and crew's view improved by deleting the upper centreplane and integrating the upper and lower wing roots into the fuselage in the manner of the Gloster IV racing biplane designed for the Schneider Trophy contest of 1927. The overall span was reduced to 37 ft and the folded width to under 12 ft, but the Handley Page tender was rejected, the five O.22/26 prototypes actually ordered being two Short Gurnards and one each of the Blackburn Nautilus, Fairey Fleetwing and navalised Hawker Hart; the last-named went into production as the Hawker Osprey and no further development of the H.P.37 took place, although some of its features reappeared in the H.P.41 design to specification M.5/28, described later.

H.P.37 (original)

(Rolls-Royce F.XIS)

Span 40 ft (12·2 m); length 28 ft 9 in (8·76 m); wing area 312 sq ft (29 m²). Maximum weight (est) 3,900 lb (1,768 kg). Speed (est) 186 mph (300 km/h); ceiling (est) 28,000 ft (8,660 m).

H.P.37 (revised)

Span 37 ft (11·29 m); length (landplane) 27 ft 3 in (8·31 m), (seaplane) 30 ft (9·15 m). Maximum weight (est) 4,250 lb (1,930 kg). Ceiling (est) 25,500 ft (7,900 m). Crew two.

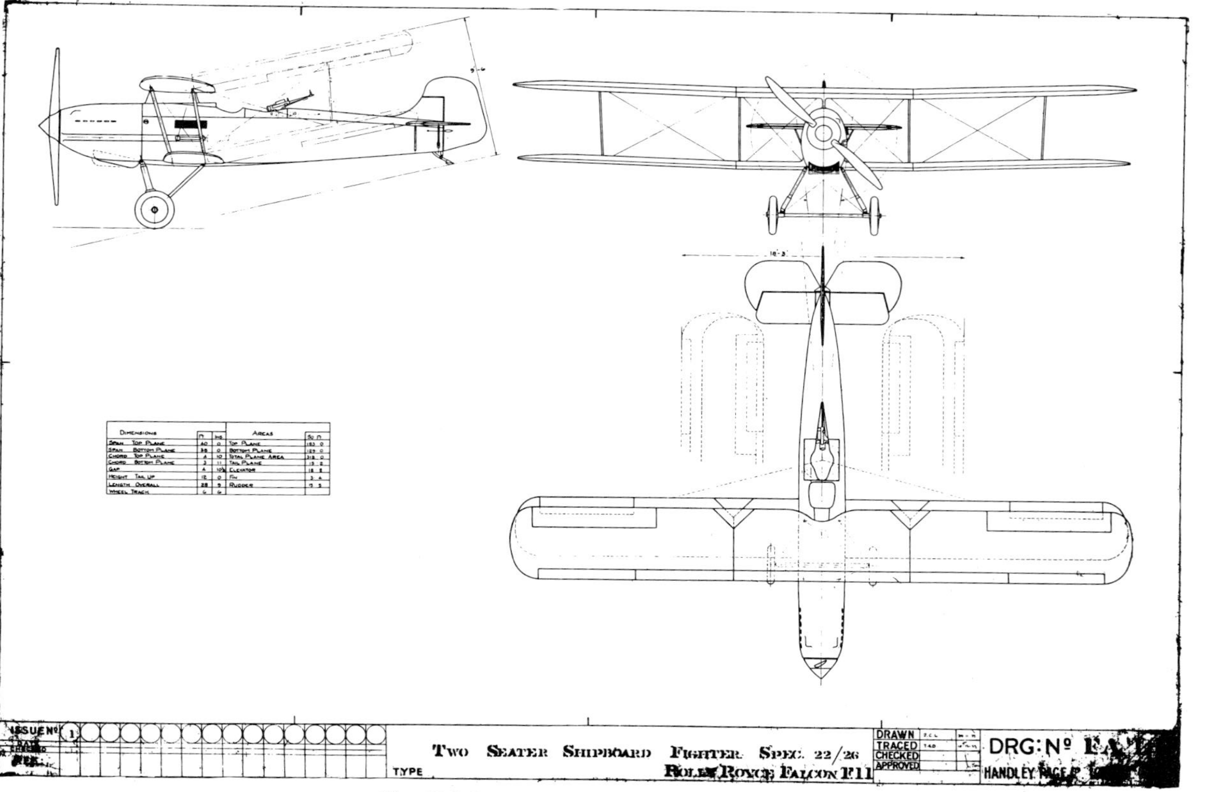

DIMENSIONS	FT	INS	AREAS	SQ FT
SPAN TOP PLANE	40	0	TOP PLANE	183 0
SPAN BOTTOM PLANE	38	0	BOTTOM PLANE	127 0
CHORD TOP PLANE	4	10	TOTAL PLANE AREA	312 0
CHORD BOTTOM PLANE	3	11	TAIL PLANE	13 2
GAP	4	10½	ELEVATOR	18 8
HEIGHT TAIL UP	12	0	FIN	3 4
LENGTH OVERALL	28	9	RUDDER	13 3
WHEEL TRACK	6	6		

First H.P.37 tender to specification O.22/26.

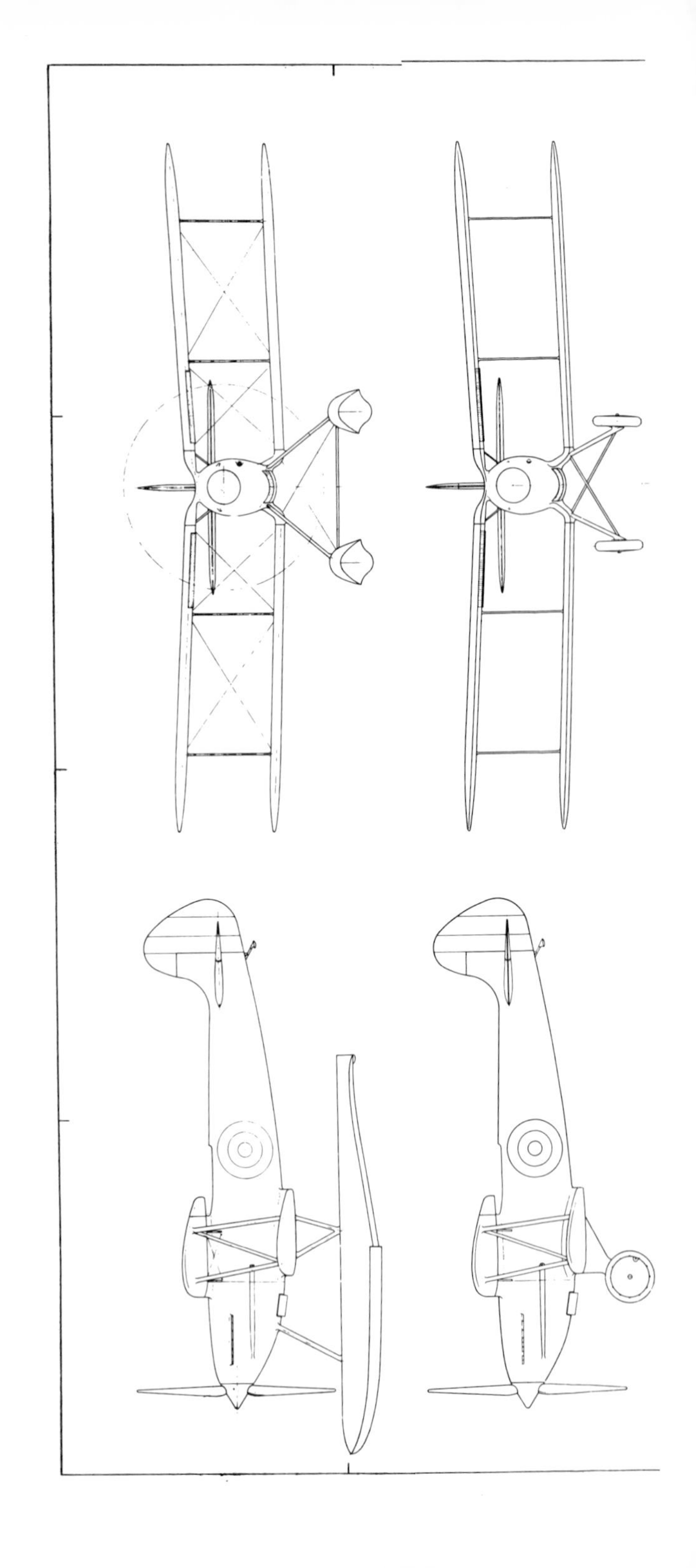

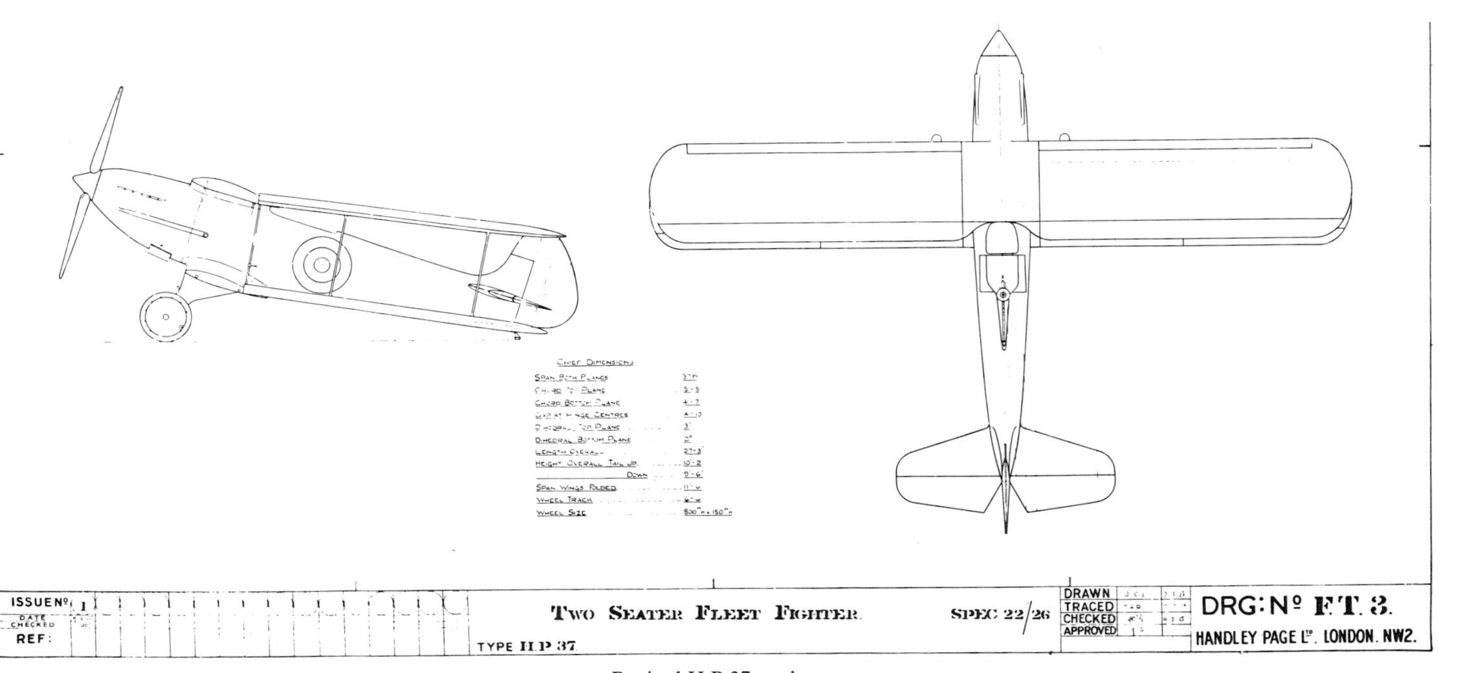

Revised H.P.37 tender

Gugnunc (H.P.39)

In January 1926 Daniel Guggenheim, president of the vast American copper-mining empire of Guggenheim Brothers and described as 'a millionaire among millionaires', inaugurated the Daniel Guggenheim Fund for the Promotion of Aeronautics with deeds of gift totalling more than $2·5 million. The Fund aimed at promoting 'airmindedness' throughout the United States and furthering the development of commercial aircraft 'as a regular means of transportation of both goods and people', and was administered by trustees under the presidency of Daniel's younger son, Harry F. Guggenheim; the trustees included William F. Durand, Charles Lindbergh and Orville Wright.

On 20 April, 1927, the Fund announced a Safe Aircraft Competition, whose object was 'to achieve a real advance in the safety of flying through improvement in the aerodynamic characteristics of heavier-than-air craft, without sacrificing the good, practical qualities of present-day aircraft'; a first prize of $100,000 and five 'Safety Prizes' of $10,000 each were offered and entries were invited between 1 September, 1927, and 31 October, 1929. The original rules were comprehensive and stringent, comprising qualifying requirements which included full compliance with the US Department of Commerce airworthiness regulations and a top speed of at least 110 mph, and a schedule of safety tests and demonstrations of ability

(a) to fly level with engine on at not more than 35 mph.
(b) to glide for three minutes with engine off at not more than 38 mph.
(c) to land over a 35-ft barrier within a total distance of 300 ft with ground run not more than 100 ft, and
(d) to take off in a ground run of 300 ft and thereafter to clear a 35 ft barrier 500 ft from the starting point.

The prize was to be awarded for the most marks scored in accordance with a scale totalling 200 bonus marks; in addition the aircraft had to achieve a flattest gliding angle of 8 degrees and a steepest gliding angle of 16 degrees without exceeding 45 mph, to demonstrate stick-free stability from 45 to 100 mph at any throttle opening, and ability to recover from abnormal conditions including an engine cut during take-off from a plot 500 ft square surrounded by a 25-ft barrier within which the subsequent 'dead-stick' landing had to be made.

Handley Page saw the competition as an excellent shop-window for demonstrating the slotted wing and proposed to build a high-wing two-seat monoplane on the lines of the Beardmore Wee Bee, winner of the Air Ministry's light aeroplane trials at Lympne in 1924 and itself derived from German glider practice. He sought advice from the RAE on optimising this design, but in January R. McKinnon Wood replied with a preferred layout for a biplane; simultaneously Armstrong Siddeley Ltd offered to lend a 150 hp Mongoose engine. This offer was accepted and in March it was decided to build a wooden biplane, H.P.39, with strutted wing bracing similar to the Hare's and incorporating the best structural features of the

Avro Avian and D.H.Moth; the undercarriage featured a divided axle, long-stroke oleo-pneumatic shock struts and American Bendix wheels and brakes.

Detail design began in June and the fuselage drawings were issued to the experimental shop in August. The Fund's British representative, Major Robert Mayo, went to the competition venue, Mitchel Field, Long Island, in September to sort out anomalies between the British and American airworthiness regulations and by 14 November, 1928, the aeroplane was ready for erection at Cricklewood. The Mongoose engine was promised for mid-December, but in fact arrived a month later. Although the rules called for dual controls, it was agreed in February to save time by omitting them until preliminary flight tests had been cleared and the final design standard was sealed on 27 March, 1929, the primary aim being to earn as many bonus marks as possible for short take-off and landing performance. By this time the cumbersome title 'Guggenheim Competition Biplane' had been shortened by the editor of *Flight* to 'Gugnunc'—a catch-word taken from Bertram Lamb and Austin Payne's popular 'Pip, Squeak and Wilfred' strip cartoon on the children's page of the *Daily Mirror*; the soubriquet stuck and was eventually accepted in official reports.

When weighed on 26 April, 1929, the Gugnunc was found to be 165 lb above the estimated gross weight of 1,878 lb, but this included an increase in fuel tankage from 22 gallons to 32 gallons, 40 lb allowance for the prescribed instruments and 31 lb due to the engine being overweight. The front half of the fuselage was of mixed wood and welded steel-tube construction, with cockpit coamings of minimum size, plywood covering and three-ply luggage compartment linings; the rear fuselage was built of spruce with plywood covering, while the wings and tail unit were also all wood with fabric covering, the wing section being RAF 28. Full-span leading-edge slots were installed on both upper and lower wings, together with full-span trailing-edge flaps. The top outer control slots were free to

J. L. Cordes demonstrates slow flying in the Gugnunc at Cricklewood in June 1929.

operate automatically and the inner lift slots, together with those on the bottom wing, were connected to the flaps so as to open automatically at a predetermined angle of attack and lower all the flaps together, no manual control of the flaps being provided. Volkert made a list of the possible combinations of slot and flap operations as a guide to England, who was to test them progressively till the best compromise was found. England made the first two brief handling flights in very gusty weather on 30 April and reported all well except for initial slackness in the aileron circuit which was rectified before the second flight. On 6 May the aileron control runs were revised to reduce friction, but on the 8th England reported that the ailerons and elevators were still heavy and the tailplane incidence control too slow in operation; he asked for a 'cheese cutter' lever instead of a hand-wheel. Next day auto-slot tests were made and on the 16th Cordes flew the Gugnunc in formation with England, who flew a Moth which had a calibrated airspeed indicator, recording a top speed of 103 mph at 1,000 ft and 104 mph at sea level; the minimum level speed measured was 29 mph with slots and flaps free and engine on. To reduce drag, the large windscreen and rubber coaming surround for the pilot's (front) cockpit were replaced by a small celastoid screen and the flap hinges were sealed with fabric, but this only raised the top speed by 2 mph. Next the flaps were rigged ½-inch up, which added another 2 mph but also raised the minimum flying speed to 32 mph. Concurrently, a stress check at the actual flying weight of 2,043 lb showed the need for stronger outer front wing struts and intermediate cabane struts to cater for the inverted aerobatic case, so further weight and drag saving changes became necessary. These were

(a) 28-inch × 4-inch tyres instead of 30-inch × 5-inch;
(b) streamline tubes for the main lift struts instead of round tubes with fairings;
(c) aluminium fairings at the axle/brake drum joints; and
(d) elevator hinge gaps sealed, together with a smaller tailplane and larger elevators, without changing the total area.

Dual control was installed before the next flight on 28 June, shared by England and Cordes; both found the cockpits too draughty without the large windscreen, but agreed that its drag was excessive. The brakes were not fully effective, nor was lateral control adequate for the engine-cut-on-take-off test required by the Fund's rules, so the slots were adjusted to open earlier and elevator travel was increased.

Next, short fairings were fitted behind the Mongoose cylinders, with fabric streamers to indicate airflow direction; these showed a good deal of turbulence, which was reduced by fitting a Townend ring, when the true airspeed rose to 112 mph. Cordes tested three different Townend rings in conjunction with both wooden and Fairey-Reed airscrews, also a pyramidal fairing under the fuselage; a coupé cockpit cover was designed and made, but not tested in flight. Time was running short, but in August a revised tail incidence gear was installed, together with small cuff fairings at all strut junctions and a true aerofoil centre-section tank of 20 gallons with a separate 15-gallon tank in the front luggage compartment. The all-up weight had by now risen to 2,141 lb and on 27 August a measured mile along the LMS railway line was timed to give a top speed of 112 mph and minimum (engine on) of 30 mph.

With final recommendations and exhortations for competition flying ringing in his ears, Cordes departed with the crated Gugnunc for New York in the ss *Minnewaska*, arriving on 25 September; the Gugnunc was rigged at Mitchel Field on 1 October, then Cordes checked it out in flight and handed it over to the Fund's pilots on the 3rd. The intended interceptors on the top control slots had not been available in time, nor had there been time to delete the bottom slots and flaps, as finally recommended by Lachmann on his return from Japan just before the competition was due to begin.

Of the 27 entries in the competition, only 15 were presented at Mitchel Field and of these three were withdrawn without being tested, two crashed during practice flying and eight failed to pass all the qualifying

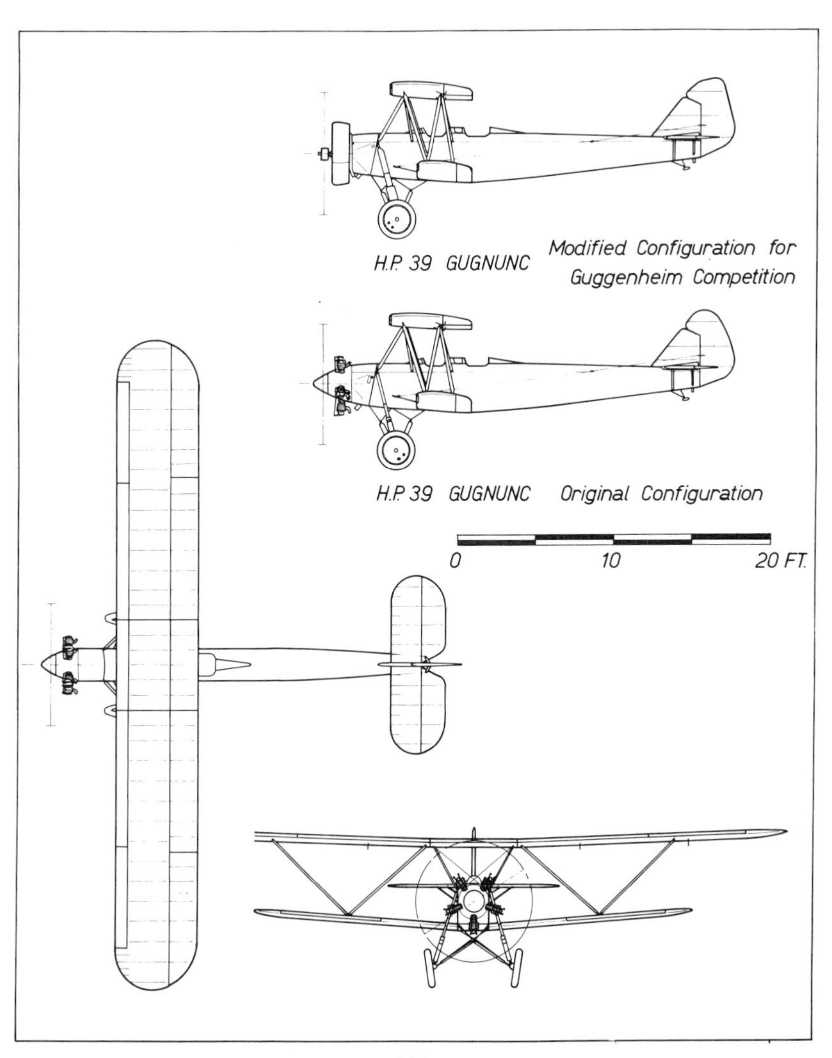

The Gugnunc with Townend ring at Mitchel Field in October 1929.

requirements. The only two allowed to complete the safety tests and demonstrations were the Curtiss Tanager and the Gugnunc, although the latter had technically failed to achieve the prescribed minimum gliding speed with engine off, when flown by the Fund's pilots. Nor could Cordes himself maintain 38 mph for a full three minutes with the engine switched off instead of only throttled back, and he cabled urgently to Handley Page, who arrived on the *Aquitania* on the 18th. Flying at Mitchel Field was much hampered by continuous bad weather and the judges had consequently extended the time allowed for the safety tests from 31 October to 18 November, which Handley Page considered unfair, although it did not affect either the Tanager or the Gugnunc. What really incensed him was the sight of the Tanager with fully-slotted wings, for which Curtiss had not paid a royalty, and he forthwith sued the Curtiss company for infringement of his patent, to which they replied by invoking Judge Chatfield's injunction of July 1920 forbidding the importation of foreign—in particular, Handley Page—aircraft into the United States. A legal battle then ensued in which expert witnesses were called for both parties, Theodore von Kàrmàn appearing for Handley Page; after eighteen months, when neither side had gained any ground and only the lawyers had profited from the affair, the Curtiss company admitted technical infringement and the action was ended by mutual consent. The Tanager had scored by having manually controlled flaps and floating ailerons, giving a slight advantage to a skilful pilot; it also provided more comfort without drag penalty by having an enclosed cabin instead of open cockpits. It was awarded the first prize of $100,000, but was destroyed on the ground by fire a few weeks later, while the Gugnunc, not even allowed a consolation 'Safety Prize' of $10,000, returned to Cricklewood for further experimental flying.

Gustav Lachmann had returned from his two years' sojourn at the Ishikawanishi works in Japan too late to make final improvements in the Gugnunc before the competition began, but he was welcomed at last on to the Handley Page design staff, which he joined formally as Experimental Engineer, primarily to develop the interceptor for lateral control at minimum speed. He recommended the immediate fitting of interceptors to the Gugnunc, also a ratchet-controlled lock for the slot across the centre section, an all-moving tailplane and a longer-stroke landing gear of wider track to permit 'pancake' landings to be demonstrated as a routine manoeuvre. The Air Ministry were interested in developing a 25 ft/sec undercarriage and had already given one contract to Vickers Ltd for a fully-slotted slow landing D.H.9A conversion; however, the best that could be achieved by redesigning the Gugnunc was 16 ft/sec, which was adequate for a completely stalled landing with full load.

On 23 May Cordes flew the Gugnunc with interceptors, a centre-section slot ratchet and a larger parallel-chord rudder and reported handling to be much improved, but when England flew it on 3 June he disagreed and said that its take-off was not as good as that of the Hawker Tomtit which he had flown recently at Radlett. On 14 June he flew the Gugnunc to Villacoublay for a demonstration to the French Air Minister, M Laurent-Eynac, staying there two days before repeating the display at Le Bourget for the benefit of

Gugnunc at Farnborough as K1908 in 1932. (*RAE—Crown Copyright*)

Gugnunc and Victor B.2 at Radlett in 1959.

French aircraft trade and press representatives. Returning on the 18th, England flew the Gugnunc in two further displays before Prince George, who formally opened Bristol Airport at Whitchurch on 31 May and then Handley Page's new aerodrome at Radlett on 7 July; on the latter occasion England started the engine inside the new large hangar and was already airborne as he passed through the doorway.

Although registered G-AACN before going to America, no C of A was applied for and in October the Gugnunc was bought by the Air Ministry as K1908 and allotted to the RAE at Farnborough for official performance testing and interceptor development, being flown by Sqn Ldr Caster and Flying Officer H. H. Leech; the latter flew it in a display at Croydon for the Imperial Conference delegates on 25 October, together with the Westland Pterodactyl IV and the Cierva C.19 Autogiro, in a strong wind which allowed the formation to fly backwards across the aerodrome. This feat became so popular that it was repeated as a kind of circus trick in several RAF Displays at Hendon, the three aircraft acquiring grotesque paint schemes which may have amused the populace but did nothing to encourage serious research into safer flying.

In July 1934 K1908 was struck off Air Ministry charge and Handley Page presented it to the Science Museum, where it remains in store, having been statically displayed, but not flown, on several occasions since 1945. In his report on the Farnborough trials (BA967, July 1932) J. E. Serby compared the Gugnunc favourably with the Autogiro on the score of speed-range and supported Lachmann's plea for further development with a longer-travel undercarriage, stating 'The moment seems opportune for a practical examination of the 'crash landing' idea, which has long been mooted, and useful information could be gained by a study of the stability and control of this aircraft with an improved interceptor.'

H.P.39

(Armstrong Siddeley Mongoose I)

Span 40 ft (12·2m); length 25 ft 9 in (7·84 m); wing area 293 sq ft (27·2 m^2). Empty weight 1,362 lb (619 kg); maximum weight 2,180 lb (989 kg). Maximum speed 112·5 mph (181 km/h); minimum speed 33·5 mph (54 km/h).

Heyford
(H.P.38 and H.P.50)

Since 1922, the British government had subscribed to the League of Nations' aim to limit armaments and if possible to make all bombing illegal; its policy on the size and role of the home-based RAF had been defined by the 'Ten-Year Rule' and 'parity' with the nearest potential enemy; the latter was France, who had occupied the Ruhr in 1923 and always maintained a large bomber force, mainly for police purposes in her widespread colonial and mandated territories. Under the terms of the Treaty of Versailles, Germany was prohibited from building aircraft with engines of more than 200 hp, although this rule was easily evaded by setting up factories in Denmark, Sweden and Switzerland, and to some extent alleviated by using two, three or four engines; in the case of civil aircraft, even though they were easily convertible to warlike purposes, the limitation applied only for the first ten years. In 1923 the establishment of the home defence (or 'metropolitan') element of the Royal Air Force had been defined as 17 squadrons of short-range fighters and 35 squadrons of unescorted day and night bombers; the optimum ratio of fighters to bombers, and of day bombers to night bombers, became a recurrent but always unresolved theme in Air Staff discussions. By 1928 the versatility of single-engined two-seaters, exemplified by the Fairey Fox and Hawker Hart, showed that one basic airframe design with suitable permutations of engine, armament and equipment, could cover all the major roles except long-range night bombing, and this was a role that both the League of Nations and the naval 'die-hards' sought to abolish, though for different reasons. So the night bomber lingered on virtually unchanged from the 1918 concept, with a maximum speed of about 100 mph and a bomb load of 2,000 lb to be carried to a target 500 miles away.

Handley Page Ltd, having produced the Hyderabad as successor to the O/400 and achieved a temporary technical superiority over the Vickers Virginia, would have been content to build wooden airframes for a long time ahead and were confident of their ability to protect timber against deterioration under extremes of climatic conditions, but the Air Ministry insisted on metal construction for all new production aircraft, so in September 1927 the Cricklewood stress office was reinforced by the arrival of Raymond H. Sandifer, a specialist in steel and duralumin applications, trained by J. D. North at Boulton & Paul of Norwich. Following the successful conversion of the Hyderabad into the Hinaidi by substituting Jupiters for Lions, Sandifer began to replace the Hinaidi's wooden structure by equivalent steel tube components from January 1928 onwards, the first steel wing spars being successfully tested by the RAE in February, although the associated duralumin ribs failed and had to be modified; concurrently a wooden Hinaidi, J9033, was equipped with welded aluminium fuel tanks in place of tinned steel. At first there was some difficulty in matching up welded tubular assemblies—for instance, at the ventral gun station—to the primary structure, because of shrinkage and distortion after removal from the welding jigs, but this and similar snags were overcome and the thirty-three production Hinaidi IIs manufactured to specification B.13/29 enabled the RAF to gain experience, particularly in ground handling and maintenance, in the differences between large wooden and metal airframes and to judge the relative merits and suitability of steel and duralumin, while the two Clive IIs proved the design under arduous tropical conditions in India.

The Hinaidi II, being obsolescent in aerodynamic layout, was no more than a stop-gap for a new generation of night bombers with much better performance designed to meet the advanced specification B.19/27 issued on 17 August, 1927, by the Deputy Director of Technical Development, Air Commodore J. A. Chamier. This demanded a good view and steadiness for precision bombing at night; adequate means of self-defence; easy maintenance; positive stability, with hands-off level cruising when trimmed; ability to hold a straight course and height with one engine dead; good manoeuvrability, and freedom from pilot fatigue. Two engines of any

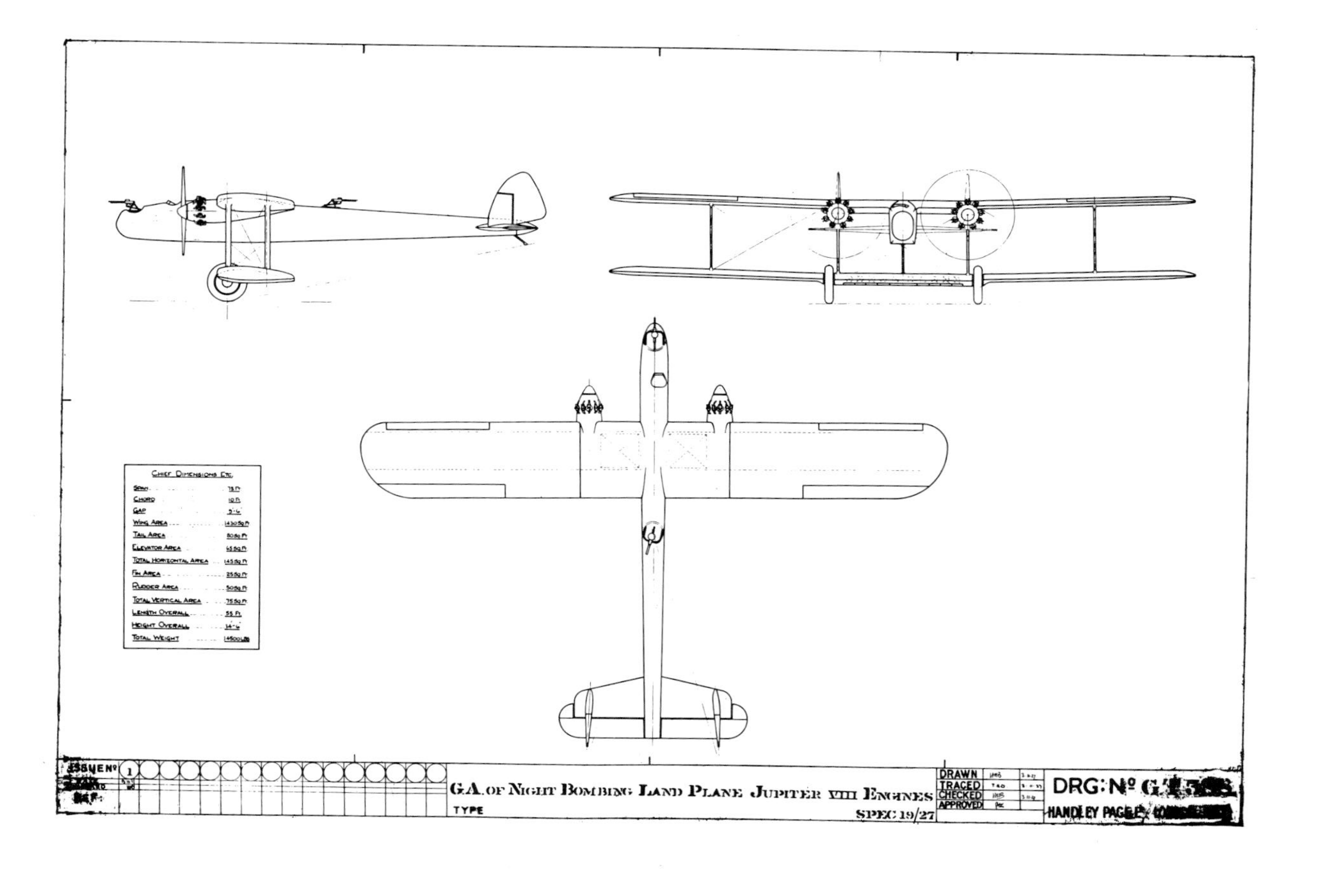
Chief Dimensions Etc.
Span 73 ft.
Chord 10 ft.
Gap 9'-6"
Wing Area 1430 sq. ft.
Tail Area 80 sq. ft.
Elevator Area 65 sq. ft.
Total Horizontal Area 145 sq. ft.
Fin Area 25 sq. ft.
Rudder Area 50 sq. ft.
Total Vertical Area 75 sq. ft.
Length Overall 55 ft.
Height Overall 14'-6"
Total Weight 14500 lbs.
Issue No 1
G.A. of Night Bombing Land Plane Jupiter VIII Engines
Type
Spec. 19/27
Drawn
Traced
Checked
Approved
DRG: No
Handley Page

approved British type were required, capable of easy removal for engine changes in the field, with swing mountings and footholds for minor repairs *in situ*; robust and non-reflective cowling and metal airscrews. Fuel tankage was required for 920 miles cruising at 115 mph at 10,000 ft after allowing for half an hour at full throttle; the main tanks could be located either in the fuselage or in the wings and preferably externally so that leaking fuel would blow clear; gravity tanks were required for half an hour at full throttle. Oil capacity was to provide the same endurance plus a reserve of 50 per cent and adequate oil cooling was required; no rubber connections were permitted in any part of the fuel system. The standard military load of 3,165 lb included a crew of four, three Lewis guns with six double drums each, wireless, P.7 camera, and a bomb load of 1,546 lb, with carriers for two 1,000-lb or four 520/550-lb, or ten 230/250-lb, or twenty 112-lb bombs, plus four 20-lb practice bombs. The maximum speed at 10,000 ft was to be better than 120 mph, landing speed less than 55 mph and service ceiling at least 17,000 ft.

Volkert, assisted by Boultbee, decided to retain the Hinaidi's overall span of 75 ft, so as to avoid any need for folding wings; they sought maximum performance through optimum aerodynamic design, particularly by avoiding any interruption of the upper wing surfaces, but this had to be achieved without sacrificing any of the military desiderata. Consequently the design tendered on 16 November, 1927, was strikingly original in layout, having the fuselage and engine nacelles closely attached under the upper wing and the undercarriage reduced to two single internally-sprung wheels inserted into the leading-edge of the lower wing. The wings were of equal span and dihedral, with only a single bay outboard of the engines, and the lower centre-section thickened to provide internal stowage for all the alternative bomb-loads; the single tailplane carried twin fins and rudders and the resulting large ground angle was expected to give a very quick take-off and short landing run, aided by automatic wing-tip slots on the upper wing. There was a choice of Napier Lions or Bristol Jupiters, but variable-pitch airscrews, though desirable and newly available, were ruled out because of the difficulty of synchronising response through their long remote control runs. Both layouts were tested in the wind tunnel, together with a third arrangement having the fuselage and Rolls-Royce F.XI engines attached to the top of the lower wing, for comparison. This layout proved inferior in drag as well as in field of fire, but showed the installational advantage of F.XI engines, so finally these were adopted in a revised high fuselage layout with wing stagger increased, which became the definitive H.P.38 in January 1928, RAF 28 wing section being chosen. A maximum speed of 154 mph at 10,000 ft with fully supercharged F.XIVS engines was estimated, but these would have needed 13 ft 6 in diameter airscrews, having only 3 inches fuselage clearance; moreover, the reliability of high-performance superchargers for long-range operation was still unproven.

Continued wind-tunnel testing overcame the initial high drag problem caused by the thickened lower centre-section, which was found to be due mainly to the leading-edge recesses which housed the internally-sprung wheels; the latter in turn had proved unduly difficult to design because of the limited travel and very narrow base available for the shock-absorbers, so normal single wheels carried in forks attached to long-travel oleo-legs

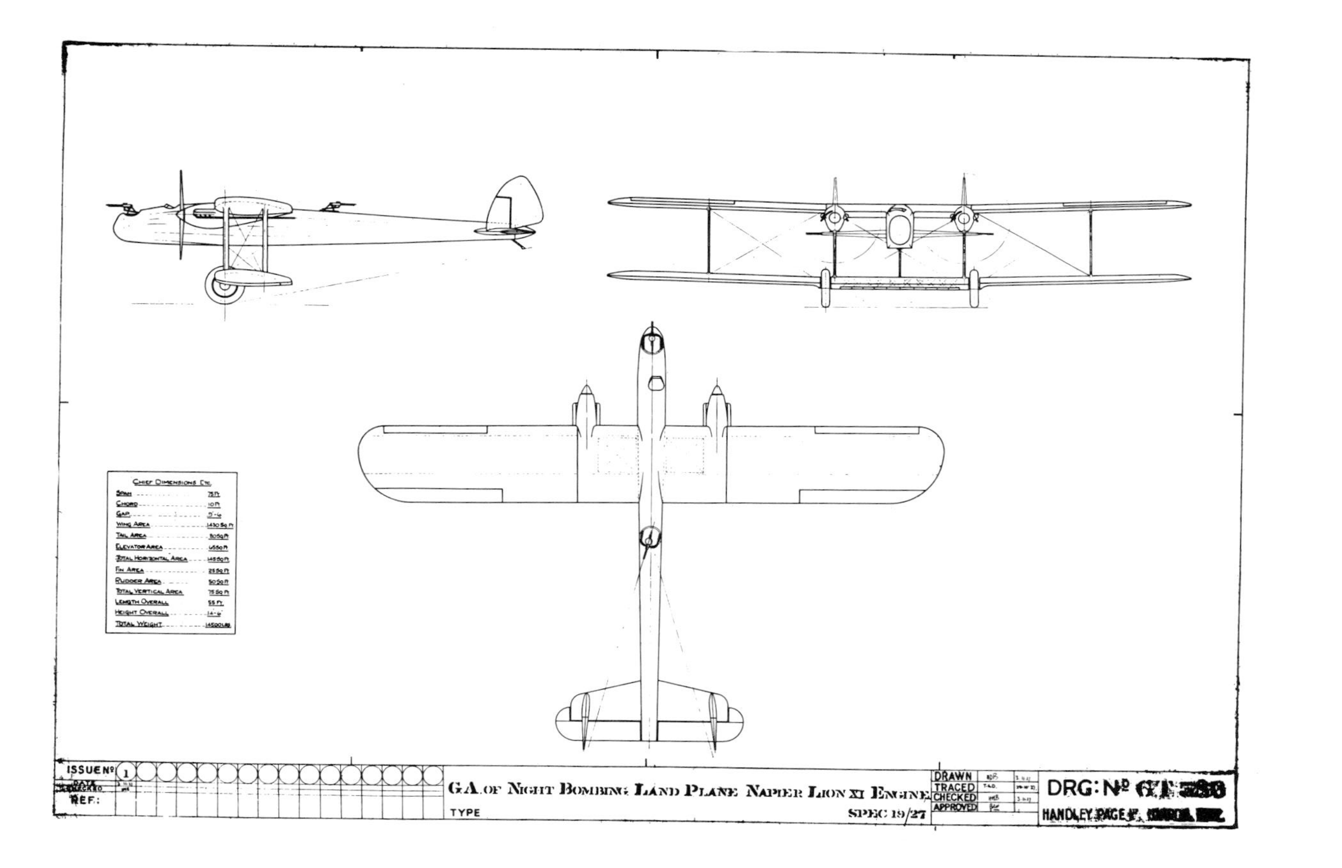
CHIEF DIMENSIONS ETC.
SPAN 75 FT.
CHORD 10 FT.
GAP 9'-6
WING AREA 1430 SQ FT.
TAIL AREA 80 SQ FT.
ELEVATOR AREA 65 SQ FT.
TOTAL HORIZONTAL AREA 145 SQ FT.
FIN AREA 25 SQ FT.
RUDDER AREA 50 SQ FT.
TOTAL VERTICAL AREA 75 SQ FT.
LENGTH OVERALL 55 FT.
HEIGHT OVERALL 14'-6"
TOTAL WEIGHT 14500 LBS.
ISSUE Nº 1
DATE
REF:
G.A. OF NIGHT BOMBING LAND PLANE NAPIER LION XI ENGINE
TYPE
SPEC 19/27
DRAWN
TRACED
CHECKED
APPROVED
DRG: Nº

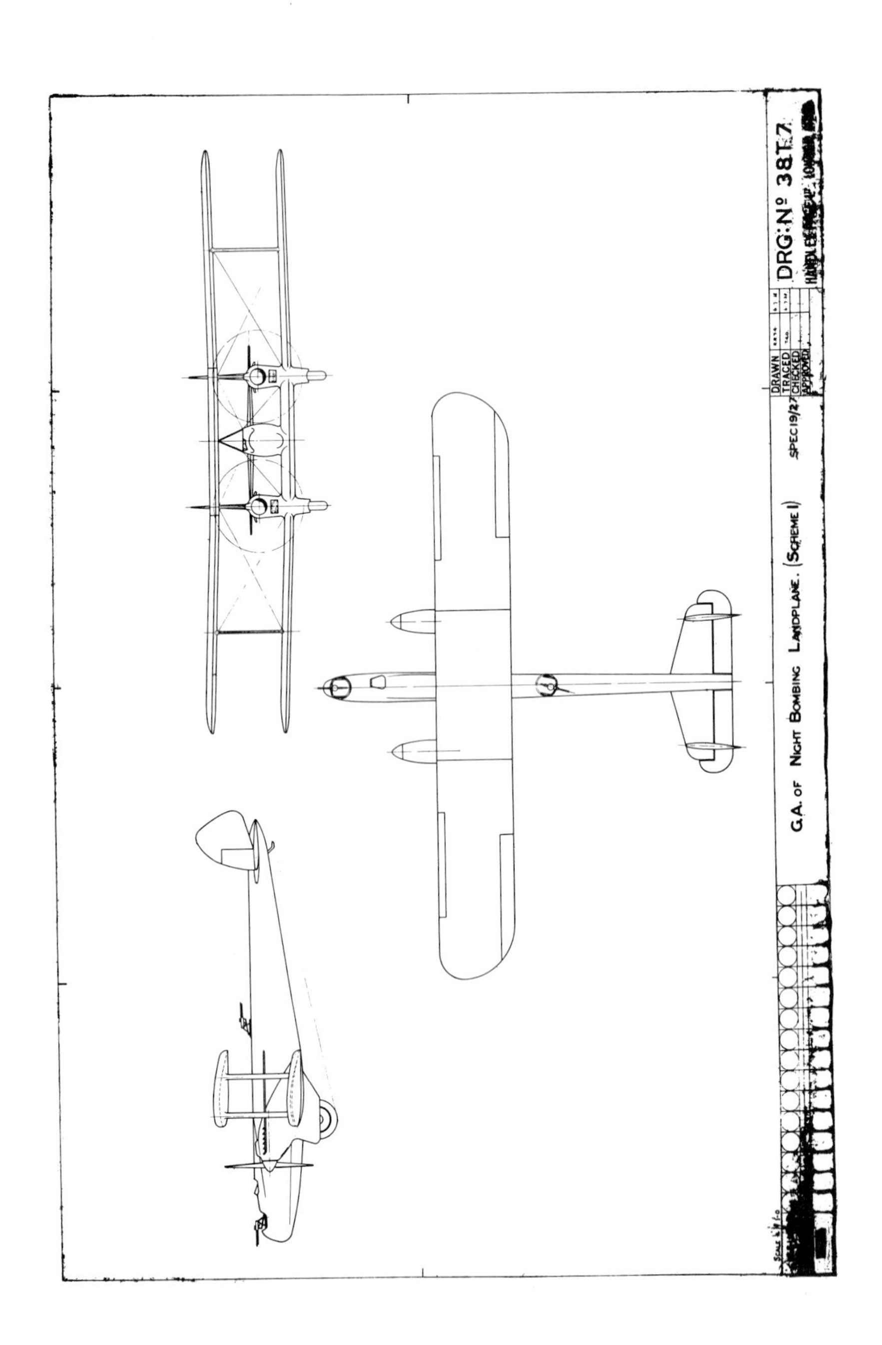

DRG: Nº 38T7
G.A. OF NIGHT BOMBING LANDPLANE. (SCHEME I)
SPEC 19/27
DRAWN
TRACED
CHECKED
APPROVED

were substituted, with fixed fairings or 'spats' blending into the leading edge. In July a full-scale mock-up was built, to enable the layout of crew stations, with instruments, equipment and armament, to be settled. Opinions on the best design of rear gunner's station were sought from Nos.10 and 99 Squadrons, who were unanimously in favour of a retractable 'dustbin' turret under the fuselage. A mock-up of this was made in less than four hours by MacRostie, who rolled up a sheet of duralumin into a tube, closed one end with a disc of wood to form a floor and suspended the other end from a Scarff ring; a working prototype was next made and, after satisfactory bench tests, was installed in the hack Hinaidi J9033 for trials by No.99 Squadron; these were not completed till March 1930, but then received a very satisfactory report. The nose and mid-upper gunners' stations were straightforward improvements on those of the Hinaidi, but employed low-drag gun-rings of smaller diameter than the standard Scarff No.7 mounting; the new Scarff No.12B ring would have been suitable but was in very short supply and eventually the Hawker 'high-speed' mounting was adopted for both stations. An oval gun-ring was also designed and made for the nose station, but when tested in Hinaidi K1063 in May 1930 it was found to be deficient in wind compensation and work on it was stopped.

With many novel features to be incorporated in its design and manufacture, the H.P.38 prototype J9130, originally ordered under contract No.790320/27 and revised by contract No.819857/28, was not completed until May 1930. The wings, tail unit and fuselage aft of the upper leading edge were conventional and derived logically from the Hinaidi II, using steel spars made by The Steel Wing Co of Gloucester, with duralumin ribs, but the forward part of the fuselage, containing the bomb-aimer's and two pilots' stations, was a duralumin monocoque shell stiffened by vertical frames internally and horizontal stringers externally. The specification had called for a gas starter for the two engines, but Volkert devised a hand-turning gear comprising a double-handled cross-shaft coupled by bevel-gearing to the lower end of a long vertical shaft plugged into the bottom of each nacelle in turn. This saved considerable weight and proved entirely efficacious. J9130 was weighed at Radlett on 15 May, 1930, and England began taxying trials a fortnight later, but found the brakes erratic and the rudder power inadequate to control excessive swing at 40 mph, so did not attempt a flight until these defects had been rectified. It fell to his assistant, Jim Cordes, to make the first two flights, both on 12 June, 1930; the first was a five-minute solo circuit and the second lasted ten minutes with W. P. Savage as observer. Cordes reported a good take-off, elevators effective but heavy, rudders light and good, and ailerons very good over a speed range of 60 to 100 mph. He noted a low-amplitude fin vibration, causing the throttles to drift back to the closed position, and found the oleo legs very stiff during taxying, with the port side harder than the starboard; there was an excellent ground cushion effect resulting in a short landing run, but the tailwheel collapsed after taxying in and turning, so no more flying could be done that day. England made his first flight in J9130 on 25 June and confirmed that its general handling was 'devoid of vice' and 'possessing all the essential features required by a night bomber'. He considered it much easier to fly than the Hinaidi and Hyderabad, but criticised the layout of the instruments and arrangement of the cockpit. Further flights on the next two days showed a rapid rise in water temperature during sustained climbs and he requested new radiators of larger area. These were ready by 15 July, together with revised rudders and extra stiffeners in the monocoque nose, and were approved by Cordes in a test flight that day. Meanwhile, on 7 July, Radlett aerodrome had been ceremonially opened by Prince George, who flew in from Northolt to join the distinguished invited guests, among them Lord Trenchard; they were permitted to see the H.P.38 taxying, but it did not fly and was in fact still very much on the Secret List. On 25 July England flew with Syd Ebel as observer, who considered that the 24-gauge duralumin skin of the monocoque should be thickened to prevent panting and resonance at low speed and also noticed tailwheel shimmy after hitting a bump while taxying at 30 mph.

By this time Handley Page was desperate to get the H.P.38 cleared to go to Martlesham Heath, where its chief rival, the Vickers Type 150, had gained a substantial time-lead and had appeared in the New Types Park at the RAF Display in June 1930. With 1 September as the latest date of arrival for participation in the B.19/27 competition, the cockpit mock-up was inspected and reported on by Sqn Ldr Mansell in August; he recommended alterations impossible to incorporate in time, but providentially the Vickers prototype crashed with a double engine failure and the competition was postponed till the following February, which gave the H.P.38 a second chance. Sqn Ldr Mansell's criticisms were investigated personally by Handley Page, who decided to increase the crew's working space

(a) in the 'dust-bin' turret by making more room for the seated gunner's knees and larger openings for his toes;
(b) by altering the front gunner's coaming to give him more headroom when seated;
(c) by widening the fuselage monocoque by five inches alongside the pilot, using bowed stiffeners instead of nearly straight ones;
(d) by reducing the first pilot's rudder travel so as to give him more leg-room and by staggering the second pilot's seat to give him enough leg-room without increasing the overall length of the cockpit.

Meanwhile the Rolls-Royce F.XIV engines still overheated on the ground and overcooled at altitude, so Handley Page sought the advice of Sydney Camm, who had had some success with steam cooling in an experimental Hawker Hart; this posed difficulties in the H.P.38, since it was impossible to locate the condenser in its ideal position above the engine, but as an interim measure new brass header tanks were installed which were equally suitable for steam- or conventional water-cooling. The Vickers 150's repairs were not completed till May 1931, but in November 1930 another B.19/27 competitor took the air—the Fairey monoplane K1695—which was the only other tender to have won a prototype contract; this too crashed early in 1931 and had to be extensively rebuilt, so once again the H.P.38 was reprieved and a final conference was held at Radlett on 24 February to clear up outstanding design questions, so as to enable contractor's trials to be completed as soon as possible.

With the take-off weight increased from 12,000 lb to 14,760 lb in October, Cordes had found the rudder power insufficient to hold a straight course with one engine dead. By February the estimated all-up weight had

H.P.38 J9130 flown by J. L. Cordes for the benefit of John Yoxall at Radlett in July 1931, with Light Series bomb racks in original position. (*Flight*)

risen to 15,270 lb, and overtime was being worked at Radlett to incorporate a spate of design improvements, notably the widened fuselage monocoque, a 25 per cent increase in rudder area (with a corresponding reduction in lower fin area), improved control runs and additional equipment including a portable engine inspection ladder stowed in the fuselage. Cordes reported a considerable improvement in cockpit comfort and ease of handling in the first flight after modification on 11 May, 1931, but next day England flew it and considered the rudder to be too heavy at speeds below 80 mph and the elevators too sluggish. All bearings in the rudder controls were eased and slack in the elevator control run was taken up; Cordes was pleased with the result on 18 May, being able to sideslip, also to hold a straight course on one engine and even turn against the dead engine; England confirmed his report next day, but suffered brake failure while landing and taxying in; so the Palmer hydraulic brakes were condemned and exchanged for a pneumatic system. Next the rudders were lightened by adding a two-inch nosing to the horn balance; the 'dust-bin' was operated up and down without any adverse effect on stability, but still the brakes were 'hopeless' even after overhaul by Palmers. On 2 June Cordes flew for the first time at over 15,000 lb and on the 10th reported better results with brake-valve pressures increased to 30 lb/sq in, also an improvement in rudder control with both fins offset $2\frac{1}{2}$ degrees to port. Next, the elevators and rudders were rebuilt and covered with new fabric, new wheel fairings were fitted and the control column was stiffened to overcome undue flexibility in pulling out from a dive. On 3 and 17 July Cordes completed partial climbs to 15,000 ft in $2\frac{1}{4}$ hours flying and on 1 August, with R. S. Stafford as observer, made three accelerate/stop runs into wind, which resulted in the starboard brake seizing solid. New brake assemblies were fitted, but on the 7th the brakes seized again after three accelerate/stop tests and the blocks were found to have melted and fused with the drums. Finally the trouble was cured by fitting Dunlop wheels and all seemed ready for J9130 to go to Martlesham, but then the Air Ministry declared the ground clearance for practice bombs on the Light Series external racks to be inadequate for the rough surface at Martlesham and insisted on urgent modification before dispatch. While this was being done, the airscrews were changed, but the new ones seemed to vibrate badly and on 9 September Cordes was unable to take off at 15,025 lb, although he was successful next day at 12,280 lb. A new tail incidence gear was fitted, lateral trim was corrected by drooping the starboard ailerons and reflexing the port, and all the sparking plugs in both engines were cleaned; this cured the vibration completely and on the 21st Cordes had no problem in taking off at 15,500 lb. On 1 October Cordes climbed to 5,000 ft, flew hands-off at all speeds between 70 and 120 mph and found no swing due to full brake application in three landing runs, so at last J9130 was cleared for Martlesham, where it had arrived and been weighed three weeks later.

The A & AEE's first criticisms, received on 10 November, were that the pilots' seats were too low and the rudder pedals too far away, with slow rate of adjustment and brake pedals unevenly placed; long exhaust pipes to prevent dazzle at night were also requested. The flying trials were completed by 1 February, 1932, followed by armament and radio trials and finally a week's maintenance trials by No.15 Squadron. On 16 February Handley Page received an anonymous but well-informed letter telling him that J9130 was the most popular of the B.19/27 competitors, with better crew comfort than its rivals; although the fuselage was narrow it was uncluttered and gave easy access fore and aft so that the pilots could change places easily. The wireless operator's seat, the 'dust-bin' turret, freedom from draughts, easy refuelling and bomb-loading were all favourably commented upon. The flying controls were considered good except the rudder control at maximum speed, when it became heavy and ineffective. In performance J9130 was equal to the best of the other competitors, though rather too stable longitudinally and directionally. The writer also commented that with the Vickers 150 being modified yet again at Weybridge, the Fairey monoplane suffering from serious tail buffeting, the Boulton & Paul P.32 and D.H.72 (both B.22/27 not B.19/27) not serious rivals, and the four-engined Vickers 163 only just arrived, 'Handley Page have every cause to feel optimistic.' The H.P.38 was flown back to Radlett from Martlesham on 17 March, 1932, and was immediately tested by England to reveal any change arising from the maintenance trials; these had been generally satisfactory apart from the excessive time needed to remove and refit a rudder or radiator. At the end of March J9130 was loaned to No.10 Squadron at Boscombe Down and in one week was flown for five hours each by five different pilots, all of whom were unanimous in their approval. Their only criticisms concerned the bomb aimer's and navigator's stations and the lack of space with dual controls fitted; they also asked for large side windows in the monocoque at the bomb aimer's station. A redesigned monocoque incorporating all available Service recommendations was authorised on 11 April and on the same day the official trials report (A & AEE M/597) was received at Cricklewood, confirming the opinions already communicated by the anonymous correspondent. England visited No.10 Squadron a few days later for further criticisms, the most serious of which was the unhappy plight of the armourer in wet grass, who got soaked to the skin while loading 20-lb practice bombs on to the Light Series racks. It had already become necessary to install external racks outboard to carry old-type 112-lb bombs, whose fins were too large for the centre-section bomb cells, as no new-type 112-lb bombs were available for trials at Catfoss, whither the H.P.38 was flown from Boscombe Down at the end of April.

With a production order at last in prospect, all components were carefully surveyed from the manufacturing and jigging aspect; at the same time possible drag reductions were investigated, but it seemed that even fully retractable wheels and vertical radiators down the front of the oleo-legs would gain only 4 mph at maximum speed and increase service ceiling by only 1,000 ft, so were not worth the cost. The production redesign affected not only the monocoque but also the tailplane, rudders, undercarriage fairings and particularly the engine nacelles, which had completely revised radiator installations and more robust duralumin fuel tanks rivetted by the de Bergue process to replace the unduly fragile welded aluminium tanks of the prototype. The revision was supervised by C. D. Holland and allotted the new project number H.P.50. A further refinement, comprising a streamlined cabin filling the gap between the fuselage and lower centreplane and accommodating both the bomb-aimer and under-turret, was tested in the wind-tunnel in May, but not taken further; a suggested change to Pegasus M.3 engines improved take-off but cost some loss of performance and ceiling above 7,000 ft, so this was turned down. The prototype's popularity with Nos.9 and 10 Squadrons at Catfoss nearly proved its undoing, for one pilot landed with only one brake applied and achieved 2½ groundloops, while another flew on for over an hour after the front gun deflector-bag had split open, allowing all the empty rounds to fall into the starboard airscrew and smash it; the pilot was unaware of this until after he had landed. Nevertheless the prototype survived these hazards to go on to No.99 Squadron at Upper Heyford at the end of May and was due to appear in the New Types Park at the RAF Display a month later; then, on 10 June, while being demonstrated to AVM Sir Geoffrey Salmond and Grp Capt Gossage at Upper Heyford, the starboard outer end of the lower centre-section front spar suddenly failed from metal fatigue, causing the starboard undercarriage to collapse; even this damage was repaired on site and J9130 arrived at Hendon on 27 June in time to take its place in the

J9130 in the RAF Display at Hendon on 27 June, 1932, showing temporary hand-made wheel spats and long exhaust pipes. (*Real Photographs*)

parade, albeit with temporary hand-made wheel-spats.

The official H.P.50 mock-up conference had just previously been held and a production order seemed imminent. Then the League of Nations at Geneva raised the question of the abolition of bombing and the Air Ministry had to hold contract action in abeyance, while Handley Page faced the prospect of laying off all his skilled hands, who had worked so hard to win the order on which their future depended. Within weeks the situation was just as unpredictably reversed: Japan invaded Manchuria, the Geneva Disarmament Conference failed to agree on bombing ethics and the Air Ministry gave 'Instructions to Proceed' with five H.P.50s, for which the revised specification B.23/32 was issued. Although formal contract action could not be taken for some months, J9130, the long-suffering single prototype, had barely won the H.P.50's place in the RAF inventory before retiring in clouds of glory, for on leaving Hendon it had gone for further armament trials with No.10 Squadron to North Coates Fitties, where on 8 July it crashed into the boundary sea wall and was destroyed by fire, fortunately without any casualties. When the production contract (25498/33) was received in March 1933 it covered not five, but fifteen, H.P.50s, K3489–K3503, and allotted the type name Heyford Mk. I, with fully supercharged Rolls-Royce Kestrel IIIS engines rated at 575 hp at 11,500 ft.

The first production Heyford K3489 was assembled by hand ahead of the remainder, to serve as a prototype after the loss of J9130; although it was

First production Heyford I K3489, showing bomb cells in lower centre-section. (*The Aeroplane*)

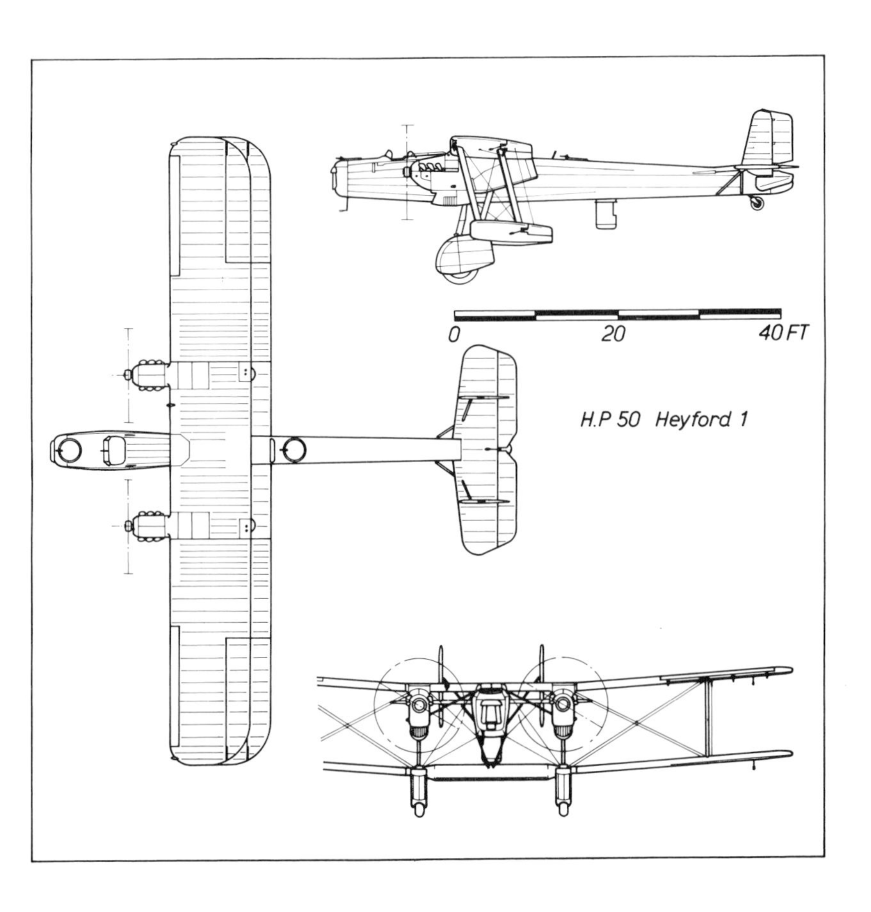

structurally a production machine, with revised oleo-legs and nacelles, it had straight exhaust tail-pipes and a few similar features which were to be changed as a result of preliminary flight tests. It incorporated improved fuel system controls, with filling points at ground level for refuelling and for replenishing oil tanks, a new bomb-loading gear with a portable winch applied to the upper surface of the lower centre-section for loading ready-fused bombs on their racks into the bomb cells. These facilities enabled ground crews to turn each bomber round ready for action within half an hour after landing from the previous sortie and justified the Heyford's claim to be called an 'express night bomber'. Final preparation went on by day and night at Radlett throughout April and May and, after last-minute delays, the first flight was made on 21 June, 1933, by Cordes; although not flown in the RAF Display at Hendon as had been hoped, it was allowed to appear at the SBAC Trade Show there on the Monday after the Display, before going to Martlesham Heath in August. Some production drawings were still awaited in the shops on 3 August, when a final mock-up conference was held; it was decided then to adopt perforated 'ram's horn' exhaust manifolds, in spite of their increased weight and drag, in the hope of achieving a lower noise level than with plain tail-pipes. Official trials at Martlesham showed that five gallons of fuel in each tank were unusable and undrainable, also that airscrew noise in the pilots' cockpit was high; so the tanks (forming the nacelle tails) were deepened and four-bladers were proposed instead of two-bladers. The second and subsequent Heyfords were all allotted to Upper Heyford to replace No.99 Squadron's Hinaidis, deliveries beginning on 14 November, 1933. On 9 December a second contract, 272083/33, was awarded for twenty-three more Heyfords, primarily to re-equip No.10 Squadron, also at Upper Heyford; these, K4021–4043, incorporated various drag and weight savings and had Kestrel IIIS-5 engines with engine-driven electric generators, so that the earlier wind-driven generators could be eliminated; they were equipped, some retrospectively, with two-piece four-blade airscrews of reduced diameter and tip speed, and were distinguished as Heyford Mk. IA; many of the first fifteen Heyford Is were later modified to the same standard. Weight saved in the wing structure by replacing steel parts with duralumin

K3490, the second Heyford I, under feint attack from a Hawker Fury during training at Upper Heyford in 1935. (*M.O.D.—Crown Copyright*)

was partly absorbed by the necessity of changing the monocoque stringers from duralumin to steel to reduce bomb-sight vibration and skin panting, and to improve crash protection for the crew.

The final Heyford of the first batch, K3503, was retained at Radlett in March 1934 as a trials aircraft for various features aimed at increasing the maximum speed to 160 mph. These included a better nacelle/wing junction, a much-improved front gun position and more powerful engines, the available choice being Rolls-Royce Kestrel VI, Bristol Pegasus III or Armstrong Siddeley Tiger, all of 700 hp. Volkert favoured the Pegasus and K3503 was set aside to await its availability, at the same time being fitted with an enclosed pilots' cockpit, a lowered forward decking and a raised coaming forward of the mid-upper gunner's cockpit. Meanwhile K3489

Heyford IA K4033 of No.10 Squadron. (*I.W.M.—Crown Copyright*)

was tested at Martlesham with vee-fronted radiator shutters, which substantially reduced drag. The choice of engines for the Heyford Mk.II remained undecided for several months. In March 1934 the Kestrel VI passed its type test, but Volkert and England hoped to take advantage of the still higher bomb-load, ceiling and range offered by the Pegasus IV, which Roy Fedden was currently testing. In October 1934 they obtained reluctant Air Ministry agreement for full Pegasus installation drawings to be put in hand, to be finished by the end of the year. Meanwhile K3503 had been flown in June with Kestrel VIs and had appeared as No.14 in the

Heyford I K3500 of No.99 Squadron with 'dust-bin' turret extended.

parade of new types at the RAF Display at Hendon; in this trial installation, not truly representative of Heyford II, the vee-fronted radiators were set back behind the oleo-legs and the engine bearers were raised 18 inches to fair the nacelles more cleanly into the leading edge; unfortunately the radiators boiled during taxying and climb after take-off, but overcooled and froze during descent from 11,000 ft. This could have been cured by redesigning the cooling system to operate evaporatively, as Rolls-Royce recommended, using condensers in the adjacent wing leading edges, had the engines been at their original height. In January 1935 K3503 was ready for conversion to Pegasus, but none were yet available, so it was decided to convert K4029 to Kestrel VI as the definitive Heyford Mk.II, of which sixteen, K4863–K4878, had just been ordered to specification B.28/34 under contract No.352860/34.

Handley Page was anxious to improve the Heyford in every possible way, because the Fairey B.19/27 monoplane, though much delayed, had reappeared in production form as the Fairey Hendon and now offered much better crew protection as well as improved performance. With the Locarno conference on the verge of disintegration and German rearmament daily more evident, a substantial expansion of the RAF was a certainty. So K4029 was fitted with an enclosed pilots' cockpit and rear gunner's coaming, similar to K3503's; it retained the original nacelles and bearers, with vee-fronted shutters replacing the original radiator scoop intakes; it had four-blade airscrews and straight exhaust tail-pipes on the inboard sides to reduce cockpit noise. In May 1935 RAF test pilots visited Radlett to try out K4029 and soon afterwards it was flown to Martlesham for full Service trials; meanwhile, as no Pegasus engines had been allocated, K3503 was refitted with Kestrel VIs, but in standard nacelles with forward radiators as in K4029. As Martlesham pilots had complained of the extreme exposure of the front gunner, particularly with the bomb-sight window open (as it had to be in order to navigate by drift sight), an attempt was made to find a means of enclosing the nose cockpit; two possible nose turrets were considered, one designed by H. J. Stieger of General Aircraft Ltd, and the other by Bert Hubbard at Cricklewood, which Trojan Ltd of

Heyford II prototype K4029 at Martlesham Heath in May 1935; the pilot's enclosure and rear gunner's raised decking were not adopted in production aircraft. (*I.W.M.—Crown Copyright*)

Heyford III K5188. (*I.W.M.—Crown Copyright*)

Croydon were to manufacture. Meanwhile, to assist navigation, side windows were provided at the bomb-aimer's station, although these were often skinned over in squadron service.

It had been necessary to derate the Kestrel VIs to the same maximum power as the Kestrel IIs because of overheating and vibration in current production Heyford IIs, but new production machines were to have wing condensers for fully-rated steam-cooled Kestrel VIs, together with rubber-bushed engine bearers. This improved standard, represented by K3503 in its final state, but without the cockpit enclosure, was defined by specification B.27/35 as Heyford Mk.III, of which twenty, K5180–K5199, were ordered by contract No.389375/35 in July 1935; the contract was later extended to include an additional fifty, K6857–K6906, before the Heyford production line gave way to a new generation of monoplanes and came to an end in July 1936. Neither the Stieger nor the Hubbard front gun turrets achieved production status for the Heyford, but development continued on K3503 in support of turret installations for later types of aircraft. In June 1935 K3489 had been severely overloaded at Martlesham when it barely survived an uncontrolled high-speed dive in a snow-storm; it was brought back to Radlett for overhaul and repair and the Air Ministry agreed that a Stieger nose turret could be installed in it before it returned to Martlesham, so that K3503 could be used concurrently for the Hubbard trial installation, which was eventually to incorporate a Frazer-Nash hydraulic control instead of Trojan's own design; the F-N gear required an engine-driven hydraulic pump, which Rolls-Royce were developing. The Stieger turret in K3489 was completed and approved at Radlett in February 1936 and went for test at Martlesham in May, but Trojan Ltd had still not delivered a trial turret for K3503 by that date and in July their contract was cancelled in favour of a new Frazer-Nash design. Later it was reinstated for a single experimental turret which Trojan had nearly completed and K3503 finally went to Martlesham with this installed on 21 June, 1937, but its trials were disappointing and K3503 was restored to Mk.III standard, together with K4029 similarly reworked, for issue to No.166 Squadron.

A total of eleven RAF squadrons flew Heyfords as front-line bombers between 1933 and 1939. As already stated, Nos.10 and 99 were the first to receive them in November 1933; in April 1935 No.7 Squadron changed to them from Virginias and No.9 did likewise in March 1936. Under the RAF expansion scheme the 'B' Flights of Nos. 99 and 10 Squadrons had respectively become two new squadrons, Nos.38 and 97, both formed on 16 September, 1935, while 'B' Flight of No.7 Squadron became the nucleus of No.102 Squadron a fortnight later. No.10 gave birth a second time, to No.78 Squadron in November 1936 and so did No.99, to No.149 in April 1937; finally No.99 re-equipped with Wellingtons in November 1938 and transferred all its Heyfords to No.148 Squadron, which kept them till the following March when their own Wellingtons arrived; No.99's 'A' Flight became No.166 Squadron in November 1936, and Heyfords were re-issued as operational trainers to Nos.3 and 4 Bombing and Gunnery Schools (Aldergrove and West Freugh) from May 1939 to mid-1940, when the last few, including K6906, were struck off charge.

Heyfords were well-liked in service, being easy to maintain, sturdy and agile; they were regularly flown across country in squadron formation and one of No.102 Squadron's Heyfords was looped with ease at the 1935 RAF Display at Hendon; although brought to readiness with full bomb-loads and armament at the time of the Munich crisis, they carried live bombs only over the ranges at Aldergrove, Catfoss and North Coates Fitties and never had to fire a round in anger, since they never went overseas, where the RAF's war went on even in peacetime. But they faced hazards hitherto encountered only by fighters, the worst of which was dense icing fog, such as that over the Pennines which assailed seven Heyfords of No.102 Squadron on 12 December, 1936, while returning in formation from Aldergrove to their base at Finningley. The leader, Sqn Ldr Attwood in K4868, successfully forced-landed at Disley near Manchester and flew on to base next day, though K6898 hit a telegraph pole nearby. Flying Officer Gyll-Murray put down K5188 near York and also flew home next day, but Sgt Otter in K6900 crashed on a hill-top near Hebden Bridge and was seriously injured, his other three crew being killed; while Flt Lieut Villiers and his crew had to bale out of K4874 near Oldham when it became uncontrollable from ice accretion. Sgt Williams wrecked K4864 in landing near Gainsborough and only Sgt Biddulph and his crew reached Finningley without incident.

This disaster drew attention to the icing hazard and in 1939 K5184, which had been retained at Farnborough for flight-refuelling experiments by the Atcherley system, was fitted with prototype TKS liquid-deicing leading-edge mats and flown by Flt Lieut A. E. Clouston, who preferred inflatable deicing shoes of the Goodrich type; K5184 was also lent to Sir Alan Cobham's company, Flight Refuelling Ltd at Ford, Sussex, after he had taken over the Atcherley patents; K5184 was later used to test the RAE's 'frictionless take-off' catapult trolley and track, being successfully launched at a weight of 12,000 lb on 22 August, 1940. On 26 February, 1935, Dr Robert Watson-Watt used K6902 from the RAE to demonstrate, in conjunction with the BBC's Daventry transmitter, a primitive radar receiver; the experiment was repeated successfully in December 1936 and a few months later he air-tested the first airborne radar transmitter, with which echoes were detected from the coastline near Harwich; this equipment was designed at the Telecommunications Research Establishment at Bawdsey by Dr E. G. Bowen and his colleagues, and marked the origin of ASV and AI radar techniques.

The Heyford was the last heavy bomber biplane to serve with the Royal Air Force. Early in 1940 at least seven yellow-painted Heyfords (K4027, 4030, 5193, 5197, 6866, 6868 and 6869) were still in use as bombing trainers, and the last two, believed to be K4029 and K5184, remained in use till April 1941 as tugs for the first secret experiments with Hotspur I assault gliders; one Heyford, probably K5184, was stored at Cardington, where it was still apparently airworthy and under armed guard in August 1944, having contributed its modest quota to the success of D-Day. Heyfords were best known to the general public for their immaculate formation flying at the RAF Displays at Hendon in 1934 and 1936, and as leaders of the massed bomber formations at the Royal Review in July 1935, when King George V inspected them at Mildenhall and took the salute at the subsequent flypast at Duxford. In 1937 they were seen and admired at Mildenhall by a German air mission led by General Milch, but his suggestion that a dozen Heyfords should be released to the Spanish government was wisely ignored by his Air Ministry hosts.

B.19/27 (early schemes)

(Two Bristol Jupiter VIII or Napier Lion XIA)

Span 75 ft (22·9 m); length 55 ft (16·79 m); wing area 1,430 sq ft (132·8 m^2). Maximum weight 14,500 lb (6,570 kg). Crew three or four.

H.P.38

(Two Rolls-Royce Kestrel III)

Span 75 ft (22·9 m); length 58 ft (17·7 m); wing area 1,470 sq ft (136·5 m^2). Empty weight 9,000 lb (4,080 kg); maximum weight 15,500 lb (7,030 kg). Bomb load 1,660 lb (745 kg). Maximum speed 140 mph (225 km/h); minimum speed 55 mph (88 km/h); range 920 miles (1,480 km); ceiling 17,000 ft (5,260 m). Crew four.

H.P.50 Heyford I

(Two Rolls-Royce Kestrel III)

Dimensions as H.P.38. Empty weight 9,200 lb (4,170 kg); maximum weight 16,750 lb (7,600 kg). Speed 138 mph (222 km/h); ceiling 21,000 ft (6,500 m).

H.P.50 Heyford IA

(Two Rolls-Royce Kestrel IIIS-5)

As Heyford I except: Maximum weight 16,900 lb (7,660 kg). Speed 142 mph (228 km/h). Bomb load 2,000 lb (907 kg).

H.P.50 Heyford II and III

(Two Rolls-Royce Kestrel VI)

As Heyford I except: Empty weight 10,200 lb (4,660 kg); maximum weight 17,000 lb (7,710 kg). Bomb load (normal) 2,660 lb (1,200 kg), (maximum) 3,500 lb (1,590 kg). Speed 154 mph (248 km/h).

H.P.42, 43 and 45

After delivering the four W.10s to Imperial Airways in March 1926, Handley Page had to wait two years for a new opportunity to compete in the field of civil aviation. The company's hopes of supplying a fleet of three-engined Middle East transports had been frustrated by Imperial Airways' preference for the Armstrong Whitworth Argosy and when that type was restricted to European routes, the contract for its replacement was won by de Havilland with the D.H.66 Hercules. Although neither of these was wholly of metal construction, both employed steel and duralumin for much of the primary structure, and Imperial Airways' rejection of the Hampstead had arisen because the makers could not guarantee prompt delivery of five more W.9s with all-metal fuselages at the specified price of £10,000 each; this compared unfavourably with £8,500 each paid for the much simpler and cheaper W.10s. In December 1926, Volkert, Boultbee, Holland, Ebel, Lewin and MacRostie all visited the Paris Salon de l'Aéronautique to acquaint themselves with the latest trends in foreign aviation technology and gleaned many new ideas, including the novel four-engined arrangement pioneered by Louis Blériot for large bombers and transports and the use by Wibault and Latécoère of corrugated duralumin for monocoque construction. These bore fruit when, in the spring of 1928, Imperial Airways invited tenders from the whole industry for a new fleet of large airliners intended to succeed the Argosy and Hercules on the Empire air-mail route to India.

Tenders were invited for four separate requirements:

(a) a three-engined aircraft for service in Europe;
(b) a three-engined aircraft for service in the East;
(c) a four-engined aircraft for service in Europe; and
(d) a four-engined aircraft for service in the East.

In each case quotations were desired for batches of three, four, five or six aircraft and the accompanying *Outline for the guidance of manufacturers* stated that the latter were to have 'the greatest possible freedom for the expression of their own ideas, while requiring the greatest safety, highest possible paying load capacity and lowest cost of operation'. The entire responsibility for the performance of the complete aircraft was to be borne by the aircraft manufacturers whether or not they were the manufacturers of the engine used. The specification assumed geared engines of about 400 hp and, while water cooling was not excluded, air cooling was strongly preferred. Imperial Airways would supply as free issues all the engines with their starting gear as delivered by the engine makers, also all electrical and wireless equipment except bonding; but tenders were to include the cost of installing the free issues. The average weight assumed for each passenger without baggage was to be 165 lb. A complete inventory of instruments, cabin fittings, furniture and equipment, also two complete sets of working drawing prints, were to accompany each tender and delivery at Croydon was to be shown as a separate item. Each aircraft was to comply with current Air Ministry requirements for a British Certificate of Airworthiness and was to be delivered with its C of A already granted. Three attached schedules listed respectively:

(a) the weights of Imperial Airways' standard electric lighting and wireless equipment;
(b) the weights and quantities required of navigational and engine instruments; and
(c) the performance tests required.

Imperial Airways would make progress payments, subject to one-third of the price of each aircraft being withheld until final acceptance. Both the European (Western) and Eastern types were to have a stalling speed not greater than 52 mph, to be capable of being trimmed to fly hands- and feet-off either with all engines on or with any one engine out. With one engine out, the Eastern type was to maintain a height of 6,000 ft in ISA conditions with full load and without exceeding the rated horsepower or normal rpm and to have tankage for a cruising range in still air of 500 miles; for the Western type the same conditions were to be met at a height of 3,000 ft for a still-air range of 300 miles; full controllability at low speeds was essential, using auto-slots if desired. Delivery dates for the Eastern type were to run from September 1930 to 1 January, 1931, and for the Western type from December 1930 to 31 March, 1931. Finally, a guaranteed minimum fuel consumption was to be expressed as 'gallons per 1,000-lb of payload-plus-crew per 100 miles at 95 mph' and the payload including crew was to be quoted for a distance of 300 miles at the above speed and consumption. A bonus would be paid for performance improvements actually achieved compared with the figures tendered and for early delivery, but corresponding penalties would be exacted for short-fall in performance and for late delivery. After careful examination, Handley Page Ltd tendered for batches of three, four or six of each of the four requirements and were gratified to receive acceptances for four Eastern and four Western aircraft, each with four engines, at prices of £22,200 and £23,000 respectively without engines.

Since the specifications had been compiled by H. G. Brackley and George Woods Humphery, now working together in Imperial Airways as they had formerly done in Handley Page Transport, it was predictable that the four-engined requirement would bear some resemblance to an improved all-metal version of the V/1500, which in its day had been an optimum load-carrier over the same range at much the same speed. So Volkert, assisted by Boultbee in the early layout stages, took the V/1500 as his starting point, chose a high-lift aerofoil section (RAF 28), arranged the four engines as a Blériot-type cluster of co-planar tractors pitched as close together as airscrew tip clearance would permit, and adopted the all-strut Warren-girder wing bracing already proved practical in the Hare as a means of reducing the cost of rigging maintenance, which had proved prohibitive in the copiously wire-braced V/1500. This in turn dictated a sesquiplane layout with a flat upper wing of slightly greater span than the V/1500's and a lower wing of reduced span and chord, with 4 degrees dihedral outboard of the engines. The fuselage was to be a duralumin monocoque for two-thirds of its length, the remaining tail portion being a fabric-covered wire-braced welded steel tube girder; it was hoped that a

Interior of H.P.42 airliner.

two-wheeled landing gear would be feasible, although four wheels could be provided if necessary. The fuselage was of good streamline form and wind-tunnel tests confirmed that a negligible drag penalty would be incurred if it were made slightly 'sagging' in side elevation, so as to increase the ground angle and bring the main passenger entrance door as low as possible, making tall entrance steps unnecessary; this feature later gave the aeroplane the nickname 'Flying Banana'. The crew were to occupy an enclosed cockpit with unobstructed forward view in the extreme nose and the passengers were to have two large and luxuriously appointed saloons in the best Pullman-car tradition, well ventilated, warmed and sound-insulated, with the galley, toilets and baggage compartment located in the vestibule between the saloons which lay in the plane of the airscrews and was therefore too noisy for continuous occupation by passengers. The ultimate refinement in this inspired layout was the pronounced anhedral angle of the lower centre-sections inboard of the lower engines, which allowed the root junction with the fuselage to be made above the saloon ceiling trim and gave all the passengers an uninterrupted view of the passing scene without making the undercarriage taller than necessary. This geometry had been the subject of Oswald Short's patent No.190576 in October 1921, but he had neither exploited it then nor paid a renewal fee in 1927, so it had lapsed and Volkert was free to use it; the same arrangement was employed by Hessell Tiltman in the Airspeed Ferry and H. P. Folland in the Gloster T.C.33.

A conference held at Cricklewood on 26 January, 1929, (after Boultbee had left the firm) reviewed all the proposed design features and laid down the basic experimental and manufacturing programmes. The choice of monoplane or biplane tail was to be decided by wind-tunnel results and a cabin ventilation model was also to be tested in the wind-tunnel. The possibility of a free-wheel airscrew drive to save the drag of a wind-milling dead engine was to be investigated; this was found to give no advantage with four engines, though possibly worthwhile with three or two. The engine mountings and nacelles were to allow the choice of either Bristol Jupiter or Armstrong Siddeley Jaguar engines, since four Jaguars were 300-lb lighter than four Jupiters. The pilots' control wheels were to be as large as possible (as on the V/1500) and Volkert preferred the W.8 symmetrical aileron nose shape to the Frise balance, which was inclined to snatch on both the Argosy and H.P.38. A full-size cabin mock-up was being made for working out details of the interior layout and furnishings and this was to be finished to exhibition standard for the Olympia Aero Show in July. On the structural side, the choice of steel or duralumin wing spars had to be made and the depth of the central longitudinal keel below the fuselage floor was thought to be excessive, unless the space each side of it could be used for payload. The airframe structure drawings were to be complete for issue to the shops by the end of September and particular attention was to be paid to the limiting dimensions for handling during manufacture at Cricklewood and transport thence to Radlett; for instance, the chord of the upper wing (15 ft 6 in) was marginal for handling in and out of the dope shop. A mock-up wing was made to decide the size of the largest sections that could be transported by road from Cricklewood to Radlett; when the 50-ft fuselage monocoque first made this journey on a special trailer towed by a Morris van, it became stuck at the Brockley roundabout and several trees had to have branches lopped to get it clear; thereafter the police insisted on having prior notice of oversize loads, which had to be escorted by outriders.

By April, stability calculations showed that an increase in overall dihedral was necessary to counteract the effect of the inboard anhedral of the lower wing, so the upper wing was given 2½ degrees and the lower 4½ degrees. The overall incidence was 5 degrees, with the upper engine thrust-lines at plus 3 degrees and the lower parallel to datum. The resultant raising of the wing-tips increased the overall height in the tail-down position by 2 ft 6 in to over 25 ft, but this was just within the limits set by the new maintenance hangars at Croydon Airport; at Karachi the large airship hangar would be available and elsewhere maintenance would be done in the open air. Since the Eastern version was required before the Western, its detail design was given priority, and it was recorded as H.P.42; the structure was the same for both versions, but the choice of Jupiter or Jaguar engines remained open; however, Woods Humphery decided to standardise fuel tankage of 500 gallons for both versions and this was conveniently distributed between four equal tanks, which fitted within the RAF 28 aerofoil section and permitted a simplified fuel system. With so large an airframe, component testing to confirm stress and weight calculations was extremely important; the primary test pieces were (a) a corrugated duralumin wing spar, (b) a wing lift strut, (c) a wing drag strut, and (d) a monocoque specimen. After seeing the H.P.38 monocoque nose under construction, Volkert decided that the H.P.42 fuselage must have longitudinally corrugated thin skin to save both weight and excessive rivetting, as well as to improve appearance; the Junkers and Latécoère fuselages used corrugated panels of only 30 swg and saved more than 70 per cent of the rivets that plain panels would have needed, and were free from panting or drumming. To obtain reliable buckling data, test panels were made up comprising one bay of the top of the fuselage shell loaded in compression and a side panel loaded in shear.

Meanwhile, the Air Ministry had issued specification C.16/28 for a three-engined bomber-transport to supersede the Clive and Vickers Victoria. It had to carry thirty fully-armed troops or an equal weight of stores, bombs, spares or fuel for at least 1,200 miles; for ambulance duties it had to accommodate twelve stretcher cases, and a large hatch and internal hoist were required for loading heavy cargo such as a spare engine. With the three-engined Eastern transport proposal no longer wanted by Imperial Airways, Volkert produced a layout combining the wing and engine arrangement already schemed with a monocoque fuselage having nose and tail gun positions and a monoplane tail with twin fins and rudders similar to the H.P.38's. In the brochure describing this design, the following points were emphasised:

(a) all engines were clear of the fuselage, so both the front and rear gunners had good fields of fire for self-defence; each engine was readily accessible and the mountings could be made suitable for Jupiter, Jaguar or Mercury engines; refuelling from ground level was provided, also a gas-starter, and any oil spilled from the engines would blow clear of the fuselage;

(b) with no bracing wires, maintenance costs were minimal and the slotted wings were divided by transport joints into the preferred lengths for transportation;

(c) the pilot and navigator enjoyed a good view all round and along the fuselage sides from an enclosed side-by-side cockpit with a separate adjacent wireless cabin, where detachable dual controls were stowed ready for quick fitting to the navigator's position; wing tanks for 500 gallons could be supplemented by four 125-gallon auxiliary tanks in the cabin to give 2,000 miles range.

The design was well-received by the Air Staff, but they preferred the familiar braced tubular fuselage construction of the Clive and Hinaidi, with fabric covering and gauze windows, so the design was altered to suit and was recorded as H.P.43. In due course, contract No.935510/29 was received for one prototype, J9833, which was built concurrently with the H.P.42 and the two Clive IIs, beginning early in 1930. In passing, it may be noted that the Vickers 163, with four Kestrels in tandem pairs closely following the original V/1500 arrangement, was tendered to both the C.16/28 and Imperial Airways civil landplane requirements, but not accepted for either; nevertheless it was allowed to compete as a private venture in the C.16/28 class, in which the only other prototype ordered was the Gloster T.C.33, J9832, after the specification had been widened to include four engines as an option.

In July 1929 the fully-furnished wooden fuselage mock-up of the H.P.42 was towed from Cricklewood along Edgware Road, Park Lane, Knightsbridge and Kensington High Street to Olympia, where the Aero Exhibition was to be opened by the Prince of Wales. The convoy, which included also an all-metal Hinaidi airframe without outer wings and eighteen men under MacRostie, left the works an hour after midnight and

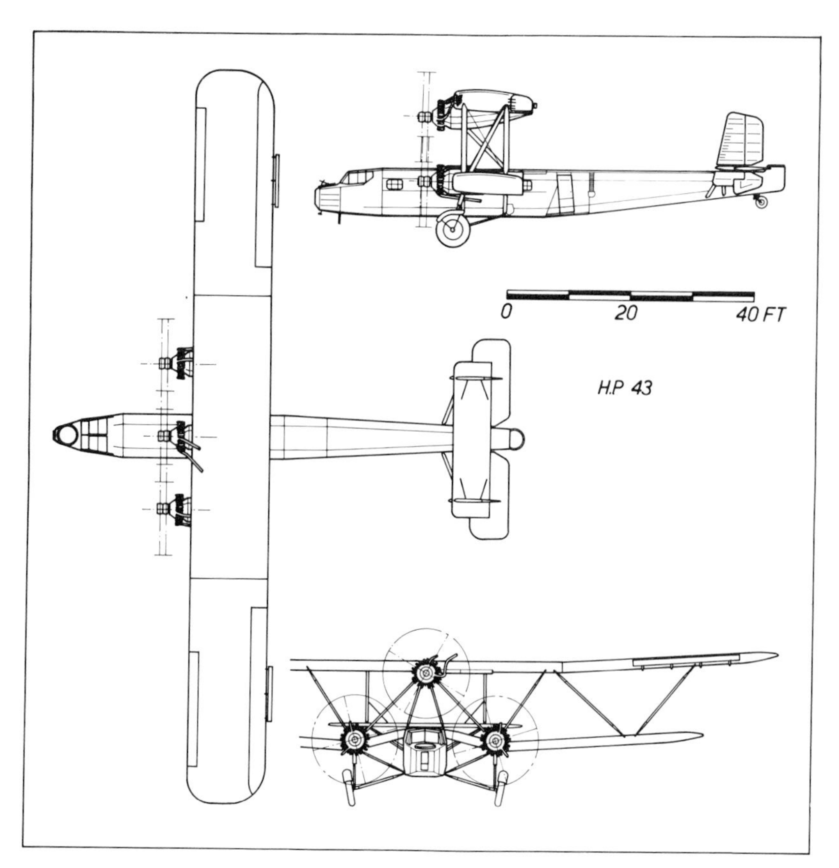

arrived in the hall at half-past four, having occasioned much ribaldry from taxi-drivers and caused consternation to all-night revellers *en route*. The mock-up included a cocktail bar, which attracted favourable notice during the exhibition, and a scale model of the complete aeroplane was shown alongside. By this time the Dunlop company had gained approval for large wheels and tyres suitable for aircraft of 30,000 lb gross weight, having overcome the setbacks experienced with the experimental wheels made for the Beardmore Inflexible prototype some years earlier. This was a very large all-duralumin stressed-skin monoplane, designed initially by Dr Rohrbach in Germany, and was not a success, although it gave valuable experience to those involved in its construction at Dalmuir. Volkert had taken a passing interest in it soon after his return from Japan and had met one of the Beardmore engineers, James Hamilton, whom in 1929 he recruited into the Handley Page team to tackle the problems of assembly and interchangeability that arose on the H.P.42. Like R. S. Hubbard, in the early days of the V/1500, Hamilton had begun as a Clydeside ship-builder and soon showed his ability as both organiser and designer, having a particular flair for jig and tool manufacture, always with simplicity and economy as his guide-lines; typical of his ideas were the hand-operated 'mangles' for corrugating fuselage monocoque panels and rolling wing spar booms and webs.

In connection with these spars, Handley Page was threatened with legal action for alleged infringement of patents owned by Aircraft Technical Services Ltd, a consortium formed by the Armstrong Whitworth, Boulton & Paul and Gloster companies to pool their patents on metal construction, particularly those relating to continuously rolled and drawn corrugated high-tensile steel strip. Handley Page resisted their claim on the grounds that his spars were wholly duralumin and that he had substantially improved on the ATS design by introducing flat surfaces to which ribs could be more easily attached. Observing at the Olympia Aero Show that Short Brothers were using a similar duralumin spar, but without the flats, Handley Page invited Oswald Short to join him in opposing the ATS action on a fifty-fifty basis, but Oswald Short declined, whereupon Handley Page fought the action through the courts alone and eventually won on appeal to the House of Lords; no doubt he was well-advised by his younger brother Theodore, who had been called to the Bar like their eldest brother, Arthur, who by then had settled in Burma after being appointed a judge there.

After the Olympia show, the mock-up was revised with a new pilots' cockpit, to suit the requirements of Captain Wolley Dod, who had returned from Cairo on exchange with Brackley for three months. Wolley Dod's views were rather different from Brackley's; in particular he insisted on the bottom edge of the windscreen being straight, not curved, and that the nose should fall away steeply below the windscreen so as to be invisible to the pilots and incapable of reflecting sunlight into their eyes. It had been Imperial Airways' custom in the Argosies to use upholstered seats in Europe, but to replace the cushions by cane backs and seats on the African routes. Brackley had approved cane chairs for the Eastern H.P.42, but Wolley Dod preferred three-ply with kapok-stuffed cushions in washable cloth covers. By October 1929 nearly all the component structural tests had been completed and the issue of drawings was well ahead; it was decided to assemble the first fuselage without waiting for the other seven sets of parts or final details of the interior trim, the chosen engine being the low-compression unsupercharged Jupiter XIF already in production at Filton. Meanwhile careful estimates of performance for the Western type were based on the record of Jaguar VIs with Townend rings (in the later Argosies), which were preferred to Jupiters, but in December 1929 Imperial Airways revised the specification for the Western type, calling for Jaguar Majors (civil Panthers) and a payload of 5,000 lb at an all-up weight of 24,500 lb, associated with a cruising speed of 90 mph and a stalling speed of 47·5 mph. The interior furnishing, including bar and galley units, was sub-contracted to Heaton Tabb & Co and fireproof sound insulation and upholstery were specified, with particular attention to the front saloon, where smoking was to be permitted. The first fuselage was taken to Radlett early in 1930 and completed without interior trim and equipment by the end of May, when it was found to be 96 lb heavier than the estimated weight of 3,050 lb. This was noted with some concern and close attention was paid to rigorous weight-saving in the other components, with the result that when the complete but untrimmed aircraft was weighed on 23 October, 1930, it proved to be 23 lb below the estimate.

Imperial Airways' preference for Panther engines, together with the changes in payload accommodation, although not affecting the primary airframe structure, introduced enough alterations affecting interchangeability to warrant a new type designation for the Western version, which became H.P.45 in the design office, although Imperial Airways had already begun to use the terms H.P.42E and H.P.42W in their public announcements and these remained in general use by the technical press throughout the operational life of the aircraft and for some years afterwards. The Panthers, like the Jaguars, were to drive two-blade airscrews in contrast to the Jupiters' four-bladers, and it was hoped to reduce drag and fuel consumption by installing them in long-chord NACA cowlings, but the nacelles were already being manufactured and were too wide except for short-chord Townend rings. The engine development timescale remained fluid during the first half of 1930, but in the autumn the supercharged Jupiter XFBM was approved for production and finally adopted for the four H.P.45s after satisfactory experience of three of this type in the last Short Calcutta G-AATZ. These engines were chosen also for the Short Kent flying-boats and their increased power for take-off permitted the H.P.45's all-up weight to rise to 29,500 lb, with a corresponding increase in payload, which was finalised as eighteen passengers in the forward saloon and twenty in the aft, plus two stewards. The passenger complement of the H.P.42, originally six forward and twelve aft, was increased to twelve in each saloon, with 500 cu ft of baggage and mail space between saloons—twice the capacity of the H.P.45.

On 30 September, 1930, Brackley, Captain W. Armstrong and G. W. Hall of Imperial Airways visited Radlett to inspect the first H.P.42, registered G-AAGX, in its final stages of completion; they agreed that crash-proof tanks were not required, but asked for cane seats to be reconsidered for the Eastern version. On 31 October Tom Harry England began solo taxying and handling tests at 20,150 lb, at which weight he found that the upper engines could be opened up before the lower with no tendency to nose over; later, however, the throttle controls were gated to prevent this being done inadvertently. He found the elevators and rudders somewhat heavy, but the ailerons light and effective, and in several straight runs into wind at 1,600 rpm the aircraft was airborne in less than three times its own length. The usual crop of 'first flight snags' was reported and mainly cured before England continued handling tests, including short straight hops, on 11 and 12 November, this time with 700 lb of ballast forward and 800 lb aft. The first true flight away from the aerodrome was made on 14 November with both England and Cordes at the dual controls and with 400 lb of ballast forward and 1,100 lb aft. Handling in gentle turns at speeds ranging from 60 to 118 mph was excellent and produced very little vibration or structural flexure. Handley Page kept the press and public waiting no longer and on 17 November (widely but erroneously quoted as the first flight date) England and Cordes gave an impressive demonstration of handling at low altitude in somewhat poor visibility, leaping off the ground in sixty yards, turning and banking under a low cloud base, and throttling back first the starboard lower engine and then both upper engines. After landing in a ridiculously short run, England stopped the two starboard engines, taxied in on the two port engines, turned to port through 180 degrees and finally turned to starboard through 90 degrees to stop in front of the hangar, all on the same two engines. This strained the tailwheel, but it did not collapse and a modified unit was put in hand at once. Before this flight a dummy horizon bar had been fitted in front of the windscreen at England's request as an aid to accurate low flying. For the next fortnight bad weather prevented useful test flying and the opportunity was taken to change the tailwheel unit and fit mudguards and oleo fairings to the main landing gear. With the gross weight increased to 22,680 lb, England and Cordes resumed trials on 29 November, when the very rough and gusty conditions caused visible flexure of the upper wing-tips, but this seemed to have no effect on the controls. On 2 December the weight was again increased, ballasted with 1,300 lb forward and 2,120 lb aft, to 25,750 lb including four passengers; one of them was Brackley, who took a turn in the right-hand seat and expressed satisfaction with the controls. On the 8th England and Cordes flew at the full weight of 25,750 lb, finding the elevator and rudder controls very heavy, although the ailerons were light and responsive. Thereafter two flights were made at 21,000 lb with several passengers moving progressively forward from frame 16 to frame 3 to check the effect of various c.g. positions; in another flight on 13 December to check wing flexure, a full-load stall was elicited with c.g. aft and on landing the tailwheel fork collapsed; the mainwheel tyres were also found to have been badly cut because the mudguards were too close and had trapped stones against the treads. By Christmas Eve these snags had been corrected and plate glass windscreens had been fitted to meet England's complaint of optical distortion, but in a series of taxying runs and short hops he found no improvement and attributed the trouble to reflection from bright parts on the instrument panel which should have been painted matt black.

Early in 1931 Imperial Airways began to advertise their forthcoming new fleet, which was already four months late in entering service, and announced individual aircraft names in accordance with their new policy of using history and mythology instead of geographical locations. The four Eastern aircraft, starting with G-AAGX, were to be named *Hannibal, Hadrian, Hanno* and *Hecate*, while the four Western variants were to be *Heracles, Horatius, Hesperides* and *Helena*. Handley Page, as always well-briefed in classical allusion, objected to the hell-fire implications of *Hecate* and Imperial Airways themselves had second thoughts about repeatedly spelling out *Hesperides*; a happy solution was reached by substituting the names *Horsa* and *Hengist*, since these had been well-known cross-Channel travellers in earlier times, renowned for the regularity of their frequent sorties. Flight testing continued at Radlett whenever the weather permitted and on 1 February England and Cordes, on their twenty-second joint flight, took up Handley Page's wife and three daughters in the course of short take-off and landing tests. After their flight, Cordes escorted them back to Handley Page's office and, looking back at *Hannibal*, was disconcerted to see that both ailerons appeared to be drooping together. He managed to draw Handley Page's attention to this phenomenon without actually saying anything and quickly took the visitors away from the hangar, while Handley Page himself had *Hannibal* towed into it and the hangar doors closed. There the aileron hinge outriggers were found to have buckled, presumably under inertia loading during the 'circuits and bumps'. Longer and stronger brackets were at once made up and Handley Page took away the defective ones; it is said they were used to reinforce the concrete bottom of a lily-pond he was making in the grounds of his home at Limes House, Stanmore, and he later hinted that they might be dug up by future archaeologists seeking the burial place of Queen Boadicea, reputed to be close to that spot. England and Cordes flew *Hannibal* again a fortnight after the mishap and manufacturer's trials went on without a hitch until, after the twenty-ninth flight on 4 April, England pronounced it ready for C of A trials at Martlesham Heath. It was flown there on 17 April by Sqn Ldr Goodwin, Flt Lieut Horrex and Flt Lieut Lucas, with Stuart Scott-Hall as technical observer, and returned to Radlett on the 22nd. In a demonstration to a party of Imperial Airways pilots two days later, rain was found to be leaking into the flight deck, so care was taken to seal all skin joints before completing the saloon trim and final weighing on 4 June, 1931.

Next day *Hannibal* was granted a full certificate of airworthiness and, since the Air Ministry considered it to be the 'type' aircraft and the other seven 'subsequent' aircraft for airworthiness purposes, the obligatory civil constructor's numbers were recorded in the British Civil Aircraft Register as H.P.42-1 to H.P.42-8 inclusive, notwithstanding the maker's own designation H.P.45 for the four Western versions. That day England flew *Hannibal* for its thirty-fifth flight on delivery to Imperial Airways at Croydon in heavy rain, for which the windscreen wipers were ineffective at maximum speed. These were adjusted before its first public appearance on 6 June, wearing its name and owner's title painted on the polished aluminium fuselage in dark blue lettering; the registration marks on the rear fuselage and the wings were in black on aluminium-doped fabric. On the same afternoon it was flown to Hanworth Air Park to be inspected by members of both Houses of Parliament, who were allowed into the saloons

Hannibal at Croydon on 25 June, 1931, embarking passengers for a flight chartered by the *Daily Mail*, showing original outer wing struts and elevator balance tab.

but not given flights; they were impressed by the excellence of the furnishings and the subsequent brief flying display by Brackley and Captain Walters, who started proving flights to Le Bourget next day, but had further tailwheel trouble there on the 18th. On the 25th *Hannibal* was chartered by the *Daily Mail* for brief flights from Croydon over London with invited passengers and on 10 July a party of newspaper reporters was flown to Paris and back by Captain Wilcockson. Fare-paying passengers were carried from 11 July onwards on the proving flights, which ended abruptly on 8 August when a loose fastener from an engine cowling damaged one blade of the port lower airscrew, which disintegrated and spread havoc to the two upper airscrews. Captain F. Dismore managed to put *Hannibal* down safely in a small field at Tudeley near Tonbridge, but the tail was broken off by a tree-stump at the last moment in trying to avoid telephone wires; none of the passengers was hurt, and the damage was repaired at Croydon after *Hannibal* had been salvaged by road. Meanwhile the second Eastern machine, G-AAUE *Hadrian*, had been delivered to Croydon on 8 July after vicissitudes of its own.

Hadrian was completed and weighed at Radlett on 19 June and found to be 215 lb lighter than *Hannibal*, which spoke well for Hamilton's insistence on rigorous weight control. Cordes attempted its first flight on the 23rd, but the engines were misfiring and leaking oil, so the resident Bristol engineer spent all night putting them right for England to fly the next day, this time without incident. Five more test flights, with various aileron settings to correct a low starboard wing with hands-off, and finally a revised rudder balance setting, led to the seventh flight on 29 June, when England and Captain Walters flew together and Walters complained of aileron snatch when banking to port. Next day Cordes flew for some time with hands-off before executing a steep turn, but could discover no snatch, so on the ninth flight on 1 July Walters, with Cordes in the right-hand seat, applied full port aileron in an attempt to elicit the condition, since he considered such a manoeuvre to be necessary for landing in patchy fog; this time the starboard outer diagonal wing strut buckled and collapsed, leaving the

Hannibal in service at Basra after modification of wing bracing and deletion of elevator balance tab.

Rolling out G-AAXC *Heracles* at Radlett for a test flight in August 1931.

lateral control very sloppy but just adequate for a gentle return to base; Cordes declined absolutely to share the blame with Walters, who had, in his opinion, taken an unjustifiable risk with so large an aircraft. In consequence of this incident, the diagonal struts of both *Hadrian* and *Hannibal* were replaced by crossed streamline tie-rods; the same modification was applied to the other six aircraft before they flew and there was no more trouble. After three more flights in which he could find no sign of snatch, Cordes cleared *Hadrian* for delivery and flew it to Croydon on 8 July, on which date Hamilton agreed revised delivery dates for the remainder, although these proved impossible to achieve and penalties for late delivery cost the company almost the full price of the last of the fleet, *Helena*, which arrived at Croydon on 31 December, 1931, nine months behind the original contract date and nearly four months behind the revised schedule. Some of the delay was occasioned by the initial rough running of the Jupiter XFBM engines installed in the Western version; the first, G-AAXC *Heracles*, flew excellently, with light controls, in seven flights between 13 and 26 August, 1931, except for this trouble, which was only partly cured by extending the exhaust tail-pipes of the upper engines further back above the wing. Hitherto all the aircraft had been fitted with two-piece airscrews, because of the Air Ministry's insistence that integral four-bladers were too costly to transport and store overseas. However, on 9 September, when *Heracles* was delivered to Croydon, the Air Ministry agreed to the use of integral four-bladers on the four Western versions only and on 27 October Brackley flew *Heracles* with Short Kent airscrews and with the elevator mass-balance removed, finding its handling much improved in this condition; approval was then given to delete this balance (in front of the leading edge of the upper tailplane) on all eight aircraft, beginning with *Hengist* and *Helena*. The latter handled so well that all its eight test flights were completed by England in two days, 30 and 31 December. Handley Page had wanted to attempt a height record with *Helena*, hoping to reach 4,750 metres (15,500 ft) with a useful load of 5,000 kg, but this would have raised the take-off weight to 31,000 lb and

G-AAXE *Hengist* climbing out of Heliopolis in 1937. (*J. Sewell*)

there was not enough time in hand to get permission for this overload. Meanwhile Brackley conducted fuel consumption tests at Croydon with the repaired *Hannibal* and delayed its departure to Cairo to join the others: *Horsa* had left Le Bourget on 10 November and arrived at Cairo on the 16th, *Hadrian* left Marseilles on the 23rd and arrived on the 26th, while *Hanno*, leaving Marseilles on 30 November, was temporarily diverted on to the South African route and took up station at Cairo on 4 January, 1932. To replace *Hannibal*, the newly-commissioned *Helena* was temporarily converted to Eastern interior layout so as to carry urgent mail to Cairo, leaving Croydon on 20 January. In all respects other than payload accommodation, *Helena* remained a Western variant, with integral airscrews and Jupiter XFBM engines, and returned to Croydon for regular inspection and maintenance. When visiting Croydon *Helena* shared the heavy London–Paris traffic with *Heracles, Horatius* and *Hengist*, which carried the main burden at all times, as well as fitting in special flights such as the much-publicised stunt 'race' between *Heracles* and the *Flying*

G-AAXF *Helena* at Croydon in July 1933. (*Commercial Motor*)

Scotsman express from London to Edinburgh on 20 May; Captain O. P. Jones maintained radio contact with the train but barely gained the lead on it. A month later, on 19 June, *Heracles* was flown to the Royal Aeronautical Society's Garden Party at Hanworth to add weight to the display and take up guests for joy-rides at 5/6d a time; unfortunately Captain Rogers was unaware of the existence of a drainage culvert across the grass aerodrome and on the last joy-ride of the day the port mainwheel broke through the surface and *Heracles* subsided on to its port wing-tip, having to be lifted out by Beck & Pollitzer's mobile crane and spending some weeks being repaired on the aerodrome boundary.

Heracles being salvaged at Hanworth after coming to grief at the Royal Aeronautical Society's Garden Party on 19 June, 1932.

After this early misdemeanour *Heracles* led an extremely profitable and blameless life and during the ensuing nine years carried more than 100,000 passengers in 13,000 flying hours; in 1935 it was airborne on 361 days, being serviced and maintained by the Croydon night-shift under Jock Stirling. Jock was extremely conscientious in maintaining total airworthiness in these large aircraft, but once had a daily certificate of safety refused by the resident AID inspector, who reported a split-pin missing. Jock said 'Tell me where—I'll see to it myself' but got the reply 'I found it—now you bloody well find it!' The snag was in the aileron control circuit in the upper wing and the AID inspector was Tommy Rowntree, who had taken the blame for the loss of the Short Crusader at Venice in the 1927 Schneider Trophy race, due to crossed aileron cables; he became head of the AID before retiring. *Heracles* and *Horatius* were the only two of the Western fleet to retain their original furnishings, for in 1933 *Helena* was permanently converted to Eastern standard and *Hengist* followed suit in 1935; in 1937 *Hanno* was damaged by a gale while picketed out and during rebuilding was converted to Western standard to replace *Hengist*, which had been destroyed by fire in the airship hangar at Karachi in May. *Hannibal* itself was out of commission for some weeks in 1932 after being overturned in a gale at Tiberias, but the only real technical trouble encountered was fatigue cracking which developed in the original welded aluminium fuel tanks. Captain Horsey first met this trouble when he flew *Hanno* to Karachi, where the RAF made up replacement tanks from tinned steel; it was cured by introducing de Bergue rivetted duralumin tanks for all eight aircraft and an extra tank was added to the Eastern versions in September 1932, to cater for the longer stages imposed by the re-routing of the Basra–Karachi sector through Kuwait, Bahrein and Sharjah when the 1929 three-year agreement with Persia expired. The first mail over this

The Captain goes aboard G-AAUD *Hanno* before leaving Croydon for Le Bourget on 26 August, 1937. (*K. A. Winkley*)

G-AAXD *Horatius* embarking passengers at Croydon on 3 August, 1938. (*K. A. Winkley*)

route was carried by *Hanno* in the first week of October 1932; a month later *Hanno* began flying the African service from Cairo to Kisumu after the spongy cotton-soil landing strips at Juba and Malakal had been sealed and strengthened by the Shell Oil Company's treatment; so effective was this process that in the rainy season pilots of H.P.42s taking off from Juba were said to watch the height of their bow-waves instead of their airspeed indicators.

At the other extreme of climate along the Arabian side of the Persian Gulf there was often no water when it was most needed. On 22 August, 1935, *Horsa* left Basra for Bahrein after sunset, but its departure signal was not received by Bahrein, so the landing lights were not lit for the arrival; *Horsa* overflew the dark landing ground and ran out of fuel 100 miles further south, but forced-landed without injuries to crew and passengers, who were found next day by a search party mounted by No.84 Squadron RAF, Shaibah, after some parched and uncomfortable hours in a shade temperature rising to 140 degrees F. One of the passengers was the American authoress Jane Smith, who autographed her camiknickers, the only garment she was wearing when rescued, and presented them to the squadron as a memento. At the enquiry into the accident it was revealed that the captain had already flown eighteen hours without a rest and still had some hours of duty ahead. Although they cruised little faster than airliners of ten years earlier, the H.P.42s and 45s carried more than three times the payload of their predecessors and were extremely safe; no passenger was killed in one up to the beginning of the war in 1939 in a total fleet mileage of 2·3 million, and the standard of comfort and cuisine was unsurpassed, for seven-course dinners could be served from the galley by the two stewards, though four-course meals were the rule. In the busy summer season they each made as many as four return flights a day from Croydon to the Continent and the ease with which they landed, taxied to the apron and unloaded was a delight to see. In days when duty-free luxuries were much sought after, some stewards found that silk stockings could be slipped through the galley partition into the gas-starter compartment, which had an external door; so when the passengers had left the saloons and the Customs men came aboard, a steward leaving his galley would pause beside the starter bay door before taking his galley stock and 'empties' into the terminal building; naturally this convenient facility was unknown to the management and manufacturers alike.

Early in 1933 Imperial Airways asked Handley Page to supply two additional H.P.42s, with such improvements as Tiger II engines in Townend rings, a monoplane tail and wheel spats, all without any reduction in payload. Major Mayo had already suggested replacing the Jupiter XFBMs with cowled Tigers, also reducing the upper wing chord from 15 ft 6 in to 11 ft 6 in with full-span slots and flaps to maintain a high lift co-efficient at a low landing speed; he estimated that a top speed of

Horatius leaving Croydon for Paris on 3 August, 1938. (*K. A. Winkley*)

145 mph would be possible, but Volkert predicted a weight increase of over 600 lb for the wing structure, which would have raised the all-up weight to 31,500 lb. Handley Page was in favour of going still further and converting existing H.P.42s as well as two new ones into monoplanes with Tiger or Pegasus engines for delivery in 1935, but Imperial Airways were not willing to discuss this; Handley Page quoted a price of £42,000 each to build two new H.P.42s and Imperial Airways then ordered two landplane versions of the Short Kent flying-boat, which, as *Scylla* and *Syrinx*, filled the immediate need, but were never the equal in comfort or flying qualities of the H.P.42, whose cost had averaged £21,000 each in 1931.

In July 1937 *Heracles* became the first commercial aircraft in the world to have flown one million miles in passenger service and a select party, including Sir Samuel Instone, celebrated the event in a flight over southern England piloted by Captain Dismore, who left the controls to his First Officer while he came into the saloon to share an iced cake depicting the Short flying-boat *Caledonia* in which Captain Wilcockson had just pioneered the

Heracles in July 1939 after flying one and a quarter million miles mostly between Croydon and Le Bourget. (*Graphic Union*)

transatlantic air-mail route from Foynes to Botwood. At this time George Woods Humphery wrote to Handley Page: 'These aircraft have given us excellent service and have set up new standards of reliability and comfort in all weather conditions. These factors are responsible to a large extent for the great increase in the number of passengers we have carried. So far as we are able to judge from their present condition, they will, in the mechanical sense, be fit for several years' service from the time they are withdrawn because their type is obsolete. We may say that our confidence in placing with you an order of such magnitude, for aircraft of a type so far in advance of anything then in use, has been fully justified.' But in fact they never were withdrawn, and the seven survivors after the loss of *Hengist* remained in service up till the outbreak of war.

Hadrian in service in 1940 with No.271 Squadron as AS982 (*F. G. Swanborough*)

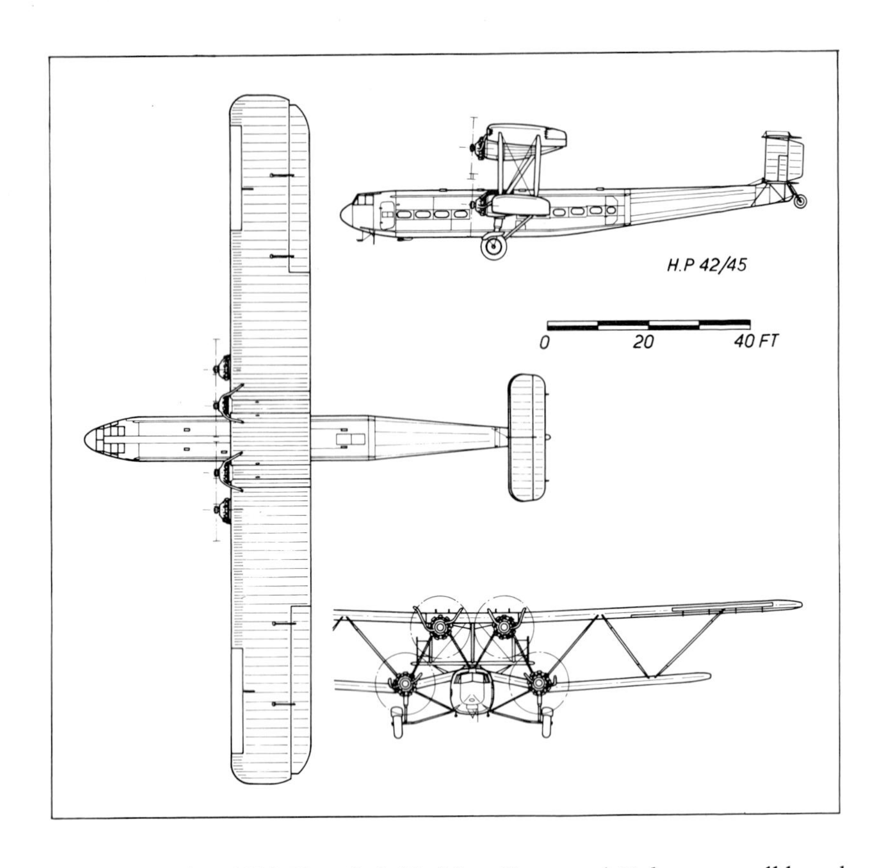

In September 1939 *Hannibal, Hadrian, Horsa* and *Helena* were all based at Cairo, with only *Hanno, Heracles* and *Horatius* remaining at Croydon. These three, together with *Scylla*, *Syrinx* and some other four-engined landplanes, were dispersed to Whitchurch (Bristol) and Exeter, whence they operated under the aegis of National Air Communications in a trooping and cargo service for the British Expeditionary Force in France. Returning from one of these sorties on 7 November, 1939, *Horatius* was wrecked while attempting an emergency landing on Tiverton golf course; on 1 March, 1940, *Hannibal*, with four passengers and a crew of four, en route from Jask to Sharjah, was lost without trace over the Gulf of Oman and the three other H.P.42s at Cairo were then flown back to Whitchurch to join the pool, which, after Dunkirk, maintained essential communications with Scotland and Northern Ireland. On 19 March a sudden gale sprang up at Whitchurch and all available staff ran out to attempt to save the tethered aircraft dispersed round the aerodrome, *Heracles* and *Hanno* being the most vulnerable. Two ground crew, Griffiths and Caseley, reached *Hanno* in time to climb aboard, but *Heracles* was already kiting backwards with tethering pickets pulled adrift and was soon blown through the boundary barbed-wire fence, to be wrecked in the field beyond. Caseley and Griffiths managed to start *Hanno's* two upper engines, but a final violent gust blew the machine backwards in a flying attitude to collapse beside *Heracles*. The three survivors, *Horsa, Hadrian* and *Helena* were impressed into RAF service with No.271 Squadron as AS981–AS983 respectively, in April, May and June 1940, but on 7 August *Horsa*, en route from Ringway to Stornoway, caught fire in a forced landing at Moresby Park, Cumberland, and was burnt out; while on 6 December *Hadrian* was torn loose from its moorings at Doncaster Airport by a gale gusting to 100 mph and cart-wheeled on to an adjacent railway track. *Helena* had been grounded after being damaged in a heavy landing on 1 August at Donibristle while carrying a detachment of troops on a training exercise. The port lower wing and undercarriage were renewed and the port lower engine was repaired early in 1941, when a successful test flight was made, but the station engineer officer condemned the aircraft because of widespread corrosion and it was dismantled on site, the monocoque fuselage being mounted on trestles as an office for the Royal Naval Air Station, Donibristle. Each of these eight gentle giants had logged over 12,000 hours at a fraction of the operating cost of their successors and contemporary rivals.

The single prototype H.P.43 already referred to had a much shorter career in its original form, but had the distinction of forming a link in the aviation evolutionary chain by being converted into a cantilever monoplane. As a biplane, it was manufactured at Cricklewood during 1930 and 1931, with many delays through indecision by the Air Ministry on the choice of engines and equipment. Eventually it had three Bristol Pegasus I engines (for which Townend rings were intended but never fitted), an RAE gas-starter, a tailskid like the Hinaidi's, gauze-covered windows like the Clive's and a twin-fin monoplane tail like the Heyford's. The enclosed cockpit accommodated pilot and navigator side by side, with the wireless station immediately aft, but no heating or insulation was installed because the RAF did not expect to use it operationally and were already looking ahead to a monoplane troop-carrier. It had Scarff No.12 gun rings at the nose and tail and a bomb-aimer's window in the nose similar to the Heyford's. As an insurance against delay in delivery of Pegasus engines, an alternative layout with three Kestrel IIIs was drawn, but not officially approved. It was erected in skeleton at Cricklewood in June 1931, before being covered with fabric and transported to Radlett for completion. It was ready for flight on 19 December, 1931, after last-minute alterations to the tail unit, but further changes were then called for and it was not flown till 21 June, 1932, when Cordes made preliminary flight trials in the hope of clearing it for the RAF Display at Hendon that year; but in fact it needed further modification and did not appear at Hendon till June 1933. There it was flown briefly by visiting pilots from Martlesham Heath and criticised as unsatisfactory because its performance was poor and its controls were heavy and badly harmonised, although it was stable with hands- and feet-off. It was flown back to Radlett, where it was inspected by the Deputy Chief of the Air Staff on 7 November, with drawings of a proposed twin-engined monoplane conversion alongside for comparison. This was the H.P.51 project, which the company had already tendered to specification C.26/31, and in December the Air Ministry gave instructions for this to proceed. The final contract price agreed in January 1934 for the H.P.43, including its conversion to H.P.51, was £41,250, although Handley Page

H.P.43 at Radlett in July 1932. (*Flight*)

claimed that costs incurred on the H.P.43 alone had amounted to £54,840 by the end of 1932.

H.P.42

(Four Bristol Jupiter XI)

Span 130 ft (39·62 m); length 92 ft 2 in (28·1 m); wing area 2,989 sq ft (278 m²). Empty weight 17,740 lb (8,050 kg); maximum weight 28,000 lb (12,700 kg). Maximum speed 120 mph (193 km/h); minimum speed 51 mph (82 km/h); range 500 miles (805 km). Crew four. Passengers 18–24.

H.P.43

(Three Bristol Pegasus IM3)

Span 114 ft (34·8 m); length 75 ft 9 in (23·1 m). Empty weight 13,550 lb (6,150 kg); maximum weight 22,500 lb (10,210 kg). Speed 118 mph (190 km/h); range 1,200 miles (1,930 km). Crew three–four. Thirty troops.

H.P.45

(Four Bristol Jupiter XFBM)

As H.P.42 except: Maximum weight 29,500 lb (13,760 kg). Maximum speed 127 mph (204 km/h). Passengers 38.

3MR4, M.5/28 and M.1/30 (H.P.40, 41 and 46)

In the spring of 1927, Mitsubishi Shoji Kaisha of Nagoya was one of three Japanese aircraft manufacturers invited to tender for a new carrier-borne torpedo-reconnaissance biplane to replace the Mitsubishi Type 13 (B1M1) then in service with the Imperial Japanese Navy. Mitsubishi, having noted the current keen competition between Blackburn and Handley Page to supply deck-landing torpedo-bombers for operation from the Royal Navy's aircraft carriers, invited both companies to tender for the design of prototypes to specification 3MR4; the winning design was to be built and tested in England, with subsequent production, if any, by Mitsubishi at Nagoya. Mitsubishi had just begun to manufacture Hispano-Suiza engines under licence and specified the 650 hp Type 51-12Lb for the 3MR4, which was to be an all-metal three-seat biplane with doped fabric covering and a gross weight of 7,500 lb.

Concurrently, Tom Harry England, who combined the duties of chief test pilot and technical adviser to Handley Page on Air Staff requirements, picked up advance information about the Air Staff's so-called 'Mark III torpedo-bomber', to be used on the Royal Navy's new aircraft carriers *Courageous* and *Glorious*, which had stronger flying decks and larger lifts, permitting the operation of slightly heavier aircraft with the limiting span increased from 46 ft to 50 ft. After a visit to the Air Ministry on 15 December, 1927, England reported that the new torpedo-bomber would have to attain at least 136 kt, stall at less than 50 kt, carry a Mk.X torpedo and a crew of two, and that an air-cooled radial engine was not favoured. These requirements were formally promulgated three months later in specification M.5/28. There seemed to be enough similarity between the British and Japanese formulas for both projects to be evolved in parallel within the existing design office capacity, so tenders for both were submitted as H.P.40 for Japan and H.P.41 for the Fleet Air Arm. Both tenders faced strong competition from similar Blackburn projects and in June 1928 the Japanese government decided in favour of the Blackburn 3MR4, so Handley Page ceased work on the H.P.40. No drawings of it seem to have been preserved and only a few records of estimated performance and weights have survived in the Handley Page archives; with an all-up weight of 7,500 lb and a 13 ft 6 in diameter airscrew, the maximum speed at sea level was estimated as 134·5 mph and the service ceiling as 16,000 ft with both wings of Clark YH section, or 16,500 ft with an upper wing of RAF 31 and a lower wing of RAF 28 section. Wind-tunnel tests to decide the choice of aerofoil were about to begin when the project was cancelled.

With only the H.P.41 going ahead, the choice of engines lay between the Napier Lion XII and the Rolls-Royce F.XIVS (Kestrel III). The Lion seemed to promise a marginally better performance, but it was an obsolescent design, so the tender was based on the Kestrel and covered both wheeled and float undercarriages. Since the pilot's view for both torpedo attack and deck landing was a governing factor, two alternative layouts were tendered in September 1928, one being a conventional single-bay type with moderate gap and aspect-ratio, bearing signs of derivation from the H.P.37; the other had narrower wings of equal span and reduced gap, with the upper wing roots merged into the fuselage below the pilot's forward decking; in both, the centre section spanned about 10 ft and the lower wing roots were downswept to increase the gap. The engine was neatly installed, with an underslung radiator in a tunnel with vertical shutters, and drove a two-blade Fairey-Reed duralumin airscrew of 13 ft 4 in diameter, with the hub faired by a pointed spinner as in the Fairey IIIF.

On 23 October, 1929, England was informed that, while the Air Staff had been favourably impressed by the H.P.41 tender, the pilot's view was still not good enough and that the specification was being revised to delete floats and catapulting, an increase of all-up weight to 9,000 lb being permitted. A revised tender was submitted, to be discussed at an Air Ministry conference on 13 January, 1930, England being invited to attend. As a result of this meeting, specification M.5/28 was cancelled and a new specification, M.1/30, was approved by Air Commodore F. V. Holt (DTD) on 22 March, 1930, for a 'two-seat torpedo-bomber ship-plane for Fleet use' to carry a 1,866-lb Type K torpedo or a 2,000-lb bomb with a maximum all-up weight of 9,300 lb, the suggested engines being the Rolls-Royce H.10 (later Buzzard) and the Armstrong Siddeley Leopard, both of 825 hp. The limiting dimensions were span: 50 ft, length: 44 ft, height: 14 ft and folded width: 23 ft, defining a larger aeroplane than the H.P.41; so the latter was abandoned and a new design, H.P.46, was tendered in April 1930, in competition with Blackburn and Vickers-Armstrongs submissions. The Air Ministry agreed to order one prototype with a Buzzard engine from each of the three contestants, allotting the serials S1640–S1642 to the Blackburn B-3, Vickers 207 and H.P.46 respectively.

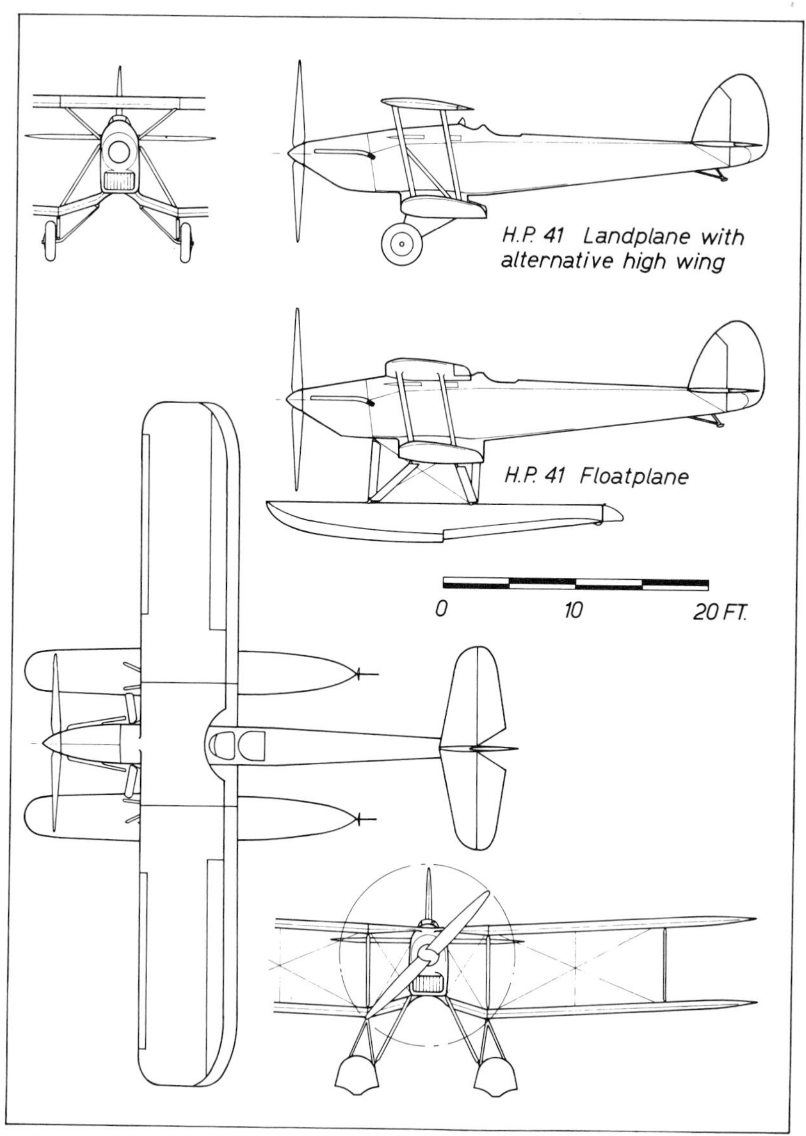

The required performance comprised a maximum speed of not less than 130 kt at 4,000 ft, landing speed not greater than 55 kt, service ceiling of 16,000 ft, oil and water for 8 hours cruising and fuel tankage for half an hour at full throttle at sea-level plus 7 hours cruising at 100 kt at 4,000 ft, while carrying a military load of 2,874 lb. Other features specified were an all-metal structure, with a metal airscrew also preferred, full protection against sea-water corrosion by the use of stainless steel, cadmium-plating or anodising (as appropriate), slinging gear and flotation gear (preferably a watertight fuselage), all fuel tanks readily drainable and the main tank fuel jettisonable. Approved slot and aileron controls were to be fitted to ensure good controllability at low speeds for take-off and landing on a carrier deck; also required were good positive stability and capability to fly level hands-off when trimmed, good manoeuvrability and means of self-defence and, finally, very good fields of view and steadiness for both precision bombing and torpedo-dropping. The crew of two were to be located close together to ensure excellent co-operation, with the pilot aiming and releasing the torpedo and the gunner having access to a prone bombing position on the floor. The pilot was to be armed with a fixed synchronised Vickers gun on the port side and the gunner with a single Lewis on a high-speed mounting. The alternative weapon loads were one torpedo (Type K or Mark VIII or Mark X), or one 2,000-lb or 1,000-lb bomb, or two 520-lb bombs, or eight 230-lb or 250-lb bombs, plus four 20-lb practice bombs in each case; an effective torpedo installation was not to be prejudiced by the provisions for a 2,000-lb bomb.

This proved on examination to be virtually an impossible goal to achieve, since with the specified total load of 4,456 lb and an installed powerplant weight of 2,250 lb there was only 2,590 lb available for the entire structure weight, representing 28 per cent of the maximum specified gross weight, whereas the best that could be expected was 29 per cent, giving a gross weight of 9,600 lb with the Buzzard or 9,900 lb with the Leopard and a Townend ring. If a Kestrel engine were used, the gross weight could be held down to 8,300 lb for the required range, but the essential performance could not be attained; if the Buzzard had to be used to get the required performance and 9,300 lb was the absolute weight limit, the weight available for fuel would allow only 4½ to 5 hours cruise instead of 7 hours. England put this assessment of the situation in a personal visit to the Air Ministry on 24 April and was told that Blackburn and Vickers also considered the 9,300-lb weight limit impossible to achieve, estimating their gross weights as 9,500 to 10,000 lb with structure weight at 30 to 31 per cent; the Air Staff all agreed with them, except Captain Liptrot, who maintained that a structure weight of 28 per cent was feasible. Eventually a tolerance of 200 lb was agreed to, but the Admiralty could not modify the carrier lifts, which had a top load limit of 9,500 lb, nor could the specified range be reduced. In view of the difficulties involved, the final date for acceptance of revised tenders was extended to 10 June.

Since by this time Boultbee had resigned from Handley Page Ltd, and Volkert and Hamilton were fully preoccupied with both the H.P.38 and the H.P.42, the return of Gustav Lachmann from Japan in 1929 and his acceptance of a staff appointment at Cricklewood as experimental design engineer offered the only real chance of success, by an optimum application of slots, interceptors and full-span droopable ailerons to improve lift coefficient and controllability without exceeding the weight limit. On 13 August Handley Page, Volkert and Lachmann examined the M.1/30 proposals in detail and laid down a programme of testing and analysis to determine the best aerofoil and strut profiles, with particular attention to obtaining the minimum interference drag at wing-root and strut junctions. A novel arrangement of the main fuel tanks as an integral part of the down-swept inboard section of the lower wings, together with internally-sprung mainwheels, was expected to save 100 lb of structure weight compared with

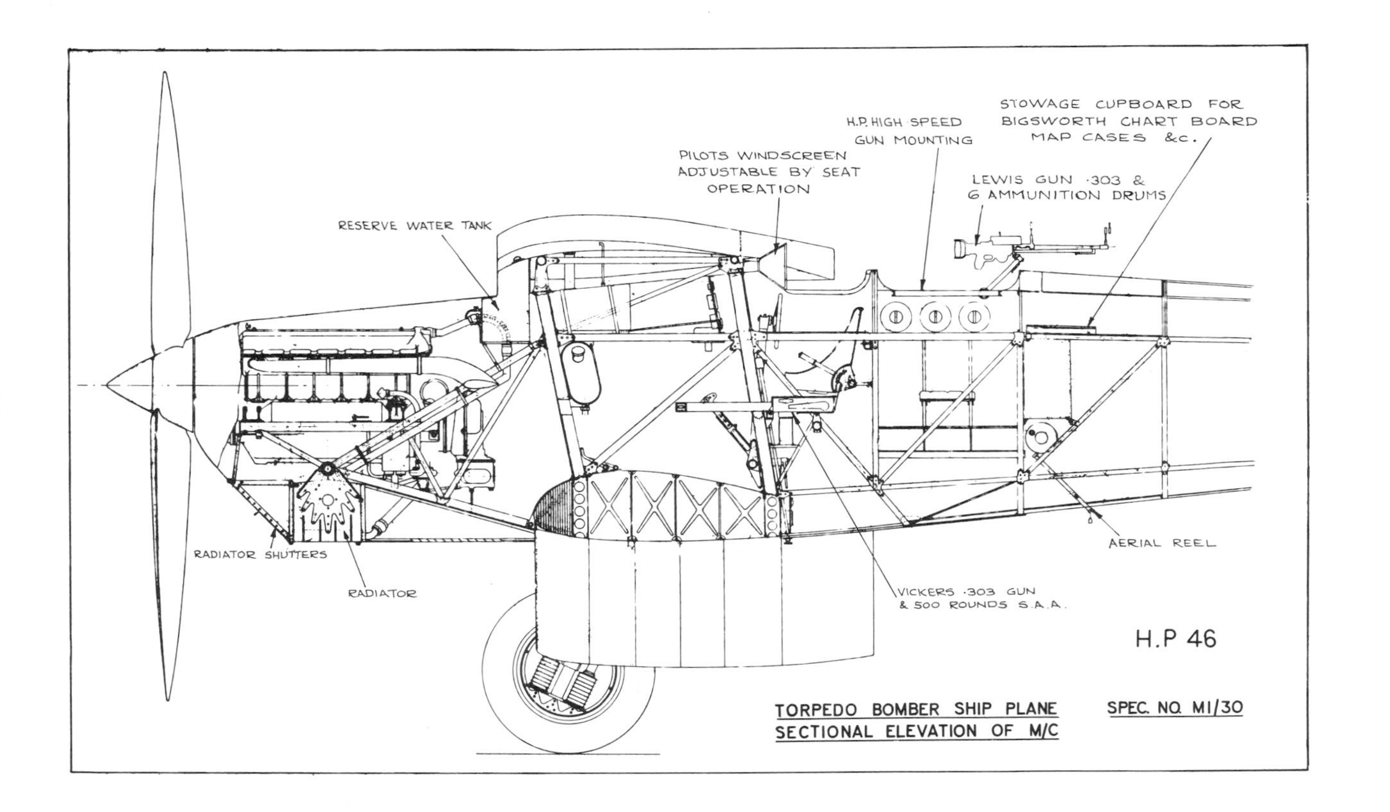

STOWAGE CUPBOARD FOR
BIGSWORTH CHART BOARD
MAP CASES &c.
H.P. HIGH SPEED
GUN MOUNTING
PILOTS WINDSCREEN
ADJUSTABLE BY SEAT
OPERATION
LEWIS GUN ·303 &
6 AMMUNITION DRUMS
RESERVE WATER TANK
RADIATOR SHUTTERS
RADIATOR
AERIAL REEL
VICKERS ·303 GUN
& 500 ROUNDS S.A.A.
H.P 46
TORPEDO BOMBER SHIP PLANE
SECTIONAL ELEVATION OF M/C
SPEC. NO. M1/30

conventional wing-mounted fuel tanks and divided undercarriages, while careful attention to the dimensions and balance areas of control surfaces would keep drag losses to a minimum and would be checked on a large-scale wind-tunnel model. The tank/undercarriage assembly was to be designed and stressed as an independent component and a full-scale half-assembly was to be made to test leakage under all static and dynamic loadings; also the proposed 'bat's-wing' trailing edges at the wing-fold hinges were to be mocked up to ensure optimum design. The features already discussed and agreed were RAF 34 wing section, duralumin wing structure and a welded steel-tube fuselage structure.

The official contract, AM 55828/30, was signed on 23 September and a week later Lachmann reported the results of his analysis, giving an estimated all-up weight of 9,322 lb, of which the structure weight took up 29·1 per cent. The possible weight saving by changing from duralumin to high-tensile steel wing-spars was too small to justify the resulting change in manufacturing methods, but he thought the welded steel-tube fuselage was too heavy and could be constructed more economically by using steel and duralumin square tubes joined by fish-plates and tubular rivets. An internal mock-up conference was held on 29 December in preparation for the first official one on 26 January, 1931. The drawings were scheduled for completion by 15 March and a second official mock-up conference was held on the 5th to inspect the prone bombing position, which was approved with some reservations on the 28th. On 3 September the Air Ministry approved the equipment layout, but introduced new stressing cases for a revised arrestor gear using a tail hook. This effectively postponed the original contract delivery date of 23 December and it was not until April 1932 that the last date for delivery to Martlesham Heath for the M.1/30 flying trials was fixed at 1 September, 1932.

Long before this, the design had run into numerous troubles, particularly with weight increases in all components and with delay due to non-delivery of castings and machining of parts for the internally-sprung main wheels, which Dunlops had declined to undertake. Already the wheels had been made larger than the aircraft weight required simply to give longer shock-absorber travel; then the Air Ministry had insisted on the main fuel tanks being made removable, which destroyed the advantage of integral monocoque construction as a means of saving weight. Now a movable bombing platform was demanded, together with evaporative cooling for the engine, which entailed a revised cooling system with condensers and header tanks in the upper centre-section leading edge. As this could not be arranged without excessive delay and the existing radiator was considered to be inadequate, a much larger one had to be accepted, which spoiled the neat lines of the nose entry and interfered with the torpedo position, although this had already had to be tilted nose-down to avoid losing ground clearance with tyres deflated and oleos fully compressed. These changes, added to those already estimated in May 1931 to have brought the all-up weight to its limit at 9,448 lb, were found by January to have raised it to 9,760 lb, of which the powerplant accounted for an increase of 327 lb and the fuselage structure 166 lb. Lachmann's suggestion to save 200 lb by making the engine cowling and seats in magnesium alloy and fuel pipes in aluminium was vetoed because of the risk of corrosion from sea-water, so the redesign of the landing gear to use conventional oleo-legs carrying small twin wheels at a weight cost of 120 lb seemed worth while to save development work and time, and in February 1932 the internally-sprung wheels were abandoned. Only much later did Handley Page learn that a successful similar design had been patented and developed by George Dowty at Glosters for the Kawasaki company in Japan, on the strength of which he had set up his own firm, which eventually grew into the vast Dowty Group organisation. Major Buchanan, Deputy DTD, was very concerned to hear of the drastic undercarriage changes, in view of earlier trouble with the H.P.38 landing gear, and expressed doubts to England on the reliability of the Handley Page tenders to new specifications then being considered.

On 22 February England paid a visit to the carrier *Ark Royal* to see how existing Blackburn, Fairey and Hawker aircraft stood up to the savage handling traditionally meted out to them by the Fleet Air Arm's Royal Navy deckhands. He returned with many useful tips, but considerable gloom concerning damage to wing-tips by boat-hooks, and to locked control surfaces and fluttering slats due to parking on deck tail to wind, all of which inevitably meant more weight increases. A month later Lachmann expressed concern over longitudinal stability and recommended an all-moving variable-camber tailplane with interconnected tail incidence and bias gear, so that as bias was applied the tailplane movement would be increased for a given control column movement; this would combine a light and powerful control at stalling speed with a restriction of loading at high speed; similar variable gearing had been successfully applied to the Gloster IV Schneider Trophy racing seaplane in 1927. In October 1932, when the assembled prototype was at last delivered from Cricklewood to Radlett for final installations to be completed before flight, the all-up weight estimated from actual component weighings had arisen to 10,300 lb and the last date for competing at Martlesham had gone by.

By this time Handley Page realised that he had caught a tiger by the tail, because cutting his losses at this point would have meant surrendering all chances of competing in the single-engined classes projected for RAF and FAA re-equipment. Already the M.1/30 requirement was being combined with the parallel S.9/30 reconnaissance/fleet-spotter role by Gloster and Fairey, eventually to mature as the S.15/33, and the Air Ministry would have cancelled the H.P.46, but for its research value as a sophisticated application of slots and flaps for high lift and low-speed control. Its planned flights were therefore to continue, although there was less urgency for military equipment to be installed.

The complete aircraft, unmarked and doped only in its red-oxide undercoat, was weighed at Radlett on 24 October, 1932, its corrected all-up weight being found to be 10,438 lb, and Lachmann suggested saving up to 800 lb by deleting the bomb-aimer's cradle, various structural refinements, a return to steam cooling and deletion of the 1,866-lb Type K torpedo in favour of the 1,460-lb Mk.X or 1,420-lb Mk.VIII* only. England made the first flight next day at a weight of 7,443 lb, with the slots locked shut and Percy Cooper (RTO) observing in the gunner's cockpit; after some preliminary taxying he took off, but landed after only a short straight hop with a long list of snags to be rectified, including an unsatisfactory hand-brake lever, elevator too light and general sponginess of the controls; he pointed out that when the slots were free to operate, the drooped lower

H.P.46 at Radlett in 1934 showing lower ailerons fixed and upper ailerons drooped with slots open. (*B. Cornthwaite*)

ailerons could touch the ground while taxying, and that the root-hinge 'bat's-wings' were too flexible. He also asked for the diagonal outer wing struts to be replaced by crossed Rafwires, as had been necessary in the case of the H.P.42. After the brakes had been adjusted, and mass-balances and a dashpot damper had been fitted to the elevators, England made a second test flight, with slots locked open, on 2 November. The take-off was much quicker than with slots closed, but there was no feel or feed-back from the floating elevators, which tended to flutter at a very low frequency in resonance with the much too flexible control column: England disliked Lachmann's 'flying tailplane' and asked for a conventional adjustable tailplane and normal elevators; he complained again of erratic braking and refused to fly the H.P.46 again until this had been put right.

For the third flight, on 16 November, with Cordes as passenger, the tailplane was fixed and the slots were again locked open. There was still no elevator response, but the aircraft took off and landed safely in a three-point attitude with very little run, and the control column, when tested on the ground with the elevator rear control lever clamped, was found to have four inches free movement due to 'whip'. England flew solo on 6 December, but landed after a single circuit, since the aircraft was now nose-heavy and still without effective elevator control, so that fore-and-aft trim could be obtained only by varying the throttle opening. The slots were free to operate, but failed to shut at high speed, and above 85 kt the whole aircraft vibrated excessively. Before the fifth flight, on 16 January, 1933, a fixed tailplane with larger elevators had been fitted; on a short flight at 7,715 lb with slots locked open, England found the aircraft still very nose-heavy, though the ailerons had improved and the new elevators gave adequate control for landing. A completely new assembly of tailplane and elevators was next manufactured, after six months of bench-testing to reduce friction and backlash throughout the control system; England's next flight was consequently delayed until 14 July, 1933. He found the new tail unit quite steady at all speeds up to 130 kt, but there was some mainplane vibration and 'bat's-wing' flutter, also insufficient roll control with slots closed. The ailerons and elevators were now almost frictionless and felt too light in the air, so England asked for increased gearing for the ailerons and slight friction damping for the elevators; he found no tendency for the elevators to overbalance, but the rudder needed excessive pressure with the right foot in order to fly straight and a manually controlled rudder bias was requested. Lachmann had the fin offset two degrees to port, replaced the 'bat's-wings' by rigid sheet metal fairings, and increased the length of the aileron lever without changing the differential setting. The H.P.46 was then flown on 25 July by England and Cordes in turn for ten minutes each; they asked for the fin offset to be increased to three degrees, agreed that the windscreen was useless at all speeds, and reported that just before touch-down the slots opened suddenly and lowered the flaps, causing a strong nose-down trim change, which the pilot could not control because the elevator was still ineffective at low speeds. By this time the H.P.46 had cost £30,650 (including £800 for the new tail unit) and Handley Page wanted the Air Ministry to take it off his hands and continue the high-lift testing at the RAE, but they declined to do so.

Alternative handling flights by England and Cordes continued on 14 August, after further modifications to reduce friction in the interceptors, and the ailerons were found to be effective with slots closed at 65 kt and above, but remained ineffective near the stall even with the windscreen removed altogether, proving that the latter was not creating turbulence over the tail as had been suspected; to add insult to injury, the pilot's seat collapsed as England was landing and he was very much annoyed. Nevertheless he made a further flight, with Cordes as passenger, on 29 August, when the seat collapsed again and he refused to go on flying until the seat-adjusting mechanism had been improved. This was ready by 23 December, together with a modified elevator control; England took off with the full automatic slot and flap gear working satisfactorily, but found difficulty in flying level because of tail-heaviness, so confined himself to straight flying only. On 13 January, 1934, the H.P.46 was still very tail-heavy, and even after further adjustments Cordes found it impossible on 23 March to gain speed above 90 kt; it was still the same on the 28th, when alteration of the tail-trimming gear had failed to make any improvement, although the aircraft would glide at 60 kt and fly hands-off with power on down to 55 kt; but lateral control was so lacking that this time he had to fly on to the ground with slots open and touch down in order to regain an even keel. Cordes tested a Flettner servo-tab on the elevators in April, with R. S. Stafford recording rates of descent with an air-log, and on the 20th attempted a stalled glide with c.g. aft from 7,000 ft, but had to abandon this test because of turbulent air. On 16 March all further design and modification work on the H.P.46 had been stopped until further advice was available from the RAE on how to cure the instability about all axes due, apparently, to blanketing of the tail surfaces; on 18 April Lachmann reported the air-log glide results. After waiting for calmer weather, England tried a general handling flight once more on 2 May, 1934; the controls were fairly well harmonised at cruising speeds of 70–100 kt, but useless below 55 kt and it was impossible to use the rudder for taxying, or to counteract torque reaction from a sudden burst of throttle by means of the ailerons. So he condemned the H.P.46 as too dangerous for deck-flying and Handley Page sought an immediate interview with Major Buchanan (D/DTD), who met him on 17 July to discuss future action.

After a visit to Cricklewood by H. L. Stevens of the RAE and having considered a detailed history of the case submitted by Handley Page on 8 November, 1934, the Air Ministry agreed to take delivery of the H.P.46 at the RAE and to pay the balance of the contract price, subject to the expression of 'DTD's dissatisfaction.' Whether or not the RAE intended to investigate the tail unit in their full-scale 24-ft wind-tunnel is not recorded, but it seems that no such work was done. The H.P.46 left Radlett for Farnborough by road in April 1935 and was no more seen, to the relief of all concerned; its total flying time had amounted to only 5½ hours and it had cost Handley Page over £36,000—nearly twice the contract price.

With today's hindsight, it seems that the RAE relied too heavily on wind-tunnel results in ignorance of the magnitude and uncertainty of local vortex formation at low Reynolds Numbers; consequently they derived and recommended misleading scale-effect data, and none of the aircraft industry's aerodynamicists—not even Prandtl's pupil Lachmann—knew any better. Only the more conventional biplanes among the M.1/30, F.7/30 and S.9/30 prototypes were in any degree successful, e.g. the Blackburn M.1/30 and the Gloster and Hawker F.7/30s, while the less orthodox

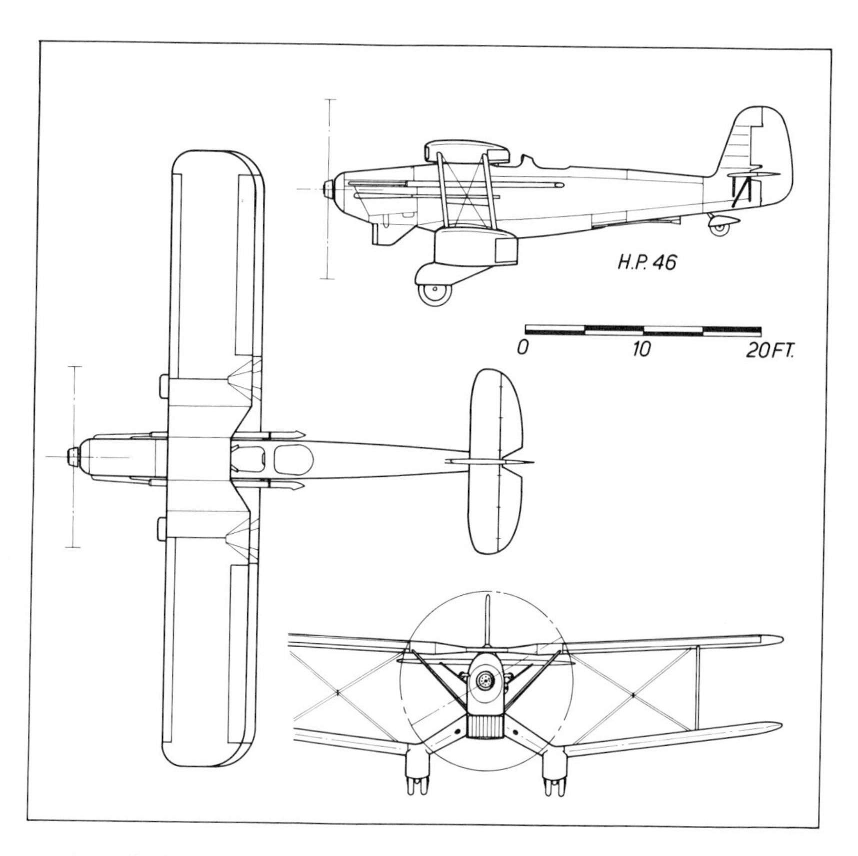

projects, including the H.P.46, Blackburn F.7/30 and Bristol 123, were all problem children, incurable in the state of the art in 1933. The H.P.46 was the last biplane to be designed by Handley Page Ltd and one of their last types to employ doped fabric covering for components other than flying control surfaces. No description was ever released to the press of the day and no official photographs have so far been discovered in the archives; the snapshots reproduced here were taken unofficially (and no doubt illegally) by Bert Cornthwaite while working at Radlett as an apprentice.

H.P.41

(Rolls-Royce F.XIVS)

Span 50 ft (15·25 m); length landplane 36 ft (10·97 m), (seaplane) 37 ft (11·29 m); wing area 610 sq ft (56·7 m^2). Maximum weight (est) 7,250 lb (3,287 kg). Speed (est) 140 mph (225 km/h).

H.P.46

(Rolls-Royce Buzzard III)

Span 50 ft (15·25 m); length 39 ft 5 in (12·45 m); wing area 656 sq ft (61 m^2). Empty weight 6,250 lb (2,837 kg); maximum weight 10,600 lb (4,800 kg). Speed 140 mph (225 km/h). Crew two.

G.4/31
(H.P.47)

In the early years of his association with Handley Page, Dr Gustav Victor Lachmann had acted not only as aerodynamic consultant on slot development, but also as correspondent on German progress in structural design, particularly of cantilever monoplane wings, which he studied at Darmstadt and Göttingen. He was instrumental in arranging for Handley Page to receive, on behalf of the Air Ministry, samples of current German metal monoplanes released for research purposes by the Allied Armistice Commission, and Handley Page Ltd obtained contract cover to rebuild a Junkers-F 13, a Dornier Komet and a Dornier Delphin III for evaluation, with the serials J7232, J7276 and N176 respectively; the first two were tested at Farnborough in 1923 and the last at Felixstowe in 1924. But the potential aerodynamic efficiency of the monoplane could not outweigh its initial disadvantage in structure weight, even in the largest sizes exemplified by the Beardmore Inflexible and Dornier Do X, although the later Junkers-G 38 enjoyed more success. Lachmann was among the first to study the tension-field theory advanced by Herbert Wagner of the Rohrbach company (published in German in 1928, but not translated into English—by NACA—till 1931) and he was eager to apply it to cantilever wing design. In 1926 he had gone to the Ishikawajima works at Tokyo as technical adviser, after a somewhat frustrating experience of the limited post-war German aircraft industry, although his neat single-engined Albatros L 72a biplane, designed specifically for Verlag Ullstein to speed deliveries of their newspaper *Berliner Zeitung am Mittag*, had achieved a remarkable speed range by means of interconnected leading-edge slots and flaps inboard of the ailerons on both upper and lower wings; no slots were provided in front of the ailerons, possibly because Lachmann knew that Handley Page was still in difficulties with slot-and-aileron gear in 1925. In his twin-engined Albatros L 73 eight-passenger cabin biplane, he discarded leading-edge slots altogether, relying solely on full-span slotted ailerons for increased lift at low speeds; this was contemporary with the Handley Page Hamlet, already described as a derivative of the Type 'X' monoplane tested by Lachmann in the Göttingen wind-tunnel.

In Japan Lachmann was required to design a light biplane with a Cirrus engine, on the lines of the Avro Avian and D.H. Moth, primarily to advertise Ishikawajima's entry into the aviation field, and he was not unduly dismayed when, on completion, he was expected to fly it himself, since no other test pilot had been engaged. This biplane performed well and in 1931 was flown across Siberia and Russia to Germany; but this event occurred two years after Lachmann had returned to Europe and had accepted Handley Page's invitation to join the company's staff to co-ordinate and extend the work of the wind-tunnel and experimental departments, under G. C. D. Russell and S. G. Ebel respectively. In one of his earliest memoranda to Handley Page, on 17 December, 1929, he scarcely endeared himself to his new colleagues by criticising the design of the H.P.42 and predicting the risk of one airscrew exploding and damaging all the others, but his foresight was acknowledged when this accident actually happened to Captain Dismore in *Hannibal* on 8 August, 1931. During 1930 he had taken over performance and weight estimation from Oswald and he had a major share in designing the unlucky H.P.46, originating both the cantilever fuel tank/undercarriage unit and the all-moving tailplane in response to the urgent problems of weight restriction and low-speed controllability. Although his careful analysis was partly invalidated by the unreliable data then available on the RAF 34 aerofoil, he was quick to appreciate the advantage of a high-lift wing section having a small variation of centre of pressure with incidence for a monoplane wing with a single spar at the mean c.p. position. In January 1931 his chance came, with a much-delayed invitation from the Air Ministry to tender for a high-speed mailplane to specification 21/28, whose prime requirement was ability to carry 1,000 lb of mail for 1,000 miles at a cruising speed of 150 mph.

Artist's impression of Mailplane tendered to specification 21/28 in January 1931.

Assuming that a single-engined aircraft was expected, Lachmann proposed a low-wing cantilever monoplane with a uniformly tapered wing of RAF 34 section, a very clean fuselage of oval cross-section with a single enclosed cockpit well aft of the c.g. and a low-drag tail unit similar to that of the Supermarine S.6 Schneider Trophy seaplane; the undercarriage had large 'trouser-leg' wheel fairings and divided swing axles. Four types of engine were available: the Rolls-Royce H.10 (Buzzard) and Armstrong Siddeley Leopard in the 850 hp class, and the smaller but more economical Rolls-Royce Kestrel V and Bristol Jupiter XFBM in the 600 hp class. The Buzzard was preferred to the Leopard, but the Kestrel, in its steam-cooled version, promised the best fuel economy, although the reliability of steam-cooling for long-range operation was still unproven; the Buzzard was chosen for the tender design, which had a span of 58 ft, wing area of 425 sq ft, all-up weight of 8,300 lb and an estimated true air speed at sea level of 190 mph. Handley Page took this tender personally to Captain Liptrot at the Air Ministry and was astonished to be told of the official preference for a twin-engined biplane with a cruising speed of 130 mph and a landing speed of less than 50 mph. On hearing this, Lachmann revised his design to a lower all-up weight of 6,500 lb using a Jupiter XFBM with a Townend ring, which gave a maximum speed of 182 mph at 5,000 ft; this was submitted on 14 February, 1931, but the Air Ministry still preferred a twin-engined biplane and awarded the contract for a single prototype to the Boulton-Paul P.64; the Handley Page project, provisionally designated H.P.47, was terminated as a mail-carrier, but revived in June when specification G.4/31 was issued for a single-engined general-purpose military aircraft.

This combined three roles: (a) to replace the Vickers Vincent in the Middle East and India; (b) as a day and night bomber to operate from unprepared aerodromes in any part of the world; and (c) as a land-based torpedo-bomber to operate from average tropical aerodromes, particularly in the Aden, Persian Gulf and Singapore areas. In each role a crew of two was required, the pilot having a fixed synchronised Vickers gun and the gunner/bomb-aimer a single Lewis gun on a high-speed mounting; the gunner was to have the best possible field of fire aft and an alternative forward prone bombing station where he could be seen by the pilot, the bomb-sight being mounted in a draught-free slot with a range of vision from 85 degrees forward to 10 degrees aft of the vertical. In the general purpose role the total military load of 1,653 lb included either desert equipment with thorn-proof wheels and brakes, or marine distress signals and dinghy stowage with provision for a twin-float undercarriage. Bomb carriers were required for at least twenty 20-lb bombs, or four 112-lb GP, or four 250-lb GP, AS or SAP bombs, or two 450-lb AP, 500-lb GP, AS or SAP, or 520/550-lb old-type bombs, or a single 1,000-lb GP or 1,500-lb AP bomb; these were alternative loads for the day and night bomber role having a total military load of 1,436 lb, but additionally, in the torpedo-bomber role, provision was required for a K-type (1,870-lb), Mk.VIII* (1,420-lb), or Mk.X (1,460-lb) torpedo, all of 18-in diameter; in the torpedo role the military load was 2,919 lb. The bomber version was to attain at least 140 mph at 5,000 ft with a service ceiling of 20,000 ft, and to land no faster than 53 mph, while the torpedo version was to be capable of climbing at 500 ft/min and landing at 60 mph.

Lachmann had already designed the wing before the specification was issued, incorporating a stressed-skin torsion-box formed by the leading edge and single main spar, aft of which the wing had a tubular rib structure with doped fabric covering, bounded by an auxiliary spar carrying the aileron and flap hinges. The centre-section was entirely metal-skinned and enclosed the main fuel tanks, so as to leave the interior of the fuselage free for carrying the several military loads, which included various stores and cargo items, or three seated passengers, or two stretcher cases for casualty evacuation. The front portion of the fuselage was semi-monocoque with thin skin stiffened by horizontal corrugations in the Junkers manner; the pilot sat high behind and above the engine bay, with a completely unobstructed view upwards and a downward field of vision of nearly 270 degrees; a side door gave easy entry to the cockpit and rapid exit in emergency, even with the aircraft inverted after a crash landing; aft of the wing, the gunner's cockpit was set low and well sheltered from the slipstream, while an exceptional field of fire was assured by tapering the rear fuselage to an oval-section small-diameter boom carrying the cantilever tail unit and tailwheel. The main undercarriage comprised two long-stroke fixed oleo-legs each carrying a single spatted wheel and braced outboard by a diagonal strut to the outer wing spar; this left the whole underside of the centre-section free for torpedo and bomb racks. In designing the flying controls, Lachmann incorporated his preferred all-moving tailplane and one-piece elevator with variable elevator gearing, ailerons inserted into the full-span flaps, and full-span leading-edge slots in three sections, the two inboard being linked to the flaps and the outer being automatic, with interceptors connected to the ailerons. The fin and tailplane, rudder and elevator all had corrugated stressed skins, only the ailerons and flaps being fabric-covered. Located a little forward of, and above, the tailplane, the fin and rudder moved together to give a graduated change of camber with minimum screening of the elevator. In the G.4/31 tender submitted on 2 November, 1931, equivalent monoplane and biplane versions were compared, with a choice of either the Rolls-Royce Kestrel IIIMS or Bristol Jupiter XFBM engine, the latter being preferred for tropical service, but in February the Air Ministry specified a Bristol Pegasus IM3 of slightly greater take-off power; on 13 April contract No.174760/32 for a single prototype, K2773, was signed, the price being £9,250 and delivery date 13 April, 1933. The mock-up was first inspected by Wing Cmdr Maund and Sqn Ldr Mansell on 4 February, 1932, and Major Buchanan agreed to order an additional wing and a specimen tail-boom for structural testing by the RAE; the first formal mock-up conference was held on 30 June and meanwhile an accurately dimensioned and weighted 1/24-scale model was made for spinning tests in the RAE's new vertical wind-tunnel.

With the prototype officially ordered, both England and Cordes became concerned at the current lack of experience of monoplanes in the RAF, and recognised that Service pilots would have to be convinced that the H.P.47's controls were much better than the Hare's had been. As England pointed out to Handley Page, the problem was twofold and comprised (a) the handling difference between biplanes and monoplanes, and (b) the handling of a fully slotted and flapped aeroplane. He suggested buying a second-hand light aeroplane for conversion to a fully-slotted monoplane of the same wing-loading as the H.P.47 for familiarisation and demonstration to the squadrons, but Lachmann opposed this suggestion and recommended the purchase of a Heinkel He 64 specifically designed for slow landing and quick take-off. The RAE supported this proposal as a continuation of the low-speed research begun on the Gugnunc, and in December the Air Ministry purchased the special Gipsy-engined He 64C with long-travel landing gear which, as D-2305, had performed well in the short take-off and landing competitions of the Europa Rundflug. Transferred to the British civil register as G-ACBS, this was loaned to Handley Page Ltd for six months and thereafter taken on charge by the RAE as K3596. England and Cordes gained a useful amount of handling experience, enabling them to suggest improvements in the H.P.47 during its construction.

In September 1932, after a second formal mock-up conference had been held and the design features agreed, Handley Page suggested several possible derivatives, including (a) a civil transport using the same wing and

H.P.47 under construction, with round-topped rudder and forward-sliding pilot's hood.

tail, with a larger fuselage and either a single Pegasus or twin Mongoose engines; (b) a torpedo-carrier to specification M.1/30, with the span reduced to 50 ft and longer oleo-legs for deck-landing; and (c) a similar deck-landing fleet spotter to specification S.9/30, with still smaller wing area and lighter weight. Project numbers H.P.48 and H.P.49 were reserved to cover the possibility of these variants going forward, but in the event were never used, the small-winged project being referred to simply as the 'H.P.47 Junior'. The initial strength tests at the RAE on the D-spar and tail-boom in December 1931 had revealed marginal ultimate factors, so these components were modified and strengthened, and the opportunity was taken to introduce flush rivets for the wing skin. In February 1933 the new tail-boom was approved, but meanwhile the spinning tests of the 1/24th model in the RAE vertical tunnel had shown undue reluctance to recover from a flat spin. Lachmann had therefore lengthened the tail-boom by 20 inches, leaving the fin and rudder in their original position so as to avoid all risk of blanketing of the rudder by the tailplane. This had only improved recovery time by a small margin, considered insufficient to counteract the effect in the c.g. aft condition of the outer wing-tip slot being open and the inner one closed, unless the ailerons were assisted by using the interceptors. Several modifications were tried out on the model, including increasing the horizontal tail area by 20 per cent and inclining the rudder hinge forward both with the vertical area unchanged and with an increase of 40 per cent; also the enlarged elevator was tested with different shapes of horn balance. By mid-June, when the spinning report (RAE B.A.1048) was issued, the H.P.47 was virtually complete at Radlett, awaiting arrival of its Pegasus IM3 engine; it was due to fly in August, six months behind schedule, and among the minor novelties could be seen the Junkers-pattern round-topped parallel-chord rudder with horn balance, the brakes on the outer faces of the mainwheels and the sliding hood over the pilot's cockpit, which opened forward over the windscreen, partly for structural reasons and partly to ensure that in a crash violent enough to shear the rack and pinion gear, the hood would jam open rather than shut. The engine arrived at the end of July but, as expected, caused too much vibration throughout the metal fuselage, especially torsional whipping of the tail unit, to be acceptable for flight. Bristols had anticipated this trouble and had already completed a 45-hr hangar test on a Pegasus IIM3 mounted on Lord rubber-bushed bearers, but, to take advantage of this, the first flight date had to be further put back to October 1933. None of the other G.4/31 competitors was any further forward than the H.P.47. Of the two ordered officially, the Vickers 253 biplane K2771 did not fly till August 1934, nor did the Parnall biplane K2772 till October 1934, but two of the private ventures, the Armstrong Whitworth A.W.19 biplane and the Westland P.V.7 monoplane, completed their contractors' trials and arrived at Martlesham in July 1934, notwithstanding the official ruling given in October 1933 that no entries could be accepted after 31 January, 1934.

The H.P.47 was prepared for flight on 11 November and externally painted all over with one coat of aluminium, with the new standard 'cockpit green' inside the pilot's station and the remainder of the interior, including the gunner's cockpit, finished in white gloss. It was hoped to complete

H.P.47 at Radlett before first flight in October 1933.

H.P.47 at Radlett in March 1935 with flaps extended. (*Flight*)

contractor's flight trials by the end of the year and to hold the final conference in mid-January, so as to meet the Martlesham dead-line. The first flights were in fact achieved on 27 November, two by England at weights of 5,930 lb and 6,110 lb respectively, followed by Cordes solo at the latter weight. They agreed that the elevator was too heavy, the oleo-legs too soft, the brakes unequal in effect and the tailplane incidence impossible to trim. Both complained that maximum effort was needed to slide the cockpit hood open against the slipstream, although no goggles were needed with the hood closed. After immediate adjustments to the oleo-legs and brakes, England flew again on the 29th, but refused to continue until a new windscreen with side wings and no hood had been made and fitted. Flight trials were pressed ahead as vigorously as the weather would allow and by 9 March, 1934, England had made thirteen flights and Cordes nine. In May, England reported tailwheel shimmy and he also asked for the interceptors to be removed since lateral control was adequate without them, but the tail controls were still unsatisfactory. Lachmann then decided to extend the rudder height and chord with plywood, including a larger servo-tab, to fit external mass-balance weights to the elevator, to improve but not delete the interceptors, and to limit oleo-leg travel still further to check wallowing while taxying. To reduce drag overall, wheel spats and strut fairings were installed and a new design of Townend ring, incorporating the exhaust manifold in the leading edge, was ordered from Bristols; a three-blade Fairey-Reed duralumin airscrew was ordered for comparison with the standard Watts two-blader, also Lockheed hydraulic flap operating gear. The Townend ring and flap gear arrived together on 5 January, 1935, enabling both to be flight-tested in time for the final design conference on the 11th. By this time Cordes was in sole charge of flight testing, England having handed over to him on 31 August after his twentieth, and Cordes' fortieth, flights in the H.P.47.

Full Service equipment was then installed, including a new Pegasus IIIM3 engine with long exhaust pipes, and torpedo gear, concurrently with a major inspection, which was completed during February and March. At last, on 20 April, 1935, K2773 reached Martlesham Heath and climbed on the 23rd to 12,900 ft with full torpedo load of 9,244 lb. Handling trials were done mainly by Flt Lieuts Bilney, Carr and Horrex during May and the full performance was measured with both bomber and torpedo loads. A & AEE report M.674 criticised its inherent longitudinal instability and the extreme sensitivity of the tail-trimming gear, which made it difficult to trim at any speed with engine on; it also noted a vibration in the control column at all speeds except between 110 and 120 mph and called for both these faults to be corrected before beginning squadron trials. The steep landing with flaps down was, as England had predicted, a novelty to RAF pilots which they soon accepted as an advantage, but they disliked the change of trim during flap operation and considered it dangerous in the event of an overshoot; they suggested interconnecting the flap gear and tail trimmer. On 29 May, when all the G.4/31 trials ended, the seven surviving competitors were inspected by AVM H. C. T. Dowding (AMRD) and Air Commodore R. H. Verney (DTD); the Vickers 253 biplane was considered superior to the H.P.47, but the latter was preferred to the Blackburn B-7. The Westland monoplane had crashed a year earlier and the Parnall failed to arrive in time, but although a production contract was awarded to the Vickers 253, its makers had the order transferred to their newer monoplane, which went into squadron service as the Wellesley.

H.P.47 flying in June 1935. (*The Aeroplane*)

Had the H.P.47 been ordered into production, Lachmann intended to improve the monocoque and wing spar, increasing the dihedral from 4½ degrees to 6 degrees, eliminating the centre-section wing joints, replacing the corrugated skin by heavier gauge smooth skin, increasing the tail-boom cross-section, replacing the undercarriage 'tripods' by cantilever oleo-legs with low-pressure 'doughnut' wheels, enclosing the pilot's cockpit with a single-piece sliding canopy, and fairing in the gunner's cockpit as on the Westland P.V.7—but it was not to be, although a revised wing-root fairing was made and flown in September as a sequel to observations of wool-tufts by R. S. Stafford and C. O. Vernon in August; this was reported to have cured control column vibration, but in November the original root fairing was restored without adverse effect. Lockheed then became unsure whether the proposed flap/tail-trim linkage was feasible and at Handley Page's request the Air Ministry agreed to take delivery at the RAE without further tests at Martlesham; Cordes cleared the mandatory pre-delivery diving tests in his seventy-ninth and final flight in the H.P.47 on 5 March, 1936, and it was ferried to Farnborough by Flt Lieut Fraser of the RAE three weeks later. During the next three months Fraser investigated its slow-flying qualities, reporting slight lateral instability with tip slots open, main

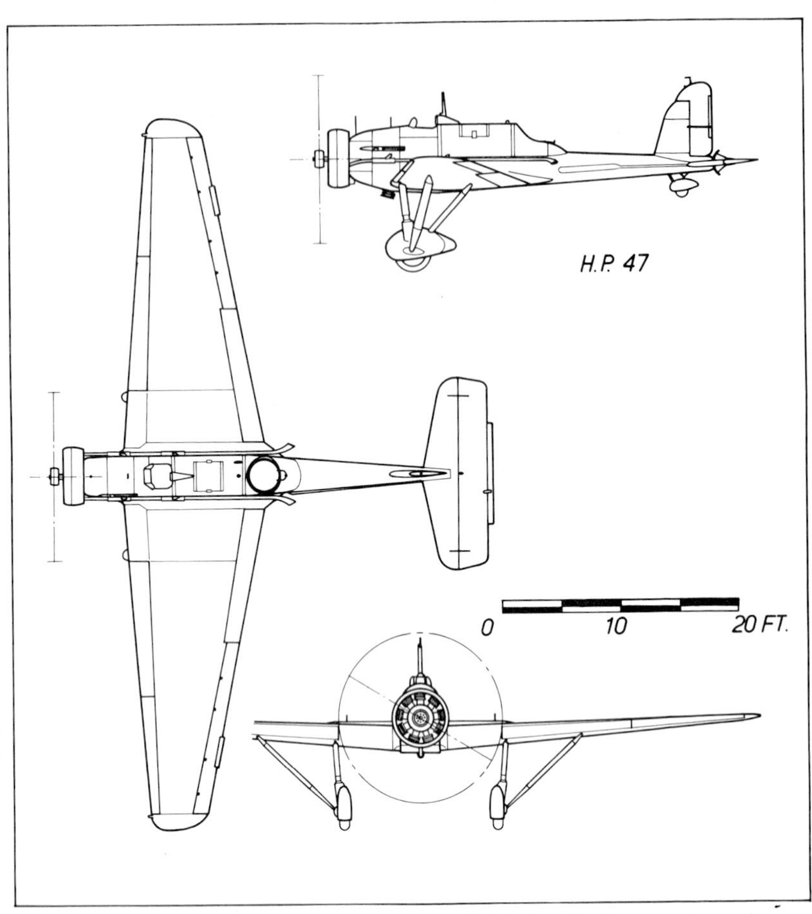

slots closed and flaps up, but fully controllable by the interceptors; it was more unstable with flaps down and main slots closed, but very stable with flaps down and main slots open; the change of trim on lowering the flaps was less than he had expected and was easily held by the elevator while retrimming. Thereafter the H.P.47 was flown mainly for engine development, because interest in steep and slow landings had been forced to give way to the quest for more engine power in preparation for the impending struggle with Hitler's rapidly expanding air fleet; K2773 was finally struck off charge and scrapped in May 1937.

H.P.47

(Bristol Pegasus III)

Span 58 ft (17·7 m); length 37 ft 7½ in (11·51 m); wing area 438 sq ft (40·7 m²). Empty weight 5,362 lb (2,435 kg); maximum weight (General Purpose and Bomber) 7,708 lb (3,500 kg), (Torpedo) 9,244 lb (4,190 kg). Speed 161 mph (245 km/h); range (General Purpose) 1,250 miles (2,150 km), (Bomber) 550 miles (885 km), (Torpedo) 400 miles (645 km); ceiling 19,900 ft (5,940 m). Crew two.

C.26/31 (H.P.51)

The failure in 1932 of the C.16/28 competition to elicit any better a replacement for the Vickers Victoria than its derivative the Pegasus-engined Valentia led to the issue in April of that year of a new specification, C.26/31, for a twin-engined bomber-transport monoplane for use principally in tropical countries at higher altitudes than the Valentia could attain. Within an all-up weight limit of 18,000 lb it was to be capable of carrying a military load of 3,050 lb (including at least ten fully-equipped troops in addition to the crew of two) for a range of 920 miles, cruising at 10,000 ft and not less than 95 mph at normal engine rating. Emphasis was laid on easy maintenance and repair in the field under desert conditions and on a wide range of maximum loads including:

(a) 24 men with full military equipment, or
(b) at least three aero-engines each weighing 1,000 lb, or
(c) an equivalent load of fuel or water, for which suitable tanks were to be supplied, or
(d) ten stretcher cases, or
(e) an equivalent load of miscellaneous cargo.

The crew of two were to share between them the duties of pilot, navigator, W/T operator and bomb-aimer, and gunner's stations were to be provided in the extreme nose and tail, each with a Lewis gun on an approved mounting and five double drums of SAA; the nose station was also to provide for navigation and bomb aiming, with a chart-board and tip-up seat adjacent. The pilot's enclosed cockpit was to provide the best possible view in all directions and to permit the crew to change places easily during flight; an auto-pilot and dual control conversion set were to be provided, and the W/T station was to be close to the pilot, but as free from noise as possible. Both passenger and cargo doors were required, also one or more parachute exit hatches in the fuselage floor, and at least five emergency exits (including break-out windows) for rapid evacuation by passengers after a crash on land or sea. Furnishings were to be adequate but as light as possible, and bomb carriers and releases were required for eight 250-lb GP bombs and eight 20-lb practice bombs. Low-pressure thorn-proof tyres were specified, together with wheel-brakes, a tailwheel, detachable mud-guards or wheel fairings, and provision for buoyancy bags.

To Handley Page and Lachmann, this was an answer to an urgent prayer, for the H.P.43 was a failure and the Air Ministry were reluctant to take delivery or pay the contract price for it. As soon as the structural tests at RAE on the H.P.47 wing spar had confirmed the validity of the design assumptions, Lachmann began the design of a similar wing of 90 ft span to which the H.P.43 fuselage and tail unit could be adapted. The wider root chord of the monoplane wing required a corresponding increase in tail arm and this was readily obtained by splicing in an extra 31-inch length of parallel section between the original front and rear portions of the H.P.43's fuselage. The original tail unit was retained, with the fin and rudder chord increased by extensions of the leading and trailing edges. By June 1933 the preliminary weight estimate and stability diagram had been drawn and Handley Page Ltd had submitted a tender for converting the H.P.43 to a monoplane designated H.P.51, having chosen Armstrong Siddeley Tiger II engines installed in long-chord Townend rings in preference to Bristol Pegasus IM3. All the drawings for the conversion were to be complete by November and the H.P.51 was to be built in the experimental shop at Cricklewood. Air Ministry permission to dismantle and convert the H.P.43 had not been received by 12 December and the final drawing issue was delayed till March 1934 to allow investigation of a possible Nash & Thompson turret for the nose station and any alterations arising from wind-tunnel tests in progress. The latter were generally promising, but the tailplane was found to be badly placed in relation to the downwash from the wing and Handley Page, having no more money available for alterations not absolutely essential and urgent, refused to allow Lachmann to design a new larger tailplane with taller fins, which would have solved the problem.

H.P.51 at Cricklewood during conversion from H.P.43.

By November 1934 the H.P.51 airframe was complete except for its fabric covering and was photographed thus at Cricklewood before being dismantled for transport to Radlett. Handley Page had already discussed with George Woods Humphery the possibility of converting Imperial Airways' H.P.42s, one at a time, into four-engined monoplanes, using the original fuselages, or of supplying a civil version of the H.P.51, and in July Imperial Airways had invited a tender, but a price and delivery date could not be agreed. In October Major Buchanan (Deputy DTD) was asked to approve the substitution of Pegasus engines for Tigers, but he refused and would agree only to using Tiger VIs instead of Tiger IVs. Meanwhile Lockheed hydraulic flap operating gear was ordered and Tampier Bloctube engine controls were agreed upon. The H.P.51, which retained the H.P.43's original serial J9833, was completed at Radlett in April 1935 and first flown there on 8 May by Cordes. He found it vastly improved from the H.P.43 and Handley Page decided to start the design of a fully-productionised

H.P.51 as first flown in May 1935 with Tiger engines and original tail unit.

version, H.P.54, which would be more likely to win the C.26/31 competition against the Armstrong Whitworth and Bristol contenders, single prototypes of which had been ordered in March 1933 and began flying in June 1935. Cordes confirmed that Handley Page's insistence on economy over the tail unit was ill-advised and strongly recommended the new tail unit which Lachmann had designed in direct defiance of his managing director's veto. Lachmann said in later years that Handley Page never really forgave him for 'disobeying orders' in spite of the improvements that ensued. After being tested in the Cricklewood wind-tunnel, the 1/32-scale model of H.P.51 had been sent to Farnborough for investigation of the gliding characteristics resulting from use of the half-span slotted flaps, which impaired the elevator response. The results of these tests in January 1935 (RAE report No.B.A.1184) enabled Lachmann to finalise the tail unit for the H.P.54; the latter retained the H.P.51's tapered wing of RAF 34 section and similar slats along the outer semi-span of the leading edge and slotted flaps along the inner semi-span of the trailing edge. The fuselage was lengthened and improved in shape by rounding-out the fabric covering with numerous stringers, and by installing enclosed gun turrets at the nose and tail, together with a hemispherical cupola for a mid-upper gun mounting above the wing. The latter was fabric-covered aft of the single main spar, as were the tailplane and all control surfaces, but the fins were stressed-skin cantilever structures. It was a matter of urgency to confirm the wind-tunnel results by full-scale flight tests, so the existing tail surfaces of the H.P.51 were extended to the H.P.54's outline, thus increasing the areas by 70 per cent. Since the fins and tailplane could not easily be strengthened internally to match the increased bending moments, they were braced as necessary by external struts and a new wooden elevator was made in February 1936, at which time two Bristol Pegasus III engines were allotted to replace the Tigers; these had two-piece four-blade airscrews of opposite rotation to the Tigers and were aerodynamically representative of the variable-pitch metal three-bladers scheduled for the Pegasus Xs of the H.P.54. The Pegasus engines needed Lord rubber-bushed mountings, which delayed completion till August 1936; the H.P.51 was flown by Cordes with Pegasus IIIs and the original tail early in September, after which the new tail was fitted.

The H.P.51 was withdrawn from the C.26/31 competition, which was won by the Bristol 130, because the H.P.54 was chosen to replace the

H.P.51 with Pegasus engines and revised tail unit at Farnborough in March 1937. (*RAE—Crown Copyright*)

long outmoded Virginia as an interim bomber crew-trainer until the new generation of high performance bombers came into service. Just as the last batch of Heyfords was being completed at Cricklewood, a contract* was awarded 'straight off the drawing-board' for one hundred H.P.54s to be equipped as night-bombers to specification B.29/35, with a crew of four and power-operated turrets at nose and tail. George Volkert, who had lately spent some months in the United States studying American production methods, planned a rapid and efficient assembly line using jigs and templates designed by James Hamilton and on 10 October the first of the batch, K6933, officially named Harrow, was flown at Radlett by Cordes, who had also been invited to fly the Bristol 130 at Martlesham; the firm was allowed to retain the revised H.P.51 for a short time for familiarisation and various equipment trials. J9833 went to Martlesham Heath in January 1937 for brief performance tests and was transferred on 11 February to the RAE, where Aero Flight undertook extended handling and acceptance trials in March 1937. In May it was allotted to Radio Flight for general radio equipment development, which was interrupted on 10 June when it was loaned to the War Office for five days for troop-carrying exercises on Salisbury Plain. It returned to this task on 28 and 29 July, but meanwhile transferred to Instrument and Photographic Flight for a preliminary fuel tanker installation with which it flew to Flight Refuelling Ltd at Ford, Sussex, on 28 June, returning to Farnborough next day. After improvements, this installation underwent full flight trials at Ford between 9 and 29 August. In October the H.P.51 was handed back to Aero Flight for

* No.435062/35.

further longitudinal stability trials in preparation for blind landing trials in February and April 1938. These were done by I and P Flight, who also tested artificial horizons in February 1939, followed in April by contact lighting trials at Hendon; between these dates Radio Flight used J9833 for trials of throat microphones, intercom, TR9D and other VHF sets, lasting till November 1939.

J9833 was still being flown at RAE in January 1940, but seems to have been struck off charge soon afterwards.

H.P.51

(Two Armstrong Siddeley Tiger IV or two Bristol Pegasus III)

Span 90 ft (27·45 m); length 78 ft 4 in (23·9 m); wing area 1,170 sq ft (157·9 m²). Empty weight 12,000 lb (5,445 kg); maximum weight 18,000 lb (8,160 kg). Speed 188 mph (302 km/h); range 950 miles (1,530 km). Crew five.

Hampden and Hereford (H.P.52) and Swedish Seaplane (H.P.53)

When Japan invaded Manchuria in 1932 and the Geneva Disarmament Conference failed to agree on the ethics of bombing, the Air Staff realised that the RAF's existing biplane bombers were much inferior in performance to the best contemporary civil monoplanes. Although two monoplane projects had been submitted to meet specification B.19/27 and a few Fairey Hendons had been ordered in consequence, their handling at higher wing loadings had raised problems and doubts as to the wisdom of abandoning biplanes too soon. However, the Vickers 246, Westland P.V.7 and H.P.47 monoplanes had shown up well in the G.4/31 class at Martlesham, holding their own with biplanes in quick take-off and short landing run as experience was gained in the use of slots and flaps. None of the G.4/31 entries had the speed and range needed to carry bombs larger than 500 lb to the nearest most probable target, which by October 1932 was seen as Germany rather than France, following Adolf Hitler's rise to power in the recent elections. If, as expected, the Disarmament Conference raised the tare weight limit for bombers to 6,500 lb, there would be an urgent demand for a high-performance day bomber to replace the Hart and Sidestrand, and this would inevitably be a twin-engined monoplane with a retractable landing gear. All this information had been gleaned by Tom Harry England in a personal visit to the Air Ministry on 30 October, 1932, and he had also discovered that a new specification, B.9/32, already existed in draft and was due to be issued to the manufacturers at the end of February, unless delayed by the League of Nations.

Handley Page at once instructed Lachmann to make a very thorough analysis of all existing and notable earlier designs and to derive therefrom an optimised replacement for the Sidestrand, then the only twin-engined day bomber in RAF service. It was to incorporate metal monocoque construction throughout, with fabric covering restricted to control surfaces only, variable-pitch airscrews and a retractable undercarriage—all features still on the fringe of technical feasibility in 1932. As soon as a basic layout had been decided, what in those days amounted to a massive sales drive was directed at the Air Ministry to persuade them to order at least one complete squadron for trial; a descriptive brochure was urgently written and sent to AMSR and DTD, while a preliminary wind-tunnel model was tested and the results were passed to Captain Liptrot and Frank Cowlin of the Ministry's technical staff. By Easter 1933 a mock-up was ready to be shown to a group of RAF officers from several day-bomber squadrons then flying Hawker Harts and expecting to be re-equipped with Hinds; also some from No.101 Squadron, who had already gained several years of twin-engined experience and were looking forward to receiving Overstrands with powered nose turrets. The B.9/32 specification laid down the tare weight limit of 6,500 lb then permitted by the League of Nations and a maximum span of 70 ft; the performance required was a top speed of 190 mph, service ceiling of 22,000 ft, ability to take off and climb to 60 ft in 600 yards and a maximum landing speed of 60 to 65 mph. Preliminary estimates in December 1933 predicted maximum speeds of 208 mph with Bristol Aquila II engines, 220 mph with Mercury IVs or 230 mph with Mercury VIs, the corresponding all-up weights being 10,100 lb, 10,900 lb and 11,450 lb respectively. In May 1934 a stressing weight of 11,300 lb was established and in July Handley Page discussed the project with Major Buchanan, who asked for maximum performance, if necessary at the expense of cockpit space, and suggested using the higher power available from the Bristol Pegasus IV instead of the Mercury, with the possibility of changing to the sleeve-valve Perseus when this went into production; with these engines the all-up weight would exceed 12,000 lb and top speed would be at least 250 mph. Of the four designs tendered to B.9/32, the Bristol 131 and Gloster proposals were declined and only single prototypes were ordered from Handley Page and Vickers. Both firms complained of the restrictive effect of the Geneva weight limit and offered large increments in performance in return for an increased tare weight; the H.P.52, as the new bomber was designated, was slightly enlarged in anticipation of this further weight increase, the wing area going up from 560 sq ft to 600 sq ft and the fuselage being lengthened by 27 inches, as well as being made one inch higher and two inches wider, but this was the maximum dimensional growth that the performance attainable with two Pegasus IVs could allow.

A preliminary mock-up conference was held at Cricklewood in January 1935, as a result of which it was agreed to replace the Pegasus IV by a similar engine with two-speed supercharging, then known as the P.E.5-SM but subsequently produced as the Pegasus XVIII. Meanwhile a 1/20th-scale model was made for testing in the 5-ft and 7-ft wind-tunnels at the RAE and results obtained by March 1935 confirmed the generally excellent behaviour of the chosen design after the lines of the wing-root fillet had been improved (RAE report B.A.1199). The geometry thus established as aerodynamically satisfactory comprised a flat-sided forward fuselage, approximately rectangular in side view, set on a straight tapered mid-wing with most of the taper on the trailing edge and a constant dihedral from root to tip of 2¾ degrees, with a slender tapered tail-boom carrying an elliptical tailplane with a one-piece inset elevator and two elliptical vertical surfaces just inboard of the tips in the slipstream of the two engines; this was a logical extension of the H.P.47 design principle and made room below the tail-boom root for a Heyford 'dust-bin' turret mounted permanently in the lowered position; the wing carried automatic slots along the outer half of the leading edge and 20 per cent chord slotted flaps along the inboard half of the trailing edge, which could be lowered to 40 degrees for maximum lift and drag at touch-down. About this time Imperial Airways invited Handley Page to quote for a civil version of the H.P.52, with either Pegasus or Perseus engines, an all-up weight of not more than 13,300 lb and a crew of two, to carry 3,000 lb of freight for 670 miles at a cruising speed of 200 mph; although attractive as a counterblast to the German civil Junkers-Ju 86, the Air Ministry refused the firm permission to tender, although an unsuccessful tender with Pegasus IVs to the Finnish government's SE/F.370 reconnaissance requirement was not frowned upon. In May 1935 AVM Dowding (AMRD) urged Handley Page to get the prototype into the air as a flying shell as quickly as possible, and this reflected the change of policy forced upon the Air Staff by the overt intervention of Hitler's Germany in the Spanish civil war, ostensibly to support the Nationalist forces against the Communist rebels, but in fact to provide the expanding Luftwaffe with valuable operational training in actual warfare; the effectiveness of new pseudo-civil designs such as the Junkers-Ju 86 and Dornier Do 17 in their real role as bombers showed up the serious inadequacy of the RAF's single-engined day bomber biplanes in quality as much as in quantity, and Lachmann compared the all-up weight needed to carry 1,500 lb of bombs for 1,000 miles in the cases of the H.P.52 and the best available biplane (the Boulton-Paul Superstrand project) with the same two Pegasus IV engines; the H.P.52 at 13,800 lb cruised at 200 mph against the B-P's 150 mph at 15,000 lb. In September, further wind-tunnel tests at the RAE evolved a tail unit of improved shape, with two triangular fins carrying constant-chord horn-balanced rudders mounted on a straight-edged tapered tailplane with a rectangular elevator inset, the horizontal surface area being increased by 15 per cent (RAE report B.A.1241). This improved longitudinal and directional stability and was provisionally adopted for the prototype, K4240.

Although only one prototype H.P.52 had been ordered, a nearly identical second prototype was begun concurrently, in response to an order for a coastal patrol seaplane from the Swedish government; this machine, H.P.53, was primarily a torpedo-carrier and a forward-firing 20-mm Bofors cannon in a nose turret was specified, together with an 8-mm dorsal Colt gun for self-defence. The initial request, for two aircraft, was made by Flygstyrelsen on behalf of Flygvapnet on 30 October, 1934, and called for interchangeable float, wheel and ski landing gear, an Eagle IV camera, a Holmes telecompass and two Harley dipping searchlights, all being essential for winter operations in the Baltic Sea and Lappland. The engines were to be Nohab-built Pegasus IIs, known in Sweden as Mercury VIIs, with short-chord Townend rings to avoid the overheating, during prolonged taxying on water, that occurred with long-chord NACA cowlings. England went to Sweden in December to discuss the contract, but details had still not been finalised by July 1935, when all the drawings common to H.P.52 and H.P.53 were due to be completed, so Handley Page decided to take his summer holiday in Stockholm, to get contractual decisions on items already technically agreed at a design conference held at Cricklewood on 27 May. Bofors 20-mm gun drawings were received in September, but not the sample Colt gun which had been dispatched by

Flygstyrelsen at the same time. A mock-up conference was held on 17 October, when Flygstyrelsen asked for NACA cowlings with removable rear panels, but Bristols were unable to undertake their design because of work already in hand. In November 1935 England resigned from Handley Page Ltd and was replaced by Grp Capt R. B. Maycock, who had just retired from a distinguished career in the RAF, including long experience of testing and evaluating large flying-boats as well as heavy bombers. Bob Maycock took vigorous action with Flygstyrelsen to end the delay in finalising their requirements and in January 1936 Flt Lieut Blomberg of Flygvapnet was appointed to act as resident inspector at Cricklewood; meanwhile additional equipment requested by Flygstyrelsen had shifted the c.g. beyond the aft limit and Volkert proposed to move the engines forward one foot to restore the balance, but this entailed local strengthening of the nacelle attachments to the wing and the resulting extra structure weight would have needed larger floats than Short Brothers had already put in hand. The Swedish impasse dragged on for another six months, when a new senior inspector, Bjarnholdt, replaced Blomberg; but, being a civilian, he was not allowed by the Air Ministry to have access to the H.P.52 prototype, which was classified Secret. Eventually decisions were reached to install Pegasus XX engines and to provide for Swedish 100-kg bombs, but doubt then arose over the 8-mm dorsal gun, for which there was a choice of Colt or Oerlikon.

The H.P.52 armament situation was equally uncertain, because progress and trials of the alternative nose turrets suitable for so narrow a fuselage had proved abortive in every case; both the Stieger and Trojan mountings tested in Heyfords K3489 and K3503 had failed to win approval at Martlesham and a later Cricklewood design by Hubbard was begun too late for consideration at the final design conference on 15 September, 1936, which decided that K4240 should go to Martlesham for trials without a nose turret. Both the H.P.52 and the H.P.53 had been given larger tail units, in which the rudders were taller with increased horn-balance area at the top, while the former one-piece elevator was divided by a lengthened tail cone into two separate surfaces of increased chord, to provide for possible installation of a remotely controlled tail-defence gun, which Boulton-Paul were developing; the new rudders and elevators incorporated adjustable Flettner trim-tabs inset into their trailing edges and the tail-boom had been torsionally stiffened as a result of further structural testing at the RAE. Cordes began flying K4240 on 21 June, 1936, and in a series of brief handling tests gained sufficient familiarity and confidence to fly it to Martlesham for a review of new prototypes by King Edward VIII on 6 July, a week after its first public appearance in the New Types Park at the RAF Display at Hendon; it was also on view at the SBAC trade show at Hatfield on the following Monday. For these occasions it was finished all over in glossy grey-green, apparently concocted by mixing Nivo and Cockpit Green with gloss varnish; the 'parade number' 8 was borne in white on each side of the nose for the RAF Display and on the tail-boom for the trade show. It had three-blade D.H.-Hamilton duralumin v-p airscrews and Bristol-NACA cowlings with integral leading-edge exhaust manifolds, but no exit gills. It was C. G. Grey, founder and first editor of *The Aeroplane*, who remarked to Cordes after a press demonstration: 'It looks like a flying suit-case', to which Cordes replied: 'Oh yes, it's a perfect Revelation!' This

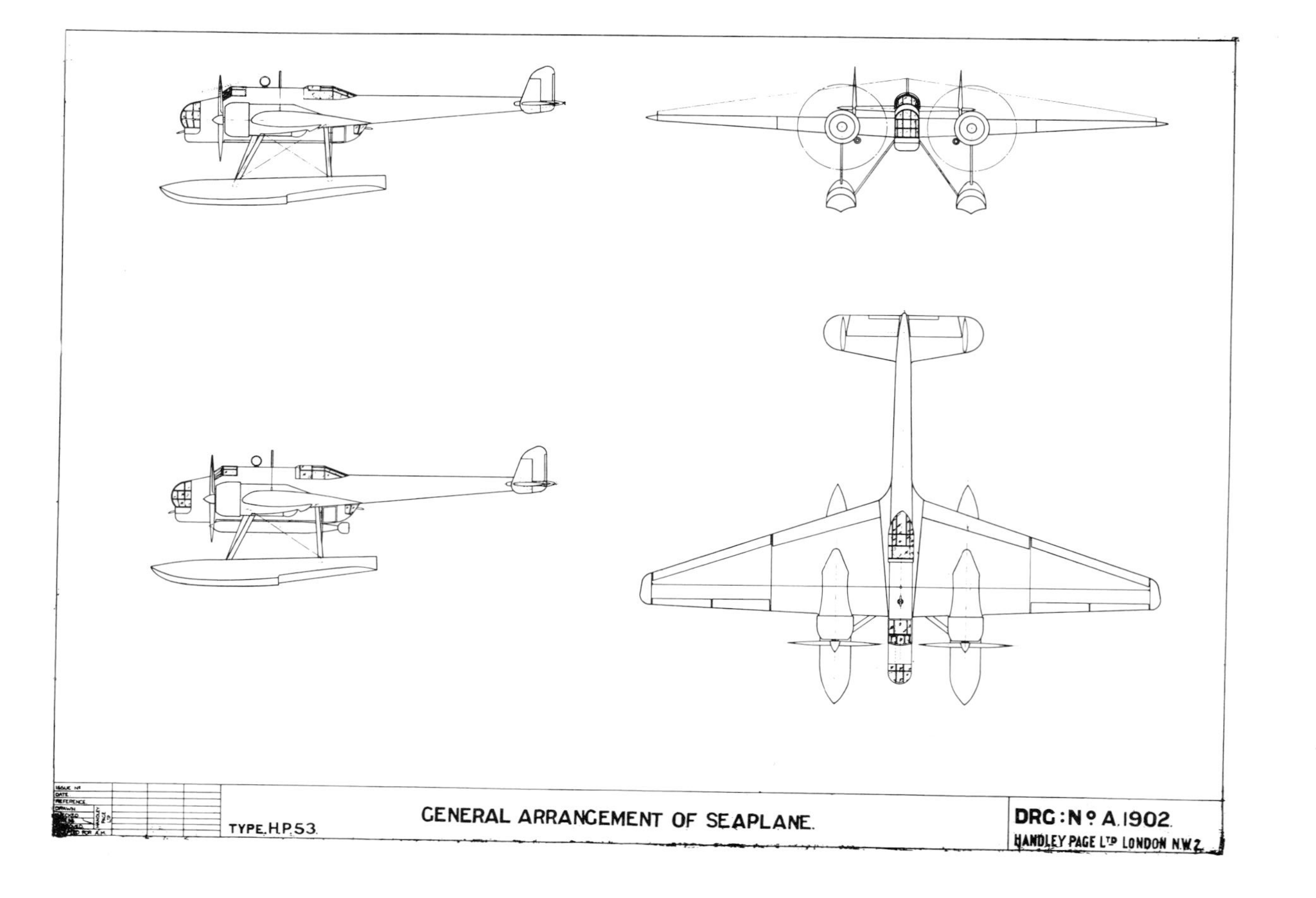

TYPE. H.P.53.
GENERAL ARRANGEMENT OF SEAPLANE.
DRG: Nº A.1902.
HANDLEY PAGE LTD LONDON N.W.2

H.P.52 in July 1936 showing original small dihedral and extended tail-cone with divided elevators. (*Flight*)

description was particularly apt because the temporary glazing of the nose had been replaced by sheet aluminium to hide its interior from unauthorised eyes; full transparency was restored in time for flight trials to be resumed at Radlett on 23 July, and Cordes flew it back to Martlesham for speed trials between 27 and 31 July. Three more intensive flight tests in August cleared the way for a preliminary production conference at the Air Ministry on 8 September, a final design conference at Radlett on the 15th, with the final production conference there on the 18th and an armament mock-up conference at Cricklewood on the 25th. These covered all the major decisions needed to begin production of one hundred and eighty H.P.52s to specification B.30/36 ordered in August. A further one hundred were to be ordered from Short Brothers Ltd, to be built in a new shadow factory at Queen's Island, Belfast, by Short & Harland Ltd, a subsidiary formed jointly with Harland & Wolff Ltd, with 60 per cent of the capital owned by Shorts and 40 per cent by Harland & Wolff. The Air Ministry had just set up a Directorate of Aircraft Production (on parallel lines to the AID) under Colonel H.A.P. Disney, who wrote on 5 August to both Shorts and Harland & Wolff confirming the intention to order one hundred H.P.52s to specification B.44/36, but intimating that an alternative engine to the Pegasus would have to be found; this emerged in March 1937 as the Napier Dagger VIII and was to be supplied as an interchangeable power-plant designed by A. E. Hagg.

H.P.52 prototype taking off from Radlett in July 1936, showing modified Heyford ventral turret. (*Flight*)

At Radlett K4240 made rapid progress in further flights, all by Cordes in October, usually with R. S. Stafford recording as flight observer in the still embryonic nose station. On 5 November the landing gear warning buzzer switch failed and no replacement was available, but the last flight in the series remained to be done urgently; reluctantly the RTO allowed one flight only to be made with the buzzer circuit disconnected, since there had been no malfunction hitherto. Cordes made an apparently normal landing, but as he turned to taxy back, the starboard undercarriage, evidently not fully latched at touch-down, collapsed and Stafford complained mildly to Cordes: 'There's a hell of a strong smell of grass in here!' as the prototype settled on to its belly; but it was not badly damaged, apart from a broken mainwheel and buckled airscrew, and was flying again on 13 January, 1937,

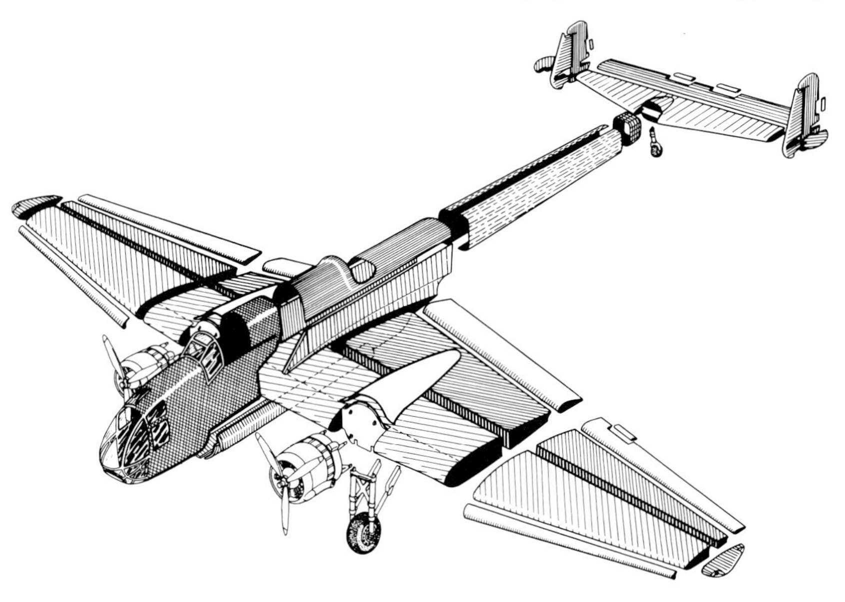

HAMPDEN SPLIT CONSTRUCTIONAL COMPONENTS

when the replacement starboard engine shed its reduction gear and airscrew over Elstree, gashing the fuselage just aft of the pilot's cockpit. Cordes managed to land safely at Radlett on the port engine alone and telephoned the police in case damage had been caused to any person or property, but the airscrew had fallen in a ploughed field and was only found when smoke was seen rising from a crater in which only the tip of one blade was visible. After a second engine change K4240 suffered no further setbacks, completing vibration tests at Farnborough in February and full-load performance and handling trials at 16,000 lb in July and September 1937 at Martlesham; it returned to Radlett on 30 September for minor changes and adjustments before final dispatch. On completion of these, it was test-flown at Radlett, in the temporary absence of Cordes, by Hubert Broad and ferried to Martlesham on 9 November. It returned to Radlett in January

1938 for local reinforcement of the tail-boom attachment joints and improvement of the elevator tab control, and flew back to Martlesham on 28 February; in July the tailwheel collapsed and the resulting damage had to be repaired at Radlett before redelivery to Martlesham on the 14th.

On 4 October, 1937, the final mock-up conference had decided on a new transparent nose, with a fixed Browning gun instead of a turret, for production H.P.52s, all of which were to have Pegasus XVIII engines instead of Pegasus XXs in the first twenty as at first proposed to avoid delay. Meanwhile the Air Staff had changed the role of the H.P.52 from day-bombing to day-and-night bombing, with increasing emphasis on the latter, but it was still seen by its makers as having an exceptional performance and ability to evade enemy fighters in spite of being too slender for any of the new powered turrets to be installed in such a way as to bring effective fire to bear on the beam. This slenderness was the main reason for its very high performance, but was also the source of many problems in both production and operation. The production aspects were ingeniously dealt with by Hamilton and Volkert, who introduced a system of split assembly in which the left and right halves of the tail-boom were completely fitted out with control runs, pipes and electric cables before being joined along the top and bottom centrelines—a familiar enough procedure today, but an important innovation in 1936. The wings and tail unit were similarly broken down into sub-assemblies, with the one-piece centre-section as foundation for attachment of outer wings, nacelles, fuel tanks, undercarriage assemblies and front and rear fuselage. Up to seventy draughtsmen worked fifty hours a week in 1936 to redesign the H.P.52 for rapid production and the new assembly line was laid out in the original Cricklewood South Shop, which O/400s had similarly occupied in 1918 and whence its erstwhile motor industry tenants had been given notice to quit.

A few changes in shape were made in the production H.P.52 in addition to the revised crew stations; the outer wing dihedral was increased to $6\frac{1}{2}$ degrees in order to improve lateral stability and reduce the effects of rough air, which had made the prototype tiring to fly over long distances; the Boulton-Paul 'tail-sting' project was cancelled in November 1937, when the horizontal area was further enlarged to improve longitudinal stability and reverted to a one-piece elevator; the rudders were given small lower horns containing mass balances below the tailplane and the fins were slightly extended upwards to shield the upper horn balances, which effectively removed a troublesome source of vibration in the tail at certain critical speeds. The proposed Hubbard nose turret with Frazer-Nash power controls, deleted by the mock-up conference, was applied only to the H.P.54 Harrow, the H.P.52's armament being reduced to a single Vickers gas-operated K-gun on a manual mounting at the bomb-aimer's station and at each of the upper and lower rear-gunner's stations; the original lower turret was replaced by a fairing with side windows behind the deepened bomb bay, which could now carry two long 2,000-lb SAP bombs or 1,500-lb mines as an alternative to eight 500-lb bombs. At the mid-upper position, the gunner had a pivoted transparent cupola, which slid inside the fuselage when open, but gave good protection and low drag when closed, without limiting the field of view. The pilot remained alone in his fighter-like cockpit, with its flat central windscreen panel and single fixed Browning gun ahead on the port side.

'Fighter-like' pilot's cockpit of the Hampden. (*M.O.D.—Crown Copyright*)

In September 1935 a proposal had been tendered to specification M.15/35 for a shore-based twin-engined torpedo-bomber of 13,600 lb all-up weight employing H.P.52 wings and tail grafted on to a wider fuselage with room for a mid-upper circular turret; the tail-boom was of larger cross-section near its junction with the main fuselage and the largest size of torpedo could be carried internally. This tender was declined by the Air Staff in favour of the Bristol 152 and no H.P. project number was assigned to it. The H.P.52 final design conference on 15 September, 1936, had failed to agree on a type name, although 'Huntley' was proposed by the Air Ministry and objected to by Handley Page as unnecessary publicity for the biscuit industry, which was not notably warlike. Suggestions were then invited from all departments at Cricklewood and Radlett and among those received were several which later became famous in relation to other types of aircraft. Maycock fancied 'Hotspur', the inspection department proposed 'Harrier' and 'Hastings', while the production shops preferred 'Havoc' and 'Halifax'. The Air Ministry, while upholding their established rule that the name of a town with historical associations in the British Empire must be used for a twin-engined bomber, dismissed 'Hastings' and 'Halifax' for reasons best known to themselves and declared the others ineligible by definition, although suitably aggressive. Honour was finally satisfied by bending the rule to admit the small Buckinghamshire village of Hampden as a suitable place-name, because of its association with the outstanding seventeenth century defender of civil liberty of the same name, so the H.P.52 became officially the Handley Page Hampden. (It may be noted that the Hampden's predecessors, Sidestrand and Overstrand, were named after two totally peaceful and historically obscure villages in Norfolk, making the rule ridiculous.)

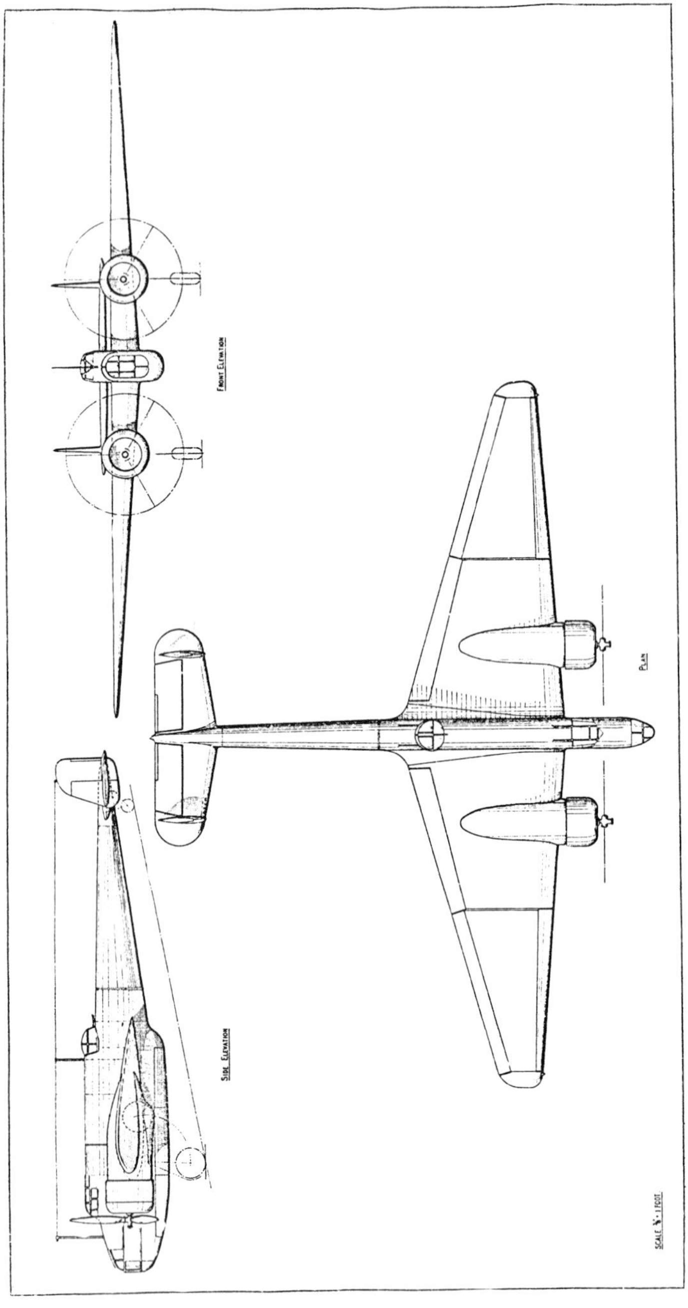

M.15/35 proposal

H.P.53 L7271 with Pegasus engines during its first flight on 1 July, 1937. (*Flight*)

Progress on the H.P.53 continued slowly while K4240 was completing its trials at Martlesham, but in February 1937 Flygstyrelsen accepted a suggestion from Maycock that two production Hampdens should be supplied bare instead of the two H.P.53s ordered, so that they could be modified to Swedish requirements after delivery. After some discussion over the financial terms, the Swedish government agreed to cancel the existing contract and surrender their deposit in return for a single production Hampden valued at £12,000, which was to be the fifth off the line. This relieved the firm of the necessity of assembling the second H.P.53 and on 28 May, 1937, the Air Ministry agreed to buy the first H.P.53 as a Dagger-Hampden development prototype for £25,000—its cost to date being nearly £34,000. Taken on charge by the Air Ministry as L7271, the only completed H.P.53 was first flown with Pegasus XX engines on 1 July, 1937, by Cordes, with Stafford as observer in the nose station, which had been built with a somewhat wider and blunter outline than on K4240 so as eventually to accommodate a Hubbard or Frazer-Nash turret. It had the production type of ventral gunner's fairing, but featured a low-profile sliding hatch designed to accommodate the Swedish dorsal gun mounting; it retained divided elevators but incorporated the shielded rudder horn balance of the production Hampden. As in the case of K4240, it had the original small wheels and undercarriage doors, which had been enlarged in the production Hampden to permit a higher all-up weight, and the original wing dihedral of 2¾ degrees. Cordes flew it over the SBAC trade show during its first flight, but did not land, and completed handling tests at 11,412 lb on 6 July before ferrying it to Farnborough, where short performance trials were completed by an RAE Aero Flight pilot on the 13th. Meanwhile Short & Harland Ltd had received contract No.68075/37 for 'development work on H.P.53 aircraft' and L7271 was flown from Farnborough to Sydenham (Belfast) on 16 July by Wing Cmdr Hilton, who had instructions to familiarise Shorts' test pilots John Lankester Parker and Harold Piper with it. The H.P.53 was then taken into the incomplete Queen's Island factory across the old wooden Connswater bridge after a great deal of reinforcement with steel plates, removal of handrails, lamp-posts and traffic signs, and not least, issue of indemnities to the Belfast Harbour Commissioners and several oil companies who owned the

L7271 with Dagger engines as Hereford prototype on Connswater bridge at Queen's Island, Belfast, in February 1939. (*Shorts*)

pipelines on an overhang of the bridge, on which one of the aircraft's wheels had to run because its track was wider than the carriageway; after this brief but quite hazardous journey on 28 July, the Harbour Commissioners presented a bill for £10 for permanent alterations to the bridge and £118 for repairing the roadway.

The Pegasus XXs were removed during the first week in October and Short & Harland were appointed as design authority for the production Dagger-Hampden in December. This cumbersome name was officially superseded on 5 February, 1938, by 'Hereford Mark I', the H.P.53 conversion being styled 'Hereford prototype' thereafter. The latter definition, taken out of context, seems to have been pounced upon by some aviation writers as evidence that H.P.53 was the recognised project number for all Herefords, but it belonged only to the Swedish prototype, which retained it fortuitously after being converted to the Hereford prototype, the change of engine type being irrelevant to the project number. The reason for giving the Hereford a new name instead of treating it as a Hampden variant seems to have been the extent of non-interchangeability outside the primary structure. Handley Page personally regarded the Dagger installation with well-founded distrust and would have liked to dissociate his company from it, but had to accept responsibility for the Hereford's wing structure in order to avoid having to give Short & Harland a copy of the Hampden Type Record. Assembly of the first two Dagger powerplants began on 9 March, 1938, the final conference was held on 9 September and first engine runs began three weeks later. 'Pip' Piper made the first flight in L7271 with Daggers on 6 October, 1938, at a weight of 12,860 lb, flying again on the 8th and 10th at 13,260 lb and finally on the 17th at the full weight of 16,000 lb. Then began a long history of cylinders overheating while taxying, and temporary cooling gills were added to the rear of the cowling to cure it, but on 28 October and again on the 31st L7271 subsided into soft patches in the grass aerodrome, which had been created on land reclaimed from Belfast Lough by dumping city refuse from 1928 onwards. On the second occasion, the tail-boom was damaged during salvage and the opportunity was taken to exchange the Daggers, which were nearly time-expired, while the boom was being repaired. Controllable gills were installed with the new engines and Piper flew it again on 14 February, 1939, but in the air the gills vibrated to the closed position and could not be re-opened in flight, so Piper made a bee-line for Aldergrove, where he landed with cylinder temperatures soaring. After attention to the gill controls, Piper flew L7271 back to Sydenham next day, but the trouble persisted and in the six months up till 31 March, 1939, Piper logged only 5½ hours' flying on the prototype. Meanwhile the 100 production Herefords were making good progress in the works and engine installation began in February, although the first Hereford I, L6002, did not fly till 17 May, 1939. The H.P.53 eventually flew to Martlesham Heath for acceptance trials in May, but during the next three months it was serviceable on only about eight days and was not flown after the first two production Herefords L6002 and L6003 arrived there on 23 and 29 August respectively; L7271 was then grounded permanently, becoming instructional airframe 2057M.

Structural testing of the production Hampden by the RAE was completed early in March 1938, the lower front gun mounting and bomb-aiming panel were approved by Martlesham armament specialists in April and the final conference was held at Radlett on 14 June, by which time the first two production Hampdens, L4032 and L4033, were ready for first flight; Cordes took L4032 into the air on 21 June, 1938, and, after clearing contractor's trials at Radlett, it was delivered to Martlesham Heath for full acceptance trials, together with L4033, in August. By 1938, the Hampden's tare weight had risen to 11,780-lb—nearly twice the 1932 Geneva limit—and the maximum permissible all-up weight to 21,000 lb, putting it well into the 'heavy' bomber category as defined four years previously by specification B.3/34. On 6 August a new direct contract for 75 Hampdens was awarded to English Electric Ltd at Preston, thus reopening their aviation department, which had closed down after delivering the last of six Kingston flying-boats from Lytham to Felixstowe in March 1926. The third Hampden from Radlett, L4034, went first for handling trials at the Central Flying School, Upavon, and thence on 20 September to No.49 Squadron at Scampton, Lincs. The fifth Hampden off the Radlett line was taken, unequipped, to fulfil the revised Swedish contract and was modified to Flygstyrelsen's special requirements, including the installation of Pegasus XXIV engines, but not the dual controls they had asked for. This

Fifth production Hampden in Swedish markings at Heston on 24 September, 1938.

Hampden, marked with the triple crowns of Sweden and serial I-90, was flown to Heston Airport on 1 September for full load tests by Wing Cmdr Enderlein of Flygvapnet, which were completed on 22 September at 18,000 lb and it was flown to Sweden two days later; this aircraft, designated P.5 by Flygvapnet, was the longest lived Hampden of all, surviving in Flygvapnet service till declared obsolete in 1945; it was sold in November that year to Svenska Aeroplan Aktiebolaget as a test-bed for electronic equipment and was flown by SAAB for two years with the civil registration SE-APD, being finally withdrawn from use on 17 November, 1947.

J. L. Cordes flying production Hampden I L4143 in 1938 showing increased dihedral and revised crew stations.

On 26 October, 1938, the first Hampden, L4032, was transferred from Martlesham to the RAE for engine development, while L4033 was joined at Martlesham by L4035 and L4037 for Service trials, including development of Lorenz blind-flying radio equipment, which was to be installed in six Hampdens as soon as possible. Deliveries to the RAF mounted rapidly as production got into its stride and by the end of 1938 thirty-six had been supplied for the initial equipment of Nos.49 and 83 Squadrons at Scampton, followed by No.50 Squadron at Waddington, which was also the headquarters of No.5 Group, based in Lincolnshire and south Yorkshire. The last five of the first contract were reserved as pattern aircraft for other contractors, L4207 being allotted to English Electric and L4208–L4211 being shipped to Canadian Associated Aircraft Ltd, a consortium of seven major engineering companies which in 1938 set up two final assembly plants at Malton, Ontario, and St Hubert, PQ, with a peacetime production capacity for 200 bombers, to be flown across the Atlantic on delivery to the United Kingdom. In November 1938 CAA were awarded a first contract for eighty Hampdens, of which half (P5298–P5337) were to be built by the Quebec group and half (P5338–P5346, P5386–P5400 and P5421–P5436) by the Ontario group; the first contract was later extended to include twelve more Hampdens (AJ988–AJ999) and supplemented by a final contract for sixty-eight (AN100–AN167). The scheme was slow in getting started and only nine Hampdens were completed up till the end of 1940, but the full quantity of 160 eventually emerged by the summer of 1942; at one time there was a risk that Bristol Pegasus engines might not reach Canada because of increased U-boat activity, so Wright Cyclones were considered as a substitute; L4032 was re-engined with two of these by the RAE and a new Preston-built machine X3115 was similarly converted for test at Boscombe Down as the

Hampden II X3115 with Wright Cyclones at Boscombe Down in January 1941.

definitive Hampden II (H.P.62) prototype in 1940, but the supply of Pegasus to Canada was never cut off and X3115 later saw service with No.408 Squadron, RCAF, as a standard Hampden I. As with the English Electric and Short & Harland contracts, CAA had to request many concessions at first and early Canadian-built Hampdens could be recognised by the external chordwise reinforcing stringers on their tailplanes.

Hampden production at Cricklewood and Radlett continued with a second batch of 200 and a final batch of 120, before ceasing with the 500th delivery in July 1940, while English Electric, having flown their first Hampden, P2062, at Samlesbury on 22 February, 1940, delivered the last of 770 (in five batches) on 15 March, 1942. Meanwhile Short & Harland, having completed their first batch of 100 Herefords on 8 June, 1940, continued with a further fifty, the last of which, N9106, was flown to Hawarden on 24 September, 1940; all these left Belfast with Dagger engines, but some time later twenty were converted to Hampdens with Pegasus engines by the Maintenance Units of No.41 Group to which they had been ferried from Sydenham. The first Canadian-built Hampden, P5298, was flown by Gp Capt J. H. Lymburner, RCAF, at St Hubert on 9 August, 1940, and by October the monthly production rate had built up to fifteen from the two assembly plants taken together; Canadian Hampdens were ferried via Iceland and Aldergrove or Prestwick to Finningley, where they were aggregated with British-built Hampdens for issue to No.5 Group squadrons as required.

During 1939 No.44 Squadron had joined No.50 at Waddington and Nos.61 and 144 Squadrons had been equipped with Hampdens at

Production Hereford L6056 at Cottesmore in 1941.

Hemswell; by 3 September six squadrons were fully operational on Hampdens (Nos.44, 49, 50, 61, 83 and 144) and two more (Nos.7 and 76) were working up at No.5 Group Pool at Finningley, with No.185 in reserve at Cottesmore, shortly to be joined by No.106 from Evanton; altogether 212 Hampdens were on RAF charge when war broke out. Herefords were issued to No.35 Squadron for initial training at Finningley in the early months of 1940, and temporarily equipped one flight of No.185 Squadron at Cottesmore, but only one ever flew an operational sortie; the Dagger engines always overheated during taxying and overcooled when cruising at altitude, so Herefords had to be restricted to crew training and eventually equipped only No.14 OTU at Cottesmore and No.16 OTU at Upper Heyford. Nevertheless, Short & Harland's production line became invaluable in 1941 when English Electric were unable to provide spares to the Hampden Repair Organisation without robbing its own final assembly line and, after a check on interchangeability, Belfast-made components were supplied direct to Tollerton Aircraft Services and the LMS Railway Works, Derby, who were mainly responsible for Category 'B' repairs for No.43 Group.

Initially deployed in their daylight role on armed reconnaissance against German naval units, the Hampdens' first major encounter came on 29 September, 1939, when eleven from No.144 Squadron searched the coast of Heligoland Bight, flying in two formations. The first section of five aircraft, led by Wing Commander J. C. Cunningham, C.O. of the squadron, was destroyed by fighters from the Frisian Islands, but the other six, led by Sqn Ldr Lindley, attacked two destroyers and all returned safely to base. This setback convinced the Air Staff that Hampdens could not defend themselves against shore-based fighters in daylight and they were switched to night operations in December, sharing with No.4 Group's Whitleys continuous security patrols to discourage German mine-laying seaplanes by bombing their flare-paths; in March 1940 these activities were extended to long-range sorties ('Nickels') into Germany to gain navigational experience and drop propaganda leaflets, since the War Cabinet shrank from bombing centres of civilian population. Only one Hampden was lost during the 123 'Nickels' flown up to the end of 1940. Meanwhile the Admiralty's magnetic sea-mine had been adapted for air-dropping, using a tail parachute, and eventually developed into the 2,000-lb HC bomb, which the Hampden was modified to carry as an alternative to the 2,000-lb SAP bomb. The mines were laid in large numbers in German coastal waters by Nos.44, 49, 50, 61 and 144 Squadrons as soon as the Nazi invasion of Norway began in April 1940, and No.5 Group had laid over 700 mines in the course of 1,200 sorties for the loss of twenty-one Hampdens when the year ended, but attempts to re-employ them on daylight operations during the Norwegian campaign had proved disastrous and only very vigorous unofficial action by the AOC 5 Group, Air Commodore A. T. Harris, succeeded in doubling the rear defence fire-power; this was achieved by fitting twin-K-gun conversion mountings designed and made very rapidly by Alfred Rose & Sons, agricultural engineers of Gainsborough, but still the ventral position was very cramped and the two front guns were useless. Hampdens had exchanged leaflet bundles for real bombs in March 1940, when on the night of the 19/20th they attacked the mine-laying seaplane base at Hornum on Sylt Island. Their first big raid on the German

Twin Vickers K-guns on Rose mid-upper mounting of Hampden in 1940. (*Flight*)

mainland came on 11/12 May, when they attacked railway yards at Mönchen-Gladbach; this raid was shared between eighteen Hampdens of No.5 Group and the same number of Whitleys of No.4 Group. During the summer, Hampdens repeatedly bombed invasion barges being assembled in occupied French and Belgian ports along the Channel coast and on 1/2 July it was L4070 of No.83 Squadron, flown by Flying Officer Guy Gibson (of later 'Dam-Buster' fame), which first dropped a 2,000-lb SAP bomb on Kiel during an attack on the battle-cruiser *Scharnhorst*. On 12/13 August Flt Lieut R. A. B. Learoyd of No.49 Squadron, flying P4403, attacked and destroyed an aqueduct on the Dortmund-Ems Canal, and on 15/16 September Sgt John Hannah in P1335 of No.83 Squadron fought single-handed and extinguished a very severe fire during a raid on barges at Antwerp, thereby saving his pilot and navigator, who brought the badly damaged aircraft back to base; both Learoyd and Hannah were awarded Victoria Crosses for their conspicuous individual bravery.

Twelve Hampdens of Nos.61 and 144 Squadrons took part in the first RAF bombing of Berlin on 25/26 August, 1940, and in the first industrial area attack on Mannheim on 16/17 December, but early in 1941 the Battle of the Atlantic claimed priority over the Ruhr targets and Hampdens were diverted to mount repeated attacks on the battle-cruisers *Scharnhorst* and

Night-camouflaged Hampdens of No.44 Squadron in 1941. (*I.W.M.—Crown Copyright*)

Gneisenau at Brest. In May No.44 Squadron scored a direct hit on the *Gneisenau* with a 2,000-lb SAP bomb and soon afterwards the *Scharnhorst* moved temporarily to La Pallice, while the cruiser *Prinz Eugen* joined the *Gneisenau* at Brest; on 24 July Hampdens combined with Wellingtons and Fortresses to attack the three ships in daylight; two Hampdens were shot down and the type reverted to night operations until 13 December, when three from No.44 Squadron, in daylight and unescorted, laid mines in Brest harbour to prevent the warships from putting to sea; two Hampdens got back with extensive damage from 'flak' and the third, flown by the squadron's CO, Wing Cmdr Misselbrook, failed to return. They were also used at night as intruders, concentrating on shipping, and on 3 November, 1941, Flt Lieut Craig of No.144 Squadron, flying AE309 from North Luffenham, sighted and attacked a convoy of ten merchantmen near the Frisian Islands, setting the largest on fire and fortuitously killing a German military observer on board, who proved to be Major-General Varda, in command of the western anti-aircraft defences. By this time Hampdens were being superseded as night bombers and their performance had been further spoiled by such necessary additions as armour-plate and exhaust flame-dampers. The Hampden's original neutral longitudinal stability (necessary at first because of the limited power of the early auto-pilot) tended to become negative as the tare weight increased and although it retained the low stalling speed of 73 mph at 18,500 lb, it also had an unfortunate trick of dropping the starboard wing if the engine on that side stopped. This could be corrected if noticed in time, but under attack at night or in cloud, the unchecked bank quickly developed into a spiral dive from which recovery was difficult, if not impossible; it could be flown straight with the port engine dead and the auto-slots seemed to make little difference to the onset of the stall, but could make the situation worse if they opened asymmetrically in a flat turn; so when barrage-balloon cable-cutters and armoured leading edges became necessary the slots were locked shut permanently with little loss of lift; this was first done on P4335 and became a retrospective modification in No.5 Group. After participating in the massive raid on the Renault works at Billancourt on 3/4 March, 1942, and in the 'Thousand Plan' raids on Cologne, Essen and Bremen in May and June, Hampdens were withdrawn from the front line of Bomber Command, their last operation being made from Balderton by No.408 Squadron, RCAF, who bombed Wilhelmshaven on 14/15 September, 1942. While under training in 91 Group, air crews of No.408 Squadron had taken part in the raid on Essen on 1/2 June and one Hampden, piloted by Wing Cmdr H. R. A. Edwards, had got back to Norfolk on one engine after the other had failed at 11,000 ft over the target area; he crossed the Dutch coast at only 1,000 ft, but managed to climb to 2,000 ft after jettisoning as much equipment as possible; the second engine failed near East Harling, where Wing Cmdr Edwards made a belly landing on a partly-built runway without injury to any of his crew. This was one of the few occasions when spiral instability was successfully countered by an experienced pilot, but illustrated how slight a survival margin remained for twin-engined night bombers in face of German defences in 1942.

Obsolescence as a night bomber by no means ended the Hampden's operational history, for its success as a mine-layer led in the spring of 1942 to trials of six aircraft equipped as torpedo-bombers, at the Torpedo

Development Unit, Gosport. The Hampden T.B.Mk.I (in effect a revival of the rejected M.15/35 project) was suggested by Dr P. B. Walker of the RAE at whose request R. S. Stafford submitted outline sketches on 22 December, 1941, showing (a) one torpedo, and (b) two torpedoes. Scheme (a) was preferred because it required minimal structural alteration and had little effect on performance, whereas take-off suffered severely with Scheme (b). The existing 2,000-lb bomb attachments carried an adaptor for a Mk.XII torpedo, whose bottom line came only 3½-in below the existing level of the closed bomb doors, so the centre bomb-doors were removed complete with jacks, and the hinged side flaps were fixed; at the same time, the main frame immediately ahead of the ventral gunner's station had 12 inches removed from its base, with corresponding modification of the gunner's fairing. Although the open bomb-cell caused a small drag increment, the torpedo blended well with the fixed side-flaps and at an all-up weight of 23,500 lb the range was 1,960 miles. The Gosport trials were successful and in April 1942 No.144 Squadron was transferred to Coastal Command, together with No.455 Squadron, RAAF, which had been formed earlier at Swinderby, initially as a bomber squadron; both these squadrons were re-equipped with the Hampden T.B.Mk.I, which also carried two 500-lb bombs on under-wing racks. The whole of the design work for this modification was undertaken by Boulton-Paul Aircraft Ltd and the final complete trial installation on P4369 was inspected and approved at Park Street on 16 October, 1942. Altogether 144 Hampden T.B.Is were converted from bombers, including N9106, which had started life as the last Hereford delivered from Belfast to Hawarden. Both Nos.144 and 455 Squadrons trained in their new role at Leuchars, using sand-filled concrete pipes as dummy torpedos, which they launched at practice targets off the Isle of May; when operational they attacked enemy shipping along the Norwegian coast and were joined by No.408 Squadron, RCAF, at Lindholme, and by No.415 Squadron, RCAF, and No.489 Squadron, RNZAF, which had both been formed a year earlier at Thorney Island as torpedo units equipped with Beauforts and changed to Hampdens based at Wick in March 1942. Nos.144 and 455 Squadrons each supplied sixteen Hampdens to protect the Murmansk convoys in 1942, and both were based

Hampden T.B.I AN127 of No.489 Squadron RNZAF at Skitten in July 1942.
(I.W.M.—Crown Copyright)

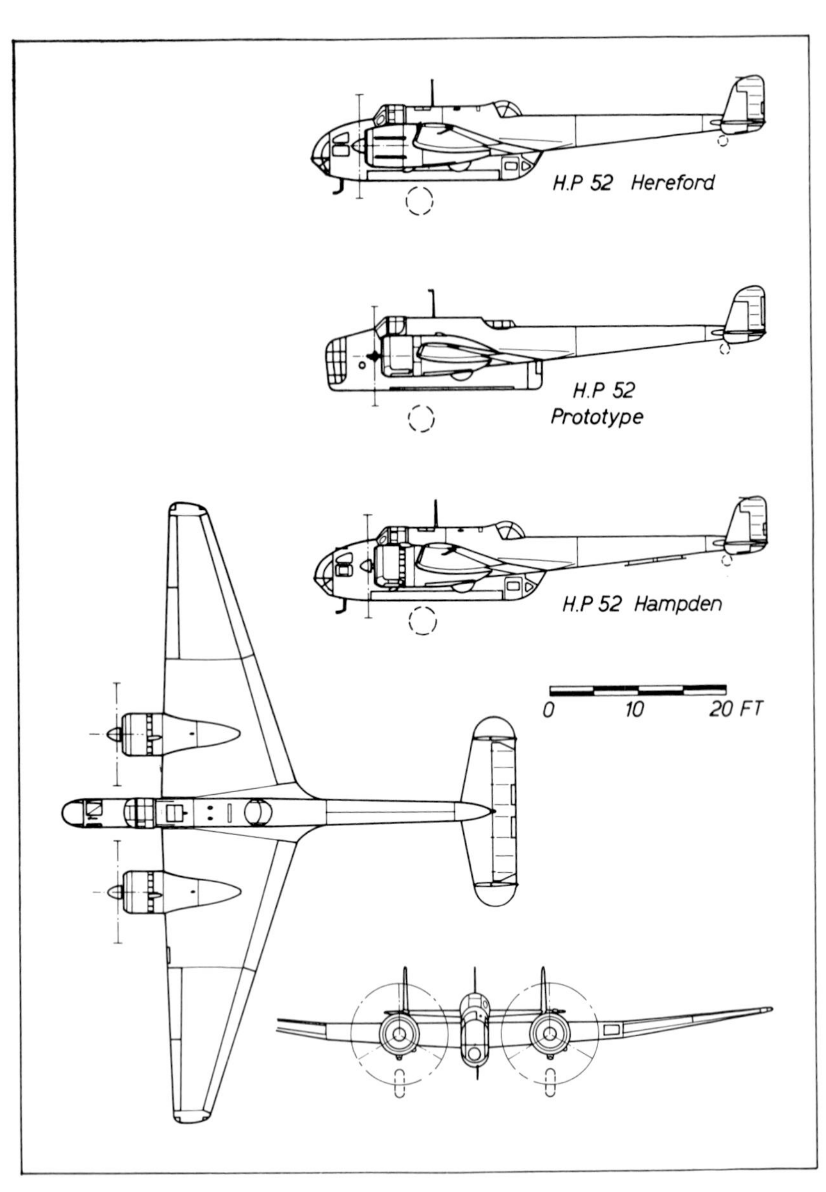

for a time at Vaenga, where they were at first at risk from their trigger-happy Russian allies as well as from the real enemy. Nine Hampdens were lost en route including one which crashed in Russia near Murmansk and two which landed in Norway. At the end of this operation the remaining Hampdens were handed over to the Soviet air force and their personnel returned by sea. Hampden torpedo-bombers were replaced by Beaufighters when the 'Torbeau' strike wings were formed in 1943 and, on being phased out of the front line, 200 Hampdens were ferried to Canada by RAF Transport Command for use as crew trainers; apparently only one, flown by American ferry-pilot Captain Robert Coffman, was lost en route in October 1943, having flown for an hour on the port engine alone after the starboard engine failed near the Greenland coast on the Keflavik–Goose Bay stage. Fighting the inevitable spiral dive, Coffman managed to ditch in the lee of an iceberg fifteen miles short of Greenland and the crew of three paddled their rubber dinghy to the rock island of Umanarsuk, where they were found by the Norwegian whaler *Polar Bjørn* after having existed for ten nights and days, in sub-zero temperatures, their only food being the chocolate and malted-milk tablets packed with the dinghy. Other Hampdens, modified for meteorological reconnaissance as Hampden Met.Is, were flown by Nos.1403, 1404 and 1408 Flights, which later became Nos.521, 517 and 519 Squadrons operating from Gibraltar, Manston and Wick till the end of 1943.

Although the Hampden was not developed to the same extent as the Wellington, proposals were made in November 1938 for a variant with a wider fuselage and either Merlin XX or Hercules engines, to carry 2,000 lb of bombs at an all-up weight of 21,000 lb and maximum speed of 315 mph. When Handley Page offered to produce this variant by arrangement with Textile Machinery Ltd in Lancashire and Briggs Bodies at Dagenham, Tedder replied that 'the Air Staff would leap at such a bomber if available immediately, but could not wait 15–18 months before delivery, so they declined the offer; what they wanted as early as possible from Handley Page was plenty of Halifaxes.' Later proposals by Handley Page for a Hampden development to meet specification B.7/40 were similarly refused. One Hampden was retained at 71 MU, Bicester, for the Air Historical Branch until 1955, when it was scrapped to save storage space—a most regrettable decision in view of the subsequent establishment of the Royal Air Force Museum at Hendon.

H.P.52 Hampden I
(Two Bristol Pegasus XVIII)
and
H.P.52 Hereford I
(Two Napier Dagger VIII)

Span 69 ft 2 in (21·07 m); length 53 ft 7 in (16·35 m); wing area 668 sq ft (62·1 m²). Empty weight 11,780 lb (5,345 kg); maximum weight 18,756 lb (8,505 kg). Maximum bomb load 4,000 lb (1,813 kg). Speed 254 mph (409 km/h); ceiling 19,000 ft (5,880 m); range 1,885 miles (3,160 km) with 2,000 lb (907 kg), or 1,200 miles (1,930 km) with 4,000 lb (1,813 kg). Crew four.

H.P.53
(Two Bristol Pegasus XX)

As for Hampden I but length of seaplane 71 ft (21·64 m).

H.P.62 Hampden II
(Two Wright Cyclone G.102)

As for Hampden I.

First Harrow I K6933 flying in November 1936.

Harrow and B.1/35 (H.P.54 and 55)

In spite of a persistent but unfounded legend, the revised production version of the H.P.51, which appeared in 1935 as the H.P.54, was never tendered to meet specification B.3/34, which called for a stressed-skin fuselage and a retractable landing gear. Handley Page intended it as a last-minute bid for the C.26/31 bomber-transport competition, the Air Staff having already adopted the Armstrong Whitworth A.W.38 Whitley as the heavy-bomber constituent of the RAF expansion programme; this had been decided in 1934, when the Cabinet increased the strength of the Metropolitan Air Force from 52 to 84 squadrons. Then, in March 1935, came Hitler's own statement to Anthony Eden and Sir John Simon that Germany's air strength was already thirty per cent higher than the Air Staff had calculated, but the development of the B.9/32 medium bomber could not be forced nor could Whitley production be accelerated; nevertheless Scheme C of May 1935 called for 68 bomber squadrons instead of 41, to be formed within two years, so 'stop-gap' types suitable for rapid production had to be ordered, although known to be obsolescent in terms of front-line performance.

Specification B.1/35 had already been issued for a more advanced twin-engined heavy bomber than the Whitley, and in June specifications 28/35 and 29/35 were written to cover orders 'off the drawing board' for production batches of the Bristol 142M (Blenheim) and Handley Page H.P.54 (Harrow) respectively. Selection of the latter to operate as a heavy bomber, in what had originally been the secondary role of C.26/31, demanded a number of structural changes, including the provision of internal under-floor stowage for 3,000 lb of bombs in sizes up to 500-lb, in spite of which it had to retain its former capability of accommodating twenty fully-equipped troops as a standby transport. Ordered in August 1935 in a single batch of 100, the Harrows were very fully planned for quick manufacture, employing the methods recently studied by Volkert at aircraft and automobile plants in America and translated by James Hamilton into a sub-assembly flow system which brought finished components together on the final erection line and achieved rapid throughput of completed aircraft combined with excellent practical training for the apprentices and the many new recruits to the industry (as Handley Page put it 'baptism of both infants and those of riper years'). It also introduced new features such as variable-pitch metal airscrews, exhaust-heated steam boilers for cabin heating and Hubbard gun-turrets at nose and tail with Frazer-Nash powered controls; these had fixed cupolas, the guns traversing in a slot which was closed by a belt carried on follow-up spools at each end like a typewriter ribbon; the traverse and elevation controls were hydraulic and linked to the gun-sight, the weight of the twin Lewis or Vickers K-guns being balanced in see-saw fashion by the seated gunner. For bomb-aiming, the nose turret incorporated a slightly

F.N.15 rear turret of a Harrow. (*Flight*)

protruding optical flat panel with a course-setting bomb sight mounted above it. The mid-upper gunner's station was not strictly a turret, since it was not powered, although the cupola rotated with the mounting ring to which it was attached as in the Anson and Whitley; at first it was hoped to use the Trojan mounting, which lagged in development and Armstrong Whitworth could not spare the time to take it over for quicker completion, although they agreed later to manufacture a similar mounting designed by Barr & Stroud as their type ARM.103/A.W.15.

Harrow production followed on closely as the last Heyfords were cleared from the shop floor and was phased in before the commencement of H.P.52 production, which advanced the split-assembly concept still further. As any delay would have imperilled the later programme, the first Harrows completed were delivered for squadron training without turrets, which allowed more time for sorting out the snags that had arisen with hydraulic pumps and relief valves; after several months' testing at Martlesham Heath, Rolls-Royce-designed Integral pumps were adopted and the gun-turrets went into production as F.N.14 (nose) and F.N.15 (tail). The first Harrow, K6933, was flown by Cordes on 10 October, 1936, after waiting several days for fine weather, and the Harrow Final Conference was held ten days later. K6933 was delivered to Martlesham Heath for service trials on 30 November, 1936, and was followed in January by K6934, which was fitted with Pegasus XXs and fully-equipped for armament trials with prototype Hubbard-F.N. turrets, and had K-guns installed. While both aircraft were at Martlesham together comparative tests were made with Serck oil coolers on one and Robertson oil coolers on the other. In March 1937, the disastrous forced landings of seven Heyfords in bad weather led to a demand for improved navigator's stations on new types of bomber, and a new blind-flying panel with improved instrument lighting was introduced as an urgent modification on all Harrows. K6934 completed full A & AEE trials in October 1937, during which eight-hour duration trials had shown the need for a crew rest seat with oxygen, improved heating and ventilation of the tail turret (with a fuselage bulkhead), a pilots' emergency exit above the chart table, extra oil tankage and provision for 2,000-lb bombs. Fuselage protection from ice thrown by airscrew blades was to be provided from the forty-first aircraft onwards and steam-heating from the seventy-first. Nearly all the production flight testing was done by Hubert Broad and by November 1937 the first fifty Harrows had been delivered without turrets and all but seven of the next thirty-five had turrets allocated. Trial installations continued at Martlesham on K6934 and Dunlop wing and tail deicing had been installed on K7028 for trials at the RAE.

Harrows were the first Handley Page aeroplanes to appear in the new brown and green camouflage finish. Deliveries to No.214 Squadron commenced with the arrival at Scampton of K6935 on 13 January, 1937, followed by K6936–K6945 by the end of March. Of these, K6940 survived less than 13 hours before colliding with a St Pancras–Manchester express, whose 60 mph passage along the LMS mainline at Napsbury on 25 March coincided with the Harrow's final approach to Radlett, with eight RAF personnel on board; though they were all slightly injured and the aircraft was wrecked beyond repair, nobody on the train was hurt, but the kitchen-car lost most of its roof. No.37 Squadron at Feltwell received

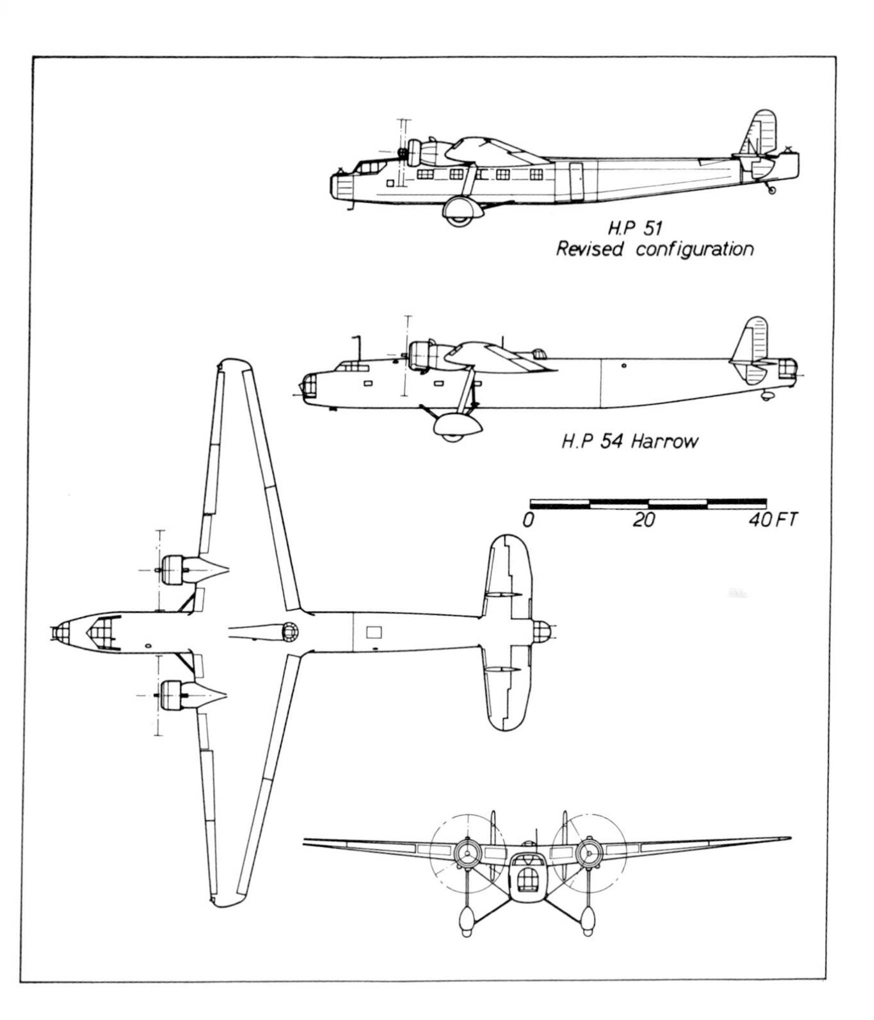

K6946–K6952 during March and April; all these had Bristol Pegasus Xs and were designated Harrow Mark I. Subsequent Harrows had Pegasus XXs and were known as Mark II, K6953 going to the RAE for auto-pilot development, while K6954 and a few others went to Nos.214 and 37 Squadrons, before equipment began of three more squadrons, No.115 at Marham in June, No.215 at Driffield in August and No.75, also at Driffield, in September. The production line ended with the completion of K7032 in December 1937. Harrows remained in service as night bombers till the end of 1939, when they were replaced by Wellingtons soon after war began; during this period they saw no active service, although brought to full stand-by during the Munich crisis in September 1938, and were best known for their public appearances in formation over various cities on Empire Air Day 1938. Only the first six Harrow Is were retrospectively modified to Mk.II by installing Pegasus XXs.

First Harrow II K6934 with turrets installed for armament trials at Martlesham in 1937.

Harrow II of No.214 Squadron in 1938. (*The Aeroplane*)

In 1938 K6933 was overhauled at Radlett and converted into a tanker for Flight Refuelling Ltd at Ford, Sussex, together with K7027 and K7029. All three were transferred to the civil register, K6933 and K7029 as G-AFRG and G-AFRH respectively in April 1939, and K7027 as G-AFRL in July at the special request of Sir Alan Cobham, who saw the opportunity of incorporating his company's initials in the registration mark. They were equipped with fuselage tanks of 1,000 gallons capacity and the necessary valves for controlling rapid fuel transfer through long hoses which could be reeled out and back by powered winches, also large observation transparencies in the front fuselage fabric covering. The first two were then shipped as deck cargo to Montreal on the Canadian Pacific ss *Bedford*, to refuel the transatlantic Short Empire Boats *Cambria* and *Caledonia* after taking off from Botwood, Newfoundland; they were re-erected by Fairchild Aircraft at Longueuil and thereafter based at Hattie's Camp (later Gander). Both were impressed into the RCAF at Rockcliffe, Ottawa, the first becoming 794, while the other was dismantled for use as spares. G-AFRL was based at Rineanna (later Shannon Airport) and refuelled the Empire Boats after take-off from Foynes; it was normally flown by Flt Lieut G. A. V. Tyson, who later resigned from the RAF to become assistant chief test-pilot to Short Brothers at Rochester. G-AFRL returned to Ford when the airmail flights ended and was destroyed there in an air raid on 18 August, 1940, along with others of the Flight Refuelling fleet.

Third Harrow tanker G-AFRL refuelling Short S.30 *Cabot* during trials over Southampton Water in July 1939.

G-AFRG as RCAF 794 at Rockcliffe in 1940.

In March 1940 many of the Harrows stored at No.19 MU, Kemble, after withdrawal from bombing squadrons were converted to their secondary role as transports and issued to No.1680 Flight of Fighter Command at Doncaster Airport on 28 March, 1940. After being transferred to Bomber Command on 27 April, No.1680 Flight became No.271 Squadron on 1 May, 1940, and shared in general transport operations between bases at Doncaster and Down Ampney and units of the Advanced Air Striking Force in France and Belgium. After the evacuation of Dunkirk, they carried aircrews and equipment between southern English bases and Scotland and Northern Ireland; on occasion they went as far afield as Gibraltar. Some retained their nose and tail cupolas but others were given nose and tail fairings and were nicknamed 'Sparrows'; among these were K6937, K6984, K6987, K6988, K6993, K6997, K6999, K7001, K7011 and K7032. After D-Day, they were equipped for casualty evacuation, first from the beach-heads and later from reoccupied aerodromes, particularly the Brussels Airport at Evère, to which casualties from the Arnhem battle were brought for the Harrows to fly them home to England. Unfortunately a number of them were congregated at Evère on New Year's Day 1945 when the Luftwaffe attacked many aerodromes simultaneously in an attempt to disable the Allied Air Forces at a critical phase in the Battle of the Ardennes; the Harrows at Evère were too easy a target to miss and seven were destroyed on the ground. A month later No.271 Squadron's Harrow Flight began changing over to Dakotas and the last Harrow in service was K7000, which returned damaged to No.19 MU, Kemble, at the end of April 1945.

'Sparrow' transport of No.271 Squadron in 1940. (*I.W.M.—Crown Copyright*)

Apart from their principal wartime use as transports and ambulances, Harrows were employed for crew training at Nos.2, 7, 8, 9 and 10 Air Observers' Schools (at Warmwell, Stormy Down, Evanton and Penrhos), No.7, 8, 9 and 10 Bombing and Gunnery Schools at the same stations, and No.8 Air Gunners' School, Evanton. A dozen were on the strength of the RAE at Farnborough, with others at A & AEE, Boscombe Down, and single Harrows were attached to No.1 Air Armament School, Manby, the Parachute Training School, Ringway, and No.42 OTU, Andover; none appear to have been used as glider tugs. One unique role they played was with No.420 Flight (later No.93 Squadron) at Middle Wallop during the winter of 1940–41, when five were equipped to carry 'Long Aerial Mines' in 'Operation Mutton'. These LAMs consisted of numerous small explosive charges suspended from parachutes with 2,000 ft of piano wire trailing below, and these were jettisoned in quick succession into the path of approaching enemy bombers; the latter, on flying into the wires, were expected to dislodge the charges, which then slid down the wires to explode on the aircraft. No.420 Flight was formed in October 1940 under the command of Wing Cmdr Homer and its pilots flew solo in their Harrows at 17,000 ft with 200 LAMs in their bomb bays. Guided towards the enemy formation by GCI radar, they climbed above it and turned steeply across its path, in the hope of entangling and destroying some of the bombers. Each operation had to be reported to Fighter Command HQ, and four or five kills were officially credited, although these were many fewer than the hits sustained by the Harrows themselves; in fact, only one pilot, Flying Officer Hoy, avoided 'blowing himself up', although there were no serious casualties. This was in some degree due to the Harrows' fabric fuselage covering, which stripped off easily without real structural damage, but the tattered results were nicknamed 'Steam Chickens' and the standard greeting after a safe return was 'Look—no feathers!' Had the Harrow trials promised better success, the LAM technique was to have been widely exploited by specially adapted Douglas DB-7s, code-named 'Havoc-Pandora', but it was abandoned after three months' trial.

Just before the Harrow was chosen as an immediately available stop-gap bomber, the Air Ministry had invited tenders for a larger twin-engined bomber as a long-term replacement for B.3/34, which was itself a stop-gap derived from the Armstrong Whitworth A.W.30 designed for the Czechoslovak government. Specification B.1/35 was issued by Air Commodore R. H. Verney (DTD) on 8 May, 1935, and called for a heavy bomber of not more than 100-ft span to carry 2,000 lb of bombs over a range of 1,500 miles at a cruising speed of not less than 195 mph at 15,000 ft, using two approved British engines of 1,000 hp, such as the Armstrong Siddeley Deerhound, Bristol Hercules or Rolls-Royce Merlin; it was intended to perform by night what the B.9/32 had, at that date, been intended to perform by day. Tenders were received from Airspeed, Armstrong Whitworth, Handley Page and Vickers-Armstrongs, and in September contract No.441975/35 was awarded to Handley Page Ltd for one prototype H.P.55, K8180, with Hercules ISM engines; single prototypes were also ordered of the Vickers 284, K8178, and the Armstrong Whitworth A.W.39, K8179, but not from Airspeed, and an advisory design conference was held by Air Commodore Verney on 13 September to discuss the tenders. DTD considered that the H.P.55 design complied well with the specification, although its performance was not as high as the others, the estimate being a top speed of 240 mph, cruising speed 200 mph, service ceiling 26,000 ft and still air range 2,000 miles on 800 gallons of fuel, which brought the all-up weight to 25,000 lb. The crew stations were similar to the Harrow's and the landing gear was an up-rated version of the Hampden's; the wireless installation was similar to the Hampden's and so at first was the armament, with nose, dorsal and ventral turrets mounting single K-guns; but DTD insisted on the ability to fire on the beam and downwards over the fuselage sides as well as under the tail, which indicated the need for a tail turret as in the Harrow. The original straight tapered wing had therefore to be swept back outboard of the engines to compensate for the weight of the tail turret and the resultant layout was virtually a Harrow-shaped fuselage and tail combined with the low-set parallel centre-section and swept outer wings of a Douglas DC-2, which Volkert had recently seen and admired. DTD wanted the span to be as small as possible, so the wing would have to be designed with two spars instead of one, with fuel tanks and bomb stowages between the spars. After agreement had been reached on these points, the contract was formally signed on 23 October, with mock-up completion scheduled for February 1936 and delivery on 23 July, 1937.

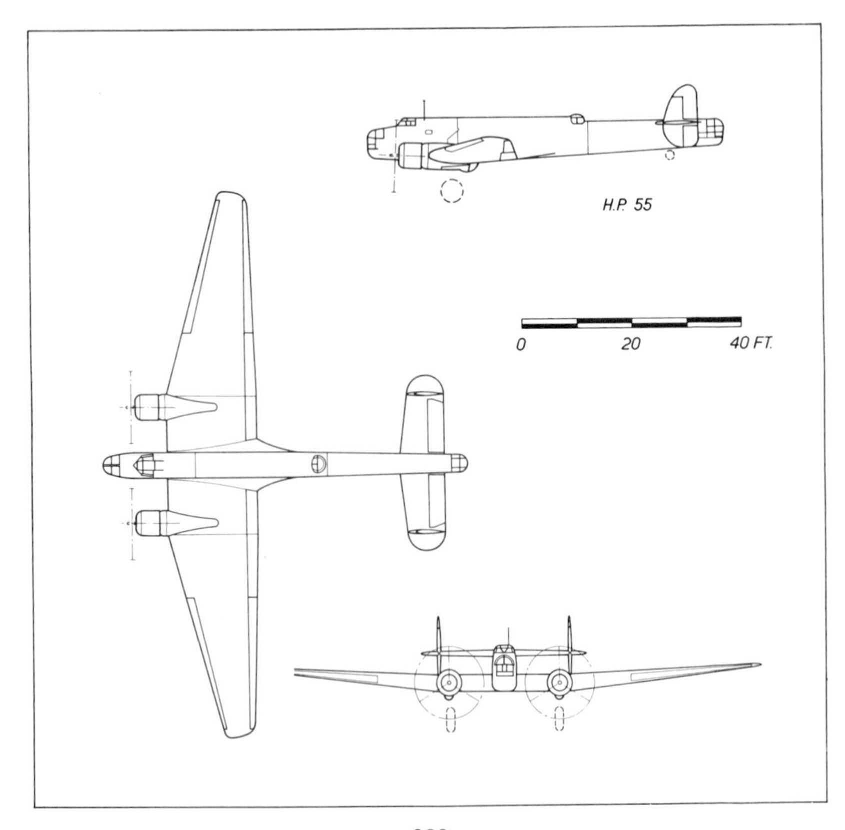

Every effort was made to reduce drag and improve performance, and by April 1936 wind-tunnel results indicated top speeds of 237 mph with two Merlin Es, 251 mph with two Hercules HE-I-SMs, or 250 mph with two Deerhounds. Volkert was very concerned at the loss of performance caused by heavy armament and estimated a gain of 16 mph if the tail turret were deleted, since its diameter (43 in) was of the same order as that of a Hercules engine (52½ in), but the only change allowed by DTD was from Hercules to Merlin XX engines of 1,200 hp in May 1936. The mock-up with Merlins was shown informally to Air Commodore Verney on 11 July, but on the 22nd he returned for a second look, with so many criticisms that the official mock-up conference was indefinitely postponed and work was stopped while the possibility of accommodating a much bigger bomb-load was investigated. This led to a meeting between Handley Page and Verney on 14 September, when a new draft specification was discussed, the proposed engines being up-rated Hercules, although it was hoped that Rolls-Royce Vultures of still higher power would be available in three years' time. Volkert thereupon prepared an enlarged design, H.P.56, with two Vultures—but that is another story.

H.P.54 Harrow I
(Two Bristol Pegasus X)
and
H.P.54 Harrow II
(Two Bristol Pegasus XX)

Span 88 ft 5 in (27 m); length 82 ft (25·1 m); wing area 1,090 sq ft (101·2 m²). Empty weight 13,600 lb (6,760 kg); maximum weight 23,000 lb (10,450 kg). Bomb load 3,000 lb (1,362 kg). Speed 200 mph (322 km/h); range 1,250 miles (2,150 km); ceiling 23,000 ft (7,110 m). Crew four.

H.P.55
(Two Bristol Hercules ISM or Rolls-Royce Merlin XX)

Span 95 ft (29 m); length 65 ft 3 in (19·9 m). Speed (est) 251 mph (404 km/h); range (est) 2,000 miles (3,220 km). Crew four.

Halifax Prototypes and Early Production (H.P.56, 57, 58, 59 and 63)

In February 1936, the Air Staff's Scheme C of May 1935 was superseded by Scheme F, which called for the same number (68) of bomber squadrons, but equipped with much heavier aircraft, as defined by specifications B.12/36 for a four-engined heavy bomber of 55,000 lb and P.13/36 for a twin-engined medium bomber of 45,000 lb. Not only were these two new types to carry double the previous bomb-load, but they were to be very well protected with armour and improved gun-turrets, without sacrificing cruising speed and ceiling in spite of a 50 per cent increase in range. Air Staff requirements were circulated on 28 August, 1936, and specification P.13/36, dated 8 September and issued in November, set out in considerable detail the very high standard of achievement expected. In view of the Luftwaffe's continuing expansion, which showed no signs of slowing down, the Air Staff had accepted the technical risk of specifying the Rolls-Royce Vulture engine of nearly 1,700 hp although this still needed three years of development to ensure reliability for squadron service. Everything depended on the integrity of this engine, which had twenty-four cylinders of Kestrel size arranged as four banks of six in X formation, and all was staked on the quality of its lubrication system and of the bearings for its enormously highly-stressed single crankshaft; but the engine specialists of the Air Ministry were confident and Rolls-Royce had an unequalled reputation borne out by their current success with the Merlin, itself derived from the Schneider Trophy racing engines of 1929 and 1931.

The principal Air Staff requirements for P.13/36 were (a) world-wide use, (b) exploitation of the alternatives between long range and a very heavy bomb-load made possible by catapult take-off assistance in the overload condition, (c) high cruising speed to ensure minimum time spent over enemy territory, (d) all-round self-defence by means of nose and tail power-operated turrets, (e) suitability for operating by day or night, (f) best possible bomb-aiming and navigational facilities, (g) good facilities for maintenance in the open, and finally (h), if possible, the combination of medium bomber, general reconnaissance and general purpose (including troop-carrying) roles in a simple basic design which could be readily adapted to each specific role during manufacture. The P.13/36 was to cruise at not less than 275 mph at 15,000 ft on two-thirds of maximum power, to reach a service ceiling of 28,000 ft, to fly level at 10,000 ft with one engine stopped, and to cover 1,000 miles with 1,000 lb of bombs after taking off in 500 yd, or 2,000 miles with a 3,000-lb bomb load in the overload case after taking off unassisted in 700 yd or, with accelerated take-off, to fly 2,000 miles with a maximum bomb load of 8,000 lb, the normal tankage being adequate for 3,000 miles with 4,000 lb of bombs.

The crew of four was specified as two pilots (one acting as navigator, bomb-aimer and front gunner), one wireless operator and one rear gunner, with rest stations on long flights for one relief pilot/navigator and one extra wireless operator/gunner. The nose turret was to mount two guns with 1,000 rounds per gun and the tail turret four guns with 1,500 rounds per gun, with a reserve of 4,000 rounds fed from within the fuselage. Stowage was required for sixteen 250-lb or 500-lb bombs, or four 2,000-lb AP bombs, or two 18-in torpedoes 18 ft 3 in long, all to be carried internally in horizontal tiers without modifying the structure or reducing performance. Other requirements included enough manoeuvrability at high speed for dive-bombing, using flaps as dive-brakes; a good all-round view (including rearward) for the pilot; very full radio and blind-flying equipment; oxygen, cockpit heating, auto-pilot, camera, dinghies, flare-launching tubes, sound-proofing, sun-blinds, and at least one parachute hatch in the floor for supply-dropping. The design was to be suitable for easy quantity production, with the centre-plane span and longest fuselage section limited to 35 ft, any other section of wing or fuselage to 22 ft and all other components to 21 ft, and each engine change was to be possible in under two hours.

The tender, based on general arrangement drawing GT3058 dated 1 January, 1937, was drafted in February and submitted in March; Volkert and Stafford also considered Napier's estimated weights and performance for a proposed new engine of 2,000 hp (the Sabre) as an alternative to the Vulture and suggested a 10 per cent chord split flap for dive-bombing at 30 degrees flight path, while on 15 March Handley Page himself telephoned Air Commodore Verney, objecting to the four-gun tail turret and stating his preference for upper and lower turrets amidships, which promised substantial weight-saving and higher speed. In reply, DTD asked for an outline drawing and statement for discussion prior to the advisory design conference. The latter was held on 23 March and on 5 April Volkert recommended the incorporation of integral fuel tanks in the wing structure, to ensure the stiffness that would otherwise be lost if the tanks were made detachable. The concept of deleting the tail turret was carried still further in May 1937 by Volkert's proposal to design a 37,000-lb unarmed P.13/36 with two Sabre engines and a crew of three, having an estimated top speed

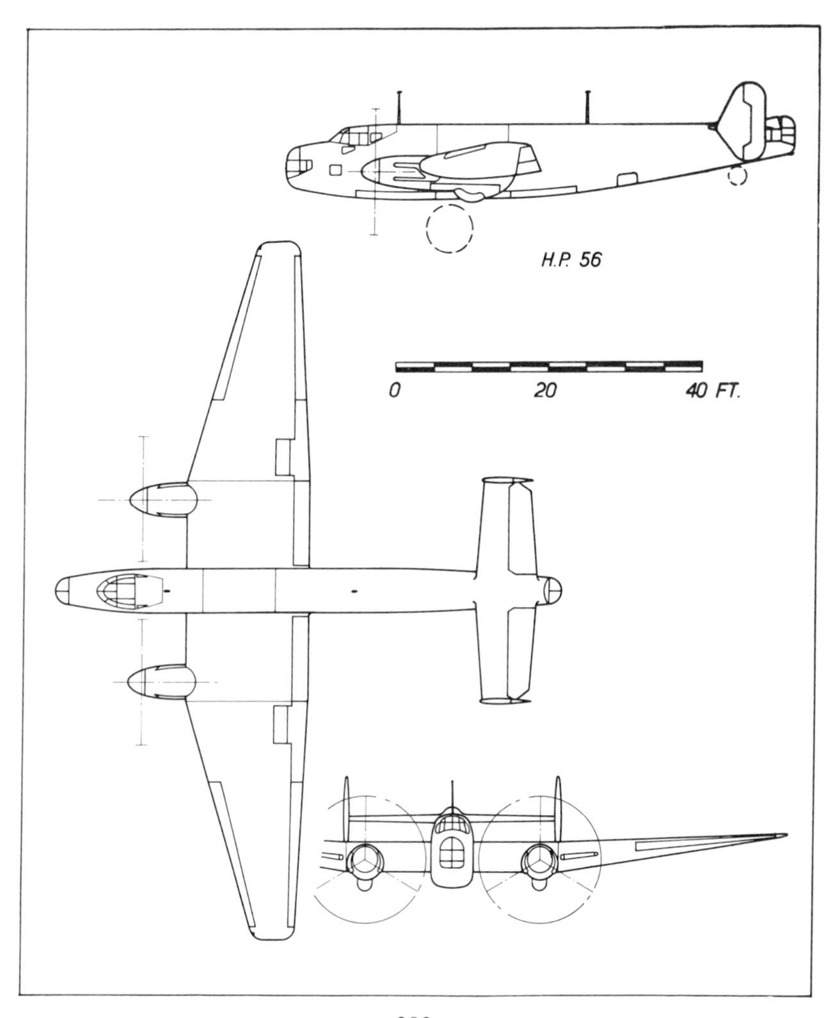

of 380 mph at 16,000 ft with a wing-loading of 30 lb/sq ft, or 400 mph with 39 lb/sq ft in the normal load case. This was considered carefully by the RAE performance specialists, who reported that the drag assumptions were optimistic in view of the skin-friction and interference effects likely to be achieved in the best production airframes. So Volkert's unarmed bomber project was declined, but is of interest as having begun a train of thought which, independently pursued by de Havillands against all official opinion (other than Air Marshal Freeman's), resulted in the production of the Mosquito. On 30 April, 1937, contract No.624972/37 was awarded for two prototypes of the H.P.56, serialled L7244 and L7245, both with Vulture engines.

Several incompatibles in the specification came to light as design work proceeded, and the Air Ministry agreed to reduce the dive-bombing angle to 25 degrees because of the structural complication involved in ensuring clearance at steeper angles. At the same time, the original requests for Light Series bomb-carriers and a message-hook, both out-dated survivals from the biplane era, were cancelled, and the maximum number of bombs was reduced from sixteen to fifteen, which enabled the bomb bay to be shortened by 4 ft and released space in the fuselage underside for either a parachute exit hatch or an under-defence turret. A preliminary mock-up inspection at Cricklewood was called for 8 July, on the eve of which Cordes had a private view and protested vehemently against the choice of a Dowty flap and undercarriage gate control with the lever moving horizontally, instead of vertically in a natural sense; nevertheless the conference upheld the horizontal arrangement and Cordes had to make an even stronger protest before having his view accepted on 15 July at the full mock-up conference, of which the chairman was Wing Cmdr McEntegart, accompanied by Air Commodore Evill representing Bomber Command; on this occasion they warned the firm of probable delay in the Vulture development programme and advised provision for Hercules as an insurance. Stafford then estimated the effect of changing from two Vultures to four smaller engines, the choice lying between Taurus, Kestrel, Dagger and Pegasus. In every case there would have to be a substantial weight increase because of the heavier engine installation, higher fuel and oil consumption, and lower cruising speed due to increased drag. For the same total horsepower, take-off would be slightly better in all cases except with Kestrels, but landing runs, at the same wing loading as with Vultures, were just outside the specified maximum.

On 19 July the Air Member for Research and Development (Air Marshal W. R. Freeman) asked Handley Page for comparative G.A. drawings of the twin-Vulture and four-Taurus versions, which were sent to him next day. The four-Taurus P.13/36 had 20 per cent greater wing area than the twin-Vulture, in order to keep the wing loading unchanged, and the lines of the inner nacelles were unavoidably spoiled by having to enclose the larger landing wheels required at the increased weight. Some relief was given when the torpedo requirement was deleted on 30 July and further investigation by Stafford revealed that, with four Merlins instead of Taurus, take-off would be so much improved that, even with an 8,000-lb bomb load and fuel for 2,000 miles, the all-up weight would not exceed 47,000 lb, at which catapulting would not be needed if the engines could be slightly up-rated for 5-minute take-off periods. In September 1937 this was provisionally agreed and at the same time the dive-bombing requirement was cancelled altogether, so that slotted flaps deflected to 60 degrees could be used solely to shorten the landing run; with four Merlins the wing span would be increased from 88 ft to 99 ft, which was still within the 100-ft limit set by the standard hangar doors then in use.

On 3 September, 1937, the contract was amended from two Vultures to four Merlins, the prototype serials being unchanged. By this time there was some risk that the Frazer-Nash nose and tail turrets chosen for both the H.P.56 and the Avro 579 would only be available in sufficient numbers for the latter, which was being urgently ordered into production as the Avro Manchester. Haynes visited Boulton-Paul Aircraft Ltd at Wolverhampton and reported that their proposed four-gun tail turret would fit the lines already drawn for the F.N.4A, but that the B-P two-gun nose turret required fuller lines than had been laid out to suit the F.N.5. The chief problem in using B-P turrets was that they needed a 2kW 24V electrical supply instead of hydraulic, and that four 500W engine-driven generators weighed 200 lb more than the equivalent hydraulic pumps. All these and many other points were discussed at the Air Ministry design conference convened on 11 October under Major Buchanan's chairmanship to ratify the change from H.P.56 with two Vultures to H.P.57 with four Merlin Xs.

To save time, it was agreed that both prototypes should be hand-assembled, the first being completed quickly as a flying shell for trials at Martlesham Heath, while the fully-equipped second followed up as soon as possible for full Service trials, but the second was not to be delayed to check production jigs. There was some argument before cancellation of the catapulting requirement was agreed and the tyre pressure was confirmed at 39 psi, but fuel-jettisoning was called for because the maximum fuel weight for take-off was 14,500 lb compared with a maximum bomb-load of 8,000 lb. To ensure maximum lift for take-off, it was agreed to install leading-edge auto-slots extending from the wing-tips as far inboard as the outer ends of the flaps. Originally the H.P.56 had its outer wings swept back to give a straight trailing edge from tip to tip, as in the H.P.55, but the change to four engines brought the powerplant centre of gravity forward; so the outer wing sweep of the H.P.57 was reduced enough to straighten the rear spar in plan view, which also simplified stress distribution at the spar joints. The new intermediate wing bay, between the inner and outer nacelles, was designed with an integral fuel tank between the spars in order to achieve the necessary torsion and bending stiffness outboard of the landing gear without incurring too great a structural weight penalty; the outer wing tanks also were integral, the total fuel capacity being 1,980 gallons. In December the Air Ministry Works and Buildings department caused temporary consternation by demanding an immediate reduction of maximum permissible tyre pressures to 17½ psi to save wear and tear on grass aerodromes, but this arbitrary decision was firmly disputed by Air Commodore Verney, who pointed out that from time immemorial camels had walked freely on shifting sand with a foot-print pressure of 25 psi. So he ruled that 35 psi was an acceptable maximum tyre pressure for grass runways, which had to be retained for the time being because concrete or tarmac was more costly than installing two catapults per aerodrome, which had already been disallowed by the Treasury. By the end of 1937 Dunlops had confirmed that 35 psi was a safe tyre pressure, even after the overload all-up weight had risen to 49,000 lb due to additional equipment and revised turrets, so the need for still larger tyres and wheels was averted.

On 7 January, 1938, a production order was awarded for the H.P.57, as defined by specification 32/37, and an official name was sought; eventually 'Halifax' (earlier suggested and rejected for the H.P.52) was agreed by the Air Ministry; the contract (No.692649/37) initially covered one hundred Halifax Mk.I, beginning with a batch of fifty, L9485–L9534. Soon afterwards, in response to information on Merlins given by Rolls-Royce, the firm proposed to provide a separate flight engineer's station and included it in the revised Halifax mock-up, but on 18 March the official mock-up conference deleted it; this meeting also failed to agree on the fuel jettison layout and eventually this problem was solved rather untidily by adding three external pipes under each intermediate wing, arranged to deflect with the flaps so as to throw fuel clear of the tail unit, with its inherent risk of ignition by static electricity. The question of turrets for production Halifaxes remained undecided; the Air Ministry wanted to expand Boulton-Paul's output to compensate for the overloading of Nash & Thompson's factory resources, but only one four-gun B-P tail turret had so far been made because of the firm's preoccupation with the low-profile dorsal turret designed specifically for their Defiant fighter. In July 1938 the Merlin X powerplant installation was approved after flight trials in a Whitley V, and the Messier hydraulic system engineered by Rubery Owen was accepted. In particular, a massive but lightweight cast magnesium portal arch for the main undercarriage, designed by Messier, had been found by the RAE Structures Department to have ample strength under side loading, which allayed any fears arising from the first Short Stirling's ignominious collapse after its maiden flight on 14 May.

Assembly of the two prototypes had begun in March in the Cricklewood experimental shop and a revised works layout for production was planned by Hamilton to extend the split-construction principle still further. Concurrently Volkert pioneered a most important innovation in the drawing office, adapted from American naval architectural methods; this was 'photo-lofting', or photographic reproduction to any desired scale of master lines accurately drawn on prepared metal plates. Not only could exact full-scale replicas be made at any time but, where appropriate, the original lines could be reproduced directly on jigs, templates and sheet material, without time-wasting or marking-out errors.

Under the Air Ministry's production Scheme K, which superseded Scheme F in April 1938, 250 Halifaxes were to be produced by April 1942 and in October 1938, after the Munich crisis, this programme was doubled by Scheme L. Even with the very wide sub-contracting made possible by split assembly and unit construction of components, with interchangeability assured by photo-lofting, it was impossible for all the 500 Halifaxes envisaged to be ordered directly from Handley Page Ltd, so English Electric were given a direct contract for Halifaxes to succeed Hampdens on the Preston assembly line, which was started early in August when full sets of assembly jigs and fifty men were sent there from Cricklewood. Numerous design changes were made to adapt the structure for rapid and reliable production by sub-contractors and to simplify maintenance in service; one of these was the provision of detachable self-sealing fuel tanks in the intermediate and outer wing bays, although the two prototypes were already too far advanced for their intermediate bay tanks to be altered.

The first Halifax prototype, L7244, was completed at Cricklewood on the eve of war, but both the firm and the Air Ministry agreed that so large a new aeroplane ought not to be flown for the first time from Radlett, where the east-west distance was less than 750 yards and provided no safety margin if wet grass caused the brakes to lock the wheels on landing. The nearest non-operational RAF aerodrome was No.13 OTU at Bicester, where there were full-sized hangars and all facilities for re-erection and flight testing. So the components were taken there by road and a picked team of Radlett flight-shed personnel, under McPhail and Salmon, worked in strict secrecy in a hangar allocated for the repair and maintenance of training aircraft, which Cordes visited at frequent intervals in a Miles Magister, thereby keeping in touch with the prototype's progress and supporting the illusion that the work in hand was of little interest to the enemy. When the Halifax eventually emerged for taxying trials, the officially preferred Lockheed hydraulic brakes proved to be so slow-acting that, after one brief taxi-run, Cordes bluntly refused to fly until they had been exchanged for Dunlop pneumatic brakes, which he had always found reliable. On hearing this, Handley Page set out for Bicester in his recently-acquired Rolls-Royce limousine, being overtaken en route (no mean achievement) by C. D. Holland in his small Ford Popular; Holland arrived in time to contact Joe Wright, the Dunlop representative, who at once telephoned his base at Coventry for a complete pneumatic brake installation, just before Handley Page stormed in demanding instant action. Wright and his assistant Jackson worked round the clock for three days and nights to complete the installation, but it was not possible to fit an

First prototype Halifax L7244 at Boscombe Down in 1940. (*I.W.M. Crown Copyright*)

extra Heywood air compressor in time for the first flight, so the system had to rely initially on a pair of precharged air bottles carried in the fuselage; both Wright and Jackson were promoted by Dunlops in recognition of their initiative. A second necessary improvisation was the installation of temporary fuel tanks in the fuselage bomb bay, because the normal integral fuel tanks between the inner and outer nacelles were to be used to carry water ballast for the full-load and overload trials; these loads exceeded the maximum permissible landing weight and in the event of an emergency descent soon after take-off it would have been necessary to dump the water as quickly as possible.

During these few days of intense effort to get the prototype flying before local rumour could take notice, Handley Page was not too popular in his role of 'Big Brother' and, seeking to lighten the atmosphere, gave Cordes a lift across the aerodrome in his Rolls-Royce, which was furnished with strong brass hand-grips inside the rear doors; Cordes, invited to admire these, commented tersely but undiplomatically 'Looks like a bloody hearse!' But on 25 October all went well on the Halifax's first flight, with the undercarriage locked down. Cordes had studied the local topography very carefully from his Magister, so as to be able to land with minimum damage in an emergency, so he was greatly puzzled, as he took off, by the appearance of a river or canal where no such feature should have been; but as he came in to land he saw that the apparent watercourse flanking the aerodrome was in fact sunlight reflected from the windscreens of a rank of parked cars along the boundary hedge—so much for security in face of local gossip! Before leaving Bicester, Cordes completed all the preliminary handling tests, with E. A. ('Ginger') Wright as flight observer; on one occasion one of the elevators fractured along the line of the spar, but Cordes was able to retain enough control to make a normal landing, thanks to the c.g. being near the middle of its range.

With its early flights accomplished, L7244 returned to Radlett, where the second prototype L7245 was being completed with full equipment and armament. The latter was to include a twin-gun nose turret and a four-gun tail turret, both made by Boulton-Paul, with individual electrically-driven hydraulic pumps incorporated in each turret and control mechanism developed under licence from the French basic design by de Boysson; this system, by eliminating long hydraulic lines and local recuperators, reduced vulnerability to enemy attack, but cost a substantial weight penalty. The

Second prototype Halifax L7245 in 1941. (*The Aeroplane*)

nose turret, Type C, was the same as that developed for the Lockheed Hudson, while the tail turret, Type E, was similar in layout, but with four guns and servo-fed ammunition supply through chutes from the fuselage. L7244 had de Havilland two-position variable-pitch airscrews with duralumin blades, but for comparison L7245 had constant-speed Rotols with Schwartz wooden blades and these, though not fully-feathering, were chosen for production aircraft. The second prototype, with fuel in its integral wing tanks and water ballast tanks in the fuselage bomb bay, was first flown at Radlett by Cordes on 17 August, 1940, being camouflaged like the first, but painted yellow underneath instead of matt black; its serial was prominently displayed under the wing in large black characters in accordance with the current style for experimental aircraft flying from the A & AEE, now at Boscombe Down, whither it was delivered after brief flight tests at Radlett. The two prototypes were followed into the air on 11 October by the first production Halifax I, L9485, which went to Boscombe Down after only two days at Radlett because of the risk of air raids in the London region; to achieve this rapid dispersal, only the minimum work necessary for a safe delivery flight was completed, but this was not at first understood by the A & AEE staff, who complained bitterly of Handley Page's incompetence in sending them so ill-prepared an aeroplane for test. Explanations and apologies ensued and the outstanding work was quickly completed at Boscombe Down by a Radlett working party. L9486, completely finished at Radlett in exemplary fashion, went to Boscombe Down in December and was allotted for initial crew familiarisation.

The first Halifax squadron, No.35, had been mustered at Boscombe Down on 5 November under the command of Wing Cmdr R. W. P. Collings and began training on L7244, which had been fitted temporarily with dual controls. The squadron moved a little later to Leeming, Yorkshire, taking L7244 and L9486 on loan, and thence on 5 December to its new operational base at Linton-on-Ouse, where it received L9487 and L9489 and began full training of aircrews, who now included flight engineers. With six crews competent by March 1941, the squadron made its first night sorties to Le Havre on 10/11 March and found the target with some difficulty; one Halifax returned with flak damage, but L9489 was unfortunately misidentified and shot down by a home defence night fighter over Surrey; nevertheless two more Halifaxes attacked Hamburg the following night. In April 'C' Flight of No.35 Squadron was expanded into No.76 Squadron, which was officially formed at Linton-on-Ouse on 1 May and, after moving to Middleton St George, went into action against German oil refineries on 12 June, sharing with No.35 a succession of night raids on Kiel, Duisberg, Hanover and Hüls.

The first fifty Halifax Is were followed by twenty-five, L9560–L9584, with structural modifications permitting an increase in all-up weight from 55,000 lb to 60,000 lb, the maximum permitted landing weight (and fuel jettisoning requirement) remaining unchanged at 50,000 lb. To distinguish these batches, the first fifty were called Halifax I series 1 and the next twenty-five, series 2; the latter were equipped with Vickers K-guns mounted in pairs to fire on the beam through side hatches amidships, so as to cover blind spots hidden from the nose and tail turrets' field of fire by the wings and tail unit. With this increased armament the Air Staff hoped that the Halifax could defend itself by day, but on 30 June, 1941, No.35

Squadron lost two out of six Halifaxes making their first daylight raid on Kiel; on 24 July fifteen Halifaxes of Nos. 35 and 76 Squadrons scored five direct hits in daylight on the *Scharnhorst* at La Pallice, but lost five aircraft in the action and Halifaxes were thereafter restricted to night raids for six months. On 25/26 July their target was Berlin, and six weeks later they moved to Stradishall whence, on 10/11 September, they made their first sorties across the Alps to bomb Turin. For this long-range operation they carried extra fuel tanks of 80 gallons each at the two rest stations amidships, as well as up to three tanks of 230 gallons each on the main racks in the fuselage bomb bay. The normal fuel capacity of the Halifax I series 1 and 2 was 1,392 gallons, carried in two No.1 tanks of 247 gallons each inboard, two No.2 tanks of 100 gallons each in the inner wing leading edges, two No.3 tanks of 188 gallons each between the spars of the intermediate bays, and two No.4 tanks of 161 gallons each outboard of the No.3 tanks.

From the seventy-sixth Halifax I onwards, larger oil coolers were installed to provide for Merlin XXs instead of Merlin Xs and the normal fuel capacity was increased to 1,636 gallons by the addition of two No.5 tanks of 122 gallons each inboard of the outer nacelles; one, two or three optional 230-gallon bomb-bay tanks could still be carried in place of bombs, but the rest-station tanks were deleted, except to special order. With these alterations, Halifaxes from L9600 onward were known as Halifax I series 3, but only nine were completed with Merlin Xs, the remainder having Merlin XXs installed, together with B-P Type C twin-gun mid-upper turrets instead of beam guns and additional No.6 fuel tanks of 123 gallons each outboard of the No.4s, raising the normal fuel capacity to 1,882 gallons. On Mk.I series 1 and 2, each inner engine drove a 24V electrical generator, but on series 3 a third generator was added on the port outer engine; from L9495 onward all were equipped with T.1154/R.1155 radio in place of the T.1082/R.1083 of the first ten production Halifaxes. In the final production form Halifaxes from the eighty-fifth on were named Halifax II series 1; the last Halifax I, L9608, completed on 12 September, 1941, was officially named at Radlett by Viscountess Halifax; it served later in No.76 Squadron as MP-H.

Originally the name Halifax II had been reserved in February 1939 for the H.P.58, a heavily-armed day-bomber capable of defending itself against cannon-armed fighters at long range. It was to have been equipped with four 20-mm Hispano cannon mounted in pairs amidships in two turrets located as in the Hampden; this allowed a relatively low-drag installation of Boulton-Paul Type H dorsal and Type O ventral turrets, with the fuselage faired and tapered to a pointed tail. Contract cover for one rear fuselage (to convert L7244 on completion of its flight trials) was placed on 25 July, 1939, (ITP 10713/39) with the intention of phasing it in after the tenth production aircraft, and the mock-up was inspected at Cricklewood on 15 December, 1939, but wartime difficulties in developing the turrets caused successive delays. On 19 August, 1940, Handley Page wrote to W. S. Farren (DTD) suggesting that, to avoid seriously holding up production, the cannon armament should be changed to twin 0·5-in Brownings in dorsal and tail turrets, which could be temporarily replaced by two and four 0·303-in Brownings respectively; this resolved itself into simply adding a twin-Browning dorsal turret to the basic Halifax I fuselage, with minimum dislocation of the production line. On 5 September, 1939, N. E. Rowe (who had succeeded Farren as DTD) defined two further stages in Halifax armament development, first replacing the four-gun B-P Type E tail turret by a similar twin 0·5-in B-P Type D turret and finally reinstating the twin-cannon dorsal turret, but the last stage was in fact never reached and the B-P Type D tail turret did not become available until 1944. Consequently the name Halifax II was switched to the revised production version with 0·303-in guns throughout and listed as H.P.59. The 200 Halifaxes ordered from English Electric were all built to this standard, as were the additional 100 ordered from the parent firm in April 1940.

In spite of unduly high casualties, due to the short effective range of their guns, in their early daylight raids, Nos.35 and 76 Squadrons had proved the reliability of the Halifax for long-range night bombing and Handley Page's early reluctance to change from two to four engines had turned into crusading zeal to persuade Bomber Command to re-equip all its disappointed Manchester and Stirling squadrons with nothing but Halifaxes. But if the better is the enemy of the good, so is the best the enemy of the better and Handley Page's ace was trumped by Roy Chadwick's rapid conversion of the Avro Manchester into the Lancaster by taking advantage of the ready availability of the slim Merlin XX powerplants designed for the Beaufighter II. In due course the Lancaster gained and held the leading position in aircrew popularity, mainly because of its superb flying qualities inherited from the Anson. Meanwhile the Halifax had plenty of potential for development in armament and performance and a number of Halifax Is became test-beds for trial installations. Although both the prototypes and the first fifty production Halifaxes had been built with leading-edge slats, these were found to contribute less to quick take-off and short landing than increasing to 70 degrees the maximum deflection of the narrow-chord slotted flaps and, since armoured leading edges and balloon cable-cutters had become obligatory, the slats were locked shut on Halifax I series 1 and 2 and deleted from series 3 onward. After returning from No.35 Squadron, L7244 was flown at Boscombe Down mainly for armament and equipment trials and came to grief there later in 1941 when it shed three of its DH airscrews during a take-off run and was grounded as instructional airframe 3299M. L7245 had narrowly escaped disaster on 13 October, 1940, when the starboard undercarriage failed to retract fully after take-off and further attempts to lock it up caused the adjacent hydraulic accumulator to burst, through the level of liquid being too high; the undercarriage was then lowered safely by hand-pump and L7245 survived, with permanent dual controls as a crew trainer, to become grounded as 3474M in August 1942 when its engines became time-expired.

The first production Halifax L9485 served long at Boscombe Down as an armament 'guinea-pig' and at one stage was flying with B-P Type C turrets at the nose and mid-upper stations, a B-P Type E tail turret, beam gun hatches and a twin-gun F.N.64 ventral turret, eventually being grounded as 3362M. Only Handley Page Ltd built Halifax Is and the accelerated production programme of 1941–42 was based on the Halifax II, first flown in prototype form by Cordes at Radlett as L9515 on 3 July, 1941, and in production form from English Electric's Samlesbury factory as V9976 on 15 August, followed from Radlett by L9609 in September. By this time Flt

The first production Halifax I L9485 became an armament 'guinea-pig' at Boscombe Down and is seen here with additional Boulton-Paul Type C dorsal turret, hatch for beam guns and F.N.64 ventral turret.

Lieut James R. Talbot had become the company's chief test pilot, because Cordes had resigned on 31 July to take charge of No.7 Aircraft Assembly Unit, RAF, at Hawarden, Flintshire, where incoming Canadian and American-built aeroplanes of many varieties were to be assembled, modified to British requirements and tested before dispatch.

In October 1941 the third Halifax squadron, No.10, was formed at Leeming and received mainly Halifax IIs with only a few Mk.Is, but several of the latter went to No.28 Halifax Conversion Flight (later No.1658 Heavy Conversion Unit) on its establishment at Riccall during the same month. On 18 December eighteen Halifaxes (six from each squadron) joined Stirlings and Manchesters in a renewed daylight attack on the *Scharnhorst* and *Gneisenau* at Brest; the fighter defences shot down only one Halifax, but spoiled the bombers' aim, so the attack was repeated on 30 December by Halifaxes alone, three out of eighteen being lost. In spite of its

English Electric built Halifax II series 1 W1245 of No.78 Squadron showing turrets and external fuel jettison pipes. (*I.W.M.—Crown Copyright*)

increased power, the Halifax II's performance at full load was no better than the Halifax I's and at the higher wing loading its lateral stability had deteriorated. Furthermore, its excessive exhaust glow, visible from dead astern over the wing, made it an easy target for cannon-armed night fighters, which could attack while still out of range of the small-bore tail turret guns. With large numbers of unarmed American-built 'cash-and-carry' bombers arriving in 1941, all requiring British armament to be installed before they could enter RAF service, the availability of turrets became even more difficult and 0·5-in and 20-mm turrets were virtually non-existent except as prototypes. One successful trial installation of a low-drag mid-upper turret was the four 0·303-in Bristol B.12 Mk.I installed in Halifax II R9375, intended as a precursor to the twin 0·5-in B.12 Mk.II of identical dimensions, but the latter, like the equivalent Boulton-Paul Type T, was never available in production form, being reserved for newer types than the Halifax.

Halifax II series 1 R9375, formerly of No.76 Squadron, at Filton during trials of Bristol B.12 dorsal turret.

There were several operational and manufacturing difficulties associated with landing gear. Messier tailwheels were designed to be retractable, but at first their self-centring was unreliable and they had to be locked down to prevent damage in landing at night when their position could not be checked visually. Although excellent in other respects, the Messier main gear was slow in retraction, which reduced take-off performance, and even slower to manufacture, which seriously hampered the accelerated production schedules. The Dowty system of the Manchester and Lancaster was both quicker in operation and easier to make in quantity. Handley Page discussed these problems with George Dowty, who proposed a completely new levered-suspension landing gear and hydraulic system to suit the Halifax, similar to one already designed for the Lancaster. On 11 April, 1941, DTD agreed that L9250, already allotted to Rotols for airscrew deicing trials at Staverton, should remain there for trial installation of the Dowty system. Unfortunately the Messier system used castor-oil based fluid (D.T.D.391) with natural rubber seals and glands, while the Dowty system used mineral oil (D.T.D.44) which necessitated synthetic-rubber seals, so it was impossible to achieve full compatibility and interchangeability without a long development and test programme, although the same geometry and structural pick-up points could be used.

At a meeting with DTD on 9 May, 1941, it was agreed to develop an improved hydraulic system for future Halifaxes, using D.T.D.44 in Messier jacks with neoprene seals, but this could not relieve the immediate shortage of production landing gears. The only solution was to install Dowty systems in certain batches of Halifaxes, which would be distinguished by a new DIS and Mark number. The Air Ministry was already discussing a projected Hercules-engined Halifax III (H.P.61), and an alternative development of Halifax II with Merlin 60s had been unofficially named Halifax IV (H.P.60A), so the Halifax II with Dowty landing gear and hydraulics became Halifax V (H.P.63); in all other respects it was identical with Halifax II. L9250 first flew as the Halifax V prototype in October 1941, but was damaged in crash landing a year later. Had the Dowty landing gear used forgings as originally intended, it would have given very good service, but a calculated risk was taken to substitute castings, which were quicker to make, but proved to be liable to brittle fracture at high stress levels; this was found out too late for the production programme to be changed, so it became necessary to limit the Halifax V's maximum landing weight to 40,000 lb. For this reason Halifax Vs were mainly assigned to meteorological reconnaissance and other coastal duties and also proved valuable as tugs for training airborne troops and glider pilots, although they were flown for a time as bombers by six Canadian squadrons of No.6 Group, commencing with No.408 Squadron, RCAF, at Leeming in October 1942, also by No.76 Squadron and briefly by the Free French squadrons Nos.346 and 347. Halifax Vs were built only by Rootes Securities Ltd at Speke (Liverpool) and the Fairey Aviation Co Ltd at Errwood Park (Stockport). One of them, Rootes-built DG399, was flown to Canada as a pattern for the proposed manufacture of Halifax Vs by Canadian Associated Aircraft, to follow Hampden production, but this plan was cancelled when the shortcomings of the Dowty undercarriage became evident; production of this gear ceased in December 1943, after which only Messier units were available, so Halifax V production also had ended by January 1944 after 904 of this variant had been delivered.

Both Halifax II and V contributed to, and benefited from, further improvements in design and performance evolved during the development of Halifax III and IV, and those applied retrospectively included both improved armament and substantial drag reductions achieved through refining the fuselage nose and nacelle lines. During the early flights of L7244, pilots had complained of a fuselage oscillation, which had been traced to vortex-shedding from the inner nacelles. The Halifax II prototype, L9515, was tested with long-tailed inner nacelles and doors which completely enclosed the landing wheels. Although not adopted for production aircraft, these improved nacelles cured the buffet and substantially reduced drag, so they were standardised for the Halifax IV and three more Halifax IIs (HR679, HR756 and HR876) were later similarly modified for flight trials. Early in December 1941 N. E. Rowe (DTD) held a conference to discuss the possibility of deleting the nose and mid-upper B-P Type C turrets, which would achieve a net weight saving of 1,450 lb alone, while the drag reduction would improve top speed by 16 mph, equivalent to a further saving of 840 lb in fuel and oil over a range of 1,800 miles. Handley Page was all in favour, having long held that turrets were needed only for self-defence by day and were not worth the resulting loss of

Rootes-built Halifax V series 1 DG235 with Dowty undercarriage and hydraulic system at Boscombe Down in October 1942. (*I.W.M.—Crown Copyright*)

Rootes-built Halifax V series 1 (Special) DG395 glider tug in North Africa before the invasion of Sicily in July 1943. (*I.W.M.—Crown Copyright*)

Halifax V series 1A of No.644 Squadron about to take-off with a Hamilcar at Tarrant Rushton in May 1944, showing ventral windshield at paratroop exit. (*I.W.M.—Crown Copyright*)

performance by night. The improvement in speed and range was very urgently needed by the Special Operations Executive for fast long-range sorties across Germany to Poland to supply the Polish resistance movement with arms, equipment and special agents for liaison tasks. These were to be flown by No.138 Squadron, based at Tempsford, to whom three cleaned-up Halifax IIs were to be delivered as quickly as possible; the first to be converted was W7774, which was flown at Park Street on 15 August, 1942, subsequent conversion kits being made up and installed at the Rawcliffe repair depot on Halifaxes flown in from the squadrons. Thus came into being the 'Tempsford nose' (Mod 398), aircraft so converted being designated Halifax II series 1 (Special), although the new nose fairing was applied generally throughout No.4 Group and not restricted to the SOE squadrons. At the same time the external fuel jettison pipes were deleted (because the former landing weight restriction no longer existed) and various improved flame-damping exhaust shrouds were tried out, though without much success at first.

Halifax II series 1 (Special) JB211 of No.77 Squadron taking off from Elvington in July 1943; the parked Halifax shows a Boulton-Paul Type A Mk.III dorsal turret with raised fairing. (*I.W.M.—Crown Copyright*)

Concurrently, a new streamlined fuselage nose had been designed for future production. This was first made in metal for aerodynamic testing on L9515, to which also a Defiant-type Boulton-Paul Type A four-gun mid-upper turret was fitted, having much less drag than Type C. The slightly longer low-drag nose provided a sitting position for the bomb-aimer as well as additional stowage space for radio and navigational equipment. The first fully transparent nose fairing (Mod 452) was installed at Hucknall for trial on W7814, but this crashed at Coningsby on 23 September, 1942, and a second trial installation had to be made on DG276; this was approved in December for future production Halifax IIs and Vs, designated series 1A when also fitted with low-drag nacelles derived from the Beaufighter II; in these, rectangular Morris block radiators replaced the bulky Gallay twin drums inherited from the Whitley V via Halifax I. The fully-modified prototype Halifax II series 1A, HR679, first flew at Radlett on Christmas Eve 1942, proving 10 mph faster than the basic Halifax II W7922 even when the latter's mid-upper Type C turret had been removed. The new nose incorporated a 0·303-in hand-held K-gun known as the 'scare-gun', which many crews regarded as little more than an ornament, although Coastal

Halifax G.R.II series 1A JP258 at Boscombe Down in April 1945. (*I.W.M.—Crown Copyright*)

Command G.R.IIs, G.R.Vs, Met.IIs and Met.Vs carried a 0·5-in Browning belt-fed scare-gun which was capable of spoiling the aim of a submarine's gunlayer in a low-level attack. Coastal Command Halifaxes were converted from Rootes-built bombers by Cunliffe-Owen at Eastleigh, who also installed F.N.64 ventral turrets and 690-gallon long-range tanks in the fuselage bomb-cells, as well as special radar and meteorological equipment according to role. The first G.R.II series 1A was JP258 and the first Met.II series 1A was DG344; another Coastal Command trial installation was of rocket projectile rails under the front fuselage of JD212; this was not adopted for service, although twin 0·5-in remotely-controlled Browning guns were installed in ventral blisters in HR909 and NA137 for operational trials in place of F.N.64 turrets, the first of the latter having appeared on W7650 in September 1942. The twin 0·5-in Brownings were prone to overheating and eventually the Preston-Green mounting for a single under-defence 0·5-in Browning was adopted for service, being more effective at long range than the F.N.64. In late Halifax IIs and Vs Rolls-Royce were able to provide Merlin 22 engines using 100-octane fuel at plus 7 psi boost and these increased the permissible all-up weight to 65,000 lb (including 4,000 lb more useful load) with practically no new design work; furthermore, Merlin 22s were much less prone than Merlin XXs to coolant leaks.

A total of 299 Halifax IIs series 1A came off the Cricklewood line, nearly all with Boulton-Paul Type A Mk.VIII four-gun mid-upper turrets; initially the Air Staff had insisted on having 10 degrees depression for this turret, which then needed a raised deck fairing, resulting in a higher drag than with the same turret installed straight on to the deck with zero depression and no fairing; opinions gleaned from squadrons in Nos.4 and 6 Groups showed that deletion of the mid-upper turret was unpopular and that a series 1A fuselage with a B-P type A turret at deck level had no more drag than a series 1 (Special) fuselage with the mid-upper turret deleted. Both Cricklewood's and English Electric's Halifaxes were equally well liked by crews, but the London Group's were not, while Mk.Vs from Rootes and Fairey suffered from the shortcomings of the Dowty landing gear, with its insufficiently damped rebound characteristic; however, the positive Dowty flap control was preferred to the Messier, in which the flaps had to be locked 'up' mechanically before selecting power 'off'. A further

Halifax II series 1A HR861 at Radlett in 1943 with revised nose and flush-mounted Boulton-Paul Type A Mk.VIII dorsal turret. (*I.W.M.—Crown Copyright*)

series of modifications concerned the fuselage bomb-doors, which originally had been made compatible with either an H_2S radome or a ventral turret, but could not enclose bombs larger than 2,000 lb. These were metal-skinned doors (Type A) which had to be replaced by faired wooden doors on steel carrier frames in order to enclose a 4,000-lb bomb. Trial doors (Type B) were made by Phillips & Powis to suit V9985, but proved unacceptable, so the original Type A doors were fitted with new hinges and side flaps (becoming Type D) to make them interchangeable with new Type C doors being manufactured by Evans Bellhouse for Halifax III, which would not fit Halifax II and V. With Type D doors, V9985 successfully dropped dummies of the 4,000-lb 'block-buster', to be carried by Halifax IIIs in conjunction with H_2S ground-mapping radar, and the first operational 8,000-lb block-buster, comprising two 4,000-lb cases joined in tandem, was dropped on Essen by R9457 of No.76 Squadron during the night of 10/11 April, 1942. The H_2S radome was first mocked-up at Radlett on W7711, the first full scanner equipment being installed by TRE at Hurn on V9977, but this Halifax crashed early in 1942, killing a number of key radar technicians on board. It was replaced by W7808 and W7823, further radar development being continued on W7851 and HR815/G; the final service installation was approved on Halifax III HX238.

The last major modification to the Halifax II and V was the introduction of enlarged vertical tail surfaces, because of rudder stalling which caused spiral instability with two engines dead on one side and had led to many crashes on final approach at night. The original (A-type) rudders of the Halifax I had proved to be overbalanced at large deflections and this had been cured by means of a bulbous leading edge (B-type), which in turn had caused 'hunting' in straight level flight. Hunting was preventable by cutting back the leading edge for two inches and increasing the balance-tab movement (C-type), but this caused 'trailing' in sideslip. Meanwhile enlarged fins and rudders, symmetrical above and below the tailplane (E-type) had been designed for the Halifax III and IV, but these too were overbalanced at large deflections. Cutting back the E-type's leading edge, as for the C-type, produced the F-type, which again trailed in sideslip, so the F-type's nose balance was cropped at the top and bottom ends, to result

Leavesden-built Halifax II series 1A JP228 with D-type fins and H_2S radome. (*I.W.M.—Crown Copyright*)

in the G-type, which was satisfactorily flown in December on DG281. Meanwhile, independent wind-tunnel investigations had evolved the combination of a C-type rudder with a rectangular fin of 50 per cent greater area. This, when tested on DK145, was found to have eliminated both overbalance and trailing and, as the D-type, was standardised on all production Halifax IIIs, with retrospective application to late Merlin-engined variants, particularly those with H_2S or with Merlin 22s and four-blade airscrews.

The total number of Merlin-engined Halifaxes (Mks.I, II and V) produced was 1,967, of which 701 (including the two prototypes) were manufactured at Cricklewood by the parent company, who built all the Mk.Is but none of the Mk.Vs; one of the twelve Rootes-built Mk.IIs,

Leavesden-built Halifax II series 1A JP246 of No.148 (S.D.) Squadron at Brindisi in 1944, taking on supplies for Polish Resistance fighters during the Warsaw uprising. (*J. D. Oughton*)

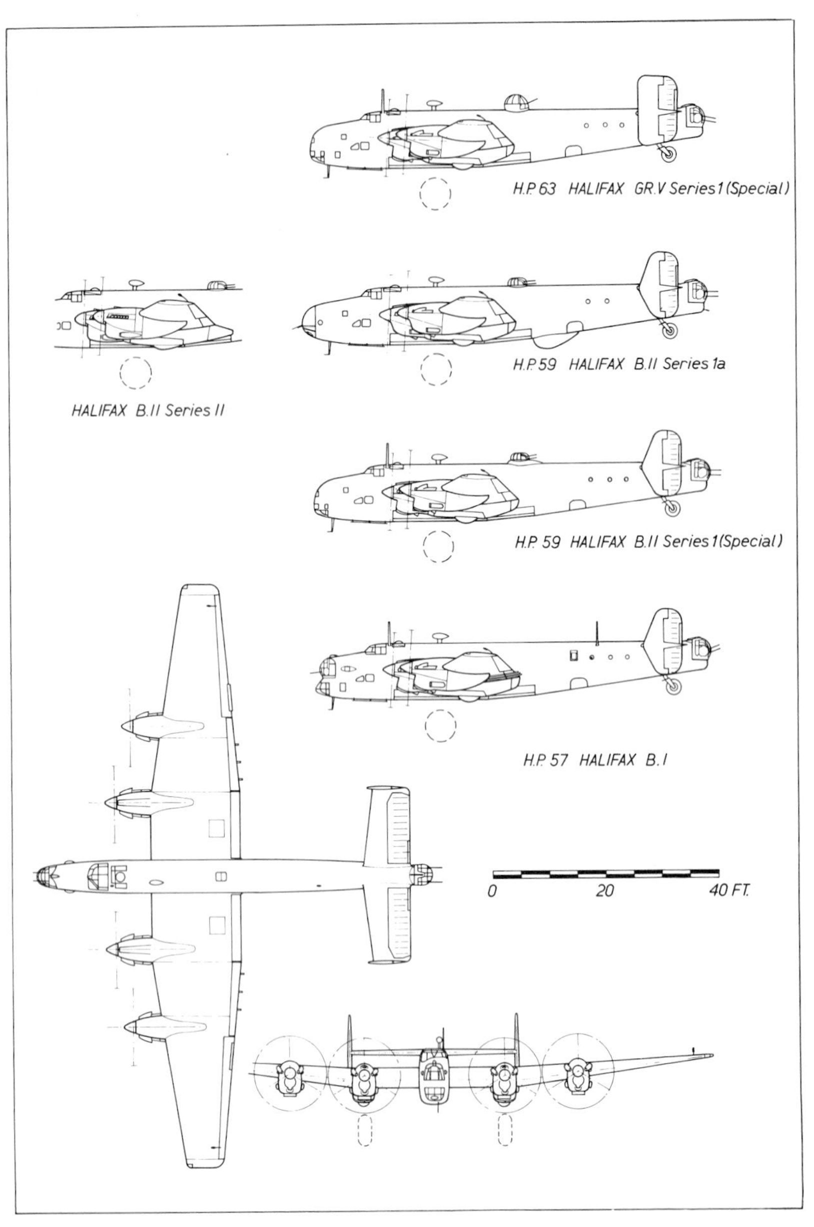

DG223, crashed on test at Speke and was not delivered, and 900 and 450 Mk.IIs respectively were made by English Electric at Preston and London Aircraft Production Group at Leavesden. Of the Mk.Vs, 246 were made by Fairey at Errwood Park and 658 by Rootes at Speke. Their contribution to the war effort was prodigious, but their operational history is too big a

Fairey-built Halifax G.R.V. series 1A LK688 of No.518 Squadron at Tiree in 1944
(*Philip Moyes*)

subject to be adequately discussed in this book. It may, however, be noted that Halifax IIs and Vs were the only British-built four-engined heavy bombers to serve in North Africa and the Middle East during the early war years under extreme tropical conditions, for which neither the Stirling nor the early Lancaster could be made suitable.

By a fortunate trick of fate, one Halifax II series 1, English Electric-built W1048, was recovered almost intact during June 1973 by skin-divers from 90 ft of fresh water in Lake Hoklingen, Norway, where it had crashed on ice after being shot down during its first sortie with No.35 Squadron in low level attack on the battleship *Tirpitz* sheltering in a branch of Trondheim Fjord on 27/28 April, 1942. With relatively little corrosion during its 31-year immersion, it was hoped to restore this unique survivor for permanent preservation in the RAF Museum at Hendon.

H.P.56

(Two Rolls-Royce Vulture X)

Span 88 ft (26·85 m); length 66 ft 6 in (20·1 m); wing area 975 sq ft (90·5 m^2). Empty weight (est) 26,300 lb (11,880 kg); maximum weight (est) 39,000 lb (17,700 kg). Speed (est) 320 mph (515 km/h); range (est) 3,000 miles (4,830 km) with 4,000 lb (1,813 kg) bomb load; ceiling (est) 28,000 ft (8,660 m). Crew four.

H.P.57 Halifax I

(Four Rolls-Royce Merlin X)

Span 98 ft 10 in (30·2 m); length 70 ft 1 in (21·4 m); wing area 1,200 sq ft (111·5 m^2). Empty weight 36,000 lb (16,320 kg); maximum weight (series 1) 55,000 lb (24,950 kg), (series 2 and 3) 60,000 lb (27,200 kg). Bomb load 13,000 lb (5,900 kg). Speed 280 mph (450 km/h); range 3,000 miles (4,830 km). Crew six.

H.P.59 Halifax II and H.P.63 Halifax V

(Four Rolls-Royce Merlin XX or 22)

As for Halifax I except: maximum weight (Mk.II) 60,000 lb (27,200 kg) with Merlin XX, 65,000 lb (29,450 kg) with Merlin 22, (Mk.V) 63,000 lb (28,600 kg).

Halifax II series 2 HR756 with Merlin 65s at Hucknall in 1943. (*I.W.M.—Crown Copyright*)

Halifax Bomber Development—Halifax III, IV, VI, VII and B.27/43 (H.P.60A, 61, 65, 66 and 69)

With the aim of using the Halifax effectively as a day bomber, the Air Staff encouraged Handley Page to develop a high-altitude version with either Bristol Hercules VIII or Rolls-Royce Merlin 60 engines, both having two-stage superchargers giving a maximum power rating at 30,000 ft. These engines were being urgently developed for the pressure-cabin Wellingtons V and VI respectively. The Hercules VIII suffered from incurable supercharger surging and was abandoned, but the Merlin 60, 61 and 62 went into production for Spitfires and Mosquitos and were proposed for the Halifax IV, which was to have had a strengthened bomb floor and enlarged bomb-doors to enclose 4,000-lb and 8,000-lb bombs, together with extended wing-tips, which increased the span to 104 ft, also enlarged symmetrical (E-type) fins and rudders. Handley Page himself wanted the Merlin 60 to be given priority over the Hercules and had set aside HR756 as the Halifax IV prototype, but although it was built with Merlin 60 powerplants, only Merlin XXs were available for initial flight tests in March 1943 and with these installed it was called Halifax II series 2. It was intended to fit Merlin 60s when available to bring it up to Halifax IV standard, but it was allotted to Rolls-Royce Ltd at Hucknall for engine development work and retained its original 99-ft span all its life, although Merlin 61 and 65 engines were eventually installed at various periods.

On 5 August, 1941, Handley Page had written to Air Marshal F. J. Linnell (Controller of Research and Development) recommending the early introduction into production of some of the Halifax IV features, but in September CRD had countered with a request for the introduction of Bristol Hercules VI or XVI engines on current production aircraft at the earliest opportunity; with structural modifications to raise the permitted all-up weight to 64,000 lb, this variant, Halifax III (H.P.61), was estimated to be capable of 307 mph at 21,000 ft and it was hoped to substitute

Halifax III prototype R9534 converted from Halifax II series 1 (Special) in October 1942, with F-type symmetrical fins and rudders. (*I.W.M.—Crown Copyright*)

improved Hercules 100 (HE-10SM) engines later to compensate for the failure of the Hercules VIII. In reply, Handley Page protested that he was already being asked for a whole host of modifications which would severely interfere with production unless they could be deferred until the 201st Halifax. They included such diverse provisions as target towing, paratrooping, heavy-gauge protective engine cowling, multiple flare chutes, revised ammunition tracks to the tail turret to clear the paratroop exit cone, a revised dual-control pilot's seat, rocket gear for short take-off and arrestor gear for short landing, none of which seemed to Handley Page to be likely to improve the Halifax's efficiency as a bomber, although he agreed with the proposal to fit a B-P Type A mid-upper turret and F.N.64 ventral turret for daylight operations. Linnell replied that he could not promise a clear run without any further modifications through to the 200th aircraft, but could defer all outstanding modifications except exhaust flame dampers, engine rear armour, astrograph and D/F loop, fixed fittings for 4,000-lb and 8,000-lb bombs, increased electrical generation and glider towing. These Handley Page accepted with good grace and even offered Rawcliffe aerodrome for the first towed flight trials of the new Slingsby

Halifax III HX238 at Boscombe Down in 1943 during trials of Boulton-Paul Type D rear turret with two 0·5 in Browning guns and A.G.L.T. radar, code-named 'Village Inn'. (*I.W.M.—Crown Copyright*)

A production Halifax III with tailwheel retracted.

Hengist paratroop glider, being built nearby at Kirkbymoorside, although these were eventually done by the Airborne Forces Experimental Establishment at Sherburn-in-Elmet.

In January 1942, R9534, just completed as a prototype Mk.II series 1 (Special) with a Tempsford nose and B-P Type C mid-upper turret, was chosen for the trial installation of Hercules VI engines; it thereby became the first prototype Halifax III and was first flown on 12 October, 1942, wearing daylight camouflage above and 'trainer yellow' below. In December the B-P Type C turret was replaced by a Defiant-type B-P A Mk.III; further performance improvement was gained by retracting the tailwheel and fitting Beaufighter-type Hercules cowlings in February 1943 in preparation for the approval of Cricklewood's 700th production Halifax, HX226, as the first true MarkIII, which was flown by Talbot in August 1943. More Halifax IIIs were built than of any other variant, production being shared by all five main assembly groups and amounting finally to 2,127, of which 2,091 were delivered before VJ-Day; among their many refinements was a return to a retractable tailwheel after the persistent trouble of shimmy on runways had been overcome. Halifax IIIs were first issued in November 1943 to No.433 Squadron, RCAF, and No.466 Squadron, RAAF, subsequently equipping forty-one operational squadrons, apart from numerous training and experimental units. At least four Halifax IIIs from No.4 Group each completed 100 or more sorties over enemy targets:— LV907 of No.158 Squadron, famous as *Friday the Thirteenth*; LV937, which served in both Nos.578 and 51 Squadrons, and LW587 and MZ527, both of No.578 Squadron. Only one Victoria Cross was won in a Halifax; this was awarded posthumously to Pilot Officer Cyril Barton of No.578 Squadron, captain and pilot of Halifax III LK797, which was severely damaged by night fighters while approaching Nuremberg on the night of 30/31 March, 1944. With intercom destroyed, one engine damaged and gun turrets inoperable, Barton's signal to open the bomb doors was misinterpreted by the navigator, bomb-aimer and radio-operator, who all baled out by parachute. Unable to call up the remaining three crew members, Barton pressed on to the target, released his bombs single-handed and struggled home to make a landfall 90 miles north of his base, with fuel nearly all gone and two engines dead. Being too low to bale out, he ordered his crew to their crash stations and, as the third engine failed, just managed to clear houses in the final crash landing, in which he was killed but his three comrades survived.

Halifax III MZ954 of No.425 'Alouette' Squadron RCAF at Tholthorpe in 1944, with single 0·5 in Browning gun in Preston-Green ventral mounting.

By February 1944, the Bristol Hercules 100 was at last in production as a self-contained powerplant and offered very greatly increased performance, using 100-octane fuel in conjunction with RAE-Hobson injector carburettors. These required a high-pressure fuel supply, so a completely revised fuel system was designed with seven flexible main tanks in each wing, arranged in inboard and outboard groups, with each engine fed from its adjacent group and all fuel cocks located on the flight deck, instead of behind the front spar. The permanent fuel capacity was 2,190 gallons, to which could be added 690 gallons in three fuselage bomb-cell tanks, giving a maximum overload tankage of 2,880 gallons. With this fuel system, larger Gallay oil coolers, the Graveley cabin heating system using four exhaust heaters, and all retrospective modifications including extended wing-tips, the Halifax became Mark VI with Hercules 100s and Mark VII with Hercules XVIs. Hercules 100 development engines were installed at Filton in the trial installation Halifax III, HX234, and in the Mk.VI prototype LV776, which was first flown at Radlett on 19 December, 1943, and thereafter with various airscrew blade root cuffs and cooling fans, before going to Filton for further development in March 1944.

The first production Halifax B.VI was NP715, first flown on 10 October, 1944; it survived some months of operational service before becoming a trial installation aircraft at Radlett. During 1946–47 it undertook flight tests of a novel lateral control system using curved spoilers moving in and

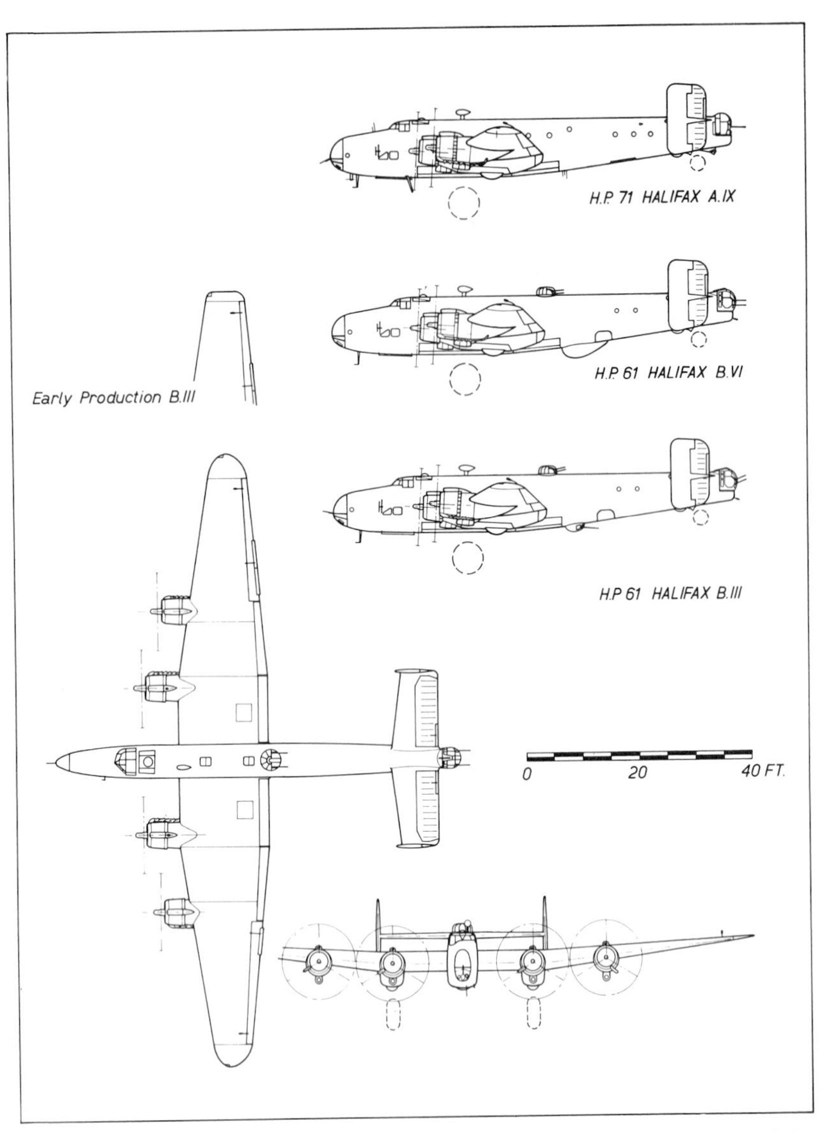

out of slots immediately in front of the ailerons, in the upper surface of the wing. These tests offered no promise of any better control than could be obtained with conventional ailerons and the aim of greatly reducing aileron area was not achieved, so in 1948 NP715 was flown to Filton, where it was grounded for use as a fire test rig during 1949 and 1950. The Halifax VI and VII were the last bomber variants in production, being built by both the parent company and English Electric; in addition, the Halifax VII was built by the Merseyside factories of Fairey and Rootes; 457 Mk.VI and 423 Mk.VII were delivered, others in progress being cancelled after VJ-Day.

Halifax B.VI RG867 of No.347 'Tunisie' Squadron French Air Force in 1945.

Most of them were fully tropicalised and several were already operating as long-range radar post detectors in South East Asia Command against the Japanese, in support of the main assault by 'Tiger Force', which was called off when the Hiroshima and Nagasaki nuclear bombs ended hostilities. After the war, several Halifax VIs were presented to the French Air Force, who operated them on long-range colonial missions until 1947, while one of several flown by the RAF Empire Radio School at Debden, RG815 *Mercury*, became famous when it flew 25,000 miles on a world-wide demonstration of radio and radar aids and equipment. Some 40 per cent of all the heavy bombers produced in the United Kingdom during the war years were Halifaxes and they flew a total of 75,532 sorties carrying 227,610 tons of bombs to enemy targets.

During the war, the Halifax programme was constrained by the two conflicting demands of quantity production and military necessity to maintain a maximum output of bombers, with the fewest possible major design changes. Nevertheless, research was vigorously pursued into higher performance and efficiency, in spite of Dr Lachmann's internment under Defence Regulation 18B, and his deputy in the Research Dept, Godfrey Lee, was later in touch with him. Lachmann was allowed to work

Halifax VI RG815 *Mercury* of the Empire Radio School, Debden, on return from a 25,000-mile three months' tour of Palestine, Iraq, India, Burma, Singapore, Australia and New Zealand on 21 November, 1946.

only on problems of basic aerodynamics and structural design and the more urgent aspects of improving bomber effectiveness had become Lee's direct concern in December 1941, when he reported on the optimisation of high-altitude bomber design. Lee suggested an aircraft of Halifax size, but of much better aerodynamic shape and lower drag, with four Merlin 60 engines mounted transversely in pairs, buried in a forward extension of the centre-section leading edge, with each pair geared to a contra-rotating coaxial airscrew unit mounted in a slender nacelle at each end of the centre-section, thereby combining the power and reliability of four engines with the low drag of a half-submerged twin powerplant installation. This project would have been heavily defended with nose, dorsal and ventral turrets, and would have had a nosewheel and a sideways-retracting main undercarriage. Lee's proposal was too advanced and idealistic for immediate implementation in 1942 and he did not attempt to design the structure in detail, but concurrent experience with the Consolidated B-24 Liberator had shown the benefit of choosing a high aspect ratio.

The Halifax itself had by no means reached the end of its development potential and in June 1943 Volkert proposed a 'Super-Halifax', having a greater bomb-load and capacity, longer range, higher cruising speed and better operational height than existing types. This improvement was to be achieved by combining the standard Halifax III fuselage (with larger bomb-doors and a stronger bomb-floor) with low-drag high aspect ratio wings, turbo-supercharged powerplants and a revised low-drag landing gear. Designated H.P.65, the new bomber featured a NACA 66 series laminar flow wing profile and the 113-ft span wing (aspect ratio 11) tapered uniformly from centreline to tip; it was to be constructed round a single spar at 40 per cent chord, using heavy-gauge skin free from waviness and with rivet lines as far as possible chordwise only; in this it resembled the Davis wing of the Consolidated Liberator, which Handley Page Ltd had briefly fostered early in the war. All four powerplants were to be in nacelles on the 55-ft span centre-section, to which 29-ft outer wings were attached. The wing structure incorporated integral fuel and oil tanks lined with flexible bags, also leading-edge deicing by hot air from the powerplants. The Hercules 38 exhaust-turbo-supercharged engines were to have leading-edge duct entries for carburettor air intakes, oil coolers and intercoolers, and the single-leg twin-wheeled main landing gear was to be totally enclosed when retracted, the tailwheel also being retractable. The fuselage was standard, being modified only in respect of the wing-root attachments, larger bomb-doors and the stronger bomb-floor, which could take bombs up to 12,000 lb without a detachable carrier, these being completely enclosed within the bomb-doors. The armament proposed was a Boulton-Paul Type T dorsal turret and a B-P Type D tail turret, each with two 0·5-in Browning guns. There was no provision for a ventral turret, but the standard Halifax III nose with a K-type 'scare-gun' was retained. With a nominal fuel capacity in the wings of 2,500 gallons, the H.P.65 was estimated to cruise at 240 mph at 20,000 ft for 3,710 miles and to attain a maximum speed of 350 mph at 27,200 ft.

By October 1943, it was apparent that Hercules 38 engines were unlikely to reach production status and furthermore that very comprehensive jigging and tooling would be needed to manufacture the single-spar wing to 'laminar flow' tolerances; at a meeting with the firm to discuss this

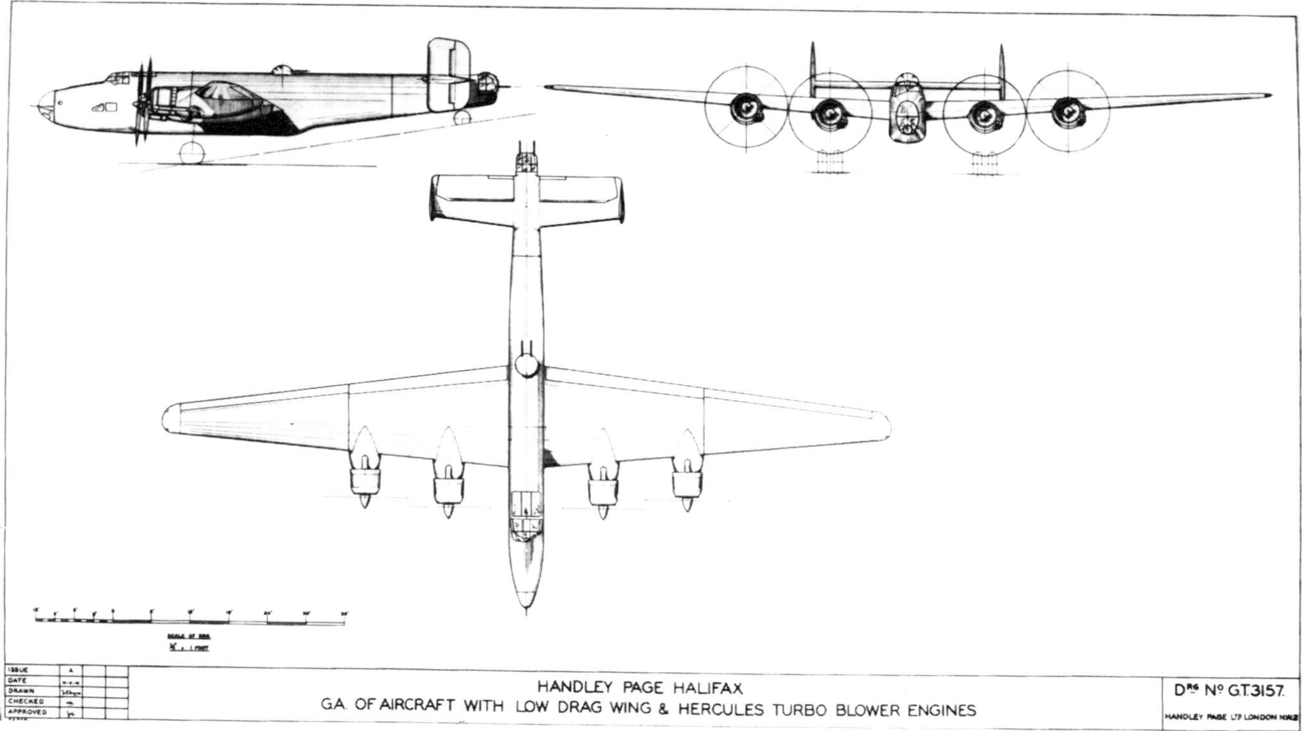

H.P.65 project.

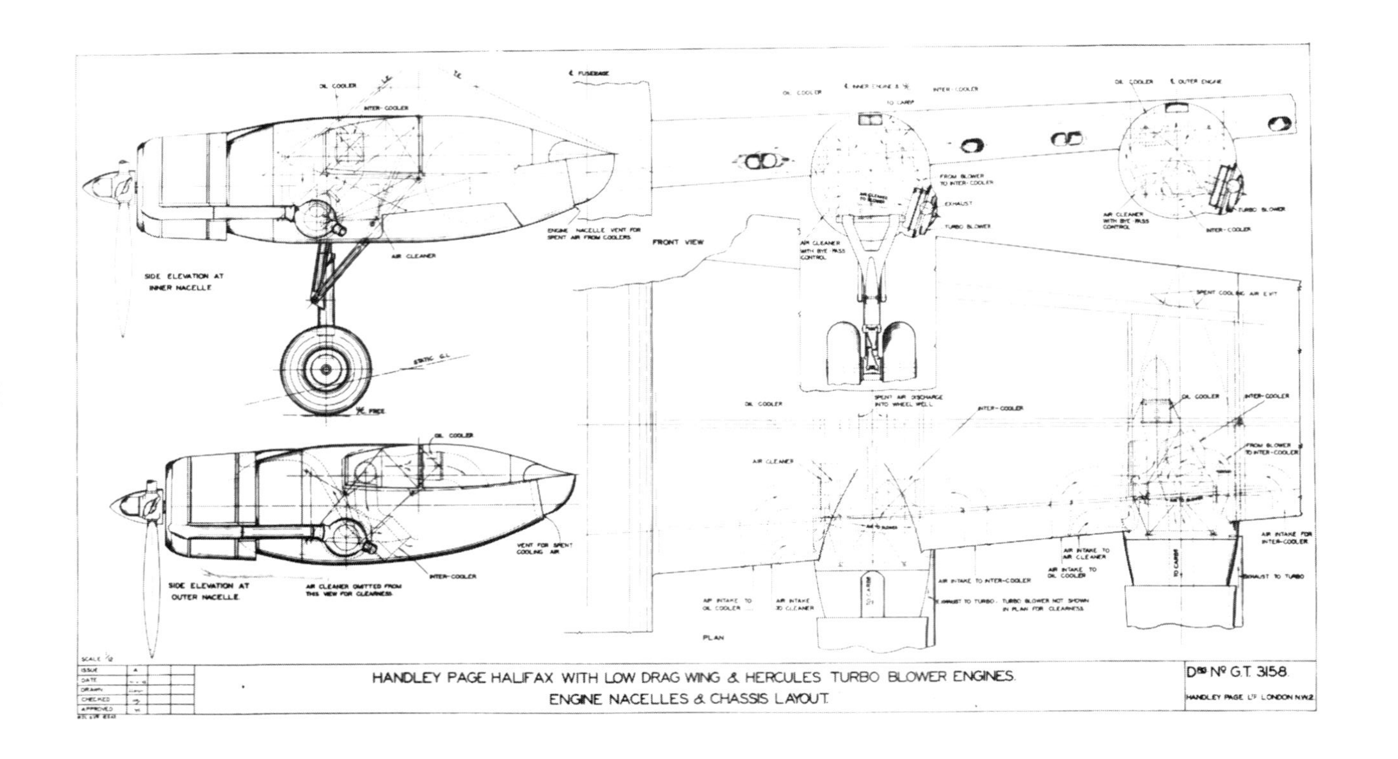

SIDE ELEVATION AT INNER NACELLE
SIDE ELEVATION AT OUTER NACELLE
FRONT VIEW
PLAN
OIL COOLER
INTER-COOLER
AIR CLEANER
ENGINE NACELLE VENT FOR SPENT AIR FROM COOLERS
VENT FOR SPENT COOLING AIR
AIR CLEANER OMITTED FROM THIS VIEW FOR CLEARNESS
FROM BLOWER TO INTER-COOLER
EXHAUST
TURBO BLOWER
AIR CLEANER WITH BYE-PASS CONTROL
SPENT AIR DISCHARGE INTO WHEEL WELL
AIR INTAKE TO OIL COOLER
AIR INTAKE TO CLEANER
AIR INTAKE TO INTER-COOLER
EXHAUST TO TURBO
AIR INTAKE FOR INTER-COOLER
HANDLEY PAGE HALIFAX WITH LOW DRAG WING & HERCULES TURBO BLOWER ENGINES.
ENGINE NACELLES & CHASSIS LAYOUT.
DRG Nº G.T. 3158.
HANDLEY PAGE LTD LONDON N.W.2.

problem, N. E. Rowe (DTD) suggested that the H.P.65 should be abandoned in favour of a conventional two-spar wing having a 55-ft span centre-section to which standard extended Halifax outer wings could be attached. Since the required freedom from waviness could not be attained with existing production techniques, the slightly lower efficiency of a wing with a nearly rectangular centre-section would be insignificant. Details of this project were further discussed with DTD and DOR on 27 November, 1943, when the design was registered as H.P.66 and defined by specification B.27/43. Three prototypes were ordered and on 21 January, 1944, the name 'Hastings' was proposed by the firm; the first two prototypes, with Hercules 100, would be Hastings B.Mk.1 and the third, when fitted with exhaust-turbo-blown HE-15MT powerplants, would be Hastings B.Mk.2 with the new type number H.P.69. As an insurance, Merlin 65s, in cylindrical RAE 'idealised' powerplants interchangeable with Hercules, were also envisaged for the H.P.66, following trial installations (with four-blade airscrews) in Halifax II DG296 and Halifax III LV795; these had already been standardised for the Avro Lincoln and Vickers Windsor. It was hoped that production of 200 Hastings bombers would follow on at Radlett after delivery of the 1,440th production Halifax, due in May 1945, but in April 1944 priority was transferred to 200 Halifax A.IX transports urgently needed by the Airborne Forces in Europe, so the H.P.69 was shelved, although the two H.P.66 prototypes remained on order. With the arrival of VJ-Day, the B.27/43 long-range bomber was no longer needed and emphasis was switched to the H.P.67 transport, to which the name Hastings was also transferred.

In its ultimate bomber development as the H.P.65 and 66, the Halifax had, in effect, attained most of the objectives of the B.1/39 'Ideal Bomber' specification to which Volkert had successfully tendered the H.P.60 design in May 1939. This would have been a low-drag four-engined shoulder-wing monoplane designed to combine a high cruising speed with a very powerful gun defence, arranged amidships in two large-diameter Boulton-Paul low-profile turrets each mounting four 20-mm Hispano cannons. From among the half-dozen designs tendered, the Air Staff proposed to order prototypes of the H.P.60 and Bristol Type 159, on condition that both types were operationally interchangeable, with identical crew stations and instrument layout; furthermore, all large forgings or castings, e.g. for the nosewheel landing gear, were to be the same in both designs, as were the major components of the flying controls, wheels, brakes, hydraulic, pneumatic and electrical systems; the turrets were to be installationally interchangeable as complete units and Boulton-Paul and Bristol armament designers were to collaborate to attain this end. Both the H.P.60 and Bristol 159 had reached the stage of being mocked-up in some detail by the end of 1939, but then priority for fullest production of existing types of aircraft overrode all longer-term plans and, with Lord Beaverbrook's appointment as Minister of Aircraft Production in May 1940, the B.1/39 was suspended and then killed stone-dead. The contract would have called for a 9/20th-scale flying model to prove stability and handling qualities, as Short Brothers had already done with their half-scale Stirling; this would have had four Pobjoy Niagara engines and was labelled H.P.59A, presumably to conceal the identity and existence of the H.P.60 project, but work on it never started.

H.P.60 (B.1/39)

(Four Rolls-Royce Griffon or Bristol Hercules)

Span 114 ft (36·7 m). Maximum weight 70,000 lb (31,750 kg). Crew five.

H.P.60A Halifax IV

(Four Rolls-Royce Merlin 65)

Span 104 ft 2 in (34·2 m); length 71 ft 7 in (21·85 m); wing area 1,275 sq ft (118·3 m²). Empty weight 39,000 lb (17,700 kg); maximum weight 65,000 lb (29,450 kg). Bomb load 13,000 lb (5,900 kg). Speed 300 mph (483 km/h); range 2,350 miles (3,780 km); ceiling 24,000 ft (7,770 m). Crew six.

H.P.61 Halifax III

(Four Bristol Hercules XVI)

Span 98 ft 10 in (30·2 m); length 71 ft 7 in (21·85 m); wing area 1,200 sq ft (111·5 m²). Empty weight 38,900 lb (17,620 kg); maximum weight 65,000 lb (29,450 kg). Bomb load 13,000 lb (5,900 kg). Speed 282 mph (454 km/h); range 2,350 miles (3,780 km); ceiling 24,000 ft (7,770 m). Crew six.

H.P.61 Halifax VII

As for Halifax III except span 104 ft 2 in (34·2 m); wing area 1,275 sq ft (118·3 m²).

H.P.61 Halifax VI

(Four Bristol Hercules 100)

Span 104 ft 2 in (34·2 m); length 71 ft 7 in (21·85 m); wing area 1,275 sq ft (118·3 m²). Empty weight 38,900 lb (17,620 kg); maximum weight 68,000 lb (30,820 kg). Bomb load 13,000 lb (5,900 kg). Speed 312 mph (502 km/h); range 2,350 miles (3,780 km); ceiling 24,000 ft (7,770 m). Crew six.

H.P.65

(Four Bristol Hercules 38)

Span 113 ft (36·6 m); length 71 ft 7 in (21·85 m); wing area 1,450 sq ft (134·7 m²). Empty weight 38,900 lb (17,620 kg); maximum weight 68,000 lb (30,820 kg). Bomb load 13,000 lb (5,900 kg). Speed (est) 350 mph (564 km/h); range (est) 3,710 miles (5,970 km); ceiling (est) 30,000 ft (9,275 m). Crew six.

H.P.66 Hastings B.1

(Four Bristol Hercules 100)

As for H.P.65 except wing area 1,408 sq ft (131·6 m²).

H.P.69 Hastings B.2

As H.P.66 with Bristol Hercules 15MT.

Halifax C.III NA195 with extended wing-tips in April 1945. (*I.W.M.—Crown Copyright*)

Halifax Military Transports, C.VIII, A.IX and A.X (H.P.70 and 71)

One of the original requirements in specification P.13/36 had stated 'consideration shall be given in the design for the provision of light removable seating for the accommodation of the maximum number of personnel in the fuselage', which established the Halifax's secondary role as a potential troop-carrier; in this it followed the tradition of its precursors, the Harrow and H.P.55 bombers. In February 1938 the newly amalgamated independent airline, British Airways, had enquired whether a civil variant of the H.P.57 could be evolved, with four Perseus, Pegasus XVIII or Dagger engines, to carry either 25 passengers over a stage of 1,000 miles between London and Copenhagen, or 1,600 lb of mail over 2,500 miles between London and Bathurst. In reply, R. S. Stafford had estimated that this would be possible at a gross weight of 38,000 lb, but considered the wing loading of around 30 lb/sq ft to be too high for civil aircraft operating from British grass aerodromes. Under wartime conditions, no transport role for the Halifax was considered until September 1941, when glider-towing and paratroop roles were called for, because the RAF were then committed to provide a substantial airborne expeditionary force by July 1942. In fact the first three paratroop Halifax II series 1 (Special) aircraft, with 'Tempsford' noses, exit cones and retracting tailwheels, were issued to No.138 (Special Duties) Squadron on 20 August, 1942. Simultaneously Handley Page proposed a 'Freighter-Bomber' Halifax using the standard 99-ft span wing, D-type tail unit, standard landing gear and either Merlin XX or Hercules VI powerplants in conjunction with a new circular-section streamlined fuselage with a diameter of 9 ft 6 in and parallel portion 26 ft long; the Halifax mid-wing layout was retained to equalise the stowage space above and below the floor. No change in the inner engine centres was needed to accommodate the new fuselage because of the existing large clearance, a legacy from the original twin-Vulture H.P.56 design.

The intended roles included (a) freighter for Halifax spares or for bulky general stores; (b) aerial tanker, with 1,800 gallons of fuel in three very large under-floor tanks in addition to the normal Halifax wing tankage of 1,880 gallons; (c) troop-carrier for 36 fully-equipped sideways-facing troops, with a paratroop exit cone just aft of the bomb cell and a four-gun dorsal turret if needed; (d) unpressurised short-range bomber with exceptionally large bomb stowage capacity; and finally, at a later stage of development (e) pressurised high-altitude bomber with relatively few structural changes. The rear fuselage was to have a large roof-loading hatch for bulky freight in addition to side doors. This proposal was discussed on 17 August, 1942, with Air Marshal F. J. Linnell (CRD), but was turned down. Nevertheless Handley Page made further proposals for a civil Halifax transport which were submitted to MAP on 11 January, 1943, on the formation of the first committee set up under Lord Brabazon of Tara to investigate British post-war air transport policy. Though not encouraged by the Brabazon Committee, Handley Page began preliminary design work and allotted designation H.P.64 to the transport project, which differed from the original Freighter-Bomber mainly in changing from mid-wing to low-wing layout. In May, wind-tunnel tests on the H.P.64 showed that an increase in fuselage diameter from 9 ft 6 in to 11 ft had little effect on wing stressing or overall drag, and Hercules powerplants were selected in preference to Merlins. The project was discussed from the airworthiness angle with Walter Tye and Harold Roxbee-Cox (later Lord Kings Norton) on 11 August, 1943, and with BOAC a fortnight later; on the latter occasion, R. S. Stafford was able to view the Curtiss-Wright CW-20 *St. Louis*, which was the first (and at that date, only) example of a pressurised, thermally insulated, sound-proofed and air-conditioned civil transport to be seen in Britain. Handley Page Ltd were not allowed to undertake design work which would in any way reduce the war effort, so could not give any priority to the H.P.64, but Flight Refuelling Ltd had temporary drawing office and factory capacity and agreed to design and manufacture a rear fuselage for static testing. This was opposed by MAP, because a parallel Air Staff exercise had shown that a quicker and cheaper way of producing an interim military transport was to strip all armament and military equipment from a standard Halifax bomber; so in December 1943 the H.P.64 project was put on low priority under the label 'Transport C', while approval was given to 'Transport A' (a stripped Halifax III, VI or VII bomber) and 'Transport B' (an unarmed production version of 'Transport A', for which the Transport Command Development Unit had designed a pannier of 8,000 lb capacity to replace the bomb doors).

The trial installation of the pannier was made at Farnborough on Halifax III LV838 in February 1945, but meanwhile many bombers were converted (by Mod. 1105) to carry freight or nine stretchers or eight passenger seats in addition to the normal crew rest bunks, which could seat six; in these all guns, the dorsal turret, the H_2S scanner and radome, the tri-cell chute and 'Monica' radio were removed and the aircraft became Halifax C.III, C.VI or C.VII, but only the last carried the pannier apart

Halifax C.VIII PP285 bright-polished and without pannier for speed and economy trials at the Transport Command Development Unit, Brize Norton, in April 1945. (*The Aeroplane*)

Halifax C.III LV838 with trial installation of bomb-cell pannier at Farnborough in February 1945.

The penultimate Halifax C.VIII, PP337, was sold to Norway as LN-OAT for Vingtor Airways in August 1947, returning in October 1948 to become G-ALEF of Eagle Airways.

G-AHDU *Falkirk*, the first Halton conversion for BOAC, was delivered to Bovingdon from Short & Harland at Belfast on 12 July, 1946. (*BOAC*)

from LV838, since this involved modifications during manufacture. The need for high-capacity freighters was met by ordering 100 of a new variant, Halifax C.VIII, in which all the 'Transport B' features were incorporated, including Mod.1192 to carry freight or ten stretchers or eleven passenger seats together with a paratroop cone, also the 8,000-lb pannier (Mod.1377) and special radio and radar (Mod.1401); a total of 160 panniers was ordered from Handley Page Ltd, who sub-contracted 60 to Evans Bellhouse, and a further 144 were supplied to MAP under direct contract by D. M. Davies Ltd. The Halifax C.VIII received the new type designation H.P.70 and was normally flown by a crew of five, with dual control for the pilot and navigator; C.VIIIs were issued initially to Nos.108, 296, 297, 301 and 304 Squadrons, the last two being Polish units based at Chedburgh and formed from the survivors of No.148 (Special Duties) Squadron who took part in the siege of Warsaw in July 1944; during this operation SOE Halifaxes flown from Brindisi to drop supplies to patriots in the city lost 32 aircraft (90 per cent of their strength) in two months. The first Halifax C.VIII, PP225, flew in June 1945 and the variant remained in RAF service until the summer of 1948, when it was phased out into storage, to be brought back on to the British Civil Register in time to play a major part in

The second Halton, G-AHDM *Falmouth*, at Queen's Island, Belfast, on 18 July, 1946. (*Shorts*)

Halifax A.VII NA366 paratroop transport at Boscombe Down in April 1945. (*I.W.M.—Crown Copyright*)

the Berlin Air Lift, which began in August that year. Civil registrations were allocated to ninety Halifax C.VIIIs, including twelve true Halton airliners for BOAC, which were fitted out and furnished for ten passengers by Short & Harland Ltd at Belfast, after primary structural modifications had been made at Radlett; the most notable of these were larger rectangular cabin windows, an outward-opening cabin door and deletion of the transparent nose in favour of a 'solid' nose containing a baggage hold. Many other Halifaxes were converted to near-Halton standard, including a special luxury model for the Gaekwar of Baroda, but all these retained the bomber nose.

In parallel with the Halifax transports, a second line of development produced a series of conversions for No.38 Group's Airborne Forces, for glider towing and paratrooping in the final assault on occupied Europe. Following thirty A.IIIs built by Rootes, the Halifax A.VII was an interim version produced in limited numbers by the parent company's Rawcliffe Repair Depot and by the two Merseyside factories; in this variant the dorsal turret was deleted, a glider-towing hook was fitted and seating and strops for twelve paratroops were installed, the existing paratroop cone and static bar being retained. Rootes built one hundred and twenty A.VIIs, Fairey sixty-nine, Handley Page forty-nine and English Electric eight; they were flown not only in the European theatre but also in the Middle East by

Fairey-built Halifax A.VII PN244 of No.148 (S.D.) Squadron with bomb-cell pannier at Brindisi in 1945. (*J. D. Oughton*)

Halifax A.IX RT796 as a development prototype in 1946.

Nos.620 and 644 Squadrons, and in the Far East by No.298 Squadron from May till August 1945 against the Japanese, being retained till the end of 1946 for photographic-reconnaissance, troop-carrying and famine relief in Indo-China, Burma and India. To follow the A.VII in Europe, a more thorough conversion of the Halifax VI was put into production at Cricklewood as the A.IX (H.P.71), the design work being sub-contracted in February 1945 to Boulton-Paul Ltd at Wolverhampton. This involved deletion of the existing port side entrance door and paratroop cone, and substitution of a new strong floor aft of the bomb cell incorporating a large rectangular, inward and upward opening, paratroop exit door, together with a rail and twenty launching trollies, with two strop-retrieval winches on the rear spar. Folding seats were provided for twelve paratroops, six a

Halifax A.VII PP350 with Universal Freight Container being prepared for a Combined Services demonstration at the Royal Military College of Science at Shrivenham on 6 March, 1951. (*P.A.—Reuter*)

side, aft of the rear spar, and the tail turret was a Boulton-Paul Type D with two 0·5-in Browning guns; the front 'scare'gun' and Mk.XIV bomb-sight were retained, but there was no dorsal turret, so that a crew of six was sufficient. The fuel system was the same as the Halifax VI's except that the No.2 replenishment tanks were reduced in capacity from 150 gallons to 90 gallons each. Most of the A.IX development flying was done on LV999/G, which had already spent many hours as a 'guinea-pig' for radar trial installations. Production of A.IXs with Hercules XVI powerplants began at Cricklewood and would have been extended to a further batch with Hercules 100s named Halifax A.X., had not the contract been curtailed after VJ-Day, one hundred and forty-five A.IXs being delivered and fifty cancelled. Halifax A.IXs replaced A.VIIs in Nos.620 and 644 Squadrons in the Middle East in 1946, these units being renumbered 113 and 47 respectively in September of that year. One Halifax A.VII, PP350, made extensive operational trials with a much enlarged pannier known as the Universal Freight Container, designed to carry bulky loads and to be dropped by eight 42-ft diameter parachutes at the same time as the paratroops. As glider tugs, Halifax A.IIIs and A.VIIs towed Hamilcar tank-carrying assault gliders into action in the later stages of the invasion of occupied Europe, and were the only aircraft to do so over the battlefield. Halifaxes continued to serve with Coastal Command on meteorological reconnaissance duties for many years, the final sortie being flown from Gibraltar by No.224 Squadron on 17 March, 1952; as late as 1954, a single Halifax was still employed for parachute testing at Henlow, the last in service of 6,176 produced.

G-ALON, formerly RT763, was one of two Halifax A.IXs converted by Aviation Traders at Southend in June 1949 for operation by Bond Air Services on the Berlin Air Lift; both retained their tail turret cupolas. (*A. J. Jackson*)

Only two Halifax A.IXs were operated (as G-ALON and G-ALOS by Bond Air Services) in the Berlin Air Lift, but thirty more were allotted civil marks and registered to Aviation Traders at Southend-on-Sea; nine of these were sold to the Egyptian Air Force in 1950, but the remainder were broken up in 1951. BOAC's twelve Haltons, having entered airline service in September 1946 between London and Cairo, began operating the London–Karachi route from July 1947 and the London–Accra trans-Sahara route three months later, until 1 May, 1948, when they were withdrawn and quickly sold to other operators when the Berlin Air Lift commenced on 4 August. Including the Haltons, forty-one Halifax civil

G-AHZJ of London Aero & Motor Services was one of four Halifaxes (PP244–PP247) delivered as A.VIIs with Hercules XVIs but converted later to C.VIIIs with Hercules 100s; seen here in dark blue livery as *Port of Marseilles* in December 1946 at Stansted while importing fruit from Spain, France and Italy. (*A. J. Jackson*)

G-AIHV *Air Trader* of Lancashire Aircraft Corporation at Squire's Gate in April 1947.

PP278, temporarily G-AHVT, at Gatwick awaiting delivery to France on 21 September, 1947, as F-BCJR. (*E. J. Riding*)

One of several Halifax C.VIIIs converted for bulk transport of diesel fuel, G-AKBB crashed in a night landing at Schleswigland on 11 February, 1949, during the Berlin Air Lift. (*I.W.M.—Crown Copyright*)

Captain Villa of Eagle Airways flew G-AIAP on 15 August, 1949, on the last civil sortie of the Berlin Air Lift. (*E. J. Riding*)

Bulkiest load carried by a civil Halifax was a crated Humber car flown from Bovingdon to Madrid by British American Air Services on 7 May, 1948; ground clearance at the start of take-off was only one foot. (*Planet News*)

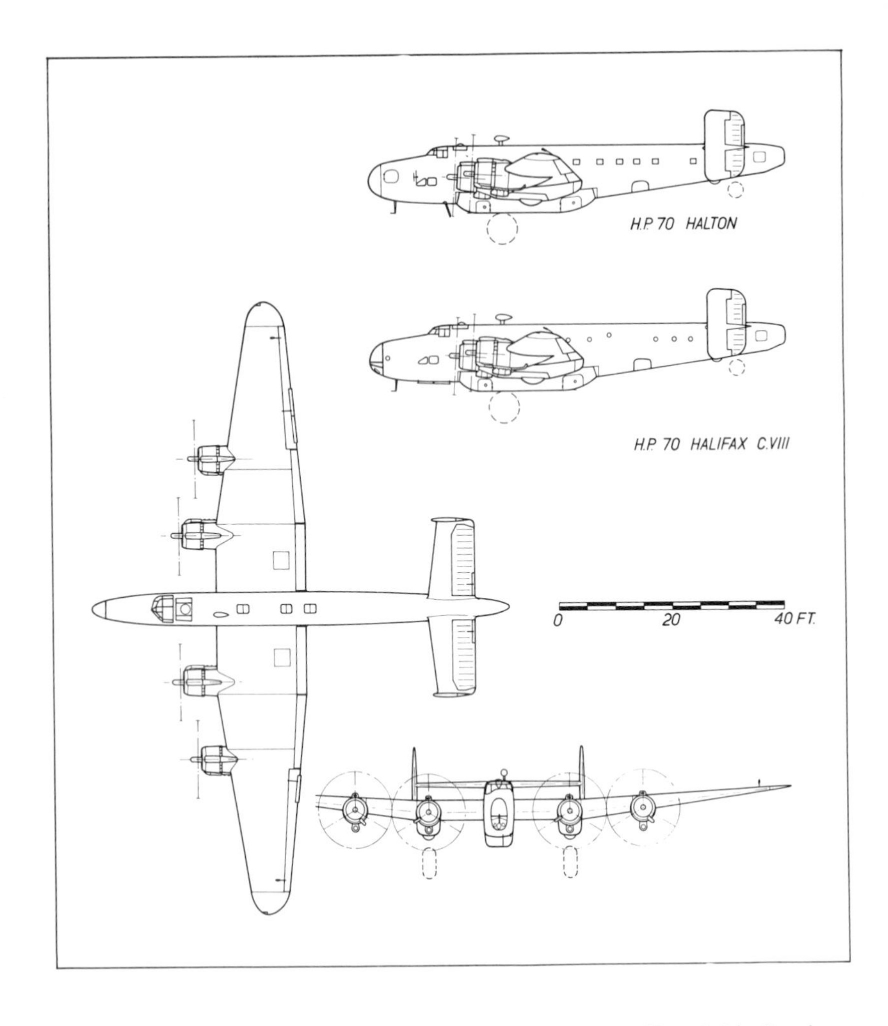

transport conversions operated by seven contractors (Bond Air Services, British American Air Services, Eagle Aviation, Lancashire Aircraft Corporation, Skyflight, Westminster Airways and World Air Freight) flew more than 8,000 sorties in the Berlin Air Lift, carrying nearly 54,000 tons in some 22,000 flying hours, a typical load being 6½ tons of coal or flour per sortie; seventeen of the Halifaxes were equipped with 1,500-gallon lorry tanks to carry diesel transport fuel; the last civil flight of the Berlin Air Lift on 15 August, 1949, was made by Halifax G-AIAP of Eagle Aviation flown by Captain Villa. To keep the Halifax C.VIIIs flying, thirty-three Halifax VIs were recovered from storage and ferried in civil marks to Bovingdon and Stansted to be reduced to spares; six more were sold to the Pakistan Air Force in 1950, one of them being equipped to carry a spare Hercules powerplant suspended from its bomb-carrier. Other outsize loads included a crate containing a Humber motorcar for delivery from Bovingdon to

Madrid in May 1948 and a 17-ft ship's propeller shaft urgently flown from Heathrow to Calcutta in July 1947 for the *Photinia*.

So the Halifax bridged the gap from war to peace in 1946 just as the O/400 had done in 1919, and in due course was superseded by the purpose-built Hastings and Hermes, in the same way that the W.8 family had replaced the O/400 thirty years before.

H.P.70 Halifax C.VIII

(Four Bristol Hercules 100)

Span 104 ft 2 in (34·2 m); length 73 ft 7 in (22·45 m); wing area 1,275 sq ft (118·3 m²). Empty weight 37,750 lb (17,100 kg); maximum weight 68,000 lb (30,820 kg). Speed 320 mph (515 km/h); range 2,530 miles (4,070 km); ceiling 21,000 ft (6,500 m). Crew five. Passengers eleven.

H.P.70 Halton

As Halifax C.VIII furnished to civil standard for twelve passengers.

H.P.71 Halifax A.IX

(Four Bristol Hercules XVI)

Span 104 ft 2 in (34·2 m); length 71 ft 7 in (21·85 m); wing area 1,275 sq ft (118·3 m²). Empty weight 37,830 lb (17,350 kg); maximum weight 65,000 lb (29,450 kg). Speed 320 mph (515 km/h); range 2,050 miles (3,300 km); ceiling 21,000 ft (6,500 m). Crew five. Paratroops 12–15.

Tailless Research Aircraft (H.P.75)

In designing the H.P.47 and H.P.52, Gustav Lachmann had taken the first step towards eliminating the structural weight and drag penalties of the conventional tail unit, which in his view was a totally parasitic appendage, capable of being reduced or even deleted by improved design of an automatically stable wing. With the H.P.52 accepted for production as the Hampden and Volkert once more in charge as chief designer after his visit to America, Lachmann suggested to Handley Page on 21 April, 1936, a programme for the development of tailless aircraft, to investigate four main problems: (a) longitudinal stability and control, (b) directional stability and control, (c) taxying stability and optimum arrangement of landing gear, and (d) means to compensate the nose-heavy moment due to the lowering of high-lift underwing flaps. He outlined his proposal for a small moderately swept tailless monoplane and estimated that wind-tunnel tests on a model could be completed by the end of 1936, with a view to building a complete aircraft by June 1937. In a further memorandum drafted on 14 July, 1936, he discussed the possibility and advantages of a new landing technique with such an aircraft, describing it as 'Autogiro-like descent'. This was an extension of the 'crash-landing' method already suggested by flight experience with the Gugnunc and H.P.47. On 16 July he visited the RAE with Cordes to enquire about results obtained with the H.P.47 and Airspeed Courier during slow-flying trials in accordance with ADM 293 and had discussions with Major Stewart, A. E. Woodward-Nutt and F. B. Alston, as well as Flt Lieut Fraser of Aero Flight.

The upshot of this enquiry was that Lachmann was released from day-to-day design responsibility in order to concentrate on aerodynamic research and by December 1936 had planned a new research department with its own separate drawing office, manufacturing shop and material stores at an estimated total capital cost of £3,300 and an annual salary and wages bill of £7,500, excluding the cost of wind-tunnel and laboratory work in which co-operation was sought from, and assured by, the existing organisation. On 16 March, 1937, Lachmann and Cordes visited the Westland works at Yeovil for a discussion on the successful Pterodactyl designs with Harald Penrose and Bill Widgery, but by that time Teddy Petter, the new chief designer, was anxious to dispose of the tailless project since Geoffrey Hill, its initiator, was no longer associated with Westlands; so the Pterodactyl was somewhat played down and Lachmann gained the impression that its main disadvantage was that it needed a larger wing area than normal, so that its extra wing weight and profile drag cancelled out the saving gained by deleting the tail. In view of the problems associated with flap-lowering and optimum choice of dihedral, needing both wind-tunnel and full-scale testing, Lachmann asked W. S. Farren (DTD) for assistance, but was told that both the RAE and NPL wind-tunnel facilities were heavily overloaded; Farren was surprised that no direct approach had been made to Geoffrey Hill, who was then Kennedy Professor of Engineering at University College, London, but it seems that Handley Page was reluctant to call on his former test pilot for advice as a consultant. In spite of this lack of official enthusiasm, Lachmann was allowed to set up his separate Research Department during May and June 1937, at Nos.5 and 6 Promenade Chambers, Edgwarebury Lane, Edgware, with easy access to both Cricklewood and Radlett, but Handley Page was not prepared to disrupt the Hampden and Halifax assembly lines to make room for a small hand-built prototype and insisted on its being manufactured elsewhere, preferably by a small firm with low overheads, such as Martin-Baker Ltd at Denham, Bucks, who were approached in August but declined the invitation. Meanwhile the powerplant had been discussed with de Havillands, who recommended the use of two 140 hp Gipsy Major II engines installed as pushers and driving two-blade variable-pitch propellers through flywheels and flexible extension shafts; the latter were ordered from the Manganese-Bronze Co and a nosewheel landing gear was ordered from the Turner Manufacturing Co. Handley Page protested that fixed-pitch wooden propellers were adequate, but Lachmann held his ground and obtained D.H. size 1000 constant-speed propellers after pointing out the dangers of directional instability with no control surfaces in the slipstream. Major F. B. Halford of de Havillands agreed to design suitable air intake scoops and baffles for the pusher installation and by April 1938 the design of the aircraft in three-ply wood had been finalised, but still no manufacturing contract had been settled.

The tailless monoplane was of simple construction, with a stubby semi-monocoque fuselage (or rather, nacelle) of good streamline shape and elliptical cross-section accommodating the pilot in front of the wing spar and the flight test observer facing aft. The pilot's transparent canopy and the observer's tail cone were both jettisonable in emergency. The parallel centre-section carried the two engines, with the forward-retracting main undercarriages inboard, while the castering nosewheel (which at first used a commercial wheel-barrow tyre) was not retractable. The slightly tapered sweptback outer wings had leading-edge slots and trailing-edge elevons operated from a normal control column through a differential pulley system. End-plate wing-tip rudders were operated by rudder pedals and split flaps of 10 per cent wing chord were hinged under the centre-section and outer wings along the 80 per cent chord line.

At last, in July 1938, the small firm of Dart Aircraft Ltd, founded at Dunstable by B. Zander and A. R. Weyl to make sailplanes and ultra-light aeroplanes for enthusiasts, agreed to construct the Handley Page tailless monoplane, provided all duralumin parts were supplied from Cricklewood, since Dart had no normalising facilities; these parts included the slats, slat-tracks and windscreen frame. Steel parts and brazed or welded components were sub-contracted to Grice & Young at Dunstable, but Dart Aircraft were soon in financial difficulty with insufficient working capital and underestimated overheads; by mid-October Weyl was having to meet current expenditure out of his own pocket and had no funds with which to pay future wages, while Grice & Young were unpaid for work already completed. Handley Page was forced to bail Dart out with a subsidy of £200 in order to get the aircraft built by the end of 1938, a year and a half behind schedule, but in spite of his personal supervision from then on, it was estimated that 21 weeks' work was still needed in March 1939 to get the aircraft into the air.

On 2 January, 1939, patent No.497969 was granted jointly to Handley Page Ltd and G. V. Lachmann in respect of a controllable fore-plane, which Lachmann had evolved as a means of ensuring longitudinal stability when employing a split flap under the wing, with a smaller weight and drag penalty than incurred by the conventional fore-plane and elevator of a classic *canard* design. Lachmann's 'rider-plane', as he called it, was pivoted about a horizontal axis so as to float freely at an angle of incidence controlled by servo-tabs operable by the pilot and was arranged to compensate for spontaneous changes of the mainplane angle of incidence caused by either gusts or by flap operation. The rider-plane had its own slot and flap gear to provide high lift at low speed without becoming stalled and Lachmann claimed that full control and manoeuvrability could be attained with a much lower lift coefficient on the rider-plane than would be required on a conventional foreplane. The elevons functioned as both ailerons and normal elevators and taxying stability and ground steering were ensured by a steerable nosewheel and brakes on the main wheels. To save weight, the rider-plane servo-controls and some ancillary services were to be powered by the Theed vacuum system, but on 18 April, 1939, Handley Page instructed Lachmann to complete the monoplane as a 'straight' aircraft, without the rider-plane, which was still only half-constructed; this enabled the vacuum system and its installational problems to be deferred until after some preliminary flying had been done and the final arrangement of the rider-plane could be appraised. Stafford considered that Radlett was adequate for initial test flights and the monoplane was delivered there from Dunstable soon after the outbreak of war, but too late to fly before Lachmann, being technically still a German citizen, was interned under Defence Regulation 18B and transported to Canada, whence he was brought back, after special pleading on his behalf by Colonel J. T. C. Moore-Brabazon, who convinced the Home Secretary that he would be just as harmless and far more useful if interned in the Isle of Man; before internment, Lachmann had been investigating an improved split flap layout to increase effective lift and minimise the accompanying nose-down trim change. An avenue of communication was set up via the RAE and from the end of 1943 Frank Radcliffe and Godfrey Lee were able to visit Lachmann regularly.

With maximum priority essential for Halifax trial installations and production, progress of the tailless monoplane was necessarily slow after war began, but it was ready for initial engine runs in mid-October and it was weighed at Radlett on 9 November, 1939. With pilot only and the observer's seat removed, the monoplane was overweight at 3,300 lb with petrol for one hour's flight (15 gallons); this was reducible by 46 lb if the starter battery were discarded, or to 3,184 lb by removing also the starters with their relays and cables; a small lightweight battery had still to be carried for the instrument supply. On 29 February, 1940, Cordes made the first taxying runs at Radlett on a wet day with fine drizzle under a cloud-base of 1,000 ft in a moderate northeast wind. Cordes decided to leave the cockpit canopy off, because the wing-tips could not be seen and he had found the quick-release inoperable from inside; he insisted on this being rectified before flight and asked for small perspex windows to be inserted in the underside so that the flight observer could check the action of the oleo-legs while taxying. The nosewheel oleo was too soft and allowed porpoising to develop above 20 mph but this damped out at 50 mph when there seemed to be no response from any of the flying controls. In better weather on 5 March, Cordes made three more runs at 60 mph, 70 mph and 80 mph respectively, with 'Ginger' Wright as observer on the first. At the highest speed there was slight lateral response to full elevon movement, but none in pitch or yaw. Lee considered that there had been some pitch response which could not be felt by the pilot because of the rough ride given by the close-coupled landing gear over the uneven surface of the Radlett grass aerodrome. Cordes did not attempt to fly it again because in March 1941 the inspection department insisted on the leading edge of the wing being stripped to permit examination of the glued joints of the main spar, which were by then two years old.

This led to the discovery of extensive deterioration and a year elapsed while both upper and lower wing surfaces were renewed; during this reconditioning, the remaining Theed vacuum pipes in the wing were removed and the front spar was reinforced. Lee spent the intervening time in investigating the effect of anhedral in improving stability, particularly with one engine dead. The NPL advised the addition of a single central fin on the fuselage tail and Lee visited Westlands on 22 August, 1941, for further advice from Penrose and Widgery, from which he concluded that the existing dihedral was safe but that a rider-plane would be essential for more extended research. On 9 March, 1942, he attended a discussion at the RAE on possible jet-propelled tailless projects and recommended that, of the three tailless configurations (a) Pterodactyl, (b) *Canard* and (c) Lachmann's rider-plane, the last was to be preferred for a fast bomber with buried engines and heavy rear armament; this was because (a) was capable of only a limited increase of lift coefficient from under-wing split flaps because of the difficulty of trimming; (b) could match a conventional tailed monoplane in lift increment, but needed a fore-plane of at least 20 per cent of the mainplane area to avoid foreplane stalling; whereas (c) required a fore-plane of only 15 per cent of the wing area and could be trimmed with only a moderate lift co-efficient on the fore-plane, which need never reach stalling incidence; with a leading-edge slot and slotted flap on the fore-plane, the latter's area could be reduced to only 10 per cent of the wing area. Lee found that Lachmann's original rider-plane was inherently prone to flutter when too close to the mainplane leading-edge and suggested a necessarily less simple arrangement of trimmers on outriggers, which nevertheless promised better success in the long run; but RAE wind-tunnel tests on a 1/10-th scale model did not confirm his theory and he was therefore keen to have a rider-plane built for flight test on the tailless monoplane.

Concurrently a Tailless Aircraft Committee had been set up at the RAE under DTD's chairmanship, primarily to combine the advantages of jet propulsion and American-designed 'laminar-flow' aerofoil sections in a high-speed long-range bomber, for which elimination of the tail had obvious attractions. The first tentative design on these lines was Major F. M. Green's A.W.50 all-wing four-jet monoplane, which was discussed at a meeting at Farnborough on 2 June, 1942, attended by Lee and Handley Page's wind-tunnel engineer, F. R. C. Hounsfield; this was estimated to be capable of carrying 4,000 lb of bombs for 1,600 miles at 400 mph, with a take-off weight of 30,000 lb. Lee extolled the advantages claimed for the rider-plane, which the RAE undertook to test, and the Tailless Panel requested him to tender a 20,000-lb project to follow the small monoplane already in being. The latter had been overhauled and fitted with a central fin and larger-chord elevons; it resumed taxying trials at Radlett on 12 September, 1942, in the hands of Talbot's assistant, J. F. Marsh, with Ashworth as observer. By this time the monoplane had been allotted the Class B registration mark H-0222 and was painted in standard day camouflage with a yellow underside; Cordes had given it the nickname 'Manx' in his two taxying-trial reports, but this name was not officially adopted until later, when it was first shown to the Press in 1945. It was not

Manx at Radlett in September 1942 ready for taxying trials by J. F. Marsh, showing original fixed undercarriage and 'wheel-barrow' nosewheel tyre. (*Real Photographs*)

yet cleared for flight and Marsh intended to taxy at increasing speeds up to 75 mph, which Lee estimated as the stalling speed, mainly to test the brakes, which still needed to be made more powerful. On his second run, the machine hit a bump and took off inadvertently to a height of 12 ft from which Marsh eased it down with moderate engine power, but then it began porpoising after touching down and the nosewheel fork broke away from the oleo-leg; Marsh said there was virtually no control response while airborne and he could not keep the machine on the ground after the first touch-down, even with the stick hard forward. Lee recommended an improved retraction gear, which C. D. Holland designed, and trials recommenced on 14 December, but were again cut short when a fitter, after starting the engines and removing the chocks, stepped backwards into one of the propellers and sustained fatal injuries. The propeller shaft and bearings had to be renewed and Talbot strongly criticised the slack supervision and some unsatisfactory workmanship, for which he demanded urgent corrective action.

First engine installation in Manx in September 1942. (*Flight*)

So the tailless monoplane's next excursion was delayed till May and during the early weeks of 1943 Lee assisted Volkert in tendering outline schemes to the Air Staff for both orthodox and tailless heavy bombers of 70 tons all-up weight. These were designed to use laminar-flow wings, for which it was considered essential to eliminate slipstream turbulence by locating the propellers behind the trailing edge. It was found impossible to balance the orthodox monoplane even with a very long fuselage ahead of the wing, but the *canard* layout was more amenable and promised success with either four developed Napier Sabre engines of 3,000 hp or eight turbojet engines. At an all-up weight of 157,000 lb in each case, these aircraft would have carried a maximum bomb-load of 48,000 lb at a wing-loading of 72 lb/sq ft, the wing area being 2,190 sq ft. The Sabre-engined bomber would have taken off unassisted in 1,700 yards and cruised at 354 mph at 30,000 ft, while the jet version needed assisted take-off, but would have cruised at 500 mph at 40,000 ft. In each case the wing was swept back through 22½ degrees, the span being 155 ft for the piston-engined version and 130 ft for the jet, the fuselage length for both being 67 ft. The Handley Page 70-ton bomber proposals were considered by

MAP to be underpowered at just over 13 lb/bhp and the firm then proposed a similar but smaller tailless bomber with four Merlin 61s, or two Sabres, with an all-up weight of 60,000 lb, maximum speed of 440 mph and range with 8,000 lb bomb-load of 3,000 miles at 360 mph or 4,000 miles at 300 mph.

On 14 May, 1943, H-0222 was ready for general ground handling prior to flight testing by Talbot, who found the brakes improved, though still inadequate for manoeuvring on the ground. In a first run up to 70 mph the nosewheel lifted and the aircraft seemed ready to fly off at a slightly higher speed; it was very steady directionally and had no tendency to porpoise. In the second run, the nosewheel began to shimmy at 60 mph so the aircraft was brought to a halt, but the port tyre collapsed just before stopping. A new twin-wheel main undercarriage was then installed and a friction shimmy damper was fitted to the nose oleo-leg; two fast taxying runs were made by Talbot on 11 June on the new Radlett runway at speeds of 70 mph and 80 mph without any sign of nosewheel shimmy, and the monoplane was almost airborne on the second run but still showed no control response in pitch. The throttle control was eased and the pitch control bracket stiffened, and on 25 June Talbot took off in 350 yards at 75 mph without warning when passing over a slight rise in the runway at full throttle. He climbed away at 100 mph finding elevons effective in both pitch and roll, but at 100 ft the pilot's canopy blew off, also the propeller pitch control was faulty, so he landed after ten minutes, making a flat approach and touching down without bouncing or porpoising. Before the second flight, on 24 August, a new latching mechanism was fitted to the pilot's canopy, a new nosewheel and fork were installed, elevon tabs were fitted to correct a tendency to fly port wing low, and the propeller pitch controls were improved. Taking off in almost still air, Talbot found the climb sluggish and top speed in level flight no more than 105 mph; rudder power was not enough to hold the aircraft straight with one engine throttled and the port wing still dropped; correct turns were difficult because of fore-and-aft sensitivity combined with slow rudder response, so he landed after 26 minutes. In September an external hand-rail was fitted to the fuselage, the rear fairing emergency release was modified, propeller pitch settings were changed and new air intakes and engine cowlings were installed to prevent overheating on the climb at full throttle. Talbot flew again for half an hour on 9 October, when he found that, with the c.g. moved one inch forward, porpoising began when taxying fast on rough ground. Fore-and-aft control was heavier and less sensitive and, after climbing to 2,000 ft in just over 2 min the oil temperatures were still rising; there was too much general vibration for the flight to be continued. No further flights were made in 1943 and at the end of the year Lee concluded his analysis of the revised rider-plane for transmission to Lachmann, who was now accessible in the Isle of Man and allowed to resume work for the firm.

In March 1944 Sir Frederick Handley Page made a statement of design policy on tailless projects, proposing that next the firm should build an aircraft of 25,000–30,000 lb, which would not be too big a jump from 3,500 lb for control problems to be foreseen, but big enough for practical study of fuselage layout and accommodation. The drawing office effort involved would only be justified if the project had a military or civil application and was, if possible, directly comparable with either the

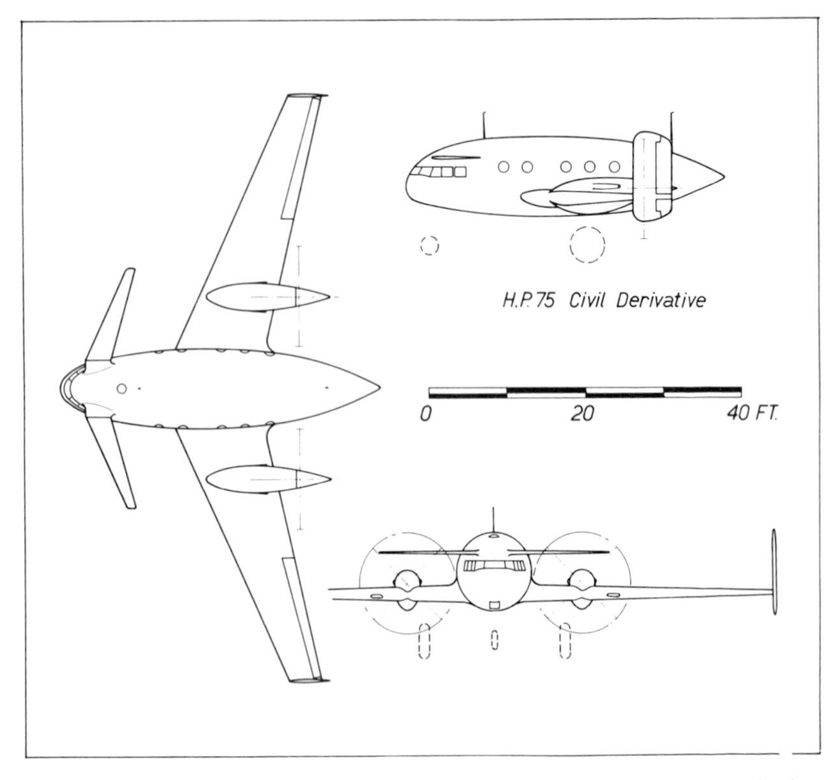

Mosquito or the DC-3. In particular, it was necessary to find out whether tailless aircraft had any real advantage over orthodox, in relation to the problems of c.g. travel and buried engines. On 13 April, 1944, Frank Radcliffe and Godfrey Lee attended a meeting at the RAE, at which design studies were suggested for (a) all-wing, (b) Handley Page tailless and (c) orthodox post-war civil projects of 150,000 lb all-up weight, in order to assess the merits of the Handley Page type over the other two and to justify the fat body of the Handley Page type, but the following day the Tailless Aircraft Committee met at MAP and decided to recommend development of an all-wing aircraft with low-drag aerofoil section and jet propulsion. This, in effect, rejected the earlier Handley Page proposal for a tail-first 70-ton bomber and any later proposal to derive a civil aircraft from it to match the Brabazon Committee's recommendation for a post-war transatlantic airliner; the only project favoured was John Lloyd's all-wing A.W.52, for which Armstrong Whitworth were to receive a contract for two prototypes to specification E.9/44.

Since so few woodworkers were available at Radlett, the improved rider-plane for H-0222 and its control gear were sub-contracted to Percival Aircraft at Luton, who also undertook the design and installation of a larger split flap under the wing. In May 1944 a 30,000-lb tailless civil project was tendered to MAP and discussed with H. M. Garner, Deputy Director of Scientific Research, who thought the Handley Page structure weight estimate was too low and the lift co-efficient claimed too high; the RAE estimated the range with 4,000 lb payload to be only 1,850 miles instead of the brochure figure of 2,950 miles, so the project was referred to Lachmann for detailed analysis; meanwhile D/DSR was prepared to discuss ordering two prototypes for a fixed price of £300,000, but advised against using the rider-plane before it had been thoroughly tested and proven on H-0222, which was once again ready to be flown after being fitted with a new

Rear-facing observer's station of Manx in October 1944, showing hinged tail-cone which could be jettisoned in emergency, also faired fixed nosewheel, retractable twin-wheel main undercarriage and fuselage hand-rail. (*Associated Press*)

retractable main undercarriage and long fairing over the nosewheel, which remained non-retractable. On 29 June, 1944, Talbot flew it for 20 min and recorded 122 mph with gear retracted. Retraction and extension functioned easily from a hydraulic hand-pump and the slight change of trim could be comfortably held on the stick alone. Lateral control seemed heavier than previously, but directional stability was excellent, although the elevon was very light in pitch, especially in rough air; the nosewheel fairing did not keep the wheel straight before landing, as intended, and tended to float at 20 degrees to starboard, to correct which a small plate fin was added later. On 30 June Talbot flew H-0222 for the first time with E. A. Wright as observer, the take-off weight being raised to 4,103 lb. After half an hour, with severe vibration throughout the flight, Wright reported that the port engine cooling fan was running eccentric and beginning to break up. Talbot flew the next two tests solo on 4 August and 10 October, on the latter date with larger spinners fitted, but could report no improvement in general performance, with climb still inadequate. Talbot and Wright flew together on 15 October and Sqn Ldr Robert Kronfeld of the AFEE was invited to give an opinion on handling at an early date.

This he did after three solo flights at Radlett on 1 and 2 November, 1944, and reported that H-0222 compared well with other tailless aircraft he had flown, although it could benefit from increased fore-and-aft damping; he considered the undercarriage to be the only satisfactory one of any tailless aircraft he knew, and landing and take-off behaviour in a cross-wind to be better than that of most of the orthodox types of aircraft. On 4 November he continued handling trials, with Wright as observer; during this flight his true air speed was checked by formating on a Halifax III fitted with a calibrated airspeed indicator and the position error of H-0222's indicator was found to be plus 20 mph at 120 mph IAS, so the true speed was 140 mph after all. Kronfeld and Wright made a 50-minute flight on 10 November, when Wright moved as far forward and aft as possible to assess change of trim with varying c.g.; this was found to be completely normal. During this flight, Kronfeld formated on the A & AEE's Oxford V3569, which had a calibrated Mark VIIIC pitot-static head, to check position error over the speed range from 90 to 125 mph. Kronfeld did not like the complication of the proposed rider-plane and thought most pilots would cope with the longitudinal sensitivity after a reasonable period of familiarisation.

Before the 14th flight on 5 December, 1944, the cooling fans were removed from the powerplants and new underside cowling panels were installed; this not only saved weight but was found to increase speed by 10 mph, although oil temperatures were still critical during take-off and climb on a warm day. Talbot and Wright continued to explore performance and handling in March 1945, after a spell of bad weather during which Talbot flew only once (solo) for a short demonstration on 5 February. Continuing bad engine vibration, even after deletion of the cooling fans, suggested the alternative of flying H-0222 as a glider, using a Halifax as a tug for take-off, and Talbot put this to Kronfeld, who considered it practicable. Ground vibration tests were made by de Havillands after modified engine mountings, front engine cowlings and inter-cylinder baffle-plates had been fitted and Talbot found that these measures had alleviated the trouble when he flew with observer J. Steele on

Manx flying at Radlett in June 1945 with nosewheel trailing to starboard.

18 June, 1945; at about this date H-0222 was for the first time designated H.P.75. Four days later, Talbot and Wright measured full-throttle climbs to a service ceiling of 10,470 ft. After this, they began handling with one engine throttled back and found that the central fin allowed full directional control to be retained; Kronfeld was invited to check this for himself, in view of his expressed doubt of the adequacy of the existing fins and rudders in the event of an engine failure. When he flew again with Wright on 17 July he was pleased to find a considerable improvement in handling and thought the vibration level to be reasonable. In preparation for level speed trials, the nosewheel fairing was given a larger fin-plate, since it still trailed to starboard and it was hoped later to remove the fuselage fin altogether to reduce drag. By 7 September, level speed and stick-free stability trials had been satisfactorily completed and on the 12th and 18th Talbot demonstrated the H.P.75 to the Press in flights number 26 and 27, when the name Manx was adopted for publicity purposes, having long been current in the works. Two further flights on 27 October and 27 November established a maximum true air speed of 146·5 mph; this was almost the same performance on the same power as had been reached by the H.P.21 monoplane over 21 years previously! Up to 30 November, 1945, twenty-nine separate flights had been made in a total of 16 hours 53 minutes, but a few days later both Talbot and Wright were killed in the crash of the

Manx in September 1945 with enlarged fin on nosewheel fairing. (*Keystone*)

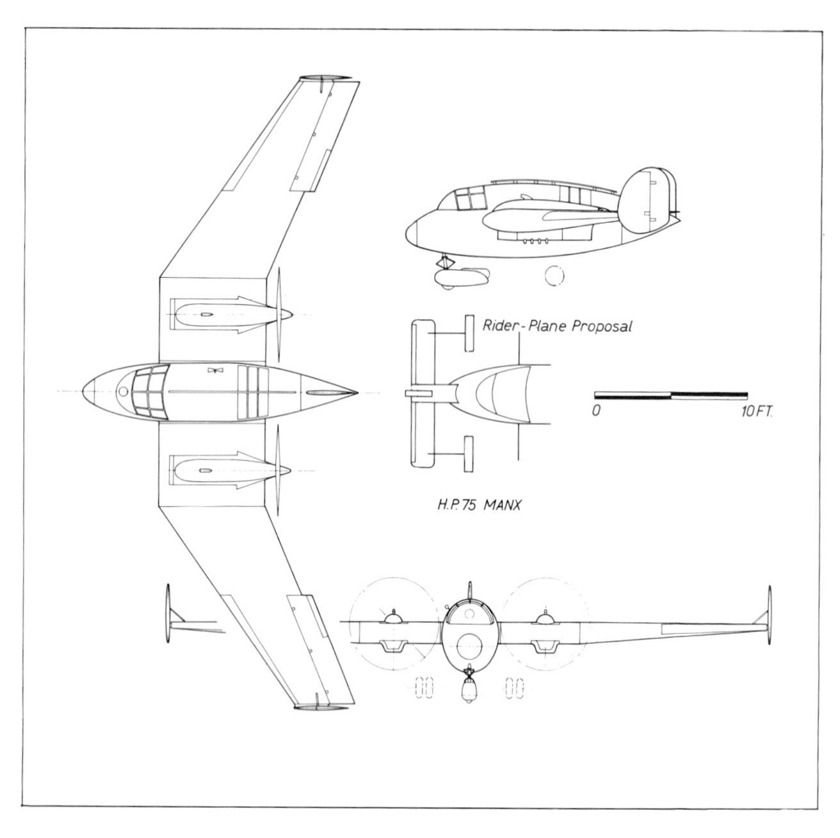

prototype Hermes I G-AGSS. Thereafter the H.P.75 was flown only twice more, on 2 April, 1946, by Kronfeld for 40 minutes with Noel Brailsford as observer and next day for ten minutes by Kronfeld with Steele. In May it was grounded as the result of a defect report by the inspection department and all further work on it was stopped in December; its remains were stored at Park Street till 1952, when they were burned as scrap.

The rider-plane for H-0222 was completed and delivered by Percival Aircraft in June 1945, but was never flown. By then a simpler and sturdier method of obtaining adequate longitudinal trim had been made necessary to take care, not only of the low-speed effects of lowering large flaps, but also of compressibility effects as the speed of sound was approached, which caused the centre of pressure of the wing to move rearwards, resulting in a very large nose-down moment, for which a controllable all-moving tailplane was the only safe solution. A preliminary scheme for a four-jet high-performance tailless bomber or transport with rider-plane control, designated H.P.75A, was discarded in favour of a 'hybrid' project with a small all-moving tailplane and swept wings with tip-rudders, at first disguised as H.P.72A but in April redesignated H.P.80; this was to become the Victor bomber—as brilliant an heir to the Halifax as was the Halifax itself to the original 'Bloody Paralyser' of 1914.

H.P. Manx

(Two de Havilland Gipsy Major II)

Span 39 ft 10 in (12·19 m); length 18 ft 3 in (5·59 m); wing area 245 sq ft (22·75 m^2). Empty weight 3,000 lb (1,360 kg); maximum weight 4,000 lb (1,813 kg). Speed 146·5 mph (235 km/h); ceiling 10,500 ft (3,250 m). Pilot and observer.

Tailless Twin Engined Transport

(Two Rolls-Royce Merlin 61)

Span 72 ft (21·95 m); length 41 ft (12·49 m); wing area 600 sq ft (55·7 m^2). Empty weight (est) 16,730 lb (7,590 kg); maximum weight (est) 30,000 lb (13,600 kg). Maximum speed (est) 400 mph (640 km/h); range (est) 3,300 miles (4,800 km). Crew three. Passengers 24–28.

Hastings I-VI, Hermes I and IA and C.15/45 (H.P.67, 68, 72, 73, 89, 90, 94 and 95)

The H.P.64 ('Transport C') project was discussed with the Air Staff in the summer of 1943, not only as a possible post-war interim civil airliner but also as an immediate successor to 'Transport B', the Halifax C.VIII, in the role of troop carrier and military freighter. In December 1943, following a visit to Cricklewood by DTD and DOR, Volkert had announced the priority order for new projects, as follows: (1) H.P.66, (2) H.P.64 Passenger Version (Civil), (3) H.P.64 Freighter Version (Civil), (4) H.P.64 Military Transport ('Transport C'), (5) Halifax Conversion, Retrospective ('Transport A': Halifax C.III and C.VII), and (6) Halifax Conversion, New Production ('Transport B': Halifax C.VIII). According to this programme, the first H.P.64 prototype was to be built to specification 15/43 as a passenger aircraft, flying initially as an unfurnished shell and later fully equipped to airline standards; the second prototype was to be built and equipped as a civil freighter with a large loading door in the port side; the third was to be nearly identical with the second, but with an extra parachute exit door in the starboard side and provision for carrying twelve store-containers externally, together with modified cockpit and instrument layouts to suit the RAF and rearward-facing adjustable seating for paratroops. Production civil passenger aircraft were to be pressurised, but freighters with large doors, both civil and military, would not be.

On 28 April, 1944, Volkert urged Sir Frederick Handley Page to settle future production policy in favour of either the H.P.66 bomber or the H.P.64 transport, since it would be impossible to manufacture simultaneously at Cricklewood two different aeroplanes, each of 70,000-lb all-up weight, after the Halifax line came to an end. He considered that an even better plan would be to go into production with a new transport project, H.P.67, combining the H.P.64 fuselage with the H.P.66 wing, as recently proposed to and agreed by MAP; furthermore, he recommended that the H.P.67 should have a single fin and rudder to reduce interference drag from the large-diameter fuselage. In the same month the Air Ministry issued specification C.3/44 to define a multi-purpose RAF transport combining

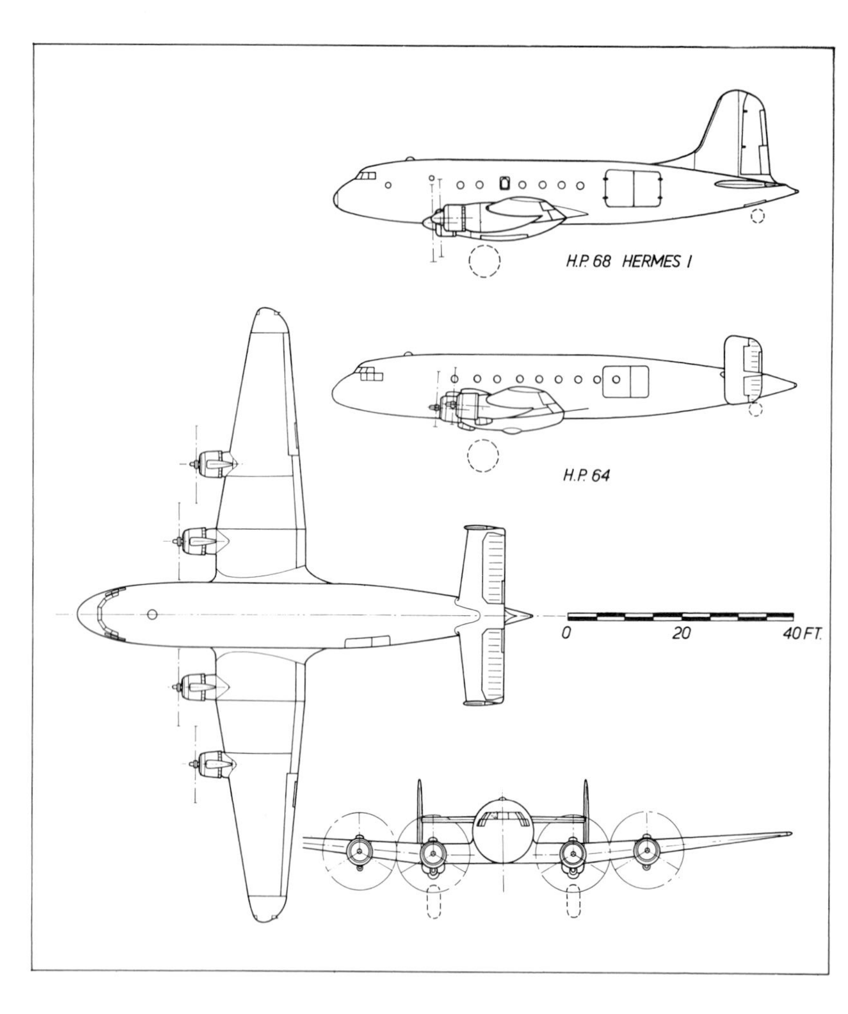

the roles of both Halifax C.VIII and A.IX; this closely matched the H.P.67, which was tendered with virtually no further alteration. The tender was accepted for two prototypes, serialled TE580 and TE583, and soon afterwards the two H.P.66 prototypes were cancelled and the name Hastings C.1 was officially approved for the H.P.67.

It was obvious that the Hastings, with full Service equipment, would take longer to build than the 'flying shell' civil passenger transport; it was also highly desirable to obtain the earliest possible confirmation in full-scale flight of drag and stability data acquired by wind-tunnel tests, so two civil prototypes, to be built entirely at Radlett, were ordered against specification 15/43, which defined the H.P.64 and was amended to cover the change of wing and tail unit. In the early stages of both the civil and military versions there was a serious shortage of draughtsmen at Cricklewood, so the design of the new single-fin empennage was sub-contracted to Blackburn Aircraft Ltd at Brough. The main assembly jigs were designed to suit both the Hastings and its civil counterpart, for which Sir Frederick chose the name Hermes; the latter was designed from the start for pressurisation and received type number H.P.68, its mock-up conference being held at Cricklewood on 9 November, 1945, and attended by representatives of BOAC and Rumbold & Co. By incorporating the nearly-completed outer wings of the first H.P.66, rapid progress was achieved with the first Hermes, which was registered G-AGSS and commenced taxying trials at Radlett on 1 December, 1945. These should have occupied several days, but next morning Sir Frederick received word from Filton that the prototype Bristol Freighter had just made its maiden flight; the prototype Avro Tudor had already become, in June, the first British post-war airliner to fly and Handley Page urged all concerned to

Hermes I at Radlett on 1 December, 1945.

ensure that the Hermes should be the next. Anxious to waste no time, Talbot and Wright took off just after 4 p.m. on Sunday 2 December, but were at once in trouble with severe longitudinal instability. In spite of determined efforts by Talbot to control a succession of alternate dives and stalls immediately after take-off, before safety height had been gained, the Hermes finally climbed steeply, stalled, and plunged upside-down into a field at Kendall's Farm, three miles south of the aerodrome, narrowly missing Radlett village. Both Talbot and Wright were killed instantly and the wreckage was almost totally destroyed by impact and fire. After a searching investigation of the accident, with only limited evidence available, the Ministry of Civil Aviation concluded in March 1946:

'1. It is considered that the accident was the direct result of elevator overbalance; this brought about flight conditions the nature of which caused the pilot to lose control.
2. Although the porpoising motions set up by the overbalanced elevators would have been expected, the final manoeuvre of the aircraft, in climbing suddenly, cannot be satisfactorily explained.
3. It seems certain, however, that at different trimmer settings, reversal of stick forces would have occurred with which the pilot could not have kept in phase as the loads increased.'

In the aftermath of this disaster, work was slowed down on the second prototype Hermes, G-AGUB, which was to be pressurised and fully furnished, all available effort being directed towards identifying and eliminating the cause of instability, while Cricklewood works completed the two prototype Hastings, which the RAF, after early doubts in Air Staff circles, now urgently needed and for which a production order had been promised for one hundred. The tailplane span was increased by 8 ft, with a small matching increase in fin area, and the trimmer and balance-tab areas were modified to increase the positive stick-free stability margin. Production of the Hastings at Cricklewood followed BOAC's twelve Haltons in the summer of 1946, but before its standard of equipment was finally agreed there was much discussion and exploration of RAF Transport Command's wide-ranging post-war commitments and requirements, including a strategic long-range transport to complement the essentially short-range tactical role of the Hastings C.1, which had been designed to carry a maximum payload of 16,000 lb at a mean cruising speed of 265 mph, with an all-up weight of 75,000 lb.

The new strategic role was defined by specification C.15/45, to which Handley Page Ltd tendered two different projects, the H.P.72 with a very large volumetric capacity and direct vehicle loading through a nose door, and the H.P.73 'Hastings Series II', which was to be a stretched version of the Hastings C.1, having an all-up weight of 80,000 lb and the parallel section of the fuselage lengthened by 80 inches forward of the wing and 50 inches aft of the wing, so as to accommodate a large under-belly hatch and hoist for direct loading of Army vehicles. On the face of it, the H.P.73's gross volumetric capacity of 3,535 cu ft was a significant increase on the Hastings C.1's 2,750 cu ft, but in real terms, taking into account additional equipment and structure weight, and the loading restrictions imposed on the longer fuselage by c.g. limits, the advantage in achievable payload was little more than 2,000 lb on average sectors, so the extra volume could be filled only by cargo of lower than average density. Consequently the Air Staff declined to support the H.P.73 in the form proposed and design work on it was stopped at an early stage. By contrast, the H.P.72 was the subject of a great deal of investigation, commencing with the original proposal of July 1945 for a shoulder-wing high capacity long-range military transport with four 2,000 hp Bristol Centaurus powerplants, a nosewheel landing gear and a Boulton-Paul Type D tail turret. At maximum all-up weight of 130,000 lb it was to carry a maximum payload of 35,000 lb for 2,000 miles at an economical cruising speed of 238 mph or 15,000 lb for a maximum range of 4,275 miles at 244 mph. The required long range and two- and three-engined climb necessitated the very high aspect ratio of 12, for which a single-spar wing similar to the H.P.65's was envisaged, together with a spoiler-cum-aileron system of lateral control and double-slotted 30 per cent chord trailing-edge flaps. The Air Staff had specified minimum cargo-hold dimensions of 28 ft 6 in long, 12 ft wide and 10 ft 6 in high, and asked for payloads of 16,000 lb over 4,275 miles and 22,000 lb over 800 miles; these were difficult to reconcile except by producing an unnecessarily large aircraft with a span of 156 ft. In August 1945 the firm suggested that if the criterion was ability to carry the Army's largest indivisible loads, including a 4·5/5·5-inch gun and a 6-ton lorry, as well as items more than 20 ft long, very little would be sacrificed if the hold dimensions were reduced to 24 ft by 8 ft by 10 ft 6 in, when the all-up weight could be reduced to 105,000 lb and the span to 139 ft.

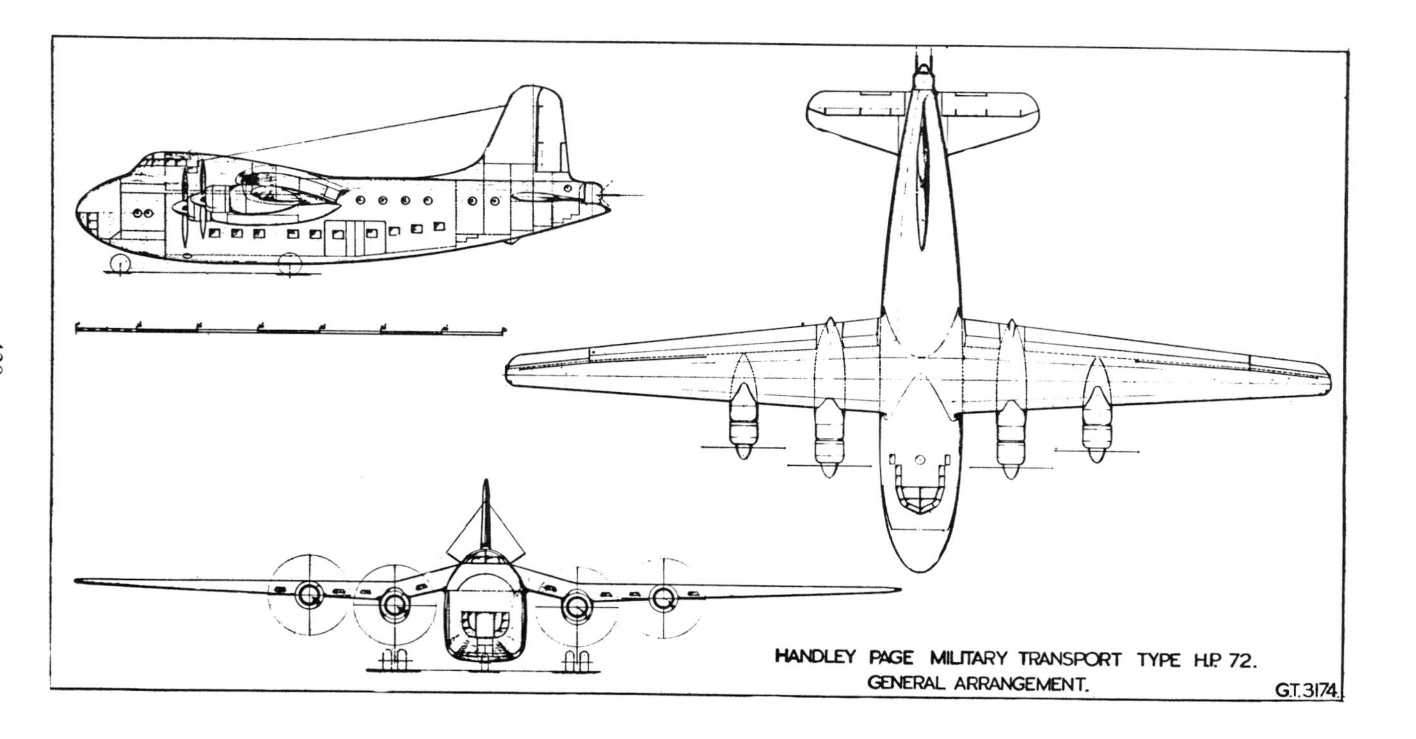
HANDLEY PAGE MILITARY TRANSPORT TYPE H.P. 72.
GENERAL ARRANGEMENT.
G.T. 3174.

This proposal was declined, but further study resulted in a slightly smaller aircraft with Hercules 130 engines, all-up weights 85,000 lb (normal) and 100,000 lb (overload), span 135 ft, fuselage maximum depth 19 ft, fuselage width 13 ft 6 in and overall height 32 ft 6 in. The landing gear comprised two mainwheels retracting backwards into the inboard nacelles, the length and weight of the gear being minimised by cranking the wing downwards between the fuselage and inboard nacelles and underslinging the latter. The nosewheel unit was installed in the hinged fuselage nose and swung sideways with it for cargo and vehicle loading, after built-in jacks in the main fuselage had been lowered to permit a loading ramp to be used. The flight deck, basically of Hastings layout for a crew of five, was located high up above the cargo hold roof ahead of the wing root, and the fin, rudder, tailplane and elevators were more or less standard Hastings components. In addition to the nose door, there were large side loading doors aft of the wing, with paratroop doors inset in them. The fuselage hold had a volume of 6,000 cu ft and a total length of 48 ft, within which was provided the specified rectangular box section measuring 28 ft 6 in by 12 ft by 10 ft 6 in. As a passenger transport, more than 60 aft-facing seats could be installed five abreast with two gangways; for mixed loads, heavy cargo or vehicles could be carried forward, with passengers aft. The wing contained 4,700 gallons of fuel in crash-proof flexible tanks and thermal deicing was provided for the wing and tail unit leading edges. Both the flight deck and the hold were sound-proofed, thermally insulated, heated and ventilated. At the end of September 1945, the Air Staff decided not to proceed with the H.P.72 because the firm's estimates were thought to be optimistic and to rely too much on forecasts of engine performance to be expected in three years' time; preliminary design work already begun at Cricklewood was abandoned after a brief study of a deeper rear fuselage providing double-deck accommodation, also of the possibility of improved performance by using submerged Rolls-Royce Pennine engines of 2,500 hp; the Pennine was an air-cooled sleeve-valve twenty-four-cylinder X engine intended as a civil counterpart to the military Eagle liquid-cooled H engine, but never achieved flight status.

For its early handling flights, the first prototype Hastings, TE580, was considered to need a longer runway than Radlett's, so permission was obtained for it to be taken to Wittering, alongside the Great North Road south of Stamford, for final assembly and initial flight trials. The firm had not yet appointed a successor to Talbot as chief test pilot and the RAF loaned Sqn Ldr Maurice Hartford for the preliminary tests, which commenced on 7 May, 1946, and were completed in just over ten hours, finishing with a two-hour handling and demonstration flight on 23 May, without any setbacks being encountered. On 4 September, 1946, TE580, having flown back to Radlett, was formally named *Hastings* in a well-publicised ceremony performed by the Mayor of Hastings. The second prototype, TE583, was flown at Radlett by Hartford on 30 December, 1946, and after completing contractor's flight tests was flown to Boscombe Down on 17 January, 1947, to join TE580 for full Service acceptance trials by the A & AEE. Meanwhile manufacture had begun at Cricklewood of one hundred production Hastings C.1s, whose major components were conveyed by road with police escorts, for final assembly at Radlett. The first, TG499, was flown on 25 April, 1947, by Sqn Ldr H. G. Hazelden, who

Hastings first prototype TE580 at Wittering in May 1946.

had just resigned from the RAF to join Handley Page Ltd. and was appointed chief test pilot three months later. On this maiden flight, tail vibration was encountered, but was quickly cured by cording the rudder trailing edge; TG499 was then allotted to the Airborne Forces Experimental Establishment at Beaulieu for paratroop trials. TG500 flew early in May and was retained at Park Street on CS(A) charge for trial installations of modifications, while TG501 was allotted to Boscombe Down to replace TE580, which returned to Radlett for investigation of longitudinal instability at 78,000 lb with c.g. aft.

On 22 May, 1947, TE580 was flown with its powerplant thrust-lines tilted up 2½ degrees, but this brought no improvement. It was then flown to Hatfield, where a new tailplane with 10 degrees dihedral was fitted, returning to Park Street on 8 June. Next day it was flown first with flaps normal and then with the centre flaps rigged 5 degrees down and later 10 degrees down. On 25 June a 15-degree dihedral tailplane was fitted and the elevators and centre flaps were interconnected to provide trim compensation at touch-down; a second set of parts for a 15-degree dihedral tailplane was made up for test on TG501, which retained its normal thrust-line. TE580 was flown several times up to 18 July with the 15-degree dihedral tailplane and blunt-nosed elevators, but without any improve-

TE580 at Radlett on 9 June, 1947, with fin-mounted camera and tailplane with 10 degrees dihedral. (*Eric Watts*)

ment in the power-off stall characteristic; meanwhile TE583 began towing trials with a Hamilcar glider on 25 June, completing the first series in September, and was then modified on site by a working party to permit a higher towing all-up weight than 65,000 lb. Next, TG501 was flown with semicircular extensions to the inner flaps and then with elevator horn balances added, all without avail. After further wind-tunnel testing, TE580 reappeared on 19 September with a new tailplane having 10 degrees anhedral, which gave stable trim curves at lift co-efficients up to 1·05 with c.g. aft—a significant improvement. On 25 October it was flown again with the anhedral reduced to 5 degrees, but this was restored to 10 degrees before dispatch to Boscombe Down on 29 October. By this time, TG499 had completed dropping trials of dummy paratroops and containers and, having survived an overshoot landing on 9 October with only superficial damage, remained at Beaulieu for live paratroop trials.

TE580 at Radlett on 19 September, 1947, with 10 degrees anhedral on tailplane. (*Eric Watts*)

TG501 went to Boscombe Down in November 1947 for full handling trials and was progressively modified to meet criticisms arising from TE583; the changes included a bulbous elevator nose, altered elevator-tab gearing with spring bias, and interconnected elevators and flaps for automatic trimming at low speeds. By March 1948 the addition of a manually operated port aileron tab, together with torsion-bars to limit aileron up-float, a rudder torsion bar, reduced trim-tab ratios on elevators and rudder, and a stall-warning indicator, enabled the Hastings to be released to service on 1 June, after trials at 75,000 lb gross weight with c.g. aft and one engine failing during take-off. The A & AEE reported that in most manoeuvres it was pleasing and safe to fly, but still needed better longitudinal stability in the climb with c.g. aft, also lower stick forces and reduced trim change for landing, together with a more positive stall-warning with power on. In July 1948 the East German ban on surface traffic to and from West Berlin created a crisis which cut short the Hastings' acceptance trials, and a synthetic stall-warning (Mod.361) was introduced as a stop-gap safety measure to permit the first Hastings C.1 squadron to be formed in October. This was No.47 at Dishforth, which, after converting from Halifax A.IXs, flew to Schleswigland to take part in Operation 'Plainfare', as the RAF's part in the Berlin Air Lift was code-named. A second Hastings squadron, No.297, was formed soon after No.47 became operational and in August 1949 relieved No.47 at Schleswigland; it continued to ferry fuel supplies of coal and petrol (both aviation and motor transport) between Schleswigland and Gatow until 'Plainfare' ended on 6 October, 1949, being joined briefly by a detachment of the third Hastings squadron, No.53, during the final weeks of the emergency.

Although the Berlin crisis caused some contraction of the intended Hastings flight development programme, and brought to light additional operational problems needing urgent solutions, it did not affect the main objective of proving the Hastings as a medium-range tactical and assault transport. TE583 continued glider-towing trials at Beaulieu until November 1948, when clearance was given for a Hastings at 68,000 lb to tow a Hamilcar loaded to 37,500 lb under temperate summer conditions. TE580 came to grief at Boscombe Down after only two flights with the 10-degree anhedral tailplane and returned to Park Street for repairs to its buckled centre-section on 22 December, 1947; these kept it grounded till the following March, when trials were resumed, but it was not liked as well as TG501 with a standard flat tailplane and bulbous-nosed elevators. TG502 completed radio trials at Farnborough in January 1948 and went on to radar trials at RRE, Defford, returning to RAE early in February. It was then flown back to Park Street on 10 February for the tailplane to be lowered 16 inches to the fuselage centreline, its incidence being increased by 2 degrees at the same time. Thus modified, it flew again on 19 April, 1948, and was found to handle much better than TE580, remaining stable almost to stalling point, but the A & AEE pilots were not entirely satisfied with its handling on final approach and in June decided to retain it at Boscombe Down for further radio trials. On 3 June, TE580 returned to Park Street for a standard tailplane to be refitted, after which it went to Hatfield for airscrew vibration tests and then to Boscombe Down for resumed contractor's trials in November. In August, Mod.436 was introduced to extend the span and area of the tailplane in its standard position, and this was flown as a trial installation on TG501 on 12 October, but was found to be very sluggish in response, although effective in improving stability. The wide tailplane was then transferred from the standard position on TG501 to the low position on TG502, and was flown on 23 October with substantially improved handling, which was enhanced when an asymmetric elevator nose-balance was added. Further stalling tests were made on TG501 with a standard tailplane and bulbous wing-root nose fillets, but these were found less effective than a sharp-edged fillet already tested at Boscombe Down in January and adopted as a means of ensuring adequate warning of a 'power-on' stall; 'power-off' stall-warning could only be obtained synthetically and, from among several systems, the 'Safe-Flight' device was adopted for all Hastings in squadron service.

The fifth production Hastings, TG503, was delivered in December 1947 to Boscombe Down for fuel jettison trials, after which it was demonstrated there to BOAC on 19 January, 1948, before starting an intensive route-flying programme. This was also to be a sales promotion exercise and took the form of a flight to Australia and New Zealand and back, in view of interest there in both military and civil cargo-carrying aircraft. Agreement was reached with the ARB and the Directors of Civil Aviation in Australia and New Zealand on the modifications necessary to enable the Hastings to obtain an unrestricted C of A and these were numerous enough to require

Hastings C.1 TG503 in New Zealand in April 1948.

the Hastings to be redrawn as the Hermes IA (H.P.90) with a new Type Record. Carrying the first air-portable sectional ramp for loading and unloading vehicles through its port side cargo door, TG503 left Lyneham on 11 March and flew via Malta, Habbaniyeh, Mauripur, New Delhi, Negombo, Singapore and Darwin to reach Sydney on the 18th. It then toured Australia and New Zealand for a month, attracting much favourable attention and being captained throughout by H. G. Hazelden. On 20 May TG503 left Sydney for Darwin on the return flight and arrived back at Radlett on 5 June, having diverted to Bretigny for a demonstration to the French Air Minister. Meanwhile TG500 had commenced H.P.90 airworthiness performance tests at Boscombe Down on 27 April, but in the event no customers for the Hermes IA showed up, so this type remained a 'paper aeroplane'. Before being diverted to C of A tests in aid of the H.P.90, TG500 had begun trials at RAE with carrier beams (Mod.26) for heavy external loads to be dropped by parachute. It first flew at Farnborough with two Jeeps attached to the beams on 14 January, 1948, and successful drops were made between 16 and 23 March. Meanwhile TG499 began live paratroop trials at Beaulieu on 5 February and thirty troops were dropped on the 17th from the port and starboard exits simultaneously, fifteen from each side. Design of a Universal Freight Container, developed from that tested on Halifax PP350, began at Cricklewood in January 1949, to carry 13,500 lb. Four UFCs, later named Paratechnicons, were ordered and on completion of the paratroop trials TG499 went back to Park Street for incorporation of Mod.26, using the beams from TG500, which itself received new beams adapted to carry a Jeep and its 10-cwt trailer and, later, a Jeep and a 6-pounder field gun. On 4 December, 1948, TG500 flew to Hatfield for the Jeep and trailer to be attached for dropping trials at Boscombe Down in January; these were successful and TG500 returned to Park Street to receive the Jeep and field gun for dropping trials at Beaulieu. A third Hastings, TG533, was fitted with a gravity roller conveyor for launching 350-lb panniers for paratroops, the first drop of four panniers being made at Beaulieu on 27 January, 1949; by 24 February twenty-four panniers had been successfully dropped in 4½ seconds and TG512, retained for training purposes at Brize Norton, was being equipped with a TCDU-designed twin-rack roller conveyor for a further series of trials. In June it had been intended to send TE583 to Shaibah for tropical towing trials with the Hamilcar, after normal tropical and high humidity trials had been completed by TG509 at Negombo in November and Khartoum in December 1948, but TE583, being a prototype, could not be brought up to the necessary modification standard in time, so TG533 went to Shaibah in its place. Concurrently TG506 had flown to Canada for winterisation trials at Edmonton, Alberta; on its return a year later, it was allotted to the RAE Parachute Test Unit and a ventral chute was installed under the rear fuselage; based on Farnborough and Henlow, it was later painted in a distinctive colour scheme of black-and-yellow diagonal stripes under the outer wings, all-black under the centre-section, rear fuselage and tail, and orange-red 'dayglo' fluorescent patches on the upper surface of the wing-tips and on the sides of the nose and fin. The second Hastings to cross the Atlantic was TG568, which left TCDU Brize Norton on 1 April, 1949, on a goodwill tour of the USA and Canada.

The Sapphire-Hastings at Radlett in 1953 prepared for Victor crew escape trials, with leading-edge profiles marked on rear fuselage. (*D. C. Clayton*)

On 5 February, 1949, TE580's contractor's trials were again interrupted at Boscombe Down by a landing accident in which the starboard undercarriage failed to extend because the jack piston-rod had collapsed; it was repaired on site and finally flown to Hatfield in April 1951 for use by the de Havilland Propeller Company Ltd, remaining there till scrapped some years later. On 14 June, 1949, TE583 was returned to Park Street from Beaulieu on completion of its temperate climate programme, to become a flying test-bed for the Armstrong Siddeley Sapphire turbojet engines chosen for the new H.P.80 bomber. In fact the two Sapphires which replaced the outboard Hercules of TE583 were early Metrovick Sa.2 engines with non-standard mounting points, so the nacelles had to be redesigned and TE583 did not fly again until 13 November, 1950. After agreed handling trials at Radlett, including jet efflux measurements, it was delivered on 30 May, 1951, to Farnborough for research flying by NGTE (National Gas Turbine Establishment) Pyestock, whence it returned to Park Street in January 1953 for installation of a mocked-up H.P.80 crew door in place of the starboard paratroop exit; this was used by RAE to evaluate H.P.80 crew escape procedures.

The first one hundred Hastings C.1s were serialled TG499–537, TG551–587 and TG601–624 and with this contract approaching completion, Sir Frederick Handley Page pressed the Air Ministry for a follow-

Hastings C.1 TG520 landing at Filton in 1950.

on order to avoid interrupting the Cricklewood production line. At first tentative agreement was reached for sixty-five Hastings C.2s to be built to specification C.19/49, but later this quantity was reduced to twenty-five. From the firm's point of view, the Hastings C.2 was a standard production aeroplane incorporating modifications to increase the range and to bring the all-up weight to 80,000 lb, so it retained the type number H.P.67; the modifications included the low wide tailplane approved on TG502 and three additional flexible fuel tanks in each outer wing, bringing the total fuel capacity to 3,172 gallons. The new contract, awarded in March 1949, covered twenty-five Hastings C.2s, WD475–499, to which was added WD500, a specially equipped and furnished variant for operation by the VIP Flight of No.24 Squadron. This had been discussed (as Hastings IIA) since March 1948 and was finalised, with enlarged crash-proof fuel tanks (to give a still-air range of 4,250 miles) and hydraulic folding entry stairs on the port side, as Hastings C.4, type number H.P.94.

The first Paratechnicon was completed and flown on TG499 at Hatfield on 13 May, 1949, and at Radlett the following day, when the loss of speed due to its extra drag was found to be 24 knots. It was flown to Farnborough on 27 June, briefly surveyed by RAE engineering staff and transferred for flight trials to Boscombe Down, but crashed on Beacon Hill nearby on 26 September. The third Paratechnicon was attached to TG533 on its return from Shaibah, but after the loss of TG499 further flight trials on the scheme were abandoned. A more radical solution to the heavy cargo carrying role (already investigated for the H.P.72 and H.P.73 projects) was the Hastings VI (H.P.89), which originated late in 1947 as the 'Hastings new development' with a nosewheel landing gear, increased wing area, choice of Centaurus or developed Hercules engines and either under-belly ramp loading or direct ramp loading through doors under the tail unit. The project was discussed with War Office and Air Staff representatives at Cricklewood on 10 June, 1948, and with DOR on 15 November; in January 1949 the rear-door 'straight-through' layout was adopted, with Centaurus engines and four-wheeled bogies on the main landing gear. The NPL was asked to advise on the optimum height for the tailplane and a sweptback fin was schemed, but in March the Air Staff expressed a preference for a twin-boom tail as in the Fairchild Packet and declined to order the H.P.89. A layout was then drawn for a Hastings C.1 with minimum alterations to accommodate a tail loading ramp, for which the type number H.P.73 was revived as the Hastings III; this reached the stage of being mocked-up before being stopped by DOR in March 1951, but the official preference for the twin-boom layout did not find tangible expression till seven years later, when the Armstrong Whitworth A.W.660 was ordered as the Argosy C.1 and replaced No.114 Squadron's Hastings in 1962.

First production Hastings C.1 TG499 at Radlett on 14 May, 1949, with Paratechnicon installed for trials in June at Farnborough and Boscombe Down. (*Eric Watts*)

Proposed rear loading doors for H.P.73 project of 1951.

The final six aircraft of the Hastings C.1 contract were not delivered to Transport Command on completion, but were modified for meteorological reconnaissance duties to replace the Halifaxes of No.202 Squadron at Aldergrove; the original 'Met' assessment had been made on TG503 on its return from Australia, but it had then reverted to C.1 for handling trials at 78,000 lb in 1950. In addition to the six already mentioned (TG616, TG620–624), four others (TG504, TG517, TG566 and TG567) were converted to Hastings Met.1s to make up the squadron's initial equipment, using modification kits manufactured by Flight Refuelling Ltd at Tarrant Rushton. They operated sorties of nine hours' duration over the Atlantic from both Aldergrove and Gibraltar, each sortie comprising two periods of three hours at 100 ft above the sea, separated by one hour at 18,500 ft; they each carried two sets of five Lindholme emergency dinghy containers, so as to be available in the air/sea rescue role during the low-level phases of each sortie.

From late 1950 the Hastings replaced the Avro York and thus became the RAF's only strategic troop-carrier in addition to its primary tactical role. During the Malayan anti-terrorist campaign and the Korean war it was the mainstay of the trunk route to Singapore and Japan, carrying reinforcements and supplies to the East and returning with aircrews on home leave and casualties from the battle areas. One fatal accident on this route proved beyond all doubt the safety of Transport Command's rearward-facing seating, when on 20 December, 1950, TG574, returning from Singapore with a flight crew of six and 28 aircrew passengers going

The original Hastings Met.1 TG504 in service with No.202 Squadron. (*R. T. Riding*)

Hastings Met.1 TG618 of the Meteorological Research Flight with storm-warning radar pod under nose. (*M.O.D.—Crown Copyright*)

Hastings Met.1 TG623 on No.202 Squadron's last meteorological flight from Aldergrove on 31 July, 1964. (*M.O.D.—Crown Copyright*)

Hastings Met.1 TG616 taking off from Filton in 1953.

home for Christmas, took off from El Adem, Cyrenaica, at about 8 p.m.; two hours later, one blade of the starboard inner airscrew came adrift and sliced into the crew rest station, where the co-pilot, Flt Lieut Bennet, was asleep, injuring him and severing the elevator, rudder and elevator-trimmer controls. Severe vibration quickly wrenched the wrecked engine from its nacelle and the first pilot, Flt Lieut Tunnadine, could only maintain level flight by varying the speed and power of the remaining three engines. Nevertheless he retained control and found that limited manoeuvre was possible, so he called up Benina and prepared to make a 'wheels-up' landing on the runway there; by sheer bad luck the aircraft undershot by a few dozen yards and hit boulders, which tore off the starboard wing, the aircraft coming to rest inverted. None of the passengers was seriously injured except a medical officer, Sqn Ldr Brown, who had left his seat to attend to Bennet; he recovered in hospital to receive the George Medal and the two surviving flight crew members were awarded the King's Commendation for Valuable Services in the Air, but Tunnadine, Bennet and two others of the flight crew were killed.

Hastings C.2 WD493 of No.114 Squadron.

When the Hastings C.2s entered service, their increased tankage proved so advantageous that fifty of the earlier variant were brought as nearly as possible up to the same standard. It was not feasible to increase the internal tankage in existing outer wings, as requested in June 1951 by Transport Command, but at a meeting on 26 October the firm undertook to investigate the provision of modification kits for Hastings C.1s to increase their total fuel capacity to that of the C.2, and to introduce Mark 9 auto-pilots and winterised oil tanks. Both wing-tip and underslung wing tanks were considered, and the latter were chosen because they were less prone to accidental damage during ground-handling. The first trial installation, using de Bergue-rivetted drop-tanks, was made on TG501, temporarily withdrawn from the Empire Test Pilots' School in February 1953, the stub fittings being approved as Mod.958 and the removable tanks themselves as Mod.1021. Tropical trials early in 1952 with WD476 had already cleared all

Hastings C.1A TG537 of No.47 Squadron in 1953, with under-wing tanks fitted.

marks of Hastings to fly at an all-up weight of 80,000 lb and with the long-range modifications incorporated the early Hastings became known as C.1As.

The tactical paratroop-carriers of Nos.24 and 47 Squadrons shared a base at Abingdon, while the long-range transports of the Far East trunk route were flown by Nos.53, 99 and 511 Squadrons based at Lyneham, their crews being trained by No.242 OCU at Dishforth; Nos.36, 59, 114 and 116 Squadrons also re-equipped with Hastings; and finally No.70 Squadron in Cyprus and No.48 Squadron of the Far East Air Force at Changi (Singapore) exchanged their Valettas for Hastings. In 1951 twenty-four more Hastings were ordered before the Cricklewood production line came to an end. These comprised three more C.4s (WJ324–326) which

Hastings C.1s and C.1As of No.70 Squadron dropping supplies near Akrotiri in May 1962.

Hastings C.2 of No.24 Squadron, Colerne. (*M.O.D.—Crown Copyright*)

Hastings C.4 WJ324 of No.24 Squadron's V.I.P. Flight (*M.O.D.—Crown Copyright*)

Air-stair on Hastings C.4 WJ324. (*M.O.D.—Crown Copyright*)

joined WD500 to enter service in the VIP Flight of No.24 Squadron in September 1951; then followed three Hastings C.3s (NZ5801–3) for No.41 Squadron, RNZAF, and seventeen Hastings C.2s (WJ327–343); the last of these left Radlett on 17 October, 1952, followed by the fourth Hastings C.3 (NZ5804) which was the last new Hastings off the production line. Hastings C.3s operated regularly over the 12,000-mile route between Whenupai and Lyneham and differed from C.2s in having more powerful Hercules 737 engines with single-speed blowers, giving them better take-off performance at the expense of cruising economy at high altitude; they also had extensive instrument and radio changes which entailed registration of the variant as H.P.95. NZ5801 first flew on 3 November, 1952, and NZ5803 was entered and flown in the 1953 London to Christchurch Air Race, but did not complete the course.

An exceptional variant was WD480, which was specially modified and equipped for sonobuoy trials at the RRE, with a long pannier-like nacelle under the fuselage having a retractable ASV radome amidships and sonobuoy stowages with doors fore and aft. After completing the

The fourth Hastings C.3 NZ5804 of No.41 Transport Squadron RNZAF at Filton in 1953.

Hastings C.2 WD480 at Farnborough after completion of sonobuoy trials at the Royal Radar Establishment. (*R. T. Riding*)

WD480 carrying press photographers during a flight from Farnborough at the SBAC flying display preview on 31 August, 1970, photographed from a Short Skyvan. (*Shorts*)

Hastings T.5 TG511 of Bomber Command Bombing School at Lindholme in 1960.

sonobuoy trials in great secrecy, it was transferred to RAE Farnborough for general experimental flying and before the 1970, 1972 and 1974 SBAC exhibitions was used as a 'camera ship' for press photography of the new aircraft flying at the show. WD482, too, served at RRE Defford (later Pershore), succeeding TG503, which had been allotted in 1951 for trials with H_2S Mk.9 radar and was equipped with a fixed ventral radome aft of the wing. When the H_2S trials ended, TG503 went to the Bomber Command Bombing School at Lindholme for assessment as a replacement for the Lincolns then used to train V-bomber aircrews on radar bomb-sights and was found to be particularly well-adapted for this role; it was then approved as the prototype Hastings T.5, and nine more were converted at Radlett by working parties from Airwork Ltd at Blackbushe, the first, TG505, being delivered to Boscombe Down on New Year's Day 1960. Two Hastings, TG560 *Iris II* and WJ338 *Iris III*, were successively employed by the Central Signals Establishment at Watton and two others, WD494 and WD499, were flown from the RAF Flying College at Manby on long-range navigational training sorties over the Canadian Arctic territories. No.24 Squadron also flew WD492 to the Arctic, to drop supplies to the British North Greenland Expedition in 1952; WD492 crashed during a low pass and was replaced by WJ327, but is likely to remain for many years 'in preservation', though inaccessible under many feet of ice.

On 5 November, 1956, Hastings of Nos.70, 99 and 511 Squadrons based at Nicosia, Cyprus, together with three Valetta squadrons, dropped paratroops of the 16th Parachute Brigade to occupy Gamil aerodrome during the short-lived Anglo-French emergency intervention (Operation 'Musketeer') in the Israel-Arab offensive which closed the Suez Canal. In the same year Nos.47 and 53 Squadrons at Abingdon exchanged their Hastings for Beverleys and in 1959 Nos.99 and 511 Squadrons at Lyneham replaced theirs with Britannias; the remaining home-based Hastings squadrons, Nos.24, 36 and 114, were thereafter based at Colerne to form the nucleus of the revived No.38 Group. In 1962 No.114 re-equipped with Argosies, followed by No.36 in July 1967 and No.70 in Cyprus in

November 1967. The Hastings' demise was hastened by fatigue failures, initially of the wing lower spar-booms (which then had to be renewed every 4,000 hours) and latterly of the elevator outer hinge-bolts, which had first been diagnosed when TG602 crash-landed at Fayid in January 1953. Modification action seemed to have eradicated this trouble for over ten years, but on 6 July, 1965, TG577 of No. 36 Squadron crashed at Abingdon with six aircrew and thirty-five RAF and Army parachutists on board; all were killed and all Hastings were grounded on 8 July for fatigue checks and further modifications, which occupied several months and brought forward the date of the Hastings' obsolescence and replacement by Lockheed Hercules, as soon as the latter became available from America. The Hastings was finally withdrawn from squadron service on 5 January, 1968, when No. 24 Squadron flew ceremonially in formation from Colerne to the 16th Parachute Brigade's headquarters at Aldershot and back before standing down. Apart from twenty-seven allotted as ground instructional airframes, the only Hastings thereafter remaining on charge were one for VIP transport duties in Cyprus, six at various experimental establishments and ten T.5s at Lindholme and later Scampton. None apart from the four C.3s of No. 41 Transport Squadron, RNZAF, served outside the Royal Air Force until No. 70 Squadron's last Hastings, TG551, with a total log of nearly 10,000 hours, was presented for training purposes to the Royal Malaysian Air Force and flown in October 1967 from Akrotiri to Kuala

Hastings C.1 TG602 paradropping a pair of Jeeps over the Suez Canal in 1956. *(M.O.D.—Crown Copyright)*

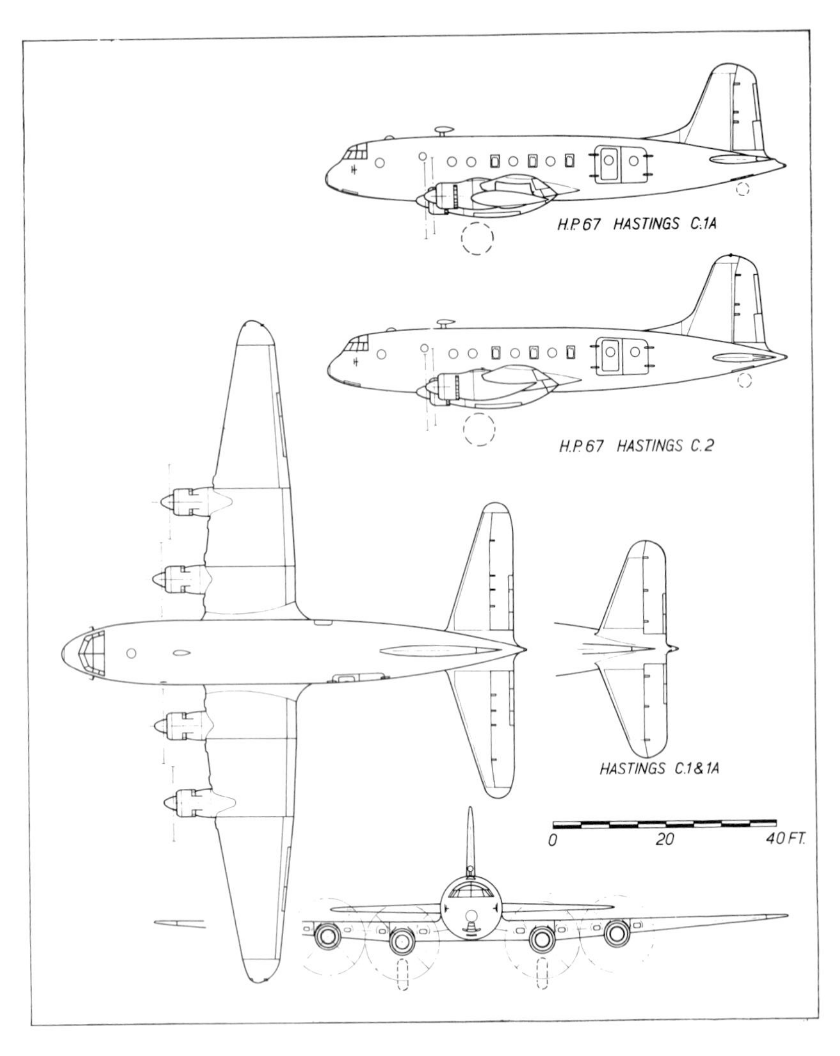

Lumpur via Bahrein, Masirah, Gan and Changi. A few months later WJ336 of the Far East Air Force Communications Squadron at Changi was the last Hastings to fly to Hong Kong and back, before being scrapped. Fortunately, two Hastings have been preserved: TG528 can be seen at the Skyfame Museum, Staverton, Gloucestershire, not far from Sir Frederick Handley Page's birthplace, and TG536 was stored at its former base, Colerne, until moved to Shawbury at the end of 1975.

During the decade 1949–1958 Hastings were the mainstay of RAF Transport Command and throughout their twenty years of front-line service they flew more than 150 million miles, carrying nearly 1½ million passengers and 180,000 tons of cargo, in climates ranging literally 'from Greenland's icy mountains to India's coral strand.'

H.P.68 Hermes I

(Four Bristol Hercules 100)

Span 113 ft (36·6 m); length 81 ft 10 in (25 m); wing area 1,408 sq ft (131·6 m^2). Empty weight 37,642 lb (17,080 kg); maximum weight 70,000 lb (31,750 kg). Speed 340 mph (547 km/h); range (est) 2,000 miles (3,220 km). Crew seven. Passengers 34–50.

H.P.67 Hastings C.1

(Four Bristol Hercules 102)

Span 113 ft (36·6 m); length 82 ft 8 in (25·25 m); wing area 1,408 sq ft (131·6 m^2). Empty weight 37,750 lb (17,100 kg); maximum weight 75,000 lb (34,000 kg). Speed 354 mph (570 km/h); range 3,260 miles (5,250 km); ceiling 26,700 ft (8,250 m). Crew five. Passengers 50 (or 30 paratroops).

H.P.67 Hastings C.1A and C2

(Four Bristol Hercules 106)

Dimensions as for Hastings C.1. Empty weight 48,427 lb (21,965 kg); maximum weight 80,000 lb (36,250 kg). Speed 348 mph (560 km/h); maximum range 1,690 miles (2,720 km); ceiling 26,500 ft (8,200 m). Crew five. Passengers 50 (or 30 paratroops).

H.P.95 Hastings C.3

(Four Bristol Hercules 737)

Dimensions as for Hastings C.1. Empty weight 48,600 lb (22,045 kg); maximum weight 80,000 lb (36,250 kg). Speed 350 mph (564 km/h); range 3,280 miles (5,270 km); ceiling 26,500 ft (8,200 m). Crew five. Passengers 50.

H.P.94 Hastings C.4

As for Hastings C.2 except range 4,250 miles (6,840 km). Crew five. Passengers 12–30.

H.P.72 (C.15/45)

(Four Bristol Hercules 130)

Span 135 ft (41·1 m); length 87 ft 6 in (25·7 m); wing area 1,520 sq ft (142 m^2). Empty weight (est) 55,000 lb (24,950 kg); maximum weight (est) 101,500 lb (46,000 kg). Cruising speed (est) 261 mph (420 km/h); range (maximum load) 800 miles (1,290 km), (maximum fuel) 4,275 miles (6,880 km). Crew five.

Hermes II at Radlett before first flight on 2 September, 1947.

Hermes II–VII and M.R.E.
(H.P.74, 79, 81, 82–86, 91 and 92)

The decision to build two prototype Hermes Is at Park Street was taken in February 1945, with the first (G-AGSS) being completed quickly as a flying shell and the second (G-AGUB) being fully furnished and equipped with thermal insulation and air-conditioning as a passenger airliner; both were H.P.68s, structurally designed for pressurisation, unlike the H.P.67 Hastings. As a result of the issue of specification C.15/45 a lengthened version of the Hastings was proposed as H.P.73 and in June 1945 a similarly extended Hermes II was projected as H.P.74. After the loss of G-AGSS in December 1945, work was temporarily stopped on the half-completed G-AGUB and in February 1946 a possible turboprop version of H.P.74 was considered for the first time, in the hope of obtaining an additional contract for one prototype. In March DOR decided against ordering the H.P.73, but agreed to an assessment of a Theseus-powered H.P.74, provided this work yielded priority to the urgently-needed H.P.80 turbojet bomber. In May the assessment was extended to include (a) a nosewheel version of the Theseus—H.P.74 and (b) the possibility of converting G-AGUB into a prototype H.P.74. By 27 May it had been agreed to extend G-AGUB by 160 inches (80 inches forward and 80 inches aft of the wing) to overcome a balance difficulty encountered on the H.P.73, which would have been nose-heavy. The nomenclature Hermes I for H.P.68, Hermes II for H.P.74 and Hermes III for H.P.74 with Theseus was agreed and a seating layout for 64 passengers, mainly five abreast, was proposed. On 25 June official approval was given to lengthen G-AGUB by 160 inches, but the seating was reduced to 52 and the outer wings were to be modified to incorporate Marflex fuel bags; at the same time the Hermes III was given type number H.P.79. G-AGUB's completion would have been delayed a full year by conversion to a nosewheel layout, so this was ruled out, but in September 1946 a new variant, Hermes IV (H.P.81), with the nosewheel, was offered for BOAC's consideration, as an improvement on the Hermes II and civil Hastings (Hermes IA). On 11 September Charles Joy discussed with MoS and MCA the performance of Hermes IV over the critical Nairobi–Johannesburg sector of BOAC's African trunk route. It was agreed that the Hermes IV's landing gear should have twin main and nose wheels on single oleo-legs and that a turboprop variant would be called Hermes V (H.P.82). It was not found practicable to furnish G-AGUB to represent the Hermes IV layout because BOAC had insisted on the galley being installed at the forward end of the cabin, which would have made the Hermes II nose-heavy. In the Hermes IV this was corrected by locating the wing 20 inches further forward, so that the extra fuselage length was distributed 60 inches forward and 100 inches aft of the wing. On 5 October production of a batch of Hermes IVs, together with one prototype Hermes V, was authorised. MCA still intended to rely on Avro Tudor IIs for main fleet requirements in 1947, but welcomed the Hermes IV and V as possible future replacements. In November a draft specification (33/46) for Hermes II was issued, calling for G-AGUB to be completed as a flying shell for general research purposes, but fitted with carpets and soundproofing to enable realistic heating and ventilating measurements to be made; it was to have a Special Category C of A, but no trial installation of turbines was now proposed, because two prototypes of Hermes V were to be ordered to specification 32/46, issued in January 1947.

Official instructions to proceed with the two Hermes Vs were received on 4 February, 1947, and for production of twenty-five Hermes IVs on 19 March; all the latter were to be manufactured at Cricklewood and the two Hermes Vs entirely at Park Street. Specification 37/46 covered Hermes IV production, but concurrently specification 2/47 had been issued for a Constellation replacement, or Medium Range Empire aircraft, for BOAC, to which tenders were invited by 28 April. In reply, Handley Page Ltd proposed three alternative Hermes developments: H.P.83 with four Centaurus 663 piston engines, H.P.84 with four single Proteus turboprops and H.P.85 with a single-spar wing and two Coupled-Proteus turboprops of the type developed for the Brabazon Mk.II and Saro Princess; for all of these a new design of high-lift double-slotted trailing-edge flap was proposed in order to obtain the specified take-off and landing performance without drag penalty in cruise. Meanwhile Handley Page's leading competitor, the Bristol Aeroplane Co, had tendered not only its own Type 175 design but also a Centaurus-engined variant of the Lockheed Constellation 749, which could easily satisfy specification 2/47 provided the Treasury would allow dollars to be spent on it. A further variant, H.P.86, was therefore submitted urgently in a brochure on 18 June in time for consideration by a joint MoS/MCA/BOAC technical meeting on 23 June; the H.P.86 combined the single-spar wing of H.P.85 with the four Centaurus 663s of H.P.83, but Sir Henry Self's committee, which met on 14 July to decide on the 2/47 tenders, finally recommended the Bristol 175 as the 'best buy' and this went into service as the Britannia. Although none of the four Handley Page tenders to specification 2/47 was successful, the lessons of these design studies were applied to Hermes development, mainly with a view to reducing structure weight and improving performance. The double-slotted flap was later tried out on the Hermes V and a preliminary design began in November 1947 for a lightened Hermes with a single-spar wing. This emerged in March 1948 as Hermes VI (H.P.91) with up-rated Hercules 783 engines and an alternative version with civil Griffon engines was also investigated as Hermes VII (H.P.92) for comparison with the Canadair-built DC-4M with Merlin engines adopted by BOAC as the very successful Argonaut. The Griffon installation showed advantages over the Hercules provided that a low-drag wing radiator could be developed, but in December 1948 this had been stopped by military demands on Rolls-Royce's drawing office capacity, so the Hermes VII was abandoned and on 18 March, 1949, official support for the Hermes VI was also withdrawn.

Chocks away from Hermes II on 2 September, 1947.

Meanwhile Hazelden had made a successful maiden flight in G-AGUB at Radlett on 2 September, 1947, and, when flown on 17 September with c.g. aft, it was found to be more stable at high lift coefficient than the Hastings. A month later, as a result of trials on Hastings TG502, it was decided to lower G-AGUB's tailplane to the fuselage centre-line; this work began on 29 November and G-AGUB flew again, with lowered tailplane, bulbous-nosed elevators and locked trim-tabs, on 18 January, 1948. By the end of February it had completed 40 hours of trouble-free handling, needing only an increased trim range to cater for power off with landing gear and flaps fully extended. On 25 March, 1948, it underwent handling tests by an ARB pilot at Woodbridge, while ballasted to the Hermes IV gross weight of 75,000 lb. On 15 July G-AGUB was flown to Boscombe Down for stability tests at full load with c.g. aft, which were completed on 8 August; after further handling with c.g. forward, it returned to Park Street on 13 August and received its C of A on 4 September, 1948. In October it was grounded for its outboard Hercules 130 powerplants to be replaced by Hercules 763s as specified for Hermes IV. Engine runs with these began in December and it was loaned to BOAC at Hurn on 9 May, 1949, for development flying and crew training, which included tropical trials at Castel Benito, Libya, in August, from which it returned to Park Street in March 1950.

Hermes II flying at Radlett on 17 September, 1947.

The first Hermes IV, G-AKFP, made steady progress at the head of the Cricklewood production line while final specification details were still being discussed with BOAC in February 1948. After final assembly at Park Street, its pressurisation tests began on 2 July and were satisfactorily cleared at 7·33 psi a month later. Undercarriage retraction tests began on 20 August, it was weighed on the 28th and taxying began on the 30th. Two days later, as speed was increased, violent nosewheel shimmy occurred because of insufficient friction damping between the two wheels, so they were positively coupled and this cured the trouble. Hazelden made the 75-min maiden flight on 5 September and went on to accumulate the qualifying hours for a first public appearance at the SBAC show at Farnborough, whence he returned on the 10th. Modifications to improve the landing gear and undercarriage doors were completed in a week and Hazelden demonstrated the Hermes IV to invited guests and the Press at Radlett on the 18th. Next day he flew it to test longitudinal stability with

The first Hermes IV G-AKFP landing at Radlett after its maiden flight on 5 September, 1948.

c.g. aft, but had to land early at Fairlop because of failing daylight; he returned next day to Radlett and was able to turn away his employer's wrath (at having to pay an unnecessary landing fee) with fair words. The stability test was repeated at an increased weight of 65,000 lb with c.g. aft on 26 September, when Hazelden landed at Hatfield, where he continued handling tests at 70,000 lb on 3 and 4 October before returning to Park Street. The weight was next increased to 75,000 lb and a new type of spring-loaded trim-tab was fitted to the elevator, but this nearly caused a disaster on 22 October when the tab fluttered so violently that one side of the tailplane began to break up; Hazelden managed to retain control and landed safely, after which a new standard tailplane was fitted. G-AKFP was flown at 80,000 lb on 8 November and at 82,000 lb on the 17th and 21st, all from Hatfield, where the aircraft remained for airscrew strain-gauge tests, returning to Park Street on 18 December for a new design of bulbous wing-root fillet to be incorporated. Development flying continued into the later months of 1949 and in mid-February Hazelden flew G-AKFP to Khartoum for tropical trials, returning to Hurn on 9 March after 55 hours' flying.

The first Hermes V, G-ALEU, was built entirely at Park Street and, like G-AGUB, was completed as a fully sound-proofed, but otherwise unfurnished, flying shell. Structurally it was similar to the Hermes IV apart from the nacelles and powerplants. These, being Theseus turboprops without heat exchangers, were lighter than the Hercules 763s of the Hermes IV and were located further forward, leaving room in the nacelles for later installation of heat exchangers in addition to the bifurcated jet-pipes which proved later on to be a constant source of unserviceability. The oil tanks and systems were integral and removable with the powerplants. It had been hoped to provide thermal deicing for the wings and tail surfaces, and double-skinned leading edges were incorporated for this purpose, but the output from the exhaust-heat exchangers on the first prototype proved inadequate and it was found necessary to install BTR-Goodrich deicer sleeves as already adopted for the Hermes IV. The Hermes V retained the basic fuel system of the Hermes IV,

The first Hermes V G-ALEU at the SBAC display at Farnborough in September 1949.

with additional outer wing tanks to increase total capacity to 3,512 gallons. The high fuel consumption, low reliability and doubtful production status of the Theseus had already led to a search for alternative turbo-props; variants with Proteus or Double-Mambas were proposed as early as January 1949, but were declined by the Director of Civil Aircraft Research and Development in the Ministry of Supply. G-ALEU was at first equipped with DH feathering airscrews which were made lighter than for piston engines of equivalent power because of the presumed absence of torsional vibration in turbines, but it then transpired that blade flutter could impose higher stresses than expected, so the initial airscrews were subject to a life limit of only ten hours. Nevertheless these and other difficulties were overcome in time for Hazelden to make G-ALEU's maiden flight from Radlett on 23 August, 1949, and once again to complete the qualifying hours for its appearance at the SBAC show at Farnborough in September. At that time, with a maximum speed of over 350 mph and a design gross weight of 85,000 lb, it was the fastest and largest turbine-engined airliner yet flown. So Sir Frederick Handley Page had a success story to tell, to compensate for the less happy progress behind the scenes of the Hermes IV.

G-ALDM *Hero* in BOAC livery.

Although not officially designated as a prototype, G-AKFP was recognised as one *de facto* and the MCA, acting as purchasing agents for BOAC, had agreed that it would require weight-saving modifications before being accepted for airline service. In order to save delay in starting flight trials, G-AKFP had made limited use of Hastings components and moreover incorporated *ad hoc* modifications to the wing/fuselage junction arising from the forward shift to compensate for the galley location specified rather late in the day by BOAC. This had increased the structure weight beyond the upper limit of the contract guarantee. Unfortunately the next six Hermes IVs off the production line were found also to be overweight to a lesser degree and BOAC declined to accept delivery when they were offered, but later agreed to do so to avoid holding up crew training and route-proving, on condition that weight reductions were achieved before final acceptance into fleet service. BOAC's somewhat tough attitude came as an unwelcome surprise to Sir Frederick Handley

Page, but stemmed partly from their disappointment with the Avro Tudor's failure to measure up to the standard set for transatlantic airliners by the Lockheed Constellation (of which they would gladly have bought more had the Treasury been able to allocate enough dollars) and partly from their satisfaction with the early delivery and high reliability of the Canadair Argonaut fleet, which had arrived in time to fill the gap left by the Tudor and so reduced the urgency to bring the Hermes into service. In the event, G-ALDA, 'DB and 'DC were rejected and 'DD was accepted in December 1949 for crew training at Hurn, together with G-ALDF, the first to have lightened floor members, but this crashed on take-off from Hurn on 1 May, 1950, and took two years to repair on site. The first Hermes IV to be accepted, on 22 February, 1950, was G-ALDE, which had been waiting for completion of its air-conditioning system and was joined in March by G-ALDG and 'DH for route-proving trials on the West African sector in June. Not until 6 July, 1950, did the tenth Hermes IV, G-ALDI, obtain a full C of A with tropical endorsement, to become the flagship of the Hermes fleet, with the name *Hannibal* bestowed by Lord Pakenham in a handing-over ceremony at Heathrow on 11 July. All twenty-five Hermes IVs were allotted names; the list included those formerly borne by the eight H.P.42s plus the earlier rejected name *Hesperides*, though *Hecate* was not revived in this second round-up. Last in the production sequence, G-ALDY *Honor* was handed over in January 1951, but the last delivery was of G-ALDL *Hector* in February. The Hermes IV entered service with BOAC furnished for 40 first-class passengers and on 6 August, 1950, G-ALDJ *Hengist* took over the London–Tripoli–Kano–Lagos–Accra schedule previously flown by Avro Yorks. On 24 September the Hermes fleet replaced Short Solent flying-boats on the East African route by operating four times weekly to Nairobi via Rome, Cairo and Khartoum, with an additional call at Entebbe on two flights a week. BOAC's remaining Solent services ceased when Hermes IVs extended the Sahara route from Kano to Johannesburg, flying three times a week via Brazzaville and Livingstone; the first service from Heathrow to Johannesburg was flown by G-ALDR *Herodotus* on 7 November, 1950.

The second Hermes V, G-ALEV, incorporated full thermal deicing of all leading edges with hot air supplied by additional Daniell combustion heaters burning kerosene turbine fuel. Hazelden first flew it at Radlett on 6 December, 1950, and after brief handling trials it was fitted with high-lift double-slotted flaps for comparison with the standard ones. These were to be assessed by the A & AEE concurrently with performance trials for a Special Category C of A with DH airscrews, and G-ALEV flew to Boscombe Down to begin this programme on 21 February, 1951. Concurrently G-ALEU was overhauled and on 5 February flew to Moreton Valence for flight testing of a strain-gauged Rotol airscrew, after which it went to Boscombe Down for six hours' handling trials for Special Category C of A and MoS acceptance. It should then have continued performance trials with DH high-camber airscrews and comparative tests of anti-skid wheel-brake systems, including the Goodyear Hytrol and Dunlop Maxaret devices. This programme was frustrated when three engines failed simultaneously (apparently from fuel starvation caused by acceleration) forcing Handley Page assistant test-pilot William Burton to make a 'wheels-up' landing just short of the runway of the disused

Double-slotted flaps on second Hermes V G-ALEV.

Chilbolton aerodrome on 10 April, 1951. G-ALEU was salvaged and carried into the aerodrome in the hope that repairs on site would enable it to be flown out again, but a full survey showed this to be uneconomical and it was then dismantled, the tail-box of the centre section being removed for use in repairing Hermes IV G-ALDU *Halcyone* which had burst a tyre on take-off from Kano in May; but that damage was repaired from local resources and G-ALEU's tail-box was used instead to repair G-ALDB (formerly *Hebe*) which, together with 'DA, 'DC and 'DF, was to be leased to Airwork Ltd for a trooping charter to the Suez Canal Zone; for this role these four Hermes were refurnished with 68 aft-facing seats stressed to withstand a horizontal acceleration of 9g; the original heavy floor members of 'DA, 'DB and 'DC were adequate for this loading, but 'DF's lightened floor was not, and had to be reinforced. Before being modified for Airwork Ltd, G-ALDA *Hecuba* was equipped with braking airscrews, which were approved by ARB in February 1951 for all Hermes IVs; they were installed

G-ALEU on its belly at Chilbolton on 10 April, 1951, showing single flap.

on the last three (G-ALDX, 'DY and 'DL) before delivery to BOAC and retrospectively on the remainder of the fleet; this allowed the maximum take-off weight to be increased to 86,000 lb and the landing weight to 78,000 lb, a useful gain on short sectors. G-ALDA had also gone to Khartoum for tropical performance trials which lasted from 7 to 22 May, 1951, and G-ALDB *Hebe* was temporarily put into service on 12 June, but later rejected because of its payload limitation and returned to Park Street.

G-ALEU was deleted from the MoS contract in June 1951 and G-ALEV then had to undertake the Hytrol and Maxaret trials in addition to its own double-slotted flap trials. First, however, it was allowed a few hours of glory when it was awarded a Special Category C of A (but limited to one month because of Theseus unreliability) on 28 May for a demonstration to French civil aviation authorities and operators on 5 June, when Douglas Broomfield flew it from Heathrow to Orly in 46 minutes with eighteen invited passengers distributed luxuriously among the seventy-four Hermes IV seats installed for the occasion. The ground speed was exactly 300 mph, somewhat better than currently achieved by the only other turbo-prop airliner ordered for airline service, the Viscount. Unfortunately a bearing failure on the starboard inner Theseus cut short the demonstration after four flights and G-ALEV was grounded till this powerplant had been changed on 15 June, when it flew back to Park Street without incident. It was evident that no production of the Hermes V could be promoted unless a more reliable engine than the Theseus could be found, and performance calculations were made for the projected Hermes VA (Napier Elands) and enlarged Hermes VB (Bristol Proteus 3); the latter would have had a gross weight of 100,000 lb, span increased to 117 ft 6 in, a taller landing gear to permit use of 14 ft 6 in diameter airscrews and a taller fin of increased area to take care of asymmetric thrust with two engines failed on one side. A variant with Napier Nomad compound engines was also considered; this would have had a better maximum range than the others, but, because of its high installed weight, would have suffered a payload penalty on stages shorter than 3,500 miles. At Park Street G-ALEV was equipped with a Maxaret braking system and demonstrated this very effectively at the SBAC show in September 1951; in the following month it completed more than twenty landings without defect and this satisfied BOAC as to the

G-ALEV landing at the SBAC display at Farnborough in September 1951, with double-slotted flaps lowered. (*Flight*)

reliability of the device for their new Britannia fleet, so the Hytrol programme was cancelled in favour of further development of the Maxaret. The final tests were made at the RAE, with ARB and BOAC observers present, on 27 June, 1952, after which G-ALEV was permanently grounded as a fatigue test airframe, being finally broken up at Farnborough in September 1953.

G-AKFP finally completed its extended performance tests at Boscombe Down and returned to Park Street on 5 March, 1952, to be laid up for some weeks while modifications were incorporated to reduce the structure weight by more than 200 lb to a figure acceptable to BOAC; in the end it was not offered back to BOAC because Airwork took it off the makers' hands at a higher weight than BOAC had specified. The A & AEE test programme had shown that by setting the flaps at 20 degrees instead of 40 degrees for take-off the initial rate of climb was increased by 150 ft/min. During planning for Airwork's trooping contract, it had been found difficult to provide advance stocks of the 115-octane fuel required by the Hercules 763, so a version of this engine modified to use the more plentiful 100-octane fuel, Hercules 773, was chosen and had the incidental advantage of reducing the powerplant weight. With these engines, the aircraft became Hermes IVA and required new performance trials for revision of the flight manual and issue of a revised Type C of A. G-ALDB began these tests at

G-ALDA in Airwork livery near the Isle of Wight in 1952.

Boscombe Down on 23 April, 1952, and was cleared to land at 82,000 lb when using methanol-water injection for take-off and baulked-landing climb. The temperate climate certification tests were completed in just over 24 hours' flying time and a Special Category C of A was issued on 16 May to allow G-ALDB to begin tropical trials, for which it was flown to Entebbe by Hazelden and Captain Stenner of Airwork on 19 May, returning to Blackbushe on 6 June. Unrestricted Cs of A were issued to G-ALDC on 17 June and to G-ALDB on 18 June and both went into service on the trooping contract forthwith. G-ALDF, which had been employed for crew training after receiving its new landing gear in May, joined them in July, but G-ALDA was still held up awaiting modified engines. For political reasons they were operated as military aircraft, with standard RAF markings and serials WZ838–WZ841, but on 23 July WZ839 (G-ALDB) crashed at

Pithiviers and was burned out, the cause being fatigue fracture of a crankshaft web in one engine. A similar failure of both inner engines caused the loss of WZ841 (G-ALDF) in the sea off Trapani, Sicily, on 25 August, when six passengers and a stewardess were drowned. Necessary modifications to Hercules 773s delayed the entry into service of WZ838 (G-ALDA) till 14 October, when it received its long-delayed first C of A. This depletion of Airwork's fleet cut short the modification of G-AKFP to meet BOAC's weight guarantee and in February 1953 it was delivered to Airwork as a Hermes IVA, XD632, reverting to civil marks a year later when Airwork won a contract for trooping between Blackbushe and Singapore, to carry 10,000 Service personnel during a period of 2½ years.

BOAC's Hermes IVs continued to fly the African and Eastern routes during the early months of 1952, being diverted via Tripoli–Khartoum and Nicosia–Damascus during the Cairo riots in January and February, but they were partly replaced by Comets on the Johannesburg route from May and entirely superseded by Argonauts on 1 October, 1953, after Comets had released these from the Far East route in April. During this period G-ALDI *Hannibal* shed a starboard airscrew blade during take-off from Tripoli in February 1952; a safe landing was made in spite of severe damage to the fuselage skin alongside the galley, but this was patched up on site and the aircraft was ferried back unpressurised to Park Street for permanent repairs in March. More serious was the loss of G-ALDN *Horus*, which went astray at night through a navigational error after leaving Tripoli for Kano on 25 May. After eleven hours' flying on a too-westerly course, it was forced by fuel shortage to land in the open Sahara desert 150 miles southeast of Port Etienne, French West Africa (now Mauritania), in the early hours of 26 May. None of the passengers was any the worse for the ordeal after being rescued, but one crew member died and it was impossible to rescue the Hermes from the constantly shifting sand waves, in which it may still lie buried.

In March 1952 the RAE carried out fatigue tests on six samples of spar booms removed from Hastings and estimated a provisional safe fatigue life of 4,000 hours for the Hermes, pending the availability of accelerometer records from fatigue-meters in five of the Hermes flying the Eastern routes during the monsoon season. In May the first Hermes withdrawn from the Johannesburg route, G-ALDJ *Hengist*, was returned to Radlett for major inspection after 3,500 hours and the opportunity was taken to renew the centre-section and inner wing lower spar booms so that the time-expired material could be further tested. In August, on the basis of these tests and after examining 78 v-g recordings, the ARB agreed to increase the allowable inner-wing fatigue life to 7,000 hours, but BOAC insisted on a minimum of 8,500 hours, after which they were prepared to withdraw the Hermes from service; if 8,500 hours could not be allowed, they would agree to all nineteen Hermes having their booms renewed, provided at least ten (including G-ALDJ and 'DK) were returned to service by March 1954 and the remainder as soon as possible afterwards. Originally BOAC had planned to dispose of all their Hermes fleet as soon as Argonauts and Comets had replaced them, but this intention was frustrated by the loss of one Comet near Calcutta in May 1953 and two others over the Mediterranean early in 1954, the latter due to pressure-cabin fatigue. Hermes IVs had begun new tourist-class services between Heathrow and

Sudan, Uganda and Kenya on 17 November, 1952, using a 56-passenger high-density layout at a fare 28 per cent lower than first-class, extending the route to Dar-es-Salaam on the 21st. These continued until Argonauts replaced Hermes in October 1953, when all nineteen Hermes IVs were offered for sale to independent charter operators—a step which met with opposition from BOAC's maintenance staff at Heathrow, whose trade unions placed a ban on their members servicing Hermes for other operators; so the Cocooned fleet lay idle at Heathrow till May 1954, although sold in March to Airwork (three), Britavia (six) and Skyways (ten). By this time the entire Comet fleet had been grounded and had to be replaced by Argonauts on the main trunk routes, so four Hermes were de-cocooned for the weekly tourist services to Nairobi and Dar-es-Salaam, to which they returned as 56-seaters on 18 July, 1954, until their final withdrawal from BOAC use early in December. The first five to be sold were G-ALDJ *Hengist* in May 1954, G-ALDI *Hannibal*, G-ALDK *Helena* and G-ALDP *Homer* in June, all to Britavia Ltd, and G-ALDE *Hanno* to Lancashire Aircraft Corporation in September. Seven more, G-ALDD *Horatius*, G-ALDS *Hesperides*, G-ALDT *Hestia*, G-ALDV *Hera*, G-ALDW *Helios*, G-ALDX *Hyperion* and G-ALDY *Honor* all went in February 1955 to Skyways, who also took G-ALDR *Herodotus* in April, G-ALDL *Hector* in May and G-ALDH *Heracles* in June. Trek Airways bought G-ALDM *Hero* in September 1956, Britavia added G-ALDU *Halycone* to their fleet in December 1956 and Airwork finally acquired G-ALDG *Horsa* in July 1957, leaving only G-ALDO *Heron* unsold, to fall under the breaker's axe at Blackbushe in March 1959.

All were re-engined with Hercules 773s, making them Hermes IVAs, and the Britavia fleet began trooping contracts to Cyprus and Nairobi in July 1954, in military marks with serials XJ267 ('DX), XJ269 ('DP), XJ280 ('DU), XJ281 ('DK) and XJ309 ('DI). On 4 March, 1956, Skyways' G-ALDW was blown up on Nicosia aerodrome by an EOKA saboteur, while on 5 August Britavia's G-ALDK landed by mistake at Drigh Road, where it crashed without serious injury to its 72 passengers and crew returning from Singapore; its pilot believed he had arrived at Karachi Airport and the landing gear collapsed on reaching the end of the very short runway. More serious was the night crash of Britavia's G-ALDJ at Blackbushe on 5 November, 1956, when seven persons were killed and one seriously injured,

G-ALDU, formerly *Halcyone* of BOAC, in Kuwait Airways livery in 1956 while on lease from Britavia.

the aircraft being destroyed. Airwork's veteran G-AKFP, temporarily operated as XD632, met its end by landing on top of a taxying Dakota at Calcutta on 1 September, 1957, and Skyways' G-ALDV was burnt out after a fatal crash at Meesden Green, Herts, on 1 April, 1958. On the credit side, Britavia's G-ALDU became the first Hermes to fly the North Atlantic, when it was chartered to carry a ship's relief crew of 39 men from Blackbushe to New York on 14 November, 1955, via Shannon and Gander, returning with the relieved crew via Gander; its flight time westward was 17 hr 15 min and eastward (overflying Shannon) 16 hr 9 min. After supplies of 115-octane fuel had improved in 1957, many Hermes IVAs reverted to Hermes IVs with Hercules 763 engines and from June 1959 five of Britavia's fleet, including G-ALDM, operated in Silver City Airways livery on the 'Silver Arrow' service between Manston and Le Touquet till April 1960. Other new charter operators acquired Hermes for inclusive tours; of these Falcon Airways at Southend flew G-ALDA, 'DC and 'DG during 1960 and on 9 October 'DC overshot the wet runway at Southend on to the adjacent railway track as a result of 'aquaplaning' with locked brakes. Three of Skyways' Hermes, G-ALDE, 'DL and 'DT, operated on the Bahamas Airways Nassau–Miami route as 78-seaters during 1960, as VP-BBO, 'P and 'Q, and were bought in 1961 by Air Safaris Ltd, which already owned G-ALDA and 'DM. Finally, G-ALDA, converted to carry 82 passengers, operated from Gatwick in Air Links Ltd ownership from December 1962 to 13 December, 1964, being scrapped at Southend early in 1965. Apart from the three Bahamas Airways aircraft, the only Hermes to carry foreign registrations were G-ALDT and 'DY, while short-leased in 1956 to Middle East Airlines as OD-ACB and 'CC, to carry pilgrims to Mecca from Baghdad, Beirut, Cairo and the Persian Gulf.

During the Hermes IV's fourteen years of activity in commercial aviation, the solitary Hermes II enjoyed a less active but none the less useful life, first as G-AGUB and, from 2 October, 1953, as VX234. After returning to Radlett from BOAC's aircrew training base at Hurn in March 1950, it was reserved for experimental flying on basic scientific research programmes, for which purpose in January 1951 a large optically-flat window was installed for aerial camera development by the Department of Scientific and Industrial Research. Its wiring was also calibrated for magnetic interference prior to installation of a magnetic anomaly detector for the World Geophysical Survey programme. On 19 April it was flown with this equipment to Lee-on-Solent to assist in the search for the missing submarine *Affray* and was found to be capable of detecting large metal objects 200 ft below the surface of the sea—in fact, fifteen uncharted wrecks were located in five days—before it returned to Park Street to resume concurrent tests on auto-pilot stability. In July 1951 it was waiting to test a new F.83 camera for the RAE, which did not materialise before it was grounded for six weeks in January for a major overhaul, after which it was prepared for the installation of the Elliott Sun Compass to be used in the Geophysical Survey. It took a year to complete the fixed fittings for this instrument, which was highly sensitive and mounted on frictionless air bearings, but the F.83 camera was still not available, so a standard F.20 was installed instead. On completion of the Sun Compass trials, which entailed many flights overseas, VX234 was flown to Airwork Ltd's base at Lasham

Hermes II as VX234 at Radlett having the Elliott Sun Compass installed in 1952, showing lowered tailplane. (*D. C. Clayton*)

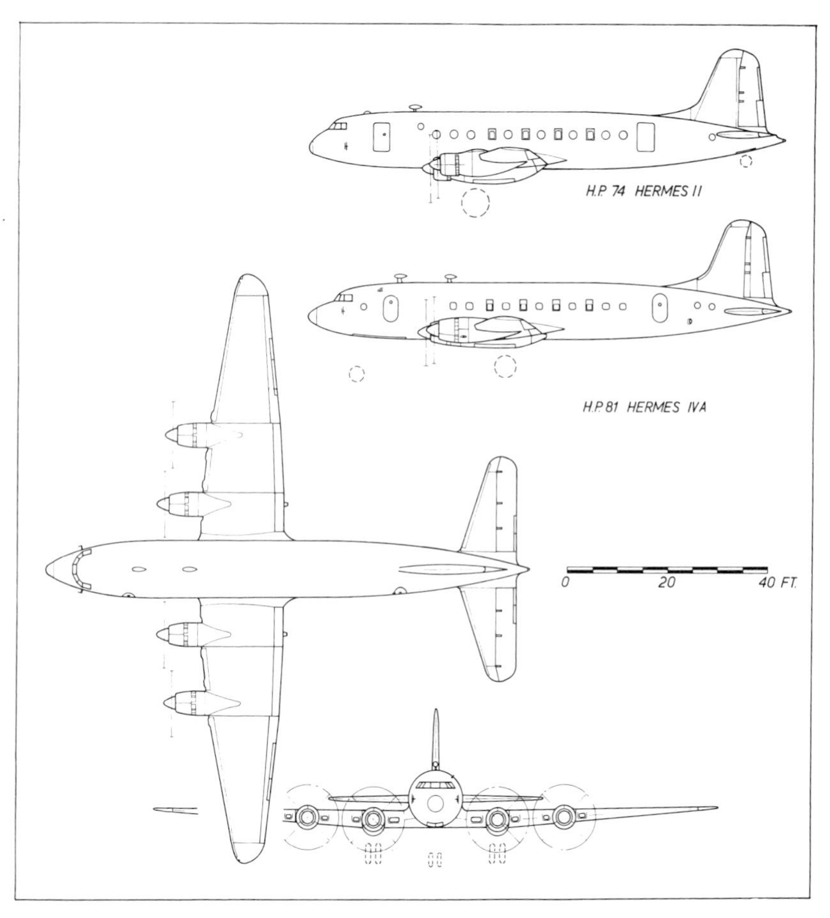

for overhaul in December 1956, during which four Hercules 106 powerplants (as for Hastings C.2) were substituted for the two Hercules 130s and two Hercules 763s previously installed. In June 1958 it was allotted to the Royal Radar Establishment at Pershore for trials of new radar equipment, including the SLR (sideways-looking radar) developed for the T.S.R.-2 supersonic bomber, the antennae being housed in a long slender radome below the centre-line of the fuselage. By the beginning of 1966 the Hermes II had logged over 1,000 hours and it was finally written-off charge and scrapped at Pershore in 1969, having become the longest-lived Hermes of all.

H.P.74 Hermes II

(Four Bristol Hercules 130 or two Hercules 763 and two Hercules 130 or four Hercules 106) Span 113 ft (36·6 m); length 92 ft 2 in (28·09 m); wing area 1,408 sq ft (131·6 m^2), Empty weight 41,700 lb (18,900 kg); maximum weight 80,000 lb (36,250 kg). Speed 350 mph (564 km/h). Crew seven. Passengers 52–64.

H.P.81 Hermes IV

(Four Bristol Hercules 763)

Span 113 ft (36·6 m); length 96 ft 10 in (29·55 m); wing area 1,408 sq ft (131·6 m^2). Empty weight 55,350 lb (25,100 kg); maximum weight 86,000 lb (39,000 kg). Speed 350 mph (564 km/h); range 2,000 miles (3,220 km); ceiling 24,500 ft (7,580 m). Crew seven. Passengers 40–82.

H.P.81A Hermes IVA

As Hermes IV except engines were Bristol Hercules 773.

H.P.82 Hermes V

(Four Bristol Theseus)

Dimensions as for Hermes IV. Empty weight 50,900 lb (23,100 kg); maximum weight 85,000 lb (38,550 kg). Speed 351 mph (565 km/h); range 2,500 miles (4,020 km); ceiling 28,600 ft (8,850 m). Crew seven. Passengers 74.

Brabazon Type 2B Projects (H.P.76, 77 and 78)

At the end of 1942 the Cabinet appointed an interdepartmental committee under the chairmanship of Lord Brabazon of Tara to examine requirements for post-war civil aviation and to recommend the types of transport aircraft on which the British aircraft industry should concentrate, when the need for maximum production of military aircraft ceased to be dominant. This programme was deemed essential to prevent a sudden collapse of the industry when the war came to an end, and to provide home-built aircraft to replace the many American transports, chiefly DC-3 and DC-4, which would be recalled when the Lease-Lend scheme ended, or have to be bought with dollars which, in turn, would have to be earned by exporting merchandise and services, not least in the field of air transport. On 9 February, 1943, the Brabazon Committee reported to the Cabinet with a recommendation for five types of aircraft, ranging from a transatlantic express airliner to a small feeder transport for internal services. The latter was classed as Brabazon Type 5 and a larger short/medium-range airliner for European services was classed as Brabazon Type 2. Specifications 25/43 and 26/43 were issued to define Type 2 and Type 5 respectively and in each case two piston engines were specified. Handley Page Ltd, committed up to the hilt with Halifax production and development, did not submit tenders and in due course prototype contracts were awarded to Airspeed Ltd for the A.S.57 (Ambassador) and de Havilland for the D.H.104 (Dove), intended as post-war successors to the DC-3 and D.H.89 Rapide respectively. Concurrently there had been a move to up-date the pre-war International Commission for Air Navigation (ICAN) and a Provisional International Civil Aviation Organisation (PICAO) was in the process of being set up at Montreal when the war came to an end in August 1945. This body issued draft requirements for *inter alia* performance and safety of new civil aeroplanes which would have become mandatory by the time the Ambassador and Dove entered service; in the spring of 1945 the improved prospect of lightweight economical turboprops of 1,000 ehp being available led to the second Brabazon Committee, after discussions with Armstrong Siddeley, Armstrong Whitworth, Napier, Rolls-Royce and Vickers, defining a four-engined Brabazon 2B requirement as a turbine-powered complement (and possible successor) to the Ambassador, which was then reclassified as a Brabazon Type 2A. The impetus for this development came from Reginald Pierson of Vickers, who proposed the VC2, a pressurised low-wing monoplane for 24 passengers powered by four Rolls-Royce Darts, and from John Lloyd of Armstrong Whitworth, whose generally similar A.W.55 with four Mambas was championed by the Ministry of Civil Aviation. The advantage offered by the Brabazon 2B concept was that total loss of power from one engine at the most critical point of take-off, as required to be demonstrated to satisfy PICAO, resulted in only 25 per cent reduction of power as against 50 per cent for

Brabazon 2A; the latter's two engines were held by some to facilitate operation by a crew of two, but it was expected that four turboprops would not entail a higher workload than two piston engines, so this factor was no longer significant and was far outweighed by the safety factor of having three out of four engines available after a single failure.

Sir Frederick Handley Page became aware of the main features of the Brabazon 2B proposals some twelve months before they were formally defined by specification 8/46 and in December 1944 had received installation drawings of the proposed Rolls-Royce Tweed twinned-turboprop around two of which was drafted a low-wing European airliner designated H.P.76, to carry 34 passengers; with a pressurised fuselage of 8 ft 6 in diameter, nosewheel landing gear, sophisticated high-lift slotted flaps for short take-off and slow landing, together with lateral

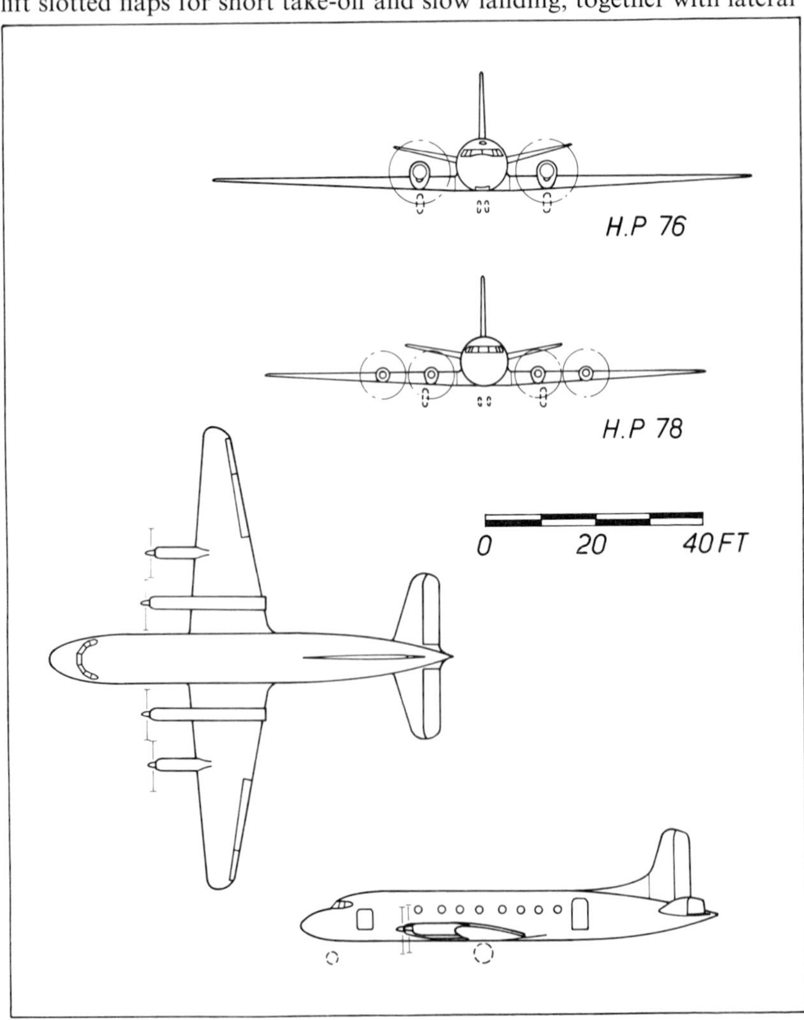

control by lift-spoilers in front of small-area ailerons, it aimed at a better cruising performance than the Ambassador. A cabin mock-up was begun and on 15 January, 1945, the diameter was increased to 9 ft and the all-up weight was established as 34,000 lb. Soon afterwards the Rolls-Royce Tweed project was abandoned and for some months the availability of any suitable turboprop remained in doubt; this problem was discussed with both Rolls-Royce and Armstrong Siddeley in November 1945, when the former offered only the single Dart, but the latter could provide the Mamba in both single and twin forms. The Twin-Mamba was chosen for the next stage in the development of the H.P.76, whose diameter was again increased, in February 1946, to 10 ft 6 in. By this time there was no question of reverting to piston engines, but alternative turboprops were sought in view of the similar needs of the Hermes V; the Napier E.128 (Naiad) would have given better cruising economy than the Mamba, but at a lower speed, while the substitution of two improved Bristol Theseus seemed a possibility, since these were being produced in limited numbers for the Hermes V. In March 1946 the H.P.76 with two Theseus was designated H.P.77; a month later specification 8/46 defined the Vickers VC2 and was followed in May by 16/46 to cover the A.W.55, which had been ordered as an insurance against failure of the VC2, whose Darts had run into development difficulties. Having failed to elicit any financial support from MoS for the H.P.76 and 77, the firm again revised the project to provide 32 seats, three abreast, in the slightly longer cabin of a new variant, H.P.78. This was to have a redesigned wing with four single Mambas in separate nacelles; later the wing span and ailerons were enlarged, because the lift-spoiler device had not lived up to expectations when tested on Halifax NP715. By this time, the chances of successfully competing with the VC2 had receded, while the emergent H.P.80 bomber demanded increasing priority in the design office, so on 25 June, 1946, all work on the H.P.76, 77 and 78 was suspended and Handley Page's interest in any airliner smaller than the Hermes seemed to have been extinguished, to be unexpectedly revived after two years, when Sir Frederick was encouraged to come to the rescue of the Marathon, for which Miles Aircraft Ltd had won a production contract in the Brabazon Type 5 class, but were unable to raise sufficient capital to finance it.

H.P.78

(Four Armstrong Siddeley Mambas)

Span 100 ft (30·5 m). No other data available.

First production Marathon I G-ALUB during short take-off and landing trials at Woodley in October 1950. (*Sport & General*)

Marathon (H.P.R.1 and H.P.R.5)

In November 1947, with the Hermes IV in limited production, but little prospect of its further development after the Bristol 175 had scooped the M.R.E. contract from the H.P.86, Sir Frederick turned his attention to the sorry plight of Miles Aircraft Ltd at Woodley, near Reading, which had been forced into liquidation by its creditors, but was available for purchase as a going concern. The Ministry of Supply was anxious not to disperse the Miles expertise and organisation, because the company had been awarded a production contract for its M.60 Marathon feeder-liner for use on internal services in the United Kingdom and by BOAC's domestic subsidiaries overseas. The Marathon had not been included in the Brabazon Committee's first project list because, like Type 2, the Brabazon Type 5 had been recommended only in twin-engined form. However, some months before the VC2 was put forward as a four-engined complement to the Ambassador, George Miles had suggested a need for a modern four-engined equivalent of the D.H.86, which was not really covered by the much smaller Rapide replacement, the Dove. So in the spring of 1944, specification 18/44 was issued for a high-wing monoplane with four 330 hp Gipsy Queen engines, seats for fourteen passengers and ability to land in and climb out of the very small aerodromes which were often the best available, particularly in the Hebrides, Orkneys, Shetlands and Channel Islands; on the Brabazon Committee's list this became Type 5A, while the Dove became Type 5B. Miles's tender, the M.60, was their first all-metal design after many years of experience built up from small beginnings with wooden aeroplanes.

The difficulties of the Miles company in satisfying its official customers on the detail design of the M.60, as well as building three prototypes in unfamiliar materials, have been fully described at first hand by Don L. Brown in the companion volume *Miles Aircraft since 1925*, and need not be repeated here. Suffice it to say that the design was fixed, after much conflict, in April 1945. The first prototype (U-10, later G-AGPD) was first flown at Woodley by Ken Waller on 19 May, 1946, and the second, G-AILH, on 27 February, 1947, during the exceptionally cold weather which was a crucial factor in accelerating the company's bankruptcy, since the resultant power-cuts ruined most of the plywood components being manufactured for other aircraft then in progress. G-AGPD went to Boscombe Down for official temperate performance trials, which were completed without setbacks between 26 August, 1946, and 15 January, 1947. After this good reception, Miles Aircraft expected a production order to follow without undue delay, but the price had still not been agreed when, on 10 May, 1948, A & AEE test pilot Brian Bastable omitted to re-trim the adjustable fin incidence after take-off, with the result that G-AGPD's tail unit became overstressed and failed in the air near Amesbury, both Bastable and his flight test observer being killed. Within days the firm's financial position became untenable, with its principal creditor, Barclay's Bank, demanding repayment of £600,000 overdraft. At this point Sir Frederick Handley Page was urged by MoS to renew his interest in short-range civil transports by assuming responsibility for the Marathon production line. Eventually, on 5 July, 1948, Handley Page Transport Ltd, dormant since April 1924 but still legally alive, was reconstituted as Handley Page (Reading) Ltd to acquire all the aircraft assets and goodwill of Miles Aircraft Ltd at Woodley, with the primary object of agreeing terms for a production contract for fifty Marathons to be purchased by MCA as agents for BOAC and BEA. The latter had also requested a turboprop version of the Marathon with two Mambas, for which specification 15/46 had been issued on 19 May, 1947; one prototype of this M.69 Marathon II had been ordered, but had not flown by July 1948, although it was well advanced.

Under its chief designer, Edwin W. J. Gray, the Handley Page (Reading) drawing office carefully appraised the Marathon production drawings and modified the design to take advantage of split-assembly, photo-lofting and other Cricklewood production techniques. At the same time the interior layout was revised to accommodate eighteen passengers instead of fourteen. These changes increased the empty weight by 500 lb but enabled the contract price and delivery schedule to be agreed without sacrificing too much performance. The unpressurised semi-monocoque fuselage was built in five sections and the floor was reinforced for high-density loads, with the freight hold stressed for 200 lb/sq ft. The wing also was made in five sections and contained crash-proof flexible fuel tanks between the two spars, extending between the four nacelles carrying underslung engines. The all-metal tail unit comprised two end-plate fins and rudders, also a fixed central fin, which was at first deleted from the second prototype, but restored later to meet engine-cut airworthiness criteria. All control surfaces were metal covered, with electrically-actuated trim-tabs, and dual controls were provided. The large-area Miles-patented retractable flaps were pneumatically operated, as were the wheel brakes, nosewheel steering and landing gear retraction, by a system supplied from Heywood compressors driven by the two outer engines; the inner engines each drove a 24V 50A d.c. generator. G-AGPD had completed temperate trials at Boscombe Down before its loss and in October 1949 G-AILH went to Khartoum and Nairobi for three months for tropical trials, when some cylinder-head and oil temperatures exceeded the maximum permitted, even with the cooling shutters fully open. During these trials a number of minor defects were reported and taken care of in the production design, which was registered as type No. H.P.R.1.

The first production Marathon I, G-ALUB, was assigned as a sales demonstrator and on 14 January, 1950, it left Woodley, flown by Hugh Kendall and Grp Capt A. F. Bandidt, on a 40,000-mile tour to Australasia. 'Bush' Bandidt had been the Air Ministry overseer at Woodley during the early war years and had made the first post-war solo flight to Australia at the end of 1946 in a Miles Gemini; returning to Britain just before the Miles company's liquidation, he had been appointed sales manager to Handley Page (Reading) Ltd and had an intimate knowledge of the needs and prospects of air transport in Australasia, particularly in his native Queensland, where aircraft utilisation was for many years the highest in the world. The places visited on this tour included Lyons, Rome, Malta, Athens, Cyprus, Baghdad, Basra, Karachi, New Delhi, Calcutta, Rangoon, Penang, Singapore, Jakarta, fifteen towns in Australia, six in New Zealand, Norfolk Island, a diversion to New Guinea, also Sharjah, Bahrein, Beirut, Cairo, Luxor and Benghazi on the return flight. Later in the year a second tour, to Johannesburg, Durban and Pretoria, took in Jeddah, Khartoum, Nairobi, Lusaka, Salisbury and Bulawayo on the way out, and Lourenço Marques, Luanda, Lobito, Benguela, Libreville, Lagos, Accra, Monrovia, Freetown, Dakar, Casablanca, Lisbon, Madrid and Brussels on the way back to Woodley. In May 1951 G-ALUB was delivered to Northolt for acceptance tests before entering service on the Scottish 'Highlands and Islands' routes as the first of the 'Clansman' class. BEA found it unable to match the versatility and economy of the ageing D.H.89 Rapide and reduced their order from twenty-five to seven. It was flown at London Airport in September in BEA livery, with the name *Rob Roy*, but in February 1952 BEA cancelled their Marathon order entirely, having already rejected the Mamba-powered Marathon II after brief trials of the prototype G-AHXU. This was first flown by Hugh Kendall at Woodley on

Mamba-Marathon flying as VX231 at the SBAC display in September 1951.

21 July, 1949, when the port undercarriage jammed in the 'up' position, but was released by skilful application of 'g' before landing. It was exhibited at the SBAC show in September 1949 and flown for Special Category C of A trials between 4 and 12 January, 1950, again by Hugh Kendall. Contrary to expectation, the cabin noise level was higher with Mambas than with Gipsy Queens, which caused BEA to refuse it, and it was also deficient in an adequate stall-warning, but this was provided by adding small spoilers on the wing-root leading edge, which proved satisfactory when tested by D. J. Broomfield on 6 April, 1950. It was again shown at Farnborough in September 1950 and flown by Hugh Kendall into seventh place in the *Daily Express* air race from Hurn to Herne Bay on 16 September at just over 280 mph. Early in 1951 it was taken on MoS charge as VX231 and allotted to de Havilland Propellers Ltd to become the first turbine reversible-pitch airscrew test-bed, commencing flight trials at Hatfield on 23 July, 1951, and demonstrating backward taxying at the SBAC show that year.

Meanwhile, production of the Marathon I for MCA continued and BOAC endeavoured to interest its various subsidiary local airlines in adopting it as a feeder-liner, while the interior was rearranged to accommodate up to twenty-two passengers in economy seating. In March 1951 the twelfth production machine, G-AMEO, was lent to the West African Airways Corporation as VR-NAI for route-proving on the regional services in Nigeria, Gold Coast, Sierra Leone and Gambia; late in 1952 WAAC ordered six Marathon IAs with Gipsy Queen 70-4 engines in

Twelfth Marathon I, G-AMEO, leased to West African Airways Corporation at Lagos for two months in 1951 and sold to Germany in 1955 as D-CFSA.

place of 70-3s, but these were replaced in 1954 by D. H. Herons and were then returned to the UK for storage. In July 1952 three more Marathon IAs equipped with increased fuel tankage (G-AMIA, 'IB and 'IC) were sold to Union of Burma Airways at Rangoon for their Akyab, Bangkok, Calcutta and Singapore services, as XY-ACX, 'Y and 'Z. The second prototype, G-AILH, had been transferred to MoS in 1951 as VX229 for use as a communications aircraft and in January and February that year the second production machine, G-ALVW, equipped with reversible-pitch airscrews, was flown at Boscombe Down to determine the optimum flap settings for short take-off and landing, using reverse thrust from all four airscrews and from the two inboard airscrews alone. Comparative tests between January and April 1951 showed that the eighth production Marathon, G-AMDH, with standard non-braking airscrews, had nearly twice as long a landing run, but was nevertheless within the specification guarantee, so MCA could not on this account refuse to accept the aircraft it had ordered, even though no customers were available; whilst supporting the Marathon with increased sales promotion, Sir Frederick made it perfectly clear that the company's sole contractual responsibility was to manufacture the Marathon—not to sell it—but agreed eventually to close the production line on completion of the 40th aircraft, after MoS had accepted a proposal for twenty-eight of them to be modified into navigational trainers for the RAF, with the new designation Marathon T.Mk.11.

Second Marathon I, G-ALVW, after rejection by BEA, became Marathon T.11 XA250, seen at Woodley before delivery to RAF Training Command in 1952, with Charles Joy standing beside it. (*D. C. Clayton*)

The prototype of this variant was VX229, whose external shape was modified by the addition of an astrodome aft of the wing and two 'peardrop' observation windows on the starboard side, without changing the interior layout. In this form VX229 was flown at Boscombe Down between 1 July and 13 August, 1952, to assess handling with c.g. forward and c.g. aft at 18,000 lb in extension of the performance trials already done on G-AMDH. Meanwhile the twenty-eight Marathons were furnished with three plotting tables and aft-facing seats for a navigation instructor and two pupils in the cabin, in addition to the pilot and radio-operator on the flight deck, and were allotted serials XA249 to XA276 inclusive. XA249 was first flown at Woodley on 29 August, 1952, in time to be exhibited at the SBAC show a week later. After further handling trials at the RAF Flying College, Manby, Marathon T.11s were issued in 1953 to the Air Navigation School at Hullavington, which later divided into No.1 ANS, Topcliffe, and No.2 ANS, Thorney Island, both equipped with Marathons. It had been hoped to sell the last two Marathon Is G-AMHY and 'HZ to Burma, for which reason they had not been modified to T.11s, but in 1953 this option was cancelled and a year later they were sold to Far East Air Lines at Nagoya, Japan, to become JA-6009 and JA-6010. On 30 September, 1954, the twenty-fourth production Marathon, XA271 (ex G-AMGT), crashed at Calne, Wiltshire, when its wing-tips became detached, all five on board being killed, but apart from this accident Marathon T.11s gave good service in RAF Training Command till they were superseded by Vickers Varsities in March 1959.

G-AMHY in July 1954 awaiting delivery to Far East Air Lines in Japan, where it became JA-6009.

Fifteen of them were then offered for sale, four (XA250, 252, 269 and 274) being bought by F. G. Miles Ltd at Shoreham for overhaul and possible resale, and two more (XA262 and 265) by Derby Aviation Ltd to back up G-AMGW (ex VR-NAN) and G-AMHR (ex VR-NAR) which they already operated as *Millersdale* and *Monsaldale* from Burnaston on internal scheduled services to the Channel Islands, Isle of Man and Scotland. Two others, VR-NAS and 'T, which had been transferred to the RAE in March 1955 as XJ830 and XJ831 for communications duties, were sold four years later to Air Navigation & Trading Co Ltd at Squire's Gate, Blackpool, where XJ831 was overhauled and sold to Canada in 1961 as CF-NUH. The twelfth production aircraft G-AMEO, after returning from Lagos as VR-NAI, was sold in August 1955 to the German Civil Aviation Board as D-CFSA, for radio calibration duties. The thirty-fourth, formerly G-AMHW and VR-NAU, was converted into the personal transport of King Hussein of Jordan, to whom it was supplied in September 1954 as VK501 of the Royal Jordanian Air Force; while the twenty-eighth, G-AMGX, after returning from Lagos as VR-NAO in 1955, was converted at Southend by Balfour Marine Engineering Co Ltd into a flying show-room for juke-boxes, for a projected sales tour of America, planned to begin with a transatlantic flight via Iceland on 18 August, 1956, but this was frustrated and the aircraft was scrapped at Southend in 1962, by which date all the others, apart from the two in Japan, had suffered the same fate.

G-AMGX flew with WAAC for nearly three years as VR-NAO before returning to Southend for conversion into a flying show-room for juke-boxes. (*Associated Press*)

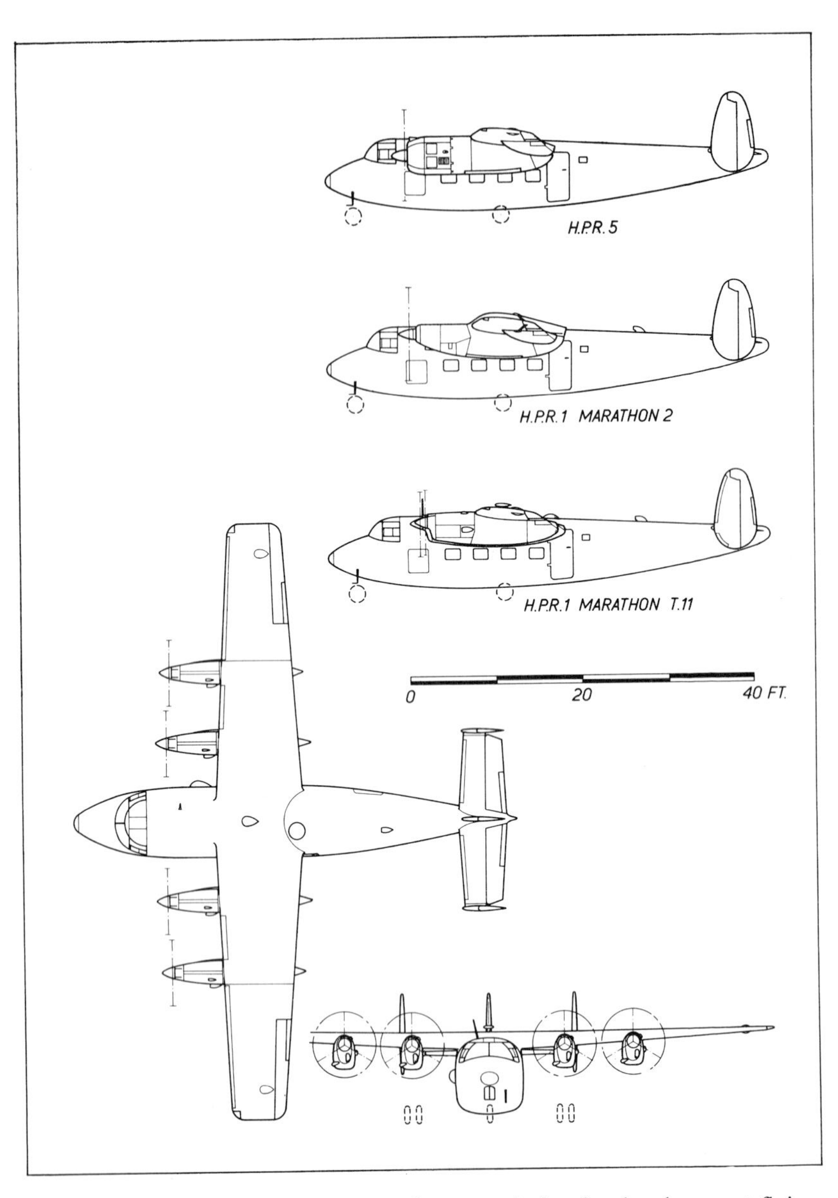

The sole Marathon II, VX231, after completing its development flying with de Havilland Propellers Ltd in 1953, went to the Empire Test Pilots' School at Farnborough, whence it was returned to Woodley in 1954 to be modified as a test-bed for the new double-row Alvis Leonides Major engines being developed in powerplant form for use in the H.P.R.3 short-haul 'branch-liner', subsequently named the Herald. The powerplant was evolved in close co-operation with the RAE, whose 24-ft wind-tunnel was

VX231 converted to H.P.R.5 at Woodley in March 1955. (*Flight*)

employed for pre-flight tests. With two Leonides Majors, VX231 was redesignated H.P.R.5 and flew at Woodley on 15 March, 1955; after 13 hours' flying at Woodley, it was transferred in May to Alvis Motors Ltd at Baginton till the Leonides Major ceased development in 1958, when it moved its base a few miles to Bitteswell on loan to Armstrong Siddeley Motors Ltd for trials of their P.181 free-shaft turboprop, but this in turn was cancelled a year later when the firm merged with Bristol Aero-Engines Ltd to become Bristol Siddeley Engines Ltd, so VX231 was scrapped at Bitteswell in October 1959.

H.P.R.1 Marathon I

(Four D.H. Gipsy Queen 70-3 or 70-4)

Span 65 ft (19·84 m); length 52 ft 3 in (15·93 m); wing area 498 sq ft (46·4 m²). Empty weight 11,688 lb (5,300 kg); maximum weight 18,250 lb (8,280 kg). Speed 232 mph (373 km/h); range 935 miles (1,500 km); ceiling 18,000 ft (5,570 m). Crew two. Passengers eighteen.

H.P.R.1 Marathon T.11

As for Marathon I except Empty weight 13,358 lb (6,160 kg). Range 1,100 miles (1,770 km); ceiling 15,000 ft (4,640 m). Crew two, Instructor one, Pupils two.

H.P.R.5 (ex M.69 Marathon II)

(Two Alvis Leonides Major)

Dimensions as for Marathon I. No other data available.

H.P.R.5 at Baginton in January 1956. (*Alvis*)

First H.P.R.2, WE496, with original canopy at Woodley in May 1950.

Handley Page (Reading) Basic Trainer (H.P.R.2)

With their intensive redesign of the Marathon for production completed by the end of 1948, Eddie Gray's design team at Reading looked around for a new project of suitable size and were helped in their search by 'Bush' Bandidt. Miles Aircraft Ltd had earlier sketched out a three-seat trainer in response to specification T.23/43, but had decided not to compete with Percival Aircraft Ltd, whose design was adopted by the RAF in 1946 as the Prentice. This had not been entirely successful in service and in August 1948 the Air Staff issued OR 257 for 'a single-engined two-seater cabin type basic trainer landplane for world-wide use'. Further details were set out in specification T.16/48, which was issued to the industry in November, and after a visit to the Air Ministry Bandidt recommended on 8 December to Sir Frederick that Gray's team should prepare a design, although tenders had not yet been invited. The trainer was to seat instructor and pupil side by side under a sliding canopy capable of being opened under all flight conditions and of being jettisoned in emergency; the undercarriage was to be fixed, but a dummy lever and lights were required to simulate retraction. A radial engine was recommended because of the width of the cockpit, but in any case engine cooling was to be suitable for long periods of ground running during 'circuits and bumps'; the structure was to be robust, easily maintained by semi-skilled personnel, with repair by easy replacement, and the powerplant was to have a time between overhauls of 800 hours and to be easily changed in 12 man-hours. The maximum speed was to be at least 110 kt, stalling speed 55 kt and endurance at least 2 hr and preferably 3 hr; the design was to be fully aerobatic (including the battery) and to provide adequate stall warning, preferably by natural buffeting.

Bandidt considered the Armstrong Siddeley Cheetah XV engine to be the best choice because it was already approved for 800 hours between overhauls, but likely alternatives were the D.H. Gipsy Queen 71 and the Alvis Leonides; John Parkes of Alvis Motors Ltd visited Gray to press the claims of his engine and told him that Percival and Fairey were also considering tenders to T.16/48. The mock-up was first made to suit a Gipsy Queen 71, since this had been the Percival Prentice's engine, but was changed after 12 March, 1949, when Handley Page (Reading) Ltd tendered for two prototypes with Cheetah 17s. Parkes then pressed for a third prototype to be built as a private venture to test the Leonides, but Sir Frederick declined to build it without official contract cover; nevertheless he urged Alvis Motors Ltd to design a suitable powerplant interchangeable with the Cheetah installation and amended the tender to this effect by a letter on 27 May. An advisory design conference was held at Thames House on 20 June at which the possible third prototype was discussed and on 19 July, 1949, the amended tender was accepted by contract No.6/Acft/4903/C.B.9(a) for the design and supply of three H.P.R.2 aircraft at a total fixed price of £103,100 ex works; the first was to be delivered eleven months from date of contract, the second two months later and the third one month after the second. A wind-tunnel model was ordered from Blackburn & General Aircraft Ltd and manufacture of the first two prototypes, WE496 and WE505, commenced at Woodley on 8 August, 1949. The first was completed and weighed on 23 April, 1950, and D. J. Broomfield began taxying tests there on 1 May. After a preliminary run at 4,000 lb, fuel was loaded up to 55 gallons, bringing the all-up weight to 4,270 lb for final taxying and the first hop. The first run, to 55 kt IAS with canopy closed, was satisfactory except for a slight swing to starboard. For the first hop, the canopy was again closed and the flaps were lowered to 30 degrees, but just as the trainer became airborne the canopy broke loose and flew off, fortunately missing the fin and rudder. Broomfield completed

WE496 with tall fin for spinning trials at Farnborough in September 1950.

Second H.P.R.2, WE505, with Leonides at the SBAC display in September 1950. (*Flight*)

a normal circuit at 500 ft, finding the controls very heavy, with insufficient elevator power and trim available for a normal three-point landing, but landed into wind with a 'wheeler'. The canopy catch was improved and two days later Sir Frederick invited selected RAF pilots to fly the H.P.R.2 at Woodley and listened to their spontaneous comments. They had already had an opportunity of flying the rival Percival P.56 prototype, which they liked for its easy flick-roll and ability to land itself; by comparison, the H.P.R.2 landed 'like a brick' and had to be deliberately flown, but this might be a factor in making it 'less forgiving' and therefore a better trainer. Sir Frederick replied that Percival Aircraft had had the advantage of experience with the Prentice, but Handley Page were glad not to have gained the Prentice's reputation; a proposal to provide a quickly interchangeable Leonides powerplant was well received and this would save waiting for the third prototype, which was then in abeyance and later cancelled.

The original Cheetah 17 engine failed a few days later and a second one was installed, which developed less power than the first, when Hugh Kendall resumed flying between 9 and 18 May. Meanwhile a model of the canopy was 'tufted' in the Reading wind-tunnel and its lines were refined until a less turbulent flow was obtained; at the same time the undercarriage legs were faired. The canopy structure was redesigned by deleting the original crash arch and substituting a plain tripod with a disc at its apex, at the same time making the rear part of the canopy a fixture. This enhanced both the appearance and the performance of WE496, and WE505 was completed to the same standard. In June two new fins were made for WE496, one having the tip chord reduced by six inches and the other by nine inches; the original area was preserved by extending the height in each case and the wing dihedral also was increased by 2 degrees. The purpose of these changes was to overcome the difficulty reported by Kendall in

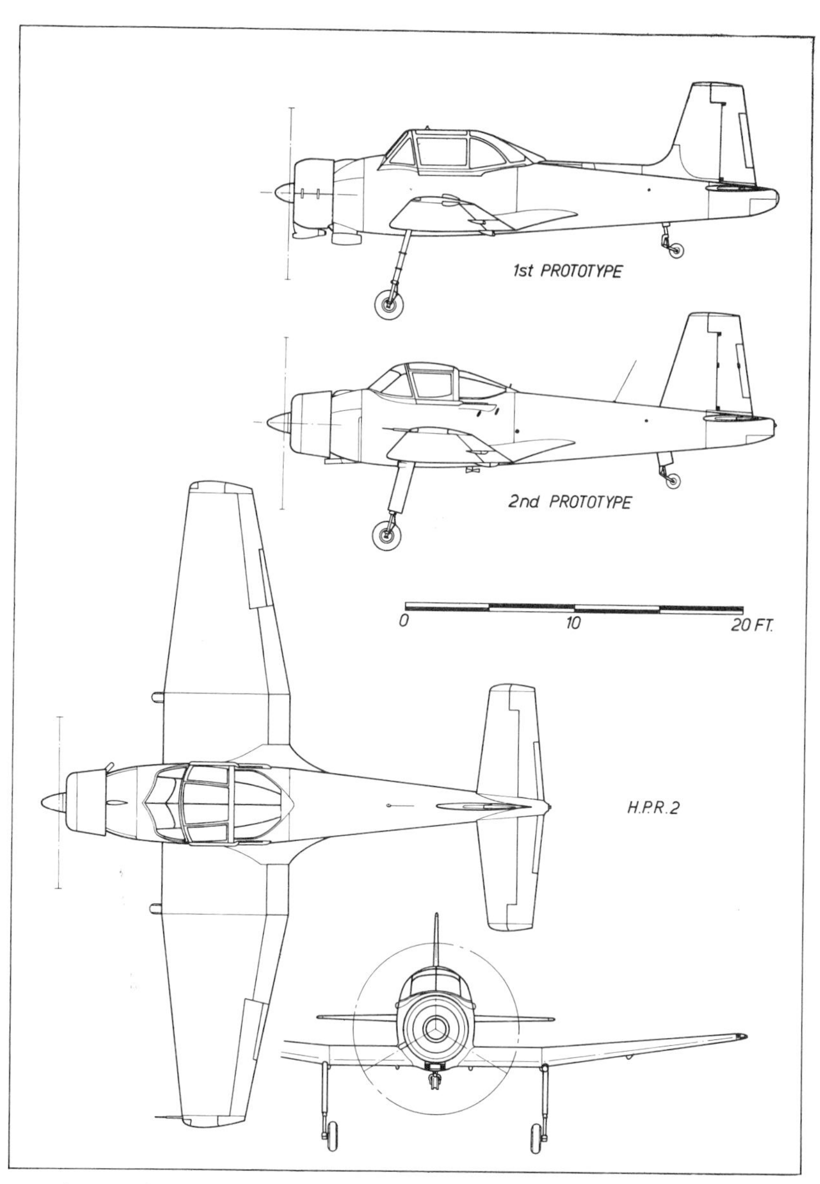

entering a spin and in obtaining a stall warning buffet; cylinder cooling was also marginal. Next, wing-tip auto-slats were installed and Kendall checked them out in a flight on 18 September before delivering WE496 to RAE Farnborough for spinning trials with the two modified fins. Meanwhile WE505 had been flown at the 1950 SBAC show with the Alvis Leonides, which improved overall performance slightly, although it was not yet acceptable to RAF Training Command on the score of reliability

WE505 with Cheetah 18 as submitted for test at Boscombe Down on 30 October, 1950.

and maintenance. On its return WE505 was fitted with a new Cheetah 18; Hazelden and Kendall flew it together on 13, 15 and 17 October, finding control effectiveness and stability satisfactory but stick-force rather high in a dive and much too high in a baulked landing; the rudder also was too heavy and taxying was difficult because of a strong tendency to swing. On 18 October comprehensive handling trials were flown on WE505 by A. E. Gunn, who was Boulton-Paul's chief test pilot, with long experience of the larger, but otherwise similar, Balliol trainer; finally WE505 was delivered to Boscombe Down for official trials on 30 October, 1950. These confirmed the A & AEE's recommendation to order the Percival P.56 into production as the Provost, and MoS declared both H.P.R.2s surplus to their requirements and returned them to Woodley with a request for all embodiment loan items, including the Cheetah engines, to be sent back to RAF Stores. To this Sir Frederick replied with an equally peremptory request for a 'submission for test' payment of £52,000 (half the contract price) to which he claimed the company was entitled, but the archives do not record whether he obtained it.

H.P.R.2

(Armstrong Siddeley Cheetah 18)

Span 37 ft (11·29 m); length 29 ft 11 in (9·14 m); wing area 223 sq ft (20·7 m²). Maximum weight 4,350 lb (1,970 kg). Speed 175 mph (282 km/h); endurance 2·84 hr. With Alvis Leonides engine: Length 30 ft 5 in (9·16 m). Maximum weight 4,363 lb (1,980 kg). Speed 190 mph (303 km/h).

Victor (H.P.80) and its Derivatives (H.P.87, 88, 93, 96, 97, 98, 101, 104, 111, 114 and 123)

As the war in Europe neared its end in the spring of 1945, British aircraft designers were already preparing to extend the application of jet propulsion from fighters, such as the Gloster Meteor and de Havilland Vampire, to bombers, and specification B.3/45 had just been issued to define a twin-engined jet-propelled day bomber to succeed the de Havilland Mosquito. Four prototypes of English Electric's successful tender to B.3/45 were ordered on 7 January, 1946, as the Canberra, its Rolls-Royce AJ.65 turbojets being concurrently named Avons. Confident that a similar replacement for the Avro Lincoln heavy bomber would be needed in five to six years' time, Sir Frederick Handley Page issued on 14 June, 1945, a private and confidential memorandum addressed to R. S. Stafford, Frank Radcliffe and G. H. Lee; in this he requested an immediate investigation of two classes of bomber, one of 100,000 lb all-up weight with four turbojets of the size of the AJ.65 (or two of twice that size), the other a 60,000 lb bomber with two AJ.65s; he suggested that both types should have their wings swept back 40 degrees, making use of the experience gained with the small tailless H.P.75 monoplane. In the course of the next few months Lee was able to visit Germany as a member of an Allied technical intelligence mission and there he learned of progress made during the war, notably by Arado, in the application of swept wings as a means of delaying the onset of compressibility effects near the speed of sound.

Victor prototype WB771 in silver finish early in 1953.

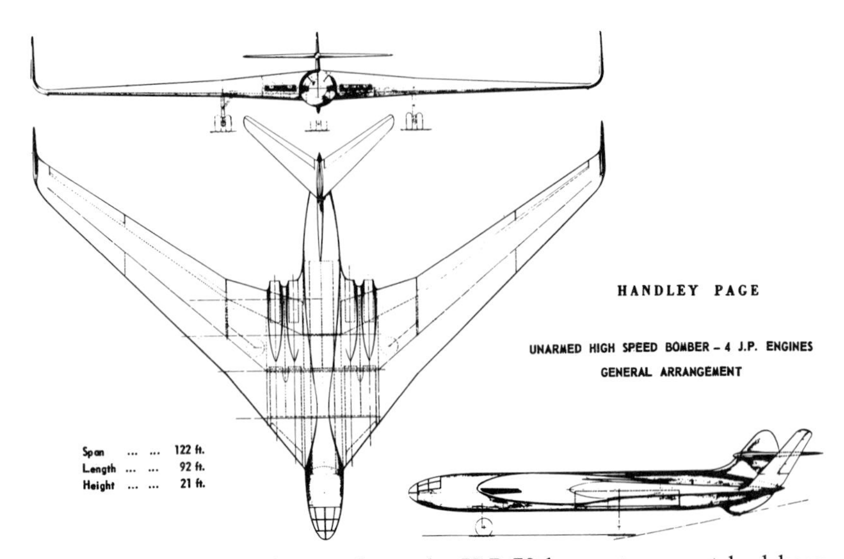

In January 1946, after work on the H.P.72 heavy transport had been abandoned, the designations H.P.72A and H.P.75A were used as a cover for Lee's investigations into a possible jet-propelled high-speed bomber of 90,000 lb all-up weight, having an alternative transport role and powered by four Avons. The H.P.75A with front rider-plane was quickly ruled out in favour of the H.P.72A with 45-degree swept wings and wing-tip rudders, having a small swept tailplane and elevators to balance nose-down pitching moments caused by either flap-lowering at low speed or compressibility (centre of pressure rear shift) at high speed. With no operational requirement yet promulgated by the Air Staff to guide him, Godfrey Lee put forward an inspired proposal, on 25 February, 1946, for a design of 2,100 sq ft area, 122 ft span, aspect ratio 7 and wing loading 43 lb/sq ft, to carry a 10,000 lb bomb load at 520 knots true air speed over a still air range of 5,000 statute miles; the wing root thickness/chord ratio was to be 16 per cent, with a 9 ft diameter body accommodating a crew of four in a pressurised nose compartment. Avon engines were somewhat larger than the ideal size for this aircraft and Lee suggested scaling them down to 5,600 lb. Two days later, Stafford approved this proposal and instructed C. F. Joy, recently appointed chief draughtsman, to prepare a brochure for submission to the Principal Director of Technical Development (Stuart Scott-Hall) by the end of March; this brochure was to demonstrate the project's effectiveness as a bomber and to include additional studies in the freighter and military or civil passenger transport roles; at this stage the new type number H.P.80 was allotted. The brochure was completed and issued to the Director of Operational Requirements (Grp Capt Silyn-Roberts), and his deputy, Grp Capt Cooper, visited Cricklewood on 19 July to discuss the third draft (issued in June 1946) of Air Staff requirements for a long-range bomber mainly derived from the firm's proposal, but containing several operational innovations. These included a visual bombing station, as an insurance against delay in availability of radar bomb-sights, an engineer's station unless the engine controls could be simplified, an electronic countermeasures operator in a separate pressure cabin near the tail, reached by a tunnel from the main cabin, and, if possible, a jettisonable main pressure cabin. A bomb load of 30,000 lb was to be carried with normal tanks full, but bomb-bay tanks were permissible to achieve maximum range with a bomb load of 10,000 lb.

On 2 November members of the TRE staff visited Cricklewood to discuss radar equipment, the main feature of which was the H_2S Mark 9 scanner, 6 ft long and rotating on a vertical axis within a large radome below the flight deck floor; in addition were Gee and Rebecca Mk.4 for short-range navigation, IFF and ECM, the latter requiring a tail parabolic scanner of 18-inch diameter facing aft; the estimated total weight of radar equipment was 1,500 lb and all aerials were to be suppressed. TRE initially wanted the H_2S scanner to be pressurised, but this posed such unsurmountable problems that they gave way on this point. A later discussion between Charles Joy and Grp Capt Cooper disclosed that DOR insisted on the crew's cabin being as small as possible to reduce vulnerability, even at the expense of crew comfort, and that the whole pressure cabin must be made as a jettisonable module because the use of ejection seats at 50,000 ft and 500 mph was considered likely to be fatal; the whole cabin would be let down on large parachutes with the crew strapped in 25g seats, falling nose first and relying on collapse of the nose structure to absorb the shock of impact. Two pilots were required and it was agreed that locating the ECM operator aft was impracticable because of the large size of the proposed nuclear weapon, which might be 6 ft in diameter and up to 30 ft long. The Air Staff's intentions were further elucidated by Scott-Hall when he visited Cricklewood on 25 November, 1946; they wished to replace the Avro Lincoln in five years' time with a four-jet bomber capable of delivering a 10,000 lb nuclear weapon at 500 mph from a height of 45,000 ft, the still air range being 3,500 miles; as a later development, the range would have to be increased to 5,000 miles and the operational ceiling to 50,000 ft; these data were being formally promulgated as Air Staff Operational Requirement No.230. Lee estimated the required all-up weight to be 90,000 lb for 3,500 miles using a swept wing, but 121,000 lb with a conventional straight wing; specification B.14/46 had already been issued to define the conventional bomber, for which Short Brothers had been given a prototype contract as an insurance against delays in developing the optimised bomber. A further meeting was held with P/DTD on 14 January, 1947, after the firm had submitted their proposals to meet OR 230; the official view was that both the firm's structure weights and drag estimates were optimistic, so that the design cruising speed would not be realised. DOR now wanted the cruising speed to be raised to 575 mph which meant that the all-up weight also would have to rise to 100,000 lb in order to attain 3,500 miles still-air range, or 120,000 lb for 4,000 miles. Consequently competitive tenders would be called for to meet the revised specification B.35/46, which had been finalised on 1 January, 1947, and was issued with OR 230 in March. In view of the very large wind-tunnel test programme involved, the prototype H.P.80 could not be expected to fly until 1951; apart from exploration of new problems of tip-stall, high-lift sections, stability and various methods of boundary layer control, a firm choice between tailed or tailless types had still to be made. Joy proposed to begin the drawing office programme on 1 October, allowing 21 months to June 1949 for the basic layout and 30 months to March 1950 for completion of the powered flying control system. All drawings for the first prototype as a flying shell would be completed by June 1951 and extra drawings for the fully-equipped prototype would be issued by March 1952, giving first flight target dates for the first prototype of March 1952 as a flying shell and September 1952 fully equipped. It was a stupendous programme for a relatively small design organisation, but not impossible, so the H.P.80 tender was duly submitted, to compete with six others, from Armstrong Whitworth, Bristol, English Electric, A. V. Roe, Shorts and Vickers-Armstrongs. On 28 July, 1947, Sir Frederick received a telephone call from Scott-Hall to say that prototypes were to be ordered of the H.P.80 and Avro 698, subject to confirmation in the high-speed wind-tunnel of test results to prove the theoretical basis of the designs.

The revised H.P.80 design, as tendered, featured four axial-flow Metrovick F.9 turbojets nominally rated at 7,500 lb static thrust, with provision for Avons as alternatives when developed to give the same thrust at the same specific fuel consumption. It retained a circular-section fuselage, now of 9 ft 10 in maximum diameter, and wing-tip fins and rudders, but the wing itself was of novel plan form. Instead of having a constant sweep angle, the inboard third was swept back at 48¼ degrees, the middle third at 37½ degrees and the outboard third at 26¾ degrees (measured at quarter chord); the taper ratio was 3 and the aspect ratio 5, with 14 per cent thickness/chord ratio at the root and 8 per cent at the tip. The span of this so-called 'crescent wing' was 100 ft and area 2,000 sq ft. The all-moving tailplane, swept at 45 degrees, was small at 150 sq ft but was intended only for trimming purposes, lateral and longitudinal manoeuvres being controlled by large elevons occupying the outer halves of the wing trailing edge, with leading-edge slats in front of them, to give a good low-speed stalling characteristics combined with a high critical Mach number. All the flying controls were to be power-operated by two independent all-electric systems with hydraulic servo-actuators adjacent to the surfaces; neither mass-balance nor mechanical feed-back was to be provided. The landing gear comprised steerable twin nosewheels and large inward-retracting single mainwheels having a track of 43 ft 2 in. The normal fuel capacity was 3,092 gallons contained in two 310-gallon tanks in the wing centre-section and five tanks in each wing; four auxiliary tanks of 310 gallons each could be installed in the fuselage above the bomb bay and all tanks were to be of Marflex lightweight crash-proof construction; additional tanks of up to 1,500 gallons could be carried in the bomb bay for very long range ferrying. A total of 2,000 gallons could be jettisoned from the wing tanks and all tanks were pressurised by a nitrogen purging system to prevent boiling at high altitude; pressure refuelling points were located on both sides of the fuselage. The electrical system was similar to that of the Hermes IV, with four engine-driven 30 kVA alternators providing 120 V direct current via rectifiers, with a secondary 24 V supply through transformers and rectifiers, together with one 15 kVA alternator driven by an aircraft auxiliary powerplant arranged to run continuously, with remote control from the engineer's station. It was proposed to employ high-pressure pneumatic operation of wheel brakes, landing gear retraction, nosewheel steering, fuel jettisoning and bomb-door actuation, the system being supplied by two engine-driven pumps, with five air storage bottles.

H.P.80 wind-tunnel model in 1947 showing crescent wing with upturned tip-rudders and all-moving slab tailplane.

The crew's pressure cabin was the subject of much investigation; the Air Staff had shown a clear preference for a jettisonable capsule, but the tender design provided ejection for all five crew members—two pilots, two navigator/bomb aimers (taking turns at the H_2S radar plan position indicator) and a radio communications and countermeasures operator; there was also a prone visual bombing station with a gyro-stabilised bomb-sight and optically flat aiming panel in the extreme nose, below the cloud and collision warning radar scanner. The first pilot's seat on the port side was staggered in relation to the second pilot's which was placed slightly aft on the starboard side, each having a full set of dual controls; the two navigator/bomb-aimer/radar operators controlled the navigational and bombing computer from forward facing seats behind the second pilot, while the radio/ECM operator also faced forward in a separate seat on the port side, slightly ahead of the navigators; all the seats were on the same level and lightweight armour-plate shields were proposed to give personal protection from fighter attack from astern. The Air Staff had many criticisms of this layout and clung to their desire for a jettisonable pressure cabin as the best method of safeguarding the crew in emergency. A contract had already been placed on the M.L. Aviation Co Ltd for dynamic separation tests at 210 knots on a 1/30th-scale model of a similar pressure cabin designed for the Short B.14/46 bomber, which were to be performed at the RAE in 1947–48. This programme was to be extended in 1949–50 with 1/15th-scale dynamic models of the Avro and Handley Page B.35/46 cabins, for which a launching catapult was designed by M.L. Aviation and ready for use in March 1949, priority in testing being given to the H.P.80. First tests of the Short capsule showed the need to prevent tumbling after separation, before deploying drogues or parachutes, and folding fins were proposed for the H.P.80 capsule to bring it into a favourable attitude for drogue deployment. In an attempt to meet the Air Staff's criticisms of the flight deck layout, the nose profile was swept up, with each pilot occupying a separate fighter-type blister canopy, giving a 'bug-eye' appearance; later the nose was slightly swept down and a larger windscreen, flush with the fuselage streamline shape, was found to give satisfactory vision for both pilots sitting side by side; finally the cloud and collision warning scanner was deleted from the nose, which was extended to a sharp point to reduce kinetic heating. Structural provision was made in the prototype for separation of the pressure cabin by means of explosive bolts; this would have eventually required more than 600 Breeze-type plug and socket connectors for electric circuits, raising severe problems of weight, space, accessibility and reliability, but the capsule concept was abandoned in 1950 after unsuccessful RAE trials of a $\frac{1}{4}$-scale cabin and fuselage fitted to a 32 ft span M.L. target glider; the electrical installation was then simplified by using in-line crimped connectors instead of plugs and sockets.

The official preliminary design conference was held on 23 December, 1947, when the overall design was approved in principle and no significant new requirements were raised, apart from the question of the jettisonable crew cabin. Close liaison was maintained with RAE Farnborough on structure and equipment weights, low- and high-speed wind-tunnel testing, and aero-elastic problems, taking into account Dietrich Küchemann's concurrent work there on aerofoil design; Lachmann and Lee were particularly concerned with flutter effects on the wing-tip fins and rudders and defended the carefully blended junction curve, although some RAE opinion considered that this would pose a manufacturing difficulty without any aerodynamic advantage over the structurally simpler end-plate; it was also hoped to design an unswept tailplane thin enough to achieve the same critical Mach number as the wing, to avoid the complication of sweep in an all-moving tailplane. The fuselage design was conventional, with frames and stringers stiffening a single skin, but the possible application of sandwich construction to the front fuselage was to be investigated. For the wing, it was hoped to develop a satisfactory form of thick-skin sandwich construction. The crew ejection seats were to be replaced by fixed seats whether or not cabin jettisoning proved to be practicable; the possible advantages of using a tandem landing gear in the fuselage, with wing outriggers, were to be examined and a powered flying model was required, to prove the crescent wing and all-moving tailplane in free flight. In view of the large amount of high-speed wind-tunnel testing needed, Stafford visited the RAE on 12 December, 1947, to discuss with the Director, W. G. A. Perring, the possibility of building at Radlett a Nene-powered transonic wind-tunnel similar to that built at Hucknall by Rolls-Royce Ltd and in due course this was approved. After a visit to the Supermarine design office at Hursley Park, Stafford agreed to use the Attacker fuselage as the basis of a flying test model having H.P.80 wings and tail scaled down to 0·4 full size. On 14 January, 1948, it was decided to delete the wing-tip fins and rudders, to increase the span from 100 ft to 110 ft and to add a central fin and rudder on the fuselage, in spite of a weight penalty of 500 lb, thereby establishing a more conventional shape for the flying model and wind-tunnel models. At the end of February the Supermarine Swift fuselage was substituted for the Attacker because its fuel tanks were compatible with 45 degrees sweep at the wing-root and on 12 March specification E.6/48 was agreed for contract purposes. There was insufficient drawing office capacity at Cricklewood to undertake detail design of the 0·4-scale wing and tail, so it was sub-contracted to General Aircraft Ltd of Feltham, Middlesex, the aircraft being allotted type number H.P.88, in succession to a design study for a towed one-third-scale glider, H.P.87, which had been abandoned. Meanwhile, a four-wheeled bogie main undercarriage, retracting rearwards outboard of the outer turbojets in each inner wing, was found to be 300 lb lighter than the single-wheel design of the tender, thus regaining some of the weight-saving lost by deleting the wing-tip rudders; each wheel had twin tyres to reduce overall depth for stowage in the inner wing, whose chord was slightly increased by straightening the trailing edge and root fillets were then found to be unnecessary. General Aircraft's weight estimates for the H.P.88 were agreed on 26 April and two days later MoS awarded contract No.6/Acft/1875/CB6(a) to build two H.P.80 prototypes, WB771 and WB775, with Metrovick F.9 engines; the first was to fly in May 1952 and the second six months later. During May 1948 tests on sample sandwich panels using Alclad skins bonded to a Dufaylite plastic honeycomb core were so promising that it was decided to make a pair of sandwich wings of laminar section for full-scale flight and structural testing on a Miles Messenger at Woodley, under the designation H.P.93. On 3 June Lachmann, after studying RAE Tech Note Aero 1928, recommended raising the H.P.80 tailplane to the top of the fin, which brought up the question of a suitable junction 'bullet' and Dr Küchemann's advice on its shape was obtained.

In the spring of 1948 production of the Metrovick F.9 turbojet was transferred by MoS to Armstrong Siddeley Motors Ltd at Coventry, with Metropolitan-Vickers retaining control of the first few experimental engines and thereafter remaining available as consultants. About the same time Rolls-Royce Ltd undertook further development of the Napier-designed E.132 by-pass turbojet to specification TE5/48; it was designed initially for 7,500 lb static thrust and, though heavier and larger than the F.9, it had a lower specific fuel consumption and was expected to reach 9,000 lb s.t. early in development; Rolls-Royce redesigned it at Barnoldswick as the RB.80/1 and later it was named Conway. Meanwhile the Coventry version of the F.9 was named Armstrong Siddeley Sapphire and its first runs confirmed that it could be scaled up by 25 per cent to give 9,000 lb s.t. also; it was chosen for production as the powerplant for the H.P.80 in May 1948 and in June construction of one prototype H.P.88, VX330, was authorised. On 1 January, 1948, General Aircraft Ltd merged with Blackburn Aircraft Ltd and Fred Crocombe and his design staff moved from Feltham to Brough, Yorkshire, taking the H.P.88 project with them, so it was Blackburn & General Aircraft Ltd that received the manufacturing contract for VX330, recorded in the Blackburn type list as Y.B.2. VX330's wing plan form reflected that of the H.P.80 in 1949, with the trailing edge straight from root to outer 'kink' and a thinner tip section, which raised the critical Mach number to 0·83. This gave satisfactory stability with Krueger nose flaps, adopted instead of leading-edge slats to avoid transition from laminar to turbulent flow at the slat trailing edge because of the unavoidable discontinuity, where suction had failed to provide a remedy. Later, in 1950, after the H.P.88 wings had been manufactured, the H.P.80's wing-root thickness was modified to increase the critical Mach number to 0·86, but this reduced stability until the outer kink was moved inboard; the final design of the wing had thickness/chord ratios of 16 per cent at the root, 10 per cent at the inner kink, 8 per cent at the outer kink and 6 per cent at the tip. The H.P.88 fuselage was delivered by road from Hursley Park to Brough on 25 February, 1950, being slightly damaged during unloading. With a Nene engine and a tailwheel, it was basically an Attacker fuselage with Swift wing roots, fuel system and instrument layout, designated Supermarine Type 521. By this time the all-moving tailplane and elevons had been discarded from the H.P.80 in favour of normal ailerons and elevators, actuated irreversibly by Hobson electro-hydraulic power controls, as was the rudder, but the H.P.88 retained elevons and 'slab' tailplane.

Construction of the two H.P.80 prototypes began at both Cricklewood and the new experimental shop at Park Street early in 1951, Joy having revised the design office programme to complete WB771 as a flying shell in March 1951 and WB775 fully equipped in September 1951, with first flights following twelve months later. All non-H.P.80 work at Radlett was relegated to Colney Street and manufacture of the ailerons, elevators, rudder and outer flaps was subcontracted to Woodley, to use capacity available there previously reserved for possible production of the H.P.R.2.

With the wing design finalised by September 1950, two transport variants of the H.P.80 bomber were proposed, using the same wings, powerplant and tail units combined with new fuselages. The first of these was the H.P.96 military transport, with the fuselage diameter increased from 10 ft to 11 ft 6 in, the overall length from 100 ft 10 in to 115 ft and the span from 110 ft to 111 ft 6 in. The H.P.96's 4,000 cu ft capacity aft of the wing centre section was arranged in two cabins separated by toilet compartments, and swing-tail loading was proposed for an alternative layout which could provide cargo stowage 40 ft long, 7 ft 6 in wide and 6 ft high. As a passenger transport, 85 troops (25,500 lb payload) could be carried 2,750 nautical miles with Sapphire engines or 3,100 nm with Conways; alternatively, with payload reduced to 40 troops (12,000 lb payload) the range with tanks full was 3,850 miles with Sapphires or 4,550 miles with Conways. The second variant was a civil airliner, H.P.97, having a span of 126 ft including wing-tip tanks, overall length of 126 ft 3 in and a double-bubble fuselage 11 ft wide and 15 ft 6 in high. The all-up weight of the H.P.96 was estimated at 136,000 lb and of the H.P.97 at 190,000 lb; the latter was held in abeyance until enough flight experience had been obtained with the H.P.80 to support serious promotion to airline operators; in both projects eight-wheeled bogies were proposed for the main undercarriage.

In June 1951 the H.P.88 was completed at Brough, with a 5,100 lb s.t. Rolls-Royce Nene 3 turbojet installed; it retained the Krueger nose flaps, elevons and all-moving tailplane of the 1948 H.P.80 design, also large Fowler trailing-edge flaps, and was expected to attain Mach 0·9 in level flight. After satisfactory taxying trials at Brough by Blackburn's chief test pilot, G. R. I. Parker, it was finished overall in glossy royal blue and taken to the long runway at Carnaby for a first flight of 5 minutes' duration on 21 June, 1951. After necessary adjustments this was repeated on 7 July, when Parker reported that the tailplane was over-sensitive to very small stick movements; a 'bump' set the aircraft pitching and any attempt to correct this made it worse and set up low amplitude porpoising, which could be

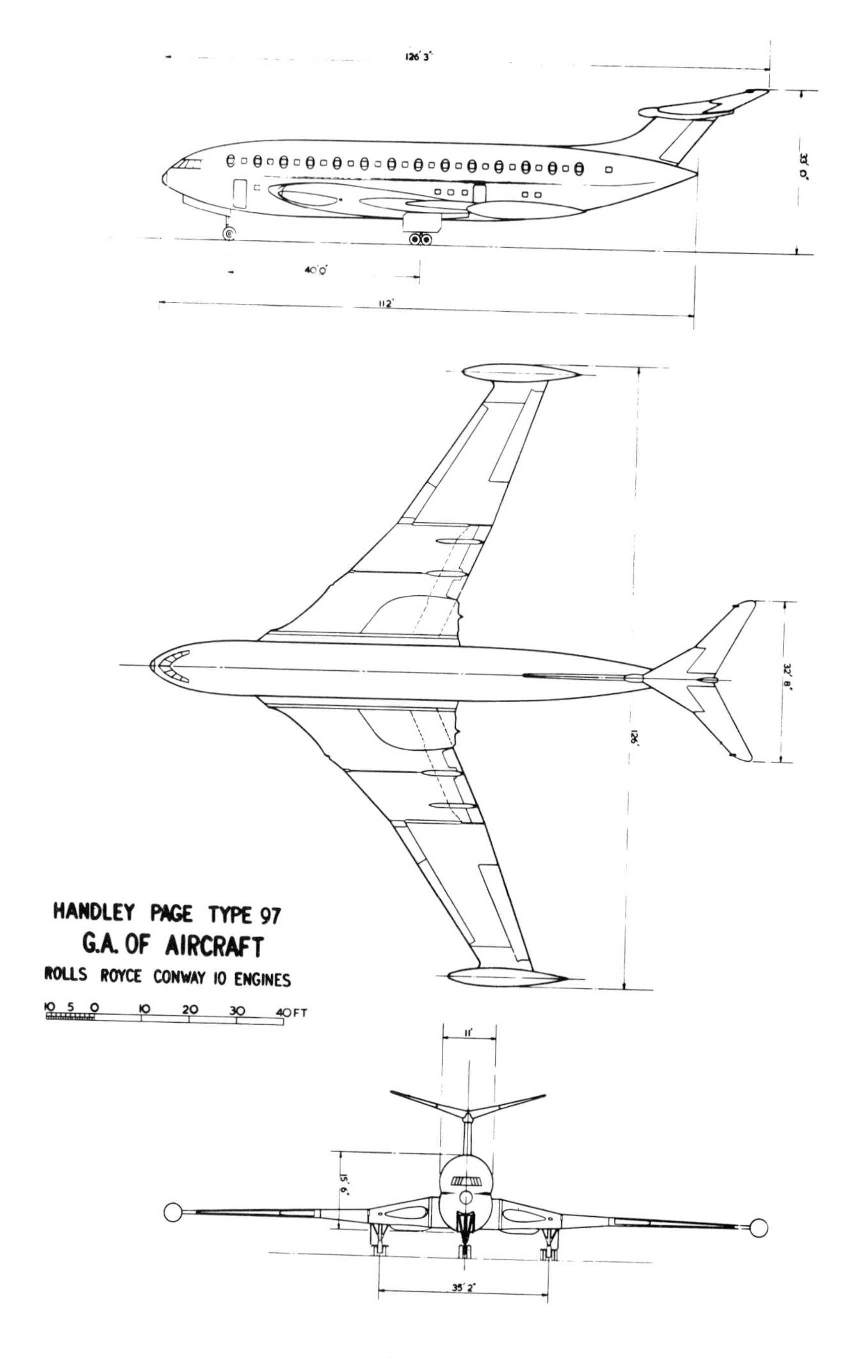
126' 3"
33' 0"
40' 0"
112'
32' 8"
126'
HANDLEY PAGE TYPE 97
G.A. OF AIRCRAFT
ROLLS ROYCE CONWAY 10 ENGINES
10 5 0 10 20 30 40 FT
11'
15' 6"
35' 2"

Royal blue H.P.88 at Carnaby in June 1951 with Krueger nose-flaps, elevons, Fowler flaps and slab tailplane. (*Blackburn & General*)

quickly damped out by holding the stick fixed. After two more flights he had established that longitudinal sensitivity became serious at 230 kt and on 25 July, in the fifth sortie, the H.P.88 became difficult to control in pitch at 255 kt and worse as speed increased. Angle strips were then added progressively to the tailplane trailing edge, first to the upper surface, then to the lower, until on the seventeenth sortie on 5 August it was possible to fly steadily up to 450 kt, the aircraft pitching for two cycles before the porpoising was damped out by steady backward pressure on the stick; 'chasing' the oscillation had to be avoided. Next day Duggie Broomfield from Radlett confirmed Parker's assessment after a searching test flight and accepted the H.P.88 for ferrying to Stansted, Essex, on its twenty-seventh flight, clearance having been obtained for progressive increases from 450 kt to 550 kt EAS, subject to a limiting Mach number of 0·85. Broomfield was scheduled to fly the H.P.88 at the SBAC show and took off at Stansted on 26 August for a series of airspeed calibration flights; after ten minutes' flying he had begun the first straight run at 300 ft when the H.P.88 broke up in the air about halfway along the runway; Broomfield ejected too late and was found dead in the ejection seat which was thrown ahead of the main debris. All the evidence pointed to structural failure through overstress and this was the Accident Investigation Branch's verdict, but MacRostie disagreed vehemently and maintained that very high accelerations could have arisen from instability in the hydraulic flying control system. The H.P.88's total flying time was 14 hours, but its loss had relatively little effect on the progress of the H.P.80, whose two prototypes

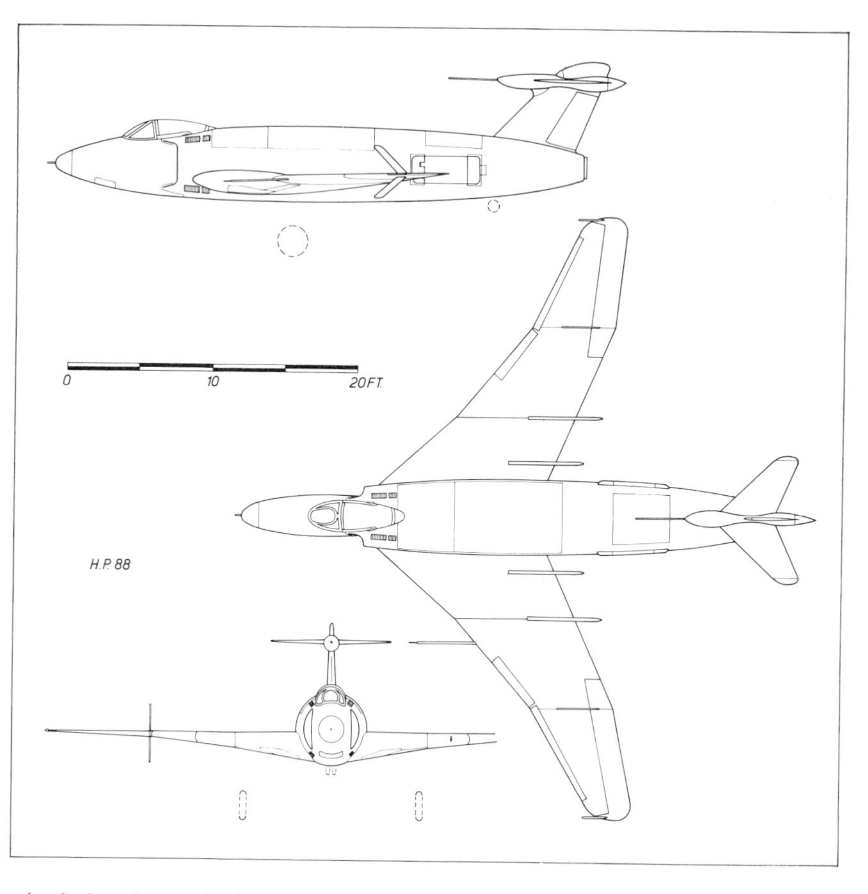

had already reached a later stage of development and were well-advanced in assembly at Park Street.

In November 1951 a target-marker (pathfinder) variant of the H.P.80 was proposed to the Air Staff as H.P.98; structurally this was identical with the H.P.80, retaining the same bomb bay and doors, and could revert to the bombing role at short notice, but was armed with remotely-controlled radar-sighted tail guns for low-altitude operation and powered by Rolls-Royce Conway 3s rated at 11,500 lb s.t. plus 20 per cent with water injection for take-off and limited duration acceleration; alternatively, Bristol Olympus engines could be installed. The Air Staff declined the H.P.98 in favour of the Vickers Valiant B.2, of which one prototype was ordered. The Valiant B.1 could not attain the range required by specification B.35/46 but had a nearly equal performance in other respects, so was more promising than the Short SA.4 as an interim nuclear jet bomber, and twenty-five production Valiants had been ordered in April 1951, to specification B.9/48, as the first of what Sir Winston Churchill named the 'V-Bombers'. The Avro 698 had been accepted as meeting B.35/46 in November 1947 and was six months in advance of the H.P.80;

due to fly early in 1952, it had been named Vulcan B.1. Meanwhile the RAF's elderly Lincolns, reinforced by Boeing B-29s on loan from the USAF, remained a somewhat fragile bulwark against the threat of attack from beyond the Iron Curtain and actual warfare in Korea. In June 1952, before the prototype Vulcan had flown, production orders were given for initial batches of twenty-five each of both the Vulcan and the H.P.80; the latter received the official name Victor B.1—a happy choice much appreciated by Gustav Victor Lachmann. The first prototype, WB771, had been completed at Cricklewood and on 24 May was ready for transport by road to Boscombe Down, where MoS had made a hangar available as a flight test base adjacent to a 10,000 ft long runway with ample overshoot.

A team of sixty Park Street men was detailed to reassemble the prototype at Boscombe Down, fourteen of them, including MacRostie in charge, travelling with the convoy. The route from Radlett to Boscombe Down was carefully surveyed, in seven journeys, to study all points where the fuselage might have marginal clearance and two critical T-junctions had to be temporarily bypassed with the aid of bulldozers. The fuselage was mounted tail-first on a powerful tractor to form an articulated trailer supported by a reinforced London Transport bus axle; to conceal its identity, it was camouflaged with white canvas sheeting, on which was painted the purported ship's name *GELEYPANDHY-SOUTHAMPTON*, the sign-writer's error in substituting an extra *Y* for the final *A* serving to confuse those who might otherwise have solved the anagram. By coincidence, the towing vehicle's registration number was OMV 80; it was manned by the company's veteran driver J. Wheeler, with transport manager Gardner as mate. Leaving Radlett one evening, with a rest stop near the Great West Road, the convoy continued along A30 to reach Andover after dawn, only to find one of the T-junction by-pass cuttings occupied by the bulldozer which had been digging it; it resisted all attempts to start its engine, so the track had to be widened with spades to allow the load to edge past. It had been hoped to fly WB771 in time to appear at the SBAC show alongside the Vulcan prototype, but this target was frustrated by the discovery after reassembly that the centre of gravity was well outside the permitted aft limit and could only be compensated by ballasting the empty radar scanner bay with half a ton of scrap iron plates, bolted up under the flight-deck pressure floor. The second prototype had to be similarly ballasted, as it was too far advanced to incorporate the permanent remedy of lengthening the forward fuselage by 40 inches applied to production Victors during manufacture. A further lengthy hold-up occurred after fire broke out in the hydraulic system in the rear fuselage during a functioning test; three fitters working inside were burned by flaming hydraulic fluid while escaping and one of them, electrician Eddie Eyles, died in hospital sixteen days later.

Hazelden had spent many flying hours since November 1950 learning to handle the Metrovick Sapphires installed in place of the two outboard Hercules in the second Hastings prototype, TE583, which on occasion he flew at 170 kt on the power of one Sapphire alone; he also flew a Sapphire-engined Canberra 2 to gain high-speed engine handling experience, but had been deprived of the possible lessons to be learnt from the H.P.88. A week before Christmas he taxied WB771 for the first time, from the hangar to the compass-swinging base, and found that it handled well in spite of the gale blowing that day. Two days later he began fast taxying on the main runway, but did not attempt to lift off because heavy rain restricted visibility. On Christmas Eve the sky was clear at last and the wind had dropped to a light breeze straight along the runway, with visibility up to twenty miles, so Hazelden and his flight test observer Ian Bennett went aboard soon after midday for an uneventful maiden flight of 17 minutes, making a trial approach and overshoot before coming in to land, to test the ground effect of the combination of swept wing and high tail. Handling trials continued at Boscombe Down for two months, while the Radlett runway was being extended northwards towards Napsbury to make it suitable for flight testing of production Victors. On the fourth flight, on 9 February, 1953, during which several landing gear extensions and retractions had been made to measure buffeting, all sixteen tyres on the mainwheels burst after touch-down; this was found to be due to an arrangement for interlocking the parking brake and retraction controls in order to check wheelspin during retraction, which was forthwith altered to prevent a recurrence. Towards the end of its stay at Boscombe Down, WB771 visited Cricklewood and Radlett to show off its paces to its builders and on 25 February Hazelden flew it away from its temporary Wiltshire quarters to land on the new concrete of its permanent base at Park Street. In April disaster was narrowly averted when the port bogie skipped and jammed in the vertical position, but Hazelden made a successful 'tip-toe' landing on the four rear tyres without damage; after cameras had been temporarily installed under the belly to record the undercarriage reaction at touchdown, the bogies were fitted with rotation dampers. At the same time, small Perspex rain deflectors were fitted to the windscreen to improve visibility for take-off in wet weather.

Although briefly glimpsed from the RAeS Garden Party in June, the Victor first appeared in public during the Queen's Coronation Review fly-past at Odiham on 15 July, 1953. A week later, at the official opening of the new Park Street Test House and transonic wind-tunnel on 21 July, Hazelden flew WB771 with Air Chief Marshal Sir John Baker, Chief of the Air Staff, on board in a temporary 'jump-seat' installed between the two pilots; he was very impressed with the Victor's manoeuvrability, but thought the pilots' view somewhat restricted. At the end of this flight, Hazelden demonstrated the Victor's ability to land itself 'hands off'; this had been predicted by Stafford before the maiden flight and was due to the high tail being out of the wing downwash with flaps down, so that ground effect started the round-out and runway reaction brought the nose level when the throttles were closed. Other privileged passengers during September included the ARB's chief test pilot, Lt-Cmdr D. P. Davies; Lord de l'Isle and Dudley VC, the Air Minister, and his Under Secretary of State the Hon George Ward MP (himself a former Handley Page apprentice); also Whitney Straight and Captain R. M. Alderson of BOAC. For the 1953 SBAC display WB771 was repainted in matt black with a narrow red cheat line, the wings and tail surfaces being silver-grey; incidentally, Hazelden's demonstration at Farnborough was made entirely on three engines, including take-off, because one igniter plug failed at the last moment.

Both prototypes had a sandwich double-skin wing structure which, in refined and lightened form, was adopted for production. Experimental panels made from two stress-bearing skins separated by honeycomb

WB771 taking off at Farnborough in September 1953, showing black fuselage with red cheat line.

material such as Dufaylite had not been successful, because available adhesives were unreliable and made quality control difficult in manufacture and repair. An alternative method was devised by R. H. Sandifer in which accurately contoured outer skins were spot-welded by the Sciacky process, which left minimum indentation of the skin surface, to corrugated sheets forming the core; after X-ray inspection of the spot-welds, the inner flanges were blind-rivetted to inner skins where surface finish was less important; the double-skinned panels thus formed needed no stringers and could be easily rivetted or bolted to wing ribs and fuselage frames. The rectilinear corrugations had to be formed to very close limits and D. C. Robinson, works superintendent, had developed brake presses for single-curved panels and stretch-presses for more complex shapes having double and reverse curvature. Using photo-lofted templates for frequent checks on profile, sandwich panels were quickly manufactured to a high standard of interchangeability; these panels, being self-supporting to an unusual degree, could be joined into sub-assemblies without needing the usual large array of jigs and fixtures. These components, in turn, could be joined up at final erection after fitting out in the well-established split-assembly manner, again with the use of fewer final assembly jigs than normal; moreover a substantial weight saving was gained in addition to the economy in labour resulting from the elimination of thousands of rivets and the holes for them in the outer skin. Apart from many ingenious detail design features, such as the compact skew levers on the control surfaces which converted linear into rotary motion without backlash or friction, the Victor had a Mach-trimmer to compensate shifts of centre of pressure due to compressibility by automatically moving the elevators and later acquired a yaw-damper on the rudder to cancel out the effects of 'dutch-roll' instability at high altitude.

The production specification, B.128P, was discussed and approved at a design conference at Cricklewood on 22 August, 1952, with Air Commodore Silyn-Roberts in the chair. The company had previously tendered Victor developments, for both bombing and photographic-reconnaissance roles, embodying some features of the H.P.98 including the tail-defence guns with radar sighting and remote control; these aircraft would have been structurally strengthened to accept first 9,700 lb s.t.

Sapphire 9s or, later, 11,500 lb s.t. Conway 3s, the respective normal all-up weights being 160,000 lb and 180,000 lb and overload weights 180,000 lb and 210,000 lb. While the internal fuel tankage remained 4,840 gallons in all cases, the Sapphire version would also have carried underwing tanks of 2,000 gallons; the Conway version was to carry larger external tanks of 5,000 gallons. The Air Staff was not yet convinced that Rolls-Royce's estimates for the Conway 3 would be achieved in practice and ruled that the twenty-five production Victors would all be supplied with Sapphire 7s and without tail guns, although the rear fuselage was to be strengthened to accept the alternative tail-cone if needed later. A photographic-reconnaissance conversion kit, comprising ten cameras mounted in a preloaded trolley, was to be installable within one working week and provision was to be made for launching 'Window'. Only the two pilots were to have ejection seats; the three other crew members were to have fixed aft-facing seats with adequate means of parachute escape through the normal entry door, which was to be fitted with a suitable wind-break. The first five production Victors were to be allotted for acceptance and operational trials extending over nine months. The target date for delivery of the first was March 1955, with delivery of eight during the next twelve months and the remaining seventeen by March 1957. To achieve this programme, the Cabinet was being asked to give super-priority for materials in short supply, also capital assistance for extra floor space at Colney Street; to help Victor production to get under way, the existing contract for 150 Canberras was to be reduced to 100, and in the event this was further cut back to 75.

Flight trials of WB771 progressed smoothly and by 15 October, 1953, Hazelden had flown it to 50,000 ft without encountering buffet; next day a true Mach number of 0·83 was reached at 47,000 ft while still accelerating, and on 3 November his assistant test pilot, K. W. Dalton-Golding, reached Mach 0·88 at 47,500 ft and obtained smooth deceleration on extending the rear fuselage dive-brakes, which had had larger strakes added to reduce turbulence. Although he reported poor damping in yaw at high altitude, he considered that compressibility drag-rise had not yet been reached. A few days later Hazelden reached Mach 0·91 at 47,500 ft and noticed a slight nose-down trim change; by the end of 1953, WB771 had logged 50 hours flying time, including demonstrations at the SBAC display and on Battle of Britain Day. Hazelden's only complaints were of a tendency to roll to port after take-off due to insufficient aileron movement, which ought to be increased by a factor of 2 or 3 before sending the Victor for A & AEE trials; also of a noise above Mach 0·75 and 38,000 ft, which he described as varying between a flute-like note and the roar of an Underground train. This elusive phenomenon was traced to air-conditioning ducting under the flight deck floor and proved difficult to cure; the NACA-type flush ramp intakes in the nose were extended by 'nostril' scoops and blanked-off in turn without avail, but the trouble disappeared when small vortex generators or 'turbulators' were fitted in front of the ramp intakes. Reducing approach speed to 115 kt had shortened the landing distance from 50 ft, as Hazelden demonstrated on 14 November, when Grp Capt Broad and BOAC Captains Field and Majendie flew in turn as second pilots. By the end of February 1954 Hazelden was able to report Mach 0·925 at 45,000 ft with no compressibility effects other than an easily held nose-down trim change between

Mach 0·90 and 0·91; steep turns at Mach 0·88 were free from buffet, but there was a satisfactory natural stall warning. Increased aileron rate was needed for take-off and landing in a 25 kt cross-wind and the existing single 13-ft Gregory-Quilter tail arrestor parachute was inadequate, so three of 8 ft each were to be used in future. In November and December successful trials were made with parachutes on the crew's escape hatch to make sure this would lift clear of the tail when jettisoned in an emergency and on 31 December WB771 shed its port inner flap during a test flight; with no apparent increase in drag, the crew were unaware of its loss till this was noticed after landing. At the end of February WB771 had logged 60 hours and was temporarily laid up for a thorough inspection, with alterations to permit the flight envelope to be extended and new operational equipment to be developed. Just before being grounded, the prototype had nearly broken the sound barrier when John Allam had inadvertently reached Mach 0·98 and this had strained the tailplane, causing slight permanent skin buckling. The completed tailplane of WB775 was therefore borrowed, to save time while WB771's own was stripped and rebuilt for incorporation in WB775; WB771's lay-up was expected to occupy three months till the end of May, priority alterations being increased aileron rate and revised throttle controls.

On completion of this work, Hazelden flew WB771 for one and a half hours at 99,000 lb on 14 June and logged 24 hours' flying time during the ensuing month; he began a schedule of airspeed calibration flights at Cranfield, where the College of Aeronautics had facilities for accurate ground speed measurement not then available at Park Street. On 14 July he had to break off these trials to take charge of an important Marathon presentation at Woodley which he could not delegate, so he assigned the Victor flights that day to his deputy, since they were essentially of a routine nature. Dalton-Golding had regrettably been killed earlier in the year during a production test-flight of Canberra WJ622 when its flying controls jammed and it flew at high speed into the railway embankment on the Radlett aerodrome boundary. His replacement, Ronald Ecclestone, latterly an RAE test pilot, had gained experience on the Victor and Hazelden had no doubt of his competence to continue the Cranfield flights during his brief absence at Woodley. Ecclestone, with Ian Bennett, Bruce Heithersay and Albert Cook as crew, had completed several low-altitude passes along the Cranfield runway, but as he began the next, ground observers saw the tailplane part company with the top of the fin, to flutter down on its own, while the Victor, deprived of longitudinal trim, nosed slightly down and exploded on hitting the runway at high speed. All four on board were killed instantly as the aircraft disintegrated into minute fragments of metal in a pall of black smoke. With no direct evidence available of the source of the defect which had caused this catastrophe, the staff of the Park Street Test House under Ken Pratt joined forces with the New Design department in a day-and-night programme of testing and theoretical analysis. On 3 August Stafford, Lee and Sandifer reported to Sir Frederick their findings and recommendations; it appeared that fatigue cracks around bolt holes in the fin had allowed the three bolts securing the tailplane to loosen and shear in quick succession. The cure was to reduce local stress concentration by spreading the load over four bolts and to employ corrugated sandwich construction in production fins. Using

WB771's original tailplane after repair, the second prototype, WB775, was completed as quickly as possible in the same black and silver-grey finish as its predecessor and was allowed by the Resident Technical Officer to make a 57-minute maiden flight on 11 September without its main undercarriage doors, in order to qualify for a fly-over appearance the same afternoon in the SBAC display at Farnborough. While WB775 continued the interrupted contractor's trials at Radlett and Boscombe Down, intensive investigation went on at Park Street into the Victor's flutter characteristics at high subsonic and transonic speeds, using flexible wind-tunnel models of ingenious and novel design which closely reproduced the aero-elastic modes of the full-size aircraft; this work was supervised by C. O. Vernon, who had succeeded Lee as chief aerodynamicist on the latter's appointment as assistant chief designer (aerodynamics), after Stafford's promotion to the Board as technical director; Vernon's assistant specialising in aeroelastic and flutter problems was J. C. A. Baldock, who had analogue computers at his disposal. He confirmed that the corrugated sandwich fin would be safe for all foreseeable conditions, provided it could be reduced in height to avoid flexural resonance, so the fins of production Victors were shortened by 15 inches, the dorsal fillet and equipment-cooling air intake being deleted at the same time. As this was difficult to incorporate in WB775, the latter was grounded in December 1954 for special one-piece skins to be incorporated in the fin; these, being larger than any held in stock by Handley Page, were obtained from Vickers-Armstrongs at Weybridge who had suitable sheets available from Valiant production. WB775 flew again on 1 February to begin trials with the large 'internal roll-up' main bomb bay doors open; some buffeting had been expected in this condition, but this was within acceptable limits until, on 2 March, the flash-bomb compartment doors also were fully opened. Fortunately the Air Staff had already cancelled the requirement for flash-bombs, so these doors were deleted from production aircraft and permanently locked and sealed on WB775. The main bomb bay was fitted with a new collapsible aft bulkhead to reduce buffet still further and this improved the Victor's ditching characteristics with bomb doors open. Contractor's trials completed, WB775 was flown to A & AEE Boscombe Down on 14 March, 1955, and clocked up eight hours in the hands of three Service test pilots during the first week. After a satisfactory night-flying assessment, it went to Orfordness for bombing trials in June; it was considered to provide a good bombing platform with auto-stabilisation, but was tiring to fly for long periods without, although a bombing run in this condition was still possible. The three handling test pilots found that initial over-control was soon corrected by familiarisation and concurred that the Victor 'was easy and pleasing to fly, with trim changes small at all times in all configurations'; Mach 0·95 was reached twice during the trials and the rear fuselage air-brakes were effective throughout the entire range of speed and altitude and free from buffet, the low buffet level with bomb doors open being particularly noted. The stall warning was considered good, with an adequate manoeuvrability stall margin at Mach 0·873 and 47,500 ft, when buffet began at 1¼g and did not build up fast; this could well be exploited by installing more powerful engines and the existing speed restriction should be cleared to a higher Mach number as soon as possible.

This report confirmed MoS predictions into the capability and performance of the production Victor B.1 when extrapolated to take advantage of increases in thrust and all-up weight. At its initial production standard, the Victor B.1 had a normal all-up weight of 160,000 lb and cruising speed of 500 kt; for a maximum altitude over the target of 50,800 ft with a 10,000 lb bomb its still-air range was 4,360 nm, using 95 per cent maximum thrust. Alternatively, range could be increased to 4,850 nm at a reduced height over target of 48,000 ft. Taking off at an overload weight of 190,000 lb, the range was further increased to 6,170 nm with height over target of 50,200 ft. The Victor's bomb bay was nearly twice the size of the Vulcan's and Valiant's, giving greater versatility for shorter ranges with the tanks partly filled. It could carry, as alternative loads to the bulky 10,000 lb nuclear weapon, one 22,000 lb 'Grand Slam', two 12,000 lb 'Tallboys', three 10,000 lb HC bombs, or no fewer than thirty-five 1,000 lb bombs or seventeen 2,000 lb Type S mines; the number of 1,000 lb bombs could be increased to sixty-three if fourteen were carried in each of two under-wing pods, which were schemed but never, in fact, detailed and manufactured for trial. All bomb-loading was done by hydraulic jacks from a fuselage gantry, making pits or ramps unnecessary, and a 10,000 lb bomb could be loaded in only 10 min, while a full internal load (35) of 1,000 lb bombs needed 30 min. For the overload case, take-off distance could be reduced by 800 yd in ISA conditions (or 1,100 yd at 25 deg F above ISA) with the help of two 8,000 lb s.t. de Havilland Spectre rocket units mounted one each side under the wing on the ribs between the two Sapphires and jettisoned by parachutes after take-off. For a weight penalty the standard bomber's range could be increased for ferrying by installing two large 'long-range' tanks in the Victor's main bomb bay. External wing tanks totalling 3,400 gal and feeding the normal system were a further possibility. The crew's cabin was pressurised to maintain a cabin altitude of 8,000 ft while cruising at 47,000 ft, but the cabin altitude would be limited to 25,000 ft for combat, to minimise the effects of enemy action. Standard electronic equipment comprised H_2S with navigation and bombing computer plus radar bombsight; H_2S with NBC plus Doppler navigator, 'Gee', radio compass, radar altimeter and periscopic sextant for navigation; a Mk.10 electronic autopilot and ILS for blind approach and landing. For the alternative photographic-reconnaissance role, fifteen cameras could be installed in crates in the bomb bay after removal of the doors, together with 150 eight-inch photoflashes internally and 110 photoflashes on external carriers for night PR or survey.

The first twenty-five Victor B.1s had been ordered in June 1952 under contract No.6/Acft/8441/CB6(a) and were serialled XA917–XA941, the price per aircraft, less embodiment loan items, being later agreed at £450,000, compared with the total paid for the two prototypes and associated test specimens of £3½ million. There had been a great deal of Treasury pressure on the Air Staff to choose between the Vulcan and the Victor and then to order only one type into production, but the Air Staff insisted on having twenty-five of each type for comprehensive squadron trials, in view of the vital importance of the 'V-Bomber' force in the nuclear age. Favourable A & AEE reports soon led to negotiations for a further batch of Victors and in February 1955 the company submitted priced tenders for either thirty-three or fifty Victors, with proposals for increasing performance with more power and enlarged wing area, although from the production viewpoint it was preferable to continue the run of Victor B.1s. The Air Staff wanted more height over the target as a priority and claimed that this could be obtained initially by using improved Sapphire 9s of 14,000 lb s.t. in conjunction with a span of 115 ft, and later Conways or Olympus in a new centre section giving a total span of 137 ft; these were known as the Phase 2 and Phase 3 development stages, the latter being virtually a new design listed as H.P.104. Stafford looked into various schemes and recommended that Phase 3 could be achieved more quickly by using six Sapphire 9s instead of four Olympus; he considered that four Conways would not give the required ceiling without much more development. The 'Blue Steel' supersonic Stentor rocket-powered nuclear missile was being developed by A. V. Roe & Co for later versions of the Vulcan, and the Victor seemed likely to be able to carry it also; this could be launched at a point 200 miles short of its target, to which it continued by inertial navigation at Mach 1·6; it was expected to be operational soon after 1960.

On 14 June, 1955, Grp Capt Wheeler (D/DOR1) flew WB775 and thought the Phase 3 Victor with Olympus engines might well be superior to the developed Vulcan with the same engines, but that to order fifty immediately would entail too much disruption of the existing Victor B.1 production line. In July WB775 appeared at both the RAE Golden Jubilee Open Day and the Paris Aero Show; next it was fitted with vortex generators along the outer wings, their effectiveness being checked by wool-tufts filmed from a ciné-camera mounted in the tailplane bullet; a single 32-ft G.Q. ring-slot arrestor parachute was also adopted because of frequent failures of the 8-ft chutes used three or four at a time. By 29 August flight tests with these had been cleared and WB775, with 120 hours on its log, appeared once more at Farnborough in the SBAC flying display in September, to the disappointment of those spectators who had hoped to see at least one production Victor. At the SBAC dinner on the eve of the show, Sir Frederick took the opportunity of telling Lord Hives (of Rolls-Royce) that the Victor's predicted ceiling with Conways was not good enough, in spite of its low fuel consumption, and was the chief reason for MoS delay in placing follow-on orders. This theme was taken up by Stafford with AVM Satterley (ACAS/OR) in a meeting on 29 September: A & AEE pilots had flown WB775 to 50,950 ft and at Mach 0·95; at Radlett the Victor's buffet boundary had been still further improved as the result of some wind-tunnel testing which had been confirmed by a searching programme of flight-trials by the company; Stafford and the RAE agreed that the existing airframe only needed more thrust in order to fly higher. The respective merits of the Conway and Olympus were discussed, but the Air Staff still had reservations about Rolls-Royce's latest claims for the Conway and preferred the Victor Phase 3 with either four Olympus or six Sapphire 9s, which, as Stafford pointed out, was a new aircraft from the production angle, with a drastically revised centre-section. Stafford then proposed an intermediate Victor development, Phase 2A, having Conways in a minimally modified wing of 120 ft span and a normal all-up weight of 170,000 lb for the next production batch, with Phase 3 to follow later if the Conway achieved its promised performance; if the Conway failed, it could be replaced retrospectively in Phase 2A by Olympus, but Conways could not replace Sapphires in Phase 2. In October it was agreed to supply the first eight of the second batch as Victor B.1s with Sapphire 7s and the next twenty-five as Phase 2 with Sapphire 9s; this was confirmed in February 1956 by amendment to contract No.6/Acft/11303/CB6(a) for thirty-three Victors already ordered in May 1955 as XH587–XH594, XH613–XH621, XH645–XH651 and XH667–XH675, at the reduced price of £244,000 each.

The first production Victor B.1 XA917 was first flown at Radlett on 1 February, 1956, and was allotted to Park Street for development trials, starting with the deicing system. Then on 9 February Stafford discovered, while visiting Air Commodore Rutter, that the Ministry of Defence had decided to cancel further Sapphire development, including all Sapphire 9 production, and to order Conways instead. By this time Victor B.1s were beginning to emerge from the Colney Street assembly line at fairly short intervals and WB775 completed satisfactory bombing trials with the 'large store' in April, with 180 hours on its log. XA918 flew on 21 March and began flight flutter tests at Park Street, but XA919 was reserved as the 'conference airframe' and was towed to Park Street on 11 April; it did not fly till 13 March, 1957. When a new extension, 675 ft long by 150 ft wide, to the Colney Street assembly hall was officially opened on 26 March by the Minister of Supply, Reginald Maudling, two more Victors, XA920 and XA921, had joined the first three. Four were finished in standard RAF lightweight aluminium, but XA921 was all-white with standard red and blue national marks, but retaining black serial numbers on the fuselage sides and under the wing; this was a new anti-flash scheme intended to reflect the intense heat-flash radiated from a nuclear explosion; in a later high-reflectivity scheme the serials also were pale blue. XA921 was first flown on 20 June and went a month later to Marham, where it was a static exhibit on 23 July for the Queen's Review of Bomber Command, when the massed formation fly-past included three Victors and three Vulcans

Eleventh production Victor B.1, XA927, in anti-flash white finish in December 1956.

following eighteen Valiants and seventy-two Canberras. XA920, having flown on 12 May, commenced handling trials at Boscombe Down in mid-November and the tenth Victor B.1 to fly was XA927 on 29 December, 1956. Meanwhile the prototype WB775 undertook various equipment trials at Boscombe Down, including the photographic-reconnaissance conversion, being repainted cerulean blue all over and appearing thus at the 1955 SABC show. The first production Victor, XA917, appeared, at last, in the 1956 show. Early in 1957 a faster and higher-flying Victor, Phase 4, was discussed with DOR, but turned down because, although capable of transonic level flight, it was unable to carry a missile equivalent to 'Blue Steel'. In March 1956, minor modifications to the Sapphire 7 had enabled it to clear a new type test to 11,000 lb s.t. and in November the Air Staff decided to continue Victor B.1 production through the first twenty-five of the second contract up to XH667 inclusive, with the last eight, XH668–XH675, being delivered to Phase 2A standard as Victor B.2s with

WB775 in cerulean blue finish at the SBAC display at Farnborough in 1955. (*Flight*)

Rolls-Royce Conway Co.11 by-pass engines of 17,250 lb s.t. To avoid the cost and delay of introducing new centre-section assembly jigs at Colney Street, the Victor B.2 retained the existing engine-bay rib pitch with the air intakes deepened, but not widened, to cope with a future mass flow for 20,000 lb s.t. The centre-section span was increased by 3 ft by the insertion of 18 inch stubs at the roots; the port stub housed a Freon unit for cooling additional ECM equipment, while the starboard stub accommodated a Blackburn-Turboméca Artouste turbine auxiliary powerplant made necessary for engine starting and low-altitude emergency power supply by the redesign of the electrical system for constant-frequency a.c. generation; for high-altitude emergency generation, two Rotax ram-air turbo-alternators were installed in the rear fuselage and had retractable intake scoops forward of the fin root. The wing-tips were extended by 3 ft 6 in each, the outer ends of the ailerons being inset. The fuel system was revised and all equipment was improved to ensure reliable functioning at 65,000 ft. Uprating the Sapphire 7 to 11,000 lb s.t. had cleared the Victor B.1 for 185,000 lb normal all-up weight and 205,000 lb overload with wing drop-tanks fitted. The Victor B.2's normal all-up weight was the same, but overload was 200,000 lb. In the course of redesign for the B.2 type record, the earlier zinc-bearing forging alloys D.T.D.687 and 683 were deleted in favour of zinc-free L.73 and L.65 to eliminate the risk of stress-corrosion fatigue cracks, particularly in the centre-plane/outer wing butt joint forgings, known as 'pipe-joints' by analogy with the bolted flanges of high-pressure steam and hydraulic pipes. Tests on these components three years previously had shown that a permanent short-grain stress-level above 15 tons/sq in caused failure in D.T.D.687 in under 70 days; anodising had no effect, but application of lanoline prolonged fatigue life indefinitely and had been used in manufacture; the untreated pipe-joints of the two prototypes had been replaced early in 1954. The Victor B.2 had provision for optional installation of the 'Blue Steel' missile and two de Havilland Spectre rocket boosters for take-off at overload weight.

A follow-on contract for a further eighteen Victors to the then undefined Phase 2A standard had been awarded in January 1956, but excluded specific cover for a Victor B.2 prototype; XH668 was therefore brought forward on the production line and transferred to Park Street at the earliest possible stage. Rolls-Royce Ltd supplied two development Conways for ground-running trials in a rig built at Park Street from a Victor B.1 engine bay; during the first runs in May 1957 the Conways overheated and surged because the existing Sapphire intakes were too small and, in spite of intake area enlargement by deepening (since the width was limited by rib pitch) this trouble recurred throughout the two years before XH668 itself began engine running. Meanwhile new Victor B.1s were coming off the Colney Street line at a steady rate and in December 1956 the Bomber Command training unit, No.232 Operational Conversion Unit at Gaydon, disbanded its 'A' Squadron to allow its instructors and ground crews to attend training courses at Radlett on Victor handling and maintenance. During a routine test flight in XA917 on 1 June, 1957, John Allam inadvertently exceeded Mach 1·0 in a shallow dive at 40,000 ft, the double sonic bang being heard over a wide area from Banbury to Watford; at that date the Victor was the largest aircraft to have exceeded the speed of sound and flight test observer Paul Langston, in the navigator's station, gained the distinction of being the first man to break the sound barrier backwards. No.232 OCU's 'A' Squadron reformed on 28 November, 1957, the fifteenth production Victor B.1, XA931, being delivered from Radlett to Gaydon that day, quickly followed by XA932–XA934 and, a little later, XA926. Early in 1958, XA923–XA925 were equipped at Park Street with 'Yellow Aster' reconnaissance radar and were attached to No.232 OCU for training Valiant aircrew from No.543 Squadron at Wyton, and in April these three moved to Wyton to become the Radar Reconnaissance Flight, to which was later added XA935. From June to August 'A' Squadron flew seven Victors for 1,000 hours of intensive flying trials and they were all grounded thereafter for removal and modification of the tailplanes at Radlett, the attachment points having again become suspect, but this action put an end to the trouble.

The first Victor B.1 squadron was No.10, reformed at Cottesmore on 1 April, 1958, receiving as initial equipment XA927–XA929 on 9 April and becoming operational six days later; these were joined a few weeks later by XA935–XA941. The second Victor squadron, No.15, was formed, also at Cottesmore, on 1 September, 1958, and received nine B.1s, XH587–XH594

Maintenance at Cottesmore on a Victor B.1 of No.10 Squadron, with radome detached from H_2S scanner bay. (*Flight*)

and XH613, from the second contract. A third Victor squadron, No.57, was formed on 1 January, 1959, at Honington and received XH614, XH616, XH619–XH621, XH645, XH647, XH648, XH651 and the last B.1, XH667, deliveries beginning in March. Meanwhile the Victor had begun to make news; no performance data had been released for general publication when, on 13 October, 1958, Air Vice Marshal K. B. B. (later Sir Kenneth) Cross, AOC Bomber Command, flew XA938 from Gaydon to the NATO Supreme Allied Command annual bombing competition at March, California, in three stages, refuelling at Goose Bay, Labrador, and Lincoln, Nebraska; next day, on a training exercise, Wing Cmdr D. Iveson of No.232 OCU averaged 655 mph in XA932 between Farnborough and Luqa Airport, Malta—a distance of 1,310 miles flown in exactly two hours. On the 20th AVM Cross flew back from California in XA938, covering the 2,480 miles stage from Goose Bay to Marham in one minute over 4 hours, an average of 618 mph including take-off and landing; from coast to coast, the 2,020 miles were flown in 3 hr 8 min at an average speed of 644 mph. The Victor had shown itself to be as fast as the Vulcan and soon it was to prove its capability of carrying a substantially greater load of bombs and fuel. A partial trial installation of a flight-refuelling system, with a nose probe and underwing tanks, had been scheduled for trial at A & AEE on XA921, but this Victor was diverted to bombing trials which lasted till June 1959, when it successfully dropped thirty-five 1,000 lb bombs—fourteen more than the Vulcan could stow internally. The refuelling system trials were transferred to XA930, the necessary modifications being made in stages at Park Street, where it first flew with probe and underwing tanks on 27 August, 1958. XA930 appeared thus at the SBAC display a week later and during the next twelve months was progressively modified with three different lengths of nose probe (the intermediate one being selected for Service use), bomb-bay tanks and strong points under engine bays for attachment of Spectre rocket-assisted take-off (RATO) units for use at overload weights up to 190,000 lb. After trial drops of dummy Spectre units

XA930 taking off from Hatfield on 14 July, 1960, at 190,000 lb all-up weight, assisted by D. H. Spectre rockets.

at Park Street, XA930 went to Hatfield for 'live' Spectre trials and achieved a successful series of take-offs at 190,000 lb with all bomb-bay and wing tanks full, in distances as short as 1,600 feet. Trials continued on air-to-air refuelling with the Victor receiving from Valiant B(K).1 tankers, but at that stage there was no requirement for Victors themselves to operate as tankers. At Park Street, the veteran prototype WB775, still in sky-blue, began flying with fixed-droop leading edges in place of Krueger nose-flaps, while XA917 continued auto-pilot trials and XA918 went on with vortex-generator development and routine engine trials; then WB775's flap gear was damaged and it had to be grounded, the fixed-droop tests being taken over by XA918. During the summer of 1959 XA920 underwent trials at A & AEE with the photographic-reconnaissance conversion pack, including a spectacular half-loop into inverted flight to check the functioning of the camera systems under negative gravity. As a new development, Bomber Command Headquarters had urged, in October 1958, the early introduction of electronic countermeasures on the Victor B.1 by a retrofit programme in which up to twelve aircraft at a time would be flown into Park Street, re-equipped and flown back to the squadrons, but this could not begin until the necessary trial installations had been approved, so XH587 was allotted for this purpose.

After satisfactory ground running of its Conways in conjunction with revised intakes, the first Victor B.2, XH668, took the air on 20 February, 1959, piloted by John Allam; its initial programme was mainly directed to engine trials below 30,000 ft and it logged 46 hours before its first inspection in June. All production Victors had been equipped with mechanical fuel proportioners to maintain the centre of gravity position within close limits as fuel was used up; this had become increasingly important since the Victor had shown its ability to carry more than its own empty weight in fuel alone. The fortieth B.1, XH619, was completed at Colney Street in May, with the second B.2, XH669, close behind. In June 1959 XH668, though not formally released, was lent to A & AEE for 'preview' handling by Boscombe Down pilots and on 20 August it had logged 100 hours, mostly in the hands of the maker's test pilots. It took off at about 10.35 hr BST to climb to 52,000 ft, where it was to make a series of high speed turns at up to Mach 0·94 to explore and possibly exceed the wing buffet boundary; its crew comprised two A & AEE test pilots, Sqn Ldrs R. J. Morgan and G. B. Stockman, with Flt Lieuts L. N. Williams and R. J. Hannaford, respectively navigator and radio operator, and Handley Page flight test observer Bob Williams as flight engineer monitoring the Conways; it was being tracked intermittently by a ground radar operator in Kent, although this was not part of the programme. Making a routine check nearly one hour after the trace had first appeared on his screen after take-off, this operator had just picked up the trace again at about 40,000 ft when it vanished. At about the same time the master and crew of a small coasting vessel, the *Aqueity*, off St Bride's Bay, Pembrokeshire, heard what were apparently two sonic bangs and saw a splash about eight miles south-southwest of their position, which they thought was near The Smalls lighthouse, but proved to be somewhat farther north and so closer to the position shown by the last radar record; XH668 was never seen again after leaving Boscombe Down and had maintained radio silence, but the presumption that the splash and radar plot had marked its destruction was so strong that a search for wreckage was begun by four trawlers and a salvage vessel, the *Twyford*, under the control of the RN Aircraft Direction School, HMS *Harrier*, at Dale, at the request of the RAE's Accidents Investigation Branch. Six winter months, in a notoriously stormy locality, elapsed before the main wreckage was discovered on the sandy sea-bed at a depth of 400 feet. Special trawls, consisting of rakes with tough Courlene nets attached, were designed to retrieve fragments buried in the shifting sand and by 19 November, 1960, about three-quarters of the aircraft weight had been recovered, using sixteen trawlers in the later months, together with HMS *Reclaim*, a naval salvage vessel equipped with a diving bell and underwater television; nearly 600,000 fragments were collected, ranging

The prototype Victor B.2 XH668 carried its serial only on the wind-break of the crew entry door, where it was invisible in flight. (*M.O.D.—Crown Copyright*)

from the largest piece weighing 570 lb down to a multitude of very small scraps of metal; these were reassembled on wooden frames in the RAE Structures Department at Farnborough for a searching investigation lasting eighteen months, involving a team of analysts directed by Dr P. B. Walker; to assist the investigators, WB775 was dismantled at Park Street and its major components were taken to Farnborough. An important piece of evidence was the co-pilot's wrist watch which had been stopped instantly on impact at 11.30$\frac{3}{4}$ hr BST and corroborated the Kent radar log; another was a voltmeter which was registering 200 volts when crushed and showed that the main electrical system was not at fault. At first it was thought that a pilot's roof hatch could have been lost at 50,000 ft, causing the crew to lose consciousness; XA919 had spontaneously released both hatches at 20,000 ft a fortnight after the disappearance of XH668, due to maladjustment of the quick-release catches, but when the wrecked aircraft's own hatches were later retrieved, they were only slightly damaged and appeared to have been intentionally jettisoned at below 10,000 ft, although the co-pilot's ejection seat had not been fired. When the wing-tips were recovered, the port pitot-static head was complete though crumpled, but the starboard head was missing altogether from its mounting socket, showing that it must have come adrift before the wing-tip hit the sea; vibration tests simulating buffet effects on a new wing-tip confirmed that the retaining collet could have worked loose during repeated high speed turns and allowed the head to be released. The starboard pitot-static system was especially vulnerable because it supplied not only the co-pilot's and navigator's flying instruments but also the Mach trimmer and stall detector. When the starboard pitot and static pipes became disconnected a spurious loss of airspeed would have been registered, the Mach trimmer would then have depressed the elevators to bring the nose down and the stall detector would have lowered the nose-flaps, being no longer inhibited by the protective high-speed over-ride switch; the Mach trimmer had been stopped by the negative g cut-out switch after the dive commenced, but had been running for at least five seconds before this occurred, suggesting that the starboard pitot-static head, which was never found, must have been lost at 23,000 ft or above, resulting in an inevitably catastrophic emergency which no action by the crew could have averted. It was indeed a case of 'the battle being lost for want of a horse-shoe nail'; the remedy was to lock the collet positively so that it could not vibrate loose in any circumstances. The automatic magnetic-wire recorder on the aircraft was never found and the only radio message recorded on the Victor's frequency at Boscombe Down at about 11.30 hr BST was unintelligible and apparently an inadvertent partial transmission of intercom between the pilots. In such difficult circumstances, the recovery of the wreckage, analysis of the debris and deduction of the causes of the accident must rank as an epic of detection as masterly as any in history or fiction.

The second Victor B.2, XH669, had been completed at Colney Street ten days before XH668 disappeared and on 11 August was handed over to Park Street for instrumentation and special equipment to continue the performance and handling trials begun by XH668; the third B.2, XH670, joined the trials programme and during the ensuing year XH669 and XH670 logged 70 hours and 23 hours respectively towards release for squadron service and XH669 was shown at the SBAC display in September 1960. XH671 was the Victor B.2 'conference aircraft' and did not fly until 2 March, 1960, after incorporation of electrical modifications agreed by the final conference; it then undertook radio and radar trials at Park Street and Boscombe Down, leading to development flying in 1962 at A & AEE on the navigation and bombing system and, later, on ECM. Meanwhile XH672 spent a year at Park Street on high-altitude flying to find a cure for engine surging during deceleration, the previous ground-running trouble having been eliminated on the Conway Co.11 engines. In November 1960 it began auto-pilot development and this led to automatic landing trials in 1963, though at a landing weight of 170,000 lb the Victor's earlier 'self-landing' capability had long vanished. The sixth B.2, XH673, undertook performance trials at higher weights, combined with visits to RAF squadrons already operating Victor B.1s, who were hoping to re-equip with B.2s in due course. After several weeks laid up at Park Street for incorporation of modifications and instrumentation, it resumed production flight trials on 23 November, 1960. On 5 December it took off from Radlett with John Allam in command, Sqn Ldr R. N. Bates (HQ Bomber Command Liaison Officer) as co-pilot and three test observers, R. A. Funnell, J. P. Quinn and J. Rudeforth. After climbing to 50,000 ft various functioning tests were performed, but the bomb doors jammed halfway open and the hydraulic system failed to close them. Allam decided to land at RAE Bedford, but lost VHF radio contact, although UHF contact with Radlett was regained, so he diverted there, but then found that the landing gear could not be lowered, even by the emergency system. On instructions from Radlett, he diverted to Waddington whose 'sudsmobile' foam spreader was called into action for a wheels-up landing. Allam reported that the tail-first touch down was surprisingly smooth, but the foam laid was short and fire broke out as the Victor slid off it onto the dry runway. After major airframe repairs XH673 was flown back to Radlett for repair at Colney Street and was returned to Park Street to be prepared for A & AEE trials in April 1961; meanwhile XH670 had completed its special RAE flying programme and XH671 and XH672 had been delivered to Boscombe Down. There had been one previous Victor B.1 belly-landing on a foam carpet, on 24 February, 1959, by a trainee crew captained by Flt Lieut Douglas Bryan on their final qualifying night sortie from No.232 OCU; in their case also, hydraulic failure occurred at the commencement of let-down, with fuel running low. Unable to operate the emergency system, after having made all possible checks with advice from Gaydon, Bryan climbed to 5,000 ft to enable his three rear crew members to bale out through the side door, then headed for Waddington where the foam had been laid; neither of the pilots was injured and the Victor suffered only minor damage.

The next seven Victor B.2s were also allotted for development trials, XH674 and XL161 both going for 'Blue Steel' trials at Woodford and later at the Weapons Research Establishment at Woomera, South Australia. XH675 took over photographic-reconnaissance development from XA920 in addition to overload take-off trials at 200,000 lb in October 1961. The first of the third contract, XL158, went to Boscombe Down and flew with open roof hatches at 20,000 ft in connection with the XH668 accident investigation in 1960; its first task, however, was the development of low-level reconnaissance radar, including sideways-locked H_2S and 'Red

Neck'; the latter had been flown previously on Victor B.1 XA918, which had carried the device in pods attached to the underwing fuel tank strong points. XL159 was delivered to Park Street for installation of up-rated Rolls-Royce Conway Co.17 engines of 20,600 lb s.t., while XL160, with the same installation on one side only, went to Rolls-Royce Ltd at Hucknall for full development and elimination of surging, which recurred at the higher mass flow of the new engine; the latter had a reduced by-pass ratio to match the Victor's limited rib spacing and could not achieve the full potential of the pod-mounted R.Co.22 in the VC10. XL162, the thirteenth B.2, went to Boscombe Down to share armament and radar trials. The Conway surging trouble was tracked down, with help from the RAE wind-tunnel, to vortex-shedding from the intake walls and was cured by removing these between the first and second spars, together with a spill slot in the lower lip of the intake. On completing the Co.17 acceptance trials at the end of 1961, XL159 was fitted with production fixed-droop leading edges, with which it began flying in February 1962. Only a month later, on 23 March, while being flown from Boscombe Down by 'Spud' Murphy, with Flt Lieut J. Waterton of A & AEE as co-pilot and three Handley Page test observers, XL159 went into a stable stall followed by a flat spin and Murphy told the three rear crew to bale out at 10,000 ft, but only John Tank in the port seat succeeded after four attempts; Murphy and Waterton fired their ejection seats successfully, but navigator M. P. Evans and observer P. Elwood were killed when the Victor crashed on a house at Stubton, near Newark-on-Trent, killing two women inside also. The fixed-droop leading edge was in no way responsible and was adopted for later production.

The additional production contract, No.6/Acft/12305/CB6 awarded in January 1956 for eighteen Victor B.2s, XL158–XL165, XL188–XL193 and XL230–XL233, had been increased by six, XL250–XL255, in consideration of a price reduction of £9,000 per aircraft, but in 1960 the whole defence programme of the NATO forces, including the role of the V-Bombers, had been influenced by the political decision taken in 1957 to rely on the American Thor ballistic missile for strategic nuclear retaliation, in conjunction with the introduction of 'Blue Steel' on Vulcans and Victors. Next Vulcans were to be equipped with Douglas Skybolt air-launched ballistic missiles and in July 1960 proposals were put to the Air Staff for carrying two Skybolts on the existing underwing strong points of Victors as the first stage, to be followed by a further contract for Victors with a wider centre section, large bomb-bay tanks and wing-tip tanks (Victor B. Phase 6, H.P.114). These would have had 14 hours endurance for standing patrol carrying two Skybolts, or four in conjunction with a taller and stronger twelve-wheel landing gear designed for a take-off weight of 240,000 lb. But the Air Staff, having earlier accepted a combination of 'Blue Steel' and underwing tanks at 213,000 lb for the Victor B.2, were not anxious to commit themselves to Victors with tip-tanks and Skybolts. They did, however, agree to equip some Victors of the existing contract with two Skybolts each, but on 2 August cancelled the additional six (XL250–XL255) on which assembly at Colney Street had already begun, their reasoning being that each Victor with two Skybolts could attack two separate targets per sortie instead of only one when armed with 'Blue Steel'; this may have been a partial trade-off to counter strong Treasury opposition to re-engining all the Victor B.2s with Conway Co.17s. In

December 1962 Harold Macmillan, then Prime Minister, flew to Nassau to meet President John F. Kennedy and agreed to the cancellation of Skybolt in exchange for Polaris nuclear missiles for use in four new nuclear submarines to be built in Britain for the Royal Navy. Before this three of the cancelled Victor B.2s had been reinstated as XL511–XL513 in 1961 and a fourth contract had been agreed for twenty-seven more, XM714–XM718, XM745–XM756 and XM785–XM794, subject to Handley Page Ltd merging with one or other of the two big groups, Hawker Siddeley and British Aircraft Corporation, formed in response to Duncan Sandys' demand in 1957 for rationalisation of the British military aircraft industry as a condition of the future award of contracts for the RAF. On his side, Sir Frederick was determined to obtain better take-over terms than the derisory bids, as he saw them, already offered by the two groups. He would have accepted a merger with the Hawker Siddeley Group later in 1962, but died before negotiations could be resumed after the Ministry of Defence had cancelled the last twenty-two Victors, allowing only XM714–XM718 to be completed and accepted; XM718 was finally delivered from Colney Street on 2 May, 1963.

The Air Staff had declined a suggestion in 1959 to re-engine Victor B.1s with 10,000 lb s.t. Rolls-Royce Avon RA.28s, but gave full priority to rapid conversion of the last B.1s to a new standard incorporating ECM, using equipment developed by trials in XH587; the modified aircraft were to be known as Victor B.1A and XH613 was allotted for trial installation of the retrofit modification (Mod.660), which entailed revisions to the crew stations as well as the ECM equipment itself. In the event XH617 was written off after damage on 19 July, 1960, so only twenty-four Victors were converted; the first, XH613, was flown in from No.15 Squadron to Radlett soon after the last new B.1, XH667, had been delivered from Colney Street on 31 March, 1960. It completed its flight tests on 29 July and was then prepared for the final ECM conference, by which time the second B.1A, XH618, was also ready for despatch. The ECM equipment was installed partly in the underfloor compartment and partly in the rear compartment and in a revised tail-cone terminating in a small radome for a backward-looking scanner. Its transformers handled a very heavy power load and needed to be cooled by a glycol circulating system with heat exchangers in the old flash-bomb bay area under No.12 tank and in the rear fuselage supplied with ram air from a ventral intake; this was later found to become blocked with 'Window' released from the front fuselage dispenser, and was usually blanked off internally. For this reason the Victor B.2, designed from the beginning for ECM, had its aft equipment cooling air intake located at the base of the fin. ECM development went on continuously and by April 1962 XH671 was engaged on trials of various devices with colourful code-names, for compatibility with 'Blue Steel'.

The first three Victor B.2s delivered to the RAF went to the B.2 Trials Unit formed at Cottesmore alongside Nos.10 and 15 Squadrons in September 1961, XL188 being the first on 1 November, followed by XL165 on 7 November and XL189 on 29 November. No.139 (Jamaica) Squadron was the first to re-equip with Victor B.2s at Wittering, receiving XL231 on 1 February, 1962, XL163 on 5 February, followed by XL232-233, XL511-513 and XL190-191. The second Victor B.2 squadron was No.100, formed on 1 May, 1962, also at Wittering. The B.2 Trials unit, redesignated 'C' Squadron of No.232 OCU, changed its title once again to the Victor Training Flight on 1 April, 1962, when it moved to Wittering to share servicing facilities with the two squadrons. After completing B.2 production and B.1A retrofit at the end of 1962, Colney Street embarked on a second retrofit production line for B.2s to modify and extend their ECM installations, to install Conway Co.17 engines and rapid take-off equipment, aimed at reducing 'scramble' time to one minute per aircraft, to provide for carriage and launching of 'Blue Steel', to introduce fixed-droop leading edges (already incorporated at manufacture in XM714–XM718) and to provide increased stowage for 'Window' dispensers in nacelle-like fairings attached to the upper surface of the wing just outboard of the 'pipe-joint'. These fairings, based on ideas put forward by Dr Küchemann at

Loading a 'Blue Steel' stand-off missile on to Victor B.2/BS XL158 of No.139 (Jamaica) Squadron at Wittering in 1964. (*M.O.D.—Crown Copyright*)

RAE and R. T. Whitcomb of the NACA Langley Laboratory in America, were effective in delaying the appearance of shock-waves on the wing at high subsonic speeds. This delayed separation of the boundary layer, extending the buffet boundary and improving performance, particularly at high altitude; nicknamed 'Küchemann carrots' they were also beneficial in low-altitude flying, to which Victors were committed in succession to the Valiants, which had pioneered the low-level reconnaissance and bombing roles under the radar after their allocation to the NATO forces in Europe in 1959. The first Victor B.2R, as the retrofit version was designated, was XL164 which was delivered to Boscombe Down and subsequently shown at the 1961 SBAC display with 'Blue Steel' installed. Its development programme was lengthy, but after XL161 had completed successful live firings of 'Blue Steel' at Woomera, No.139 Squadron became operational with

XL158 of No.139 (Jamaica) Squadron at Wittering showing 'Blue Steel' and ECM tail radome. (*M.O.D.—Crown Copyright*).

the missile soon after receiving its first six B.2Rs; these were finished in high-reflectivity gloss-white with pale blue and pink national marks and pale blue serials, but the seventh, XL513, was delivered from Radlett in January 1964 in grey and green upper surface camouflage for low-level operation. On 16 January No.100 Squadron received its first B.2R, XL160, also camouflaged; before retrofit this had completed Conway Co.17 trials at Hucknall in August 1962. Three Victor B.2s, XM714, XM715 and XM717, had been issued to No. 100 Squadron early in 1963, but the first of these crashed at Barnack on 20 March and was replaced on 2 May by the last Victor of all, XM718; this made a belly landing at Wittering in October and went back to Radlett for repair.

XL512 of No.139 (Jamaica) Squadron in 1964 with 'Blue Steel', long-range tanks, Küchemann 'carrots' containing 'Window' dispensers, and low-level camouflage. (*M.O.D.—Crown Copyright*)

Victor B.2 XM715 of No.100 Squadron at Wittering in 1963 with high-reflectivity anti-flash finish and pale markings, with dive-brakes extended. (*Flight*)

At Boscombe Down the photographic-reconnaissance development Victor B.2, XH675, had cleared take-off tests with overload at 206,000 lb in October 1961 and obtained full clearance at 216,000 lb in 1963 before joining No.100 Squadron as a B.2R with 'Blue Steel' on 19 February, 1964, and XL233, wearing the badges of both Nos.100 and 139 Squadrons, was on static exhibition at the 1964 SBAC show. At that time Valiants equipped the RAF's only Strategic Reconnaissance unit, No.543 Squadron at Wyton, and in accordance with NATO's revised policy of avoiding the greatly increased risk of interception at high altitude by surface-to-air missiles, began operating at low level; the only other Valiants still in service had been converted into flight-refuelling tankers which also had to operate below 20,000 ft. By August 1964 many Valiants were found to have fatigue cracks in their wing spars from flying continuously in rough air, and the future, not only of No.543 Squadron's eleven Valiant B(PR).1s, but also of sixty B(PR)K.1s and B(K).1s, was immediately placed in jeopardy; repair, though technically feasible, was uneconomic and in December 1964 all Valiants were withdrawn from service three years earlier than scheduled. To fill the gap, Victor B.1s and B.1As were converted with all possible speed

XL513 after retrofit at Radlett in January 1964 awaiting redelivery to Wittering, showing ECM radome, extended air-turbine scoops and high-gloss low-level camouflage. (*M.O.D.—Crown Copyright*)

to the tanker role; at the same time, continuous fatigue testing of a complete airframe was begun and XA919, originally the B.1 'conference aircraft' and later grounded as a fully-equipped instructional airframe at RAF Locking, was brought back to spend its remaining days in the fatigue test-rig at Park Street, accumulating simulated 'flying hours' in advance of the longest life of any Victor still in service, being repaired and modified as any points of weakness were shown up. The last nine Victor B.2Rs being converted at Colney Street were to be further modified to a photographic and radar reconnaissance variant, whose prototype was to be XL165, then serving with the Victor Training Flight at Wittering. After intensive reworking at Park Street XL165 made its first flight as a Victor SR.2 at Radlett on 23 February, 1965, before being inspected at a final conference

XM715 in 1965 after conversion to Victor SR.2 for service with No.543 Squadron at Wyton, showing fixed-droop leading edges. (*M.O.D.—Crown Copyright*)

on 19 March and going at once to Boscombe Down for full operational assessment. At Colney Street XM718, having completed repairs, became the second SR.2, following XL165 to Boscombe Down because it had retained its 'Blue Steel' capability after conversion and was thus unique; after satisfactory compatibility trials, it joined No.543 Squadron at Wyton in January 1966, XL230, XM715, XH672, XH674 and XM716 having already arrived there at intervals from 18 May, 1965, onwards, with XL161 and XL193 following, the last on 21 June, 1966; XM716 crashed at Warboys during a press demonstration on 27 June, killing its crew of four. Just previously, on 31 May, another of the squadron's Victor SR.2s had flown nonstop from Piarco, Trinidad, to Wyton, a distance of 3,896 nautical miles in 8 hr 21 min without refuelling, using its maximum available tankage. In addition to having highly developed radar mapping and sideways scanning capability, the Victor SR.2 carried a day-reconnaissance camera crate which was compatible with the two large bomb-bay fuel tanks giving 40 per cent longer range than that of the

Valiant B(PR).1; for night reconnaissance, 108 photo-flashes could be carried in the bomb bay in three canisters in addition to the camera crate, or 72 photo-flashes in two canisters with one bomb-bay tank, or 36 photo-flashes in one canister with two bomb-bay tanks. The cameras used were F.96 Mk.2 for day photography, F.89 Mk.3 for night work and F.49 Mk.4 for surveying and mapping. Each 8-inch photo-flash was of several million candle-power, but since most of the SR.2's operations were maritime it carried less comprehensive ECM equipment than the B.2R. One Victor SR.2 could photograph every ship in the whole Mediterranean in a single seven-hour sortie, bringing back 10,000 ft of exposed film for processing either at Wyton or at the Joint Air Reconnaissance Centre nearby at RAF Brampton; infra-red and 'false-colour' infra-red photography was particularly valuable and successful.

Victor K.1A XH618 of No.57 Squadron, Marham, refuelling Buccaneer S.2 XV348 of No.12 Squadron from nearby Honington. (*M.O.D.—Crown Copyright*)

Concurrently with the conversion of the nine Victor SR.2s for No.543 Squadron, Colney Street began a day-and-night programme to convert six Victor B.1As, returned to Radlett from Cottesmore by Nos.10 and 15 Squadrons after disbandment in March and October 1964, into two-point tankers using the wing-mounted Flight Refuelling F.R.20B hose-drogue pods already under trial on XA918. At first it was intended to make these units interchangeable with under-wing tanks or 'Red Neck' on the standard strong points, but this was found to bring the trailing drogues dangerously near the tail unit, so a position further outboard was chosen. XA918 had also been equipped with a retractable F.R.17 hose-drogue pack in the former bomb bay and this was incorporated in the full three-point modification applied later to 10 Victor B.1s and 14 B.1As, which became Victor K.1s and Victor K.1As respectively with bomb doors removed leaving the fuel tanks and HDU fairings as the outer surface, while the the first six two-point Victor B(K).1As retained their bombing capability, to which they could revert. The first B(K).1A to fly was XH620 on 28 April, 1965; all six went to No.55 Squadron at Marham, which became operational as a tanker unit in May and was employed in refuelling fighters after satifactory trials with the Lightnings of No.19 Squadron in August. The first K.1 three-point tanker, XA937, flew on 2 November, 1965, and subsequent K.1s were issued to No.57 Squadron at Marham, which became operational with them on 1 June, 1966, and completed successful trials using the central drogue to refuel a Transport Command VC10 of No.10

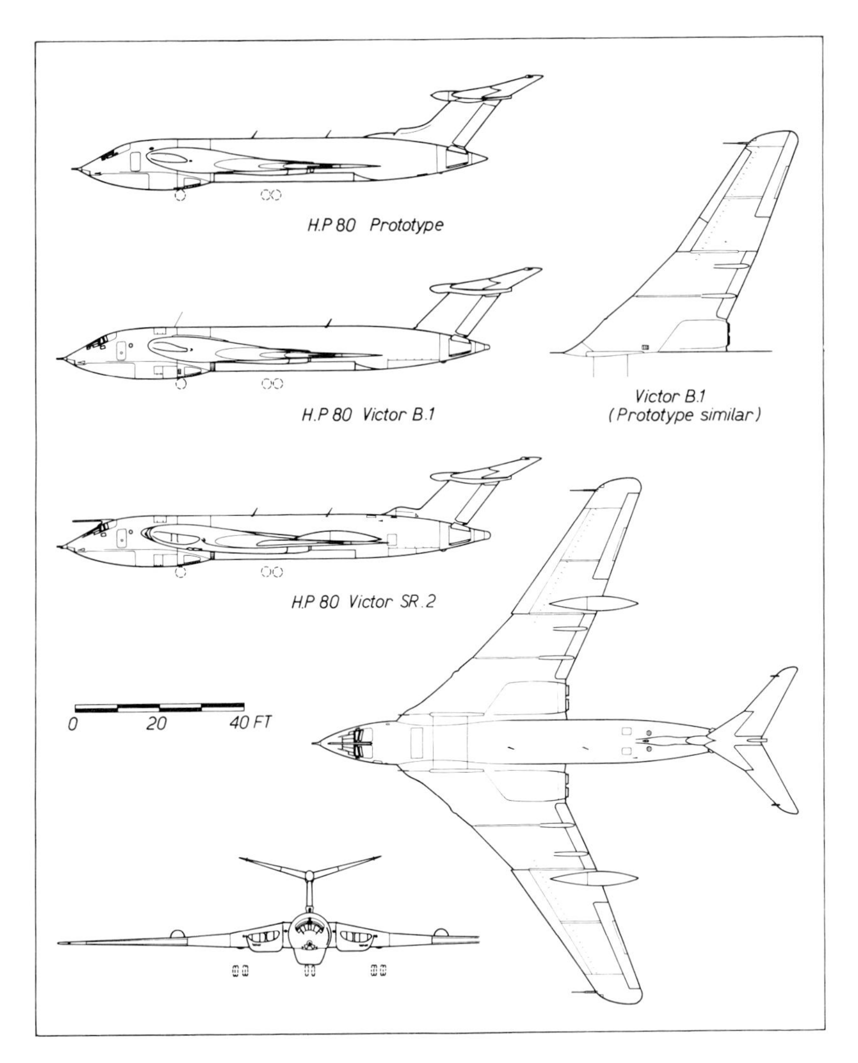

Squadron in October 1966, soon after No.214 Squadron, the pioneer of Valiant tanker techniques, had been re-equipped with Victor K.1s on 1 October. No.55 Squadron, hitherto serving as the tanker training unit at Marham, surrendered this task to the Tanker Training Flight, formed in 1965, and itself became fully operational with K.1As. XA926 of No.57 Squadron was on static view at the Queen's Review at Abingdon on 14 June, 1968, but the Victor tankers' unblemished record was marred when XH646 collided with a Canberra and crashed at Holt, Norfolk, on 19 August, 1968.

At the end of 1968 Victor B.2Rs were phased out as operational bombers, No.100 Squadron being disbanded on 1 October, when they flew their ten aircraft back to Radlett for storage; No.139 was disbanded on 31

December, flying eight of their Victors to Radlett and XL188 and XM717 to A & AEE and No.543 Squadron respectively, the latter being normally on loan to the Victor Training Flight, which also moved to Wyton. Early in 1969 No.543 Squadron's SR.2s were flown in turn to Radlett for major inspections and emerged in a new gloss polyurethene camouflage finish; in May the squadron was permitted to show its paces in public by entering two crews and Victors in the transatlantic return race between Heathrow and New York organised by the *Daily Mail* to celebrate the 50th anniversary of Alcock and Brown's first direct crossing from Newfoundland to Ireland; XL161's best time westbound was 6 hr 28 min 9 sec and eastbound 5 hr 49 min 28 sec, while XM717 did better westbound in 6 hr 16 min 54 sec but not so well on the return flight with 5 hr 55 min 31 sec, the great circle distance in each case being 3,450 statute miles. No. 543 Squadron's Victor SR.2s were scheduled to continue in service till 1971 but were then to be converted to a higher-performance tanker version, Victor K.2, having an adequate full-load performance from 'hot and high' aerodromes, where the Sapphire-engined variants were weight-limited. A Victor K.2 prototype was to be converted from XM715, which had been returned to Radlett after being damaged at Wyton in December 1967; the modifications included not only the three-point flight-refuelling conversion but also underwing tanks, improved navigation aids, structural changes to improve wing fatigue life and a revised flight deck with ejection seats for all six crew. It had been intended to convert twenty-one B.2Rs during 1969 and 1970, with the SR.2s following in 1971, but in July 1969 the Ministry of Defence decided to retain No.543's eight SR.2s in their existing role till 1973, incorporating only the essential structural and electrical modifications to permit later conversion to tankers. Before this programme could be implemented, or instructions to proceed issued, Handley Page Ltd went into liquidation on 27 February, 1970. The Victor K.2 conversion contract, technically agreed in October 1969, but limited at Radlett to initial design and feasibility studies, was awarded to Hawker Siddeley Aviation Ltd at Woodford (formerly A. V. Roe & Co Ltd), whither twenty-one Victor B.2Rs and the veteran trials B.1, XA922, were transferred in July and August 1970, when the whole of the Colney Street and Park Street complex was sold for redevelopment by the Receiver, Kenneth Cork of

XL233, the second Victor K.2 conversion by Hawker Siddeley Aviation Ltd, Woodford, was delivered to No.232 OCU, Marham, on 8 May, 1974. (*Hawker Siddeley Aviation*)

W. H. Cork, Gully & Co. Hawker Siddeley undertook future product support for the Victor K.1s and K.1As of Nos.55, 57 and 214 Squadrons and No.232 OCU, all at Marham, and for No.543 Squadron's SR.2s at Wyton till on 24 May, 1974, Vulcans of No.27 Squadron replaced Victors in the strategic reconnaissance role and No.543 Squadron was disbanded; after temporary employment during 1974–75 to monitor French nuclear tests in the Pacific, the seven remaining SR.2s were converted to K.2s. The Victor K.2 prototype, XL231, first flew at Woodford on 1 March, 1972, and was evaluated at A & AEE during late 1973. It was later returned to full K.2 standard and delivered on 8 July, 1977. The first K.2 to enter service, XL233, flew to No.232 OCU on 8 May, 1974.

No Victors ever served outside the RAF though in 1959 Australia and in 1963 South Africa showed interest in acquiring some for their home defence forces. Nos.10 and 15 Squadrons and later Nos.55 and 57 Squadrons, while at Honington, all operated detachments of Victor B.1As with the Far East Air Force at Tengah as a deterrent to Communist guerillas in Malaysia during 1964 and 1965, taking turn and turn about in spells of duty of 2½ to 3 months duration and sharing the Song Song bombing range with the RAAF at Butterworth. Here the Sapphires encountered the hazard of 'centre-line closure', or thermal contraction of the light-alloy compressor casing on to the tips of the revolving blades caused by suddenly passing from hot dry air into much colder tropical rainstorms; on the night of 24 November, 1964, XH614 of No.57 Squadron suddenly had two engines wrecked and a third flamed-out almost simultaneously while flying in cloud at 23,000 ft, but got back 40 miles to Tengah on one engine, making a safe landing after the flamed-out engine had been restarted at 10,000 ft; for this 'exceptional feat of leadership, airmanship and courage' the captain, Flt Lieut Terry Filing, was awarded the Air Force Cross.

Although none was destined to leave the drawing board, several transport versions of the Victor, both military and civil, were projected, of which H.P.96 and H.P.97 have already been mentioned. Neither of these attracted any interest from the Air Staff and BOAC respectively when proposed in 1952, shortly before the Victor's first flight, but in 1956 H.P.97 was revised and again tendered to BOAC as a British alternative to the Boeing 707, but without success in spite of vigorous personal efforts by Sir Frederick Handley Page, who made some progress with Sir Gerard d'Erlanger but failed to impress his successor, Sir Matthew Slattery. A military version of H.P.97, listed initially as H.P.101, was offered in 1956 to the RAAF as H.P.97A but was not accepted. This was followed in May 1958 by a new circular-section Victor transport, H.P.111 ('Treble One'), which employed many components common to the Victor B.2 and others proposed for the Victor B Phase 3 (H.P.104).

With span increased to 130 ft including tip-tanks, a strengthened landing gear with three-axle twelve-wheel bogies, permanent tankage for 11,500 gallons and a take-off weight of 240,000 lb, H.P.111 could carry a payload of 53,000 lb for 3,300 nm in still air with a cruising speed of 472 kt at 41,000 ft. The interior layout permitted either a double-deck arrangement or a single cargo hold 40 ft by 11 ft by 11 ft aft of the centre-section spar, with 30 seats above and forward of the wing and heavy cargo and vehicle loading through clam-shell doors from a folding ramp under the rear fuselage. The double-deck passenger layout provided six-abreast aft-facing seats for 145 troops on the upper deck and five-abreast for 55 troops on the lower; the deck could be quickly secured in the upper position or lowered to floor level by two hoists otherwise used for cargo handling. An alternative civil airliner, H.P.111C, accommodated 145 passengers on the upper deck, with a baggage and cargo hold below, or pallet-loaded freight on both decks together. The two versions were tendered to the RAF in 1958 and BOAC in 1959 respectively as alternatives to the Vickers Type 1000 and VC10, but rejected. H.P.111 had a widened centre-section to accommodate

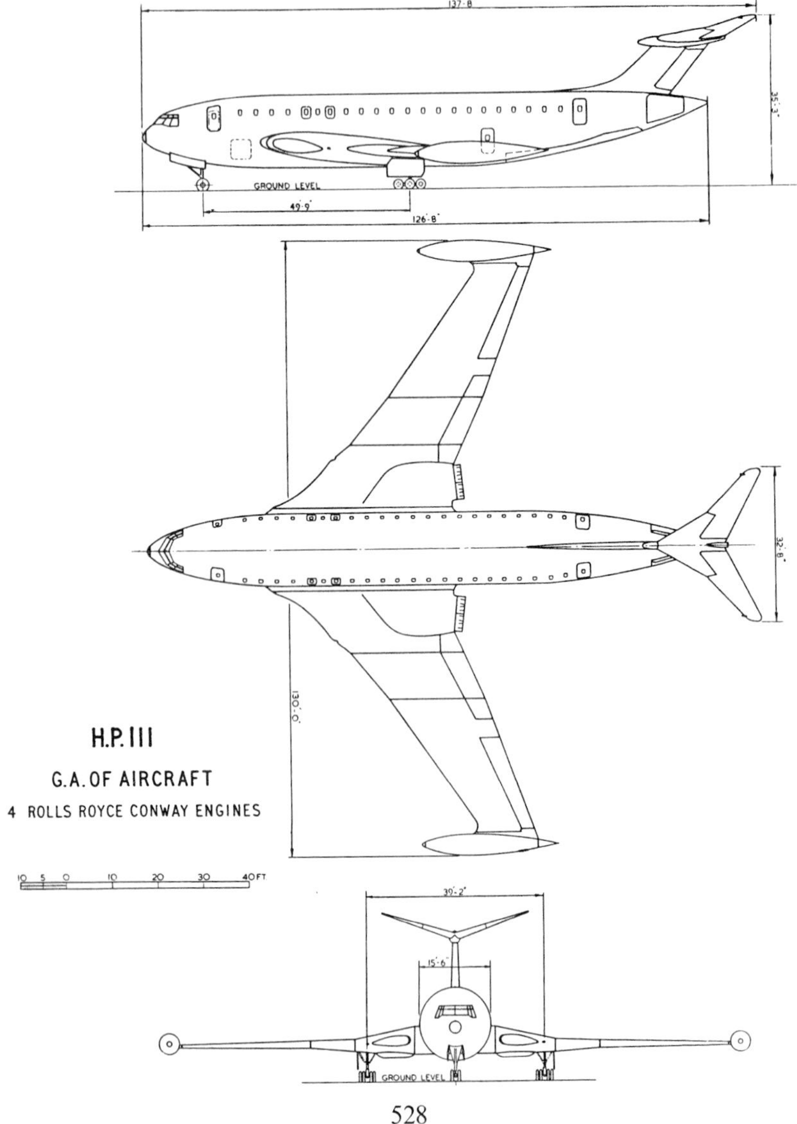

both large intakes for Rolls-Royce Conway Co.22 engines and also fuel tankage outside the pressure hull to replace the Victor's standard over-wing fuselage tanks; the fuel tanks and system in the wing were the same as the Victor's, with the addition of tip-tanks which, in effect, increased the aspect ratio by reducing end-losses. The same wing, engine installation and landing gear, combined with the Victor B.2 fuselage, resulted in the Victor B Phase 6 (H.P.114) already mentioned. H.P.111 incorporated outboard split flaps and inboard slotted flaps with boundary layer control by blown air supplied from engine-fed jet pumps. More extensive boundary layer control by flap-blowing was proposed for a military tactical freighter derived from H.P.111 and tendered as H.P.123 to Air Staff General Operational Requirement No.351, which demanded V/STOL performance. The successful GOR351 contender was the Armstrong Whitworth A.W.681, ordered in 1963 but cancelled two years later.

From 1965 and throughout the 1970s Victor K.1 and K.1A, then K.2 tankers of Marham's small but elite fleet provided a flight-refuelling service for RAF Strike Command's 'teeth aircraft' – Buccaneers, Harriers, Phantoms, Jaguars, Vulcans, Tornados and Belfasts. Victor K.2s deployed to Ascension Island during April–June 1982, refuelled Vulcans, Victors, VC10s and Hercules enabling them to operate long overwater sorties into the South Alantic area during the Falklands War. The phase-out of Victor K.2s began on 30 June, 1968, when No.57 Squadron was disbanded leaving No.55 Squadron with about 15 aircraft to continue flying, perhaps until 1990.

H.P.88

(One Rolls-Royce Nene 3)

Span 40 ft (12·22 m); length 40 ft (12·22 m). Maximum weight 14,460 lb (6,560 kg). Speed M: 0·9.

H.P.80 Victor B.1

(Four Armstrong Siddeley Sapphire Sa7)

Span 110 ft (33·55 m); length 114 ft 11 in (35 m); wing area 2,406 sq ft (223·5 m^2). Maximum weight 205,000 lb (93,100 kg). Maximum bomb load 78,000 lb (35,400 kg). Speed M: 0·95; range 6,000 miles (9,650 km); ceiling 56,000 ft (17,300 m). Crew five.

H.P.80 Victor B.2

(Four Rolls-Royce Conway Co.17)

As for Victor B.1 except for: Span 120 ft (36·6 m); wing area 2,600 sq ft (241·5 m^2). Maximum weight 216,000 lb (98,000 kg).

H.P.97 Victor Civil Transport

(Four Rolls-Royce Conway Co.10)

Span 126 ft (38·4 m); length 126 ft 3 in (38·5 m); wing area 2,680 sq ft (248·7 m^2). Empty weight (est) 95,222 lb (43,200 kg); maximum weight (est) 210,000 lb (95,300 kg). Speed (cruise) M: 0·875; range (est) 4,800 n miles (8,840 km); ceiling 50,000 ft (15,250 m). Crew eight. Passengers 134–150.

H.P.111 Military Transport

Span 130 ft (39·6 m); length 137 ft 8 in (42 m); wing area 2,827 sq ft (262·5 m^2). Empty weight (est) 110,460 lb (52,000 kg); maximum weight (est) 240,000 lb (108,900 kg). Cruising speed (est) M: 0·825; range (est) 6,300 n miles (11,600 km). Crew five. Passengers 202 (Paratroops 120).

The first H.P.R.3 Herald, G-AODE, at the SBAC display in 1955. (*Flight*)

Herald
(H.P.R.3, H.P.R.4 and H.P.R.6)

The refusal of British European Airways in February 1952 to accept the Marathon for its domestic routes did not immediately leave the Handley Page (Reading) design office without work in hand, because there was still the prospect of contracts with some of BOAC's regional subsidiaries in Africa and Asia; in the event, only West African Airways Corporation and Union of Burma Airways ordered a total of nine Marathons and meanwhile no generally acceptable substitute or replacement had emerged for the many ageing DC-3s still in service all over the world. On 20 February, 1952, Major R. E. Nicoll had reported to Sir Frederick that neither BOAC nor BEA had asked the Ministry of Civil Aviation to specify a requirement for a DC-3 replacement which would be cheaper to buy and operate than the Vickers Viscount adopted by BEA. In 1948 Miles Aircraft Ltd had almost completed the design of a larger version of the Marathon with four Alvis Leonides engines; this project, M.73, utilised the existing outer wings, nose and tail units of the Marathon, combined with new longer centre fuselage and wider centre wing sections. Since it retained the non-circular cross section of the Marathon, it could not easily be pressurised and this was deemed to be essential in future civil aeroplanes, even for short stages, to enable them to climb above stormy weather, particularly in monsoon regions and Australia. In March 1952 E. W. Gray began scheming an enlarged M.73 having a pressurised fuselage similar to the Airspeed Ambassador's, in which the basic circular cross-section was intercepted by an arc of greater radius, thus forming two chines at floor level and permitting a low sill for easy passenger entry and baggage hold loading. In May Sir Frederick authorised construction of a simple mock-up, having just received details of Canadair's proposed CL-21 high-wing feeder-liner, to be powered by two 1,450 hp Pratt & Whitney or Wright piston engines. Sir Frederick and Gray both preferred the four engine formula and were therefore compelled to rely on the only available engine of 800 hp, the Alvis Leonides Major, a fourteen-cylinder two-row version of the nine-cylinder Leonides already flown in the second H.P.R.2 trainer; the equivalent Armstrong Siddeley engine, provisionally called Cheetah-pard, existed only on paper. In July 1952 Sir Frederick allocated £7,000 for a design study and wind-tunnel programme, also authorising Gray to form a small separate design team at Reading, leaving his deputy, John Allan, to take charge of Marathon affairs; the new project was designated H.P.R.3 and by September the Reading drawing office staff had increased to eighty-five. In the same month, the Fokker company in Amsterdam announced their DC-3 replacement, to be called F.27, which was to be a high-wing monoplane of similar size to H.P.R.3, but powered with two Rolls-Royce Dart turboprops. At this time H.P.R.3 retained the triple-fin empennage derived from the Marathon, since this gave satisfactory engine-cut handling at take-off in larger aircraft including the Ambassador and Constellation, but Sir Frederick was impressed by the F.27's tall single fin and told Gray to do likewise for H.P.R.3; at first sight this seemed unacceptably large and some months elapsed before it was decided that, in spite of a weight penalty, the single fin was to be preferred to the triple layout on the score of structural simplicity and reliability. Moreover, opposition by prospective operators to four piston engines on a new aeroplane entering service in 1956 made the eventual adoption of twin turboprops almost certain. The ideal solution would have been four small lightweight turbines of less than 1,000 hp each, but these were still in the early project stage, needing at least five years to reach production.

Although George Volkert had retired in 1948, he had been persuaded to return on a part-time basis as deputy chief engineer to advise and assist Eddie Gray at Reading; in March 1953 he was urging Alvis Ltd to embark on a realistic development programme for the Leonides Major both on the bench and in flight. He was instrumental in obtaining the release of the Marathon II from the Empire Test Pilots' School for conversion into a twin Leonides Major testbed; he also investigated the performance of H.P.R.3 with two Darts, but found it unable to meet the critical case of engine-cut during take-off. To provide the largest possible span for large Fowler flaps, Gray had hoped to use very short ailerons boosted by lift-spoilers, but tests on this device were disappointing and the aileron span had to be increased at the expense of flap area. By May 1953 the Marathon II had been allotted to Reading and design of the Leonides Major engine mounting and cowling was well in hand, while the RAE had agreed to run airflow and cooling-drag tests on a complete powerplant in the 24-ft wind-tunnel at Farnborough. In June Trans-Australia Airlines issued their specification for a DC-3 replacement having two propeller-turbines, pressurised to 3·75 psi for passenger comfort at cruising altitudes above turbulence, all-up weight 30,000 lb and a cruising speed of 240 kt over stage lengths between 300 and 2,000 miles. At about the same time the Engine Division of the Bristol Aeroplane Co produced an independent proposal for using two Bristol Hercules 738 engines which, they claimed, would be cheaper than four Leonides Majors and could satisfy the critical take-off case. Sir

Frederick felt that this would show no advantage apart from first cost, while perpetuating the 50 per cent loss of power already faced by the Ambassador in the event of a single engine failure. Meanwhile the Air Staff had begun discussions with A. V. Roe & Co and Vickers-Armstrongs on a twin-engined Valetta replacement to carry 40 passengers or 32 fully-equipped troops in the tactical transport role, with full capability for rear loading of vehicles and air-dropping of weapons and paratroops. Determined, as always, to compete for military contracts, whether invited to tender or not, Sir Frederick instructed Volkert to investigate a possible rear-loading military variant of H.P.R.3 and to have a perspex model made for demonstration; this was shown to Air Commodore Kyle (DOR(A)) at Reading on 20 July, 1953, when he expressed interest but doubted whether any funds would be available for a Valetta replacement if plans matured for the Vickers V.1000 and Blackburn Beverley to replace the Hastings for the long-range and short-range roles respectively. Since the success of a twin-turboprop version seemed to be increasingly promising, a design study was begun in October of a variant with two Napier Elands, which at that date had achieved a higher degree of reliability than either the Dart or Mamba; this was designated H.P.R.4 and a few days later the Leonides Major-engined Marathon II was named H.P.R.5. On 18 January, 1954, the Board of Handley Page Ltd decided to order two prototypes of H.P.R.3, to be built at Woodley, and authorised expenditure of £1,000,000 spread over the next three years, plus £550,000 for jigs and tools, representing a 'break-even' production of 75 aircraft. Sir Frederick had already called for a type name for H.P.R.3, preferably one translatable into French and Spanish. From about a dozen possibilities, the name 'Herald' was finally chosen and was announced to 150 selected guests at a cocktail party given by Sir Frederick at Londonderry House, headquarters of the Air League, on 31 August, 1954.

Before this date, BEA had begun to show interest in H.P.R.3 for its difficult Scottish 'Highlands and Islands' services, which were non-profit-making and enjoyed government support on account of their social necessity. Peter Masefield visited Reading in May 1954 to discuss this requirement and also mentioned that BEA would soon be considering a replacement for the Vickers Viscount itself, for which as yet they had no firm specification except the ability to earn a profit on scheduled stages of 260 miles, so that cost per aircraft-mile became more important than cost per passenger-mile. Handley Page Ltd were not invited to tender, but in April 1955 Sir Frederick instructed Gray to hand over the Herald programme to John Allan (as deputy chief designer) in order to concentrate on a high-density Viscount replacement, H.P.R.6, in which the highest possible aerodynamic efficiency was to be achieved by using blown flaps of the Attinello or Breguet type on laminar-flow wings, in conjunction with four Rolls-Royce RB.109 (later Tyne) turboprops. Lachmann advised that wing suction would not be suitable for such short-range operation and Rolls-Royce reported that a blown-flap system could not be supplied with air tapped from RB.109s at the mass flow required without risk of compressor surging; they suggested instead two Conways with a swept wing; this was discussed with Peter Masefield on 22 July, 1955, but by this time BEA had chosen the Vanguard to succeed the Viscount, so the H.P.R.6 was abandoned; Gray resumed his place as leader of the Herald design team, but resigned from Handley Page Ltd six months later to join Vickers-Armstrongs; John Allan then took charge of the Herald. After some early carburation trouble with the Leonides Major, cured by changing from S.U. carburettors to RAE-Hobson injectors as Bristol had done many years earlier, the H.P.R.5 had flown 13 hours at Woodley by June before going to Alvis Ltd at Baginton. By 15 July the Herald first prototype, registered G-AODE, was complete at Reading except for engine cowlings, powerplant equipment, ailerons and elevators; it was taken by road to Radlett on 2 August for re-erection and initial flight testing by Hazelden, who made a 30-minute maiden flight on 25 August. For this occasion it had been painted in the livery of Queensland Airlines who, together with Australian National Airways and Lloyd Aereo Colombiano, had ordered a total of twenty-nine Heralds subject to satisfactory attainment of performance guarantees and an unrestricted C of A. A month later a further provisional order for six Heralds was placed by a British charter operator, Air Kruise (Kent) Ltd. Already very comprehensive market research by Grp Capt Collard, following sales tours by 'Bush' Bandidt and Wing Cmdr Slade in 1952 covering virtually all parts of the world in which DC-3s were operating, had forecast a potential market for a DC-3 replacement of over 1,000 aircraft, of which the Herald's share could be 300, so in October 1955 the Board authorised production of one hundred Heralds in four batches of twenty-five. The production Herald incorporated structural improvements to permit a twin-turboprop variant to be introduced if and when a suitable powerplant became available and took the type number H.P.R.4 originally allotted to the twin-Eland version.

G-AODE flying at Woodley in July 1956. (*Flight*)

The second H.P.R.3, G-AODF, in September 1957. (*Flight*)

The Herald was straightforward in design and made use of the techniques of corrugated sandwich construction and electric spot-welding already developed for the Victor. It was to be furnished for 36 passengers in standard Rumbold seats, or 44 in high-density seating which could be quickly folded against the cabin walls to provide space for cargo. The Electro-Hydraulics landing gear had forward-retracting main and nose units, all with twin wheels and with power steering for the nosewheels; the Dunlop hydraulic wheel-brakes incorporated the Maxaret anti-skid device tested earlier on the Hermes V G-ALEV. The first prototype was cleared for flight development as an unpressurised and unfurnished flying shell, but the second, G-AODF, was to be pressurised to 3·35 psi and fully equipped as a demonstration 'branchliner'; it was first flown by Hazelden at Woodley on 14 August, 1956, and shown at the SBAC display in a blue, white and silver colour scheme, following up the first prototype's debut the previous year. By the end of 1956 the Leonides Major was achieving good reliability, but concurrent improvement of the Dart in successive models of the Viscount had swung prospective operators more in favour of the twin-Dart formula and no more orders were offered for the Herald after the first thirty-five. Sir Frederick therefore decided to have G-AODE converted to a new variant, H.P.R.7, having a further strengthened airframe, twin Dart 527s identical with those of the Viscount 810 and a twenty-inch forward extension of the fuselage to bring the crew door clear of the airscrews in their new position. In this form G-AODE first flew at Woodley on 11 March, 1958, whereafter sales prospects for the Alvis-engined Herald virtually disappeared, the two Australian options having been cancelled by Ansett's purchase of ANA and rationalisation of their equipment with Butler's, who controlled Queensland Airlines. Both ANA and TAA opted for the Fokker F.27, by then being produced both in Holland and by Fairchild in the United States as the Friendship. The Colombian contract was frustrated by currency problems and at home Air Kruise (Kent) had been taken over by British Aviation Services. So, in spite of satisfactory demonstration of G-AODF to Jersey Airlines in October 1956, during which its short-field ability coped successfully with Alderney's tiny airport, it seemed that no operator preferred four piston engines to twin turbo-props—in particular, to twin Darts.

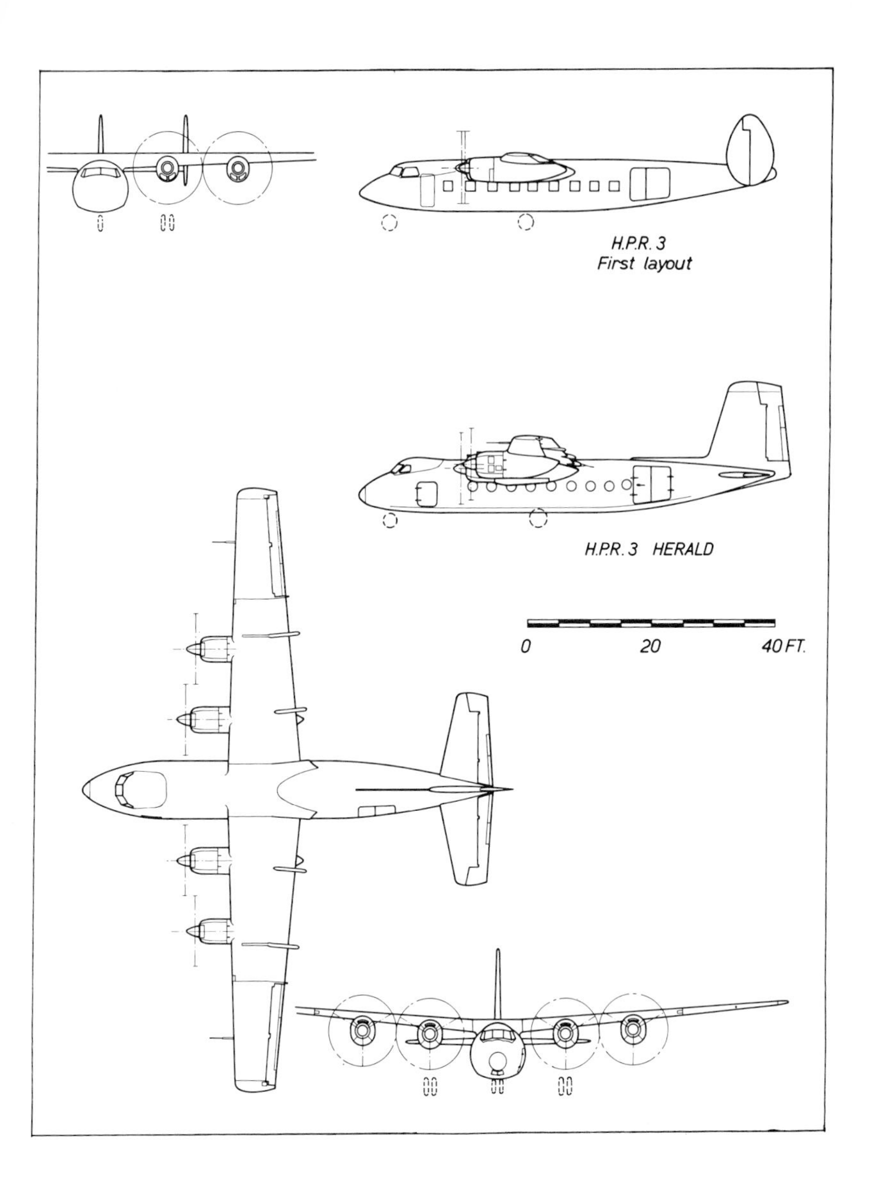

H.P.R.3 and H.P.R.4 Herald

(Four Alvis Leonides Major 701/1)

Span 94 ft 9½ in (28·89 m); length 70 ft 3 in (21·42 m); wing area 886 sq ft (82·3 m²). Empty weight 25,240 lb (11,450 kg); maximum weight 37,500 lb (17,010 kg). Cruising speed 224 mph (360 km/h); range 1,640 miles (2,640 km). Crew two. Passengers 36–44.

H.P.R.5: *see* H.P.R.1 Marathon data table.

H.P.R.6: no data available.

Dart-Herald (H.P.R.7) and its Derivatives (H.P.R.8, H.P.124, 125, 127, 129 and 131–3)

A reappraisal of the Herald with two Rolls-Royce Dart turboprops, for comparison with the Fokker Friendship, was made in July 1955; some two years earlier Viscounts had entered regular service with BEA and had also been adopted by Trans-Canada Airlines, thus initiating scheduled turbine air travel on the continent of North America. By 1955 the Dart R.Da.7 had acquired a three-stage turbine giving over 1,700 shaft hp and was being further developed beyond 2,000 ehp compared with the original civil rating of 1,130 ehp in 1947 and R.Da.5 rating of 1,690 ehp in 1953. This would enable the Dart-Herald to satisfy the most critical engine failure case of both British and American civil airworthiness requirements; Napiers had stopped producing civil Elands after supplying a limited batch to Canadair Ltd for their Convair 540s and a new generation of small turboprops was not yet in sight. There was still the possibility of a four-engined Herald being wanted in the future, so John Allan, chief designer at Reading in succession to Edwin Gray, retained the existing centre-plane geometry with strong points for outer engine mountings, although the ten H.P.R.4 airframes laid down at Woodley were now to have two Darts installed. The three-spar centre-section was further strengthened to take an increase of 30 per cent in maximum bending moment and the upper and lower flanges of the middle spar were redesigned to improve its fail-safe fatigue characteristics, partly by replacing corrugated plates with machined extrusions. It was desirable to retain the existing main undercarriage and its mounting brackets, but the Dart's 12 ft 6 in diameter airscrew needed more clearance from the fuselage side than was already provided for the Leonides Major's 11 ft airscrew; there was also the problem of arranging clearance for the Dart's large tail-pipe, from which the jet efflux contributed more than 500 ehp in residual thrust. Both these problems were resolved with typical Handley Page pragmatism by locating a Viscount-type Dart powerplant with its axis 30 inches farther outboard, resulting in an asymmetric nacelle plan form, with the tail-pipe lying alongside the retracted landing gear and the engine oil-cooler and air-conditioning intercooler occupying the available space inboard, in front of the original nacelle position. The Fowler flaps, accounting for 18½ per cent of the total wing area, retained their original tracks on the trailing edge and were operated by an improved hydraulic jack system. The fuselage had been extended by 20 inches ahead of the wing, partly to improve c.g. location but mainly to bring the combined crew's entry and forward baggage hold door well clear of the repositioned airscrews. As in H.P.R.4, the cabin windows, circular in the prototype H.P.R.3, had been enlarged to 'neutral hole' ellipses of 4 inches greater depth; the tail unit incorporated a shielded Irving balance on the rudder in place of the former horn balance and a short inverted slot in each root of the tailplane leading edge; this was introduced to cure an incipient fin stall in sideslip and had nothing to do with the asymmetry of the nacelles which, in fact, provoked no abnormal turbulence. Another major change was in the fuel system, which now included flexible bag tankage for 700 gallons in the centre-plane, with an integral tank of 160 gallons in each outer wing; the redesign of the outer wing, including spar strengthening, was undertaken by Boulton-Paul Ltd at Wolverhampton to relieve pressure in both the Reading and Cricklewood drawing offices.

Although instructions to convert G-AODE to H.P.R.7 standard had only been given in May 1957, the target date then set for its first flight was met when Hazelden took off from Woodley on 11 March, 1958; he reported a markedly improved performance and excellent handling, completing 50 hours' flying during the next five weeks including a preliminary assessment by the ARB's chief pilot, D. P. Davies. Early in the programme a dorsal fillet had been added to the fin area to preclude the risk of rudder-locking in single-engined climb; this later provided a convenient housing for the cool-air unit found necessary for air conditioning in hot climates, with a ram air intake halfway along the fillet. It was expected that a full normal C of A would be gained by the end of the year, so that production could commence in February 1959 and it was hoped that an appearance at the SBAC show in September would elicit firm orders to compensate for the loss of sales of the original Heralds. Though obviously faced with competition from the generally similar Fokker Friendship, which could be expected to claim a large share of the American market through the Fairchild connection, the Dart-Herald was initially offered at £40,000 less in first cost and hopes of expanding sales ran high on 30 August, 1958, when Hazelden took off from Woodley with eight passengers on a positioning flight to Farnborough for the SBAC show due to begin two days later, having just completed 200 hours of flight trials and needing only a few minor checks before issue of the C of A. While flying at 6,000 ft near Godalming, Surrey, there was a loud bang from the starboard engine, which immediately caught fire. The extinguishers failed to check the flames and the aileron controls began to

G-AODF after conversion to Dart-Herald H.P.R.7 commencing its maiden flight at Woodley on 17 December, 1958.

jam; then, at 1,500 ft the starboard engine and nacelle fell away and Hazelden aimed for a forced landing in a flat field he had chosen. At the last moment he saw high-voltage electrical cables in his path and, since there were trees on the far edge of the field, he forced the Herald to the ground, touching down at 130 kt and sliding under the cables, one of which made momentary contact with the fin; all nine on board were unhurt and made a rapid exit through the large hole torn in the starboard side by a tree stump, but the fire was already out. The Herald was salvaged, but was found at Woodley to be beyond economic repair; the fire had burnt off the outer half of the starboard side of the tailplane and only the fail-safe design of the wing and its external nacelle attachment had saved the wing from similar destruction. On strip-examination at Derby, the damage in the Dart was found to have originated from fracture of the hollow auxiliary gear-box layshaft, which prevented lubricant from reaching the turbine bearings; when these failed, the high-pressure turbine fouled its seals and the turbine disc broke up, cutting one of the engine mounting struts and the main fuel pipe, flooding the engine bay before the main cock could be closed. Rolls-Royce had already introduced modified layshafts and low oil pressure warning lights for the turbine main bearings in consequence of two previous identical failures, but this particular engine had escaped modification. For his exceptional skill and presence of mind in saving the lives of his companions, who included his wife, Hazelden was awarded (for the second time in his career) a Queen's Commendation for Valuable Services in the Air; Sir Frederick also expressed his personal gratitude by presenting him with a gold watch. The second prototype, G-AODF, was already in course of conversion to Darts and its first flight at Woodley by Hazelden on 17 December, 1958, enabled the flying programme to be resumed; a special category certificate was issued in March 1959 and unrestricted clearance was expected to follow within twelve months. To replace G-AODE in the development and marketing programme, the first production Dart-Herald was brought forward as quickly as possible, ahead of the other nine aircraft on the Woodley assembly line.

Sir Frederick's persistent extolling of the Dart-Herald's qualities and corroborative route analyses by the Ministry of Civil Aviation resulted on 11 June, 1959, in a fixed-price contract (£750,000) for the supply of three Dart-Heralds to MCA to be leased to BEA for operation on the Scottish Highlands and Islands services. On the strength of this order, the ten Dart-Heralds were registered G-APWA to G-APWJ inclusive and details were put in hand for a further fifteen. The new company demonstrator G-APWA took the air at Woodley on 30 October, 1959, in BEA's new black and red livery, to match G-APWB, 'WC and 'WD. Its acceptance tests were completed in three weeks, including the provision of automatic feathering actuated by the engine torquemeter, and the C of A was issued on 25 November; on 3 December 'WA flew to Nice for demonstration to Aristotle Onassis, Prince Rainier and Princess Grace of Monaco. Next it spent three days on proving flights between Inverness, Orkney, Shetland and Stornoway, making easy work of the restricted island aerodromes and returning on 18 December, to be prepared for a 30,000-mile demonstration tour in South America. Already G-AODF, in the course of three tours totalling 26 weeks and taking in 44 different countries, had visited India in April, returning via Iran, Turkey, Greece and Crete; in June, with two 330-

First production Dart-Herald 100, G-APWA, at Radlett before delivery to Sadia in May 1967 as PP-SDM.

gallon underwing long-range tanks installed, G-AODF flew via Dakar across the South Atlantic to Recife, touring Trinidad, Venezuela, Colombia, Ecuador, Peru, Bolivia, Chile, Argentina, Uruguay and Brazil during July and August, and returning in time to take part in the SBAC show in BEA colours. In October it was away again on a tour to New Zealand, arriving at Wellington for the opening of the new airport on 24 October and returning via Australia, New Guinea, the Philippines, Singapore, Malaya, Indonesia, Vietnam and Burma to reach Woodley on 18 December.

Piloted by Captain R. Shilton, on loan from Silver City Airways, G-APWA left Blackbushe for a second tour of South America on 16 March, 1960, and reached Recife from Dakar just as severe floods rose in the nearby Fortaleza district, and immediately undertook emergency relief, flying food and other supplies to the stricken area and parachuting packages to isolated groups of survivors. It went on to demonstrate its performance on typical DC-3 operations to the principal South American airlines, including Aerolineas Argentinas, Cruzeiro do Sul, Lloyd Aereo Colombiano, LADE, NAB, Panair do Brasil, REAL, Transcontinental, VARIG and VASP and the Argentine and Brazilian Air Forces. Returning to Dakar in May, Captain Shilton demonstrated 'WA in Nigeria and Ghana before heading home. During 1959 and 1960 no other Dart-Heralds were completed and these two flew more than 170,000 miles during which the schedule was delayed on only three occasions, by a burst tyre, a faulty microswitch and dirty fuel respectively. G-APWA flew at the 1960 SBAC show, on the second day of which, 7 September, Jersey Airlines ordered six Dart-Heralds after Handley Page Ltd had agreed to extend the front fuselage by 42 inches so as to increase the maximum seating capacity from 44 to 50 passengers. The BEA version was then designated Series 100 and the lengthened version Series 200; the latter immediately proved attractive to prospective customers, being competitive with the well-established Fokker Friendship and a new Japanese design, NAMC YS-11, which was to have higher powered Dart R.Da.10 engines; only one more enquiry was received for a Series 100, from a charter company, North-South Airlines of Yeadon, Yorkshire, whose order was not confirmed later. G-AODF went back into the Woodley factory during the winter for conversion to Series

200, resuming flight trials on 8 April, 1961; it then went out on a sales tour of Mediterranean and Middle East airlines via Rome, Athens, Cairo, Aden and Teheran, returning via Beirut, Amman (where King Hussein of Jordan piloted it) and Cyprus.

In August it was equipped with weather radar and appeared in the 1961 SBAC show re-registered G-ARTC and in the livery of Maritime Central Airways; this Canadian operator and its associate Nordair had each ordered two Series 200s for delivery early in 1962 and the increasing demand for Heralds led to a second production line being started at Cricklewood, as there was no room for expansion at Woodley. The Cricklewood fuselage jigs were ready in January 1961 and additional wing and nacelle jigs were set up at Radlett later in the year; this was a further stage in the progressive removal of all activity from Reading, since the Woodley site was under pressure for industrial redevelopment and was to be vacated by the end of 1962, the wind-tunnel having already been closed for this reason. During the same period the Reading and Cricklewood design departments were merged, permitting closer co-ordination with the new wind-tunnel department at Park Street on projected major variants of the Herald involving significant changes in aerodynamic shape.

With fuselage lengthened G-AODF was re-registered G-ARTC.

The first of these, and the last with a Reading type number, was H.P.R.8, tendered late in 1959 to meet Silver City Airways' requirement for a high-capacity car-ferry aeroplane specifically for the Lydd–Le Touquet and similar intensive cross-Channel services pioneered by their fleet of Bristol Freighters. Silver City specified a 'drive-on/off' payload of at least four large or six medium-sized cars together with a cabin for twenty-five passengers and a few bicycles, the passengers' baggage remaining in their cars. The aircraft had to be (a) exceptionally tough and fatigue-free to stand up to repeated take-offs and landings at intervals of less than 20 minutes, (b) fully controllable at low altitude in rough weather and bad visibility after loss of power from one engine, and (c) economical to operate both on very short hauls and over long ranges, such as Lydd or Manston to Basle or Marseilles, in expectation of a demand for car ferrying to the more popular European tourist centres. It was to be convertible to carry up to 100 passengers in simple coach seating and to this end the structure was to provide an adequate number of windows and emergency exits, although a

Artist's impression of H.P.R.8 car-ferry project. (*I.W.M.—Crown Copyright*)

pressure cabin was not necessary. John Allan's response was a larger Herald derivative of 120 ft span with a flattened oval-section fuselage providing a car-deck 45 ft 6 in long, 15 ft wide and 7 ft high; the floor-sill height was less than 3 ft above ground level for vehicle loading up portable ramps through clam-shell doors in the Bristol Freighter manner, the twin-wheel nose undercarriage being non-retractable and semi-enclosed in a low-profile fairing. The passenger cabin occupied the tapering rear fuselage, with access through side doors with built-in airstairs, and the flight deck accommodated a crew of two above the main hold ceiling level, with access by ladder and an external emergency exit hatch for ditching. The Herald's basic mainplane was retained, with suitable strength modifications, the existing port and starboard halves being joined to a new parallel-chord centre-section of 30 ft 6 in span, which also carried the standard engine nacelles and main landing gear; the latter could be fixed

Model of H.P.R.8 passenger version. (*I.W.M.—Crown Copyright*)

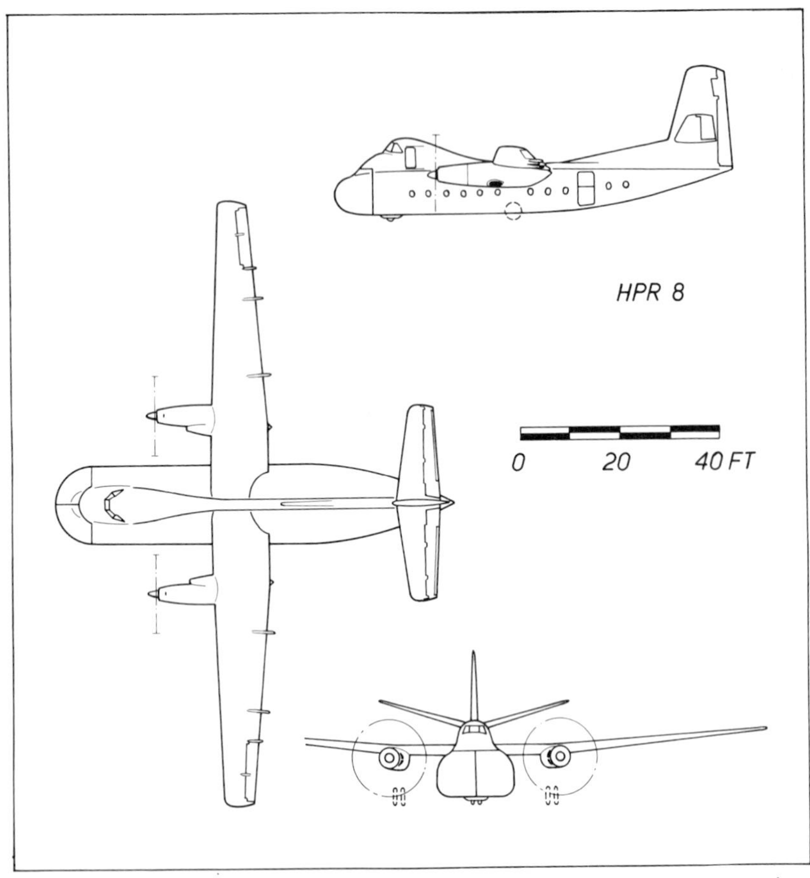

and faired for short-haul operations, saving maintenance and inspection time rather than weight, since, as in the Bristol case, the reduced weight of a permanently fixed gear was cancelled by the additional weight of fuel consumed because of its higher drag. The tail unit was similar in structure to the Herald's, but larger, and the tailplane had a span of 41 ft 6 in and 20 degrees dihedral. The main hold floor was to be of honeycomb sandwich transverse panels faced with renewable Tufnol sheet and the whole cabin and flight deck were to be soundproofed, heated and ventilated. In the all-passenger version, seating was to be arranged mainly eight abreast with a central gangway; the flight deck access was to be by fixed stairs with an adjacent light-luggage and coat compartment and toilet opposite on the port side. The front of the saloon was to be laid out as a semi-circular observation lounge with panoramic nose windows and a small bar unit, although passengers would not be permitted to occupy this area during take-off and landing. After considering the H.P.R.8 and competitive tenders from many other firms, Silver City Airways accepted the proposal of Freddie Laker's company, Aviation Traders (Engineering) Ltd of Southend-on-Sea, to convert surplus Douglas C-54 Skymasters for car-ferrying, and these went into service as Carvairs; though these were cheap in first cost, the cars had to be loaded by scissors-lift instead of a drive-on ramp.

The second major Herald variant stemmed from the Air Staff requirement, already mentioned, for a Valetta replacement in RAF Transport Command; work on it began in 1960 at Cricklewood, where it was designated H.P.124. It retained the basic Dart-Herald geometry except that the rear fuselage was swept up to permit direct loading of vehicles and other military loads through ramp doors under the raised tail unit, as proposed earlier for the Hastings VI. The Air Staff had stated a need for forty-five such tactical transports, capable of air-dropping paratroops, stores and vehicles and preferred H.P.124 to its costlier competitor, the Avro-designed H.S.780, which was a low-wing monoplane less easy to load. The prototype Herald 200 G-AODF was assessed alongside the prototype Avro 748MF in operational trials in July 1961, including landing on and taking off from a very rough airstrip at Martlesham Heath; it came through this ordeal with flying colours, but the Minister of Aviation, Peter Thorneycroft, declined to place a contract for H.P.124 except with either BAC or Hawker Siddeley, with whom Sir Frederick refused to merge unless an acceptable take-over bid were offered; he valued his company at 42 shillings per share, but Hawker Siddeley would not bid higher than 15 shillings, so no deal was made up to the time of his death on 21 April, 1962; there is little doubt that the government's political intransigence deprived the RAF of a transport ideally suited to their short-term needs and that the conflict hastened Sir Frederick's death; so ended the last duel between Sir Frederick and his oldest adversary, Sir Roy Dobson of A. V. Roe & Co. The H.P.124, like the H.S.780 which entered service three years later as the Andover C.1, would have had Dart R.Da.12 engines of nearly 3,000 ehp and a spectacular short take-off and landing (STOL) capability, which could have been further enhanced by two under-wing podded turbojets such as Vipers. An extension of the H.P.124 theme was the company's tender in 1961 to NATO Basic Military Requirement No.4 of the H.P.125 project, using under-wing pods containing eighteen vertical-lift Rolls-

Model of H.P.124 military Herald project. (*I.W.M.—Crown Copyright*)

Royce RB.162 turbojets to achieve the very stringent demands of N.B.M.R.4 for vertical climb, hovering and vertical landing. With the pods removed, H.P.125 would have been virtually the same as H.P.124 and the pods, being air-portable, could have been ferried in the cargo hold between tactical bases. In 1963 H.P.124/3 with under-wing podded RB.162 turbojets was tendered to N.B.M.R.22.

Two design studies were made at Cricklewood early in 1962 into the possible substitution of turbofans for Darts. The first of these, the H.P.127 'Jet Herald', was seen as a competitor to the Fokker F.28 Fellowship, which was due to replace the Friendship, and a model was shown on the Handley Page stand at the 1962 SBAC display, with estimated performance and payload range data when powered by two nacelle-mounted Rolls-Royce RB.183/1 Spey Juniors of 8,850 lb s.t. for take-off. The fuselage was extended forward by 11 ft to balance the rearward shift of engine c.g. and could accommodate up to 70 passengers at an exceptionally low seat-mile cost; the wing span was reduced to 80 ft, with commensurate cropping of the tailplane and an increase of fin area. Alternative to H.P.127 was the H.P.129 'Mini-Herald', using the same two Spey Juniors to carry 30 passengers faster in a shorter cabin and with a smaller wing area, the span being 57 ft 4 in. Although offered fully-equipped at a competitive price of less than £500,000, neither of these two projects attracted sufficient interest to justify substantial re-tooling for manufacture. More modest developments, capable of being built on existing jigs, were Series 300, which was a 200 with minor modifications to gain American type approval (granted by FAA in May 1962) and Series 400, a military version with a strengthened floor, aft-facing seats, inward-opening side door for paratrooping and aero-medical roles and a separate navigation station aft of the flight deck; a later development of Series 400, with Dart R.Da.12 engines, lift spoilers and nosewheel brakes, was Series 500.

Artist's impression of H.P.127 Jet Herald project.

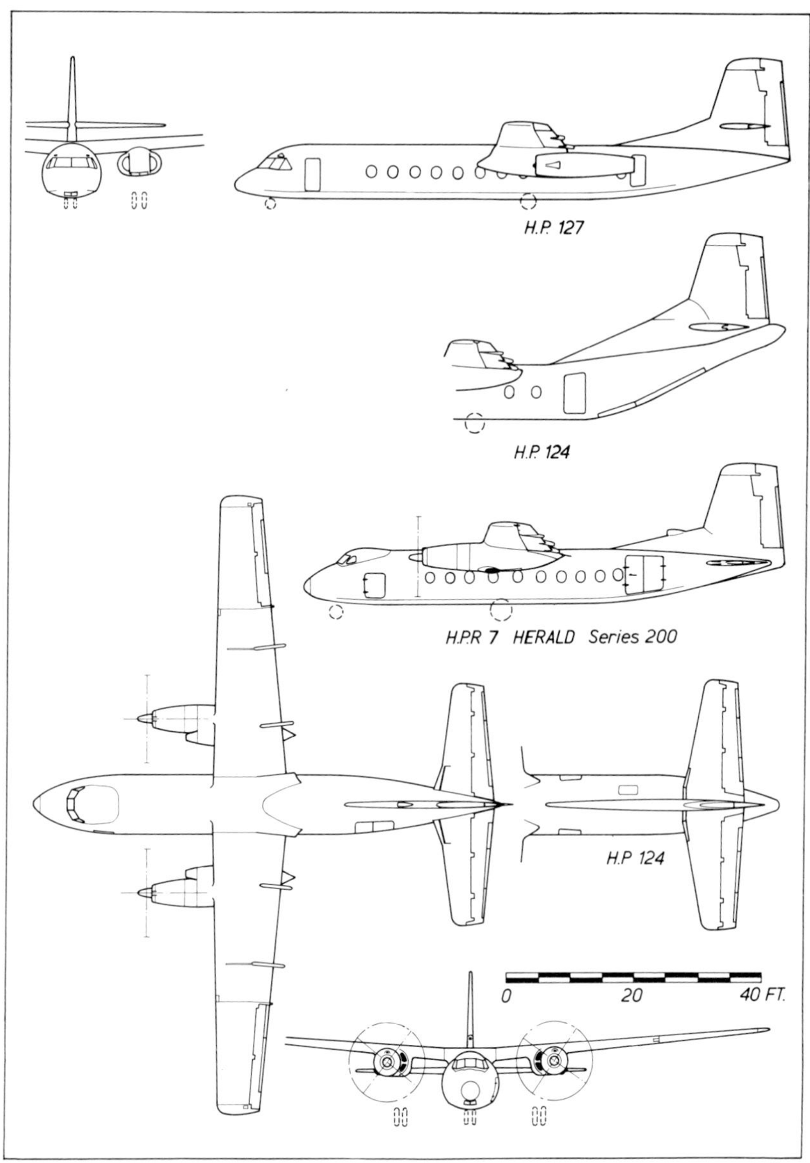

Concurrently with this project work, Dart-Heralds had begun to flow off the Woodley production line and new orders, arising from the various demonstration tours, were keeping pace. Although no new Heralds emerged in 1960, the first Series 100s for BEA, G-APWB and G-APWC, flew on 6 July, 1961, and 2 November, 1961, followed by Jersey Airlines' first series 200, G-APWE, on 13 December. G-APWA and 'WB were leased to Jersey Airlines till delivery of G-APWE on 15 January, 1962, twelve days after 'WC, which had been prepared for Prince Philip's forthcoming 19,000-mile tour of South America; he himself was to fly with his personal staff in G-APWA, which was refurnished as a 21-seat executive aircraft during January, while G-APWC, flown by Hazelden with a Handley Page crew, left Heathrow on 11 January for Jamaica, whence on 17 January Captain W. J. Johnson of BEA made a 20,000-mile three-weeks-long proving flight over the full intended route of the Royal Tour, including a call at La Paz in Bolivia, at 13,500 ft above sea level. On 5 February Prince Philip left Heathrow in G-APWA flown by Captain J. Nicolle of BEA en route for Port of Spain, Trinidad and Mackenzie Airport, Georgetown, British Guiana, where the tour officially began on 9 February. Both Heralds had two 330-gallon long-range tanks installed on under-wing pylons for the whole of the tour, whose 62 sectors included the shortest one of 11 min between Lima's two airports followed by the longest, of 4 hr 9 min from Lima to La Paz. Out of the total flying time of nearly 127 hours, Prince Philip flew G-APWA personally for 99 hours and told Sir Frederick, when the tour ended, that he 'had enjoyed every one of them'. Export deliveries of the Herald began with the two for Nordair; the first of these, CF-NAC, flew on 15 January and left Radlett, with long-range tanks fitted, on 13 February, the second, CF-NAF, flying on 2 March and departing on the 13th. Meanwhile G-APWB, overhauled after its busy season in the Channel Islands and repainted in BEA colours, had been formally handed over at Renfrew on 8 March, to join G-APWC on the Scottish routes. The third of BEA's Heralds flew at Woodley on 19 April and joined the others on the 30th. Three for Jersey Airlines followed, G-APWF flying on 29 March and leaving Woodley on 9 April, G-APWG next on 27 April and 22nd May, and G-APWH on 23 May and 6 June respectively, but the last two were held over at Jersey Airlines' request till the following year. G-APWG had indeed developed a snag during crew training near Jersey on the day following delivery and was flown back to Radlett with the starboard main undercarriage locked in the 'up' position, making a belly landing with minor damage to the fuselage underside, starboard wing and starboard airscrew. Investigation showed that the undercarriage door jack had been incorrectly assembled and action was taken to prevent a recurrence.

G-APWA, still furnished to the executive layout, was leased to the newly formed British United Airways at Gatwick in June 1962, pending delivery later of the similarly furnished G-ASBP (originally G-ASBF, but changed at the request of Air Traffic Control); among G-APWA's first charter passengers were King Hussein of Jordan and his bride Princess Muna, for their honeymoon tour to Morocco in July and August; after relieving G-APWA at Gatwick on 9 October, G-ASBP served in the executive role until March 1966; its first flight date had been 24 September, 1962, following the two Heralds for Maritime Central Airways, CF-MCK and CF-MCM on 5 July and 8 August respectively. Neither of these was delivered to Canada although 'CK flew in Maritime Central livery at the 1962 SBAC show; later it was repainted in the colours of Cruz Airways with the Philippine registration PI-C910, but this sale was frustrated by Cruz merging with Air Manila. Retaining the Cruz livery, it was registered to the makers in July 1963 as G-ASKK and leased in August to Autair International, then for a year to Sadia of Brazil as PP-ASU on 6 December, 1963; CF-MCM was

The executive Dart-Herald G-ASBP of British United Airways at Southend in 1963. (*Aviation Traders*)

sold in 1963 to the Swiss charter firm of Globe Air AG of Basle as HB-AAG *Herald of Bern* and appears to have been the last Herald manufactured at Woodley, although G-APWI and 'WJ, earlier on the line, were not flown till May 1963, being delivered to British United Airways, with which Jersey Airlines had been merged, on 28 May and 6 June respectively. During the early weeks of 1962 G-ARTC had flown to Italy for proving flights over Itavia routes in Northern Italy, with the result that the tenth of that year's Heralds, first flown on 13 November, was delivered to Itavia on 17 April, 1963, as I-TIVA, the first of a fleet of five, together with the second, I-TIVE; G-ARTC was withdrawn from use on its return from Italy in May

Itavia's second Dart-Herald, I-TIVE, was delivered from Radlett on 17 April, 1963, together with the first, I-TIVA.

1962. In July 1962, a new subsidiary company, Handley Page (Leasing) Ltd was formed with £25,000 capital, to own Heralds and lease them to new operators pending delivery of their own orders. Although G-APWA and 'WB had been leased already to Jersey Airlines and 'WA went on to BUA at Gatwick as an executive stand-in for G-ASBP, there was no provision for leasing in Handley Page Ltd's articles of association and the creation of a new wholly-owned subsidary was the simplest solution to this legal anomaly.

The eleventh and last new Herald to fly in 1962 was No.109 for the Royal Arab Air Force on 12 December; although furnished for 50 passengers, it had a strengthened floor and could be equipped with a roller-conveyor for easy freight handling, with a ball-plate platform inside the door for air-dropping; it was handed over at Radlett to the Jordanian Military and Naval Attaché in London, Brigadier Mohammed Is-Haq, on 21 January, 1963; a second Herald, No.110, joined it in July. In December 1963 both were transferred to ALIA (The Royal Jordanian Airlines) as JY-ACR and JY-ACQ to operate the routes between Amman and Jerusalem, Beirut and Cairo, and Beirut, Damascus and Kuwait. Two more Heralds for a third Canadian operator, Eastern Provincial Airways, emerged at the beginning of 1963, CF-EPI flying on 27 January and CF-EPC on 8 March, being ferried by EPA crews to Gander via Prestwick, Keflavik, Søndre Strømfjord and Frobisher; Eastern Provincial had absorbed Maritime Central Airways, to whom Nordair had sold CF-NAF, and had also bought the other Nordair Herald CF-NAC in 1962, thus becoming the sole Herald operator in Canada. In February 1964 CF-EPC was leased to Bahamas Airways for four months as VP-BCG, reverting to the Canadian register at the end of May. Globe Air had ordered a second Herald early in 1963, which flew on 25 July and was delivered to Basle in August as HB-AAH *Herald of Zürich*; in April the Royal Malayan Air Force signed a £1,500,000 contract for four military Heralds, Series 400, with an option for four more which was confirmed in June. The first of these, FM1020, flew at Radlett on 28 September and the second, FM1021, on 8 November, both being ferried to No.4 Squadron at Kuala Lumpur as 44-seaters in December by crews trained on G-APWA, which was flown to Kuala

Globe Air's second Dart-Herald, HB-AAH, at Jersey Airport on 15 December, 1966, awaiting re-registration to Jersey Airlines as G-AVEZ. (*Ian Law*)

FM1024, the fifth Dart-Herald 400, was demonstrated at the 1964 SBAC display after being handed over to the Royal Malaysian Air Force in August. (*R. T. Riding*)

Lumpur in September on lease for three months. Two more 400s, FM1022 and FM1023 left Radlett in January and February 1964 and the final four, FM1024–'27, with inward opening doors for paratrooping, were delivered between May and November. Other deliveries in 1964 were Globe Air's third, HB-AAK *Herald of Basle*, in March, Bavaria Fluggesellschaft's first, D-BIBI *Herald of Munich*, and Arkia of Israel's first, 4X-AHR, in April, followed by the second, 4X-AHS, and Itavia's third, I-TIVU, in May; finally Sadia of Brazil purchased their first, PP-SDG, which as G-ASVO had appeared at the 1964 SBAC show in Sadia livery and was flown to São Paulo on 23 October, to be followed by PP-SDH in January 1965; Sadia had previously leased G-ASKK in December 1963 as PP-ASU, then G-APWA in March 1964 as PP-ASV; these reverted to British registry in October 1964 and March 1965 respectively, but 'WA was eventually sold to Sadia in May 1967 as PP-SDM after one year's lease to British Midland Airways at Castle Donington.

Bavaria Fluggesellschaft's first Dart-Herald, D-BIBI, at Radlett before delivery in April 1964.

With eleven Heralds delivered in each of the years 1962 and 1963, and twelve in 1964, Handley Page Ltd looked forward to several more years of modest production, with three more for Sadia and one each for Globe Air, Arkia and Bavaria Fluggesellschaft already ordered for delivery in 1965, of which Sadia's PP-SDH in January was the first, releasing PP-ASU for British Midland as G-ASKK on 12 February. D-BEBE flew on 19 March, named *Herald of Bavaria*, but two days earlier CF-NAF of Eastern Provincial crashed from 11,000 ft in Nova Scotia soon after taking off from Halifax International Airport, all on board—five passengers and three crew—being killed. Investigation indicated that explosive decompression might have been the cause and while this possibility was being explored a second Herald, JY-ACQ of ALIA, crashed twenty minutes after take-off from Damascus on the night of 5 April. All Herald operators were at once warned to inspect their aircraft for suspected under-floor skin and stringer corrosion by 'bilge fluid'—an accumulated condensate containing nicotine, urine and bar spillage—and to reduce cabin pressure till further notice. The original differential of 3·35 psi had been increased in 1964 to 4·2 psi after satisfactory fatigue test evidence had been submitted to the ARB; on 15 April the ARB and the firm issued an agreed 'alert bulletin' giving recommended repair schemes and limiting cabin differential pressure to 3 psi on all Heralds up to six months old, to 2 psi on those between six and twelve months old, and zero on all more than a year old. The ALIA Herald wreckage was totally destroyed by fire, but the EPA fuselage showed signs of having split longitudinally along a spot-welded underbelly stringer in the plane of the airscrews. On inspection, the other Jordanian Herald and one of BEA's showed signs of corrosion, so all Heralds in service were recalled in turn to Radlett for their inter-chine belly structure to be renewed, reskinned and internally painted with an anti-corrosive heat-cured epoxy resin; ten had been so treated and returned to service by the end of June, leaving about twice as many still to be done. It was unfortunate that this emergency should have coincided with the conclusion of the sale to VASP of ten Herald 700s on 21 April after many months of waiting for the Brazilian Treasury to authorise payment of the overall price, including spares, of £3·75 million; this contract included options on further Heralds and was contingent on satisfactory arrangements being made for the manufacture of Heralds in Brazil; in this venture Handley Page Ltd were competing with Canadair, Fairchild and Hawker Siddeley, the last of whom already had H.S.748s in service with the Brazilian Air Force, and Rolls-Royce Ltd had set up an engine maintenance factory at São Paulo, where future Darts could be assembled. The Herald 700s were to have 2,320 ehp Dart R.Da.9 engines, 280 gallons of additional integral fuel tankage in the wings and seating for up to 60 passengers at a minimum pitch of 28 inches, take-off weight being increased to 45,000 lb. Concurrent projects included Series 800, which was the military version developed from Series 400 to the same structural standard as Series 700; and Series 600, a short-haul high-capacity version of Series 700 with the fuselage lengthened by 5 ft to accommodate up to 68 passengers, the crew door being replaced by a new combined crew and forward cabin door on the starboard side. Interest in Series 700 was shown also by Globe Air, who reserved three options, and Far Eastern Air Transport of Taiwan, who ordered one Series 700 and one Series 200. In 1965 three improved tactical assault versions of

H.P.124 were submitted to the Belgian Air Force as H.P.131, H.P.132 and H.P.133; all three would have had uprated R.Da.12 engines of 3,245 ehp and the latter two were to have gained STOL performance from two additional General Electric CF700 4,000 lb s.t. turbofans, installed at the wing-tips in H.P.132, or retractably mounted in the nacelles in H.P.133, but none of them was built.

Forty-five production Heralds had already been manufactured at Woodley and Cricklewood, and the last ten of these were due to be delivered in 1965, but the ARB insisted on a new fuselage fatigue specimen being tested in a water tank, and this was taken from the production line to save time. Globe Air's fourth Series 200, HB-AAL *Herald of Interlaken* went into service in July, but a few months later, the Swiss firm, which had been operating intensive contract holiday charters, with a utilisation of 18 hours per day, supplemented in the winter months by Safari flights to Kenya, decided to go over to four-engined aircraft and sold its first two Heralds back to Handley Page Ltd; they came on to the British register as G-ATHB and G-AVEZ, the former being sold in February 1966 to Far Eastern Air Transport as B-2001, while the latter went to Jersey Airlines in December 1966; in March 1966 G-ATHE (ex JY-ACR, bought back from ALIA after the loss of JY-ACQ) was sold to Bavaria Fluggesellschaft as D-BOBO *Herald of the Alps*. Meanwhile PP-SDJ and PP-SDL had gone to Sadia in November 1965 and January 1966, and PI-C866 had been delivered to Air Manila on 18 March, to be followed a week later by PI-C867, formerly BUA's G-ASBP, initially on lease until May while the outright sale was being negotiated; retaining Air Manila livery throughout, it was demonstrated at the 1966 SBAC show and finally redelivered to Air Manila on 3 November.

By this time it had become clear that the Brazilian Treasury would not be willing to finance VASP's ten Herald 700s and these were cancelled; six additional airframes begun at Radlett to meet this order were not completed and were later scrapped. Globe Air's option for three 700s was allowed to lapse and Far Eastern Air Transport's single option for the same variant was later satisfied by the sale in December 1968 of BUA's G-APWI

Sadia's fifth Dart-Herald, PP-SDL, was flown away from Radlett on 1 February, 1966.

as B-2009; unhappily this crashed in Southern Taiwan three months later, but was replaced on 4 March, 1969, by B-2011, which as D-BOBO had returned to the makers in October 1968, reverting to G-ATHE. Globe Air went into liquidation at the end of the 1967 season and its two remaining Heralds, HB-AAK and HB-AAL, were sold in July 1968 to the newly-formed French domestic and charter operator Europe Air Service of Perpignan, becoming F-OCLY and F-OCLZ, which were later changed to F-BLOY and F-BOIZ. Sadia was allowed by the Brazilian Treasury to buy one new Herald, PP-SDN, to replace PP-SDJ, which had been destroyed in a fatal crash into high ground at Curitiba on 3 November, 1967; but could only satisfy its outstanding order for one more by trading-in three DC-3s and a C-46 Commando, which Handley Page Ltd accepted for immediate sale in Florida as payment for their original demonstrator G-APWA, already delivered to Sadia in May 1967 as PP-SDM.

Arkia's fourth Dart-Herald, 4X-AHO, leaving Radlett on 4 April, 1968.

All aircraft manufacture had been transferred from Cricklewood to Radlett in 1966, when the old works were sold for redevelopment, leaving three Heralds still unsold until 1968, when after delivery of PP-SDN on 10 January, 4X-AHO went to Israel on 11 April to reinforce the Arkia fleet on the new routes resulting from the Six-Day War. Itavia bought the penultimate Herald, I-TIVI, delivered in June, and the last joined 4X-AHO in Israel as 4X-AHN on 16 August. Although no more Heralds were built after 1968, G-AVPN (formerly D-BIBI and owned by Handley Page (Leasing) Ltd since June 1967) was delivered to Itavia as I-TIVB as late as 2 July, 1970, after Handley Page Ltd itself had gone into liquidation and the Radlett factory in turn was up for sale by the Receiver.

With forty-four Heralds in regular service all over the world, the existing service organisation was kept in being until a new company was formed in August 1970 jointly by Scottish Aviation Ltd of Prestwick and C. F. Taylor Ltd, both Handley Page sub-contractors of many years standing; this company, Dart-Herald (Support) Ltd acquired all the existing spares and tools and was based at C. F. Taylor's factory at Wokingham, Berkshire, under the management of Keith Wilkins, formerly of Handley Page Ltd. The Herald was popular with charter operators and changed hands readily when offered on the second-hand market. In November 1966 BEA's three

Sadia's sixth Dart-Herald, PP-SDN, delivered on 10 January, 1968, was bought by British Midland Airways in April 1973 as G-BAVX and returned to Castle Donington in Transbrasil livery. (*Avia Press*)

Series 100s had been snapped up by Autair International of Luton, which in turn was acquired by Court Line in December 1969 to become Court Line Aviation Ltd; on 13 November, 1970, Bavaria Fluggesellschaft's D-BEBE was sold to British Island Airways and registered G-AYMG, to operate a twice-daily flight between Gatwick and Antwerp in co-operation with SABENA, who already flew a similar Heathrow–Antwerp shuttle; BIA's service on this route began on 1 April, 1971. In November 1970 also, Court Line's three Herald 100s, G-APWB, 'WC and 'WD, were purchased by Lineas Aereas La Urraca of Colombia and departed from Luton in a striking red livery during December 1970 and January 1971 as HK-718, '715 and '721 respectively; the first and last of these had been damaged beyond repair before the end of 1973. It appears that the two Air Manila Heralds also had been withdrawn from use before 1973, when British Midland Airways bought back from Transbrasil three of the former Sadia fleet, PP-SDG, 'DI and 'DN, as G-ASVO, G-ATIG and G-BAVX in March and April for charter work from Castle Donington, near Derby. In the same year BIA's fleet was augmented by the purchase in July of Arkia's 4X-AHR to become G-BAZJ, followed by Itavia's I-TIVA and 'VB in September and October, reverting to the British register as G-ASBG and G-AVPN, and made up to a baker's dozen with I-TIVU and 'VI, re-registered G-BBXI and 'XJ respectively on 18 January, 1974; meanwhile Dart-Herald (Support) Ltd had become Scottish Aviation (Dart-Herald) Ltd, with headquarters at Prestwick, Ayshire.

The Herald had achieved its original purpose of becoming a DC-3 replacement, on 30 May, 1974, when British Island Airways flew its one remaining DC-3 for the last time and thereafter maintained its services from Jersey and Gatwick to some twenty destinations in Europe and North Africa, carrying more than 550,000 passengers per annum, with its all-Herald fleet of thirteen aircraft.

The two Far Eastern Air Transport Heralds, reported to have been sold to Air Comores in 1974, were still without engines in Taiwan in 1975, but the first export Herald, CF-NAC, together with CF-EPI, returned from Canada to Southend to become G-BCZG and G-BCWE on 28 January and 13 March, 1975, respectively for British Air Ferries, who also received CF-EPC after repairs in Canada, to become G-BDFE on 10 July, 1975. On entering service between Southend and Basle, Le Touquet, Ostende and

Rotterdam, they were named *Rupert Keegan, Jeremy Keegan* and *Rory Keegan* after the three sons of BAF's chairman, T.D. Keegan, who in January 1976 was negotiating for a fourth Herald, from Arkia. Later G-BDFE, renamed *Janet*, went into service as a 21-seat executive aircraft.

H.P.R.7 Dart-Herald

(Two Rolls-Royce Dart R.Da.7/2)

Span 94 ft 9½ in (28·89 m); length (Series 100) 71 ft 11 in (21·92 m), (Series 200) 75 ft 6 in (23·01 m); wing area 886 sq ft (82·3 m²). Empty weight (Series 100) 24,200 lb (10,950 kg), (Series 200) 24,960 lb (11,300 kg); maximum weight (Series 100) 41,000 lb (18,580 kg); (Series 200) 43,000 lb (19,500 kg). Cruising speed (Series 100) 275 mph (442 km/h), (Series 200) 270 mph (439 km/h); range (Series 100) 1,730 miles (2,790 km), (Series 200) 1,635 miles (2,530 km); ceiling 26,700 ft (8,250 m). Crew two. Passengers (Series 100) 44, (Series 200) 50. (Series 300 and 400 as for Series 200.)

H.P.R.8 Car Ferry

(Two Rolls-Royce Dart R.Da.7)

Span 120 ft (36·6 m); length 82 ft 2 in (25·4 m); wing area 1,176 sq ft (109·2 m²). Empty weight (est) 31,350 lb (14,200 kg); maximum weight (est) 53,800 lb (23,400 kg). Cruising speed (est) 210 mph (338 km/h). Crew two. Passengers 25. Cars four large or six medium. All-Passenger version as Car Ferry except: Empty weight (est) 34,185 lb (15,500 kg); maximum weight (est) 56,800 lb (25,350 kg). Crew three. Passengers 100.

ER.197D (H.P.115) and Supersonic Projects (H.P.100, 107, 109, 110 and 128)

At the end of 1952, the Air Staff were planning the next generation of weapon systems to succeed the V-Bombers in ten years' time; their choice lay virtually between a manned supersonic bomber or an unmanned ballistic missile derived from the V 2 rocket pioneered for the Luftwaffe during the Second World War by Werner von Braun and further developed by him in the United States, and by Soviet scientists and engineers in Russia, since 1945. Either alternative was certain to be an exceedingly costly investment, but was seen as an unavoidable insurance against the threat of nuclear war. A cheaper substitute was a fast, but not supersonic, aircraft just large enough to carry a rocket-propelled nuclear missile, released before reaching a heavily-defended target and continuing at supersonic speed to the target by pre-set inertial guidance, while the manned carrier aircraft returned to base or friendly territory. The missile was expected to weigh 10,000 lb and the carrier would have to fly as fast as possible at minimum terrain-clearance altitude to escape detection by radar; a range of 5,000 nautical miles was to be attained and, to keep its wing area as small as possible, the carrier would take off with only its crew, missile and minimum fuel, taking on a full load of fuel from a tanker after reaching cruising speed. This concept was crystallised in Operational Requirement 324 and specification B.126T, issued in October 1952, to which Handley Page Ltd tendered H.P.99, a crescent-winged monoplane of 75 ft span powered by four Armstrong Siddeley Sapphire 7 turbojets, assisted for take-off either by catapult launching or by four de Havilland

Sprite rockets, which could also be used to accelerate into a half-loop 'toss' manoeuvre while releasing the missile and turning for home. Taking off at 106,000 lb, it would weigh 200,000 lb after refuelling and was to be equipped with supersonically-blown flaps and auto-throttle control for precise approach to the target, the missile's course being set immediately before release; in the event of an emergency en route to the target, the landing speed would have been as high as 220 kt, which was considered by the Air Staff to be an acceptable risk. Four other tenders to B.126T were received from A. V. Roe, Bristol, Shorts and Vickers-Armstrongs, but the whole project was cancelled early in 1954; H.P.99 was nicknamed 'Daisy Cutter' in the Handley Page New Design department. Although not itself supersonic, H.P.99 was projected concurrently with H.P.100, a supersonic reconnaissance aircraft which G. H. Lee began to investigate in January 1953 in advance of a formal operational requirement; the latter was issued as OR.330 after cancellation of B.126T, and was intended to enter RAF service ten years later.

H.P.100 was tendered in January 1955 as a slender *canard* monoplane with a mainly parallel oval-section fuselage; both foreplane and mainplane were of delta-form with 70 degrees sweepback on the leading edge; twelve under-wing Rolls-Royce RB.121 small-diameter turbojets were installed with three pairs each side sharing two common rectangular two-dimensional intakes. The landing gear was conventional, with twin steerable nosewheels retracting aft and four-wheeled main bogies

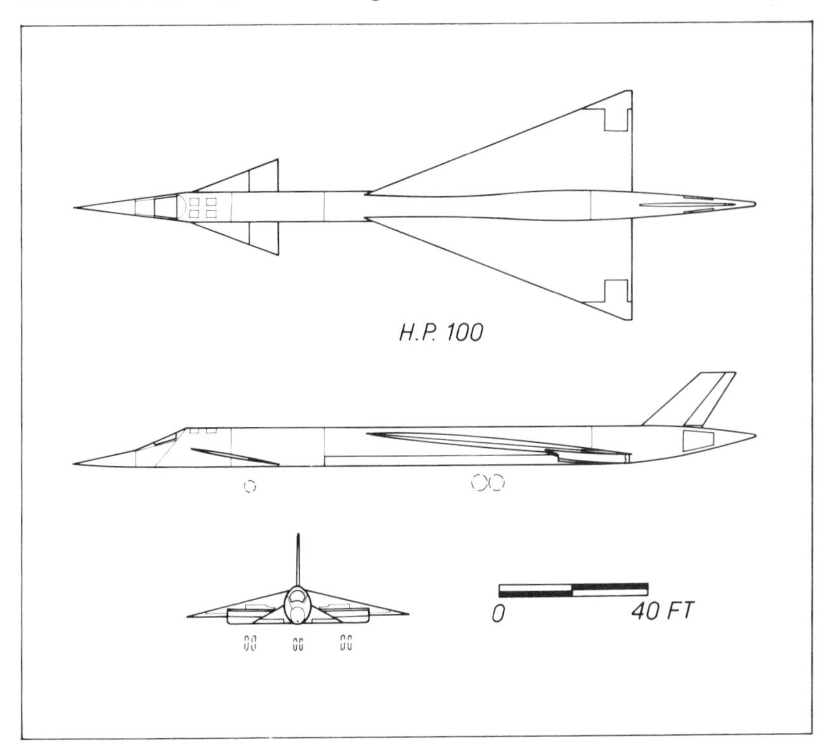

retracting inwards, while the pressure cabin for the crew of three carried a pointed 'droop-nose' with a retractable visor to improve the pilot's view at the high angle of attack needed at low speed. Immediately aft of the pressure cabin, the fuselage contained a cylindrical fuel tank 20 ft long and 7 ft 6 in in diameter, with space for electronic equipment and reconnaissance cameras in the remaining two feet of depth under the fuel tank, while the next 60 ft of fuselage length formed the bomb-bay, with internal roll-up doors like the Victor's. In addition to a comprehensive series of supersonic wind-tunnel tests at the RAE and NPL, with the leading-edge vortices made visible by oil-film technique, models were also tested at temperatures representing kinetic heating by skin friction and shock waves, and the isothermals over wings and nose were plotted. H.P.100 was required to cruise at Mach 2·5 and to attain Mach 3·0 over the target or to evade interception; much design effort was applied to means for cooling the flight deck and temperature-sensitive equipment, by using air tapped from the engine compressors and cooled by 'boot-strap' cold-air units, the bulk fuel being used as a heat sink, with secondary cooling by turbines driving electrical generators. The stagnation temperatures expected on the leading edges were too high for conventional light alloys and stainless steel was proposed for the prototypes, with the intention of changing to titanium in any production aircraft ordered; spot-welded sandwich construction, as in the Victor, would have been adopted throughout. Approximately equal in gross weight to the Victor B.2 at 225,000 lb, H.P.100 had a wing span of 59 ft 4 in and overall length of 185 ft; cruising at 60,000–70,000 ft a range of over 6,500 miles was estimated, and Elliott Bros undertook the design of the advanced navigation system. Tenders to OR.330 were submitted also by Vickers-Armstrongs and A. V. Roe, the Avro 730 being chosen, but before manufacture of this prototype could begin, the 1957 Sandys White Paper on Defence put an end to the requirement; this also ended a second Handley Page supersonic bomber project of 1955, H.P.107, of somewhat less ambitious performance and lower wing loading, powered by five Olympus turbojets.

With official defence policy swinging from manned bombers to long-range ballistic missiles, results of high-speed research at the RAE and NPL suggested the feasibility of an advanced supersonic airliner and on 5 November, 1956, the Supersonic Transport Aircraft Committee met for the first time under the chairmanship of M.B. (later Sir Morien) Morgan at Farnborough, to coordinate the necessary research effort between government establishments and the aircraft industry. Handley Page Ltd contributed design studies for a long-range airliner cruising at Mach 1·8 and a medium-range type cruising at Mach 1·3, type numbered H.P.109 and H.P.110 respectively, the former being the responsibility of New Design department and the latter that of Research department; H.P.110 was proposed in both conventional and boundary layer suction variants. By 1959 the STAC had decided to concentrate on the higher-speed long-range type, increasing the Mach number to 2·2, which represented the safe limit for kinetic heating in aluminium alloy structures; detailed design studies, with thick and thin wings respectively, were commissioned only from A. V. Roe and Bristol, the latter's eventually developing into the Anglo-French Concorde. Although slender delta wings promised to be an attractive solution to the problems of high-speed flight, it was predicted from American wind-tunnel tests that their low-speed handling characteristics would be unsatisfactory. However, W. E. Gray of RAE showed, by flying small hand-carved models from the roof of the old *Beta* airship hangar at Farnborough, that the American results were misleading and he proposed that a simple piloted glider should be built to explore the handling characteristics of slender wings at a larger scale. An outline design for such a glider was prepared by Slingsby Sailplanes Ltd; after

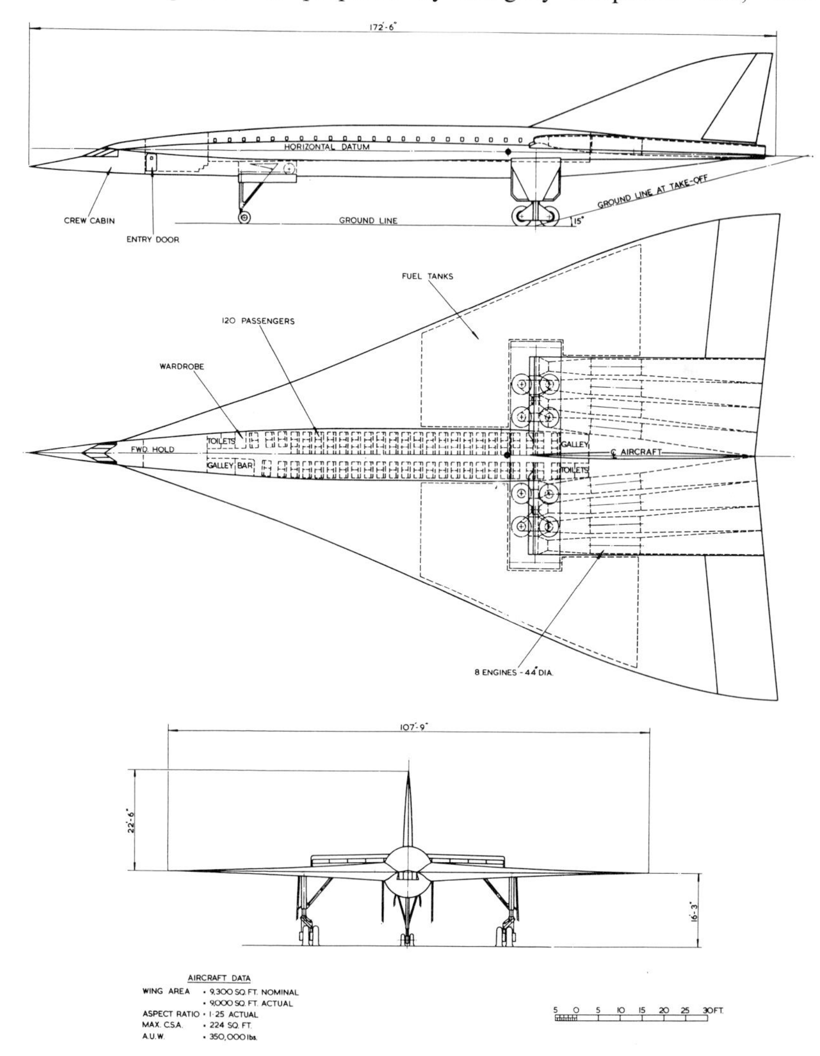

SUPERSONIC TRANS-ATLANTIC CIVIL AIRCRAFT

THIN WING VERSION

H.P.109 Supersonic Transport project.

considerable wrangling, the official specification X.197T was issued, calling for the construction of a single machine. At the same time, Fairey's were given a contract, subsequently transferred to Hunting Aircraft and then to Bristol Aircraft Ltd, to redesign the Fairey F.D.2 with a slender ogee wing for high-speed research. In spite of, or perhaps because of, his devotion to the sport of gliding, Godfrey Lee expressed a strong preference for a powered research aircraft, rather than a glider, to extend its usefulness for take-off and landing and the prolonged study of 'dutch-rolling'; furthermore, he and Charles Joy preferred metal construction because of the necessity for great strength and the non-availability of skilled aircraft woodworkers since the closing-down of Woodley seven years earlier. A revised specification was issued in December 1959 as ER.197D, concurrently with ER.193D, which defined the redesign of the Fairey F.D.2 as the Bristol 221 to cover high-speed handling; the low-speed delta was designated H.P.115, built at Cricklewood in the Wood Mill section and fitted out at Park Street during 1960, close liaison being maintained with Aero Flight Dept at RAE Bedford, where the RAE flight simulator was already in use for stability research on the Short S.B.5 and S.C.1.

H.P.115 had a symmetrical section delta wing of 40 ft mid-chord, 20 ft span, 74·7 degrees sweep and aspect ratio 1·0, with trailing-edge elevons and a 60-degree swept fin and rudder; the pilot's cockpit, with sliding canopy and Martin-Baker ground-level ejection seat, formed a small nacelle mainly below the apex of the leading edge at the forward end of a rectangular girder forming the mid-rib and terminating in the engine nacelle above the trailing edge. The powerplant was a Bristol Siddeley Viper BSV.9 turbojet of 1,900 lb s.t. and the landing gear comprised a non-retracting castering nosewheel under the pilot's nacelle and a fixed wheel and oleo-leg under each side of the wing. Perforated air-brakes were arranged as split flaps located at 50 per cent chord and were infinitely variable and pneumatically powered from a precharged air bottle. The flying controls were manually operated through a differential gearbox at the base of the control column providing the same input of 'aileron' and 'elevator' movements as the cruder chains and sprockets of the H.P.75 Manx, this system being preferred to power controls. The elevons were each approximately 8 ft wide and 4 ft in chord, with spring servo-tabs and anti-balance tabs along the trailing edge, considerable ingenuity in design being needed to obtain simultaneous optimum lateral and longitudinal sensitivity. The wheel brakes were hydraulically operated by toe pedals and the instruments comprised airspeed indicator, altimeter, yawmeter, electric turn-and-slip indicator and a suction-driven artificial horizon and directional gyro supplied from two venturis, together with an E.2A stand-by compass; no lighting was specified, so only a small battery was needed for the turn-and-slip indicator. 150 gallons of fuel were carried in three tanks located across the interior of the wing at the middle of the centre-line chord, coinciding with the centre of gravity. The normal take-off weight was 5,050 lb, including 1,170 lb of fuel for half an hour's flying. The construction of H.P.115 was of conventional aluminium alloy stressed skin throughout except for the sharp leading edges, which were of plywood and readily removable so that conical camber could be introduced by means of alternative extensions if necessary; the rudder and elevons were fabric covered. The elevons had set-back hinges and the rudder carried an

H.P.115 at RAE Bedford in August 1961. (*I.W.M.—Crown Copyright*)

external mass-balance at its tip; the fin incorporated a bullet in the upper leading edge to house a ciné-camera for filming wool tufts and, later, dense coloured smoke streams produced from generators at the leading-edge roots to make the attached vortices visible. A braking parachute was stowed at the base of the rudder above the tail-pipe, the latter being slightly up-turned at the efflux nozzle to minimise pitching moment due to thrust.

The pilot selected to fly H.P.115 was Sqn Ldr J. M. Henderson of Aero Flight, who spent many hours practising on a simulator programmed with data derived from theory, wind-tunnel tests and W. E. Gray's free-flight model tests. The control difficulties expected in so slender a delta were explored as fully as possible and the simulator was 'flown' at four speeds corresponding to the design maximum of 250 kt and at 200 kt, 120 kt and 80 kt, including simulated cross-wind landings at the two lower speeds. Simulation of the Short S.B.5 had predicted worse handling characteristics than had actually been found in flight, so the worst cases with the simulated H.P.115 were also likely to be more severe than actual handling would prove to be; these would be tolerable in fair weather, even if rolling oscillation occurred in normal banked turns as the simulator predicted. Model tests at high lift coefficient and low speed at 17 degrees angle of attack had produced a sustained dutch-roll condition which acquired the label 'Gray's instability' after its principal demonstrator. On completion at Park Street the H.P.115 received the serial XP841 and national markings, but remained otherwise unpainted except for a matt black anti-dazzle area in front of the windscreen. It was taken by road to RAE Bedford, where the Viper was installed; in addition to normal weighing and c.g. determination, the complete aircraft was suspended from three vertical wires as a free torsional pendulum to enable its yawing moment of inertia to be measured, and on knife-edge supports to determine lateral and longitudinal inertias. Two synchronised flight recorders were installed to register continuous traces of airspeed, altitude, normal and lateral accelerations, pitch attitude, angles of incidence and sideslip, control

H.P.115 flying near Bedford in 1961. (*I.W.M.—Crown Copyright*)

H.P.115 with smoke canisters at leading edge for visualisation of attached vortices. (*I.W.M.—Crown Copyright*)

surface and tab angles, angular velocities in roll, pitch and yaw, and angular accelerations in roll and yaw; later the sideslip vane proved inaccurate at high incidence and was redesigned.

Extensive taxying trials, with varying c.g. positions and control tabs locked, preceded the first flight; first brake and tyre temperatures were measured and streaming of the tail parachute was tested, then large control movements were made at speeds up to 80 kt and finally the nosewheel was lifted at nearly 'unstick' speed with c.g. at mid-range, to determine the best take-off trim. On 17 August, 1961, the weather was right and, after one more high-speed taxying run, Jack Henderson took off at 16.10 hr BST for a first flight, from which he landed after 31 minutes full of enthusiasm, which was shared by Godfrey Lee and others of the Handley Page team. Subsequent flights of about the same duration were devoted first to obtaining flutter clearance and after the ninth sortie XP841 was flown at the 1961 SBAC display, from which it returned on 11 September to resume a further $4\frac{1}{2}$ hours flying, in nine flights, to complete contractor's trials on 29 September. By this time the H.P.115 had been flown in moderate turbulence, landed in 15 kt cross-winds and proved acceptably stable at 30 kt lower than the specified minimum control speed; flutter was excited both by stick-jerking and by buffet from the air-brakes. Harmonisation of the controls, as for the S.B.5, was much better than forecast by simulation and the H.P.115 evidently had great research potential; as Jack Henderson put it in his lecture to the Royal Aeronautical Society Graduates' and Students' Section on 23 May, 1962: 'The H.P.115 has turned out to be a simple and delightful aircraft to fly and one that can be flown very accurately with a minimum of effort throughout a flight envelope that has now been extended beyond even the most optimistic of our early hopes'. During the next four years much useful low-speed handling experience was gained on behalf of the Concorde project and many flow visualisation techniques were employed, including smoke in the vortex cores and kaolin and red ink injection along the wing surface; an interesting, though rarely observed, phenomenon was the vortex condensation effect obtained by flying through thin cloud. Maximum level speed was limited to about 175 kt by the low thrust, while approach speed was usually held at 95 kt to reduce high incidence at touchdown.

The H.P.115 was used to validate a technique of investigating stability and control characteristics by flying large radio-controlled models. A quarter-scale heavily-instrumented model of the H.P.115 was dropped, first from a balloon and later from a helicopter, and its behaviour compared with that of XP841 and with predictions from smaller wind-tunnel models and simulator trials. Later still XP841 was equipped with Hartmann noise generators and was flown with these at various locations above and below the wing to investigate the problem of overhead and sideline noise from slender delta aircraft—Concorde in particular. At the end of 1973 XP841 was nearing the end of its designed flying life of 500 hours, having completed much more than its originally intended programme. On 1 February, 1974, it made its last flight from RAE Bedford to Colerne, Wilts, piloted by Flt Lieut John Rudin, to join the collection of historic RAF aircraft stored there; at the end of this flight, its log recorded a total of 493 hours. With the dispersal of the Colerne collection in 1975, XP841 went to RAF Cosford, thence to RNAS Yeovilton on 6 June, 1974.

One further supersonic project was investigated by the New Design department early in 1962 and was featured at the SBAC show later that year. This was the H.P.128 short-range airliner designed to cruise at Mach 1·15 without causing sonic bangs at ground level, over stage lengths of 500 miles. The first study was for an area-ruled fuselage of 11·5 ft maximum diameter accommodating 90 passengers, but later this was enlarged to cater for 125 passengers at 30 inch pitch. The wings and tail surfaces were to be of NACA 65 or RAE 100 section, swept back at 45 degrees on the quarter-chord line, with a span of 67·5 ft and area of 1,300 sq ft, the thickness/chord ratio being 6 per cent and aspect ratio 3·5; the trailing edges were straight and leading edges curved to terminate in pointed streamwise tips. Three turbojets each of 15,000 lb s.t. were to be installed side by side in the fuselage tail and were envisaged as Rolls-Royce Speys scaled-up by a factor of 1·45. Aluminium alloy structure would have been adopted, with thick wing skins having integrally-milled stringers and thick shear webs. For maximum lift at low speeds, the wing would have had nose flaps, with suction at the knuckle when deflected, and blown trailing-edge flaps, the control surfaces being conventional. The proposed maximum all-up weight was 117,700 lb and payload 25,000 lb; H.P.128 was estimated to save about 20 per cent in block time over 500-mile stages, for a 15 per cent increase in direct operating cost over comparable subsonic airliners. Studies continued till July 1964, but only confirmed that H.P.128 could not be competitive with large-bodied subsonic aircraft like the Boeing 727. Godfrey Lee made a brief study of the possibility of using a 'slewed' wing early in 1961, but it did not acquire a type number. He proposed a very large Mach 2 all-wing airliner with passengers accommodated within the wing and four underslung podded turbojets arranged to rotate in parallel with a crew nacelle at one wing-tip and a fin and rudder at the other wing-tip, thus varying the sweep angle from a minimum at low speed to a

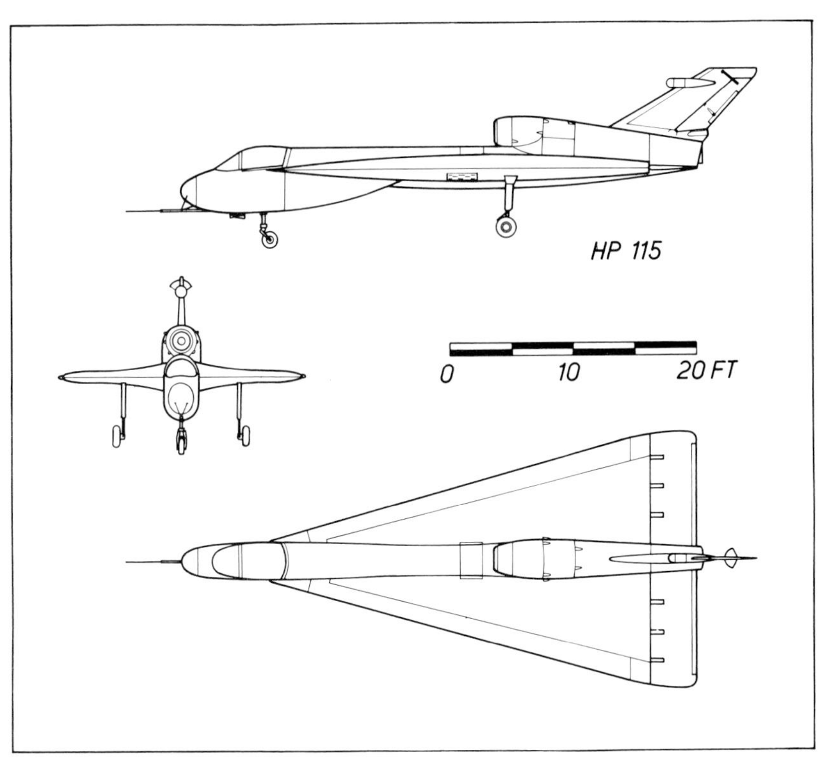
HP 115
0
10
20 FT

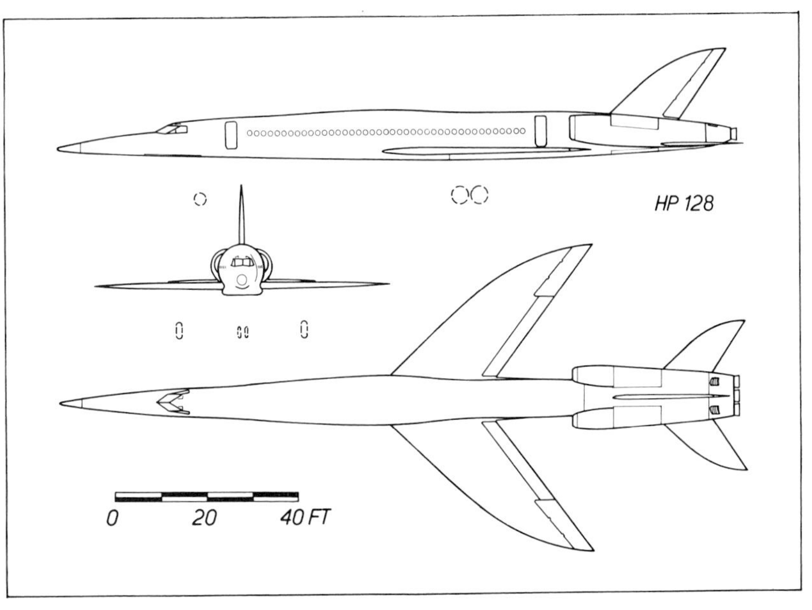
HP 128
0
20
40 FT

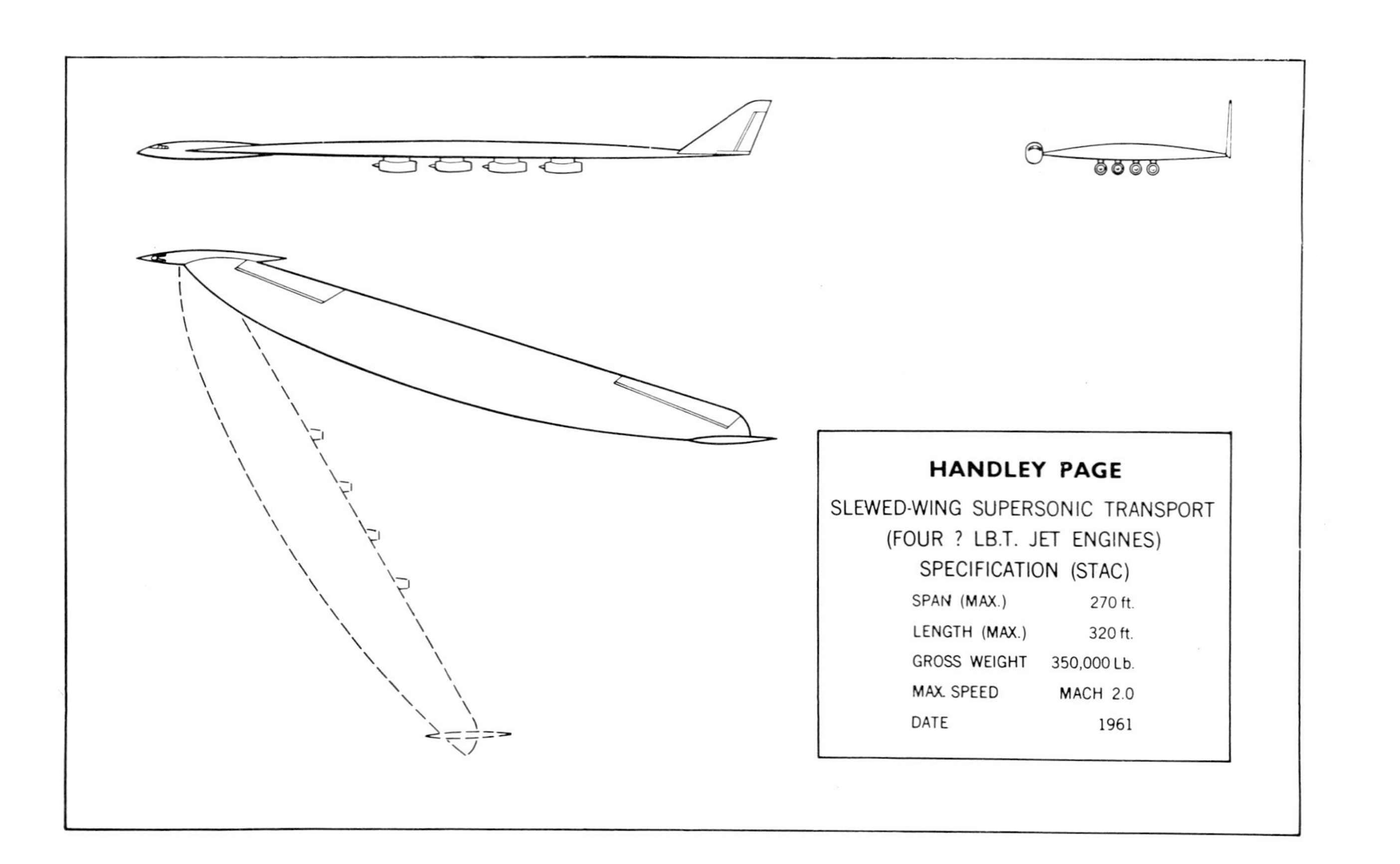
HANDLEY PAGE
SLEWED-WING SUPERSONIC TRANSPORT
(FOUR ? LB.T. JET ENGINES)
SPECIFICATION (STAC)
SPAN (MAX.) 270 ft.
LENGTH (MAX.) 320 ft.
GROSS WEIGHT 350,000 Lb.
MAX. SPEED MACH 2.0
DATE 1961

maximum of 72 degrees at high speed; the idea had originated twenty years earlier with Blohm & Voss in Germany and was also investigated in America as an alternative to Sir Barnes Wallis's Swallow project.

H.P.100

(Twelve Rolls-Royce RB.121)

Span 59 ft 4 in (18·2 m); length 185 ft (56·5 m); wing area 2,500 sq ft (232 m^2). Maximum weight (est) 225,000 lb (102,000 kg). Speed (est) M:3·0; range (est) 6,900 miles (11,100 km); ceiling (est) 70,000 ft (21,600 m). Crew two or three.

H.P.109

(Six turbojets)

Span 107 ft 9 in (33·2 m); length 172 ft 6 in (52·2 m); wing area 9,300 sq ft (864 m^2). Empty weight (est) 174,600 lb (79,200 kg); maximum weight (est) 350,000 lb (158,800 kg). Speed (est) M:2·2; range (est) 5,400 miles (8,700 km); ceiling (est) 65,000 ft (20,500 m). Crew four. Passengers 120.

H.P.115

(One Bristol Siddeley Viper BSV.9)

Span 20 ft (6·1 m); length 45 ft (13·72 m); wing area 432 sq ft (40·1 m^2). Empty weight 3,680 lb (1,668 kg); maximum weight 5,050 lb (2,300 kg). Speed 248 mph (400 km/h); endurance 40 min. Pilot alone.

H.P.128

(Three turbojets)

Span 67 ft 6 in (20·6 m); length 156 ft (47·6 m); wing area 1,300 sq ft (121·5 m^2). Empty weight (est) 74,700 lb (33,850 kg); maximum weight (est) 117,700 lb (53,400 kg). Speed (est) M:1·15; range (est) 1,000 miles (1,610 km); ceiling (est) 40,000 ft (12,360 m). Crew two. Passengers 125.

Boundary Layer Control Projects (H.P.102, 103, 105, 108, 113, 117, 119, 130 and 135)

The boundary layer was first postulated in 1897 by Frederick Lanchester and mathematically explained in 1911 by Professor Ludwig Prandtl at Göttingen. When a streamlined body moves through air, the air flows smoothly over it and the disturbance left behind is confined to a narrow wake, caused by the formation of a boundary layer along the surface of the body due to the viscosity of the air. Although the viscosity of air is very small, it is nevertheless responsible for more than half the drag of a modern subsonic streamlined aircraft. If the shape is not streamlined, the flow in the boundary layer can reverse its direction and the outer flow is then forced away from the surface. This so-called 'separation' results in a very thick wake and can also cause buffeting and, on a wing, loss of lift, or stalling. The Handley Page/Lachmann slot prevented or delayed separation, thereby enabling higher lift to be achieved and increasing the angle at which the stall occurred. It was thus the first practical form of boundary layer control for high lift, later forms of which included slot-blowing and various applications of suction. Flow reversal can only occur when the boundary layer becomes too thick and slot-blowing prevents the accumulation of the boundary layer and hence its thickening, by keeping it moving along the surface. Boundary layer control for high lift by means of suction prevents its thickening by removing some of the boundary layer through the surface into the interior of the wing or body.

Early aircraft had many components that were not well streamlined, so that flow separation occurred in many places and gave rise to high drag. In 1929, Melvill Jones gave a historically important lecture to the Royal Aeronautical Society entitled *The Streamlined Aeroplane*, in which he drew attention to the big reduction in drag and hence the improved performance, speed and economy, that could be achieved by proper streamlining. During the following decade the adoption of the cantilever monoplane, retracting undercarriage and improved engine cowling enabled streamline flow to be largely achieved; hence separation was generally avoidable and much lower drags were normal. However, all drag is undesirable, so attention was next directed towards finding ways of reducing the drag still further. Boundary layers exhibit two characteristically different states—laminar and turbulent. Typically, the boundary layer is laminar on the forward part of wings and bodies, but further back it becomes turbulent. The phenomenon of transition from laminar to turbulent conditions is very complicated and understanding has only come gradually during the last forty years, and even now is not complete. It has long been known that if flow over most of the surface remains laminar then drag will be lower and therefore ways were sought to move the position of transition from laminar to turbulent flow further aft. One way of doing this was to design the shape so that there was an extensive region over which pressure is falling, as in the low-drag aerofoils of the early 1940s, by means of which a fairly extensive laminar boundary layer region could be maintained, provided the surface was smooth enough and without blemishes. In about 1936, Dr A. A. Griffith and F. M. Meredith at RAE, Farnborough, suggested that distributed suction could be used to stabilise the laminar boundary layer and thus provide extensive regions of laminar flow. This was a theoretical suggestion and more than ten years elapsed before distributed suction was actually investigated. In 1946 a paper by Dr J. H. Preston of the NPL, entitled *The boundary layer flow over a permeable surface through which suction is applied* heralded a revival of interest in Griffith's earlier suggestion and in 1948 J. M. Kay, working at Cambridge under Professor Sir Melvill Jones, reported the results of wind-tunnel tests with distributed suction. The suction quantities required were rather higher than expected and this was later explained as being due to conditions in the wind-tunnel. Following this successful experiment, flight tests were made by Sqn Ldr M. R. Head with small model wings mounted underneath an Avro Anson, whereby the effect of distributed suction could be demonstrated at higher Reynolds Numbers than was possible in the wind-tunnel. Head later went to RAE to continue this work, using a Vampire fitted with a suction 'glove' over part of the wing, with which he succeeded in demonstrating full-chord laminar flow up to fairly high Reynolds Numbers, the results being reported in 1955 by Head, Johnson and Coxon. The kinds of suction surfaces used in these experiments were not really practical, but in 1949 Dr G. V. Lachmann suggested the application of suction through porous strips in an otherwise impervious surface. In that year Lachmann had acquired British citizenship and rejoined Handley Page Ltd as a consultant aerodynamicist working alone without a department; his concern was to develop a practical engineering solution, whereas the experiments hitherto were merely demonstrations that the theoretical possibility was also a real one. A large model made by Handley Page Ltd to Lachmann's design was tested at NPL in 1951, very good results being obtained, with very little trouble, almost as soon as the model was put into the tunnel.

Following these good results, it was decided to manufacture a glove of similar construction to fit over part of the wing of another Vampire and in fact the Handley Page glove was begun before RAE started work on theirs and there was some exchange of information resulting in similarity in the pumping equipment used in both Vampires. The difference was in the suction surfaces and here Lachmann was attempting a more difficult task by not giving himself the freedom to use a completely porous surface, confining the porosity to narrow spanwise strips. Handley Page's Vampire experiments encountered many difficulties and in fact it took nearly twenty months to complete 27 hours of test-flying. Apart from the usual causes of delay—aircraft unserviceability, bad weather, shortage of test pilots because of the high priority of the Victor programme, and mechanical trouble with the suction system—much time was spent in climbing to 30,000 ft and coming down again. Only limited instrumentation could be carried on the Vampire and the installation of the glove and suction system had necessitated removal of some of the fuel tanks, so that duration was very short; to alleviate this problem, external tanks were installed, but these aggravated the three-dimensional flow (already present because of the tapered planform of the Vampire wing) and it was some time before this was appreciated and the external tanks were removed. The Vampire first flew with the Lachmann-designed glove in 1953, but aeroelastic deformation in flight opened up the smooth joints between the porous strips and the impervious wing surface, although the design had worked well in the wind-tunnel. Instead, a single surface, with narrow spanwise bands of holes, was tried and a new glove designed on this principle was flown on the Vampire in 1955 and eventually proved successful, this programme being covered by a Ministry of Supply contract.

Meanwhile, late in 1951, W. E. Gray at the RAE, who had been studying the boundary layers formed in flight on several types of laminar wing, reported that on the A.W.52 all-wing monoplane the transition point was well aft over the unswept centre-section but very close to the leading edge over the moderately swept outer wings. Theoretical and wind-tunnel investigations of this unexpected phenomenon resulted in a prediction by the RAE that achievement of laminar flow by suction on swept wings would be very difficult and, even if successful, costly in pumping power, so that suction was no longer seen as an attractive idea for high-speed military aircraft with swept wings. Consequently Handley Page Ltd concentrated their attention, for some time, on projects having only slight sweep and therefore limited maximum speed; thus earlier hopes of applying laminar flow control to later developments of the Victor had to be abandoned and thereafter the Research Department, of which Lachmann had become

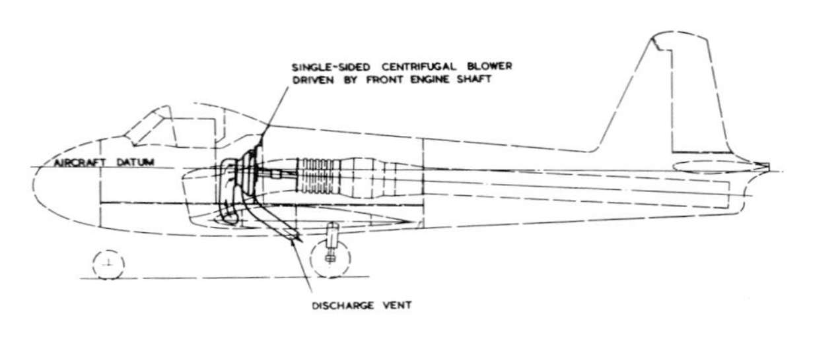

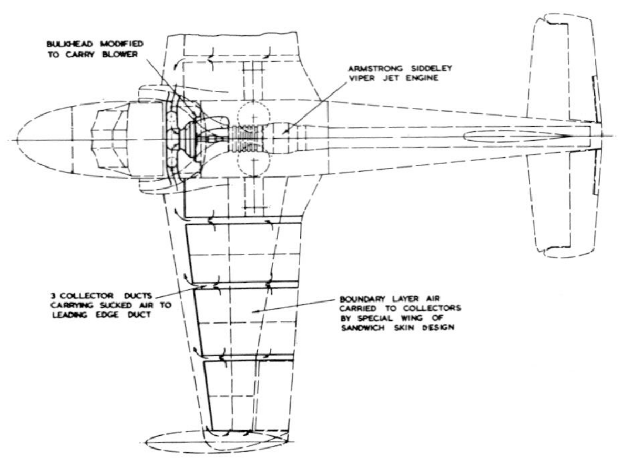

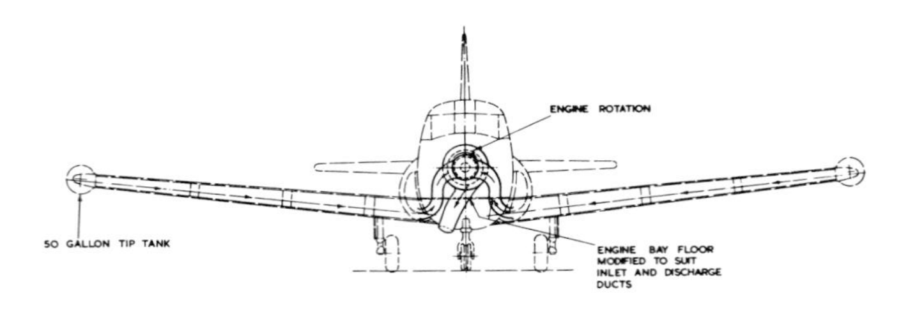

H.P. 103

ARRANGEMENT OF SUCTION SYSTEM

SCALE 0 1 2 3 4 5 6 7 8 9 10 FT.

Head in 1953, became preoccupied with civil projects. In order to demonstrate the practicability of laminar flow control in applications to civil aircraft under service conditions, a larger long-range aircraft was needed, capable of flying to all parts of the world for climatic and route-proving trials. At this time, Canberras were in production at Cricklewood and a first step would have been to manufacture a suitable set of wings for a Canberra for demonstration to airline operators, but a proposal along these lines in 1954 was not favourably received by RAE and MoS.

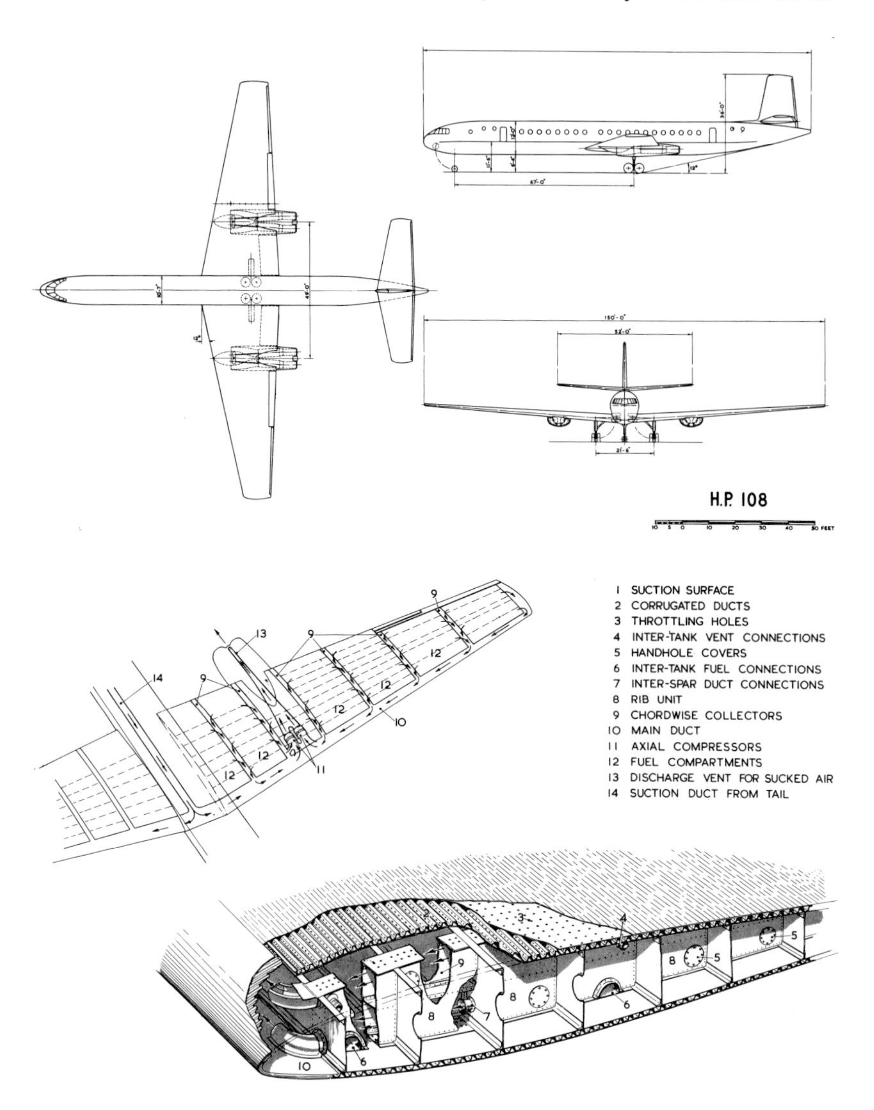

ESSENTIAL FEATURES OF WING CONSTRUCTION

Although BOAC had outlined a possible requirement for a 'Long Range Empire' airliner capable of regular operation over the same stages as the Boeing 707, no guidance was forthcoming as to the preferred size and performance of a suitable demonstration aircraft. The Ministry of Supply indicated that something bigger than a Vampire was necessary and in 1955 Handley Page Ltd submitted design studies for a straight-winged laminar flow controlled airliner (H.P.102), a generally similar military transport (H.P.105) to meet specification C.132D, and a small test aeroplane with suction wings (H.P.103) derived from the Hunting-Percival Jet Provost. Sir Frederick, however, was anxious not to waste time and effort on the H.P.103 and wanted to press on with his dream of cheap mass air travel for people of moderate means, which he was convinced that laminar flow control alone could achieve, but he was unable to persuade his colleagues and others that it would be reasonable to build a full-sized prototype of H.P.102. In January 1956 a measure of MoS support was agreed for Handley Page Ltd to design and make the wings and suction system for a single H.P.103 prototype, to be converted from the last production Jet Provost 1, XD693. While the detail design of H.P.103 went ahead, H.P.102 was reviewed and a new brochure was issued in June 1956 for an improved version, H.P.108, having four Rolls-Royce Avon RA.28 turbojets of 10,000 lb static thrust each. H.P.108 retained the tapered unswept wing and tail unit of H.P.102, with distributed suction to reduce cruising drag, and drag was to be further saved by employing ailerons, elevators and rudder of very small chord, whose effectiveness at low speeds was to be enhanced by blowing out air tapped from the engine compressors; blow-out flaps also were to be used to improve take-off and reduce landing speed. The efficacy of the suction system would have depended on the results of flight trials of H.P.103 and these had not begun a year later when BOAC ordered a fleet of Boeing 707s and lost interest in the 'Long Range Empire' project, whereupon MoS withdrew support for H.P.108.

Concurrently with the British experiments, Dr Werner Pfenninger, working at Zürich under Professor Ackeret, had used distributed suction successfully through slots and had repeated the wind-tunnel results obtained by NACA in the United States; in 1949 he joined the Northrop company, who had built several all-wing prototypes, and applied his Swiss experience to a two-seat Northrop F-94 equipped with a suction sleeve over part of the wing; in this he received very much more substantial support from the US Air Force than Lachmann could command from MoS and after an extensive investigation had been able to show that the problem of maintaining laminar flow on swept wings was more easily solved than the RAE had predicted, with a relatively small penalty in terms of the additional suction power required. This renewed the prospect of applying laminar flow control by suction at higher cruising speeds. Further studies were made of H.P.108 with moderate sweep and these, though brief, attracted renewed interest from the airlines. The prospect of redesigning H.P.103 with swept wings was frustrated by c.g. problems, so the Jet Provost conversion was stopped and for a time attention was turned to possible applications of suction to the supersonic transport aircraft studies then in progress, as mentioned earlier. In January 1957 the Research Department submitted studies for a Mach 1·2 airliner (H.P.110) both with and without laminar flow control. Concurrently Handley Page Ltd had become involved in assisting the College of Aeronautics at Cranfield with a test programme in which a Folland Midge half-wing was to be mounted vertically above the rear fuselage of a Lancaster bomber, with MoS contract cover. Handley Page Ltd undertook the design and manufacture of the root attachment for this half-wing and suggested that the same mounting could be used later to test the other half of the Midge wing after incorporation of a distributed suction system. An early scheme for doing this was submitted in March 1957 and to encourage interest a comprehensive one-day symposium on laminar flow was held at Shell-Mex House, London, in June, to which representatives from MoS, RAE, ARB, airline operators and the aircraft industry were invited, papers being presented by Dr Lachmann and J. B. Edwards of Handley Page Ltd, and Dr M. R. Head of Cambridge University. Meanwhile a start had been made with the design of a new test aeroplane, derived from the Canberra, with swept wings, designated H.P.113; when the brochure was issued in November 1957, the interest aroused exceeded that being expressed in the Dart-Herald, which had just begun flying; indeed H.P.113 had considerable appeal as a fast long-range executive transport for eight to twelve passengers and remained attractive in this role, even without suction, for shorter ranges.

H.P.113 had a 35-degree swept wing of 71 ft 3 in span and 775 sq ft area, tapering from 15 ft 4 in chord at the centre-line to 6 ft 3 in at the tips and having a thickness/chord ratio of 12·5 throughout. Two Bristol Orpheus BOr.12 turbojets of 5,250 lb s.t. each were installed side by side in the rear fuselage with scoop intakes on the fuselage sides above the centreline and aft of the rearward-folding main landing gear, which retracted into the fuselage aft of the wing root trailing edge. Each engine drove a four-stage axial fan through a forward extension shaft; normally these fans sucked air from the wing surface through ducts, but for take-off and initial climb the suction system was inoperative, to reduce wing contamination by insects and dust at low altitude, and the fans then augmented the engine mass flow through a retractable air intake in the top of the rear fuselage. A small quantity of high-pressure air, tapped from the engine compressors, was fed to the small-chord control surfaces and automatically blown out tangentially at the hinges at large deflections, on both sides of the elevators and rudder, but on the upgoing aileron only; an all-moving tailplane maintained longitudinal trim, so that the elevators were needed only for minor trim variations and manoeuvring. The cylindrical pressure-cabin was 7 ft 3 in in diameter and provided 6 ft 1 in head-room above the centre gangway; at its aft end it was closed by a hemispherical pressure bulkhead and at its forward end it was matched to the front fuselage of a Canberra bomber, using the latter type's existing nosewheel assembly, flight instruments and controls, bubble canopy and pilot's and navigator's seats; the intention was to replace the one-piece canopy later by a conventional windscreen assembly if preferred by customers. The two-spar wing structure had double-skin corrugated sandwich panels between the spars forming integral fuel tanks for 2,290 gallons from the wing root (at 8 per cent span) to the fifth main rib station (at 80 per cent span); at the root, middle (44 per cent) and outer stations the ribs formed air ducts connecting main spanwise collector ducts along the forward face of the front spar and aft face of the rear spar; these ducts passed through the wing-root fillets into the unpressurised rear fuselage without penetrating the pressure-cabin

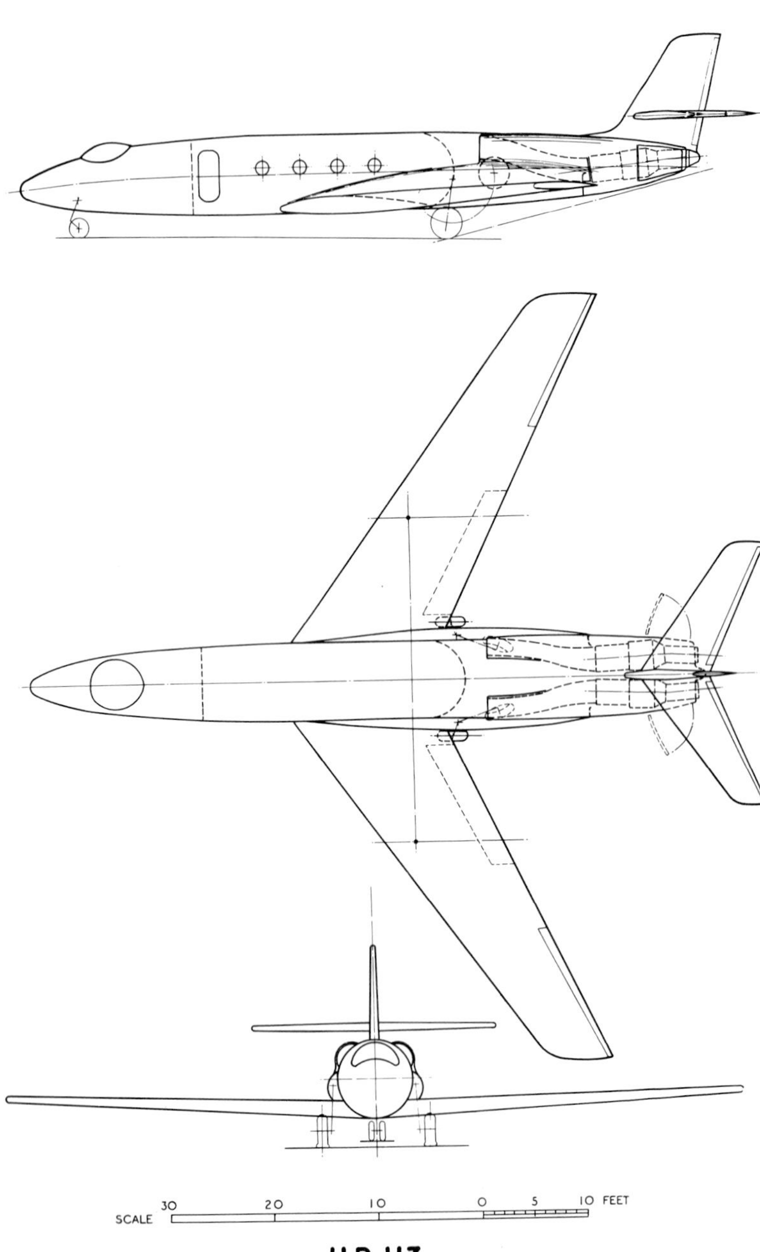

SCALE 30 20 10 0 5 10 FEET

H.P. 113

and joined a common duct feeding the suction fan intake manifold, the suction fan outflow being discharged without added drag along the sides of the fuselage at slightly more than the aircraft's flight speed; in the original design the tailplane was set halfway up the swept fin, but later it was raised to form a T-tail. Alternative cabin layouts provided five or six aft-facing seats on each side of a central gangway, with a toilet forward near the port-side entrance door and air-stairs; in an executive layout, eight seats were arranged as two facing pairs with tables, on each side of the gangway. With an all-up weight of 36,500 lb and a maximum payload of 2,520 lb, H.P.113 was expected to cruise at 530 mph over a still-air range of 5,300 miles, or 6,100 miles with tanks full and payload reduced to 1,075 lb; thus it had global range capability with not more than two refuelling stops; the cruising height would have varied from 43,000 ft to 50,000 ft as fuel was used up and the landing speed at 25,000 lb was estimated as 106 mph. Air-brakes similar to the Victor's were mounted on the rear fuselage sides, but thrust-reversers were not proposed because of their weight and cost on a small aeroplane. Sir Frederick extolled the potential of H.P.113 as a high-speed special charter aircraft and got some support in the Transport Aircraft Requirements Committee from Sir George Cribbett and Sir Gerard d'Erlanger in 1959, but no firm orders were offered, so H.P.113 was never built.

Model of H.P.113 executive B.L.C. transport project. (*I.W.M.—Crown Copyright*)

The next of G. H. Lee's projects was an all-wing airliner, with either three engines to carry 200 passengers or four engines to carry 300 passengers; this was H.P.117, proposed in April 1959 after swept versions of H.P.108 had been studied and discarded. At the first International Congress of the Aeronautical Sciences at Madrid in 1958, Lachmann had reviewed progress in Europe and America on boundary-layer suction research and summarised the results, which indicated that full-chord laminar flow could be maintained on a swept wing with suction qualities small enough to give net profile drag reductions of 70 to 80 per cent after allowing for suction pumping power. Using closely spaced narrow slits in the outer skin of sandwich panels, neither structural design for production nor weight penalties posed great difficulties; fly-accretion—held up as an insurmountable operational obstacle—could be effectively countered by spraying the leading edges with camphor or similar substances, which could be volatilised by brief application of thermal deicing heat on reaching cruising altitude in clean air; the effect of roughness decreased as altitude and speed increased, and with a rear engine installation the air intake could be arranged to swallow the suction-pump outflow or clean up pockets of turbulent flow, for instance, at the wing-body junction. The latter, of course, would not exist in a true all-wing aircraft such as H.P.117, and this was a compelling answer to the intractable problem of achieving laminar flow on the body of an orthodox aeroplane of equivalent size.

In spite of the prospect of 30 per cent fuel saving, both NACA in the United States and the RAE in England had stopped officially sponsored

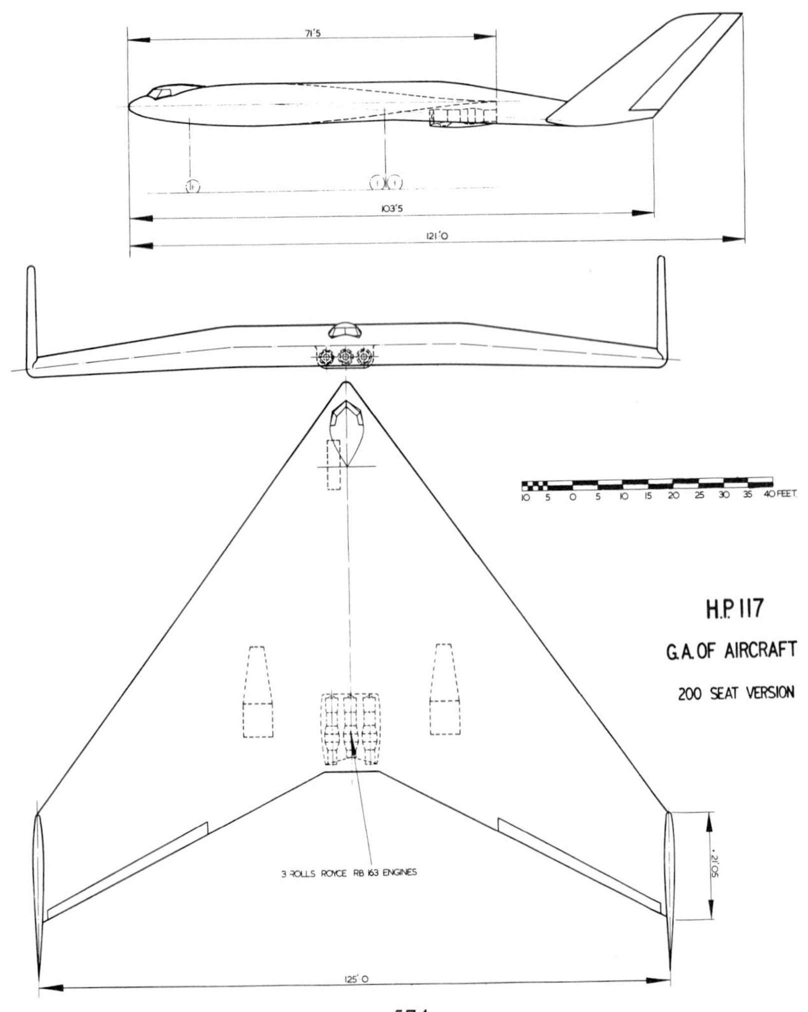

laminar flow research in 1958, because the problem of swept wings seemed then to be insuperable, but Pfenninger and his Northrop team continued their work and found that only 5 to 10 per cent more suction was in fact needed for a swept wing than for a straight one, in addition to leading-edge suction which a straight wing did not need. Northrop then received a $13 million contract to convert two Douglas WB-66Ds as laminar flow control aircraft for the USAF under the designation X-21A. Hoping that financial support might be forthcoming in Britain also, Lachmann had planned a research programme beginning with flight tests with suction on the Folland Midge half-wing mounted vertically on the fuselage of the College of Aeronautics's Lancaster PA474, followed by 50 hours' test flying of the Midge suction wing at a higher speed on a Victor, concurrently with the start of three years' flight testing of two 0·3-scale H.P.117 aircraft, to be

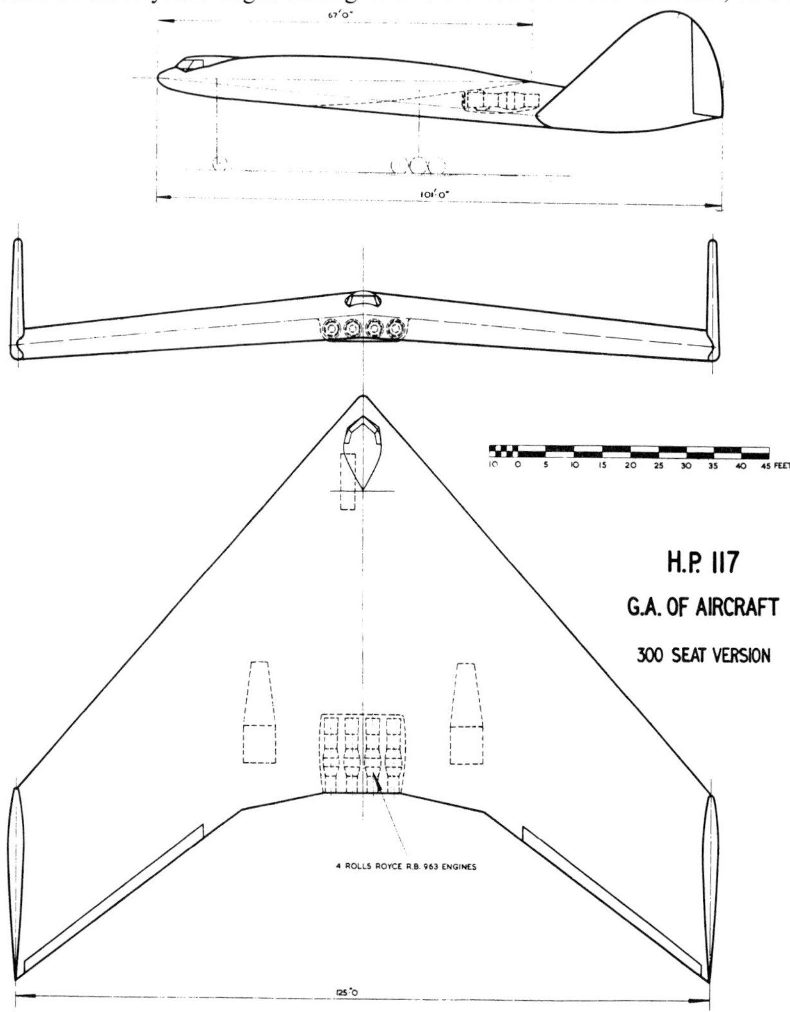

known as H.P.119s. H.P.119 was to have a maximum take-off weight of 30,000 lb and to be powered by three Bristol Siddeley Viper BSV.20 turbojets of 3,000 lb s.t., two being normally used for propulsion and the third, running at constant mass-flow, for suction. The two propulsion engines took in boundary layer 'clean-up' air through internal intakes and the centrally-installed suction engine could be used for emergency propulsion by extending a retractable ram air intake under the fuselage. The wing was to span 44 ft 8 in and was swept 50 degrees with fins and rudders at the tips. With a crew of two, instrumentation payload of 1,000 lb and 1,700 gallons of fuel, the still-air range was estimated as 5,850 nm at 458 kt and 40,000 ft. H.P.119 was discussed at intervals during 1961 with the Ministry of Aviation, but Treasury support was denied and only the trials of the Midge suction wing on the Cranfield Lancaster were approved for an initial research contract.

In its earliest form, H.P.117 was proposed as a 200-passenger airliner with three Rolls-Royce Spey turbojets in the middle of the trailing edge; apart from the intakes and tail-pipes, the only excrescence was the raised canopy of the flight deck at the apex of the leading edge. Within the overall limitations of a sweep angle appropriate to a cruise critical Mach number of 0·8 and head-room for 200 passengers entirely within the wing profile, design studies were made for three spans—155 ft, 140 ft and 125 ft—the last being chosen as the optimum. A wing was then designed to accommodate 300 passengers with the same span of 125 ft, the mid-chord sweep being 44 degrees for both; a pusher turboprop version was briefly examined, but found to be less economic than by-pass turbojets because of its lower cruising speed, which nevertheless gave no useful weight saving in structure or fuel required. The engines proposed for the 300-passenger version were Rolls-Royce RB.963s giving 12,500 lb s.t. as against the Spey's 10,400 lb. With adequate depth out to the tips, the whole span of the larger wing could provide head-room for passengers, but the smaller wing was not deep enough over the outer quarter span. When no contract cover was forthcoming to develop H.P.117, Lachmann continued to optimise the design for 300 passengers and by 1962 the span had increased to 148 ft 10 in, with increased sweep and aspect ratio; the reduced chord and depth then limited passenger accommodation to the inboard half of the span, with a central lengthened cabin for 110 passengers seated five abreast and 97 passengers in each wing-root cabin. The central pressure-cabin formed a truncated cylindrical fuselage flanked by two clusters of three Speys drawing half their air through the suction system and half in 'clean-up' air aft of the flight-deck canopy together with ram intakes; for take-off and climb below 15,000 ft, the suction system was to be inoperative except for the outer leading edges, where it was maintained to prevent tip stalling. Originally the all-up weight had been estimated as 250,000 lb and direct operating cost half that of current orthodox long-range aircraft; by 1962 the all-up weight had grown to 330,000 lb with 79,000 lb payload and 100,000 lb of fuel giving a range of over 5,000 miles with full BOAC allowances and reserves for headwinds, diversions and normal deterioration of performance in service.

The Midge wing proved more costly to convert to suction than the design and construction of an equivalent new half-wing with 45 degrees sweep at the leading edge, 13 ft tall, 8 ft 4 in root chord and 5 ft 8 in tip chord, the

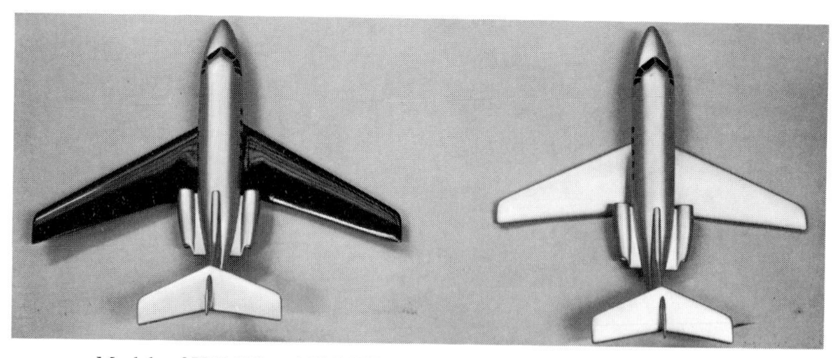

Models of H.P.130 and H.S.125 compared. (*I.W.M.—Crown Copyright*)

laminarised span being 8 ft 4 in above a boundary layer fence at the root parallel to the Lancaster fuselage. The suction installation in the Lancaster comprised two 60 hp Budworth marine gas-turbines enclosed in plenum boxes connected to the test wing by six flexible suction pipes fed with air drawn through manifolds, needle-valves and venturi-meters from numerous slits in the wing surfaces. A separate similar system collected air from the fibreglass leading edge in which the 0·005-in slits were more closely pitched. The test-wing root attachments permitted 5 degrees of adjustable offset incidence on either side of the centre-line. The installation was ready for flight testing by the end of September 1962 (more than three years after the original date) and the Lancaster with the suction-wing installed was first flown for 70 min on 2 October by Bert Russell, test pilot of the College of Aeronautics; before flight trials of the Lancaster ended it had been discovered that turbulence at the leading edge could be much reduced by a small hump near the root and the trials continued at Cranfield till late in 1965 after the suction wing installation had been improved and transferred to a Lincoln; earlier instrumentation difficulties were largely overcome by developing a hot-film technique in place of pitot combs. One small bonus from the Cranfield programme was that PA474 remained flying for some years after most other Lancasters had been broken up for scrap and thus survived to become a popular performer at flying displays from 1970 onwards, after restoration to its original wartime appearance.

In 1963 the Ministry of Aviation accepted a design tender from Handley Page Ltd for larger suction wings to be installed on a Hawker Siddeley H.S.125 twin-jet light transport, with suction provided by a small turbine in a fairing forward of the wing-root and exhausted at slightly above flight speed under the fuselage. This design, H.P.130, was technically approved by MoA in August 1964 for manufacture and conversion at Park Street under sub-contract to Hawker Siddeley Aviation Ltd, since Handley Page Ltd had not complied with the Ministry's rationalisation plan and could therefore not be given a prime contract. This programme was not completed within the twelve months specified and lapsed with Dr Lachmann's retirement at the end of 1965. His final design study in laminar flow control by suction was H.P.135, an ultra-long-range military transport designed to carry a payload of 100,000 lb at Mach 0·875 over 7,300 nm. It had shoulder-mounted swept wings fully laminarised by suction turbines pod-mounted under each wing, and a high T-tail

Model of H.P.135 global range B.L.C. transport.

laminarised from the four ducted-fan turbojets installed in the tail; the span was 205 ft and all-up weight 475,000 lb. A model of H.P.135 was exhibited on the Handley Page stand at the Paris Air Show at Le Bourget in June 1965; large though it was, the project was dwarfed by the Soviet 212-ft span, 552,000-lb, Antonov An-22 prototype, which dominated the flying display outside, though a much less advanced concept than H.P.135. Lachmann had intended to continue studying laminar flow problems after his retirement, but died in May 1966.

H.P.103

(Armstrong Siddeley Viper ASV.5)

Span 35 ft 2 in (10·7 m); length 31 ft 10 in (9·72 m); wing area 214 sq ft (19·87 m²). Empty weight 4,474 lb (2,027 kg); maximum weight 6,640 lb (3,015 kg). Speed 275 kt (510 km/h); range 440 n miles (826 km); ceiling 34,000 ft (10,500 m). Pilot alone.

H.P.113

(Two Bristol Orpheus)

Span 71 ft 3 in (21·74 m); length 71 ft 6 in (21·8 m); wing area 775 sq ft (72 m²). Empty weight (est) 19,258 lb (8,730 kg); maximum weight (est) 36,500 lb (16,550 kg). Cruising speed (est) 458 kt (870 km/h); range (est) 5,300 miles (8,500 km); ceiling (est) 50,000 ft (15,450 m). Crew two. Passengers 8–12.

H.P.117

(Four Rolls-Royce RB.963)

Span 125 ft (38·1 m); length 101 ft (30·8 m); wing area 5,820 sq ft (540 m²). Empty weight (est) 130,135 lb (59,100 kg); maximum weight (est) 330,000 lb (149,500 kg). Cruising speed (est) 458 kt (870 km/h); range (est) 5,000 miles (8,050 km); ceiling (est) 55,000 ft (17,000 m). Crew 4–6. Passengers 300.

Flying Jeep and V/STOL Freighter Projects (H.P.112, 116, 118, 120 and 122)

By 1950 gas-turbine technology had advanced to the point where it was possible to design a very lightweight simple turbojet having a thrust eight or more times its own dry weight and capable of being installed vertically so as to produce direct lift independently of wing-borne aerodynamic flight. Dr A. A. Griffith had resigned from RAE Farnborough to join Rolls-Royce Ltd as chief scientist and in 1953 had demonstrated the principle of jet lift with the Rolls-Royce Thrust-Measuring Rig, popularly known as the 'Flying Bedstead'. He then initiated the design of the RB.108 lifting turbojet of 2,000 lb s.t. with a thrust/weight ratio of 8:1 and the Ministry of Supply issued specification ER.143T for a VTOL research aeroplane, the successful tender being Short Brothers & Harland's S.C.1, two of which were ordered and built. The first of these, XG900, began flying at Boscombe Down without lift engines on 2 April, 1957, while the second, XG905, began tethered hovering flight trials at Belfast on 23 May, 1958, flying free for the first time on 25 October. Immediately, the Army became interested and invited the aircraft industry to submit schemes for enabling a light scout car to use direct lift to surmount topographical obstacles such as rivers, woodland, major roads and railways which interfered with free-ranging cross-country reconnaissance by land vehicles. The Fighting Vehicle Research and Development Establishment at Chobham, Surrey, issued specification 92/58 for an airborne reconnaissance vehicle with a crew of two and the New Design department of Handley Page Ltd made a number of exploratory studies of the 'Jumping Jeep', as did Shorts with their P.D.46, also English Electric Aviation Ltd at Preston.

The first studies, H.P.112, had to rely on the RB.108 as the only lift engine available in 1958 and the multiple installation of these small units was somewhat too complex for an acceptable operational solution, but a further design study, H.P.118,—the 'VTOL Jeep'—was begun in 1960

TYPE A
RIVER CROSSING

TYPE B EXECUTING SHORT HOP WITH WINGS FOLDED

around a larger lift engine, the RB.162 of 4,400 lb s.t.; this still had insufficient performance, but in 1961 Rolls-Royce's forecast of 11,000 lb s.t. from a developed RB.162 with an additional top (or front) fan led to a tender from Handley Page of H.P.120, offered in two variants. Type A was a simple wingless vehicle relying solely on direct lift from a centrally-installed fan-jet to permit hedge-hopping and short low-altitude flights; for normal land use it had a four-wheel drive from a 100 hp Coventry Climax F.W.B.B.6 2½-litre petrol engine, giving a cruising speed of 25 mph across country or 45 mph on average roads, with a radius of action of 230 miles. As a 'jumper' Type A had fuel capacity for about 50 hops of 1,000 yards or a still-air flying range of 45 miles at low altitude. Type B evolved as the last of five design schemes using folding wings and tail, with jet deflection to enhance the airborne performance, without encumbering land operation. Addition of a simple folding wing of 16 ft span and 144 sq ft gave no useful improvement and, in fact, reduced still-air range to 40 hops or 37 miles; limited thrust deflection of the RB.162, together with larger wings of 27 ft span and 178 sq ft only reduced performance further, to 36 hops or 35 miles in still air. Extending the range of jet deflection to permit horizontal thrust more than doubled the air miles per gallon and range went up to 79 miles without loss of hopping ability, but the need to throttle the engine in horizontal flight resulted in very poor specific fuel consumption. To avoid the latter defect, four small RB.172 aft-fan engines of 3,300 lb s.t. each were substituted for the single RB.162; this allowed the operational take-off weight to rise from 8,000 lb to 9,200 lb, keeping the maximum vertical thrust 15 per cent above the take-off weight. This combination, with the same 27-ft wings, nearly doubled the air-miles per gallon again, allowing a still-air range of 198 miles or 42 hops of 1,000 yards each, but the complexity of four engines and their intricate ducting was still an objection. The final scheme comprised one RB.162 top-fan lift engine together with one horizontally-installed RB.172 aft-fan flight engine; this gave the best operational flexibility and was the scheme tendered in October 1960, but when the RB.162 with top fan, renamed RB.175, eventually ran in 1962, its net thrust was only 8,800 lb, so the necessary margin of thrust over weight for take-off was not available and H.P.120 was abandoned.

Concurrently with the 'Jumping Jeep' and 'Flying Jeep' studies, the Air Staff had issued OR 351 for a V/STOL tactical freighter to carry a payload of 20,000 lb in a hold 40 ft by 10 ft by 10 ft. After investigating possible layouts under the heading of H.P.116, Handley Page Ltd submitted two tenders in May 1961. The second, H.P.123, has already been mentioned as the last projected Victor transport variant, but H.P.122 was an independent design relying on the 'Crouch-Bolas Effect', using distributed slipstream from large airscrews to develop vertical lift by means of leading-edge slots and trailing-edge slotted flaps. Neither was ordered, the successful tender being H.S.681, which was chosen in 1963 but cancelled two years later on grounds of national economy. Also referred to above was H.P.125, a Herald variant with eighteen lift engines, tendered to NBMR-4 in 1961.

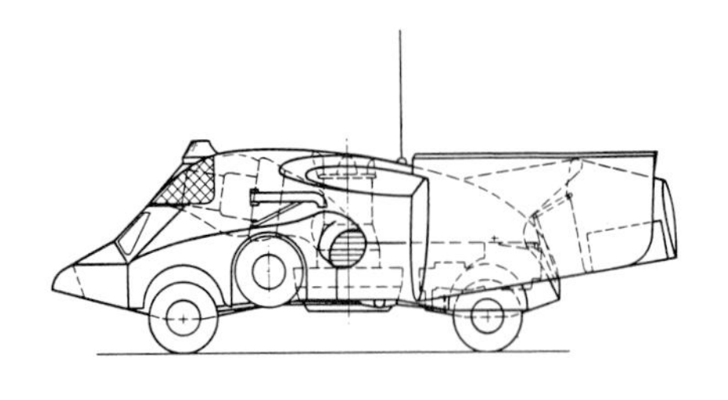

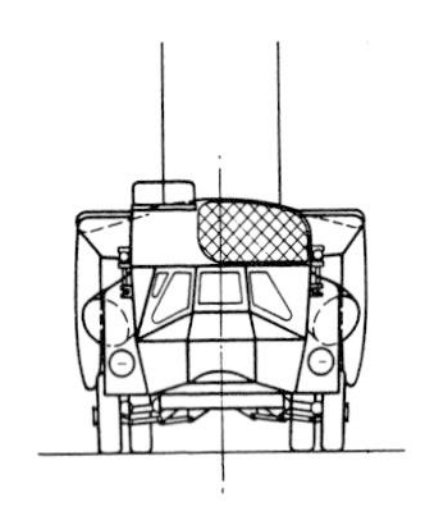

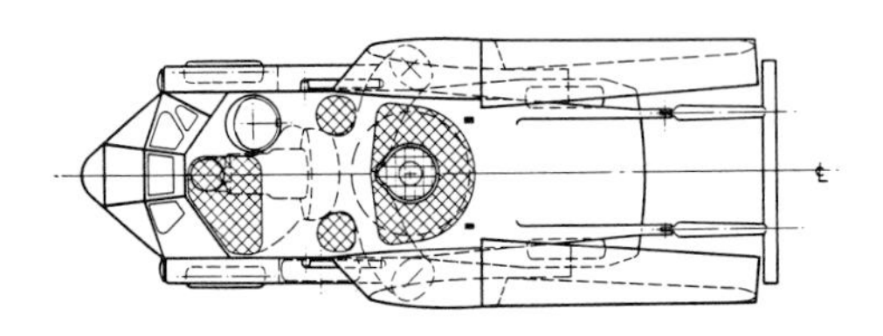

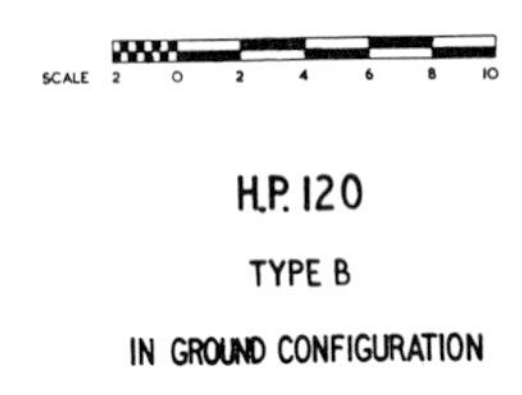

H.P.120

(Rolls-Royce RB.172 plus RB.175)

Span 27 ft (8·23 m); length 24 ft 8 in (7·55 m); wing area 178 sq ft (16·55 m²). Empty weight (est) 6,260 lb (2,840 kg); maximum weight (normal) (est) 9,200 lb (4,170 kg), (overload) (est) 10,200 lb (4,650 kg). Cruising speed (est) 200 mph (322 km/h); minimum speed (est) (wing-borne) 118 mph (191 km/h), (jet-borne) nil; range (est) normal 200 miles (322 km), overload 300 miles (483 km).

Aerobus Projects (H.P.126 and 134)

In November 1960 S. B. Gates FRS, a distinguished aerodynamicist at the RAE, wrote a memorandum urging that domestic civil aviation should be accorded the same advantages, accruing from advanced technology, as were being applied to the development of long-range high-speed aircraft. His paper *Wraps for Air Travellers* advocated an economical all-wing 'aerobus' and his arguments persuaded Dr M. J. Lighthill, Director of the RAE, to raise the matter with the Transport Aircraft Requirements Committee which, on 26 September, 1961, authorised him to form under his chairmanship a Working Party on Short-range Minimum-cost Air Transport, to include representatives of the Ministry of Aviation, SBAC, ARB, BEA, BOAC and BIATA.* Their terms of reference were 'to examine the long-term potentialities for reduction of operating costs of short range transport aircraft, particularly those arising from new ideas in

* British Independent Air Transport Association.

aircraft design, and to recommend lines of research conducive to a reduction of operating costs'; three Panels (Operational, Technical and All-wing) were formed to consider specific aspects of the problem. The All-wing Panel commissioned three different design studies, from Bristol Aircraft Ltd, Handley Page Ltd and the Whitworth Gloster Division of Hawker Siddeley Aviation Ltd respectively, of a 100-passenger aircraft to operate two consecutive 250-mile stages with normal reserves and without refuelling between stages. The Whitworth Gloster design was conventional and the other two were all-wing, Handley Page's being H.P.126 with a compound swept wing, while Bristol submitted a compound delta which received no type number. In each case an outline study of a geometrically similar aircraft to carry about 250 passengers was prepared for comparative cost estimates.

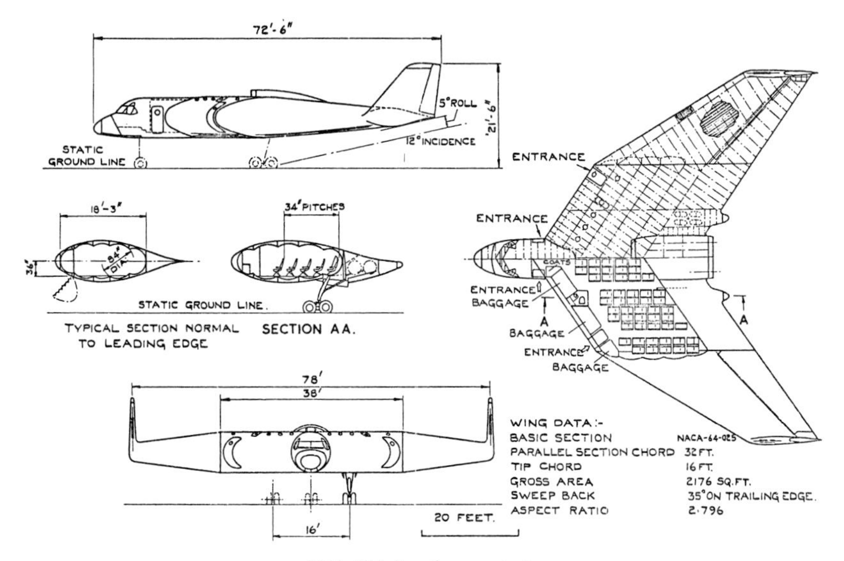

H.P. 126 Aerobus project.

The H.P.126 wing had a thick basic aerofoil section (NACA–64–025) with a constant chord centre-section of 35 degrees sweep and 38 ft span, carrying tapered outer wings of 20 ft span each with upturned swept fins and rudders at the tips, the overall span being 78 ft and gross wing area 2,176 sq ft; the centre-section chord was 32 ft and the outer wings tapered to 16 ft chord at the tip. A circular-section front fuselage contained the flight deck and forward retracting twin-wheeled nose undercarriage, while the two main undercarriages, with four-wheeled bogies, retracted rearwards into fairings in the trailing edge. Four by-pass turbojets totalling 29,000 lb s.t. were installed side by side in a central nacelle, with a combined ram intake on the upper surface of the wing; control surfaces—elevons and rudders—were conventional without blow-out, since no form of boundary layer control was economic over such short stages. H.P.126 was designed to cruise at Mach 0·70 at 20,000 ft and its all-up weight was 78,000 lb. The centre-section provided seating for 102 passengers in a cabin space constructed of five intersecting cylinders, three of 7 ft diameter flanked fore and aft by smaller cylinders, with their axes parallel to the leading edge; these wing-cabins, and the fuselage which merged into them, were moderately pressurised and the cusps of the intersections could have been joined by vertical tie-rods to permit a higher cabin pressure. The similar larger design would have had a span of 111 ft and overall length of 101 ft, with four by-pass turbojets of Conway size and accommodation for 264 passengers; its all-up weight would have been 170,000 lb. Although the larger project would have had 20 per cent lower direct operating costs than H.P.126, it was considered too large for the operations under review and was not examined in detail, nor was an intermediate size to carry 178 passengers. All three design study reports were submitted to the Working Party in March 1963; in their final report in January 1964 the Working Party concluded that there would be good market prospects in the 1970s for an aircraft with 100 to 150 seats designed specifically to offer low direct operating costs over stages less than 500 miles in the developed regions of the world. Such an aircraft would have a high usable maximum lift coefficient and sophisticated electronic equipment, but furnishing and operator's items would be reduced to minimum weight. They believed that a total reduction in d.o.c. of about 35 per cent below current short-haul figures could be achieved for an 'aerobus' entering service in 1975, but that the all-wing designs had no clear advantage over conventional layouts, though they urged the TARC to explore all-wing concepts further.

Charles Joy, as Handley Page's chief designer, was one of the SBAC representatives in the Working Party, but most of the H.P.126 design study was the work of his deputy Godfrey Lee, who, still collaborating with Barry Gates, extended it in a further project, H.P.134, which he called the Ogee Aerobus. This had an integrated thick wing and fuselage evolved by suppressing the outer wings and extending the front fuselage of H.P.126 and finally smoothing the resulting shape to an ogival plan of equal area but minimum drag, with a single central fin and rudder instead of upturned wing-tips. With three turbojets of 14,000 lb s.t. each, H.P.134 would have

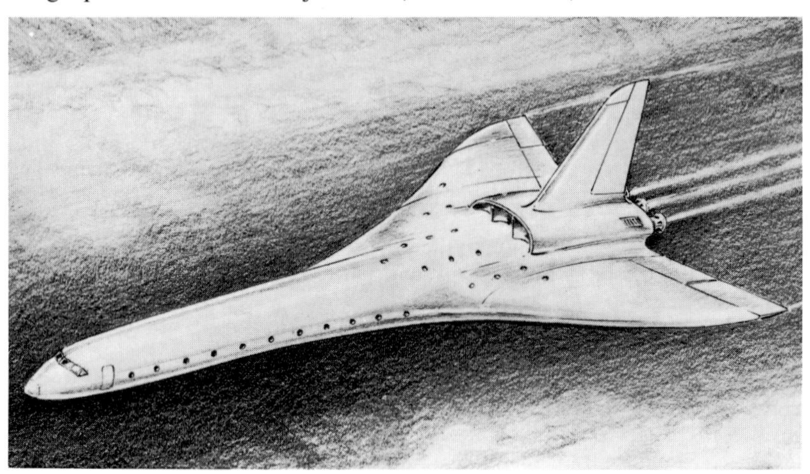

H.P.134 Ogee Aerobus project. (*I.W.M.—Crown Copyright*)

carried 154 passengers at Mach 0·80 at 20,000 ft, giving a block speed of 347 mph over 250 miles at a d.o.c. 15–20 per cent lower than conventional aircraft; with ample space available for increased fuel tankage, H.P.134 could have operated at a slightly higher take-off weight over a 1,600-mile stage for only 9d/passenger-mile, or half the d.o.c. of conventional designs. H.P.134 was described by Lee in his contribution to the All-Day Symposium on Cheap Short-Range Air Transport held by the Royal Aeronautical Society in London on 4 May, 1965, with Professor M. J. Lighthill (as he had become) in the chair.

H.P.126 Aerobus

(Four by-pass turbojets)

Span 78 ft (23·8 m); length 72 ft 6 in (22·7 m); wing area 2,176 sq ft (201·5 m²). Empty weight (est) 42,000 lb (19,050 kg); maximum weight (est) 78,000 lb (35,400 kg). Speed M: 0·7; range 500 miles (805 km). Crew two. Passengers 102.

HP.134 Ogee Aerobus

(Three by-pass turbojets)

Span 55 ft (17·7 m); length 95 ft (28·95 m); wing area 2,350 sq ft (218·2 m²). Maximum weight (est) 103,000 lb (46,700 kg). Speed M : 0·8; range 500 miles (805 km). Crew two. Passengers 154.

Jetstream (H.P.137)

Denied Treasury funding for new projects because of their decision not to merge with BAC or Hawker Siddeley after Sir Frederick's death in 1962, Handley Page Ltd had been occupied during the next three years with production of Heralds and modification and overhaul of Victors. A new Commercial Division had been formed to exploit existing facilities (including the large spot-welding machine) at Cricklewood to manufacture non-aircraft products, such as domestic oil-filled radiators, and to apply aeronautical techniques to new commercial projects, comprising the Jet Stream Airveyor factory handling system, various items of brewery plant and an all-fabric catenary-suspension portable hangar enclosing a floor area of 11,000 sq ft and capable of withstanding wind speeds up to 75 mph. This last was adopted by the RAF but the company was reluctant to become solely a supplier of ground equipment. Laminar-flow wing development had ceased after cancellation of H.P.130, following a change of government policy in 1964, and the exhibition model of H.P.135 shown at Paris in June 1965 was, in effect, a farewell gesture from Lachmann on the eve of his retirement.

British aerobus projects were overtaken by French proposals for the much larger European Airbus, but the Working Party's conclusions on the compatibility of simple structural design with sophisticated systems had been endorsed and followed up by the technical director, Reginald Stafford. The Herald faced continuing competition, not only from the Fokker Friendship and Avro 748, but also from a new generation of short-haul turbojet airliners. Furthermore, some of the many piston-engined

D.H. Doves and Herons operating local airlines in the USA had been successfully modernised by Riley Aeronautics Corporation at Fort Lauderdale, Florida, and suitable small turboprops, such as the Pratt & Whitney PT-6A and Garrett AiResearch TPE-331 in America and the Turboméca Astazou in France, were becoming available in the 800 hp class for turbine conversions. Yet no manufacturer had so far shown an interest in catering for the potential market for a 12/20-passenger turboprop transport, much cheaper to buy and operate over ranges of less than 1,000 miles than the small executive jets exemplified by the D.H.125. This was the gap in the transport aircraft spectrum that Handley Page Ltd decided in August 1965 to fill with the Jetstream, H.P.137; the next available type number, 136, was passed over because of possible confusion with the current H.S.136 project nearby at Hatfield; by mutual agreement, de Havilland had not used type numbers 117 and 124 because of their prior adoption by Handley Page, who in turn had avoided 121 when assigned to the D.H.121 Trident.

With the promulgation of US Federal Airworthiness Requirements Part 23, to permit single-pilot operation of commercial transport aircraft of not more than 12,500 lb all-up weight, and draft issue of the equivalent BCAR Section K, it was decided to optimise the Jetstream for 12,500 lb, while designing it structurally for eventual two-crew certification at 14,000 lb under FAR 25 and BCAR Section D. A genuine 'walk-around' cabin with 6 ft head room was deemed essential, necessary corollaries being a cabin differential pressure of 6·5 psi and a long fatigue life in spite of frequent landings. The structure weight was, nevertheless, to be kept low enough to ensure profitable operation either as a third-level airliner with eighteen passengers or an executive transport with eight. Market research studies were commissioned in America from business consultants Warren Kraemer and R. Dixon Speas, before distributing the specification to likely operators in October 1965, and in December discussions with Jack M. Riley at Fort Lauderdale resulted in a firm order for twenty Jetstreams from Riley Aeronautics Corporation.

In January 1966 the Board of Handley Page Ltd authorised the immediate manufacture of four prototypes, plus one and a half static airframes for structural testing, intending to provide the estimated launching costs of £2½–3 million from the company's own resources; meanwhile Lord Plowden had reported to the Minister of Aviation the findings of his committee, appointed in December 1964 to consider '. . . the future place and organisation of the aircraft industry in relation to the general economy of the country, taking into account . . . export prospects . . .' Somewhat unexpectedly, in view of earlier government commands to 'merge or die', MOA offered to provide £1½ million in launching aid, subject to prior examination and approval of the development programme and to a levy on every production aircraft sold, but without penalty in respect of any short-fall in sales before full reimbursement had been achieved; the offer was accepted and while the four prototypes took shape alongside Heralds and Victors (and still a few Hastings) in the main assembly hall at Colney Street, a Jetstream production line was tooled-up for a possible total of 500 aircraft in a completely new adjoining single-storey factory built in three blocks of 30,000 sq ft each. At the SBAC show in September 1966, the firm displayed a mock-up fuselage furnished in executive style and announced the receipt of sales options on 65 Jetstreams in USA, where the Riley concern, already renamed Riley Jetstream Corporation, had been taken over by K. R. Cravens of St Louis, Missouri, who formed the International Jetstream Corporation to handle all American sales and service. At home, CSE Aviation Ltd of Oxford had undertaken to sell twenty Jetstreams a year for five years and were appointed distributors and service agents for Europe, Asia and Africa; the Australasian franchise was to be negotiated later and the manufacturers retained only military sales for themselves; by relying on distributor networks in the same way as the automobile industry, the manufacturers relieved themselves of the task of building up a sales and service organisation specifically for Jetstream customers. A range of eight basic furnishing schemes was designed by Charles Butler Associates of New York and these were to be executed in America by Pacific Airmotive Corporation of Los Angeles, or for CSE Aviation's aircraft by Rumbold Ltd. Jetstreams were to fly away from Radlett untrimmed and unfurnished, but with all systems fully installed except avionics which, like furnishings, were buyer's options and were to be installed by the distributors; basic ferrying kits were returnable to Radlett after delivery and comprised a radio package, also long-range cabin fuel tanks where necessary for transatlantic stages.

The Jetstream was an entirely conventional, yet highly refined, twin-engined low-wing pressurised monoplane of 52 ft span and 47 ft overall length—substantially smaller than Radlett's traditional products. The wing area was 270 sq ft and the aspect ratio 10; the wing was unswept with 7 degrees dihedral, tapered uniformly from root to tip and basically of NACA 63A profile. The fuselage had a cylindrical cabin 24 ft long and 6 ft 6 in in diameter; the tailplane, like the wing, was tapered and unswept, but flat; it was mounted on the fin above the tapered rear fuselage in the lowest position where it would remain clear of the downwash from the wing and double-slotted flaps. The outer wings were attached by root-end bolts to a stub-wing built integrally with the fuselage and outside the pressure-cabin. To increase the effective elevator and rudder power, the fin was swept back at 45 degrees; although not necessary aerodynamically, this improved the visual effect and was calculated to appeal to American customers. The Frise-type ailerons were conventional and the elevators and rudder were horn-balanced, with geared trim-tabs on ailerons and elevators, and a large spring-tab on the rudder for trimming and bias in the engine-cut case. The flight deck was arranged for a crew of two side by side with dual controls; the rather long nose forward of the windscreen and front pressure bulkhead was unpressurised and carried the twin-wheeled steerable nose undercarriage, which retracted forward; the space around this was used for electrical and avionic equipment, where it was readily accessible for servicing through top-hinged doors; a nose radome was available in place of the metal nose-cap if needed for weather radar. There were seven 'neutral-hole' elliptical windows on each side of the cabin, the middle one on the starboard side being mounted in an inward-opening rectangular emergency-exit hatch. The downward-opening entrance door at the rear of the cabin on the port side was double-skinned, bottom-hinged and incorporated air-stairs. Structurally the fuselage was conventional, with frames and stringers attached to the single skin by countersunk rivets, but the skin was locally reduced in thickness by chemical milling to save weight and Bloomingdale epoxy adhesive was used as a gap-filler along all frame and stringer faying surfaces. The floor comprised a central walkway giving 71 inch headroom inside the trim line, flanked by vertical keel members supporting longitudinal standard seat-rails, all floor surfaces being metal sandwich panels with expanded plastic cores to improve thermal and acoustic insulation. A movable square-section 'floor-box' could be located along either the starboard side of the walkway to offset the footwell to port in the 18-passenger three-abreast layout, or the opposite side to give a nearly central walkway in the executive version. The air-conditioning system gave a cabin altitude of 8,000 ft when flying at 30,000 ft and the seven-panel flight deck windscreen comprised double-paned flat sandwich panels of which the two in front of the pilots were of bird-impact-resistant laminated glass, electrically heated by gold film for demisting and anti-icing; the cabin windows, central and side fixed windscreen panels and two direct-vision windows were of sandwich plastic construction with a sealed interspace. Each wing comprised a box spar having 25-ft long single upper and lower skins forming an integral fuel tank of 195 gallons divided internally by diaphragm ribs with one-way flap valves to direct fuel flow inboard, where the innermost cell formed a collector tank containing two electric booster pumps supplying the engine on its own side; the collector tanks were interconnected by a cross-feed pipe outside the pressure cabin, the low-pressure feed and cross-feed cocks being mechanically operated from the pilot's console. Protective treatment of the Jetstream airframe was thorough, with chromic acid-etch primer followed by epoxy enamels designed to leach protective chromate salts on exposure to salt water or 'bilge fluid'.

The very small-diameter Turboméca Astazou XIV turboprops were mounted on welded steel tube bearers from firewalls at the wing leading edge, with over-wing tail-pipes. The main landing gear retracted inboard, to be enclosed by fairing plates which left the single wheels flush in the wing but uncovered and, like the wheel-brakes, nosewheel steering and wing flaps, was hydraulically actuated from a 2,000 psi system powered by two engine-driven Vickers-Sperry-Rand pumps; this system was suitable for either D.T.D.585 mineral oil or Skydrol non-flammable fluid as preferred by the customer, subject to the appropriate seal materials being chosen. The double-slotted wing flaps could be selected in three flight positions for cruise, take-off and landing, the last selection giving, automatically, an extreme 'lift dump' deflection as soon as the airscrews had been selected to 'ground-fine' pitch and the nosewheel was on the ground. From take-off to landing the Astazou XIV was run at constant speed, with airscrew blade-angle and fuel flow automatically determined by the position of the pilot's 'beta-control' power lever, there being safeguards against flame-out and high turbine entry temperature. Unlike earlier models, which had been integrated with the Ratier-Figeac electric pitch-control system, the Astazou XIV drove a Hamilton Standard reversible-pitch hydraulic airscrew. The Jetstream's electrical system was powered by a 200V alternator on each engine, 'raw' a.c. being used for airscrew and windscreen deicing, with general services supplied with d.c. at 28V and instruments and avionics with controlled frequency a.c. at 115V. Electronic equipment was comprehensive and advanced, a choice of the Bendix M-4C or Collins 103 auto-pilot systems being available, with full VOR/ILS facilities for blind flying.

From the beginning, the design programme had been monitored by PERT critical path analysis, to control both cost and weight within the very tight limits imposed by the specification and there had been no serious slippage up till May 1967, when the first prototype was due to fly. By this date minor delays had begun to accumulate and G-ATXH was not finally rolled-out for fuel flow tests till the end of June; having missed its chance of a debut at the Paris Aero Show, it was then more comprehensively equipped with systems and flight-test instrumentation before beginning engine runs and taxying trials at Radlett, after a week of which it took off on 18 August for a 100-minute maiden flight piloted by John Allam and Harry Rayner with John Coller as flight test engineer. Allam found it 'a delight to fly', the only incident being partial seizure of the starboard wheel brake at touch-down, which he was able to compensate by applying full reverse thrust from the opposite engine. During the ensuing week G-ATXH, still temporarily powered by 690 ehp Astazou XIIs, was flown by seven pilots who all endorsed Allam's opinion. Two definitive 840 ehp

First Jetstream prototype G-ATXH flying in 1968. (*Aviation Photo News*)

Astazou XIVs were then installed, with which 'XH flew again on 29 November; G-ATXJ, similarly powered, was next to fly on 28 December. Development flight testing was speeded up in better weather by using the Turboméca airfield at Pau as a winter base and 'XH flew there on 14 December, followed by 'XJ directly after its maiden flight. The next prototype, G-ATXI, flew on 8 March, 1968, and the fourth, G-ATXK, assigned to International Jetstream Corporation as the US demonstrator, on 8 April, was ferried to St Louis in May.

Meanwhile the United States Air Force Source Selection Board had been considering tenders from nine firms, including Handley Page, to the CX requirement for a light twin-turboprop 'mission support' transport and had provisionally chosen the Beechcraft 99 for an initial contract for about eighty aircraft, but in December 1967 this decision was overruled by the Defense Secretary Robert McNamara and Air Force Secretary Dr Harold Brown in favour of a smaller trial batch of eleven Jetstreams, to be powered by Garrett AiResearch TPE-331s of 895 ehp; at 14,500 lb all-up this Jetstream 3M was to be certificated to FAR 25 as the C-10A utility

Jetstream 3M prototype with Garrett AiResearch TPE-331 engines near Radlett in 1969.

transport adaptable for passenger, cargo, crew training and aero-medical roles. It was to have an extra side door extending the existing passenger door, a strengthened floor for cargo and a removable jump-seat for a third crew member. At £2,400,000 for eleven aircraft, the contract price barely covered the cost of manufacture, but was accepted in expectation of further options totalling £18 million and initially fifteen USAF serials, 68-10378 to 68-10392, had been allocated. In support of this contract, a Garrett-engined fifth prototype was put in hand and flew as G-AWBR on 21 November, 1968, while G-ATXI, on its return from Pau in March 1969, was also re-engined with Garretts, with which it flew again on 7 May; it was hoped that the Garrett installation might attract further civil sales in America, as had happened in the case of the Short Skyvan, but the USAF contract provided for only a nominal down-payment and no real launching aid, so this variant lost money from the start and Handley Page Ltd had spent £5½ million on development by the end of 1968, when the first production Jetstreams began flying. In May 1968 an additional Handley Page factory had been started at Cumnock, Ayrshire, to provide three-shift employment for 300 workers made redundant by local coalpit closures; equipped with 'advanced technology' numerically-controlled machine-tools, it was to provide most of the myriad small machined parts required in Jetstream production; earlier the manufacture of all Jetstream wings had been sub-contracted to Scottish Aviation Ltd at Prestwick, Ayrshire, and complete tail assemblies were ordered from Northwest Industries of Edmonton, Alberta, together with hydraulic systems and landing gear from Electro-Hydraulics Ltd and electrical equipment from Plessey Ltd. The production programme envisaged manufacture of ten batches of fifty aircraft at a rate of fifteen per month, but this proved to be too ambitious.

The prototypes and early production aircraft were somewhat overweight and this entailed modifications which eventually proved effective, but at a heavy cost in design overtime and delay. The airworthiness certification flying programme had to be shared by G-ATXH and 'XJ alone, since 'XI and G-AWBR were committed to Garrett trials and 'XK had gone to America; of these only 'XJ was fully instrumented. The ARB insisted on a stall-warning indicator, since the natural buffet was not positive enough, and after clearing these handling trials 'XJ was damaged while demonstrating short-field landings at Hatfield on 4 September, 1968, which caused several weeks' delay. Meanwhile the company's annual profit from all sources had fallen substantially and an issue of additional share capital to raise £3,200,000 to support Jetstream production had not been successful in providing urgently needed cash flow. By January 1969 bought-out parts and sub-contracted components were arriving at Radlett in quantity and had to be paid for.

The first and third production Jetstreams, having flown as bare aircraft on 6 December, 1968, and 22 January, 1969, respectively, were ferried by Captain W. J. Bright of Terravia Trading Services to International Jetstream Corporation at St Louis, having been ordered by Sun Airlines, while the second, first flown on 2 January as G-8-4, became the CSE demonstrator G-AXEK at Kidlington. This flew daily to Le Bourget and back during the Paris Air Show in June 1969 and was then evaluated by Dan-Air Services Ltd on their Bristol–Cardiff–Liverpool–Newcastle route, but was returned to the makers when CSE, disappointed with the excess structure weight, relinquished their distributorship after completing G-8-5 and G-8-6 as G-AXEM and 'EL. The latter was delivered to the British Steel Corporation but was short-lived, crashing soon after delivery near Hunstanton, Norfolk, on 29 September. The former was re-registered D-INAH on delivery to Bavaria Fluggesellschaft of Munich, who were foremost in a race to gain approval for third-level air services in Europe.

In contrast to disappointment in the Old World, there had been a keen demand for Jetstreams in America. Although Sun Airlines had not retained its two aircraft, these had been taken up by Cal-State Air Lines of Long Beach, California, as N1039S and N1040S, in addition to four already ordered as N1035S–N1038S and the fourth prototype G-ATXK, which the airline had leased from International Jetstream for its initial operations. Following type certification in April 1969, American sales continued and by July ten more had been ferried to St Louis by Bill Bright, as well as CF-QJB to Northwest Industries at Edmonton, where Airspur Corporation took up the Canadian agency and ordered twenty. The Board of Handley Page Ltd had already been reconstituted to enable £2¾ million in cash to be provided mainly by Barclays Bank and Scottish Aviation Ltd, but the only immediate way of regaining the Jetstream's original payload/range performance was to install the more powerful Astazou XVI; this required further finance and delay in development and the new Board had no alternative but to ask Barclays Bank to appoint a receiver, Kenneth R. Cork, who attempted to interest the RAF in the Jetstream as a multi-role trainer-transport, but without initial success in spite of favourable reactions by A & AEE and Training Command handling pilots. The Jetstream 3 prototype G-AWBR had completed tropical and certification trials and the first Jetstream 3M was about to commence flying in October when the USAF cancelled the contract on grounds of delayed delivery and the future of the Jetstream was even more in jeopardy. It was saved only by the last-minute agreement of the International Jetstream Corporation's parent company, K. R. Cravens Corporation, with the assistance of the Mercantile Trust Company of St Louis, to operate a new company, Handley Page Aircraft Ltd, solely for the development and production of

Third prototype, G-ATXJ, re-engined with Astazou XVIs as a prototype Jetstream 200, at Luton in 1970. (*Brian M. Service*)

Jetstreams. G-ATXH and 'XJ were then re-engined with Astazou XVIs, the former being sent to Rolls-Royce Ltd at Filton for intensive flying, while the latter undertook certification trials at 12,500 lb as Series 200, later to be raised to 14,000 lb as Series 300. Meanwhile eleven more Jetstream 1s were ferried across the Atlantic between September 1969 and February 1970 and G-AXFV, first flown in April as G-8-8, was also re-engined with Astazou XVIs in November as the Series 200 demonstrator. G-ATXJ was completing tropical trials at Fort Lamy, Chad, and G-AXEK was on a sales tour in Queensland when, on 27 February, Cravens Corporation informed Jack Rizika, the resident deputy chairman at Radlett, that no more cash was available for development and Handley Page Aircraft Ltd in its turn was bankrupt. For nine days, pending the appointment of its own receiver by Mercantile Trust, the company virtually ceased to exist and Bavaria Fluggesellschaft, who had been operating D-INAH successfully in Switzerland, asked for an assurance that aircraft and engine product support would be maintained. No reply had been given before this aircraft caught fire in the air, following an engine failure, and crashed while attempting to land at Samedan, near St Moritz, on 6 March, 1970, killing all eleven on board, including the managing director of Bavaria Flug, Max Schwabe, who was piloting. With the cessation of continuous cumulative fatigue-testing at Park Street, the twenty-five Jetstreams in the United States and CF-QJB in Canada were permitted to continue flying only up to a limit of 2,500 hours; at least one had already reached 1,000 hours and by the end of 1970 many of them were due to be grounded. Cal-State Air Lines ceased operation in May and six other Jetstreams were flown to Airspur at Edmonton for storage.

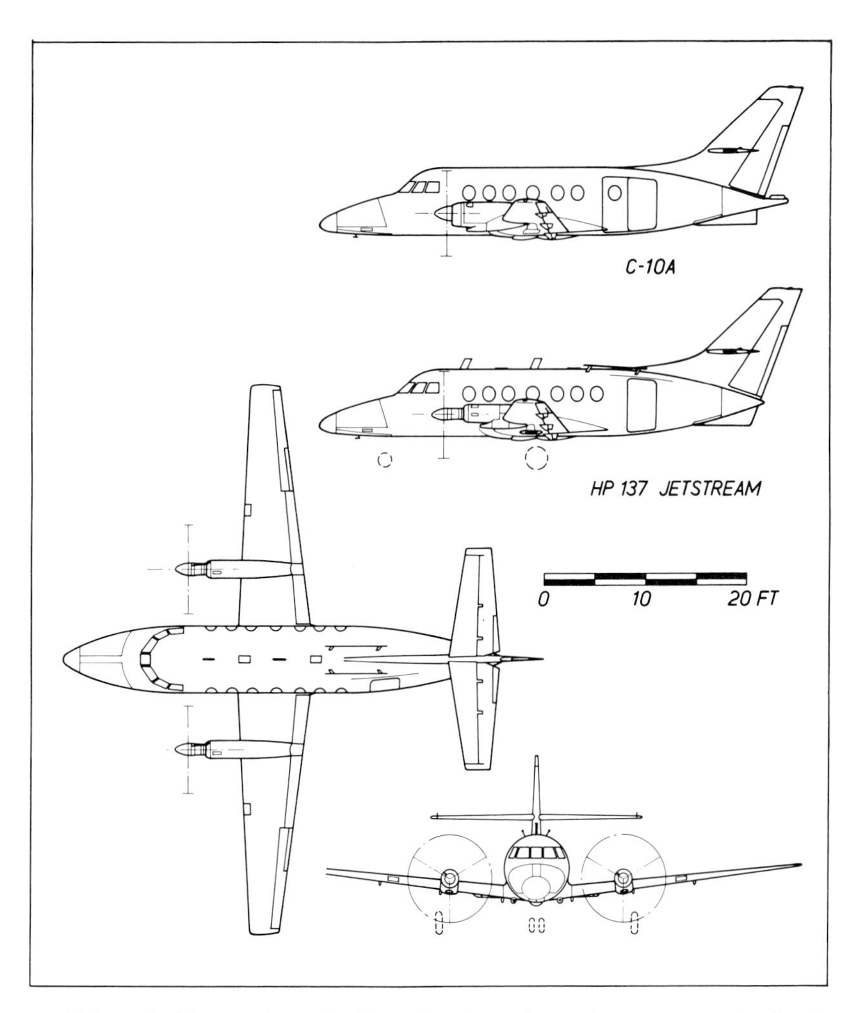

Although this was the end of Handley Page, it was by no means the death of the Jetstream, for the energetic Bill Bright was determined to keep it alive and to that end succeeded in 1971 in forming Jetstream Aircraft Ltd with the help of Terravia Trading and Scottish Aviation, after acquiring from the receiver of Handley Page Aircraft Ltd all the available spares and airframes in various stages of completion. With a flight-test and demonstration base at Leavesden and a production line at Sywell, some twenty airframes were to be completed for sale and N1035S was brought back from California as sales demonstrator. Prior to this, two Jetstreams had been moved in September 1970 from Radlett to Cranfield, where the Institute of Technology was to convert them into flying class-rooms for its own use. Cranfield was approved for the completion of additional structural test and design work required for certification of the Jetstream 200 and took G-AXFV on loan from Terravia for performance trials with

In June 1972 G-AXUI became a flying class-room for the Cranfield Institute of Technology. *(C.I.T.)*

Astazou XVIs. Having already won the *Daily Express* air race from Sywell to Biggin Hill on 12 June, 1971, in N1035S, Captain Bright competed a month later with G-AXFV in the London–Victoria, BC, transatlantic air race, from which it returned to Leavesden to be flown by John Allam to Dubai in September for tropical trials; several other key Handley Page personnel joined Terravia, others being Peter Cronbach (former deputy sales manager) and Frank Tyson (former deputy chief designer), while the former service manager, A. G. Knivett, later bought an incomplete Jetstream from Terravia and completed it at Kidlington as G-BBBV for export to America. Since neither Terravia nor Jetstream Aircraft were members of the SBAC, the Jetstream had been excluded from exhibition at Farnborough in 1970, but three were demonstrated at the Paris Air Show in June 1971.

The first Jetstream to be completed on the Sywell line, G-AXUO, was also the first to be sold in Europe by Jetstream Aircraft, becoming F-BTMI on delivery to the Franco-Belgian charter operator Air Wasteels of Metz on 26 January, 1972. On its return from Dubai, G-AXFV had gone to A & AEE Boscombe Down for assessment as the only British entrant in a competition to choose an RAF twin-turboprop pilot-trainer to replace the long obsolescent Vickers Varsity. As in the USAF CX competition, it proved superior to the Beech and other contestants and on 24 February, 1972, Mr Ian Gilmour, Minister of State, Defence Procurement, was able to announce in the House of Commons; 'We intend, subject to the conclusion of satisfactory contract arrangements, to place an order for about twenty-five Jetstream aircraft with Scottish Aviation'. This coincided with the acquisition by Scottish Aviation Ltd of all production and design rights held by Jetstream Aircraft, including all drawings, jigs, tools, components and aircraft completed or in progress at Sywell and Leavesden. Backed by their proprietors, the Laird shipbuilding and engineering group, Scottish Aviation formed a subsidiary, Scottish

G-AXUO was sold to Air Wasteels at Metz as F-BTMI after completion by Jetstream Aircraft Ltd at Sywell and Leavesden in January 1972. (*J. M. G. Gradidge*)

Aviation (Jetstream) Ltd, to manufacture fuselages at the former Handley Page factory at Cumnock, for assembly to the wings already being produced at Prestwick; they also reinstated a $500,000 subcontract for tail units with Northwest Industries at Edmonton, Alberta, who had earlier had to write off $2 million worth of work in progress when Handley Page Aircraft Ltd collapsed.

The Ministry of Defence contract was confirmed in August 1972 for twenty-six Jetstream T.1s, basically Series 200 with Astazou XVIs, but equipped with Sperry-Rand STARS flight director and Marconi

Scottish Aviation's second Jetstream T.1, XX476, formerly G-AXGL and N1037S, at CFS Little Rissington in 1973, showing modified aerials and 'eyebrow' windows. (*M.O.D.—Crown Copyright*)

AD.370BA DF systems, with an all-up weight of 14,000 lb; serials XX475–XX500 were allotted and deliveries were to begin in the spring of 1973. By reimporting N1036S and N1037S, little flown by Cal-State Air Lines before their demise, it was possible to rework these as XX475 and XX476, which were flown by John Blair and David Gates at Prestwick on 13 April and 19 June, 1973, respectively, the former going to A & AEE Boscombe Down and the latter to CFS Little Rissington for extended handling and operational trials. Five more, XX477–XX481, were reworked from the Colney Street-built but unflown airframes originally registered as G-AXXS, 'XT, 'UR, 'XU and 'UP respectively; between December 1973 and March 1974 XX477, XX478 and XX480 joined XX476 at Little Rissington, where the first eight-week standardisation course for qualified instructors on Jetstreams was completed in June, while the first all-Prestwick-built aircraft, XX482, went to No.5 Flying Training School, Oakington, on 16 May, followed by XX479 on 20 May, XX481 on 3 June and XX483 on 10 June; with the delivery of XX484 to No.5 FTS, the first advanced pilot-training course on Jetstreams began on 3 July, 1974. Conversion of the Series 200 transport into the Series 201 pilot-trainer entailed over 100 hours of development flying at A & AEE and CFS, where XX477 crash landed on 1 November and caused the temporary grounding of all RAF Jetstreams. Early stall-buffet encountered with some, but not all, individual aircraft was traced to turbulence induced by air leakage across the inner wing from the starboard nacelle and was rectified by improved sealing of the nacelle panel joints, but difficulty on landing approach persisted until the airscrew fine-pitch stop setting was modified to make the onset of braking less abrupt when the throttles were closed; this feature, designed for short-field commercial operation, had proved embarrassing to trainee pilots and their instructors alike. By January 1975 the Jetstream's problems had been resolved, but meanwhile a new programme of defence economy cuts had caused the disbandment of No.5 FTS and closure of Oakington, also the removal of CFS from Little

Rissington to Cranwell and the curtailment of multi-engine pilot-training, new Jetstreams being thereafter delivered to St Athan for storage. Production of civil Jetstream 200s had continued temporarily at Leavesden with G-BBYM (ex G-AYWR) for the Morgan Crucible Co, followed by G-BCGU (ex G-AXRI) for Arthur Guinness and G-BCWW (ex G-AXUN) for The Distillers Co Ltd, Turnhouse (call-sign, 'Whisky Whisky'); in December 1973 Captain Bright had sold his prototype G-AXFV to Gecamines in Zaïre, where it was re-registered 9Q-CTC. Production of any new civil Jetstreams at Prestwick depended on firm orders for at least fifteen Series 200s being received by Scottish Aviation before completion of the Ministry of Defence contract during 1975.

Cal-State's N1035S was returned to Biggin Hill, in December 1970, to become Terravia's demonstrator, reverting to G-AWVK when sold in 1974 to the Decca Navigator Co. Ltd. as a test-bed and demonstrator for electronic navigation aids. (*Courtesy Decca Navigator Co. Ltd.*)

In America, G-ATXK, like the three UK-based early prototypes, had been withdrawn from use before 1972, but the second production Jetstream 1 G-AXEK had been sold as N1FY to South Central Air Transport, whose intended but undelivered second Jetstream N1BE had become A. G. Knivett's G-BBBV at Kidlington. Cal-State's former N1035S, temporarily Terravia's demonstrator, reverted to its British registration G-AWVK on being sold to the Decca Navigator Co and N1039S was bought by Jack Riley as N14RJ when he re-established the Riley Aeronautics Corporation at a new base at Waco, Texas; there he converted another Jetstream, formerly Di Giorgio's N10DG, to N7RJ with Pratt & Whitney PT6A 34 engines as a demonstrator to attract the interest of those who liked the Jetstream but preferred an American power unit; this was shown at Dallas in October 1973. Seven Jetstreams remained stored by Airspur at Edmonton and others reverted to their owning finance companies after completing leases to temporary operators.

Given adequate support by Scottish Aviation and Riley, Jetstreams seem likely to continue flying into the 1980s, but new construction and development beyond the aircraft begun at Radlett are not properly Handley Page history.

H.P.137 Jetstream 1

(Two Turboméca Astazou XIV)

Span 52 ft (15·86 m); length 47 ft 1½ in (14·35 m); wing area 270 sq ft (25·05 m^2). Empty weight 8,450 lb (3,835 kg); maximum weight 12,500 lb (5,670 kg). Speed 298 mph (480 km/h); range 745 miles (1,200 km); ceiling 30,000 ft (9,270 m). Crew one or two. Passengers 18.

H.P.137 Jetstream 3M

(Two Garrett AiResearch TPE-331)

As Jetstream except:— Length 48 ft (14·64 m). Empty weight 10,000 lb (4,540 kg); maximum weight 14,500 lb (6,570 kg). Speed 300 mph (483 km/h); range 1,455 miles (2,340 km). Crew three. Passengers 12.

* * *

Further rationalisation and nationalisation of the British Aircraft Industry in 1975 brought Scottish Aviation into a major new grouping, with British Aircraft Corporation, Hawker Siddeley Aviation and Hawker Siddeley Dynamics, named British Aerospace.

On 5 December, 1978, British Aerospace Aircraft Group–Scottish Division at Prestwick, launched the 18/19-seat Jetstream 31 mini-airliner powered by two 940 shp Garrett TPE 331-10 turbines turning Dowty Rotol four-bladed advanced technology propellers. The prototype, G-JSSD, first flew on 28 March, 1980, making an 82 minutes flight from Prestwick. On board were British Aerospace test pilots Angus McVitie and J. L. S. Houston, J. R. Baker of Garrett-AiResearch and BAe flight test engineer Andrew Eldred. Three versions of the Jetstream 31 were available; an 18-seat airliner, a 12-seat Executive Shuttle and an 8/9-seat corporate aircraft. Specialist and military capabilities included flight inspection or Economic Zone patrolling, pilot/navigator training and Casevac duties.

More than 150 Jetstream 31s have been ordered by some 20 operators, including the Royal Navy. Over 50 of the earlier Astazou-powered Jetstreams have been delivered to customers, among them the RAF and Royal Navy taking 27 for multi-engined pilot training and as navigation trainers. Four Garrett-powered Jetstreams, designated T.3, serve with the Royal Navy for training maritime helicopter observers.

APPENDIX A

Handley Page Type List

Handley Page designs were identified at first by letters, but in 1924 type numbers were introduced; these continued until the firm ceased trading in 1970. From 1948 to 1960 designs originating in the former Miles Aircraft Ltd drawing office at Woodley were separately listed as Handley Page (Reading) type numbers. The complete Type Letter and Number list is given below, together with unsuccessfully tendered projects which were not given Type Numbers.

Type Letter	Type Number	Description and Name	Engine(s)	Date
A	H.P.1	Monoplane ***(Bluebird)***	Advance 20 hp	1909
B	H.P.2	Biplane	Green 60 hp	1909
C	H.P.3	Monoplane (A rebuilt)	Alvaston 25 hp	1910
D	H.P.4	Monoplane ***(Antiseptic)***	Green 35 hp	1911
D	H.P.4	***Antiseptic*** rebuilt	Isaacson 50 hp	1911
E/50	H.P.5	Monoplane ***(Yellow Peril)***	Gnome 50 hp	1911
F/70	H.P.6	Monoplane (Military)	Gnome 70 hp	1912
G/100	H.P.7	Biplane	Anzani 100 hp	1913
H/110	---	Monoplane project	Anzani 110 hp	1913
K/35	---	Biplane project	Anzani 35 hp	1913
L/200	H.P.8	Biplane (Atlantic)	Salmson 200 hp	1914
M/200	H.P.9	Biplane project	Two Salmson 95 hp	1914
MS/200	H.P.9	Seaplane version of M/200 project	Two Salmson 95 hp	1914
N/80	H.P.10	Biplane Scout project	Gnome 80 hp	1914
O/100	H.P.11	Biplane Heavy Bomber	Two Rolls-Royce Eagle	1915
O/100	H.P.11	Biplane Heavy Bomber	Two Sunbeam Cossack	1916
O/400	H.P.12	Biplane Heavy Bomber	Two Rolls-Royce Eagle VIII	1917
P/320	H.P.13	Triplane project	Sunbeam Cossack	1916
R/200	H.P.14	Biplane N.2B	Hispano-Suiza 200 hp	1917
S/400	---	O/400 Seaplane project	Two Rolls-Royce Eagle VIII	1917

Type Letter	Type Number	Description and Name	Engine(s)	Date
T/400	---	Flying-boat project	Two Rolls-Royce Eagle VIII	1917
V/1500	H.P.15	Biplane Heavy Bomber	Four Rolls-Royce Eagle VIII	1918
V/1500	H.P.15	Biplane Heavy Bomber	Four Napier Lion	1919
O/7	---	O/400 Transport Variant	Two Rolls-Royce Eagle VIII	1919
O/10	---	O/400 Transport Variant	Two Rolls-Royce Eagle VIII	1920
O/11	---	O/400 Transport Variant	Two Rolls-Royce Eagle VIII	1920
W/400	H.P.16	O/400 Transport Development	Two Rolls-Royce Eagle VIII	1919
---	H.P.17	Slotted D.H.9	Siddeley Puma	1919
W.8	H.P.18	Biplane Transport	Two Napier Lion	1919
W.8a	H.P.18	Biplane Transport project	Two Cosmos Jupiter	1919
W.8b	H.P.18	Biplane Transport	Two Rolls-Royce Eagle VIII	1921
W.8c	H.P.18	Biplane Transport	Two Rolls-Royce Eagle IX	1923
T	H.P.19	Torpedo Biplane (Hanley)	Napier Lion	1921
X/4B	H.P.20	Slotted Monoplane	Liberty 12	1921
S	H.P.21	Monoplane Scout (USN)	Bentley BR2	1922
---	H.P.22	Ultra-Light Monoplane	A.B.C. or Douglas	1923
---	H.P.23	Ultra-Light Monoplane (slotted wing)	Blackburne	1923
W.8d	H.P.24	Biplane Bomber (Hyderabad)	Two Napier Lion	1923
Ta	H.P.25	Torpedo Biplane (Hendon)	Napier Lion	1924
W.8e/f	H.P.26	Biplane Transport (Hamilton)	One Rolls-Royce Eagle IX and two Siddeley Puma	1924
W.8g	H.P.26	Hamilton rebuilt	Two Rolls-Royce F.XIIA	1929

Type Letter	Type Number	Description and Name	Engine(s)	Date
W.9	---	Military Transport project	Three Armstrong Siddeley Jaguar	1923
W.9a	H.P.27	Biplane Airliner (Hampstead)	Three Armstrong Siddeley Jaguar or Bristol Jupiter	1925
C/7	H.P.28	Biplane Bomber (Handcross)	Rolls-Royce Condor III	1924
D/4	H.P.29	Biplane Transport project	Bristol Jupiter	1924
W.10	H.P.30	Biplane Airliner	Two Napier Lion	1926
E	H.P.31	Torpedo Biplane (Harrow)	Napier Lion VA	1926
E	H.P.31A	Torpedo Biplane project (Hanwell)	Bristol Jupiter	1927
D	H.P.32	Transport Monoplane (Hamlet)	Three Bristol Lucifer IV	1926
D	H.P.32	Hamlet re-engined	Two Armstrong Siddeley Lynx	1927
D	H.P.32	Hamlet re-engined	Three Armstrong Siddeley Mongoose	1928
---	H.P.33	Biplane Bomber (Hinaidi I)	Two Bristol Jupiter VIII	1927
H	H.P.34	Biplane Bomber (Hare)	Bristol Jupiter	1928
---	H.P.35	Biplane Transport (Clive)	Two Bristol Jupiter	1928
M	H.P.36	Biplane Bomber (Hinaidi II)	Two Bristol Jupiter	1929
F	H.P.37	Ship's Fighter project (O.22/26)	Rolls-Royce F.XIS	1927
	H.P.38	Biplane Night Bomber (B.19/27)	Two Rolls-Royce Kestrel	1930
	H.P.39	Slotted Biplane (Guggenheim)	Armstrong Siddeley Mongoose II	1929
	H.P.40	Biplane project for Japan (3MR4)	Hispano-Suiza 12Lb	1929
	H.P.41	Torpedo Biplane project (M.5/28)	Rolls-Royce Kestrel	1929

Type Number	Description and Name	Engine(s)	Date
H.P.42	Biplane Airliner – Eastern	Four Bristol Jupiter XIF	1930
H.P.43	Biplane Bomber-Transport (C.16/28)	Three Bristol Pegasus IM3	1930
H.P.44	Biplane Bomber project (Hinaidi III)	Two Armstrong Siddeley Panther	1929
H.P.45	Biplane Airliner – Western	Four Bristol Jupiter XFBM	1930
H.P.46	Torpedo Biplane (M.1/30)	Rolls-Royce Buzzard	1932
H.P.47	G.P. Monoplane (G.4/31)	Bristol Pegasus III	1933
H.P.48	reservation - not used		
H.P.49	" " "		
H.P.50	Biplane Bomber (Heyford I, II and III) (last H.P. biplane design)	Two Rolls-Royce Kestrel	1933
H.P.51	Bomber-Transport (C.26/31)	Two Armstrong Siddeley Tiger IV or Bristol Pegasus III	1935
H.P.52	Bomber (B.9/32 - Hampden I)	Two Bristol Pegasus XVIII	1936
H.P.52	Bomber (B.30/36 - Hereford I)	Two Napier Dagger VIII	1938
H.P.53	Coastal Patrol Seaplane (Sweden)	Two Bristol Pegasus XX	1937
H.P.53	H.P.53 above converted to Hereford Prototype	Two Napier Dagger VIII	1938
H.P.54	Bomber-Transport (Harrow I and II)	Two Bristol Pegasus X or XX	1936
H.P.55	Heavy Bomber project (B.1/35)	Two Bristol Hercules or Rolls-Royce Merlin	1936
H.P.56	Heavy Bomber project (P.13/36)	Two Rolls-Royce Vulture	1937
H.P.57	Heavy Bomber (Halifax I)	Four Rolls-Royce Merlin X	1939
H.P.58	Heavy Bomber (cannon-armed project)	Four Rolls-Royce Merlin X	1939
H.P.59	Heavy Bomber (Halifax II)	Four Rolls-Royce Merlin XX, 22 or 24	1941
H.P.59A	Half-scale B.1/39 project	Four Pobjoy Niagara V	1940

Type Number	Description and Name	Engine(s)	Date
H.P.60	Heavy Bomber project (B.1/39)	Four Rolls-Royce Griffon or Bristol Hercules	1940
H.P.60A	Heavy Bomber (Halifax IV) project	Four Rolls-Royce Merlin 60	1940
H.P.61	Heavy Bomber (Halifax III)	Four Bristol Hercules VI	1941
H.P.61	Heavy Bomber (Halifax VI)	Four Bristol Hercules 100	1943
H.P.61	Heavy Bomber (Halifax VII)	Four Bristol Hercules XVI	1943
H.P.62	Medium Bomber (Hampden II)	Two Wright Cyclone G.102	1941
H.P.63	Heavy Bomber (Halifax V)	Four Rolls-Royce Merlin 22	1943
H.P.64	Halifax Transport project	Four Bristol Hercules	1944
H.P.65	Halifax IV development project	Four Bristol Hercules 38	1943
H.P.66	Hastings B.1 project (B.27/43)	Four Bristol Hercules 100	1944
H.P.67	Hastings C.1 Transport (C.3/44)	Four Bristol Hercules 102	1945
H.P.67	Hastings C.2 Transport (C.19/49)	Four Bristol Hercules 106	1949
H.P.68	Civil Transport (Hermes I)	Four Bristol Hercules 100	1945
H.P.69	Hastings B.2 project (B.27/43)	Four Bristol Hercules He-15MT	1945
H.P.70	Halifax C.VIII Transport	Four Bristol Hercules 100	1945
H.P.70	Halton Airliner for BOAC	Four Bristol Hercules 100	1945
H.P.71	Halifax A.IX Transport	Four Bristol Hercules XVI	1945
H.P.72	Military Transport project (C.15/45)	Four Bristol Centaurus	1946
H.P.73	Military Transport project (Hastings III)	Four Bristol Hercules	1946
H.P.74	Civil Transport (Hermes II)	Four Bristol Hercules 130	1946

Type Number	Description and Name	Engine(s)	Date
H.P.75	Tailless Experimental (Manx)	Two D.H. Gipsy Major II	1939-46
H.P.76	Civil Transport project (Brabazon 2B)	Two Armstrong Siddeley Double Mamba	1945
H.P.77	Civil Transport project (Brabazon 2B)	Two Bristol Theseus	1946
H.P.78	Civil Transport project (Brabazon 2B)	Four Armstrong Siddeley Mamba	1946
H.P.79	Civil Transport project (Hermes III)	Four Bristol Theseus	1947
H.P.80	High Speed Bomber (B.35/46 - Victor)	Four Armstrong Siddeley Sapphire or Rolls-Royce Conway	1947
H.P.81	Civil Transport (Hermes IV)	Four Bristol Hercules 763	1948
H.P.82	Civil Transport (Hermes V)	Four Bristol Theseus	1949
H.P.82A	Civil Transport project (Hermes VA)	Four Napier Eland	1949
H.P.82B	Civil Transport project (Hermes VB)	Four Bristol Proteus	1949
H.P.83	Civil Transport project (M.R.E. - 2/47)	Four Bristol Centaurus	1947
H.P.84	Civil Transport project (M.R.E. - 2/47)	Four Bristol Proteus	1947
H.P.85	Civil Transport project (M.R.E. - 2/47)	Two Bristol Coupled Proteus	1947
H.P.86	Civil Transport project (M.R.E. - 2/47)	Four Bristol Centaurus 663	1947
H.P.87	1/3-scale H.P.80 glider project	---	1947
H.P.88	4/9-scale H.P.80 wing and tail on Supermarine Attacker	Rolls-Royce Nene 3	1948
H.P.89	Military Transport project (Hastings VI)	Four Bristol Centaurus	1948
H.P.90	Civil Freighter project (Hermes IA)	Four Bristol Hercules 630	1948
H.P.91	Hermes VI project (lightened Hermes IV)	Four Bristol Hercules 783	1948
H.P.92	Hermes VII project (lightened Hermes IV)	Four Rolls-Royce Griffon	1948

Type Number	Description and Name	Engine(s)	Date
H.P.93	Dufaylite Test Wing for Miles Messenger	---	1948
H.P.94	V.I.P. Transport (C.115P - Hastings C.4)	Four Bristol Hercules 106	1950
H.P.95	Transport for RNZAF (Hastings C.3)	Four Bristol Hercules 737	1950
H.P.96	H.P.80 Military Transport project	Four Armstrong Siddeley Sapphire	1950
H.P.97	H.P.80 Civil Airliner project	Four Rolls-Royce Conway	1951
H.P.98	H.P.80 Target-marker project	Four Rolls-Royce Conway	1951
H.P.99	Low Level Bomber project (B.126T - 'Daisy Cutter')	Four Armstrong Siddeley Sapphire	1952
H.P.100	Supersonic Reconnaissance-Bomber project (R.156T)	Twelve Rolls-Royce RB.121	1953
H.P.101	H.P.80 Military Transport project	Four Rolls-Royce Conway	1954
H.P.102	Civil Airliner project (B.L.C.)	Four main and four auxiliary turbojets	1955
H.P.103	B.L.C. conversion of Jet Provost	Armstrong Siddeley Viper	1955
H.P.104	Victor Bomber Phase 3 project	Four Bristol Olympus or Armstrong Siddeley Sapphire	1955
H.P.105	Military Transport project with B.L.C. (C.132D)	various	1955
H.P.106	General Designs of Missile projects	various	1955-57
H.P.107	Supersonic Bomber project (OR 330)	Five Bristol Olympus	1955
H.P.108	B.L.C. Transatlantic Transport project	Four Rolls-Royce Avon	1956
H.P.109	Supersonic Transport project (M:2·2)	various	1956-57
H.P.110	Supersonic Transport project (M:1·2)	various	1957
H.P.111	H.P.80 Strategic Freighter project	Four Rolls-Royce Conway	1958
H.P.111C	H.P.80 Strategic Freighter project (Civil version)	Four Rolls-Royce Conway	1958

Type Number	Description and Name	Engine(s)	Date
H.P.112	Flying Jeep project	various	1958
H.P.113	B.L.C. Executive Transport project	Two Bristol Orpheus	1958
H.P.114	Victor Bomber Phase 6 project	Four Rolls-Royce Conway	1958
H.P.115	Low Speed Slender Delta (ER.197D)	Bristol Siddeley Viper	1959
H.P.116	Tactical Freighter project studies	various	1959
H.P.117	All-Wing B.L.C. Airliner project (200 passengers)	Three Rolls-Royce Spey	1960
H.P.117	All-Wing B.L.C. Airliner project (300 passengers)	Four Rolls-Royce Spey	1960
H.P.118	VTOL Jeep project	various	1960
H.P.119	3/10-scale H.P.117 project	Three Bristol Siddeley Viper	1961
H.P.120	Two-man Jumping Jeep project	Rolls-Royce RB.172 and RB.175	1961
H.P.122	VTOL Transport project (OR 351)	Four Rolls-Royce Tyne	1961
H.P.123	H.P.80 B.L.C. Transport project (OR 351)	Four Rolls-Royce Conway	1961
H.P.124	Military Herald project	Two Rolls-Royce Dart	1961
H.P.125	Tactical VTOL Herald project (NBMR-4)	Two Rolls-Royce Dart	1962
H.P.126	All-Wing Aerobus project	Four turbojets	1962
H.P.127	Jet Herald project	Two Rolls-Royce Spey Jr	1962
H.P.128	Short Range Supersonic Transport project	Three turbojets	1962
H.P.129	'Mini-Herald' project	Two Rolls-Royce Spey Jr	1962
H.P.130	H.S. 125 B.L.C. project	Two Bristol Siddeley Viper	1963
H.P.131	Projected Variant of H.P.124 for Belgium	Two Rolls-Royce Dart	1965
H.P.132	Projected STOL version of H.P.131	Two Rolls-Royce Dart and two General Electric CF 700	1965

Type Number	Description and Name	Engine(s)	Date
H.P.133	Projected STOL version of H.P.131	Two Rolls-Royce Dart and two General Electric CF 700	1965
H.P.134	Ogee Aerobus project	Three turbojets	1965
H.P.135	Global Range B.L.C. Transport project	Four turbofans	1965
H.P.137	Light Civil Transport (Jetstream 1 and 2)	Two Turbomeca Astazou	1965

Reading Design Office (1948 - 1960)

Type Number	Description and Name	Engine(s)	Date
H.P.R.1	Production of Miles M.60 Marathon I	Four D.H. Gipsy Queen	1948
H.P.R.2	Basic Trainer (T.16/48)	Armstrong Siddeley Cheetah or Alvis Leonides	1949
H.P.R.3	Herald Civil Transport	Four Alvis Leonides Major	1952
H.P.R.4	Herald Propeller-turbine project	Two Napier Eland	1953
H.P.R.5	Conversion of Miles M.69 Marathon II	Two Alvis Leonides Major	1953
H.P.R.6	Short Range High Density Transport project	Four Rolls-Royce Tyne	1955
H.P.R.7	Dart-Herald	Two Rolls-Royce Dart	1957
H.P.R.8	Car Ferry project for Silver City Airways	Two Rolls-Royce Dart	1959

Note : To avoid confusion with contemporary D.H. projects at Hatfield, Type Numbers H.P.121 and H.P.136 were not used. None of the types described as projects was built.

APPENDIX B

Production Data 1914–1974

(a) Handley Page Types

46 O/100s ordered from Handley Page Ltd, all delivered

Contract	Serials	Engine
Contract C.P.65799/15,	serials 1455-1466,	Rolls-Royce Eagle IV
C.P.69522,	serials 3115,3116,3118-3141,	Rolls-Royce Eagle IV
"	serial 3117,	Sunbeam Cossack
"	serial 3142,	Fiat A.12bis
AS.20629,	serials B9446-B9451,	Sunbeam Cossack

324 O/400s ordered from Handley Page Ltd, 211 delivered, 113 cancelled

Contract	Serials	Engine
Contract AS.27863,	serials C9636-C9785,	Rolls-Royce Eagle VIII, (all delivered)
AS.18201,	serials D8301-D8350,	" " Eagle VIII, (all delivered)
AS.18201,	serials H4325-H4424,	" " Eagle VIII, (cancelled)
35a/1052/C887,	serials F3748-F3767,	" " Eagle VIII, (11 delivered)
35a/2064/C2348,	serials J6574-J6576,	" " Eagle VIII, (cancelled)
"	serial J6578,	" " Eagle VIII, (cancelled)

Note : D8301-D8350 originally ordered from British Caudron (Contract AS.38340) but transferred to Handley Page Ltd, with British Caudron as main sub-contractor

24 O/400s ordered from Royal Aircraft Factory, all delivered

Contract	Serials	Engine
Contract AS.1198,	serials B8802-B8813,	Raf 3a or Sunbeam Cossack, (cancelled)
"	serials C3487-C3498,	Rolls-Royce Eagle VIII, (all delivered)
35a/88/C43,	serials B8802-B8813* *re-allotted	" " Eagle VIII, (all delivered)

175 O/400s ordered from Metropolitan Wagon Co Ltd, 100 delivered, 75 cancelled

Contract	Serials	Engine
Contract AS.29198,	serials D4561-D4660,	Rolls-Royce Eagle VIII, (all delivered)
AS.35429,	serials J3542-J3616,	" " Eagle VIII, (all cancelled)

120 O/400s ordered from Birmingham Carriage Co Ltd, 102 delivered, 18 cancelled

Contract	Serials	Engine
Contract AS.28201/17,	serials D5401-D5450,	Rolls-Royce Eagle VIII, (all delivered)
35a/391/C284,	serials F301-F320,	" " Eagle VIII, (18 delivered)
AS.34499,	serials J2242-J2291,	" " Eagle VIII, (34 delivered)

50 O/400s ordered from Clayton & Shuttleworth, 46 delivered, 4 cancelled

Contract AS.28197 serials D9681-D9370, Rolls-Royce Eagle VIII

100 O/400s ordered from Cubitts Ltd (National Aircraft Factory No.1), 70 delivered, 30 cancelled

Contract AS.4292, serials F5349-F5448, Liberty 12-N

(F5349 completed with Liberties, erected at Ford Junction by US Air Service; next 69 erected by Handley Page Ltd with Rolls-Royce Eagle VIIIs; last 30 cancelled)

1 O/400 ordered from Harland & Wolff Ltd as replacement for sample O/400 diverted to Standard Aircraft Corp, USA; components transferred to Handley Page Ltd for erection

Contract AS.23996/17, serial J1934, Rolls-Royce Eagle VIII (delivered)

6 R/200s ordered from Handley Page Ltd, 3 delivered, 3 cancelled

Contract AS.11217, serials N27-N29 delivered, N30-N32 cancelled

3 V/1500s ordered from Handley Page Ltd, to be manufactured by Harland & Wolff Ltd

Contract AS.22690/17, serials B9463-B9465, Rolls-Royce Eagle VIII; components delivered to Handley Page Ltd for final assembly and flight test. B9463 flown and crashed before acceptance, B9464-B9465 extensively modified, using parts manufactured by Harland & Wolff under contract AS.23996/17 and delivered by Handley Page Ltd as serials J1935 and J1936

20 V/1500s ordered from Harland & Wolff Ltd, 5 delivered, 15 assembled by Handley Page Ltd

Contract 35a/185/C74, serials E4304-E4323, Rolls-Royce Eagle VIII
E4304-E4306 assembled by Handley Page Ltd at Cricklewood
E4307-E4311 delivered by air from Aldergrove
E4312-E4323 delivered as spares, one set assembled and delivered by air from Aldergrove as J6573 with Napier Lions

50 V/1500s ordered from William Beardmore & Co Ltd, 20 delivered, 30 cancelled

Contract 35a/315/C200, serials E8287-E8306, B.H.P. Galloway Atlantic or Rolls-Royce Eagle VIII
E8287-E8295 delivered by air from Inchinnan with Rolls-Royce Eagle VIII
E8296-E8306 delivered as spares, not erected

Contract 35a/1662/C1784, serials F8201-F8230, cancelled

10 V/1500s ordered from Alliance Aircraft Co Ltd; Rolls-Royce Eagle VIII

Contract 35a/1452/C1528, serials F7134-F7143, completed and delivered by Handley Page Ltd

90 V/1500s ordered from Handley Page Ltd, 10 delivered, 80 cancelled

Contract 35a/1657/C1725, serials F8281-F8320, Rolls-Royce Eagle VIII
F8281-F8290 delivered
F8291-F8320 cancelled

Contract 35a/2064/C2348, serials J6523-J6572, Napier Lion IB, cancelled

40 V/1500s ordered from Grahame-White Aviation Ltd, all cancelled

Contract 35a/2292/C2589, serials H4825-H4864

11 O/7s built new as private venture using O/400 surplus spares

c/n	Registration	C of A	Date		Shipped	
HP-1	K-162, G-EAGN	C of A 149,	8.8.19,	shipped	25.8.19	to China
HP-2	not registered,	" 175,	25.8.19,	"	25.8.19	" "
HP-3	"	" 176,	25.8.19,	"	25.8.19	" "
HP-4	"	" 188,	6.9.19,	"	6.9.19	" "
HP-5	"	" 209,	20.9.19,	"	20.9.19	" "
HP-6	"	" 210,	19.9.19,	"	20.9.19	" "
HP-7	G-EANV	" 222,	2.10.19,	"	11.19	to Cape Town, crashed 23.2.20
HP-8	not registered,	" 236,	16.10.19,	"	11.19	" " " reg to H.P. Indo-Burmese Transport Ltd as G-IAAA, wfu 7.21
HP-9	G-IAAB,	C of A 268,	28.11.19,	shipped		to Calcutta for H.P.I.B.T. Ltd 11.19, wfu 7.21
HP-10	G-EAQZ,	C of A 297,	18.2.20,	"		" " " H.P.I.B.T. Ltd 2.21, scrapped 7.21
HP-11	G-EAPA,	C of A 275,	9.12.19,	"		" " " H.P.I.B.T. Ltd as G-IAAC, crashed 10.20

1 W.8 c/n W.8-1 G-EAPJ first flown 2.12.19, C of A 7.8.20; Handley Page Transport Ltd, ***Newcastle***, later ***Duchess of York***; crashed Poix 10.7.23

4 W.8b c/n W.8-2 G-EBBG Handley Page Transport Ltd, ***Bombay***, later ***Princess Mary***; to Imperial Airways Ltd 31.3.24; crashed Abbeville 15.2.28

W.8-3 G-EBBH Handley Page Transport Ltd, ***Melbourne***, later ***Prince George***; to Imperial Airways Ltd 31.3.24; wfu April 1929

W.8-4 G-EBBI Handley Page Transport Ltd, ***Prince Henry***; to Imperial Airways Ltd 31.3.24; wfu March 1932

W.8-5 O-BAHK built by Handley Page Ltd for SABENA

3 W.8b c/ns 1, 2, and 3, O-BAHJ, O-BAHL and O-BAHM built by SABCA for SABENA

11 W.8e c/n W.8-6 O-BAHG built by Handley Page Ltd for SABENA
c/ns not known, O-BAHN to O-BAHU, built by SABCA for SABENA

1 W.8f Hamilton c/n W.8-7 G-EBIX Imperial Airways Ltd, ***City of Washington***, converted October 1929 to W.8g, crashed Neufchatel 30.10.30

2 W.8f c/ns not known, O-BAHY, O-BAHZ, built by SABCA for SABENA

3 S for US Navy, serials A-6402, A-6403, A-6404; all cancelled

4 T Hanley; 3 ordered for RAF service trials, 2 delivered, 1 cancelled

Contract A.M.313750/20, serials N143 and N145 delivered, N144 crashed

1 built for USSR and delivered together with N144 repaired

1 X/4B H.P.20 converted from D.H.9A; Contract A.M.225504/21, serial J6914

1 W.8d Hyderabad (prototype); Contract A.M.369332/22, serial J6994

2 H.P.22 first aircraft ordered and cancelled after unsuccessful test flight

Contract A.M.446453/23, serial J7233, competition No.23; second aircraft private venture, unregistered, competition No.25, flown at Lympne 11.10.23

1 H.P.23 high speed version of H.P.22, private venture, unregistered, competition No.26, not flown at Lympne; purchased for test at A & AEE

Contract A.M.488791/24, serial J7265; delivered to A & AEE, not flown

6 Ta Hendon, all delivered; Contract A.M.452299/23, serials N9724-N9729

3 C/7 Handcross, all delivered; Contract A.M.445076/24, serials J7498-J7500

45 W.8d Hyderabad (production), all delivered in five batches

Contract A.M.517715/24, serials J7738-J7752
A.M.709618/26, serials J8317-J8324
A.M.763672/27, serials J8805-J8815
A.M.790318/27, serials J9031-J9036 (later converted to Hinaidi I)
A.M.790318/27, serials J9293-J9297

1 W.9a Hampstead c/n W.9-1 G-EBLE, first flown 1.10.25, C of A 20.1.26, Imperial Airways Ltd *City of New York*; to New Guinea as VH-ULK Jan 1929, crashed Salamaua 31.5.30

4 W.10 c/n W.10-1 G-EBMM *City of Melbourne*, del 5.3.26 Imperial Airways Ltd; sold Nov 1933 to National Aviation Day Displays Ltd *Youth of New Zealand*, crashed Aston Clinton 24.9.34

c/n W.10-2 G-EBMR *City of Pretoria*, del 9.3.26 Imperial Airways Ltd; sold Nov 1933 to National Aviation Day Displays Ltd; scrapped Malta 1934

c/n W.10-3 G-EBMS *City of London*, del 9.3.26 Imperial Airways Ltd; crashed in English Channel 21.10.26

c/n W.10-4 G-EBMT *City of Ottawa*, del 13.3.26 Imperial Airways Ltd, crashed in English Channel off Dungeness 17.6.29

2 E Harrow prototypes, both delivered

Contract A.M.528239/25, serials N205, N206

1 D H.P.32 Hamlet, c/n 1 G-EBNS, first flown 19.10.26 with three Bristol Lucifers; re-engined and flown with two Armstrong Siddeley Lynx 19.5.27; re-engined but not flown with three Armstrong Siddeley Mongoose March 1928; delivered by road to RAE Farnborough; not flown at RAE, scrapped 1929

1 H	H.P.34	Hare prototype; Contract A.M.716900/26, serial J8622
1	H.P.33	Hinaidi I prototype; Contract A.M.786340/27, serial J9030
6	H.P.33	Hinaidi I (production); Contract A.M.790318/27, serials J9298-J9303
1	H.P.35	Clive I prototype, Contract A.M.786340/27, serial J9126; registered 13.8.32 as Clive III G-ABYX, to Sir Alan Cobham 4.33; scrapped 1935
2	H.P.35	Clive II ordered for RAF India, both delivered March 1930

Contract A.M.911523/29, serials J9948, J9949

34	H.P.36	Hinaidi II, all delivered; serials J9478 (prototype), K1063-K1078, K1909-K1925
1	H.P.38	prototype to Spec B.19/27, Contract A.M.790320/27, cancelled and replaced by Heyford prototype, Contract A.M.819857/28, serial J9130
1	H.P.39	private venture for Guggenheim Safe Aircraft Competition, 1929; registered G-AACN 1929 but C of A not issued; loaned to RAE December 1930, serial K1908; presented to Science Museum 1934
4	H.P.42	ordered by Imperial Airways Ltd (as H.P.42E)

c/n 42/1 G-AAGX del 5.6.31 *Hannibal*; crashed in Gulf of Oman 1.3.40
42/2 G-AAUE del 10.7.31 *Hadrian*; to RAF May 1940 serial AS982, wrecked in gale Doncaster 6.12.40
42/3 G-AAUD del 30.7.31 *Hanno*; wrecked in gale Whitchurch 19.3.40
42/4 G-AAUC del 19.9.31 *Horsa*; to RAF May 1940 serial AS981, crashed Cumberland 7.8.40

4	H.P.45	ordered by Imperial Airways Ltd (as H.P.42W)

c/n 42/5 G-AAXC del 31.8.31 *Heracles*; wrecked in gale Whitchurch 19.3.40
42/6 G-AAXD del 13.11.31 *Horatius*; crashed Tiverton 7.11.39
42/7 G-AAXE del 10.12.31 *Hengist*; burnt in hangar Karachi 31.5.37
42/8 G-AAXF del 31.12.31 *Helena*; to RAF May 1940 serial AS983, scrapped Donibristle 1941

1	H.P.43	prototype to Spec C.16/28, Contract A.M.935510/29, serial J9833; converted January 1934 to H.P.51
1	H.P.46	prototype to Spec M.1/30, Contract A.M.55828/30, serial S1642; delivered to RAE by road April 1935
1	H.P.47	Prototype to Spec G.4/31, Contract A.M.174760/32, serial K2773; delivered A & AEE 20.4.35, to RAE 5.3.36, struck off charge May 1937
15	H.P.50	Heyford I, all delivered; Contract A.M.254598/33, serials K3489-K3503
23	H.P.50	Heyford IA, all delivered; Contract A.M.272083/33, serials K4021-K4043
16	H.P.50	Heyford II, all delivered, Contract A.M.352860/34, serials K4863-K4878

70 H.P.50 Heyford III, all delivered; Contract A.M.389373/35, serials K5180-K5199, K6857-K6906

1 H.P.51 prototype to Spec C.26/31; converted from H.P.43, retaining serial J9833 delivered A & AEE January 1937; to RAE 11.2.37, struck off charge January 1940

1 H.P.52 prototype to Spec B.9/32, serial K4240; delivered A & AEE 9.11.37

1 H.P.53 ordered by Flygstyrelsen, not delivered to Sweden but taken on charge by Air Ministry, serial L7271; delivered RAE 6.7.37, to Short & Harland Ltd for conversion to Hereford prototype 16.7.37 Contract A.M.68075/37; delivered A & AEE May 1939; replaced on Swedish contract by one H.P.52 serial I-90

100 H.P.54 Harrow; 19 delivered as Harrow I, serials K6933, K6935-K6952
81 delivered as Harrow II, serials K6934, K6953-K7032

K6933 converted to tanker for Flight Refuelling Ltd, G-AFRG; to RCAF 1939 as serial 794

K7029 converted to tanker for Flight Refuelling Ltd, G-AFRH; to RCAF 1939, reduced to spares for 794

K7027 converted to tanker for Flight Refuelling Ltd, G-AFRL; destroyed by enemy action, Ford, Sussex 18.8.40

500 H.P.52 Hampden I ordered from Handley Page Ltd, all delivered

serials L4032-L4211, P1145-P1189, P1194-P1230, P1233-P1261, P1265-P1305, P1309-P1356, P4285-P4324, P4335-P4384, P4389-P4418

770 H.P.52 Hampden I ordered from English Electric Co Ltd, all delivered

serials P2062-P2100, P2110-P2145, X2893-X2922, X2959-X3008, X3021-X3030, X3047-X3066, X3115-X3154, AD719-AD768, AD782-AD806, AD824-AD873, AD895-AD939, AD959-AD988, AE115-AE159, AE184-AE203, AE218-AE267, AE286-AE320, AE352-AE401, AE418-AE442, AT109-AT158, AT172-AT196, AT216-AT260

160 H.P.52 Hampden I ordered from Canadian Associated Aircraft Ltd, all delivered

serials P5298-P5337 (Quebec), P5338-P5346, P5386-P5400, P5421-P5436, (Ontario), AJ988-AJ999, AN100-AN167 (Quebec)

150 H.P.52 Hereford I ordered from Short & Harland Ltd, all delivered

serials L6002-L6101, N9055-N9081, N9084-N9106 (20 converted to Hampden I after delivery)

2 H.P.56 prototypes ordered to Spec P.13/36, amended to H.P.57 before delivery

Contract A.M.624972/37, serials L7244, L7245, both delivered

84 H.P.57 Halifax I ordered from Handley Page Ltd, all delivered, c/ns 1-84

Contract A.M.692649/37; serials L9485-L9534, L9560-L9584, L9600-L9608

615	H.P.59	Halifax II ordered from Handley Page Ltd, all delivered		
		Contract A.M.692649/37; serials	L9609-L9624	
			R9363-R9392	
			R9418-R9457	c/ns 85-200
			R9482-R9498	
			R9528-R9540	
		Contract B73328/40; serials	W7650-W7679	
			W7695-W7720	
			W7745-W7754	c/ns 201-400
			W7801-W7826	
			W7844-W7887	
			W7906-W7939	
		serials	HR654-HR699	
			HR711-HR758	
			HR773-HR819	
			HR832-HR880	c/ns 401-650
			HR905-HR952	
			HR977-HR988	
		serials	HX147-HX191	c/ns 651-699
			HX222-HX225	
326	H.P.61	Halifax B.3 ordered from Handley Page Ltd, all delivered		
		serials	HX226-HX247	
			HX265-HX296	c/ns 700-800
			HX311-HX357	
		serials	LV771-LV799	
			LV813-LV842	
			LV857-LV883	
			LV898-LV923	
			LV935-LV973	c/ns 801-1025
			LV985-LV999	
			LW113-LW143	
			LW157-LW179	
			LW191-LW195	
132	H.P.61	Halifax B.6 ordered from Handley Page Ltd, all delivered		
		serials	NP715, NP748,	c/ns 1075,1096
			NP752, NP753,	1100, 1101
			NP758, NP760	1106, 1108
			NP762-NP767	
			NP821-NP836	c/ns 1110-1115,
			NP849-NP895	1158-1240
			NP908-NP927	
		serials	PP165-PP187	c/ns 1264-1300
			PP203-PP216	
15	H.P.61	Halifax B.7 ordered from Handley Page Ltd, all delivered		
		serials	LW196-LW210	c/ns1026-1040

145	H.P.61	Halifax A.7 ordered from Handley Page Ltd, all delivered		
		serials	NP681-NP714	c/ns 1041-1074
			NP716-NP723 NP736-NP747	c/ns 1076-1095
			NP749-NP751	c/ns 1097-1099
			NP754-NP757	c/ns 1102-1105
			NP759, NP761	c/ns 1107, 1109
			NP768-NP781 NP793-NP820	c/ns 1116-1157
		serials	TW774-TW796	c/ns 1241-1263
			PP339-PP350 PP362-PP389 RT753-RT757	c/ns 1401-1445
100	H.P.70	Halifax C.8 ordered from Handley Page Ltd, all delivered		
		serials	PP217-PP247 PP259-PP296 PP308-PP338	c/ns 1301-1400
		(Note : PP244-PP247 delivered initially as A.7, later converted to C.8)		
195	H.P.71	Halifax A.9 ordered from Handley Page Ltd, 145 delivered, 50 cancelled		
		serials	RT758-RT799 RT814-RT856 RT868-RT908 RT920-RT938	c/ns 1446-1590

Total Halifax production by Handley Page Ltd (excluding 2 prototypes) : 1,590

860	H.P.59	Halifax II ordered from English Electric Co Ltd		
		serials	V9976-V9994, W1002-W1021, W1035-W1067, W1090-W1117, W1141-W1190, W1211-W1253, W1270-W1276	200 delivered
		serials	DT481-DT526, DT539-DT588, DT612-DT649, DT665-DT705, DT720-DT752, DT767-DT808	250 delivered
		serials	JB781-JB806, JB834-JB875, JB892-JB931, JB956-JB974, JD105-JD128, JD143-JD180, JD198-JD218, JD244-JD278 , JD296-JD333, JD361-JD386, JD405-JD421, JD453-JD476	350 delivered
		serials	LW223-LW246, LW259-LW301 LW313-LW345	60 delivered

940 H.P.61 Halifax B.3 ordered from English Electric Co Ltd

serials LW346-LW348, LW361-LW397, LW412-LW446, LW459-LW481, LW495-LW522, LW537-LW559, LW572-LW598, LW613-LW658, LW671-LW696, LW713-LW724 — 300 delivered

serials MZ500-MZ524, MZ556-MZ604, MZ617-MZ660, MZ672-MZ717, MZ730-MZ775, MZ787-MZ831, MZ844-MZ883, MZ895-MZ939 — 360 delivered

serials NP930-NP976, NP988-NP999, NR113-NR156, NR169-NR211, NR225-NR258, NR271-NR290, RG345-RG390, RG413-RG446 — 280 delivered

650 H.P.61 Halifax B.6 ordered from English Electric Co Ltd, 325 delivered, 325 cancelled

serials RG480-RG513, RG527-RG568, RG583-RG625, RG639-RG679, RG693-RG736, RG749-RG790, RG813-RG853, RG867-RG879, ST794-ST818

12 H.P.61 Halifax B.7 ordered from English Electric Co Ltd

serials RG447-RG458 — all delivered

8 H.P.61 Halifax A.7 ordered from English Electric Co Ltd

serials RG472-RG479 — all delivered

Total Halifax production by English Electric Co Ltd: 2,145

---

450 H.P.59 Halifax II ordered from London Aircraft Production Group

serials BB189-BB223, BB236-BB285, BB300-BB344, BB357-BB391, BB412-BB446, JN882-JN926, JN941-JN978, JP107-JP137, JP159-JP207, JP220-JP259, JP275-JP301, JP319-JP338 — 450 delivered

380 H.P.61 Halifax B.3 ordered from London Aircraft Production Group, 260 delivered, 120 cancelled

serials MZ282-MZ321, MZ334-MZ378, MZ390-MZ435, MZ447-MZ495, PN365-PN406, PN423-PN460

Total Halifax production by London Aircraft Production Group: 710

---

12 H.P.59 Halifax II ordered from Rootes Securities Ltd, 11 delivered, 1 crashed before delivery

serials DG219-DG230 (DG223 crashed on test flight)

658 H.P.63 Halifax B.5 ordered from Rootes Securities Ltd, all delivered

serials DG231-DG253, DG270-DG317, DG338-DG363, DG384-DG424, EB127-EB160, EB178-EB220, EB239-EB258, EB274-EB276, LK890-LK932, LK945-LK976, LK988-LK999, LL112-LL153, LL167-LL198, LL213-LL258, LL270-LL312, LL325-LL367, LL380-LL423, LL437-LL469, LL481-LL521, LL534-LL542

280 H.P.61 Halifax B.3 ordered from Rootes Securities Ltd, all delivered

serials LL543-LL559, LL573-LL615, MZ945-MZ989, NA102-NA150, NA162-NA205, NA218-NA263, NA275-NA310

140 H.P.61 Halifax A.7 ordered from Rootes Securities Ltd, 120 delivered, 20 cancelled

serials NA311-NA320, NA336-NA380, NA392-NA431, NA444-NA468 — delivered

serials NA469-NA488 — cancelled

Total Halifax production by Rootes Securities Ltd: 1,070 built, 1,069 delivered

246 H.P.63 Halifax B.5 ordered from Fairey Aviation Ltd, all delivered

serials DJ980-DJ999, DK114-DK151, DK165-DK207, DK223-DK271, LK626-LK667, LK680-LK711, LK725-LK746

326 H.P.61 Halifax B.3 ordered from Fairey Aviation Ltd, all delivered

serials LK747-LK766, LK779-LK812, LK826-LK850, LK863-LK887, NA492-NA531, NA543-NA587, NA599-NA644, NA656-NA704, PN167-PN208

108 H.P.61 Halifax B.7 ordered from Fairey Aviation Ltd, 90 delivered,18 cancelled

serials PN223-PN267, PN285-PN327, PN343, PN344 : 21 delivered as B.7, 69 delivered as A.7

serials PN345-PN362 — cancelled

Total Halifax production by Fairey Aviation Ltd: 662

Grand total Halifax production by all contractors: 6,177 built, 6,176 delivered

2 H.P.67 prototypes to Spec C.3/44, serials TE580, TE583; both delivered

100 H.P.67 Hastings C.1; serials TG499-TG537, TG551-TG587, TG601-TG624 — all delivered

41 H.P.67 Hastings C.2: serials WD475-WD499, WJ327-WJ343; — all delivered

4 H.P.94 Hastings C.4; serials WD500, WJ324-WJ326; — all delivered

4 H.P.95 — Hastings C.3; serials NZ5801-NZ5804; all delivered

1 H.P.68 — Hermes I prototype, c/n H.P.68/1, G-AGSS; crashed on first flight 2.12.45

1 H.P.74 — Hermes II prototype, ordered to Spec 33/46, c/n H.P.74/1, G-AGUB; later serial VX234, wfu 1969

1 H.P.75 — Manx tailless monoplane ordered from Dart Aircraft Ltd, serial H-0222, delivered to Radlett 1939 for completion by Handley Page Ltd; wfu 1946

2 H.P.80 — prototypes to Spec B.35/46;

Contract 6/Acft/1875/C.B.6(a), serials WB771, WB775

50 H.P.80 — Victor B.1, Contract 6/Acft/8441/C.B.6(a), 25 delivered

serials XA917-XA941

Contract 6/Acft/11303/C.B.6(a), 25 delivered

serials XH587-XH594, XH613-XH621, XH645-XH651, XH667

34 H.P.80 — Victor B.2, Contract 6/Acft/11303/C.B.6(a), 8 delivered

serials XH668-XH675

Contract 6/Acft/12305/C.B.6, 26 delivered

serials XL158-XL165, XL188-XL193, XL230-XL233, XL511-XL513, XM714-XM718

(28 Victor B.2s cancelled, serials XL250-XL255, XM745-XM756, XM785-XM794)

1 H.P.88 — prototype ordered from Blackburn & General Aircraft Ltd

serial VX330; crashed Stansted 26.8.61

25 H.P.81 — Hermes IV ordered to Spec 37/46 by Ministry of Supply for BOAC, all delivered

c/n H.P.81/1 G-AKFP ***Hamilcar***, not accepted by BOAC, leased to Airwork Ltd (XD632), sold to Airwork 2.57, destroyed Calcutta 1.9.57

H.P.81/2 G-ALDA ***Hecuba***, not accepted by BOAC, leased to Airwork Ltd (WZ838), sold to Airwork 1.57, Falcon Airways 10.59, Air Safaris 12.60, Air Links 11.62, scrapped 1965

H.P.81/3 G-ALDB ***Hebe***, not accepted by BOAC, leased to Airwork Ltd 1952 (WZ839), crashed Pithiviers 23.7.52

H.P.81/4 G-ALDC ***Hermione***, not accepted by BOAC, leased to Airwork Ltd 1952 (WZ840), sold to Airwork 1.57, Falcon Airways 6.59, crashed Southend 9.10.60

c/n H.P.81/5 G-ALDD *Horatius*, to BOAC 12.9.49, sold to Skyways 4.55, scrapped 1959

H.P.81/6 G-ALDE *Hanno*, to BOAC 7.2.50, sold to Skyways 1.55, leased to Bahamas Airways 1.60 as VP-BBO, sold to Air Safaris 5.61, scrapped 5.62

H.P.81/7 G-ALDF *Hadrian*, not accepted by BOAC, leased to Airwork Ltd 1952 (WZ841), lost off Sicily 25.8.52

H.P.81/8 G-ALDG *Horsa*, to BOAC 9.3.50, sold to Airwork Ltd 5.57, Falcon Airways 10.59, Silver City Airways 12.59, scrapped 10.62

H.P.81/9 G-ALDH *Heracles*, to BOAC 20.3.50, sold to Skyways 8.55, damaged beyond repair Heathrow 8.3.60

H.P.81/10 G-ALDI *Hannibal*, to BOAC 6.7.50, sold to Britavia (XJ309) 7.54, operated by Silver City Airways, scrapped 10.62

H.P.81/11 G-ALDJ *Hengist*, to BOAC 7.7.50, sold to Britavia 7.54, crashed Blackbushe 6.11.56

H.P.81/12 G-ALDK *Helena*, to BOAC 12.7.50, sold to Britavia (XJ281) 7.54, crashed Drigh Road, Karachi, 5.8.56

H.P.81/13 G-ALDL *Hector*, to BOAC 21.2.51, sold to Skyways 6.55, leased to Bahamas Airways 1.60 as VP-BBP, sold to Air Safaris 4.61, Skyways 12.61, Air Links 8.62, scrapped 9.62

H.P.81/14 G-ALDM *Hero*, to BOAC 17.7.50, sold to Air Safaris 11.56, leased to Silver City Airways till 12.59, scrapped 5.68

H.P.81/15 G-ALDN *Horus*, to BOAC 20.7.50, crashed in Sahara Desert 26.5.52

H.P.81/16 G-ALDO *Heron*, to BOAC 20.7.50, leased to Airwork Ltd 1952, scrapped 3.59

H.P.81/17 G-ALDP *Homer*, to BOAC 24.8.50, sold to Britavia (XJ269) 7.54, scrapped 10.62

H.P.81/18 G-ALDR *Herodotus*, to BOAC 29.8.50, sold to Skyways 4.55, scrapped 1959

H.P.81/19 G-ALDS *Hesperides*, to BOAC 6.9.50, sold to Skyways 4.55, scrapped 1.60

H.P.81/20 G-ALDT *Hestia*, to BOAC 13.9.50, sold to Skyways 4.55, leased to Middle East Airlines as OD-ACB 6.10.55, leased to Bahamas Airways 10.60 as VP-BBQ, sold to Air Safaris 6.61, scrapped 6.62

H.P.81/21 G-ALDU *Halcyone*, to BOAC 12.10.50, sold to Britavia (XJ280), leased to Kuwait Airways 7.56-1.57, Silver City Airways 1.57, scrapped 11.62

c/n H.P.81/22 G-ALDV ***Hera***, to BOAC 29.9.50, sold to Skyways 4.55, crashed Meesden Green 1.4.58

H.P.81/23 G-ALDW ***Helios***, to BOAC 30.10.50, sold to Skyways 4.55, destroyed Nicosia 4.3.56

H.P.81/24 G-ALDX ***Hyperion***, to BOAC 13.12.50, sold to Britavia (XJ267) 7.54, leased Kuwait Airways 7.56-1.57, wfu 1.60

H.P.81/25 G-ALDY ***Honor***, to BOAC 16.1.51, sold to Skyways 9.54, leased to Middle East Airlines 6-10.55 as OD-ACC, wfu 12.58

2 H.P.82 Hermes V ordered to Spec 32/46 by Ministry of Supply, both delivered

H.P.82/1 G-ALEU, allotted to Handley Page Ltd, crashed Chilbolton 10.4.51

H.P.82/2 G-ALEV, allotted to Handley Page Ltd, grounded as fatigue test structural specimen at RAE Farnborough 9.53, scrapped 1958

1 H.P.115 ordered to Spec ER.197D, serial XP841; delivered to RAE Bedford, first flown 17.8.61; to RAF Cosford 9.10.75; to FAA Museum Yeovilton

50 H.P.R.1 Marathon I ordered by Ministry of Supply; 40 delivered, 10 cancelled

c/n 101 G-ALUB not accepted by BEA, reworked as Marathon T.11 serial XA249

102 G-ALVW not accepted by BEA, reworked as Marathon T.11 serial XA250

103 G-ALVX not accepted by BEA, reworked as Marathon T.11 serial XA251

104 G-ALVY not accepted by BEA, reworked as Marathon T.11 serial XA252

105 G-ALXR not accepted by BEA, reworked as Marathon T.11 serial XA253

106 G-AMAX not accepted by BEA, reworked as Marathon T.11 serial XA254

107 G-AMAY not accepted by BEA, reworked as Marathon T.11 serial XA255

108 G-AMDH not accepted by BEA, reworked as Marathon T.11 serial XA256

109 G-AMEK not accepted by BEA, reworked as Marathon T.11 serial XA257

110 G-AMEL not accepted by BEA, reworked as Marathon T.11 serial XA258

111 G-AMEM not accepted by BEA, reworked as Marathon T.11 serial XA259

112 G-AMEO leased to West African Airways 7-9.51 as VR-NAI, sold to Germany 8.55 as D-CFSA

113 G-AMEP reworked as Marathon T.11, serial XA260, scrapped 10.58

114 G-AMER reworked as Marathon T.11, serial XA261, scrapped 2.62

c/n 115 G-AMET reworked as Marathon T.11 serial XA262, scrapped 10.58

116 G-AMEU reworked as Marathon T.11 serial XA263; scrapped 10.58

117 G-AMEV reworked as Marathon T.11 serial XA264, scrapped 10.58

118 G-AMEW reworked as Marathon T.11 serial XA265, restored 10.57 to Derby Aviation as G-AMEW, wfu 7.61

119 G-AMGN reworked as Marathon T.11 serial XA266, scrapped 10.58

120 G-AMGO reworked as Marathon T.11 serial XA267, scrapped 10.58

121 G-AMGP reworked as Marathon T.11 serial XA268,

122 G-AMGR reworked as Marathon T.11 serial XA269, scrapped 2.62

123 G-AMGS reworked as Marathon T.11 serial XA270, scrapped 10.58

124 G-AMGT reworked as Marathon T.11 serial XA271, crashed Calne 30.9.54

125 G-AMGU reworked as Marathon T.11 serial XA272

126 G-AMGV reworked as Marathon T.11 serial XA273

127 G-AMGW leased to West African Airways 10.52 as VR-NAN, sold to Derby Aviation 10.55 as ***Millersdale***, wfu 4.61

128 G-AMGX leased to West African Airways 10.52 as VR-NAO, sold to Balfour Marine Engineering Co Ltd 5.55, scrapped 1962

129 G-AMHR leased to West African Airways 10.52 as VR-NAR, sold to Derby Aviation 10.55 as ***Monsaldale***, wfu 7.61

130 G-AMHS leased to West African Airways 10.52 as VR-NAS, to RAE Farnborough 3.55 as Marathon IC serial XJ830, sold to Air Navigation & Trading Co 9.58, scrapped 1959

131 G-AMHT reworked as Marathon T.11 serial XA274, sold 6.59 to F. G. Miles Ltd, scrapped 2.62

132 G-AMHU reworked as Marathon T.11 serial XA275

133 G-AMHV leased to West African Airways 7.52 as VR-NAT, to RAE Farnborough 3.55 as Marathon IC serial XJ831, sold to Air Navigation & Trading Co 9.58, sold in Canada 3.61 as CF-NUH

134 G-AMHW leased to West African Airways 7.52 as VR-NAU, to Royal Jordanian Air Force 9.54 as King Hussein's personal transport, serial VK501

135 G-AMHX reworked as Marathon T.11 serial XA276

136 G-AMHY sold 1954 to Far East Air Lines, Nagoya, Japan as JA-6009

137 G-AMHZ sold 1954 to Far East Air Lines, Nagoya, Japan as JA-6010

c/n 138 G-AMIA sold 12.52 to Union of Burma Airways as XY-ACX, crashed 4.8.53

139 G-AMIB sold 12.52 to Union of Burma Airways as XY-ACY

140 G-AMIC sold 12.52 to Union of Burma Airways as XY-ACZ

2 H.P.R.2 prototypes to Spec T.16/48, submitted for test 1950 but rejected by MOS

Contract 6/Acft/4903/C.B.9(a), serials WE496, WE505, c/ns 142, 143

2 H.P.R.3 Herald prototypes built at Woodley as private venture

c/n 147 G-AODE first flown 25.8.55; converted to H.P.R.7 Dart Herald 11.3.58, crashed near Godalming 30.8.58

148 G-AODF first flown 3.8.56; converted to H.P.R.7 Dart Herald 17.12.58, reworked as Series 200 8.4.61, re-registered as G-ARTC, wfu 5.62, scrapped Radlett 1970

55 H.P.R.7 Dart Heralds laid down, 48 completed and delivered

c/n 149 G-APWA Series 100 first flown 30.10.59, leased Jersey Airlines 7.61, leased to SADIA 3.64 as PP-ASV, leased to British Midland Airways 3.65, sold to SADIA 18.11.66 as PP-SDM; to Air Brasil 1969

150 G-APWB Series 101 first flown 6.7.61, leased to Jersey Airlines 27.7.61, delivered BEA 3.62, sold to Autair 11.66, to Court Line 12.69, to Lineas Aereas la Urraca 11.70 as HK-718, crashed Colombia 1973

151 G-APWC Series 101 first flown 2.11.61, delivered BEA 3.1.62, sold to Autair 11.66, to Court Line 12.69, to Lineas Aereas la Urraca 11.70 as HK-715

152 G-APWD Series 101 first flown 19.4.62, delivered BEA 27.4.62, sold to Autair 11.66, to Court Line 12.69, to Lineas Aéreas la Urraca 11.70 as HK-721, crashed Colombia 1973

153 G-APWE Series 201 first flown 13.12.61, delivered Airlines (Jersey) Ltd 4.1.62, to British United Airways (CI) 3.67, to British Island Airways 5.70

154 G-APWF Series 201 first flown 29.3.62, delivered Airlines (Jersey) Ltd 4.62, to BUA (CI) 3.67, to BIA 5.70

155 G-APWG Series 201 first flown 27.4.62, delivered Airlines (Jersey) Ltd 5.62, to BUA (CI) 3.67, to BIA 5.70

156 G-APWH Series 201 first flown 23.5.62 delivered Airlines (Jersey) Ltd 6.62, to BUA (CI) 3.67, to BIA 5.70

157 G-APWI Series 201 first flown 8.5.63, delivered BUA 22.5.63, to Far Eastern Air Transport, Taiwan, 11.68 as B-1009, crashed Cheluchien 24.2.69

158 G-APWJ Series 201 first flown 29.5.63, delivered BUA 18.6.63, to BIA 5.70

159 CF-NAC Series 202 first flown 15.1.62, delivered Nordair 13.2.62, to EPA, to British Air Ferries 3.75, re-registered as G-BCZG

c/n		
160	CF-NAF	Series 202 first flown 2.3.62, delivered Nordair 13.3.62, to EPA, crashed 17.3.65
161	CF-MCK	Series 211 first flown 5.7.62, not delivered.Cruz as PI-C910, leased Autair 8.63 as G-ASKK, leased SADIA 12.63 as PP-ASU, to BMA 2.65 as G-ASKK, to BUA (CI) 12.66, to BIA 8.70
162	CF-MCM	Series 211 first flown 8.8.62, converted to Series 210, delivered Globe Air 13.3.63 as HB-AAG, to Handley Page 22.7.65 as G-ATHB, sold to Far Eastern Air Transport 2.66 as B-2001, to Air Comores 12.74
163	G-ASBP	Series 204 first flown 24.9.62, delivered BUA 9.10.62, to Air Manila 3.66 as PI-C867, wfu 1972
164	G-ASBG	Series 203 first flown 13.11.62, delivered Itavia 17.4.63 as I-TIVA, to BIA 9.73 as G-ASBG
165	109	Series 207 first flown 12.12.62, delivered 22.1.63 to Royal Arab Air Force, to ALIA 12.63 as JY-ACR, to Handley Page Ltd 26.7.65 as G-ATHE, to Bavaria Fluggesellschaft 4.66 as D-BOBO, to Far Eastern Air Transport 4.69 as B-2011, to Air Comores 12.74
166	CF-EPI	Series 206 first flown 27.1.63, delivered Eastern Provincial 1.2.63, to British Air Ferries 1.75 as G-BCWE
167	CF-EPC	Series 206 first flown 8.3.63, delivered Eastern Provincial 30.3.63, leased 2-5.64 to Bahamas Airways as VP-BCG, to British Air Ferries 7.75 as G-BDFE
168	I-TIVE	Series 203 first flown 4.4.63, delivered Itavia 17.4.63
169	HB-AAH	Series 210 first flown 25.7.63, delivered Globe Air 8.63, to Airlines (Jersey) 31.1.67 as G-AVEZ, to BUA (CI) 3.67, leased 1-4.68 to SADIA as PP-ASW, to BIA 8.70
170	110	Series 207 first flown 26.6.63, delivered 7.63 to RArab AF, to ALIA 12.63 as JY-ACQ, crashed near Damascus 5.4.65
171	FM1020	Series 401 first flown 28.9.63, delivered Royal Malaysian Air Force 21.12.63
172	FM1021	Series 401 first flown 8.11.63, delivered Royal Malaysian Air Force 21.12.63
173	G-ASPJ	Series 210 first flown 26.2.64, delivered Globe Air 3.64 as HB-AAK, to Europe Air Service 7.68 as F-OCLY, re-registered 5.69 as F-BLOY
174	G-8-2	Series 209 first flown 18.4.64, delivered Arkia 18.5.64 as 4X-AHS
175	FM1022	Series 401 first flown 3.1.64, delivered Royal Malaysian Air Force 17.1.64

c/n		
176	D-BIBI	Series 213 first flown 2.4.64, delivered 4.64 to Bavaria Fluggesellschaft, to Handley Page Ltd 22.6.67 as G-AVPN, leased to Itavia 21.7.67 as I-TIVB, sold to Itavia 7.70, sold to BIA 10.73 as G-AVPN
177	G-ATIG	Series 214 first flown 9.9.65, delivered SADIA 18.9.65 as PP-SDI, to British Midland Airways as G-ATIG 28.4.73
178	FM1023	Series 401 first flown 30.1.64, delivered Royal Malaysian Air Force 2.64
179	D-BEBE	Series 213 first flown 19.3.65, delivered Bavaria Fluggesellschaft 10.4.65, to BIA 13.11.70 as G-AYMG
180	FM1024	Series 401 first flown 30.7.64, delivered Royal Malaysian Air Force 8.64
181	FM1025	Series 401 first flown 22.9.64, delivered Royal Malaysian Air Force 10.64
182	FM1026	Series 401 first flown 18.11.64, delivered Royal Malaysian Air Force 11.64
183	G-8-1	Series 209 first flown 18.4.64, delivered Arkia 17.4.64 as 4X-AHR, to BIA 21.7.73 as G-BAZJ
184	I-TIVU	Series 203 first flown 14.5.64, delivered Itavia 29.5.64, to BIA 18.1.74 as G-BBXI
185	G-8-3	Series 214 first flown 2.7.64, delivered SADIA 23.10.64 as PP-SDG, to British Midland Airways 23.3.73 as G-ASVO, leased Air Anglia 2.75
186	PP-SDH	Series 214 first flown 5.1.65, delivered SADIA 26.1.65
187	FM1027	Series 401 first flown 11.5.64, delivered Royal Malaysian Air Force 5.64
188	HB-AAL	Series 210 first flown 11.5.65, delivered Globe Air 18.5.65, to Europe Air Service 16.7.68 as F-OCLZ, re-registered 5.69 as F-BOIZ
189	G-ATDS	Series 209 first flown 12.5.65, delivered Arkia 7.65 as 4X-AHT
190	PP-SDJ	Series 214 first flown 2.11.65, delivered SADIA 7.12.65, crashed Curitiba 3.11.67
191	PP-SDL	Series 214 first flown 15.1.66, delivered SADIA 1.2.66
192	PI-C866	Series 215 first flown 5.3.66, delivered Air Manila 18.3.66, wfu 1972
193	---	retained as structural test specimen for Series 700, scrapped 1970

c/n 194 PP-SDN Series 214 first flown 28.12.67, delivered SADIA 10.1.68, to British Midland Airways 28.4.73 as G-BAVX

195 4X-AHO Series 209 first flown 5.4.68, delivered Arkia 10.4.68

196 I-TIVI Series 203 first flown 25.6.68, delivered Itavia 6.68, to BIA 18.1.74 as G-BBXJ

197 4X-AHN Series 209 first flown 13.8.68, delivered Arkia 16.8.68

c/ns 252-257 laid down in 1964 as Series 700 for VASP, cancelled 1966

59 H.P.137 Jetstreams manufactured at Radlett by Handley Page Ltd and Handley Page Aircraft Ltd, 38 flown and delivered from Radlett, 11 cancelled and scrapped, 5 completed at Leavesden by Jetstream Aircraft Ltd, 5 completed at Prestwick by Scottish Aviation (Jetstream) Ltd

c/n 198 G-ATXH 1st prototype first flown 18.8.67, scrapped at Filton 1973

199 G-ATXI 2nd prototype first flown 8.3.68, scrapped at Radlett 1969

200 G-ATXJ 3rd prototype first flown 28.12.67, scrapped at Luton 1972

201 G-ATXK 4th prototype first flown 8.4.68, to International Jetstream Corp 5.68, wfu 1971

202 G-AWSE first flown 6.12.68, to Cal-State Air Lines 7.69 as N1039S, to Riley Aeronautics Corp 1973 as N14RJ

203 G-AXEK first flown 2.1.69 as G-8-4, to CSE 31.5.69, to South Central Air Transport as N1FY

204 G-AWVI first flown 22.1.69, to Cal-State Air Lines 7.69 as N1040S, to Acme 1972 as N11DH

205 G-AXEM first flown 10.2.69 as G-8-5, to Bavaria Fluggesell-schaft 10.69 as D-INAH, crashed Samedan 6.3.70

206 G-AWVJ first flown 23.5.69, to Cal-State Air Lines 5.69 as N1036S, to Scottish Aviation 24.5.72, reworked as Jetstream T.1 serial XX475 first flown 13.4.73, delivered A & AEE

207 G-AXEL first flown 4.3.69 as G-8-6, to British Steel Corp 9.69, crashed Hunstanton 29.9.69

208 G-AWVK first flown 17.4.69, to Cal-State Air Lines 5.69 as N1035S, to Jetstream Aircraft 12.70, to Decca Navigator Co Ltd 3.74 as G-AWVK

209 G-AXEP first flown 2.5.69 as G-8-7, to Hoover Corp 5.69 as N5V (later N5VP), to Omni Investment Corp 1972 as N74169

c/n 210 G-AWYM first flown 17.5.69 to J.R. Coson, Burbank as N62BS

211 G-AXFV first flown 24.4.69 as G-8-8, converted to Jetstream 2 prototype 11.69, to Cranfield Inst Tech 9.70 for Type Certification, to Jetstream Aircraft Ltd 6.71, to Terravia Trading Services 2.72, to W.J. Bright 4.73, to Gecamines, Zaire, 20.12.73 as 9Q-CTC

212 G-AWYN first flown 29.5.69, to National Steel Corp 7.69 as N340

213 G-AWYP first flown 14.6.69, to International Jetstream Corp 6.69 as N137HP, sold 1973 to Robert Graf Inc

214 G-AXHB first flown 12.6.69, to Northwest Industries 6.69 as CF-QJB

215 G-AXGK first flown 16.6.69, to Walter W. Selover, Burbank 7.69 as N200PA

216 G-AXGL first flown 21.6.69, to Cal-State Air Lines 28.6.69 as N1037S, to Scottish Aviation 24.5.72, reworked as Jetstream T.1 serial XX476 first flown 19.3.73, to CFS

217 G-AXHJ first flown 17.6.69, to K.R. Cravens Corp 7.69 as N12217

218 G-AXGM first flown 2.7.69 to International Jetstream Corp 7.69 as N12218

219 68-10378 laid down as Jetstream 3M (C-10A) for USAF, cancelled 1969

220 G-AXGN first flown 4.7.69, to Cal-State Air Lines 7.69 as N1038S, to N.E. Isaacson & Associates 1972 as N651KE

221 G-AXIK first flown 10.7.69, to International Jetstream Corp 7.69 as N12221

222 G-AXUI first flown 1.1.70 as G-8-9, to Cranfield Inst Tech 9.70, first flown as flying laboratory 6.72, as flying classroom with students 1.5.73

223 G-AXIL first flown 25.7.69, to Cal-State Air Lines 9.69 as N1044S, later N12223

224 G-AXIM first flown 31.7.69, to Cal-State Air Lines 9.69 as N1041S, later N12224

225 G-AXON first flown 3.10.69, to International Jetstream Corp 11.69, to Buckner Industries as N10AB

226 68-10379 laid down as Jetstream 3M (C-10A) for USAF, cancelled 1969

227 G-AXJZ first flown 21.7.69, to International Jetstream Corp 9.69 as N12227, to G.C. Murphy & Co as N510E

228 68-10380 laid down as Jetstream 3M (C-10A) for USAF, cancelled 1969

c/n 229 G-AXKG first flown 28.7.69, to USA 12.69 as N10EA, stored Airspur 1971

230 G-AXVF first flown 9.1.70, to Airspur, Edmonton for storage, sold USA

231 G-AXLO first flown 12.11.69, to Di Giorgio Corp, Burbank as N10DG, to Riley Aeronautics Corp, Waco 1972, re-engined with PT-6A as Riley Jetstream and first flown 6.73 as N7RJ ***Life of Riley***

232 68-10381 laid down as Jetstream 3M (C-10A) for USAF, cancelled 1969

233 G-AXLP first flown 18.11.69, to USA as N8943, sold to Standard Oil Corp as N815M

234 G-BBBV first flown 11.69 as G-8-12, stored Kidlington, reg 25.6.73 to Knivett Aviation Support Ltd, sold to USA 3.7.74

235 G-AXRE first flown 2.12.69, to USA as N10GA, stored Airspur 1971

236 68-10382 laid down as Jetstream 3M (C-10A) for USAF, cancelled 1969

237 G-AXRF first flown 23.12.69, to Associated Aero Leasing 12.69 as N2527, to Air Investments Inc as N666WB, stored Airspur 1971

238 G-AXRG first flown 16.1.70, to USA as N1137C, to Airspur 1971 as N10360

239 68-10383 laid down as Jetstream 3M (C-10A) for USAF, cancelled 1969

240 G-AXRH first flown 27.1.70, to USA as N4770, stored Airspur 1971; last Jetstream flown away from Radlett

241 G-AXRI first flown 12.6.74 at Leavesden after completion by Jetstream Aircraft Ltd as Jetstream 2, re-registered G-BCGU to Arthur Guinness Son & Co Ltd

242 68-10384 laid down as Jetstream 3M (C-10A) for USAF, cancelled 1969

243 G-AWYR first flown 23.4.74 as G-8-13 at Leavesden after conversion by Jetstream Aircraft Ltd to Jetstream 2, re-registered G-BBYM to The Morgan Crucible Co Ltd, Leavesden

244 68-10385 laid down as Jetstream 3M (C-10A) for USAF, cancelled 1969

245 G-AXUM delivered by road to Jetstream Aircraft Ltd, Sywell 9.70, first flown 7.71 from Sywell to Cranfield Inst Tech, refitted as flying classroom 12.74

246 G-AXUN delivered by road to Jetstream Aircraft Ltd, Sywell 9.70, first flown 7.71 from Sywell to Cranfield Inst Tech, to Leavesden 28.2.74 for conversion to Jetstream 2, re-registered G-BCWW to The Distillers Co Ltd 1.75

c/n 247 68-10386 laid down as Jetstream 3M (C-10A) for USAF, cancelled 1969

248 G-AXUO delivered by road to Jetstream Aircraft Ltd, Sywell 9.70, first flown 26.1.72, sold to Air Wasteels, Metz, re-registered F-BTMI

249 G-AXXS delivered by road to Jetstream Aircraft Ltd, Sywell 9.70, to Scottish Aviation Ltd 7.72 by road for reworking as Jetstream T.1 serial XX477 first flown 21.8.73, to CFS, crashed 1.11.74 Little Rissington

250 68-10387 laid down as Jetstream 3M (C-10A) for USAF, cancelled 1969

251 G-AXUP delivered by road to Jetstream Aircraft Ltd, Sywell 9.70, to Scottish Aviation Ltd 8.71 by road for reworking as Jetstream T.1 serial XX481, first flown 9.3.74

258 G-AWBR first flown 21.11.68 as Jetstream 3M prototype, scrapped Radlett 1970

259 G-AXUR delivered by road to Scottish Aviation Ltd 4.5.72, first flown 27.10.73 as Jetstream T.1 serial XX479

260 68-10388 laid down as Jetstream 3M (C-10A) for USAF, cancelled 1969

261 G-AXXT delivered by road to Scottish Aviation Ltd 5.72, first flown 4.10.73 as Jetstream T.1 serial XX478

262 G-AXXU last airframe completed at Radlett, delivered by road to Scottish Aviation Ltd 5.72, first flown 3.2.74 as Jetstream T.1 serial XX480

14 Scottish Aviation Jetstream T.1 built at Prestwick using Handley Page built fuselages; serials XX482-XX495

5 Scottish Aviation Jetstream T.1 entirely manufactured at Prestwick; serials XX496-XX500

(b) Other than Handley Page Types

1 Sonoda biplane manufactured at Barking and assembled at Hendon in June 1912; rolled out on 7.7.12, 5.8.12 and 28.9.12; first flown and crashed 30.9.12 by C.W. Meredith

5 B.E.2a biplanes ordered August 1912 by War Office, serials not identified; 2 delivered in 1913, 1 in 1914, last 2 cancelled

6 D.H.9A biplanes reconditioned and modified for deck trials on HMS *Eagle*, serials J6963-J6968, Liberty engines

15 D.H.9A biplanes reconditioned (airframes only), serials J7018-J7032

1 Junkers-F 13 monoplane reassembled for trials at RAE Farnborough 1923 serial J7232

1 Dornier Komet monoplane reassembled for trials at RAE Farnborough 1923 serial J7276

1 Dornier Delfin monoplane reassembled for trials at MAEE Felixstowe 1924 serial N176

150 English Electric Canberra B.2 ordered, 75 built at Cricklewood and Radlett

serials		
	WJ564-WJ582 WJ603-WJ649 WJ674-WJ682	74 delivered 1950, WJ622 crashed during test flight
	WJ683-WJ707 WS960-WS969 WT113-WT122	75 cancelled 1950

5 Miles aircraft completed and delivered from Woodley 1950-1951

M.69 Marathon II G-AHXU first flown 21.7.49, to MOS 1951 serial VX231, converted to H.P.R.5, first flown 15.3.55, wfu 10.59

c/n 141 Gemini G-ALZG, first flown 3.6.50

144 Aerovan IV G-AJXK, first flown 3.12.50

145 Gemini G-AMEJ, first flown 21.12.50

146 Messenger 2A, G-AJYZ, first flown 24.5.51

APPENDIX B, part 2

At the end of January 1987 there were 15 Heralds still in service, a further 16 aircraft, or hulks, existed but few were airworthy.

c/n			
	166	G-BCWE	British Air Ferries
	167	4Q-CAA	MMM Aero Service, Zaire
	174	G-BEZB	Channel Express Air Services
	175	G-BEYF	Air Bridge Ltd (for Elan Air)
	176	G-AVPN	Euroair (leased from Nordic Oil on behalf of Euroair)
	177	G-ATIG	Janus Airways (owned by Euroair)
	178	HK-2701	Aerosucre, Colombia
	179	G-AYMG	Securicor Air International (owned by Skyguard)
	180	HK-2702	Aerosucre
	182	TA-ALE	Aerovias, Guatemala
	185	G-ASVO	Channel Express Air Services
	187	G-BEYK	Euroair
	189	G-ATDS	Channel Express Air Services
	194	G-BAVX	British Air Ferries

APPENDIX C

Civil Transport Conversions from Bombers 1919–1949

(a) O/400 Civil Variants (excluding O/7s built new from spares, listed in Appendix B)

c/n			
HP-12	(O/7)	serial J1934 reg	G-EAPB C of A 346, 23.4.20, to India 1.21
HP-13	(O/400)	serial F5414 reg	G-EAAF C of A 1, 1.5.19, crashed Harker 12.5.19, rebuilt as O/7 reg G-EAAF C of A 165. 14.8.19, to USA 5.20
HP-14	(O/400)	serial F5417 reg	G-EAAW C of A 2, 1.5.19, wfu 4.20
HP-15	(W/400)	serial C9713 not registered, c/n transferred to W.8 G-EAPJ	
HP-16	(O/400)	serial D8350 reg	G-EAAE C of A 3, 1.5.19, wfu 8.20
HP-17	(O/400)	serial C9704 not registered, flown to Spain, crashed Durango 8.19, repaired on site, flown back to Cricklewood 6.3.20, to USA 5.20	
HP-18	(O/400)	serial F5418 reg	G-EAAG C of A 4, 1.5.19, wfu 4.20
HP-19	(O/400)	serial J2249 reg	G-EAKF C of A 160, 10.10.19, scrapped 10.20
HP-20	(O/400)	serial J2250 reg	G-EAKG C of A 161, 6.9.19, scrapped 8.20
HP-21	(O/400)	serial J2251 reg	G-EALX C of A 249, 31.10.19, wfu 10.20
HP-22	(O/400)	serial J2252 reg	G-EAKE C of A 159, 25.8.19, crashed Sweden 30.6.20
HP-23	(O/400)	serial J2243 reg	G-EALZ C of A 277, 23.12.19, wfu 12.20
HP-24	(O/400)	serial J2247 reg	G-EALY C of A 239, 17.10.19, wfu 10.20
HP-25	(O/400)	serial J2248 reg	G-EAMA C of A 258, 7.11.19, crashed Golders Green 14.12.20
HP-26	(O/400)	serial D4623 reg	G-EAMB C of A 279, 23.12.19, wfu 12.20
HP-27	(O/400)	serial D4624 reg	G-EAMC C of A 293, 28.1.20, crashed Sudan 25.2.20
HP-28	(O/400)	serial D4633 reg	G-EAMD C of A 269, 1.12.19, sold in Poland 12.19
HP-29	(O/400)	not identified, believed shipped to Argentina 3.20	
HP-30	(O/11)	serial C9699 reg	G-EASL C of A 375, 26.3.20, wfu 4.21
HP-31	(O/11)	serial C9731 reg	G-EASM C of A 374, 26.3.20, wfu 4.21
HP-32	(O/11)	serial D4611 reg	G-EASN C of A 373, 23.6.20, wfu 4.21
HP-33	(O/400)	serial D5444 reg	G-EASO C of A not issued, Napier Lions, wfu 4.21

c/n HP-34 (O/10) serial F308 reg G-EASX C of A 426, 15.10.20, sold in India 4.21

HP-35 (O/10) serial D4614 reg G-EASY C of A 376, 23.6.20, to India 4.21

HP-36 (O/10) serial F310 reg G-EASZ C of A 379, 25.6.20, to India 4.21

HP-37 (O/10) serial D4618 reg G-EATG C of A 377, 23.6.20, wfu 4.21

HP-38 (O/10) serial D4631 reg G-EATH C of A 385, 30.6.20, wfu 1924

HP-39 (O/10) serial F307 reg G-EATJ C of A 378, 25.6.20, wfu 4.21

HP-40 (O/10) serial J2262 reg G-EATK C of A 394, 15.7.20, Bristol Jupiters, scrapped 8.22

HP-41 (O/10) serial F312 reg G-EATL C of A 417, 30.8.20, wfu 4.21

HP-42 (O/10) serial D4609 reg G-EATM C of A 399, 30.7.20, crashed Berck 30.12.21

HP-43 (O/10) serial J2261 reg G-EATN C of A 389, 13.7.20, crashed Senlis 14.1.22

(b) Halifax (built by Handley Page Ltd, excluding those by other contractors)

1 B.6 c/n 1270 serial PP171 reg G-AKNL 29.11.47 Lancashire Aircraft Corp : to spares 5.48

94 C.8s (* converted to Halton 1 for BOAC by Short & Harland Ltd)

c/n 1301 serial PP217 reg G-AKJF 26.9.47 to LAMS, sold in South Africa

1302 serial PP218 reg G-AIWI 13.5.48 to LAMS, Berlin Air Lift, scrapped 1949

1303 serial PP219 reg G-AKBA 8.3.48, to Airtech Ltd, crashed Albacete 25.5.48

1304 serial PP220 reg G-AKXT 29.12.48 to LAC, *Air Rover*, scrapped 1950

1306 serial PP222 reg G-AIHU 25.9.47 to LAC, *Air Adventurer*, crashed Rhyl 5.12.47

1307 serial PP223 reg G-AKGP 10.9.47 to Airtech, to France 6.48 as F-BESE *Ker Gawler*, scrapped 1950

1308* serial PP224 reg G-AHDL 18.9.46 to BOAC *Fitzroy*, 7.48 Aviation Traders, 2.49 Westminster, crashed Gatow 1.4.49

1310* serial PP226 reg G-AHDO 13.8.47 to BOAC *Forfar*, 7.48 Aviation Traders, 3.49 Bond, scrapped 11.56

1312* serial PP228 reg G-AHDM 20.7.46 to BOAC *Falmouth*, 7.48 Aviation Traders, 2.49 Westminster, scrapped 9.50

1313 serial PP229 reg G-ALBS 14.6.48 to Hyland Automobiles (England) Ltd, scrapped 1950

1314 serial PP230 reg G-AHWN 21.6.46 to H.P.Ltd, to LAC 4.48 *Air Viceroy*, crashed Schleswigland 6.7.49

1315 serial PP231 reg G-AKBK 11.1.49 to LAC, scrapped 1950

1317 serial PP233 reg G-AKBJ 8.12.48 to LAC *Air Ambassador*, crashed Tegel 1.6.49

c/n 1318* serial PP234 reg G-AHDN 24.3.47, to BOAC *Flamborough*, 7.48 Aviation Traders, scrapped 11.50

1319 serial PP235 reg G-AIWN 23.5.47 to LAMS *Port of Darwin*, 10.47 Payloads, 5.49 Bond, wfu 5.50

1321 serial PP237 reg G-AKBB 16.4.48 to Airtech, to BAAS 4.48, crashed Schleswigland 11.2.49

1322 serial PP238 reg G-AHWM 21.6.46 intended for CADTA (cancelled 1.47), returned to 29 MU, RAF 17.3.47, then re-registered G-AJZY 4.48 to LAC *Air Monarch*, crashed Gt. Missenden 8.3.51

1323 serial PP239 reg G-AHZO 24.12.46 to LAMS *Port of London*, 3.49 Sky-flight, scrapped 6.49

1324 serial PP240 reg G-AIOH 15.5.47 to C L Air Surveys, 3.48 Bond, crashed Barcelona 30.5.47

1325 serial PP241 reg G-AIHY 19.6.47 to LAC *Air Explorer*, crashed Le Bourget 28.12.49

1326 serial PP242 reg G-AHZL 26.10.46 to LAMS *Port of Oslo*, wfu 6.49

1327 serial PP243 reg G-AIOI 16.1.47 to C L Air Surveys, 3.48 Bond, crashed Tegel 15.2.49

1328 serial PP244 reg G-AHZN 28.8.46 to LAMS, ditched off Knocke 26.9.46

1329 serial PP245 reg G-AIWR 11.47 to LAMS (SA) as ZS-BUL *Port of Durban*, crashed Port Sudan 25.11.47

1330 serial PP246 reg G-AHZK 15.11.46 to LAMS *Port of Naples*, 3.49 Sky-flight, wfu 1949

1331 serial PP247 reg G-AHZJ 18.9.46 to LAMS *Port of Marseilles*, scrapped 8.47

1332 serial PP259 reg G-AJNT 14.4.47 to Payloads, 6.47 sold in France as F-BCQY

1333 serial PP260 reg G-AHZM 17.7.46 to LAMS, wfu 16.9.46

1334 serial PP261 reg G-AHYH 24.9.46 to BOAC, returned to RAF 10.47, to LAC 29.10.48 *Air Merchant II*, scrapped 28.10.49

1335 serial PP262 reg G-AIHV 10.4.47 to LAC *Air Trader*, wfu 12.47

1336 serial PP263 reg G-AJPJ 15.10.47 to Chartair, 11.47 BAAS, hijacked to Israel 20.7.48

1337 serial PP264 reg G-AJBK 11.4.47 to Air Freight, 10.47 to France as F-BCJZ, wfu 12.47

1338 serial PP265 reg G-AIWT 3.4.47 to LAMS *Port of Sydney*, 10.47 Payloads, wfu 10.48

1339 serial PP266 reg G-AIWM 4.12.47 to LAMS *Merchant Venturer*, scrapped 1949

1340 serial PP267 reg G-AKAC 2.11.48 to Payloads, to World Air Freight, crashed near Berlin 29.4.49

1341* serial PP268 reg G-AHDP 24.3.47 to BOAC *Fleetwood*, 7.48 Aviation Traders, wfu 9.4.49

c/n 1342* serial PP269 reg G-AHDR 7.7.47 to BOAC *Foreland*, 6.48 to Louis Breguet as F-BECK

1343 serial PP270 reg G-ALBT 14.6.48 to Hyland Automobiles (England) Ltd, scrapped 8.50

1344 serial PP271 reg G-AIAN 2.9.46 to BOAC, returned to RAF 4.47

1345 serial PP272 reg G-AIAO 2.9.46 to BOAC, returned to RAF 4.47

1346 serial PP273 reg G-AKCT 1.8.47 to Payloads, to Air Globe 9.47 as HB-AIK, 12.48 to Egyptian Air Force

1347 serial PP274 reg G-AGTK 8.47 to CTAI as F-BCJX, crashed Bovingdon 13.5.48

1348 serial PP275 reg G-ALBZ 2.2.49 to LAC, crashed Schleswigland 10.5.49

1349 serial PP276 reg G-AJBL 15.9.47 to Air Freight, scrapped 6.7.49

1350* serial PP277 reg G-AHDS 24.8.46 to BOAC *Fremantle*, 7.48 Aviation Traders, wfu 7.51

1351 serial PP278 reg G-AHVT 25.6.47 to Anglo-French Distributors, to France 21.9.47 as F-BCJR

1352 serial PP279 reg G-AJNU 14.4.47 to Payloads, to Pakistan Airways 5.48 as AP-ACH

1353 serial PP280 reg G-AILO 27.10.47 to College of Aeronautics, 9.49 LAC *Air Courier*, wfu 9.51

1354 serial PP281 reg G-AIAP 2.9.46 to BOAC, 10.48 Airtech, 6.50 Eagle, crashed Calcutta 25.11.50

1355 serial PP282 reg G-AKEC 4.2.48 to LAC *Air Voyager*, crashed Squires Gate 17.12.52

1356 serial PP283 reg G-AKAD 1.3.48 to BAAS, crashed Rennes 17.5.48

1357 serial PP284 reg G-AIHW 29.4.47 to LAMS, crashed Heathrow 5.6.47

1359 serial PP286 reg G-AIWJ 15.5.47 to LAMS *Port of Athens*, wfu 6.49

1360 serial PP287 reg G-AGPC 25.10.47 to Anglo-French Distributors, to Aero Cargo 10.47 as F-BCJS, crashed Lyons 1.12.48

1361 serial PP288 reg G-AIWP 26.1.48 to LAMS, scrapped 3.50

1362 serial PP289 reg G-AKBP 16.7.47 to Payloads, to Air Globe 8.47 as HB-AIL, 12.48 to Egyptian Air Force

1363 serial PP290 reg G-AIWO 18.11.46 to LAMS, wfu 1947

1364 serial PP291 reg G-AIWL 18.11.46 to LAMS, wfu 1949

1365 serial PP292 reg G-AJNV 14.4.47 to Payloads, to Air Globe 8.47 as HB-AIF, 12.48 to Egyptian Air Force

1366 serial PP293 reg G-AIZO 18.8.47 to Union Air Services *County of Surrey*, 5.49 Bond, crashed Berkhampstead 23.5.48

1367 serial PP294 reg G-AIHX 7.6.47 to LAC *Air Merchant*, crashed Squires Gate 3.9.48

c/n 1368 serial PP295 reg G-AIWK 21.7.47 to LAMS *Port of Sydney*, scrapped Mascot 12.47

1369 serial PP296 reg G-AJNW 27.4.49 to Payloads, 5.49 Westminster, wfu 4.50

1370* serial PP308 reg G-AHDT 4.6.47 to BOAC *Fife*, 7.48 Aviation Traders, scrapped 11.49

1371 serial PP309 reg G-AHKK 21.4.47 to Anglo-French Distributors, to France as F-BCJV

1372* serial PP310 reg G-AHDU 10.7.46 to BOAC *Falkirk*, 7.48 Aviation Traders, scrapped 7.50

1373 serial PP311 reg G-AHYI 24.9.46 to BOAC, returned 7.47 to RAF, 1.48 to Anglo-French Distributors, 3.49 Skyflight, scrapped 1949

1374 serial PP312 reg G-AJNX 30.1.48 to Payloads, 2.48 Bond, to Pakistan Airways 8.5.48 as AP-ABZ

1375 serial PP313 reg G-AJPK 20.8.47 to LAMS, 8.47 Payloads, 11.47 VIP Services, wfu 10.48

1376* serial PP314 reg G-AHDV 19.8.46 to BOAC *Finisterre*, 7.48 Aviation Traders, 3.49 Westminster, 2.51 LAC, dbr Squires Gate 17.12.52

1377* serial PP315 reg G-AHDW 29.7.46 to BOAC *Falaise*, 7.48 Aviation Traders, scrapped 11.50

1378* serial PP316 reg G-AHDX 4.6.47 to BOAC *Folkestone*, 7.48 Aviation Traders, 3.50 Worldair Carriers, crashed 16.4.50

1379 serial PP317 reg G-AIID 24.9.46 to BOAC, returned 4.47 to RAF, 1.48 to Anglo-French Distributors, 3.49 Skyflight, scrapped 10.49

1381 serial PP319 reg G-ALBU 14.6.48 to Hyland Automobiles (England) Ltd, scrapped 8.50

1382 serial PP320 reg G-AITC 2.12.47 to College of Aeronautics, 3.49 World Air Freight, crashed Brindisi 20.1.50

1383 serial PP321 reg G-ALBV 12.6.48 to Hyland Automobiles (England) Ltd, scrapped 8.50

1384 serial PP322 reg G-AJNY 2.4.48 to Payloads, 4.48 Bowmaker, sold to Pakistan Airways 8.5.48 as AP-ACG

1385 serial PP323 reg G-AJNZ 26.11.47 to Payloads, World Air Freight *Trade Wind*, crashed Isle of Man 28.9.48

1386 serial PP324 reg G-AKGO 10.9.47 to Airtech, 5.48 to Stansted, scrapped 5.48

1387 serial PP325 not registered, crash-landed 9.46 while on loan from RAF to BOAC

1388 serial PP326 reg G-AIAR 2.9.46 to BOAC, 10.48 Airtech, 9.49 Chartair, 3.50 BAAS, wfu 5.51

1389 serial PP327 reg G-AIAS 2.9.46 to BOAC, scrapped 4.47

c/n 1390 serial PP328 reg G-AJOG 20.8.47 to Peteair Ltd, to Norway 6.49 as LN-OAS *Sky Tramp*

1391 serial PP329 reg G-AKBR 9.9.48 to Payloads, 9.48 Skyflight, 9.48 Eagle, scrapped 1950

1392 serial PP330 reg G-AJXD 23.6.47 to Anglo-French Distributors, to France 6.47 as F-BCJQ

1393 serial PP331 reg G-AHWL 25.10.47 to Anglo-French Distributors, to France 10.47 as F-BCJT

1394 serial PP332 not registered, to College of Aeronautics for conversion to Nene test-bed, trial installation not completed, airframe believed sold to Pakistan

1395 serial PP333 reg G-AKGN 25.8.48 to BAAS, 8.49 Chartair, scrapped 17.12.49

1396 serial PP334 reg G-AJZZ 8.7.48 to LAC, converted to tanker for Berlin Air Lift, crashed Schleswigland 21.3.49

1397 serial PP335 reg G-ALCX 18.11.48 to LAC ***Air Regent***, scrapped 1952

1398 serial PP336 reg G-AGZP 20.3.46 to BAAS, converted to Halton 2 for Gaekwar of Baroda, 4.47 to Alpha Airways (Pty) Ltd as ZS-BTA, 8.49 to LAC, scrapped 1953

1399 serial PP337 reg LN-OAT 8.47 to Vingtor Airways, to Eagle 11.10.48 as G-ALEF ***Red Eagle***, scrapped 1950

1400 serial PP338 reg G-AKGZ 28.1.48 World Air Freight ***North Wind***, crashed Gatow 8.10.48

7 C.8s c/ns 1305 (PP221), 1309 (PP225), 1311 (PP227), 1316 (PP232), 1320 (PP236), 1358 (PP285), 1380 (PP318) were not released by the RAF for civil use

2 A.9s were operated by Bond Aviation Services in the Berlin Air Lift

c/n 1451 serial RT763 reg G-ALON 1.6.49 to Aviation Traders, scrapped 6.50

1589 serial RT937 reg G-ALOS 15.6.49 to Aviation Traders, scrapped 7.49

INDEX

General

For Aircraft and Engines see p. 659

INDEX

Aircraft and Engines